# The Passions

# The Passions:
# A Study of Human Nature

## P. M. S. Hacker

Fellow of St John's College · Oxford

**WILEY** Blackwell

*Registered Offices*
John Wiley & Sons, Inc., 111 River Street, Hoboken, NJ 07030, USA
John Wiley & Sons Ltd, The Atrium, Southern Gate, Chichester, West Sussex, PO19 8SQ, UK

*Editorial Office*
9600 Garsington Road, Oxford, OX4 2DQ, UK

For details of our global editorial offices, customer services, and more information about Wiley products visit us at www.wiley.com.

Wiley also publishes its books in a variety of electronic formats and by print-on-demand. Some content that appears in standard print versions of this book may not be available in other formats.

*Library of Congress Cataloging-in-Publication Data*
Names: Hacker, P. M. S. (Peter Michael Stephan), author.
Title: The passions : a study of human nature / by P. M. S. Hacker.
Description: Hoboken, NJ : John Wiley & Sons, 2017. | Includes bibliographical references and index. |
Identifiers: LCCN 2017030690 (print) | LCCN 2017036805 (ebook) |
    ISBN 9781118954744 (epub) | ISBN 9781118952436 (pdf) |
    ISBN 9781118951873 (cloth) | ISBN 9781119440468 (pbk.)
Subjects: LCSH: Emotions (Philosophy) | Philosophical anthropology.
Classification: LCC B815 (ebook) | LCC B815 .H33 2017 (print) | DDC 128/.37–dc23
LC record available at https://lccn.loc.gov/2017030690

Cover design by Wiley

Set in 10.5/12.5pt Sabon by SPi Global, Pondicherry, India
Printed and bound in Malaysia by Vivar Printing Sdn Bhd

1  2018

*For*

*Robert and Betsy Feinberg*

# Contents

Preface                                                                 xi

Acknowledgements                                                        xvii

*Part I   Sketching the Landscape*                                        1

Chapter 1   The Place of the Emotions
            among the Passions                                            3

1.   Passions, affections, and appetites                                 3
2.   Agitations and moods                                               14
3.   Emotions                                                           22

Chapter 2   The Analytic of the Emotions I                              37

1.   The representation of emotions                                     37
2.   The language of the emotions                                       40
3.   Expressions and manifestations of emotion                         45
4.   Emotion, cognition, and the will                                   56

Chapter 3   The Analytic of the Emotions II                             60

1.   The epistemology of the emotions                                   60
2.   Emotion and reason                                                 67
3.   The place of the emotions in human life                            77

**Chapter 4    The Dialectic of the Emotions**                83

   1.  The Cartesian and empiricist legacies and their
       invalidation                                            83
   2.  Philosophical and psychological confusions: James     97
   3.  Neuroscientific confusions: Damasio and the somatic
       marker hypothesis                                      103
   4.  Evolutionary accounts of the emotions:
       Darwin and Ekman                                       111
   5.  The quest for basic emotions                           115

**Part II    *Human, All Too Human***                       129

**Chapter 5    Pride, Arrogance, and Humility**             131

   1.  The web of pride                                       131
   2.  Shifting evaluations of pride                          135
   3.  Pride: connective analysis                             140

**Chapter 6    Shame, Embarrassment, and Guilt**            152

   1.  Shame cultures and guilt cultures                      152
   2.  Shame and embarrassment: connective analysis           157
   3.  Guilt: connective analysis                             173

**Chapter 7    Envy**                                       183

   1.  Envy and jealousy: a pair of vicious emotions          183
   2.  Envy and jealousy: conceptual unclarity                187
   3.  Envy and jealousy: their conceptual roots              192
   4.  Envy: iconography, mythology, and iconology            197
   5.  Envy: connective analysis                              200

**Chapter 8    Jealousy**                                   208

   1.  Different centres of variation                         208
   2.  Iconography                                            215
   3.  Jealousy: connective analysis                          216
   4.  Jealousy and envy again                                228

Chapter 9   Anger                                            232

   1.   The phenomena of anger                          232
   2.   The vocabulary of anger                          235
   3.   Anger: connective analysis                       239
   4.   Conceptions of anger in antiquity                253
   5.   Is acting in anger warranted?                    259

Part III   *The Saving Graces: Love,*
*Friendship, and Sympathy*                                   265

Chapter 10   Love                                            267

   1.   Concepts and conceptions of love                 267
   2.   The biological and social roots of love          269
   3.   The objects of love                              274
   4.   Historico-normative constraints                  279
   5.   The phases of love                               282
   6.   The web of concepts of love                      287
   7.   The iconography of love                          294
   8.   Connective analysis I: categorial complexity     298
   9.   Connective analysis II: peculiarities of love as an emotion   304
  10.   Connective analysis III: some characteristic
      features of love                              316
  11.   Self-love                                        324

Chapter 11   Friendship                                      327

   1.   Friendship and love                              327
   2.   The roots and marks of different forms of friendship   336
   3.   Analysis of the relation                         345
   4.   Friendship, virtue, and morality                 350

Chapter 12   Sympathy and Empathy                            357

   1.   Sympathy: the historical background              357
   2.   The analysis of sympathy                         367
   3.   Empathy: from *Einfühlung* to mirror neurons     377
   4.   Empathy and sympathy                             385
   5.   Envoi                                            392

## Appendix: Moments in the History of Love                393

1.  The history of love                                        393
2.  Ancient Israel                                             395
3.  Ancient Greece                                             402
4.  From pagan Rome to Christian Rome                          410
5.  Early Christianity                                         417
6.  The deification of love                                    426

Index                                                          438

# Preface

The subject of the human passions has excited the imagination and attracted the attention of philosophers since the pre-Socratics. That is hardly surprising, given the role that emotions play in our lives. We are all subject to joy and delight, to anger and fear, to sadness and grief. That is an intrinsic part of the human condition – for we are purposive, self-conscious, goal-seeking creatures and can recognize what frustrates or facilitates our purposes, and can respond affectively to and reflect upon the achievement of our goals and the maintenance or loss of what we value. We are mammals whose offspring require years to achieve biological maturity, and we are by nature social creatures with an innate capacity for bonding. So we are given to love, loyalty, and affection, and hence also subject to grief and sorrow. We express our emotions in what we do, how we act, and what we say, and we recognize the passions of our fellow human beings in their verbal expressions and behavioural manifestations of emotion. Having a natural propensity to sympathy and empathy, we can share our emotions with others and respond sympathetically to their feelings. Any study of human nature has to investigate the passions, to elucidate our concepts of emotions, and to describe our rich affective vocabulary. For the passions and emotions, collectively and severally, present manifold conceptual problems and provide fertile terrain for conceptual confusion among both philosophers and psychologists. Our problems are not merely intellectual. Human beings are often guided by their emotions, sometimes for good and sometimes for ill. They may be masters of their emotions or in bondage to them. Clarity about the concepts of the emotions is not only a contribution to the better understanding of human nature; it also facilitates deeper reflection upon our lives and the emotions that beset us. Accordingly this book is not aimed solely at philosophers, who are concerned with the conceptual problems examined here. It is also aimed at psychologists and cognitive neuroscientists, whose conceptual confusions and unclarities are subjected to detailed analysis here. And it is equally aimed at educated readers, who are interested in understanding the nature of the emotions, and in attaining a clearer understanding of the place of emotion in their own lives.

The emotions have an immediate and patent connection with (or with what is thought to be) the beneficial and the detrimental. For we fear and seek to avoid what we perceive as harmful to us or to those whom we cherish. We feel trepidation and anxiety, or anger, at the prospect of anything that threatens our welfare and endangers the good of those to whom we are attached. So the emotions are also perspicuously connected with what is, or is thought to be, good and bad. Our emotional pronenesses and liabilities are partly constitutive of our temperament and personality. Our ability to control our emotions, to keep their manifestations and their motivating force within the bounds of reason, is constitutive of our character as moral agents. So the investigation of the emotions is a fruitful prolegomenon to the philosophical study of morality. It provides a point of access to the elucidation of right and wrong, good and evil, virtue and vice, that skirts the morass of deontological and consequentialist approaches to ethics without neglecting the roles of duties and obligations, or the role of the consequences of our actions in our practical reasoning. Unlike deontology and consequentialism, such an approach highlights the context-bound and ideographic character of much normal moral experience and decision without obscuring the role of principle in the lives of people of integrity. So this book paves the way for a subsequent investigation into axiology and morality.

Because the understanding of the role of the emotions in human life is ideographic rather than nomothetic, the deepest students of the passions are not psychologists, physiological psychologists, or cognitive neuroscientists. Science may study the endless forms of emotional abnormality and aberration, and strive to ameliorate the suffering of those subject to them. It may also investigate, as Darwin and his successors have, the expression of the emotions in animals and man, and explain, in so far as is possible, the evolutionary selection for one emotional propensity as opposed to another. But it can shed relatively little light on the diverse patterns of socialization of emotions in human communities, let alone upon the shifting history of the emotions in human cultures. For, once mankind acquired sophisticated languages, the nature and scope of emotions and their objects changed beyond anything that could be ascribed to, let alone rendered intelligible to, non-human animals. Mastery of a language made possible second-order emotions (e.g. regret for one's anger, pride in one's fearlessness), as well as objects of emotion that lie in the dated past or future, and abstract and universal objects of emotion (e.g. love of nature, hatred of injustice, compassion for mankind). Mastery of a language not only made man into a rational animal; it also brought human emotions within the scope of reason. For human emotions are normally supported by reasons, are capable of evaluation by the exercise of the faculty of reason, and are subject to control by means of the power of reason.

The deepest students of the role of the emotions in human life are the novelists, dramatists, and poets of our culture. The great novelists depict, in the most profound ways, emotional possibilities in human life, contextualized to a social and cultural form of life, and individualized to fictional characters portrayed in the round with consummate skill. The great dramatists manifest in the dialogues of their plays the roles different emotions may play in human life, the manner in which human beings may be victims of their passions and motivated by them. The great poets give refined articulate form to emotions we all feel but are incapable of crystallizing in such subtle expression. It is for this reason that I decided to illustrate my cultural and conceptual observations by reference to novels, plays, and poems, and to draw on numerous quotations from Western literature. I have not made use of the rich fund of Eastern literature, partly through ignorance, and partly because the conceptions of individual emotions that I chose to examine are conceptions manifest in Western culture, problematized in Western philosophy, and described and articulated in the literature of the West.

It does not require a great deal of reading in the extensive writings on the emotions in antiquity, in Jerusalem, Athens, and Rome (the three roots of Western civilization), to realize that the emotions have a history. They are commonly differently conceived and differently evaluated in different times and places. The extensions of *ahava*, *eros*, *philia*, *agape*, *amor*, and *concupiscentia* are not the same, nor do these terms coincide *exactly* with our concept of love, let alone with our conception of it (see chapter 10 and Appendix). Pride is a meritorious emotion and attitude of the Aristotelian great-souled man, but the deadliest of sins for the Christian (chapter 5). Shame, but not guilt, is a dominant emotion in the heroic warrior cultures depicted in the *Iliad* and in the Norse sagas, but the role of guilt, repentance, and redemption dominate Jewish and Christian cultures (chapter 6). It is, I believe, important to view the concepts of our various emotions, and indeed our emotions as we conceive them, as features of our culture and products of history. For we shall then realize that emotional phenomena may be, have been, and are differently conceived and understood in different cultures and different times. Very different forms of life rest upon the biological substrate of animal emotion. Consequently, cultural history, in addition to the history of philosophy, plays a far greater role in this book than in its predecessors.

Part I of this volume 'Sketching the Landscape' prepares the ground for the investigation of individual emotions. It presents a *distinct idea* of the emotions in chapter 1 by differentiating them from passions in general, affections, and appetites, as well as from agitations, moods, and sentiments. It delineates a *clear idea* of the emotions in chapters 2 and 3, which advance a detailed connective analysis of the concept of emotion. The fourth chapter, 'The Dialectic of the Emotions', investigates and rectifies salient misconceptions, misunderstandings, and misconstruals of the emotions by philosophers, psychologists, and cognitive neuroscientists. Part II, 'Human, All Too Human', examines a selection of individual emotions: pride, arrogance, and humility; shame, embarrassment, and guilt; envy and jealousy; and anger. Part III, 'The Saving Graces', investigates love, friendship, sympathy, and empathy. Why just this selection? It was obviously impossible to examine the whole range, or even the larger part of the range, of human emotions in one book. So selection was unavoidable. It was guided partly by philosophical considerations, and partly by my own puzzlement and curiosity. Pride, arrogance, humility, shame, embarrassment, and guilt are distinctively human emotions of self-assessment. They have been the subject of moralizing and philosophical reflection for more than two thousand years and are intrinsic features of human nature. Their discussion in a work of philosophical anthropology was imperative, and they enabled me to at least touch on a battery of related emotions, such as contempt, regret, remorse, and repentance. Envy and jealousy seemed to me to be two terrible emotions to which human beings are subject. Like arrogance, they destroy the soul of those they hold in their grip. Their differentiation appears to be increasingly difficult for the younger generation today – and so they seemed good candidates to exemplify what is, alas, human, all too human. Anger, and its cousins, rage and annoyance, are the most 'animal' of the emotions I chose to examine. I could equally well have chosen fear (and its cousins, terror, trepidation, and anxiety). Love, feelings of friendship, sympathy, and empathy are investigated in chapters 10 to 12. They are indeed the saving graces of human nature, mitigating our savagery and selfishness. They are sources of absolute value, and provide the roots of morality. Their investigation is necessary for any comprehensive study of human nature. There are many other emotions I should have liked to examine, but considerations of length were a constraint. I hope that the methods of investigation evident in this book will help others to explore, describe, and disentangle the networks of emotions that I have not discussed. Pleasure and happiness are marked by their absence. But they are not emotions. So they will be examined only in the sequel.

This book, *The Passions: A Study of Human Nature*, as its title intimates, is a study in *philosophical anthropology*. The latter term, known to anyone who has studied Kant, is not common in Anglo-Saxon philosophy. That is unfortunate, since it is needed. The subjects studied here and in the previous two volumes of this sequence of essays on human nature encompass much more than can be subsumed under the heading of philosophy of mind or philosophical psychology. The current book is the third in the series that began with the publication in 2007 of *Human Nature: The Categorial Framework*. That examined the most general categorial concepts in terms of which we conceive of ourselves and of the world in which we live: substance, causation, powers and abilities, agency, teleology and teleological explanation, reasons and rational explanation of action, mind, self, body, and person. The second volume, *The Intellectual Powers: A Study of Human Nature*, was published in 2013. It presupposed the results of the first volume, but was designed to be read quite independently of it. In the prolegomenon, it investigated the concepts of consciousness, intentionality, and mastery of a language, which completed the stage-setting for the examination of human cognitive powers – knowledge and belief, sensation and perception, and memory – which was followed by investigations of our cogitative powers, namely thought and imagination. It was my intention to complete the task I had set myself in a third volume, which I prematurely announced as *The Moral Powers: A Study of Human Nature*. It was to fall into three parts: the passions; axiology and human identity, i.e. the roots of value and the nature of good and evil, character, temperament, and personality; the *summum bonum* – happiness and the meaningful life, and the place of death in life. As I began my work on the emotions, it rapidly became clear that this plan was unrealistic if the project was to be implemented in the manner I wished. So what was intended to be a trilogy would have to be a tetralogy.

This volume, like the previous one, can be read independently of its predecessors. There is nothing here that is unintelligible without knowledge of the first two books. But the results of the previous investigations are presupposed. If a reader wishes to find the reasoning that underpins any controversial claim that is here taken for granted, cross-references to the first and second volumes are given. As in the previous volumes, I have supplied many tables, lists, and diagrams to illustrate the conceptual networks that I trace. The diagrams are not substitutes for the argument of my text, but rather offer rough pictorial representations of distinctions drawn and connective analyses elaborated. They have the merit that they can be taken in at a glance, but they do not aspire to the accuracy of the analyses they illustrate. As in the second volume of the series, I have inserted italicized marginalia to facilitate surveyability, to make it easier to follow the argument, and to assist the reader in locating topics discussed.

I hope to be able to complete this tetralogy on human nature. It was planned as a very large fresco, and I should be sorry to leave it unfinished. But only time will tell whether I shall be able to do so, or whether I have left things too late.

P. M. S. Hacker
November, 2016

# Acknowledgements

Friends, colleagues, acquaintances, and ex-students have aided and encouraged me in writing this book. Conversations with them were wonderful, blending acute criticism and helpful advice, with frequent digressions, all punctuated with much laughter and merriment.

I am grateful to Hanoch Ben-Yami, Aaron Ben-Ze'ev, John Cottingham, David Ellis, Alessandra Fussi, Edward Greenwood, Anselm Mueller, Stephen Mulhall, Dennis Patterson, Amit Sa'ad, and Joachim Schulte, who all read one or more draft chapters and gave me comments, corrections, literary references, and suggestions for improvement. They saved me from numerous mistakes. Edward Greenwood generously permitted me to print three of his philosophical poems.

I am indebted to George Barton, Anthony Kenny, Iddo Landau, Parashkev Nachev, Thomas Oehl, Herman Philipse, Dan Robinson, and David Wiggins, who read many if not all of the chapters and gave me copious comments and criticisms. I benefited greatly from their acumen and scholarship, and their encouragement helped me more than I can say. Their questions steered me down pathways that I should otherwise not have trodden and these led me to insights I should otherwise not have attained.

Hans Oberdiek read the whole book as it was being written. His criticisms and advice were invaluable. I enjoyed many dozens of hours of conversation with him, which were not only instructive and constructive, but also wonderfully entertaining and heart-warming. Discussions with Hans always replaced puzzlement by enlightenment and confusion by clarity.

I am deeply grateful to the doyenne of students of the emotions, Gabriele Taylor. She read many of the chapters of the book and discussed them with me over delightful lunches. Her comments upon my drafts displayed the subtlety and sensitivity evident in her books, as well as the wisdom of her years.

A fragment of chapter 6 on shame and guilt was presented at the meeting of the European Philosophical Society for the Study of the Emotions in Edinburgh in July 2015. I benefited from the questions of the audience and from discussions with the participants. A greatly compressed version of a part of chapter 10 on love was presented at the University of East Anglia. A selection of material was presented in a series of graduate seminars at the University of Kent at Canterbury. I am grateful to the audiences for their queries and objections.

P. M. S. H.

## Philosophy

The table shining in the sun
Against dark foliage, called you and me
To talk of what it means to be
What we should do, what we should leave undone.

We talked till dusk made contours blurred.
At last our meditations reached
The bounds of sense that can't be breached,
And still we tried to find the saving word.

The word to dissipate the weight
That lies upon one's consciousness
To lift the burdensome distress
By making all that was entangled straight.

Once the mind's idols are destroyed
Without creating any new,
Then all is open to our view
The power of illusion rendered void.

Edward Greenwood

# PART I

## Sketching the Landscape

# 1

# The Place of the Emotions among the Passions

## 1. Passions, affections, and appetites

*Emotions and what we care about*  Emotions and moods are the pulse of the human spirit. They are both determinants and expressions of our temperament and character. They are tokens of our modes of engagement with the world and with our fellow human beings. Our frame of mind is moulded by our moods, which wash our experience with their pink, grey, or black colours. Our emotions reflect what we care about and what we are averse to, what is important to us and what does not matter to us. A life bereft of emotion would not be worth living, for it would be a life without love or affection, lacking joy and delight, wanting enthusiasm and excitement. It would be driven by arbitrary wants, inclinations, and natural appetites. It would be a life in which we encountered the works of nature and of man without awe or wonder, without curiosity or admiration. There can be no happiness without such emotions. It would also be a life without pity and compassion, grief and sorrow – a life immune to empathy and to human fraternity, and to recognition of the human condition.

There can be no creature with sensibility, desire, and a modicum of cognitive powers, *a fortiori*, no creature with powers of intellect and will, that is immune to emotions. For emotions are corollaries of vulnerability (fear and anxiety, hope and relief), of success and failure

*The Passions: A Study of Human Nature*, First Edition. P. M. S. Hacker.
© 2018 John Wiley & Sons Ltd. Published 2018 by John Wiley & Sons Ltd.

in the pursuit of goals (triumph and delight, frustration and disappointment), and of conflict (rage, anger, hostility). There could hardly be creatures that reproduce sexually and whose young require prolonged care that do not feel maternal and filial bonding and affection. Nor could there be social creatures with knowledge of good and evil that were not susceptible to such emotions as shame, guilt, and remorse.

*Animal emotions*     We share both appetites and emotions with beasts. But the emotions that can intelligibly be ascribed to beasts, both in their nature and in their objects, are limited by the expressive constraints of the animal's physiognomy and physique, and by lack of a language. Without either a tensed language or a language with means of temporal reference, there can be no current emotions conceptually and cognitively linked to the past (such as present remorse for a past misdeed) or to a specific time in the future (current fear of tomorrow's danger). Without a vocabulary of emotions and the apparatus of pronouns, there can be no consciousness of one's emotions, that is, realizing what emotions beset one – that one is irritated, is becoming increasingly excited, is ashamed. And, without that, the possibility of self-conscious assessment and control of one's emotions is beyond one's reach. There could be no second-order emotions, such as anger at one's humiliation, shame for one's fear, or embarrassment for one's ill-judged curiosity. Nor could there be any emotions of self-assessment, such as pride in one's achievements, guilt for one's sins, remorse for the wrongs one has done to others. In the domain of the emotions, as with all the faculties of man, mastery of a rich language distances the horizon of what is humanly possible far beyond anything that lies within the reach of other animals. It opens the doors of felicity – and of suffering unknown to other animals.

*Feelings*     Emotions are *feelings*. The things we call feelings constitute a curious melange of categorially disparate phenomena.[1]

Feelings include *physical sensations* – feeling pain, itches, and tickles as well as sensations of overall bodily condition, such as feeling well or ill, and *somatic sensations*, such as the feeling of a distended belly, of creaking joints, and of shortness of breath. The concept of feeling subsumes *tactile perception*, such as feeling the roughness of a surface, the warmth of a fire, the shape of an object. *Hedonic feelings* are feelings of pleasure and displeasure. There are *cogitative feelings*, namely feeling – that is, opining, having a hunch or intuition – *that*

---

[1] It should be noted that not all languages share such a ramifying and heterogeneous notion of feelings.

things are thus-and-so. There are *deontic feelings*, as when one feels that one *must* act thus-and-so. None of these will be discussed here.[2] What concerns us are the feelings associated with what were traditionally conceived to be *the passions of the soul* – a category that includes the emotions and much else besides.

*Passions of the soul*    This term of art has been used to signify all that can be contrasted with the 'actions of the soul'.[3] In early modern philosophy, it was understood to encompass all receptive, rather than active, psychological attributes. These were held to include the powers of perception, taken to be no more than forms of sensible receptivity. This both distorts many of the concepts of perception and the two-way powers exercised in voluntary perceptual activities (intentionally feeling shapes, textures, warmth and cold, as well as listening to and listening for, scrutinizing, observing, watching, examining, looking for, etc.)[4] and imposes too crude a dichotomy upon the psychological attributes of living creatures. It is more fruitful and illuminating to employ the word 'passions' as a quasi-technical term to subsume the *appetites* (hunger, thirst, lust, and addictions); *felt desires*, such as urges, cravings, and impulses; some *obsessions* (obsessive emotions and compulsive obsessions); and the *affections* (agitations, moods, and emotions) of a living being.[5] These are indeed passions rather than actions: we cannot voluntarily, intentionally, or deliberately feel hungry or thirsty, feel an urge or an impulse, be compulsively obsessed with something; nor can we recklessly, negligently, or inadvertently feel excited or amazed (agitations), cheerful or depressed (moods), angry or frightened (emotions). At the same time, it is true that we can sometimes suppress our passions or bring them under control by an effort of will and self-restraint.

---

[2] Feeling in general and tactile perception in particular were examined in *The Intellectual Powers: A Study of Human Nature* (Wiley Blackwell, Oxford, 2013), pp. 278–85; doxastic feelings were surveyed in the same book, pp. 114–19.

[3] The Greeks had no word equivalent to 'emotion'. The term they used was 'pathos', meaning 'that which happens to a person or thing'. Its extension was far wider than that of 'emotion'.

[4] For discussion of perception, see *The Intellectual Powers*, pp. 286–315.

[5] There are many other different uses of 'passion' in modern English, ranging in meaning from physical suffering ('the passion of Christ') to an overpowering emotion ('passionate grief') or outburst of such emotion ('passionate weeping'), and from a fit of rage ('to fly into a passion') or an amorous impulse ('a passionate desire to kiss her') to an enthusiasm for something ('a passion for chess') or a zeal in pursuit of a goal ('a passionate quest'). Someone of a passionate nature is excitable, temperamental, or emotional. A passionate lover is amorous, ardent, and hot-blooded.

We can moderate or even eradicate them through the exercise of reason. Sometimes we can enhance them or even engender them *indirectly* by voluntary thought or action. We can also cultivate, refine, and educate our sentiments and emotions. We shall discuss the relationship between the emotions and the will in chapters 2 and 3. Note that, while sensibility, intellect, and will are faculties of human beings, there is no faculty of the passions. That is no coincidence, since 'faculty' derives from the Latin *facultas*, meaning a power to do, which does not subsume susceptibilities, liabilities, passivities, or passions.

*The goal: a distinct idea of emotion*     The first task that must be undertaken in clarifying the concept of emotion is to locate it among the concepts of the passions thus construed, and to describe the differences between emotions and other passions. This will give us a distinct but not yet a clear idea of what an emotion is. We must describe the conceptual boundaries that distinguish the emotions from other affections, such as agitations and moods; from felt desires, such as urges and cravings; from obsessions and appetites; and also from *attitudes* (see fig. 1.1). Attitudes may be of different kinds. First, *subjective axiological judgements* of liking or disliking, approval or disapproval, being pleased or displeased. Secondly, *sentiments,* which are emotionally tinged beliefs or opinions. One may agree with the sentiments of another about the merits

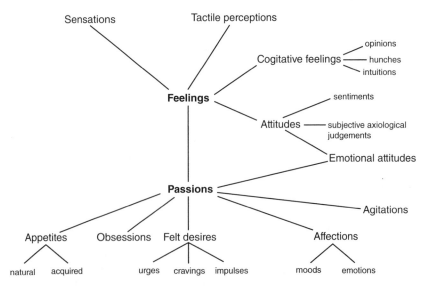

**Figure 1.1**  *The passions of the soul and their relation to other feelings*

of an object, plan, or policy but not about the truth of a mathematical theorem or law of nature. Thirdly, *emotional attitudes*, such as feelings of admiration or contempt, which differ both from mere affective judgements and from sentiments.

Appetites

The term 'appetite' (from the Latin *appertitus*) has different uses. Most generally, it is used to signify a desire to attain an object or to fulfil a purpose. Somewhat more restricted is its use to indicate an inclination, preference, liking to do, or fancy for, something. By extension, we may speak of having *no appetite* to pursue a given course of action, meaning an aversion to doing something or a reluctance to act – finding a course of action distasteful or perhaps even fearful. Much more narrowly, 'appetite' signifies hunger or desire for food, as when we speak of having a good or poor appetite, of 'working up an appetite before lunch' (meaning engendering hunger by vigorous exercise), and of 'loss of appetite' (signifying a disinclination to eat). Anything that 'whets one's appetite' stimulates one's desire for food – and by extension therefrom also signifies anything that makes one eager to enjoy something. However, here the expression will be used in a quasi-technical sense (sanctioned by usage) that is wider than mere hunger and narrower than a desire to attain a goal. Appetites – thus conceived – are common to both man and beast.

Natural and acquired appetites

*Natural appetites* are hunger, thirst, and – with qualifications – lust. *Acquired appetites* are material addictions – to alcohol and other depressants (opium, morphine), as well as to tobacco, caffeine, cocaine, and other stimulants.[6] Appetites are blends of sensations and felt desires (such as inclinations, urges, or cravings). The sensations characteristic of natural appetites have specific locations. The sensation that is partly constitutive of hunger is located in the midriff – one could not have a feeling of hunger in one's throat any more than one could have feelings of thirst in one's midriff. Constitutive feelings of hunger must be distinguished from mere accompanying sensations, such as a headache and dizziness that may occur as a consequence of lack of food. The sensation characteristic of thirst is a feeling of a dry throat. Sensations characteristic of appetitive lust are of

---

[6] Material addictions are to be contrasted with non-material addictions, such as an addiction to gambling. Non-material addictions are not appetites. The cravings of a drug addict will persist despite incarceration or hospitalisation. Not so the irresistible desire to gamble.

genital arousal. In general, the sensations associated with the appetites are *forms of unease* that dispose one to take action to satisfy the appetite and thereby to ameliorate the feeling of unease. (In the case of natural human appetites, the expectation of satisfaction of the appetite may be pleasurable. In this respect, they resemble human material addictions.) The intensification of appetitive sensations over time renders the appetite progressively more and more urgent and the craving more and more pronounced. Loss of appetites is associated with illness and old age.

*Objects of appetites*    The appetitive desire that is blended with sensation is specified or characterized by an infinitive grammatical object. To be hungry, thirsty, or lustful entails that one wants *to eat, to drink,* or to *attain sexual release*. To be hungry is to crave *food*, to be thirsty is to crave *drink*, and to be lustful is to crave *copulation* or *sexual release*. These are the *formal* objects of the appetites. The formal object of V-ing is specified by a description which *must* apply if one V-s at all.[7] The connection between V-ing and its formal object is logical, not empirical. Trivially, one can produce the formal object of V-ing by modalizing the verb 'to V': only what is edible can safely be eaten, only what is perceptible can be perceived, and only what is imaginable can be imagined. Less trivially, only what is dirty can be cleaned, only what is damaged can be repaired, only what is liquid can be drunk.

What distinguishes desires characteristic of appetites from other kinds of desire or wanting is not merely the fact that they are blended with sensation, but also that they are *fully specified* by their formal object. One might say that they have no non-formal, 'material', object. Or one might say that there is no distinction between their formal and their material object. The child who announces that he is not hungry for the main course but only for the pudding is inadvertently making a grammatical joke. The adult, who announces that he is thirsty for a gin and tonic but not for a cup of tea is intentionally making one. Lust, however, straddles the divide between appetites and desires. For, unlike hunger and thirst, lust *may* have a specific object (a man may lust after a specific woman, as David lusted after Bathsheba, and a woman after a specific man, as Potiphar's wife lusted after Joseph).

---

[7] For discussion of this valuable medieval distinction, see A. J. P. Kenny, *Action, Emotion and the Will* (Routledge & Kegan Paul, London, 1963), pp. 189 ff. Note that the formal object of an action, desire, or emotion is not the same as an internal accusative (e.g. to dream a dream, to think a thought).

Here animal lust is transmuted into sexual desire directed at a particular *person* (see chapter 10).

The intensity and urgency of an appetite are typically proportional to the intensity of the sensations. Satisfying an appetite leads to its temporary satiation and so too to the disappearance of the sensation. Of course, the glutton may still want food but no longer because he is hungry, just as the drunkard may want a scotch but not to quench his thirst. Appetites are neither constant (as love may be) nor singular (as a desire such as wanting to see Naples before one dies perforce is). Rather, they are *recurrent* in the following sense: despite their satisfaction on a given occasion, they will, other things being equal, recur naturally some time later, when one becomes thirsty again, feels hungry or lustful again. Appetites are caused by physiological conditions that are typically concomitants of bodily needs (or, in the case of lust, by hormonally determined drives) consequent upon deprivation of food, drink, copulation, or sexual release. Nevertheless, the felt need for food, drink, or copulation is not the same as wanting it.[8] Non-natural appetites are similarly caused by physiological changes consequent upon habitual consumption of the addictive substance. When the agent successfully takes action to satisfy his appetite, the desire is sated and the sensation of hunger, thirst, or lust, or the craving for the addictive substance, ceases for a time, only to recur if deprivation is prolonged.

The teleology and evolutionary warrant of the natural appetites is obvious. Hunger and thirst have the patent purpose of driving the animal to eat and drink for its own preservation. Without animal lust for copulation the species could not survive. Human beings may be moved to eat, drink, and copulate from appetite alone – from hunger, thirst, and lust. But they may also be moved by regular habit, on the one hand, and by acquired tastes and preferences, on the other. In this way the appetites are transformed into ordinary desires with specific objects. Refinement of the natural appetites is characteristic of civilized societies, hence the cultivation of cuisine and culinary taste, of connoisseurship regarding artificial beverages, and of the transmutation of lust into sexual desire and erotic love, on the one hand, and into the erotic refinements of love-making, on the other.

The criteria for being hungry, thirsty, or lustful,
*Criteria for an appetite*    or for craving alcohol or an addictive drug do

---

[8] For detailed examination of needs and their relationship to wants, see *Human Nature: the Categorial Framework* (Blackwell, Oxford, 2007), pp. 130–7.

not lie in expressive behaviour, bodily mien, or facial expression. One does not jump with hunger, as one may jump for joy; cringe with thirst, as one may cringe in terror; or smile with lust, as one may smile with tender love. The criteria for having an appetite are the appropriate conative behaviour of *trying to get*. The criteria for being possessed by an appetite – being in a frenzy of hunger, thirst, or lust – are constituted by single-minded conative behaviour to attain the object of one's appetite, and distinctively greedy behaviour in satiating one's appetite, as when one ravenously falls upon food, slakes one's thirst without pause for breath, or sates one's lust 'like an animal', as soldiers are prone to do in the sack of a city when on a rampage of rape. Satisfaction of an urgent appetite, unlike fulfilment of ordinary wants, is manifest by feelings and behavioural expressions of *relief*.

*Obsessions*    Being possessed by an appetite has an obvious kinship with *obsessions*. However, obsessions do not display the pattern of occurrence, satiation, and recurrence characteristic of the appetites. They are not bound up with bodily located sensations after the manner of the appetites. They have a non-formal, material, object in addition to a formal one. Obsessions may be *non-emotional* or *emotional*.

Obsessive collecting of Rembrandt prints, ancient Greek coins, or seashells is non-emotional. Similarly, an interest in philosophy, poetry, or genetics may become, and then be, obsessive. Though not emotional obsessions, they are likely to be emotion-involving, as is manifest in the excitement of the collector's pursuit, the joys of displaying one's collection, the delight in sharing one's enthusiasm for a subject with others. The distinctive features of non-emotional obsessions are the single-mindedness of the obsessive pursuit, the intensity and extent of the preoccupation in thought and imagination, the strength of the desire to pursue the interest, and the lengths to which one will go to engage in the obsessive activity or to attain the goal of the obsession.

Obsessive hatred, jealousy, or guilt are emotional obsessions. An emotion becomes obsessive when the agent is *invaded* by recurrent thoughts, mental images, recollections, and fantasies concerning the object of his emotion. The obsessive emotion occupies one's mind, driving out one's customary concerns and projects. This is manifest, for example, by Othello's crying out in his agony of obsessive jealousy:

> O, now for ever
> Farewell the tranquil mind! farewell content!
> Farewell the plumed troops, and the big wars
> That makes ambition virtue! O, farewell!
>
> (III. 3)

Obsessions may be directed at a person (an obsessive preoccupation with an acquaintance, with a celebrity, or with a past historical figure), a class of persons (the Nazis' obsessive anti-Semitism), a topic (an obsession with ancient history, the philosophy of Kant, or the novels of Jane Austen or with the study of barnacles (Darwin) or fleas (Miriam Rothschild)), a pursuit (collecting stamps or memorabilia, balletomania, footballomania), or an activity (gambling, playing chess or golf, running, or mountain climbing). Obsessions may be harmless and even laudable, or irrational and deleterious (sometimes involving ingrained prejudices and stereotyped thought, understanding, and interpretation that guide and pervert one's life). As obsessions become increasingly compulsive, they verge on the pathological. Carried to extremes, they involve obsessive–compulsive and ritualized behaviour, on the one hand, and pathological monomania, on the other. By and large, pathological obsessions are defects of intellect and will.

*Appetites and cravings*       Appetites have a kinship to cravings. A recurrent craving for a specific food or drink is akin to an appetite, save for the fact that it has a specific object. Like hunger and thirst, such intense desires invade one, plague one, intrude upon one – driving all else from one's mind the more urgent they become. One is beset by longing for the object of the craving. Pregnant women are given to cravings. But, of course, one may crave for something non-recurrently, in which case one's craving is no more than an intensely felt desire.

One might wonder why the felt desire to sleep is not conceived to be an appetite. After all, it is marked by sensations of lassitude and weariness (which are sensations of overall bodily condition[9]), blended with an intense desire to rest, close one's eyes, and fall asleep. Like appetites, the desire to sleep forces itself upon one. Like appetites, the constitutive desire (to sleep) is sated by its satisfaction, and the characteristic feeling (of weariness) evaporates. Like appetites, the desire to sleep is recurrent. For all that, it is not an appetite for two reasons. First, little if any conative behaviour of *trying to get* is involved (other than lying down or demanding quiet). Secondly, the desire to sleep involves no impulse *to act* but rather a desire to *cease* acting and to rest.

*Urges*       Similarly the felt desire to void one's bladder or bowels, despite its pattern of onset, satisfaction, relief, and recurrence, is not an appetite but an urge. Urges are inhibited felt desires. An inhibited appetite, when it becomes intense, *is* experienced as an urge

---

[9] See *The Intellectual Powers*, pp. 262–5.

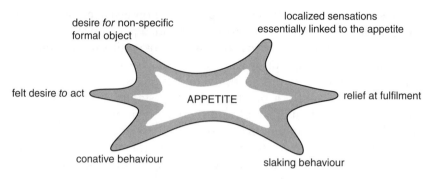

**Figure 1.2**    *Conceptual links of appetite*

to drink or eat, or as an urge to copulate or find sexual release. But there are numerous non-appetitive urges too. Some may be completely inhibited by self-control (the urge to strike another who has insulted one) or may be inhibited for a while (the urge to void one's bladder) or only for a few moments, as when one feels and finally succumbs to an urge to yawn. Sometimes they cannot be inhibited for more than a few moments despite one's best efforts, as when one tries in vain to hold back a sneeze. For a schematic representation of the conceptual links of appetite, see figure 1.2.

*Attitudes*   Attitudes, as noted earlier, may be *sentiments* – emotionally tinged beliefs, *subjective axiological judgements* – such as liking or disliking, approving or disapproving, or may be *emotional attitudes*, such as respect or contempt. Like other passions, attitudes are felt. Unlike sensations, they are neither somatically located feelings nor feelings of overall bodily condition. Unlike tactile perceptions, they are neither the upshot of the exercise of a cognitive faculty nor the result of cognitive receptivity. They have a kinship with cogitative feelings (hunches, opinions, intuitions) inasmuch as they are kinds of judgement. Emotional attitudes are estimative judgements infused with emotion, as sentiments are beliefs tinged with emotion. Emotional attitudes include respect, admiration, and reverence for another, as well as disdain, contempt, and hostility. Their objects may be individual human beings or classes of individuals, living things, the natural world, the artefacts of man, institutions, or doctrines. Emotional attitudes lay a claim to objectivity in so far as their grounds are alleged attributes of their object that are conceived to warrant the attitude. They persist or endure for a time, but, lacking what Wittgenstein called *genuine duration* (as opposed to mere duration), they are not mental states or states of mind. In so far as dispositions, pronenesses, and tendencies are defined by reference to what they are dispositions, pronenesses, and tendencies *to do*, emotional attitudes are clearly not dispositions. They are logically linked with reasons for feeling respect or contempt, admiration or disdain, rather than with categories of acts or actions that manifest a disposition. Those reasons may also provide reasons for behaviour motivated by the emotional attitude. One's contempt for someone may lead one to vote against that person, if he is running for an office for which one is an elector, but not voting for him is not contemptuous behaviour. One's respect for another may underlie one's trust in him, but trusting another is not the actualization of a disposition to respect.

*Affections*   Affections, like sensations, felt desires (urges, cravings, and impulses), and appetites, are *felt*. One feels love or hate (emotions), startled or astonished (agitations), cheerful or depressed (moods). Unlike localized physical sensations (pains, tickles, itches) and somatic sensations (of heartbeat, distended belly, tense muscles), affections do not have a bodily location and do not, save *per accidens*, inform one of the state of one's body (or what has impacted on it), even though they are sometimes linked with sensations. One does not feel pride in one's chest, although one's chest may 'swell with pride' and one may be 'bursting with pride'. One does not feel fear in one's mouth, even though one's mouth may feel dry with fear. If characteristic sensations are integrated with affections, then, unlike physical and somatic sensations, they do not, save *per accidens*, inform one of the state of one's body. One's blush of shame does not inform one of the state of one's facial arteries, although it may inform one that one is more ashamed than one thought. One's tears of grief do not inform one of the state of one's lachrymal glands, although they may inform one that one loved the deceased more than one thought. Unlike feelings that are perceptions (tactile feelings), the affections do not inform one about the world around one. They are not sources of knowledge of our environment but presuppose, or incorporate, knowledge or belief concerning the world. They are forms of response to what we perceive, know, or believe about the world around us and about ourselves. As in the earlier examples, they can be sources of knowledge about ourselves. The form of knowledge, in such cases, is realization.

The term 'affection' is here used as a term of art. Like 'passions', it has both a wide technical use and a variety of common or garden uses. Widely used, it coincides with the traditional wide use of 'passion' to signify the varieties of ways in which a human being (or beast) may be psychologically affected. In its common uses, it signifies a favourable or kindly disposition towards a person or thing, hence fondness, tenderness, and warmth of attachment. It will be used here in a narrow technical sense to signify a subcategory of the passions.

The feelings that are affections can be divided into *agitations*, *moods*, and *emotions*. The boundary lines between these are not sharp. Unlike perceptions, they often occur in blends: astonishment and joy, surprise and anger, and excitement and hope are common blends of agitation and emotion. Grief-laden depression, guilt-ridden gloom, and morose jealousy are blends of mood and emotion. Fear and anger, joy and love, hatred and rage, and shame and guilt are common blends of paired emotions. Moreover, a mood may transmute into an emotion, as when a vague anxiety is transformed into a determinate fear; an emotion into a mood, as when grief grows into depression; one emotion into another, as when affection grows into love; and an emotion into a persistent emotional attitude, for example anger with another into hostility, and disappointment in another's lack of good faith into distrust. Nevertheless, the distinctions are useful, even though they often have to be qualified by 'may be' and 'for the most part'.

## 2. Agitations and moods

*Agitations*     Agitations are short-term affective disturbances, typically caused by change, often by something unexpected. They include such affective responses as feeling thrilled, shocked, convulsed, amazed, surprised, startled, horrified, revolted, disgusted, or delighted. These too, like appetites, are commonly, but injudiciously, assimilated to emotions. Agitations are immediate consequences of what we perceive, come to know, or realize (or think we do). Because they are disturbances – often unanticipated disruptions that intrude upon us – they do not involve motives for action, as many emotions do, but rather temporarily *inhibit* motivated action. One may behave in certain ways *because* one feels startled, thrilled, or shocked. But one does not act *out of* thrill, shock, or being startled as one acts out of love, compassion, or gratitude. One may be *motivated* by love or jealousy, by compassion or envy, but one cannot be motivated by horror, amazement, or delight. This requires a brief explanatory digression.

*Motivating and adverbial emotions*

Emotions are not themselves motives – motives are not felt, do not overcome one at a given time or place, and are not pleasant or unpleasant, as many emotions are. Nevertheless, some emotions involve motives for acting, for example gratitude, jealousy, hatred, fear, and love. They involve motives in so far as the reason for the emotion and the reason for action it furnishes fit a general pattern of backward- and forward-looking reasons constitutive of a motive.[10] The backward-looking reason for gratitude is a benefit conferred upon one, which provides a forward-looking reason for thanking the benefactor in order that he may recognize one's gratitude – so 'acting out of gratitude' describes a motivated act. So too in cases of acting out of remorse (commission of an offence, wishing one had not committed it, acting to make good the evil done) or acting out of fear (something threatening and a good reason for avoiding or removing it). Similar patterns are displayed by jealousy, envy, and pity. However, emotions such as hope, despair, sadness, grief, shyness, and embarrassment do not provide motives, even though one may do something *with* hope, *in* despair, *out of* embarrassment – for in these cases there is no determinate pattern of backward- and forward-looking reasons. Rather, these emotions are manifest in the *manner* of acting – and might be deemed *adverbial emotions*.

*Criteria for agitations*

Agitations are made manifest by distinctive *modes of reaction*: one cries out *in* horror or amazement, recoils *with* revulsion or *in* disgust, is convulsed *with* laughter or paralysed *with* shock. They have characteristic forms of behavioural manifestation. These may be facial expressions, such as the wide-eyed look of alarm, amazement, surprise, wonder, the grimace of revulsion or disgust. They may be gestures – the open arms of delight, withdrawn arms of alarm, the open hands of surprise or amazement. They may be vocal exclamations, such as cries of delight and glee, and shrieks of excitement and thrill. They encompass more global behaviour, such as shrinking with revulsion or in disgust, jumping when startled, or prancing with delight. These various forms of affective reaction, in an appropriate context, constitute criteria for

[10] For discussion of motives, see *Human Nature*, pp. 162–3, 218–19; Kenny, *Action, Emotion and the Will*, ch. 4; and A. R. White, *The Philosophy of Mind* (Random House, New York, 1967), pp. 135–42, 163–4.

ascribing the agitation to a person. Of course, what in one context is a shriek of excitement or thrill (children on a helter-skelter) may in another context be a shriek of alarm or fright. What corresponds among the emotions to agitations will be denominated 'emotional perturbations'. Emotional perturbations are manifest in the clenched fists and frown of anger, the cries of joy, or the trembling of fear. We shall discuss emotional behaviour in chapter 2.

Agitations may transmute into long-standing *emotional attitudes* and *sentiments*, for example, of finding something revolting or offensive, having previously been revolted or offended by it. One may have been awe-struck by something sublime in nature, and this immediate response may give rise to the sentiment that it is awe-inspiring. One's palpable shock at encountering exceedingly shabby behaviour may yield to the sentiment that what shocked one is contemptible. Similarly, delight at good news commonly modulates into a mood of cheerfulness or into a feeling of gratitude. These are no longer agitations or disturbances.

Yet another form of affection that differs from emotion is
*Moods*   a *mood*. Feeling cheerful, jovial, or euphoric; feeling happy, contented, or tranquil; feeling bored, irritable, morose, melancholic, or depressed are moods. They contrast with agitations in various ways. They do not *need* any determinate object.[11] One can feel happy or cheerful without being happy or cheerful *about* anything, but one cannot feel surprised or alarmed without being surprised at something or alarmed by something. One may feel depressed or bored without being depressed or bored by anything in particular, but one cannot feel amazed without being amazed by anything. It is important not to confuse the cause of a mood with an object of the mood. What puts one into a good or bad mood *need not* be an object of the mood. The good news that one does not have cancer may make one cheerful. One is *relieved* not to have cancer, but one is not cheerful *about* not having cancer. Nor is one cheerful (as opposed to relieved) *that* one has not got cancer – one is just very cheerful. Persistent pain often makes one irritable, but the pain is the cause, not *the object* of erupting irritation. A relaxed afternoon in the sunshine by the sea may put one into a tranquil mood, but one is not tranquil *about* the sun and the sea. It is sometimes suggested that, while to be depressed or cheerful is not to be depressed or cheerful about anything in particular, one is depressed or cheerful about everything.

---

[11] We shall refine the notion of the object of an emotion in chapter 2.

But this is to confuse the view of the world characteristic of the mood (rosy or black, joyful or gloomy) with a putative generality of objects of a mood.

A mood is a *state of mind* or *frame of mind*.[12] One may be in a state of melancholia – possessed by undirected angst or persistent depression, or in a jovial or relaxed frame of mind. Moods are associated with having a certain view of the world: a rosy, resigned, or grey outlook, or a dark and embittered one. Anxiety and worry (*Sorge*) descend upon one, enfolding one in dank mist. But joy is a suffusion of one's whole being, as memorably expressed in Coleridge's lines:

> Joy is the sweet voice, Joy the luminous cloud –
>     We in ourselves rejoice!
> And thence flows all that charms or ear or sight,
>     All melodies the echoes of that voice,
>     All colours a suffusion from that light.[13]

Moods *colour* one's thoughts and *pervade* one's reflections. Joyous moods limn our thoughts with the rainbow; dark moods make one prey to black thoughts and blacker feelings. Moods (like emotions) are exhibited in the *manner* in which one does what one does when in a given mood, for example, cheerfully, sadly, grumpily, miserably. They are evident in one's demeanour, facial expression, and tone of voice, as well as in one's manifest (and avowed) inclinations and disinclinations to act.

Of course, moods *may* have an object (signified by a 'nominalization-accusative' (see pp. 42–3)). One may feel depressed *that* war has broken out or depressed *at the prospect* of a war, that is, depressed that war is going to break out. One may be positively euphoric *at one's stunning success* – and one's euphoria may last for days. One's euphoria is a mood, but it does not lack an object – one is happy *that one has succeeded*. A mood that has an object may pervade one's mind no

---

[12] We have defined mental states by reference to the idea of *genuine duration*, i.e. they obtain only during one's waking life, and cease with sleep or loss of consciousness, they admit of degrees of intensity, they may wax and wane, they are interruptible by distraction of attention, they can be resumed after interruption, and so on. (For elaboration, see *The Intellectual Powers*, pp. 164–8, pp. 227–30.) States of mind may be distinguished from mental states by their approximation to frames of mind. The latter not only have 'genuine duration' (and not merely duration), but they are also cogitatively invasive and colour one's outlook.

[13] Coleridge, 'Dejection: an Ode', stanza 5.

less than an objectless mood. Directed anxiety about one's kidnapped child (e.g. Mrs Trevelyan in Trollope's *He Knew He Was Right*) – designated by an 'object-accusative' – may take over one's inner life (one's thoughts and one's imagination, one's zest for life, and one's interests) no less than objectless angst.

*Mood with object compared with emotion with object* What then differentiates a mood with an object from an emotion with an object? Romeo's passionate love pervades his thoughts and occupies his imagination, but it does not gild the world as he views it *with love*. Obsessive emotions, such as Othello's jealousy, approximate moods in their invasiveness. But they still differ from moods in so far as they do not determine a frame of mind or outlook upon the world. Othello's agony does not suffuse everything he views *with jealousy*. What they commonly do is engender an all-pervasive mood, such as good cheer and a general feeling of benevolence (Pierre Bezukhov, on realizing that he is in love with Natasha) or profound depression (the upshot of Othello's jealousy and Macbeth's guilt).

*Moods as occurrent or dispositional states* The relation of mood to temporality differs from that of agitations and emotions. One may be surprised or amazed for a second or two, revolted or disgusted for a minute. One may feel a pang of jealousy or envy, a sudden flash of anger or annoyance, a momentary thrill of fear or wave of despair.[14] But one cannot feel cheerful or bored for a moment, jovial or melancholic for a minute, let alone feel a sudden flash of tranquillity. Moods must last for a while. We distinguish between occurrent moods, which are *states of mind* with genuine duration, and moods that are longer-term *dispositional states*.[15] One may feel depressed for an afternoon, but one may suffer from a depression that lasts for months. A piece of good news may

---

[14] But there are exceptions. Love is an emotion, but one cannot feel a flash of love or love someone *for* a moment, although one may fall in love *in* a moment. For love is a persistent emotion, not a momentary or passing episodic mental state (see chapter 10).

[15] The term 'dispositional state' may seem an oxymoron. How can something be both a state (an actuality) and a disposition (a potentiality)? Well, that is the concept we have. We speak of being *in* a depression or *in* low spirits for weeks, or of being *in* a cheerful mood for some days. Dispositional states are not *mental* states since they lack genuine duration. They are standing and persistent pronenesses to be in a given mental state during hours of wakefulness. The dispositional state of being in a prolonged depression is to be distinguished from the general disposition to depression.

make one feel cheerful for the whole afternoon, or one's good mood may last a few days. As a dispositional state, a mood is a disposition to feel, say, joyful, depressed, or cheerful during one's waking hours, and a proneness to respond in, say, a joyful, depressed, or cheerful manner to the people and events one encounters. Because moods guide one's thought down characteristic tracks, they are manifest in the tenor of one's expressed thoughts and judgements. Because they colour one's thought, they also affect one's inclinations and disinclinations to act and one's acceptance of something as a good reason for acting. Those who feel cheerful or joyful are prone to engage in sociable activities; those who feel melancholic and depressed are more likely to eschew company, picnics, parties, and so forth.

*Mood, temperament, and character trait*

It is unsurprising that names of moods may also serve as names of temperament, as when one is said to have a cheerful or melancholic temperament. A cheerful person is *normally* in a cheerful mood, just as a melancholic person is *normally* gloomy. It is striking that *a moody person* is one who is prone to be in a melancholic mood, to be irritable or glum, but not one who is disposed to be in a cheerful or jovial mood. Character traits are different from this: an irascible person is not someone who is normally irate, a timorous person is not someone normally frightened, and a compassionate person is not one normally engulfed by waves of compassion. Names of temperament, when they are also names of moods, signify tendencies or pronenesses. Names of traits of character, when they are also emotion names, more commonly signify liabilities and susceptibilities.

*Reasons and causes of moods*

Moods have reasons that are also causes, reasons that are not (Humean) causes, as well as overt causes that are not reasons. As noted, good news may put one into a good mood, just as bad news may engender a melancholic or depressed mood. 'What makes you so cheerful?', 'Why are you in the dumps today?', or 'What has made you so miserable?' are questions we commonly ask our friends and family. They typically respond by saying: 'I'm feeling so cheerful because we won', or 'I'm in the dumps because my girlfriend has jilted me', or 'I'm feeling miserable because I failed'. Such answers specify the cause of one's mood in a perfectly decent, common or garden sense of 'caused' or 'made happen'. It is an explanatory relation. An antecedent event is identified as the cause of one's lapsing into the mood one is in, although there need be nothing nomological about this sequence. However, in these cases the answer to the question of what *made* one feel as one feels specifies something that is also (one thinks) a *warrant* or *justification* for feeling thus-and-so. One's answer normally makes it *rationally intelligible* why one is in the mood one is in. Failing a major examination or being jilted by one's girlfriend is a *good reason* for feeling low. Here one mentions a factor that is both a cause (inasmuch as it *made* one feel thus-and-so) and one's reason for feeling so-and-so. It is one's reason not for acting or for thinking, but for feeling as one does. That what makes one feel thus-and-so or puts one into such-and-such a mood is *one's reason* is further evident from the fact that one's mood will normally evaporate as soon as one hears or discovers that what made one feel melancholic or depressed is no longer so, or, indeed, was never in fact so at all. In the latter kinds of case, one will have recourse to the explanatory pattern: 'I was depressed because *I thought that* ...'.

In other kinds of case, one's reason for being in a given mood is not an *antecedent cause* of one's mood. For one's reason for being in a buoyant mood may be a future event. Jack's reason for feeling so cheerful may be Jill's prospective arrival, but *that Jill is going to arrive tomorrow* is not the (Humean) cause of Jack's now feeling buoyant. Nevertheless, it would be perfectly correct to say that what is making Jack feel so cheerful is that Jill is going to arrive tomorrow. This reflects the pliability of our notion of making things happen and the multifaceted character of our concept of a cause.[16]

There are causes of moods that are independent of any reasons for feeling as one feels. A persistent pain or a woman's menstrual period commonly engender an irritable mood. One is not irritated *at* the nagging pain but prone to become irritated at some nuisance that intrudes upon one. One may, but need not, be aware that one's mood is caused by one's condition. In the right circumstances and in the right company, alcohol is apt to make one feel jocose (and in the wrong company or in solitude, morose). Such causes of moods are not one's reasons or justifications, although they may well be cited to excuse or explain one's irritable or jocular mood (fig. 1.3).

---

[16] For detailed examination of the multifocal character of the concept of causation, see *Human Nature*, ch. 3. To be sure, a causal theorist may argue that although one's reason – namely *that Jill is going to arrive* – is no cause, it is one's mental state of believing that she is going to arrive that is the mental cause of one's feeling. But believing is not a mental state (see *The Intellectual Powers*, pp. 227–32). Moreover, it is not *the believing* but *what is believed* that makes Jack cheerful. For a general discussion of reasons and causes, see *Human Nature*, pp. 226–30.

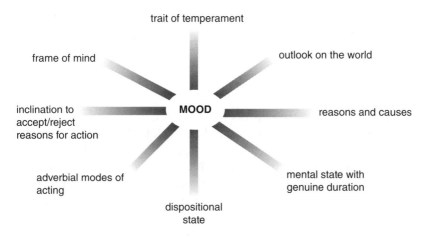

**Figure 1.3**  *Conceptual links of moods*

Of course, all moods are dependent on a neurological substrate without which one would not be in the mood one is in. Low levels of serotonin in the brain, which can be caused by dietary deficiency, are prone to cause depression. But equally, encountering something that is a good reason for feeling sad and depressed, such as bereavement, is prone to cause a fall in serotonin levels. It would be an egregious error to suppose that a reductive physiological explanation of mood could replace explanations in terms of reasons and justifications.

*Epistemology of moods* One normally has non-evidential knowledge of what put one into such-and-such a mood or what made one feel so cheerful, joyful, or depressed. In such cases, the cause of one's mood is also one's reason for being in the mood. However, one's knowledge is not infallible – one may be wrong about the reason one is moody. It may not be the unwelcome letter one received this morning that made one so depressed, but rather the harsh words one's wife or husband said yesterday evening or their failure to congratulate one for some noteworthy achievement, which upset one. The letter may occasion irritation, but the root cause of one's irritability is yesterday's distress and resultant low spirits. This is something others may notice and they may then correct one.

*Moods and the will* Not only may one err in identifying what put one into such-and-such a mood, but one may not even be aware of what brought it about. Others may notice that one has been cheerful or depressed ever since one heard that things are thus-and-so, even though one did not oneself realize this. Nevertheless, one may acknowledge the reason when it is pointed out to one. In other kinds of case, one may be in a given mood 'for no reason at all' – one may just feel low and depressed, or wake up feeling cheerful and eager to face another day. It does not, of course, follow that one's mood has no cause. It may well have a physi-ological cause.

The connection between moods and the will is importantly differ-ent from that between emotions and the will. For emotions are bound up with reasons for action, with specific patterns of intentional action, and with motives. By contrast, moods merely incline or disincline one to actions of certain kinds. Hence the idiom 'I'm not in the mood for ...' and 'I feel like ...'. That one is feeling cheerful or depressed does not give one a reason for doing anything in particular, although it makes one more likely to accept or not to accept certain facts as reasons for one to do certain things or to adopt or reject certain goals (to go out as opposed to staying home, to invite guests for the evening, or to accept an invitation, and so on).

A mood may modulate into an emotion, as when objectless angst (a mood) crystallizes into determinate fear (an emotion). Conversely, an emotion may fade into a mood, as when a fit of anger (an emotion) leaves one depressed or irritable (moods).

## 3. Emotions

*Different classifications of emotions*    Emotions are neither appetites nor agitations or moods, although the boundaries separating these three categories are blurred. Paradigmatic emotions are fear, anger, gratitude, resentment, hatred, indignation, envy, jealousy, pity, compassion, grief, hope, excitement, pride, shame, humiliation, regret, remorse, and guilt. Love, as we shall see in chap-ter 10, is, in one sense, paradigmatic and, in another sense, atypical. Emotions can be variously classified. We may distinguish reflexive emo-tions, such as self-love, self-hatred, self-pity, and self-respect, from emotions that are not thus reflexive (including love, hatred, pity, and respect). We may differentiate emotions of self-assessment, such as pride, shame, guilt, and humiliation, from emotions that do not involve self-assessment. We may classify emotions as negative or positive, according as to whether one would (normally) prefer to feel such emo-tions (delighted, excited, overjoyed, contented, amused, affection), or prefer not to be subjected to them (feeling bored, envious, jealous, frightened, sorrow, embarrassed, humiliated). We may distinguish between emotions that we share with animals (anger, fear, expectation, affection, loneliness) and emotions that are unique to humanity (pride, shame, remorse, guilt, humiliation, nostalgia). We shall have occasion, later in this book, to examine some of these distinctions.

*Etymology of emotions*      As its etymology suggests, the idea of an emotion is linked with that of *being moved* by something. In its earliest occurrences in English in the sixteenth century the word signified political agitation, civil unrest, and commotion, a usage derived from the French *émouvoir* (to stir up). By the end of the sixteenth century, 'emotion' signified a movement of peoples, a disturbance of society, or a perturbation of the body. According to the *Oxford English Dictionary*, it was only in the early seventeenth century that it came to signify an agitation of the mind, an excited mental state, or passion. The etymological association between the idea of emotion and that of motion (and impact) is embedded in our descriptions of the causes of some of our emotional responses. A scene may be 'touching', a story 'moving', a song 'stirring', and a tragedy 'shattering'. We are *moved by* or *stirred by* emotion, both in being *perturbed* by what causes us to feel what we feel (a pitiful scene, a noise in the night, an offence) and in being *moved to* act by our feelings (of compassion, fear, anger). This is the *picture* we use, the form in which we present our emotions to ourselves.

*Emotions and the heart*      Just as we associate thinking with the head (we close our eyes and clutch our head when we think hard), so too we associate emotions with the heart (many emotional episodes are accompanied by a violent felt increase in our heartbeat, and we are prone to touch our chest when declaring our passion). This association is built into numerous cardiac idioms: we may be broken-hearted with unrequited or disprized love. We may be warm-hearted if we are naturally sympathetic to other people, or cold-hearted if we are indifferent to their sorrows, travails, and entreaties. We are light-hearted when cheerful, and have a heavy heart when we are the bearers or recipients of bad news. Our heart may overflow with tenderness and melt with love. Sincere emotions are said to be heartfelt, and to reveal one's emotional responses too readily is to wear one's heart on one's sleeve. Nevertheless, despite the fact that one may love a person *with* all one's heart, the heart is not an organ of emotion in the sense in which we see *with* our eyes, walk *with* our legs, and manipulate things *with* our hands. We use our eyes in order to see, but there is nothing we can do with our heart in order to love. To give one's heart to someone is not to do anything with one's heart but to bestow one's love upon another. To love someone with all one's heart is to love them without qualification or restraint. Similarly, the heart is not the locus of emotions, for, although one may indeed love someone with all one's heart, one does not feel love, let alone have a feeling of love, in one's heart, as one may feel a pain in one's chest.

*Emotions and what we care about*

What, if anything, characterizes the emotions? Why do we collect this underdetermined range of feelings under their rubric? They are, to be sure, affections – ways in which we are affected by what we perceive, know, or believe about things and what we perceive, know, or believe about ourselves. Like other affections, episodic emotions are non-voluntary *responses* to people, animals, and things that we encounter and to how we take things to be. They manifest our *sensitivity* or *insensitivity*, our *judgements* and *evaluations* concerning the people we encounter and the situations with which we are confronted, and our *responsiveness* in expressive behaviour. Unlike agitations, which are mere spontaneous reactions, *emotions exhibit what we care about*. Hence, unlike agitations, they are intimately linked, especially in the form of enduring or persistent emotions, with intentional action and motivation to attain, conserve, and protect what we care about, and to respond to or avoid what we are averse to and what is detrimental to what we care about. And that is also why they are loosely linked in manifold ways with the pleasant and unpleasant, with the distressing and the hurtful.[17]

It is pleasing to see what we care about well protected, and distressing to see it harmed. What we care about is internally related to what is important to us. It is natural to take joy in the flourishing of what we care about, and painful to see something important to us destroyed. Some emotions, such as affection, contentment, enthusiasm, amusement, relief, and satisfaction, are in themselves pleasant to experience. Others, such as jealousy, envy, anxiety, fear, terror, shame, embarrassment, and humiliation, are intrinsically unpleasant or worse. Yet others, such

[17] In the history of the analysis of the emotions, it was Plato who inspired this link between emotions, the pleasurable and the painful (see *Philebus*, 47ᶜ). Aristotle inherited the idea (with the qualification 'for the most part' or 'in general' (*Eudemian Ethics*, 1220ᵇ12). It was duly transmitted to Aquinas and to the early moderns. But they did not explain the association of pleasure and pain with the emotions by reference to the notion of *what we care about*.

as the epistemic emotions of wonder and curiosity, need have no direct link with such reflexive hedonic/anti-hedonic features.

*Emotions and motives*     As already observed, many emotion names are often also names of motives. We do things *out of* love or hatred, jealousy or envy, compassion or gratitude – these emotions providing us with *motives* for acting, that is, systematic *patterns* of backward- and forward-looking reasons. In displaying our emotional responses to people, things, and events around us, we reveal ourselves and our nature. We show what kind of person we are, for we show what we care about, how much we care about those things, what reasons move us, and what reasons move us to action. So it is unsurprising that some names of emotions also signify traits of character and personality. One may be a loving, affectionate, compassionate, or jealous person in so far as one has such feelings and is commonly moved by such motives. But one may be an irascible, shy, timid, and anxious person even though *these* emotion names do not signify motives but feelings linked to appropriate pronenesses, liabilities, or susceptibilities. Other emotion names, such as 'guilt', 'embarrassment', 'awe', 'dread', and 'ecstasy' do not signify character traits at all.

*Caring*     To care about something is to value it or to condemn, censure, or be otherwise averse to it in one axiological dimension or other. Not to care about something is to be indifferent to it. Animals who lack the capacity to care are animals without emotions. Human beings who are generally deficient in their emotional responses are deemed to be unfeeling, unemotional, passionless. They are held to be cold, impassive, detached, aloof, or stony. This is a fault of character, for it betokens not caring about what one *should* care about. To be emotional, however, is to be sentimental,[18] excitable, and temperamental. These traits too are considered to be character failings. They display caring to excess, or caring about the wrong kinds of thing, manifesting excessive emotion, or being affectedly effusive or maudlin. One may fail to control one's emotions in contexts where self-control is called for. We are sometimes overcome by emotion or are in the grip of passion, when we should be restrained. Where the heart overrides the head and feelings override the intellect, ill-considered judgement more often than not ensues. We shall discuss this further in the chapters that follow.

---

[18] To be sentimental, in contemporary usage, is, on the one hand, associated with sentimentality. In this sense it means being extravagantly, self-indulgently, effusively, or insincerely emotional. At the same time, it is associated with sentiment, in one of the senses of the word; thus used, it signifies being tenderly nostalgic.

Susceptibility to emotion is, in general, a corollary *Roots of emotions* of vulnerabilities, liabilities, and pronenesses – of the innate desire for self-preservation and the innate tendency to sympathize with others, on the one hand, and of the pursuit of goals that may or may not be achieved, on the other. For these are primitive roots of care and concern. All moderately developed animals care for their own physical safety. However, mere avoidance behaviour and threatening displays, as exhibited by fish and reptiles, for example, are insufficient for ascription of emotion in anything but the thinnest of senses. There are adequate grounds for ascribing emotions to a creature only to the extent to which its behavioural repertoire incorporates expressive behaviour, facial and vocal expressions of emotion appropriate to occasions that warrant an emotional response. The snarl of a dog exposing its fangs, coupled with stiffened tail and ears drawn back, is, in appropriate contexts of challenge, indicative of anger and aggression. Its wagging tail and desire to lick the hands or face of its master when being patted manifest affection. The closed eyes and purring of a cat signify contentment; the arched back, erect hair, laid-back ears, spitting, and hissing signify threat or fear.[19] Most carnivores display anger (or fear) when prevented from eating their prey. Territorial animals fight with ferocious rage to protect their domain. Most animals take care of, and manifestly care for, their young during the period of their dependency, will fight to death in order to protect them, and exhibit distress (primitive grief) at the death of their young. Animals that jointly rear their young bond. These responses to the circumstances of life are the primary animal roots of caring and, by the same token, of the most primitive emotions. Social animals have, to a greater or lesser degree, capacities for group bonding, and hence for primitive forms of affection that reaches beyond their mate or offspring. They stand in hierarchical social relationships and protect their status within their social group. Relatively few kinds of animals, apart from humans, have an innate capacity for the form of caring that is constituted by *sympathy*. This, as Adam Smith and David Hume saw clearly, is one root of morality.

Emotions differ from appetites. First, many emotions, *Emotions and* such as affection, gratitude, hope, pride, and regret, *appetites* have no distinctive link with sensations at all. Some *compared* emotional occurrences, such as flashes of anger or

[19] For what is still a classic description of animal emotion, see C. Darwin, *The Expression of the Emotions in Man and Animals* (John Murray, London, 1872).

thrills of fear, are indeed associated with distinctive sensations, but the connection with sensations differs from that between appetites and sensations. One does not feel fear in one's stomach in the sense in which one feels thirst in one's throat, even though one may feel butterflies in one's stomach. One does not have a feeling of anger in one's temples, heaving chest, or tight stomach muscles, as one has a feeling of hunger in one's belly. So emotions do not have a somatic location in the manner in which appetites do. One's fear, jealousy, or longing, no less than one's hunger, may be dreadful – but not because of the feeling in one's chest or stomach. *Those* feelings are not what is dreadful.

Secondly, emotions have formal objects that restrict the range of intelligible non-formal, material, objects of the emotion. Anything that can be feared, anything for which one can feel remorse, anything that one can envy, is a potential material object of the emotion. The formal object of an emotion is the characteristic that *must apply* or must *be thought (or known) to apply* to anything towards which one feels a given emotion. The formal object of an emotion restricts the range of its possible material objects. Or, to put the same point in the formal mode, the formal object limits what expressions may intelligibly occur as the direct objects of the emotion verb. So, for example, one fears what one thinks to be frightening, harmful, or dangerous – one cannot intelligibly (non-pathologically) fear flowers, grass, or leaves. What one feels remorseful about is a misdemeanour one has, or thinks one has, committed. One cannot feel remorse for what another has done or for something one is about to do. What one envies is something one believes to be a good that is another's. One cannot feel envious of another's misfortunes or of one's own good fortune. Unlike appetites, which have *only* formal objects, emotions can have an indefinite array of objects characterized by and subsumed under the formal object definitive of the emotion.

Thirdly, the intensity of emotions is not proportional to the intensity of whatever sensations may accompany their episodic manifestation. How much one fears heights may be evident not in the intensity of the perturbations one may feel when on a high building, but rather in the lengths one goes to avoid being on it. How proud one is of one's children's achievements on prize-giving day cannot be measured by reference to any sensations (no matter how thrilled one is).

Fourthly, emotions do not display the pattern of occurrence, satiation, relief, and recurrence characteristic of the appetites.

Fifthly, emotions have a cognitive dimension that is absent from the appetites. The hungry animal wants food, the thirsty animal wants drink, the animal in rut or in heat wants to copulate, but no particular knowledge or belief is essentially associated with these appetites. By contrast, the frightened animal is afraid of something it *perceives* or *thinks* to be dangerous; a mother is proud of her offspring, *believing* them to be meritorious; the repentant sinner is remorseful, *knowing* or *believing* himself to have sinned. This cognitive dimension of the emotions will be examined later.

Sixthly, and coordinate with the cognitive dimension of emotions, is the rational dimension. For emotions are rightly evaluated in terms of their rationality or reasonableness. One may have good or poor reasons for feeling angry with someone, for feeling regret, remorse, or guilt. The reasons are related to the subsumability of the material object of the emotion under the formal object that is constitutive of the emotion, as well as to the specific circumstances of the case. It is these that make certain emotions warranted or unjustified, reasonable or irrational. The rationality of emotions will be explored in chapter 3.

Finally, many emotions are exhibited by characteristic facial expression and manifest in typical tones of voice – as in the case of love and affection, fear, anger, or hatred. The appetites are not (see table 1.1).

|  | *Emotion* | *Appetite* |
|---|---|---|
| Locus | ✗ | ✓ |
| Non-formal object | ✓ | ✗ |
| Intensity proportional to sensation | ✗ | ✓ |
| Pattern of recurrence | ✗ | ✓ |
| Can occur in blends | ✓ | ✗ |
| Cognitive dimension | ✓ | ✗ |
| Characteristic facial and tonal expression | ✓ | ✗ |

Table 1.1 *A comparison between emotions and appetites (give or take borderline cases)*

*Temporary and enduring emotions*

Just as we distinguished between moods that occur on a given occasion (feeling cheerful this afternoon) and moods that are longer lasting dispositional states (as when one suffers from a depression), so too we must distinguish between *temporary emotions* and *persistent* or *enduring emotions* (see fig. 1.4). I shall use the term 'temporary emotion' to signify an emotional response on a given occasion to some actual or imagined person, object, event, state of affairs, or putative information that has come to one's attention, either by perception (or misperception) or by hearsay that informs (or misinforms) one, or that one imagines. We can distinguish two kinds of temporary emotions by reference to their duration. A temporary emotion may be *momentary* or *acute* like a flash of anger, a pang of envy, a flush of pride, or a sudden thrill of fear that immediately dissipates. Alternatively, a temporary emotion may *last for a while*. One may feel furious with another for some actual or imaginary slight and remain angry and ill-tempered for the rest of the afternoon. One may feel frightened or terrified by a present danger and cower in terror until it passes an hour or more later. One may feel proud of one's spouse throughout the whole celebratory dinner in his or her honour. I shall refer to such temporary but continuous emotions as *episodic*. These are restricted to emotions that are felt while awake and conscious but that cease on loss of consciousness. One feels no anger, fear, or pride while one is asleep). *Temporary emotions* (momentary and episodic alike) are to be distinguished from *enduring* or *persistent emotions*. The latter persist through periods of sleep – one does not cease to love one's beloved when one sleeps any more than one ceases to know or believe what one knows or believes

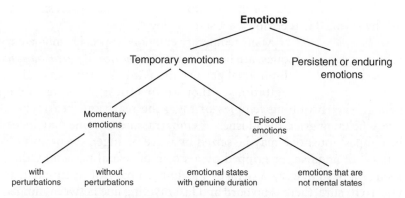

**Figure 1.4**  *Forms of emotion distinguished by temporality*

when one falls asleep). Enduring emotions may last for long periods of time, indeed, sometimes for a lifetime. A characteristic feature of enduring emotions, such as love, is that they develop over time (see chapter 10). The passion of youth develops, in a happy marriage, into the love of old age. Grief, initially unbearably intense, will gradually evolve into abiding sadness and a sense of loss that may, with time, modulate into sorrowful nostalgia. The trajectory of jealousy is commonly from doubts, suspicions, and anxieties over supposed infidelity, to anger and resentment at confirmed or supposedly confirmed infidelity, culminating *in extremis* in hatred (see chapters 7 and 8).

*Episodic emotions and mental states*    Among *episodic emotions* we must distinguish two kinds: *episodic emotions that constitute mental states*, as when one is in a state of anxiety over one's missing child all day, or excited all afternoon in anticipation of a party that evening, or bored all through a lecture. These are emotions with *genuine duration*. They obtain only when one is conscious; they commence, last for a while, and then terminate; they have degrees of intensity, and may wax or wane; they can be interrupted by diversion of attention and later resumed; they do not persist through sleep or loss of consciousness. These may be contrasted with *episodic emotions that are not mental states*, since they cannot, in the same sense, be interrupted by distraction of attention and later resumed. One may feel proud of one's child throughout a ceremony in his honour, but one cannot be said to be in a state of feeling proud, and one's feeling of pride cannot be said to be interrupted by distraction of attention. Similarly, one may envy another for some honour he receives at a ceremony one is attending, but one's feelings of envy cannot be said to be interrupted and later resumed in the way in which one's fear, boredom, or anxiety may be. Nor would one answer the question 'What kind of mental state is he in?' by saying 'He is envious/in a state of envy'.

*Momentary emotions and perturbations*    Many temporary emotions, especially momentary ones, are bound up with *emotional perturbations*. Emotional perturbations are disturbances akin to agitations – they are manifest in the trembling of fear, the throbbing temples of rage, the tears and heartache of overwhelming grief, the blushes of embarrassment. Some may indeed be tempestuous: one may be seized by wave of anger, swept away by a flood of anguish, or gripped by a storm of sexual passion. Others, such as a flash of envy, a twinge of jealousy, a pang of resentment, are not. To be sure, there is no hard and fast dividing line between momentary and episodic emotions.

Many episodic emotions involve (or need involve) no perturbations, for example, pride, contentment, curiosity, interest, wonder, trust, gratitude, and loneliness. Others may indeed involve perturbations in certain types of case but not in others. Becoming indignant or angry with someone who has insulted one typically involves perturbations, but becoming angry at what is said in an article in a newspaper or at a prime-ministerial announcement on the radio need not. Here the anger may be manifest in what one says ('That's outrageous') and does (writes a critical letter to *The Times*; resigns one's party membership) rather than in flushing red with anger, raising one's voice, shaking one's fist, and so forth.

It is primarily, but not only, temporary emotions that give rise to the stark, but often misleading, contrast between reason and the emotions (which will be discussed in chapter 3). Episodic emotions in particular (but also persistent ones) are associated with being emotional rather than rational, with an excess of sensibility and a deficiency of sense, with reckless, passionate reaction as opposed to thoughtful and measured response. In this respect, momentary emotions – *fits* of rage, *waves* of remorse or pity, *flashes* of jealousy – resemble agitations. Beset with such feelings, one may act or react spontaneously – without thinking – angrily, jealously, fearfully. By contrast, many episodic as well as persistent emotions, such as hatred, jealousy, sexual passion, and being in love, often *warp one's reason* and *distort one's judgement*.

*Persistent* emotions lack 'genuine duration'. They do not
*Persistent* lapse with loss of consciousness. So they are neither *mental*
*emotions* *states* nor *states of mind*. One may love or hate a person, an
activity, a cause, or a place for the whole of one's life. One may be proud of the achievements of one's youth or of one's children for the rest of one's days. One may be envious or jealous of a person (one's sibling, for example) for years (see fig. 1.4). One may fear for one's endangered family and friends for as long as the danger persists. One may be ashamed or guilty of one's misconduct for decades, and one's regret for one's follies may never cease. Although persistent emotions may *arise* out of emotional episodes, as when one's persistent fear of heights may originate in a particular episode of terror on a cliff face, they are not themselves such episodes. Can they, like persistent moods, be said to be *dispositional states*? It is tempting to think so. One might suppose that one's pride in one's children is a tendency *to feel proud* of them from occasion to occasion, that one's lasting remorse for some past misdeed is a proneness *to feel remorse*

from time to time, and that one's persistent jealousy of one's spouse's flirtatious relationship with another is a disposition *to feel jealous*. This is at best misleading, at worst quite mistaken.

It is misleading in so far as it suggests a sharp and perspicuous distinction between *being* angry, hopeful, frightened, or jealous, on the one hand, and *feeling* angry, hopeful, frightened, or jealous, on the other. But it is unclear whether there is any systematic difference between feeling angry and being angry, between feeling jealous and being jealous, or between feeling frightened and being frightened. Heathcliff's hatred lasted a very long time – does that imply that he hated Edgar and Isabella Linton as well as Hindley and Hareton Earnshaw for a long period, but felt hatred only from time to time? Othello and Swann were in the grip of persistent jealousy – does that mean that they were jealous for a prolonged period, but felt jealous only when awake and thinking of the woman they loved? There is a temptation to think so, but it should be resisted. We may say indifferently, 'A feels very angry with B' or 'A is very angry with B', 'A feels frightened of B' or 'A is frightened of B', and 'A feels pity for B' or 'A pities B'. Perhaps the phrases 'feels frightened/angry/pity' more readily invite the question 'What makes one feel …?', whereas the phrases 'is frightened/is angry/pities' invite the question 'Why is/does he …?' or 'What reason does he have for …?'

The relation between a persistent emotion lacking genuine duration and a temporary emotion (no matter whether momentary or episodic) is not that between a disposition or tendency and its actualization. As we have noted, human dispositions (with the exception of dispositions of health) are unlike inanimate dispositions.[20] Rather, they are traits of character or temperament. But being angry with, afraid of, or pitying someone, unlike being irascible, timorous, or compassionate, are not character traits – indeed, they may sometimes be 'out of character'. Are persistent, enduring, emotions then pronenesses or tendencies? Pronenesses and tendencies are specified by reference to what they are pronenesses or tendencies to *do*. To be sure, feeling an emotion is not a *doing*. But there seems no reason why one should not extend the idea of proneness and tendency to *feelings*. Is Othello's jealousy not a proneness to feel jealous? Is Jean Valjean's remorse not a tendency to suffer feelings of remorse? Is Achilles' anger with Agamemnon not a proneness to episodic fits of anger with him?

---

[20] See *Human Nature*, ch. 4, sections 7–9.

Is Pierre's love for Natasha not a tendency to experience floods of tenderness towards her with appropriate frequency? It should be obvious that something is awry.

We are misled by the form of words '*feeling* [an emotion]', a form that inclines us to ascribe a false quasi-substantiality to what is felt when we feel an emotion. It invites the thought that to feel an emotion is to stand in a relation to a something; or, as has sometimes been supposed, that we know what emotion we feel because we perceive it (feel it) in inner sense. To avoid this grammatical undertow, we should keep in mind the adverbial forms of emotion words, for example, to do something *angrily, fearfully, enviously*, or *affectionately*, as well as the verbal forms *to rage, to fear, to envy*, and so on. Moreover, we should reflect on what someone who is jealous, frightened, angry, remorseful, grateful, and so on is prone to *do*, and not rest satisfied with the glib tautology that he is prone to *feel* jealous, remorse, fear, angry, gratitude. For that merely provides us with a lame excuse for avoiding the question of what feeling angry, jealous, afraid, grateful, and so on can amount to from case to case.

*Emotional histories*     What is necessary is to shift focus from *momentary emotions*, which may incorporate pangs, twinges, flashes, or explosions of emotion, on the one hand, and *episodic emotions*, on the other, to *emotional histories*, in which *enduring emotions* find their place. Such histories are narratives involving manifold forms of human reaction and response, thought and intention, action and interaction.[21] We must focus upon the complex ways in which an emotion may come alive and be manifest in what one says and does. Moreover, we must not forget the manifold ways in which the emotions are active in one's inner life, torturing or tormenting one, keeping one awake at night, racking one with obsessive fantasies, delighting one in one's daydreams, and informing one's dreams. To be enraged or furious, or to have a fit of anger, are emotional episodes. Rage and fury are not persistent emotions, but anger may be. To be angry with someone for a prolonged period is not a proneness to occasional outbursts of anger with that person, but rather a lasting resentment, a persistent lack of amiability, the severance of social relations, coldness and distance on occasions of meeting, and so forth. It is to think and speak of the

---

[21] See R. Harré, 'Emotions', in R. Harré and F. M. Moghaddam, *Psychology for the Third Millennium* (SAGE, London, 2012), and P. Goldie, *The Emotions* (Clarendon Press, Oxford, 2000).

object of one's anger with disdain, to be prone to dwell upon the reason for one's anger with resentment and hurt, to rehearse imaginary dialogues in one's mind, and so forth. That is what it is to feel angry with someone over a period of time – it is not merely, or not even necessarily, to succumb to episodic outbursts of anger. Love that persists over a lifetime may grow out of falling in love at first sight, out of the emotional perturbations characteristic of erotic love and the ensuing emotional states distinctive of passionate wooing. But the constant love of a happy marriage (e.g. Pierre and Natasha) is not merely a tendency to be swept by feelings of loving tenderness or erotic passion, but rather a persistent concern for whom one loves, a standing motive for action beneficial or pleasing to the beloved, a desire for and delight in shared experience, and a persistent colouring of thought, imagination, and fantasy. What does Othello's jealousy amount to? He is racked with doubts and suspicions, tormented by distrust, writhes in self-inflicted torments. He stoops to spying, plotting, and conniving; seeks vengeance for imaginary wrongs; spends sleepless nights mocked by the 'green-eyed monster' of jealousy. The things a jealous person does out of jealousy and the behaviour that discloses persistent jealousy cannot be reduced to a determinate act-category that specifies a tendency or proneness. However, to characterize jealousy as a 'multitrack disposition' is equally misconceived.[22] For that merely masks the fact that the relation between an emotion and its ramified expression in judgement, imagination, behavioural expression, and motivated action or omission is *not* akin to the relation between a disposition (proneness or tendency) and its actualization. The hatred that Edmond Dantès bears his treacherous erstwhile friends is manifest far less in emotional perturbations and outbursts of episodic emotion than in the iron determination of his will for revenge, in the cast of his thought and fantasy, and in his motives and reasons for action over many years. The envy that moves Cousine Bette need not sweep over her every morning, but it informs her life in a multitude of ways, invades her imagination and fantasy, occupies her thoughts day and night, and motivates her plans and projects. We need to shift our focus from tendencies and pronenesses to the agent's acknowledged *reasons* for his persistent emotions and

---

[22] The idea of multitrack dispositions was introduced by Ryle in *Concept of Mind* (Hutchinson, London, 1949), pp. 44–5. For refutation of the view that belief is a multitrack disposition, see *The Intellectual Powers*, pp. 221–6.

to their constituting pertinent considerations in his imaginings and practical reasonings.

*Emotional attitudes*      It should already be evident that the boundary between temporary and enduring emotions, on the one hand, and *emotional attitudes*, on the other, is blurred. Momentary emotions often generate emotional attitudes – as one's brief flash of anger is transformed into dislike, disdain, and hostility. Similarly, episodic emotions often mutate into emotional attitudes. When someone misbehaves shamefully in one's presence for a prolonged time (he may be drunk, or have failed to control his temper, or be unctuous towards his superiors), one may react with rising feelings of contempt. One's feeling of contempt may be exhibited in one's facial expression when addressing the person who has behaved contemptibly – one looks down one's nose, curls one's lip, raises one's eyebrow. One's contempt may be long-lasting, but that does not imply that one will have recurrent feelings of contempt (facial expression and all). Rather, one's *attitude* towards the person will be contemptuous. One *judges* him to be contemptible. One will hold him in disdain, sever social relations with him, no longer speak well of him.

*Compositional and narrative complexity*      It is evident that emotions exhibit both *compositional complexity* and *contextual or narrative complexity*. Compositional complexity is patent in the manner in which emotions may involve cognitive and cogitative strands (perception, knowledge, belief, judgement, imagination, evaluation, and thought); sensations and perturbations; forms of facial, tonal, and behavioural manifestation; or emotionally charged utterances that express one's feelings; reasons and motives for action; and intentionality and causality. The contextual complexity is manifest in the manner in which emotions, in all their temporal diversity, are woven into the tapestry of life. An emotional episode is rendered intelligible not only by reference to the context and occasion in which it arises, but also by reference to a past history – to previous relationships and commitments, to past deeds and encounters, and to antecedent emotional states. The loss of temper over a triviality may be made comprehensible by reference to long-standing, but suppressed, jealousy. One's *Schadenfreude* (delight at the misfortune of another) may be explained by one's antecedent malicious envy (one's resentment at the good fortune of another) or by reference to one's standing resentment at an insult. The intensity of one's grief may be explained by reference to the passion with

which one loved. The general point is finely depicted in Edward
Greenwood's poem 'The Story':

> I glimpsed as I passed an open door
> The sight of someone else's grief,
> A visitor bent with flowers in her hands,
> Whispering words to bring relief
>
> To one who, stooped in the doorway there,
> Was a picture of distress,
> For, as she took them, she'd tears in her eyes
> From some cause I could only guess.
>
> I couldn't eavesdrop on words exchanged,
> For they shared a sorrow not mine,
> Round which a boundary was drawn
> That stopped me crossing its line.
>
> But I hovered on its threshold when
> I saw them both mourning there,
> Though both of them were unknown to me,
> There was something I could share.
>
> They made me meditate on grief,
> And I thought as I passed slowly on
> Of the one who had come to commiserate,
> And the one whose tears shone.
>
> A glance takes the part of a sorrowing heart,
> Not with what's behind the pain,
> For that you'd need to be in at the start
> And see the whole story plain.

For the most part, understanding the emotions, as opposed to explaining their cortical and physiological roots, is idiographic rather than
nomothetic, and historical rather than static. We shall explore this
thought in chapters 2 and 3.

# 2

# The Analytic of the Emotions I

## 1. The representation of emotions

*Idiographic understanding of emotions*
Inasmuch as our emotional perturbations, our temporary and our enduring emotions, show what we care about and what is important to us, they show what sort of person we are. Disregarding crowd emotions, in which people lose their individuality in waves of infectious adulation, war fever, hatred, joy, or grief, the role of the emotions in the life of a human being is highly personal and individual. Because emotions are embedded in the circumstances in which they arise, because they originate in responses to the specificity of the situations that are encountered by the individual human being, because the person's emotional response is rooted in *his* past history and in *his* present understanding of the situation that *he* confronts, understanding another's emotion is paradigmatically *idiographic* rather than *nomothetic*. Understanding Antony's love for Cleopatra is quite a different matter from understanding Dante's love for Beatrice, and understanding Heloise's love for Abelard is quite distinct from understanding Abelard's love for Heloise (which, in turn, is quite different from grasping Abelard's own later (defective) understanding of his erstwhile love for Heloise (see below, pp. 424f.)).

Of course, there is much for nomothetic investigation to clarify, both in psychology and in cognitive neuroscience. The sciences of

*The Passions: A Study of Human Nature*, First Edition. P. M. S. Hacker.
© 2018 John Wiley & Sons Ltd. Published 2018 by John Wiley & Sons Ltd.

man can discover a great deal about post-traumatic stress disorder, about the manifold phobias to which mankind is subject, about anxiety neuroses and obsessive guilt, about murderous jealousy and uncontrollable rage. And they can, sometimes, find ways of ameliorating these pathological conditions by pharmaceutical means or by means of various forms of individual or group therapy. Nevertheless, no amount of experimental psychology or neuroscience can explain and illuminate the role the manifold emotions *actually* play in the life of any given individual human being, or the role they *can* play in the lives of men and women, let alone the role they *ought* to play in a life in which the intellect, the will, and the passions are in harmony.

*Literature as deepest study of emotion*

Given the centrality of the emotions in our lives, it is no surprise that they constitute the main theme of so many of the arts of the West. For it is through the arts that we express our conceptions of human nature and of the human condition. Poetry since the dawn of culture, drama since its evolution in ancient Greece, and the social and psychological novel since its reinvention in the eighteenth century have as their main themes the loves and hatreds of men and women, their longings and disappointments, their joys and sorrows. The poets, dramatists, and novelists of our literary canon are the greatest students of human emotions, who attain the deepest insights by depiction of the particular. It is no surprise that, when we want a profound description of someone in the grip of an emotion, we go to the great dramas, novels, and poems. We learn about jealousy from Medea, Othello, Swann, and Louis Trevelyan (in Trollope's *He Knew He Was Right*); about love from Romeo and Juliet, Pierre Bezukhov and Natasha, Balint Abády and Adrienne (in Bánffy's *Transylvanian Trilogy*), Emma Bovary, and Anna Karenina; and about guilt from Raskolnikov or Prince Nekhlyudov (in Tolstoy's *Resurrection*).

Furthermore, when we are in the grips of an inchoate emotion for which we crave crystallization or articulation, we turn to the great poets who sing of the passions of the human heart. There we may find expressed in wondrous forms the love and tenderness we may be feeling, the jealousy that grips us, grief for the dead, the longing of the traveller for home, delight in nature, the weariness that overwhelms us, the joys and sorrows of life, and human attitudes towards death. Poetry gives shape to our feelings, and thereby alleviates the pressure of our emotions. It is equally important that, irrespective of our own feelings, we find the poets' expressions of emotion worthy of our closest attention and admiration. Through them we can come to understand the nuances of human passions, the depth of feeling that may overwhelm a man or woman, and the manifold modes in which mankind responds to life.

*Representation of emotion in visual arts*  It is an important feature of our culture that we are fascinated by, and take delight in, the visual representation and expression of emotions in painting (drawing and printmaking) and in sculpture. From the dawn of post-medieval art the representation of love and adoration of God, of the tender love of the Virgin for her child, of horror at the crucifixion, of lamentation at the deposition of Christ, of the grief of the pietà, and of the mourning at the entombment are major themes that occupied the hands of the greatest artists from Giotto to the Renaissance and Baroque. With the revival of the study of antiquity and the rise of neo-Platonism, mythological painting became licit in the princely courts, offering numerous further subjects of the incarnation of the passions of the gods and of man in the High Renaissance. The Baroque taste for emotional extremes opened up a veritable chamber of visual horrors for painting, from the decollations depicted by the Caravaggisti (Caravaggio himself, Artemisia Gentileschi) to the agony of Prometheus (Rubens, Daniel Rombouts), from the fear and lust of the rape of Lucretia (Antonio Bellucci, Palma il Giovane) to the blinding of Samson (Rembrandt trying to out-Rubens Rubens). Artists revelled in the portrayal of extreme emotions and hideous suffering, of fear and loathing, lust and love, or revulsion and disgust, aiming not only to mesmerize the eye, but also to horrify the viewers.

*Representation of emotion in music*  Although drama provided the opportunity for the dynamic display of human emotions, opera is the greatest expressive vehicle of passion. Love and lust, longing and grieving, rage and anger, triumph and humiliation, pride and contempt, fear and terror, pity and compassion all find a supreme expression in the synthesis of music, the expressive powers of the human voice, the acting of the protagonists, and the stagecraft of scenery, lighting, and stage effects. For those accustomed to the conventions of opera and sensitive to music none of the other arts can so stir their sensibility as opera, producing tears, pity and compassion, fear and horror, joy and delight.

Indeed, music itself has been considered to be the purest artistic expression of human emotions and of the striving of the human will. Schopenhauer, the metaphysician of music, wrote:

Melody ... relates the most secret history of the intellectually enlightened will, portrays every agitation, every effort, every movement of the
will, everything which the faculty of reason summarizes under the wide
and negative concept of feeling, and which cannot be further taken up
into the abstractions of reason. ... music does not express this or that
particular and definite pleasure, this or that affliction, pain, sorrow,
horror, gaiety, merriment or peace of mind, but joy, pain, sorrow,
horror, gaiety, merriment, peace of mind *themselves*, to a certain extent
in the abstract, their essential nature, without any accessories, and so
also without the motive for them. Nevertheless, we understand them
perfectly in this extracted quintessence.[1]

On a Beethoven symphony, he wrote:

It is a *rerum concordia discors*, a true and complete picture of the
nature of the world, which rolls on in the boundless confusion of innumerable forms, and maintains itself by constant destruction. But at the
same time, all the human passions and emotions speak from this
symphony; joy, grief, love, hatred, terror, hope, and so on in innumerable shades, yet all, as it were, only in the abstract and without any
particularization; it is their mere form without the material, like a mere
spirit world without matter.[2]

Our expressive powers are a gift of nature, evolution, and our culture.
The rich artistic tradition of the West is a gift of the genius of past
generations. It depicts and expresses the emotional life of Western
societies over many centuries, moulded by, and moulding, our changing conceptions of ourselves and our nature.

## 2. The language of the emotions

*Our goal: a clear*        Chapter 1 gave us a *distinct* idea of the emotions,
*idea of emotion*        differentiating the emotions from other psychological
                         attributes with which they are commonly conflated
or confused, and locating the concept of an emotion upon our conceptual map. Now we shall endeavour to achieve a *clear* idea of the
emotions. Without this we cannot resolve the conceptual unclarities
that bedevil our reflections on the emotions and their role in our lives.

---

[1] Schopenhauer, *The World as Will and Representation*, 2 vols, trans. E. F. J. Payne
(Dover, New York, 1966), vol. 1, III, §52.
[2] Schopenhauer, *The World as Will and Representation*, vol. 2, ch. 39, p. 450.

Are the emotions the primary source of unreason? Is reason in permanent conflict with the emotions? These questions spill over into profound ethical questions: Is reason the faculty to be invoked in mastering the essentially irrational emotions (as Platonists and Stoics held), or is reason to be the slave of the passions (as Hume suggested)? Can we know what emotion another is feeling, or are the emotions of others inaccessible to us? How do we know what emotion we are feeling? Can we be ignorant of our own feelings? Or do we have the last, *authoritative*, word on what we feel? Are there such things as unconscious emotions? If so, what is an unconscious emotion? Does an unconscious emotion stand to a conscious one as an occluded chair stands to a visible one? Do non-human animals feel emotions? If so, are there ways in which animal emotions differ from human ones? Are there emotions that we feel but that other animals not only do not but cannot? Are emotions beneficial or detrimental to human felicity? If so, what makes a given emotion the one or the other? And so on. If we are to answer these and many further conceptual and ethical questions, we must first attain a clear view of the concept of an emotion. The beginning of wisdom is to attain an overview of the grammar of emotion words and of the intentionality of the emotions.

Our emotional vocabulary is replete with abstract nouns (*anger, fear, hope, despair, envy, jealousy, curiosity, regret, pity, love*), verbs (*to fear, to hope, to despair, to envy, to regret, to pity, to love*), adjectives (*angry, hopeful, envious, jealous, curious, loving*), modal adjectives (*enviable, pitiable, regrettable, lovable*), and adverbs (*angrily, fearfully, hopefully, enviously, jealously, curiously, guiltily, regretfully, lovingly*). As already noted, in philosophical reflection the abstract nominals are misleading and one is well advised to diversify one's diet with verbal, adjectival, and adverbial forms. This will reduce one's temptation to reify the emotions, conceiving of them as 'mental *entities* (things)', or to succumb to the misconceived dichotomy of 'inner' and 'outer', conceiving of emotions as '*inner* states', named by emotion nouns, to which the subject has *privileged access*. It will mitigate the pressure to present reified emotions as causal agents – as daemons that invade a human being, forcing one to act in ways one does not will. We do indeed say such things as 'His jealousy drove him to ...' and 'Anger clouds judgement'. But the forms of these phrases – their surface grammar – is misleading. 'Othello's jealousy drove him to murder Desdemona' does not imply that jealousy is a causal agent. Rather, it identifies the motive out of which Othello acted – and

*Our emotion vocabulary*

motives, as we have seen, are not causes, but patterns of reasons. 'Anger clouds judgement' is not a causal statement akin to 'LSD causes hallucinations'. It means no more than 'When people are angry they are prone to misjudge (for they are agitated, perturbed, preoccupied with the offence they believe to have been given)'. Economizing on the abstract nouns will facilitate directing our attention to the *human being* who is angry, joyful, or frightened, to *the manner* in which his emotion manifests itself, that is, to his acting angrily, joyfully, or fearfully; to the factors *awareness* of which occupy his mind (i.e. to the offence given, the good news, the apprehension of present danger); and to *the motives* that the reasons for his feeling what he feels afford him when he acts *out of* love, jealousy, fear, and so forth. Human beings, although they have minds, brains, and bodies, are neither a psycho-physical unity of mind and body, nor a cerebral-somatic synthesis of brain and body.[3] Rather, they are living organisms with somatic features and psychological and intellectual capacities and abilities. It is the human being as a whole that is the subject of emotions (and not the mind or the brain), just as it is human beings that are sometimes motivated by their emotions (and not by the emotions of their minds or brains).

As we have suggested, the emotions distinctive of human beings, as opposed to other animals, are emotions that presuppose possession of a language and hence powers of intellect and rational will. The objects distinctive of human emotions presuppose mastery of a language and possession of rational abilities. That, as we shall see, is why our emotions can be rational, reasonable, irrational, or unreasonable. It is also why we are, to a degree, responsible for our emotions, despite the fact that we cannot feel them at will.

*Intentionality of the emotions*

The various grammatical complements of emotion verbs or verb phrases must be distinguished in order better to grasp the intentionality of the emotions. We should distinguish between the *object-accusatives* and the *nominalization-accusatives* of emotion verbs (fig. 2.1).[4] The *object-accusative* of one's emotion is a grammatical object of the emotion verb that specifies by means of a relative wh-pronoun whom or what one loves or hates, fears or pities, is angry with or envious of,

---

[3] Brain/body dualism is no improvement over mind/body dualism. See *Human Nature: the Categorial Framework* (Blackwell, Oxford, 2007), chs 8–10.

[4] For a systematic examination of intentionality, see *The Intellectual Powers: A Study of Human Nature* (Wiley Blackwell, Oxford, 2013), ch. 2, especially pp. 66–9.

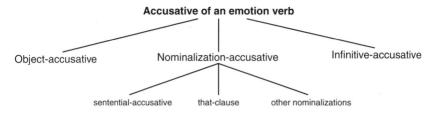

**Figure 2.1** *Accusatives of emotions (emotion verbs not being factive, their accusatives are intentional)*

and so on. Since emotion verbs are not factive, the object-accusatives of emotion verbs are intentional, that is, what is signified by the expression need not exist in order for the emotion attribution to be true. One may love or fear objects that do not exist (as people have loved or feared their gods, and as children love Santa Clause and fear ghosts) – that is to say, some object-accusative expressions in true emotion-ascriptions may not refer to anything that exists.

The *nominalization-accusative* of an emotion verb may be given in *sentential form*, or in *nominalized form*, which may be a that-clause or a variant thereof. The sentential form is exemplified by 'Jack fears *Jill is away*' or 'Jill hopes *Jack is in town*'. A common nominalized form is a that-clause, as when one fears *that one's children are in danger* or hopes *that they are safe*. But there are also other nominalized forms, for example, 'Jack fears *failure*' (Jack fears that he will fail), 'Jack envies *Jill's success*' (Jack envies Jill's having succeeded), and 'Jack is jealous of *Jill's flirting with Tom*'. The accusative of an emotion verb may also be given by means of an *infinitive-accusative*. This is exemplified by such sentences as 'I hope *to be* in London tomorrow', 'He loves *to play* golf', and 'She is afraid *to go*'.

These nominalization-accusatives and infinitive-accusatives do not signify an existent or non-existent object.[5] Rather, they specify the *content* or *intention* of an emotion. They specify the answer to such questions as 'What do you/does NN fear/hope/regret?' or 'What is Jack jealous/envious of?' Here the wh-pronoun is the interrogative 'what', not the relative 'what'. (We must distinguish between Jack being jealous of Jim (which specifies of whom he is jealous) and Jack being jealous of Jill's love for Jim (which specifies of what he is jealous), between Jack fearing Jill and Jack fearing that Jill will scold him.)

---

[5] So-called intentional objects are not kinds of objects any more than abstract objects are kinds of objects.

The nominalization-accusative gives us *the terms in which the content or intention of someone's emotion can be reported*. The content of an emotion is not a kind of thing, but rather a kind of answer to a question. Clearly, the truth or falsehood of the emotion-ascription is independent of the truth or falsehood of the sentential or nominalized intentional-accusative. Parents really are afraid that their son, who is serving in the army, will get killed in the war – his survival does not imply that they were not really fearful. Their hopes for their son's survival may be dashed, but his death does not imply that they did not hope he would survive. Desdemona's fidelity does not imply that Othello was not jealous of her love for Cassio (which never existed). It is in these terms that *he* would characterize his jealousy, and it is in these terms that we describe Othello's feeling. But, just as we report his utterances in indirect speech with the rider 'He said that …', so too, knowing as we do that Desdemona is faithful to Othello, we would describe him as being jealous of *what he believed to be* her love for Cassio.

*Learning the use of emotion words*       Given that human beings are not endowed with innate knowledge of a language, how then can a child master the rudimentary emotional vocabulary?

How might we teach a child the use of emotion words? (We are not engaged in armchair learning theory, but exploring *possible* ways of teaching in order to shed light upon what is learnt, i.e. upon the meaning of emotion words and what it is to have mastered their use.) We must teach the child the appropriate objects and intentions of the elementary emotions. We explain that there is no reason to fear *this* dog, because it is friendly and harmless; we warn the child to be careful of *that* dog, because it may bite. We gear our demonstrative uses of emotion words to the occasions that warrant the emotion, and in so doing we teach the child the appropriate objects of the emotion and the appropriate warrants for it. To master the rudiments of the emotional vocabulary of fear, the child must react with fear to certain things – on this natural fear reaction we can graft the concept of fear, that is, teach him to exclaim 'I'm frightened'. But the child must also learn what to be frightened of, that is, what are appropriate things to fear. Similarly, the child has a natural reaction of disgust to unappetizing food. On the natural reaction of disgust, we can graft the use of the emotional utterance 'That's disgusting', and in the fullness of time also 'I feel disgusted with his behaviour'. But, to be sure, the child must learn what things merit such epithets, that is, what constraints are placed on the material objects of disgust by its formal object. We teach the child to express gratitude ('Say "thank you!"') when, for example, given a gift, and we teach the use of 'grateful' and 'ungrateful' ('Don't be so ungrateful! She gave you a lovely present'). We teach the child forms of reciprocal behaviour over prolonged periods that are appropriate to one to whom gratitude is due – that is, we teach him to be motivated by gratitude. We use emotion words in association with the child's natural emotional reactions: of fear ('Did it frighten you, darling? There's no need to be afraid'), of affection ('That's a nice hug! Do you love Mummy?'), of outbursts of temper ('Why are you so angry? Don't lose your temper!'). In this way, the child learns to express and report his emotional responses by the use of emotion words. Simultaneously, the child learns how to apply emotion words to others who are manifesting emotions in emotion-eliciting situations. Moreover, we engender and cultivate new emotional reactions geared to the use of emotion words. For example, 'You should be ashamed of yourself!' presupposes the child's grasp of what he must or must not do, and the realization of unwarranted transgression. 'Are you sorry for what you have done? Will you promise not to do it again?' and so forth belong not only to the child's acculturation (morals and mores) but also to his emotional education.

*Emotional self-consciousness* Learning a rich emotional vocabulary is acquiring the ability to realize what emotion one is feeling and to articulate what one cares about in the axiological forms of the passions. Thereby one learns to become self-conscious – to reflect upon one's emotions. For that is an essential stage in learning to evaluate one's own emotions as warranted or unwarranted. It is presupposed for the possibility of feeling second-order emotions, such as feeling ashamed of one's fear or of losing one's temper, or relief at not having panicked or at not having lost one's temper. It is a precondition for the possibility of controlling one's emotion. Mastering the vocabulary of the emotions is also learning how to understand the behaviour and utterances of others. It is learning how to describe the manifestations and expressions of emotion by others, and to understand what they care about, their consequent reasons and motives for acting. Hence it is also learning to understand, to evaluate, and sometimes to predict their behaviour and to prevent it.

## 3. Expressions and manifestations of emotion

*Accompaniments and expressions of the emotions* The emotions, in particular temporary emotions, have characteristic multiple associations, manifestations, and forms of expression. We can distinguish between the neural/physiological and somatic *associations*, on the one hand, and the behavioural *manifestations* and *verbal expressions* of the emotions, on the other.[6] Neural associations are cortical and subcortical events, activities, and conditions that have been discovered to be associated with (and are perhaps causal conditions of) emotions. *Physiological associations* are such things as changes in pulse rate, blood pressure, skin conductance, hormonal changes, and so forth that have been discovered to be associated with temporary emotions. *Somatic associations* are either *sensations* (a hollow feeling in the stomach, a muscular tension, the sensation of throbbing heart) felt by the subject of the emotion, or *visible externalities*, such as changes in breathing (gasping, hyperventilating), blushing, and perspiring. Among the *behavioural manifestations* of temporary emotions (and agitations) are *facial expressions* (smiles, scowls, grimaces), *bodily manifestations* by means of gesture and mien, and more or less inarticulate vocal manifestations of alarm, fear, delight, ecstasy, amazement, amusement, disappointment, or grief (e.g. cries, gasps, groans, moans, screams, shouts, laughter, wailing). One's feelings are also made manifest by one's *articulate expressions* – spontaneous exclamations and intentional utterances – as well as by *spontaneous voluntary actions and reactions*. *Emotionally motivated actions* also make the emotion *evident*. These distinctions (see fig. 2.2) merit scrutiny, so we must look closer.

*Neural, pharmacological, physiological causes*     Neural and physiological changes that accompany temporary emotions and that play a causal role in their generation (as well as that of moods and emotional dispositions (traits)) are proper subjects for scientific investigation. It is up to neuroscientists to discover the neural events and processes that are characteristic of temporary emotions – both momentary and episodic – such as heightened activity of the amygdala and the medial frontal cortex. It is also their task to discover what neural structures and processes and changes in neural structures and processes, if any, are associated with enduring emotions. Neuropharmacologists investigate the roles of complex chemicals such as dopamine, noradrenaline, and serotonin in human and animal emotional responsiveness and responses to

---

[6] The term 'behavioural manifestation' is used here and in the rest of this book as a quasi-technical term. It includes facial responses, gestures, and mien, as well as non-verbal exclamations and cries, and the tone of voice of one's utterances. Articulate utterances that exhibit one's feelings are termed 'verbal expressions' of emotion. The two obviously overlap. What one says may express one's feelings, and the tone of voice in which one says it may manifest how deeply one feels.

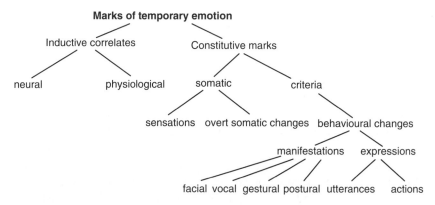

**Figure 2.2**   *Marks of temporary emotions*

emotion-eliciting situations. Physiologists investigate the operations of the endocrine system and clarify, for example, the hormonal changes during menstruation that dispose women to emotional fluctuation, or the correlation between testosterone production and young male irascibility. Such empirical facts, correlations, and causal explanations are not constitutive elements of our concepts of the emotions, nor are they logical criteria for someone's feeling an emotion. They are inductive marks of emotions (as well as moods and agitations) that are discovered by experimental investigations. Their discovery *presupposes* non-inductive behavioural criteria for the ascription and identification of emotion. Otherwise it would be impossible to make the inductive correlations.

*Somatic accompaniments*

    *Felt* somatic changes, however, differ from physiological changes. Some are somatic *sensations*: the thumping of one's heart (associated with fear or excitement), the throbbing of one's temples (commonly linked to rage), the tightening of one's throat (a common accompaniment of anxiety or passion). They belong to certain emotional syndromes, and are partly constitutive of many temporary emotions. Nevertheless, they are not *logical criteria* for others to ascribe an emotion to one, although their avowal may be. Other, *overt,* somatic changes, *in appropriate circumstances, are* criteria for ascribing an emotion to another. Shame and embarrassment are generally visibly characterized by blushes; episodic fear commonly involves hyper-ventilation; and grief and disappointment are often accompanied by tears and sobs. Someone who is enraged is prone to turn red; someone who is terrified commonly turns pallid and trembles.

Behavioural *manifestations* of emotion in an
*Forms an emotion*   emotion-eliciting context are the predominant
*may take*           criteria for ascribing temporary emotions to human
beings. Our anger is made manifest – *exhibited to
view* – in our responses to an offence or insult – in our scowl, raised
or icily controlled voice, or clenched fists. It is expressed in what we
say, and manifest in how we say it. Our love, in the company of someone with whom we are in love, may be manifest in our smile, in the
gentleness of our voice as we speak, in the manner in which we gaze
into his or her eyes. Our grief in the face of the death of someone
loved is made manifest by our tears, sobbing, or broken voice, and the
lowering of our head into the palms of our hands. Such complex patterns of behavioural response are *forms that our emotions take*. The
form an emotion may take varies. One's anger may take the form of
shouting, turning red, and shaking one's fist, or the quite different
form of stiffened upright posture, cold eye, icy voice, and contemptuous tone. One's fear may take the form of pallid face, shaking hands,
and tremulous voice, or of cowering, perspiring, and trembling, or of
taking a deep breath, controlling one's tremor, and cracking a black
joke. One's grief may be manifest in the form of tears, sobbing, and
broken voice, or in the form of frozen pallid face, toneless voice, and
rigid posture as one assimilates the shock. In some cultures it is exhibited by screams, wailings, and lamentations.

Verbal *expressions* of emotion – what we say and
*Expressions and*    how we spontaneously respond – are further behav-
*manifestation of*   ioural criteria for feeling an emotion and for having
*emotion*            an emotional attitude. However, the criteria for the
ascription of an emotion include not only the spontaneous utterances
made in response to the circumstance eliciting it, but also the consequent utterances and *actions* taken over longer periods of time that
are rooted in the emotion and may be motivated by it. They too make
our emotional state evident. For, as we have noted, many of our emotions have an evolving history. Othello's jealousy from the moment in
which Iago plants the seed of suspicion to the murder of Desdemona
is exhibited in a wide variety of actions, plans, and plots, as well as
in what he says about them. Coriolanus's pride is evident not only in
his bearing and gait, in his arrogant facial expression and manner of
speaking, but also in his plans, projects, and actions that are driven
by pride. Love may be manifest and expressed not only in the passionate encounters of Romeo and Juliet, the embraces and kisses,
the caresses and tones of voice, but also in the persistent cogitative

preoccupation with each other when separated, the daydreaming, the dwelling on memories of previous amorous encounters, the way in which they talk of their beloved to others. Mature, abiding love is exhibited in innumerable ways in daily life over many years (as in Pierre and Natasha's marriage), in mutual care and assistance, in the endless actions motivated by love and concern, in protectiveness, in intimacy and sexual intimacy, in manifest affection and fidelity, in mutual longing when separated, and in the joys and sorrows of shared experience.

*Sign: what it is a sign of/form:what it is a form of*

It is of capital importance to realize that the relation between the expression or manifestation of an emotion and the emotion expressed or manifest is *not* akin to the relation between a natural sign of something and what it is a sign of, for example the relation of clouds to rain or of smoke to fire. Rather, it is the relation between *a form* and *what it is a form of*.[7] We are prone to confuse the two quite different relations. Clouds may occur without rain, and there may be smoke without fire. So, too, someone may shed tears without feeling grief or sorrow – they may be tears of laughter or of joy. Someone may tremble and be pallid without being afraid – it may just be very cold. Someone may smile without feeling affection or amusement – it may just be a polite smile on being introduced to a stranger, a sarcastic or ironic smile. Moreover, we can pretend to feel an emotion we do not feel at all, as actors, hypocrites, and the deceitful do. So we think, perfectly correctly, that both in the case of the natural sign and the thing signified, and in the case of the behavioural manifestation of an emotion and the emotion manifest, we have a defeasible evidential relation. So we conclude, quite wrongly, that an emotion and its behavioural manifestation and expression are externally (non-logically, inductively) related. Then it will also seem that the emotion is the hidden, *inner cause* of the externally exhibited behaviour, and that the behaviour is merely an *external sign* of what is actually *concealed from sight*. The route from this misunderstanding to various forms of scepticism about 'other minds' is direct.

*The form an emotion takes makes it patent*

In thinking thus, we forget that we often see the joy, delight, or pride, and the fear, shame, or guilt in another's face. We commonly hear the love and affection, the grief and sorrow, or the

---

[7] See A. R. White, *The Philosophy of Mind* (Random House, New York, 1967), pp. 118–19.

anger and indignation in the tones of voice of others. These are not *signs* of the emotions – they *manifest* or *express* the emotions, make the emotions patent. By contrast, clouds do not manifest rain, and smoke does not express fire. We do not *infer* that someone who breaks down in tears on being told of the death of a beloved spouse is grief-stricken. But we do infer rain tomorrow from rain clouds tonight. We do not *deduce* that someone who turns red on being insulted, shakes his fist, and shouts threateningly is angry. The fact that we would adduce the behaviour as grounds warranting our judgement does not imply that the judgement was inferred from the behaviour as an illness is inferred from its symptoms. When a man loses his temper with us, we do not reason: 'He has turned red, is shaking his fist and shouting threateningly at me, so he is probably angry.' It is true that we make mistakes in ascribing emotions to others. Someone may tremble with anger or with fear, weep from sorrow or from joy, raise his voice in rage or in triumph. Moreover, one may conceal one's emotions by suppressing their manifestation and expression. But when we misascribe an emotion, our mistake is not one of inferring the wrong cause from our observation of an apparent effect. The behavioural manifestations of an emotion are not the *effects* of the emotion, but the *form* it takes.[8] So our misjudgement is not the result of a faulty inference of cause from its signs. Rather, we *misinterpret* what we observe. We take the observable behaviour to mean something other than what it actually means. So, for example, what seemed like cold indifference was in fact the controlled suppression of passionate love; what sounded like affection was no more than courtesy; what looked like grief was dissimulation.

*Pretending to feel an emotion*

One can pretend to feel an emotion one does not feel. In such cases, the behaviour one engages in is not an expression or manifestation of emotion at all – it merely looks like it. One can pretend to be angry – shout, rant, and rave – but then one is not shouting in anger, ranting in rage, or raving in fury at all. One cannot deceitfully *manifest* an emotion, only deceitfully *mimic* being angry, affectionate,

---

[8] It is therefore less surprising than it is currently held to be that paralysing the muscles on which the expression of the emotion depends (using botulinum toxin, for example) attenuates the episodic emotion itself. For, to be sure, *controlling* one's manifestations of emotion (taking a deep breath, swallowing, counting to ten before one speaks, etc.) commonly ameliorates (moderates the intensity of) one's occurrent emotion and emotional perturbation.

or sorrowful. When one pretends to be angry, one pretends to shout *in* anger – which one does not feel. When one pretends to feel affection, one pretends to smile affectionately, one softens one's tone – but not *with* affection. The anger one shows, if one shows anger rather than pretending to be angry, *is* the anger one feels – the anger is not hidden behind the behavioural manifestations and expressions of anger. The love one shows *is* the love one feels – one cannot show love and not feel it; one can only pretend to show love that one does not feel. One cannot manifest fear that one does not feel, only emulate fear with fear-like behaviour.

'Every motion of the soul', Cicero noted, 'has its natural appearance, voice and gesture; and the entire body of man, all his facial and vocal expressions, like the strings of a harp, sound just as the soul's motion strikes them' (*De Oratore*, III, §216). Cicero's distinctions merit scrutiny.

*Facial manifestation of emotion* Our emotions are made manifest by our facial expression, predominantly by means of our mouth, brow, and eyes.[9] It is crucial to the expressive powers of the human face that it is highly plastic, capable of gradual, minute alterations that modulate smoothly one into another. To this we are naturally sensitive,[10] and with experience may become highly sensitive. These biological and anthropological facts constitute a part of the background against which our rich emotional vocabulary evolves. Wittgenstein invites us to consider a humanoid face which had only five positions and changed by snapping from one straight to another.[11] Would this fixed smile really be a smile? Surely not. But why not? Wittgenstein suggests that we might not be able to react to it as we do to the smiles of others. It would not be infectious, as smiles often are. Could we understand the smile? What would manifest its meaning? We tell a joke, whereupon the face snaps into a smile. Does laughter come forth? Does this exhibit amusement? Could the eyes smile in amusement together with the mouth? We introduce someone, whereupon the face snaps into a smile. Does this show friendliness? There is no *mechanical* manifestation of friendliness, only the mechanical

---

[9] To be sure, we also wrinkle our nose in disgust or revulsion (and sometimes in laughter), and look down our nose in contempt or disdain. We grit our teeth and clench our jaw with determination. And so on.

[10] Autistic children, who avoid eye contact, are not.

[11] Wittgenstein, *Remarks on the Philosophy of Psychology*, vol. 2 (Blackwell, Oxford, 1980), §614.

pretence of it, as one smiles at the ninety-seventh guest announced and introduced to one. But the mechanical pretence of a smile is possible only for those who *can* smile non-mechanically. In Wittgenstein's imagined 'robotic' face, the face would not be *alive* with a smile.[12] Nor could the face *light up* with a smile or *darken* with anger. The lighting up or darkening of the face *requires* the possibility of smooth modulation from one expression to another.

Our facial features are not only highly plastic; they also function as an ensemble attuned to the context of reaction and coordinated with responsive behaviour. Our eyes may be bold and assertive, tender, affectionate, quizzical, angry, indignant, inviting, and alluring. They may twinkle, glitter, or sparkle; be bright or dull, soft, gentle, hard, or cold – but only in appropriate facial expressions of laughter, smiles, grins, smirks, pouts, frowns, scowls, or a poker face. 'The countenance', Cicero wrote, 'is the portrait of the mind, the eyes are its informers' (*De Oratore*, III, §59). A tender smile is accompanied by smiling eyes, a sarcastic smile by bitter eyes, a cruel smile by cold eyes. We open our eyes wide in surprise, wonder, or amazement, as well as in awe, fear, terror, or horror. We narrow them in suspicion, distrust, hesitation, puzzlement, or incomprehension.

*Context dependence of expression of emotion*

We display distinctive looks of amusement, excitement, expectation, anxiety, and trepidation, as well as quizzical looks and looks of tenderness and affection, of dislike, disgust, revulsion, and animosity. We frown in irritation or puzzlement, yawn with boredom, purse our lips with disapproval or hesitation. Our jaw drops in amazement, we lick our dry lips in trepidation, or we put our hands to our lips in surprise or wonder. These facial manifestations of emotion occur *in a context that gives them a meaning*. For the context provides the object of understanding to which the facial expression is an intelligible response, given the knowledge and belief, wants and purposes, of the respondent. A smile is an amused smile if there is something that has amused one; but the smile of the village idiot is quite meaningless. A smile is a tender smile when we look into the eyes of someone we love, not someone we hate. We screw up our face in disgust when there is something repulsive in view, or if we have eaten something we find disgusting. Remove the face from the context to which the facial

---

[12] See L. Herzberg, 'What's in a Smile', in Y. Gustafsson, C. Kronqvist, and M. McEachrane (eds), *Emotions and Understanding: Wittgensteinian Perspectives* (Palgrave Macmillan, Basingstoke, 2009).

expression is a response and it becomes as intelligible, *and as unintelligible*, as context-dependent remarks when removed from their context, for example, 'Then he got up and left her', 'It is too late now', 'Tell me when you'll do it'. This has non-trivial consequences for Darwinian investigations into the expression of emotion in animals and man, which we shall discuss in chapter 4.

Our facial expressions are bound up with manifold forms of vocal manifestations of feelings. Our amused smiles both precede and follow our laughter. We may split our sides, laugh until tears run down our cheeks; we chortle, cackle, guffaw, and roar with laughter; and we chuckle, giggle, titter, and simper. Our laughter may manifest our amusement, our joy and delight, our shyness or embarrassment. It may be an expression of congeniality, an invitation to intimacy, or an expression of derision, contempt, or disdain. We manifest our disappointment, sorrow, or grief with crumpled face and tears. We may weep in silence or we may sob, whimper, cry out, keen, or wail. We may scream with fear, crow in triumph, squeal with excitement, roar or bellow in rage, or howl in despair. These manifestations of emotion too occur in contexts that render them intelligible. If we scream with fear, we are afraid *of* something or someone in our vicinity. If we scream with excitement, we are excited by something we find thrilling. If we shout in anger, something has greatly annoyed us. Were such forms of behaviour to occur outside any legitimating context, we should find the behaviour incomprehensible and suppose the person behaving thus to be a victim of hallucinations.

*Body language as expression of emotion* Our emotions are made evident not only by our countenance and voice, but also by our posture and mien, the way we walk or sit, our gestures and gesticulations.[13] So called body language, *sermo corporis* as Cicero dubbed it, is rich and variegated, with natural behavioural roots and cultural modifications, constraints, refinements, and inventions. There is a spring in the walk of the cheerful or joyful. Aggressive masculinity is exhibited in a swagger, with elbows raised while walking – considered vulgar in earlier times, but now adopted by leading politicians. Sadness, depression, and grief are manifest in bowed shoulders and downcast head – wonderfully depicted by Masaccio's *Expulsion* in the Brancacci Chapel. The frightened may quail and cower – as do the prisoners waiting to be executed in Goya's

[13] For instructive discussion, see J. Bremmer and H. Roodenburg (eds), *A Cultural History of Gesture* (Polity Press, Cambridge, 1991).

*Third of May*. Power and arrogance may be manifested by posture, standing with legs well apart and arms akimbo – think of Holbein's cartoon for *Henry VII and VIII* or his *Sir Henry Guilford*, with thumbs thrust into girdle – but equally when seated (Ingres's *Napoleon Enthroned*) or on horseback (Verrocchio's Colleoni monument). Pride of station was (but no longer is) demonstrated by protruding elbow with the back of the hand or wrist on the hip – as in countless mannerist and Dutch portraits (Pontormo's *Duke Cosimo as a Halberdier*, Van Hoogstraten's *Mattheus van den Broucke*, or Hals's *Officers of the St George Militia Company in 1639*). Shame on the public disclosure of wrong-doing is characteristically made manifest by hanging head and submissive posture (Guercino's *Woman Taken in Adultery* or Rembrandt's *Christ and the Woman Taken in Adultery*).

*Expressiveness of hands*

Our hands, unlike the hands of other anthropoids, are capable of displaying the most refined variations of feeling. Reflect on the tenderness manifest by the hands of husband and bride in Rembrandt's *The Jewish Bride* or Rubens's *The Honeysuckle Bower*, or on the supporting hands of maternal love in numerous Raphael Madonnas. Call to mind the hands of shame clutching at a garment to conceal her pudenda and cover her breasts in Rembrandt's *Susanna and the Elders*. The hands of the *Mona Lisa* no less than her face are expressions of serenity and tranquillity. Recollect the manifestations of grief by the hands and gestures in Van der Weyden's Abegg Crucifixion, in numerous Giovanni Bellini's pietàs, and in Caravaggio's *Entombment of Christ*.

*Grammar of gesture, posture and deportment*

Throughout recorded history, posture and deportment were refined and constrained in order to differentiate the aristocracy from the demos or plebs, imperial rulers from the ruled, and men from women. Natural gestures and gesticulations of anger, defiance, triumph, submission, grief, awe, and wonder were, from one period to another, subjected to various forms of social modification and restraint to mark out the superior from the inferior, the cultivated from the uncouth. Gestures and posture were conventionalized and taught by rhetoricians in both ancient Greece and Rome for the purposes of public debate in governing assemblies, for pleading in the law courts, and for civil and military leadership. The grammar of gesture was described in detail in the Renaissance by such writers as Castiglione in *Il Cortegiano* (1528), Erasmus in *De Civilitate morum puerilium* (1532), and Della Casa in *Il Galateo* (1558) for the practical purpose of the education of the cultured aristocratic elite

(Castiglione) or of a gentleman (Della Casa), or for the cultivation of the civility to which all may and should aspire (Erasmus). Guides for the young to the posture, deportment, gesture, and forms of self-restraint persisted into the twentieth century.

*Conventional signals of emotion*  Facial expression, inarticulate vocal expression, gesture, and mien constitute collectively an orchestra of possible behavioural manifestations and expressions of agitations, of the perturbations of temporary emotions, of enduring emotions, of moods, and of emotional attitudes. In addition there are wholly conventional behavioural signals by means of which we express our feelings. These include nodding or shaking one's head, thumbs up or down, pointing with index finger or – rudely – with thumb, winking, beckoning, waving, and rude and obscene gestures of rejection, mockery, and insult. Couple them with the articulate verbal expressions of agitation, emotion, mood and attitude; the tone and speed of utterance; and the volume of voice in which one speaks (whispers, murmurs, sobs, shouts, screams, or roars), and we have a veritable symphony for the manifestation and expression of affections in general and of emotions in particular. The orchestra is normally conducted in honest concord. The various forms of discord are often marks of insincerity, which, for the unaccustomed, is difficult to mask. (It takes much skill to be a confidence trickster like Felix Krull in Mann's eponymous tale.) The eyes are the windows of the soul but also the traitors of the heart. They often betray furtive inclinations that we try to conceal with our words. A shifty look may shatter the appearance of sincerity, just as a tremor in the voice or shaking hands may belie our bold words.

*Rejecting the inner/ outer picture*  These vivid reminders are meant to break the grip of the tantalizing picture of the emotions as something 'inner', accessible only to the subject, and of the manifestations and expressions of the emotions as something 'outer', causally related to the 'real' inner feelings. One *can* wear a veil but, when one doesn't, one's features are *revealed*. That one *can* sometimes conceal one's feelings does not imply that, when one does not, it is not the very feelings themselves that are manifest – even though anger is not shaking one's fist and crying is not sadness.

Both mentalism of the Cartesian and Lockean forms and behaviourism incorporate insights. There is indeed an important asymmetry between first- and third-person emotion attributions. But the whole conception of the inner and the outer is deeply misleading. It would

be an egregious error to suppose that we must choose between viewing the emotions as something inner (mentalism) and viewing them as
something outer (behaviourism). We must repudiate *the whole picture
of inner and outer*, and reject *both* the concept of the 'inner' and the
concept of the 'outer' as they are presented in traditional thought. Of
course, there is a conceptual, logical, connection between emotions
and their behavioural manifestation and verbal expression. But feeling an emotion is not a form of behaviour. One can often feign an
emotion one does not feel and feel an emotion one does not exhibit.
Equally, when one exhibits an emotion in behavioural manifestations
and verbal expression, *there is nothing hidden*. It is not as if the real
fear is *hidden behind* the pallid face, trembling hands, sweating palms,
and shaky voice – this is the form fear takes on this occasion, not the
facade behind which it is concealed.

## 4. Emotion, cognition, and the will

*Emotions*        Behavioural manifestations and expressions of emotion
*and the will*    and emotionally motivated actions lie along a volitional
                  spectrum that ranges from the non-voluntary to the
involuntary, and from the voluntary but not intentional to the intentional and deliberate. No one can blush or turn pale at will. These are
non-voluntary doings. Few can weep to order. We *find* our eyes filling
with tears, we *burst into* tears, or we *break down* in tears. But most
people, at least in some circumstances, can stifle their sobs and hold
back their tears. So crying can be partly voluntary, partly under our
control. Facial expression, tone of voice, gesture, and posture are
often assumed, especially in the case of tempestuous emotions, without
our even being aware of them. In such cases they are not voluntary.
Sometimes the manifestations of emotion are involuntary, as when we
know that we are smiling but cannot help it, or as when we cannot
control the tremor in our voice that we hear perfectly well or the
trembling of our hands that we observe. In other cases, we know perfectly well that we are smiling or scowling, raising our voice in delight
or shouting in anger, gesturing our welcome or our irritation. These
*are* under our control. We could suppress them if we so wish and
restrain our manifestations of feeling, but we have no wish to do so.
Here our behaviour is voluntary without necessarily being intentional.
However, such behaviour may be executed intentionally and on purpose,
although no intention need be formed in advance of the behaviour

and there need be no further intent – as when we smile on meeting an acquaintance in the street, as when we thump the table to emphasize a point or in the course of an angry tirade.[14] In general, authenticity in manifestations and expressions of our feelings requires absence of instrumentality. When, in advance of acting, we form the intention to smile or to scowl, to raise our voice or to stammer, to gesture *with* a purpose, and indeed we do so *in order* to bring about a further effect, then the manifestation and expression of emotion is not spontaneous and may not be wholly sincere.

*Emotion, knowledge, and belief*
The emotions of language-users are essentially linked in complex ways with what the subject knows or believes. As noted, emotions have formal objects in virtue of which they qualify as the emotions they are. The formal object of fear is what is (or is thought to be) dangerous or threatening to oneself or to an interest one has. That of remorse is a past misdemeanour that one wishes one had not done; that of envy is the good of another that one resents and may wish for oneself; and that of pity is the misfortune of another. On pain of *irrationality* or *psycho-pathology*, a person must take the object or intention of his emotion to satisfy the formal characteristics intrinsic to the emotion. If he fears someone, or someone's action, or some forthcoming event, he must know or believe that person, his act, or that event to be a threat. Irrational or pathological fears are fears that persist despite knowledge of the harmlessness of their object. If a person pities another, he must know or believe that this person has suffered, is suffering, or is going to suffer a misfortune. If he feels regret, remorse, or guilt, he must know or believe himself to have done something unfortunate, wrong, or untoward. Irrational or pathological guilt is guilt that persists despite one's knowing that it is groundless (e.g. survivor guilt).

*Emotion and reasons*
Consequently, the subject of any given emotion must have a further array of knowledge or beliefs regarding the object of his feelings. The formal characteristics that make a certain emotion the kind of emotion it is are shared by all emotions of that kind. But one's reasons for fearing tomorrow's examinations (that one is ill-prepared and so may fail) are quite different from one's reasons for fearing one's teacher or global warming, or for fearing for one's spouse or child. So, too, the reasons that make X-ing regrettable (e.g. that, as a consequence, one will not be able to do

---

[14] For a comprehensive discussion of voluntariness and intention, see *Human Nature*, ch. 7.

something one wanted to do) are typically quite different from the reasons that make Y-ing regrettable (that, as a consequence, one will catch cold). So feeling an emotion presupposes the subject's knowledge or belief that warrants subsuming the object and intention of the emotion under its formal characteristics. The intelligibility of the emotion depends upon the cogency of the reasons. The cogency of the reasons provides an explanation or justification for what is felt, and often a motive (a backward-looking reason) for what one consequently does.

*Emotion, evaluation, and judgement*
Human emotions are suffused with evaluation of the circumstances in which one takes oneself to be and of the characteristics one attributes to the substantive object of one's emotional response. For, as we have emphasized, our emotional responses manifest what we care about (positively and negatively) and constitute our modes of engagement with our fellow human beings. We evaluate people as friendly, indifferent or hostile, trustworthy or unreliable, honest or deceitful, witty or dull. We evaluate the circumstances as beneficial or harmful, as inviting or minatory, as worthy of interest or boring, as frightening or dangerous, and so forth. Hence our emotions essentially involve our faculty of judgement – which we may exercise well or ill in our evaluations of the situation with which we are confronted.

*Emotion and imagination*
It is equally important to note the manner in which *human* emotions are commonly bound up with thought, in particular with the imagination.[15] We distinguished between the *reproductive imagination* (eidetic imagery involved in recalled experience) and the *creative imagination* (the capacity to think up new, interesting, and hitherto undreamt-of possibilities). Both are deeply involved in our emotional life. Because emotions commonly have a history, powerful emotions such as love and hate, anger and fear, and pride and humiliation engage both forms of imagination. We conjure up images of shared experiences with the beloved. These fill our daydreams, and often inform our erotic fantasies. The vividly recollected occasions of some humiliation inflicted upon us, the image of one whom we passionately hate, or the mental picture of the terror we went through may haunt us during sleepless nights, and infiltrate our dreams – making nightmares of them. The cogitative imagination is at work in the torments the jealous inflict upon themselves, thinking where and with whom their beloved is, and

---

[15] The subject of imagination was investigated in detail in *The Intellectual Powers*, ch. 11.

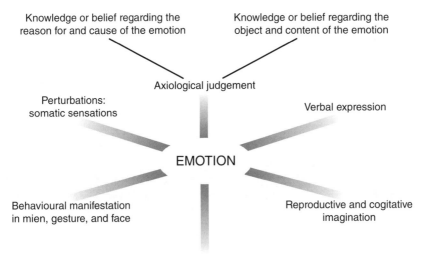

**Figure 2.3**    *The conceptual web of an emotion*

what he may be doing. Persistent hatred and anger may occupy a person's thoughts with imaginary possibilities of response, rehearsing what he should have said, thinking of what he would say if ...

The emotions therefore, although not themselves faculties, engage a plurality of human faculties. Hence our observations, in chapter 1, on their compositional complexity. Figure 2.3 provides a schematic overview.

# 3

# The Analytic of the Emotions II

## 1. The epistemology of the emotions

*Knowing emotions of others*    It should be evident, in the light of our discussion thus far, that the idea that the emotions of others are hidden from us is misguided. The conceivability of the emotions of others does not *logically* depend upon our having felt the emotion ourselves – one need not have felt jealous in order to understand Othello or Swann, or have plumbed the depths of despair in order to understand Lear's wild curses or Anna Karenina's suicide. We do not judge of the emotions of others on the basis of *analogy* with ourselves even though, in some cases, our sympathies may be more readily aroused if we have been through what others are now going through. We usually apprehend the feelings of others directly – by seeing their reactive and responsive behaviour. As previously argued, the behavioural manifestations of an emotion in a particular case are the *form* the emotion takes on that occasion, not the external signs of an inner state. The emotions of others are not *postulated* as the best explanation of their curious facial contortions and strange movements of arms and hands. For we no more see mere facial contortions and strange movements of hands than we hear mere sounds being emitted from the mouths of others when they speak in a language we understand. We *cannot* hear mere sounds when we listen to what another is saying. So, too, we *cannot* see smiles and laughter, tears and sobbing,

*The Passions: A Study of Human Nature*, First Edition. P. M. S. Hacker.
© 2018 John Wiley & Sons Ltd. Published 2018 by John Wiley & Sons Ltd.

as strange grimaces and noises. We do not *postulate* emotions as hidden causes of the manifestation and expression of emotion, we *see* the manifest emotion and hear it in the tones of voice.

*Criteria for emotions* The behaviour of others, in all its diversity and complexity, *in a context that renders it intelligible*, constitutes the *logical criteria* for ascribing emotions to them. We do not *infer* their emotions from the behavioural criteria we observe. But it is this behaviour that provides us with the logical (non-inductive) grounds for ascribing to another an appropriate emotion. The criteria are, of course, defeasible. We may have misunderstood the context and consequently misinterpreted the tears of disappointment as tears of grief. People may be insufficiently sensitive to discriminate between sincere expressions of love and deceitful emulation for the sake of lust or gain – often because their own emotions are involved (Natasha's belief in the genuineness of Kuragin's selfish passion, Kitty's inability to see the superficiality of Vronsky's flirtations, or Alice's trust in the love of George Vavasor in *Can You Forgive Her?*). The misjudgement, in such cases, is not indicative of an inductive inference or inference to the best explanation from the visible to the concealed. Nor does defeasibility imply defeat. In the absence of defeating evidence, we can, in many circumstances, have a warrant for complete certainty in ascribing an emotion to another person. For there are unmistakable manifestations of anger or rage, of sorrow or grief, and of joy or delight in appropriate settings.

*Constitutional indeterminacy of emotions* Nevertheless, the possibility of complete certainty in *some* kinds of case must not overshadow the fact that there is a degree of *opacity* and sometimes even a form of *constitutional indeterminacy* about the emotions and their manifestation.[1] Manifestations and expressions of emotion are elements of an ensemble of immediate reactive and responsive behaviour, emotion-eliciting situation, past relationships and events, persistent emotions exhibited in intentional and emotionally motivated speech and action. These elements form, and reform, highly complex patterns – but, like the patterns of tribal carpets (by contrast with the sophisticated symmetrical designs of

---

[1] This matter was discussed by Wittgenstein in his late writings on the philosophy of psychology (for references and analysis, see P. M. S. Hacker, *Wittgenstein: Meaning and Mind* (Blackwell, Oxford, 1990; paperback edn 1993), essay no. 7, 'The Inner and the Outer', §3). For further elaboration, see G. H. von Wright, 'Of Human Freedom', repr. in his *In the Shadow of Descartes* (Kluwer, Dordrecht, 1998), lecture 1, §§13–16.

Persian ones), the patterns display varying degrees of irregularity and asymmetry, which vary from rug to rug. One often cannot predict from the patterns in one corner of the carpet what the precise pattern in the opposite corner is. And no two rugs are the same. So, too, with the carpets of human passions. These irregularities are reflected in the peculiarities of the concepts and of the epistemology of the emotions.

We find that some people are transparent to us: we understand their feelings, we know what mood they are in, their responses are perspicuous, and we are sensitive to the fine nuances of their behaviour. But others may be completely opaque to us: we do not know what makes them 'tick'; we are not sure what feelings they are actually displaying, let alone what feelings they are controlling and suppressing. This interpersonal opacity is pronounced when encountering different cultures in which the forms of behavioural manifestation of emotions may be unfamiliar, and where the nuances of the verbal expressions of emotion are misunderstood. (Even a common language may mask what is meant: it takes an Englishman to know that 'That is very interesting, but ...' means 'That is totally irrelevant', or an American to realize that 'It was great to meet you! You *must* come to see us when you're in town' means no more than 'Goodbye'.) Even when we understand an alien tongue well, we may find the emotional reactions and motivations of the native speakers impenetrable. This is not because we do not know what they are saying to themselves *in foro interno*.

In some cases we cannot understand another person's feelings even though he tries his best to explain himself to us. We may not be able to grasp how such a triviality could count for so much, or why reconciliation is impossible without an explicit apology when both parties long for reconciliation. It may be unintelligible to us that rancour could last for so long, that events from the distant past may be brought up in interpersonal conflicts when they would best be left forgotten. While we *can* have complete certainty about another's emotions, and while there may be some uncertainties that could be settled if he or she opened his or her heart to us, there are also *constitutional uncertainties*. In such cases, the uncertainty about the feelings and emotionally determined motivations of another is not due to our not being able to look into their soul. They cannot look into their soul to resolve this indeterminacy either! The indeterminacy is not due to lack of knowledge or insufficiency of evidence. It is a feature of the nature of emotions and of understanding emotions.

The constitutional indeterminacy of the emotions, of their depth and authenticity, and of the motives to which they give rise is part of the human condition. It can be the source of mutual misunderstanding that may have tragic consequences. Two people, bound to each other by love, may interpret each other's emotions and emotional responses differently. Where one sincerely avows complete fidelity, the other senses wavering loyalty; where one insists upon undiminished love, the other may apprehend a weakening of fervour; where one honestly avers a certain motive for something said or done, the other sees a different motive. There need be no disagreement between them over the facts of their relationship – but one interprets the manifold nuances of behaviour and attitude one way, and the other another way. There may be no additional data to resolve the misunderstanding – all the facts are given. One person makes a pattern of their emotional life one way, the other another way. There need be no further 'fact of the matter'. Here tragedy lurks in the wings.

*Imponderable evidence*      It is noteworthy that, given the penumbra of opacity and indeterminacy surrounding the application of concepts of the emotions, there is such a thing as better and worse judgement about the emotions of others. Greater sensitivity to fine shades of behaviour is conducive to more refined insight into their hearts. Wide knowledge of mankind and openness to what people tell of themselves make for better judgement. If one knows a person well, one is more likely to be able to render his responses and reactions intelligible than if one were a mere acquaintance. One may learn to look, and come to see what others pass over. One may become sensitive to *imponderable evidence*, to subtleties of glance, facial expression, gesture, and tone of voice. One will then not have a better 'theory of the emotions' than others: one will have become a connoisseur of the emotions.

*Emotions and self-knowledge*      Let us now turn to self-ascription of emotions and its relationship to self-knowledge. It should not be surprising that we have little use for such remarks as 'I know I am afraid' (overjoyed, angry, sad, disappointed, embarrassed, etc.) save as concessive utterances in response to another's observation, 'You're frightened' (etc.). As such, they normally precede a 'but': 'I know I'm afraid, but it's jolly frightening' or '… but who wouldn't be?' This is roughly parallel to the lack of any epistemic role for the operator 'I know' affixed to avowals of pain or thought.[2] It is not an empirical coincidence that a mature language-user can normally

---

[2] See *The Intellectual Powers: A Study of Human Nature* (Wiley Blackwell, Oxford, 2013), pp. 41–6, 245–8.

say, without evidence, what emotion he feels. We don't *discover* that when someone wrongs us, is offensive to us, or humiliates us, then the feeling that regularly comes over us is anger. We do not *conclude* that what we feel must be anger, because someone just insulted us. Nor do we *correlate* the feeling of delight with being given a present we have been longing for, and we do not *infer* that what we are feeling must be gratitude. We do not reason 'This desideratum is neither certain nor impossible – it may well happen, so the feeling I have must be hope'. We do not normally identify, let alone misidentify, an emotion we are feeling. We commonly *express* our feelings, usually without any self-ascription of an emotion: 'Damn it, why did you do that?', 'Oh, how lovely! It's just what I wanted', 'Oh, I wish I hadn't done that'. But we do sometimes *report* our feelings by means of a self-ascription: 'I'm very angry with you, you know!', 'I'm so grateful!', 'I regret doing that.' Such expressions, reports, and the common *blends* of the two, are immediate. We do not normally observe ourselves, either inwardly or outwardly, and come to the conclusion that we are angry, afraid, sad, grateful, delighted, or disappointed. That is why there is normally no *epistemic* role for the operator 'I know' with respect to a wide range of emotion-ascriptions. There can be no room for 'Do you know whether you are angry?' as opposed to 'Are you angry?', or for 'Do you know whether you are afraid?' as opposed to 'Do you know whether he is afraid?' The question 'How do you know that you are anxious/disappointed/disgusted/embarrassed/sad/frightened?' would normally be met by incomprehension: 'What do you mean "How do I know?"?' That is not because, *of course*, we all know that sort of thing. Joking apart, could there be any role for 'As far as I know, I am grief-stricken', or 'To the best of my knowledge, I am grateful'?

*Ignorance and self-deception*          Nevertheless, by contrast with expressions of pain or of thought, the possibility of ignorance, doubt, or even error is intelligible in special circumstances, as indeed is self-deception. Tolstoy describes Prince Andrei as being in love before he is aware of it:

> It was late in the evening when Prince Andrei left the Rostovs. He went to bed from habit, but soon saw that he could not sleep. Having lit his candle he sat up in bed, then got up, then lay down again, not at all oppressed by his sleeplessness: his soul was so full of new and joyful sensations that it seemed to him as if he had just emerged from a stuffy room into God's fresh air. It did not even enter his head that he was in love with the little Rostov girl, he was not thinking about her but only

picturing her to himself, and in consequence all life appeared in a new light. (*War and Peace*, III. 19)

Othello combines ignorance of his own emotional response with self-deception. When Iago so patently sows seeds of jealousy in Othello's mind, he rises to the bait like a salmon to the fly, while denying adamantly that he is jealous:

> Thinkst thou I'ld make a life of jealousy,
> To follow still the changes of the moon
> With fresh suspicions? No, to be once in doubt
> Is once to be resolv'd: exchange me for a goat,
> When I shall turn the business of my soul
> To such exsufflicate and blown surmises
> Matching thy inference.'Tis not to make me jealous
> To say my wife is fair, feeds well, loves company,
> Is free of speech, sings, plays and dances well;
> Where virtue is, these are more virtuous:
> Nor from mine own weak merits will I draw
> The smallest fear, or doubt of her revolt,
> For she had eyes, and chose me. No, Iago;
> I'll see before I doubt, and when I doubt prove,
> And on the proof, there is no more but this:
> Away at once with love or jealousy.
>
> (*Othello*, III. 3)

Sometimes someone who has been deceiving herself may indeed realize that she has been so doing. Anna realizes from her disappointment at Vronsky's absence at a party that what had seemed to her displeasure at his pursuit of her was self-deception:

> At first Anna sincerely believed that she was displeased with him for having allowed himself to pursue her; but soon after her return from Moscow, having gone to a party where she expected to meet him but to which he had not come, she clearly realized, by the sadness that overcame her, that she had been deceiving herself and that his persecution supplied the whole interest of her life. (*Anna Karenina*, II. 4)

*Realization and self-ascription of emotion*

What is striking about such cases is that the form knowledge takes, when the penny drops, is *realization*. Moreover, what alerts one to one's own feelings are sometimes not criteria for the emotion at all, but rather constitutive somatic associations and feelings of pleasure or distress. There may be circumstances in which one emotion is mutating into another, as when one's excitement may turn into fear. Here indeed one may suddenly *realize* (not observe or discover) that one is afraid because one's mouth has gone dry and one's heart is suddenly racing (the elephant one has been quietly watching in the African bush starts coming towards one). Someone whom one dislikes may insult one, and one's fully controlled dislike may change: one may suddenly feel one's temples throbbing and *realize* that one is becoming angry. Similarly, when one suddenly notices that one's heart melts whenever one hears Elizabeth's voice and that one's pulses race whenever she enters the room, one may realize to one's surprise and chagrin (as Mr Darcy did) that one is falling in love.

*The place of doubt and uncertainty* — Doubt and uncertainty are, with respect to *some* emotions, and in *some* circumstances, possible. But, unlike the cases of being unsure what one thinks or what one wants, this does not betoken the need *to make up one's mind* what one feels (as one may make up one's mind, on the balance of reasons, what one thinks) or to *decide* what to feel (as one may decide what one wants). For one cannot *decide* to feel frightened or angry, joyful or grateful, to love or to hate. When one is unsure what one feels, one's emotions may be in an indeterminate state of flux. One may well say 'I don't know whether I love her' but it would be bizarre to say 'Well, either I love her or I don't. I must find out which it is'. For what is necessary to quell one's uncertainty is for one's feelings to *crystallize*. One may well ask oneself what one would sacrifice for her, but that is not an experiment to discover how things stand, but an attempt to give form to an inchoate feeling. Others may realize that one is falling in love or indeed has fallen in love before one does oneself (Casaubon's apprehension of Dorothea's feeling for young Ladislaw in *Middlemarch*).

In the main, uncertainty with respect to one's own feelings is more commonly manifest in borderline cases, and in ignorance in cases of self-deception. Am I really afraid or just a little apprehensive? Do I just dislike him or do I actually hate him? Is it just that I think he got what was coming to him, or is what I feel *Schadenfreude*? Am I enquiring merely out of curiosity, or out of genuine concern? Is my applause genuine, or is it coloured by a touch of envy? These are questions that may arise for most people at one time or another in the course of their lives. They may not be questions to which the subject can give a determinate answer. Of course, they can arise with respect to others too. A bystander may not be able to give a clear and determinate answer either. This may be because of ignorance, but it may be because of the inchoate form of the subject's feelings – an inchoateness exhibited by the equivocal behaviour that is the ground for ascribing the emotion.

However, there are cases in which the subject does not correctly characterize the emotion that besets him. One may exhibit a modest degree of hostility without really being aware that one is doing so – although an observant bystander may see it. One's restlessness and discontent may be the form that one's unacknowledged loneliness takes. A friend may see what evades one or what one is reluctant to confront. It may not seem to one that one's apprehension is a form of distrust, but this may be evident to others. It may not occur to one that one's irritation is a mark of jealousy – but one's spouse or best friend may see it immediately. What one typically lacks in such cases is not information but realization. What is necessary is to bethink oneself – to reflect, not investigate.

*Emotions and self-deception* There are cases in which one deceives oneself, and is unwilling to acknowledge one's feelings even to oneself, whereas a perceptive onlooker may apprehend the self-deception. What one tells oneself is genuine concern may in fact be, and be seen by others to be, an appetite for malicious gossip. One may readily acknowledge pity, but be unwilling to recognize that one is taking pleasure in the misfortune of the other. Avowals of contentment or happiness often mask a fundamental insecurity and disappointment with one's life that one is unwilling to admit to oneself. In these, and doubtless endless further ways, one can deceive oneself about one's feelings or fail to realize what one's feelings are.

One thing, at any rate, should be clear. There are large differences between different emotions, for they are not made to a single pattern. Generalization across emotions is unlikely to yield much truth. Each emotion that gives rise to conceptual difficulties of one sort or another needs to be scrutinized in its own right. Conceptual diversity is great and the forms of intentionality, the modes of context dependence, and the forms that a given emotion may take call out for careful attention to the particular case.

## 2. Emotion and reason

*Responsibility for emotions* It is the cognitive and evaluative features of the emotions that bring human emotions into the domain of the rational and the reasonable. For one's emotions (for the most part³) should be felt for the right reasons, directed at the right objects, made manifest and expressed on the right occasions, and felt to the right degree (Aristotle). Then one's emotions are reasonable and justifiable, even though we cannot feel an emotion at will. We are, to a degree, responsible for our emotions, just as we are, to a degree, responsible for our beliefs.⁴ We are sometimes ashamed of our feelings – as when we feel a pang of jealousy at our spouse's flirting trivially with another, or lose our temper when we should have controlled it, or persist in our hostility when we should have forgiven the offence. Equally, we are sometimes ashamed *not to feel* what we ought to feel – as when we should feel grief but do not, should feel compassion but are indifferent, or ought to feel remorse but feel none. Similarly, we blame others for feeling angry when anger was inappropriate, criticize others for not mastering their fear, castigate them for their lack of pride or for their excessive pride. We can tell others that they ought to fear global warming, but we cannot *order* them to fear it, nor can we ourselves *decide* to fear it. We commonly tell another that he *ought* to be ashamed of himself, but we cannot give an order 'Be ashamed!', only exclaim 'Shame on you!' Although we may say to a child 'Don't be so frightened!', this is not an order to do something, but an adjunct to 'There is nothing to be frightened of!' or an encouragement to control his feelings. How then can we be held responsible for feeling something when we cannot feel it at will or by design, and cannot obey orders to feel or to refrain from feeling? The answer, unsurprisingly, runs parallel to the conceptual clarification of our responsibility for our beliefs.

*Explanation of emotional responsibility*          Criticism for feeling an emotion turns on:

   (i)   A mistake in the object and intention of the emotion: for example, Hippolytus did not rape Phaedra, and Theseus's vengeful anger, directed at Hippolytus (the object of his anger), and his rage *at Hippolytus's having raped Phaedra* (the intention of his rage) were wrong. Such mistaken beliefs are capable of being corrected by reflection and further enquiry. If we jump to a conclusion about the object of our feelings or about their intention, we are answerable for our failure adequately to examine the evidence or to make further enquiries, or for taking the word of those who are untrustworthy (as Othello trusts Iago),

---

³ There are exceptions. There may be reasons for loving a person, but one rarely loves a person for a reason (see chapter 10).

⁴ For examination of responsibility for beliefs, see *The Intellectual Powers*, pp. 215–17.

or for not trusting someone we should have trusted (sometimes despite the evidence (as Othello should have trusted Desdemona).

(ii)   An inadequacy of the reasons for the emotion: for example, it is true that Hugh Stanbury wrote for the *Daily Record*, but that was not a good reason for Miss Jemima Stanbury's wrath and consequent disinheritance of young Hugh (Trollope's *He Knew He Was Right*). Inadequate reasons are subject to correction by further thought and enquiry, as Hugh's aunt comes to realize. If our reasons for feeling what we feel were inadequate, we should have considered the matter with more care. That is why we are answerable for our feeling.

(iii)  A disproportion in the intensity of the emotion: One can, to a degree, control the intensity of one's feelings through reflection and reconsideration. To fall victim to an excess of sensibility in general (like Marianne in *Sense and Sensibility*) is no less a fault than insensibility and callousness. An emotion may coil around one's mind, dominating one's life to the exclusion of all else, warping one's judgement, destroying one's life, and leading to cruelty and wrongdoing (Othello's jealousy, Heathcliff's passion, Achilles' wrath).

Criticism of an emotional episode may turn on additional factors pertaining to:

(iv)   The propriety of the manner in which the emotion is manifested or expressed: To display emotion on a particular occasion in a manner that is wholly out of proportion to the significance of its object is a form of over-reaction indicative of bad judgement and lack of self-control (Lord Chiltern in *Phineas Finn*). But one *can* control one's manifestations of emotion to a degree (bite one's tongue, count to ten, take a deep breath, allow time to lapse before venturing a response, and so forth). Equally, there are occasions on which one may be criticized for excessive self-control: one should have shown one's anger or annoyance to the young whippersnapper; or one should have shown one's love or grief, rather than keeping an iron grip upon one's feelings.

(v)    The propriety of the occasion on which the emotion is expressed: We sometimes respond to what another says or does, or to a piece of information imparted to us, with a manifestation of intense feelings inappropriate *on the occasion*. But it is, for the most part, within one's power to refrain from expressing one's feelings in public here and now, and to wait until a private occasion arises later, for example, in castigating one's wayward spouse.

(vi)    The avoidability of the occasion that gave rise to the emotion. For example, one should not start talking politics with so-and-so, as one always loses one's temper with him and makes a scene. If one does, then one is to blame, because one brought the scene upon oneself.

In the case of persistent emotions, we are answerable for further flaws despite the non-voluntariness of our feelings:

(vii)   The unwarranted duration of one's emotions: for example, that it is time to stop mourning (Queen Victoria) or to abate one's anger (Achilles).

(viii)  The irrational and obsessive character of one's emotion: for example, the hatred of Inspector Javert (*Les Misérables*), the jealousy of Louis Trevelyan (*He Knew He was Right*), the envy of Bette (Balzac's *Cousine Bette*), Philip Carey's obsessive love for Mildred (*Of Human Bondage*).

(ix)    The excessive motivating force of the emotion or the insufficiency in the motivating force of an emotion is a further ground of reasonable criticism. This is patently the case with obsessive emotions.

(x)     The unjustifiability of the intentional actions motivated by the emotion: for example, Lear's disinheritance of Cordelia out of pique, Anatole Kuragin's attempted abduction of Natasha out of infatuation and lust (*War and Peace*) or Pozdnyshev's jealous murder of his wife (*The Kreutzer Sonata*).

---

- Mistake in the object or intention of the emotion.
- Inadequacy of the reason for the emotion.
- Disproportionate intensity of the emotion.
- Impropriety in the manner of expressing the emotion.
- Impropriety of the occasion on which the emotion is expressed.
- Avoidability of the emotion.
- Unwarranted duration of the emotion.
- Obsessive character of the emotion.
- Unwarranted motivational force of the emotion.
- Unjustifiability of the intentional actions done out of the emotion.

---

**List 3.1**   *Faulting an emotion*

Emotions are reasonable to the extent to which they *Reasonableness* are directed towards what warrants the feelings, and *of emotions* to the extent that the intensity of the emotion felt is proportional to its warrant. Disproportionality indicates unreasonableness; gross disproportionality indicates irrationality. Fear in the face of danger is perfectly rational, but excessive fear may lead to cowardice, while insufficient fear may lead to rashness. In both cases, judgement is likely to be impaired. Anger and indignation are perfectly proper responses to what is incompetent or foolish (when competence is rightly expected and common sense required), wrong (instrumentally or morally), disobedient (when obedience may rightly be demanded), or offensive (insulting, humiliating, contemptible). But rage – excessive anger – deprives one of judgement and inclines one to wrong-doing. Here the reins of reason are thrown off and disaster often ensues. To express or manifest one's anger is one thing, which, if properly controlled, may not be unreasonable. To act in anger is another – for it is to act with clouded judgement. Remorse – the daughter of conscience – is the proper emotion to feel in response to one's own misdeeds and misdemeanours. One who feels remorse for his wrong-doings will strive to make good the harm he has caused (Scrooge in *A Christmas Carol*), to repent (Tolstoy's Prince Nekhlyudov), or to wipe out the disgrace and shame that he has brought upon himself (Conrad's Lord Jim). But to wallow in remorse may lead to the paralysis of the will and the abnegation of obligation. Reasonableness in emotional life is also manifest in corrective responsiveness to criticisms concerning feelings and the actions they motivate. One's misguided feelings *ought* to vanish on realization of the groundlessness of the beliefs on which one's emotion rests. Those who are capable of modifying their feelings and the manifestation of their feelings when faced with justifiable criticism are being reasonable (Plantagenet Palliser in *The Duke's Children*). They can acknowledge that their reaction was wrong or that it was excessive in relation to its object or intention or that it was inappropriate in context – and they can modify their behaviour accordingly.

There is a striking asymmetry between the criticisms for *Emotional* an excess of emotion and the criticisms for deficiency of *deficiency* emotion. This is unsurprising, precisely because feeling an emotion is not directly subject to the will. Someone who lacks emotion when emotion is meet is criticized, for the most part, for being insensitive, unfeeling, lacking in sensibility. Lack of remorse (Iago) shows callousness to those one has harmed and indifference to the harm one has inflicted. Lack of pity (Lady Macbeth) manifests a cold, unfeeling, ruthless heart. Ingratitude (Regan and Goneril) displays lack of appreciation for benefits granted and disregard of reciprocal obligations. Such insensitivity to reasons for feeling may itself be rooted in emotion, for example in hatred, jealousy, or distrust. If such responses are characteristic of the agent, then they are defects of character and personality. For the agent evidently does not care about things that he or she should care about and is indifferent to matters that demand concern.

*Irrationality of emotions*        Irrationality in the emotions is manifest when there is no reason that warrants the emotion displayed, when the reason adduced is patently false or irrelevant, or when the agent persists in his feelings despite being reliably informed of the falsity or irrelevance of his emotion-warranting beliefs. It is exhibited by obsessive emotions, such as obsessive love, hatred or envy, all-consuming jealousy or grief, and fanatical humility (such as expressed in the grovelling avowals of some of the church fathers such as Tertullian and St Augustine, in which humility, one cannot but suspect, they took pride). These border on, and sometimes even transgress, the boundaries of the pathological.

*Phobias*        Phobias are pathological fears, for they persist despite known lack of warrant. They are insensitive to reason. An acrophobe's fear of heights is not ameliorated by being shown that there is no danger of falling. An arachnophobe's fear of spiders does not vanish on being told that this dear little tarantula is quite harmless. Despite the acknowledged absence of good reasons for being afraid, the fear persists. Precisely for this reason we are *not* held accountable for such fears. The contrast with bigotry, which is primarily a doxastic rather than an affective defect, is striking. For the phobic's irrational fear is immune to reason and to reasoning, whereas the bigot's hatred (nationalist, racial, religious, sectarian) is supported by a system of beliefs and it is the *beliefs* that are insensitive or immune to reason.

*Responsibility for emotions and for beliefs contrasted*        Although we are partly responsible for both our beliefs and our feelings, there is an asymmetry between the two cases.[5] If a person accepts that his belief is false, he cannot, logically, go on believing

[5] See *The Intellectual Powers*, pp. 215–17; also S. Hampshire, *Freedom of the Individual* (Chatto & Windus, 1965), ch. 3, and J. Raz, 'When We Are Ourselves: the Active and the Passive', repr. in *Engaging Reason* (Oxford University Press, Oxford, 1999), pp. 5–21.

what he believed. There can be no 'Things are not so, but nevertheless I believe that they are so'. One may not be able to control the thoughts, including pathological thoughts, that cross one's mind – they invade one. But, once one has accepted that they are false, one *cannot* believe them. One cannot find oneself *saddled* with a belief willy-nilly. So one may say 'I know that things were not so, but I am still haunted by the thought that they were', or '... I can't help thinking (imagining) that they were', or '... I can't get rid of the idea that they were'. Emotions are unlike beliefs in this respect. One may indeed be saddled with a phobia. One may know full well that there is no danger of falling, that this spider is harmless, that mice do not usually run up one's legs – but nevertheless be frightened. Equally, one may wake up with a nameless dread, an undirected fear or objectless anxiety. Knowing that there is nothing threatening may not alleviate one's ominous feelings at all. One is then their unwilling victim, in a sense in which one cannot be an unwilling victim of one's beliefs.[6]

*Educating the emotions*        Although emotions are passions and so cannot be felt or cease to be felt at will, they are not *given*, as sensations, such as aches and pains, are. Because there are reasons and justifications for feeling emotions, because emotions can, to a degree, be suppressed, because their manifestation is, to some extent, controllable, because the expression of persistent emotions in words and deeds is largely intentional, and because our emotions provide us with reasons (and hence too with motives) for voluntary and intentional action, *emotions can be educated*. Infants doubtless come to care about things they encounter by finding out whether what attracts them gives them pleasure, whether what repels them warrants aversion, and whether what frightens them is indeed dangerous. In due course, they discover what incurs parental approval or disapproval, and their emotions are engaged (positively and negatively) in response. Children have to be taught what is worth caring about, and how much they should care about the things they do care about. They have to learn what merits an emotional response and what kind and what degree of emotional response it merits. Equally, children and adults alike need to learn to control the manifestations of their immediate and spontaneous emotional responses, as well as the expression of emotional responses

---

[6] Not all emotions are like this. The greater the doxastic component and the lesser the perturbations, the less intelligible it would be for the emotion to persist in the face of contrary grounds. One *cannot* feel remorse for something one knows one did not do or feel proud of doing something one knows one never did.

in what they say. They need to learn to reflect on the motivational warrant afforded by persistent emotions and to make reasonable and rational decisions about acting out of emotions.

Although our emotions need educating, there are, of course, no *lessons* in feeling emotions any more than there are lessons (as opposed to training) in virtue.[7] Our emotional education takes place in the white waters of life, with its rocks, eddies, waterfalls, and whirlpools. Our emotions are diurnally engaged in familial and social intercourse; in relationships with superiors, equals, and subordinates at the workplace; with members of the public at large and with officials of the bureaucratic state. They are subjected from time to time, to a greater or lesser degree, to criticism and approval – especially, but not only, in childhood and youth. As we are social creatures, our emotional education is the product of parental care (or neglect), peer pressure (in childhood and adulthood alike), responsible (or negligent) schooling, the wisdom (or bigotry) of religion, the honest (or deceitful) rhetoric of political leaders, and the mass media. All of these teach us, well or badly, what to care about and what not to care about. They are all liable to breed emotional inauthenticity. They are prone to generate prurient emotions, sentimentality (spurious and excessive emotion), hypocrisy, clichéd and stereotyped emotional responses, religious, racial and political bigotry, self-satisfaction, and self-righteous aggressive emotion. Authentic emotions require not merely an open heart, but also a critical mind – the exercise of one's own rational faculties. Mere authenticity in emotion is of little merit, let alone an excuse, in the absence of reason and understanding. Emotional maturity requires good judgement.

*Reasons and passion: 4 misunderstandings*

It should by now be obvious that the common supposition that there is a necessary conflict between heart and mind, between reason and emotion, between intellect and feeling, is misleading. It has many roots. One may well be embedded in the Homeric tradition, in which the extreme and impulsive emotions are seen as invasive daemonic powers for which the victim bears no responsibility.[8] Hence Agamemnon's *explanation* of (not apology for) his rage:

---

[7] That is one reason why critical education in literature is not a pedagogical luxury, but an indispensable part of the curriculum in any civilized society. It awakens the imagination, broadens the conception of emotion-eliciting situations, fosters the ability to appreciate different points of view, encourages the critical evaluation of emotions and emotional motivation, and invites considered judgement.

[8] The suggestion is E. R. Dodds's, in *The Greeks and the Irrational* (University of California Press, Berkeley, 1951), ch. 1.

'Mad, blind I was! Not even I would deny it ... But since I was blinded, lost in my inhuman rage, now, at last, I am bent on setting things to rights: I'll give a priceless ransom paid for friendship' (*Iliad* IX. 138–45). Later on in the epic, he repeats this explanation: 'I am not to blame! Zeus and Fate and the Fury stalking through the night, they are the ones who drove that savage madness in my heart, that day in assembly when I seized Achilles' prize – on my own authority, true, but what could *I* do? A god impels all things to their fulfilment: Ruin, eldest daughter of Zeus, she blinds us all' (*Iliad* XIX. 100–108). This conception sets up an irresolvable conflict between mankind and the afflicting passions, fixing a picture – a form of representation – of bewitching power. To be sure, that is a speculative genetic account of a form of thought. This much, however, is clear: faculty psychology, which we inherited from the Greeks, is a seedbed for four misunderstandings that bear on our concern.

First, it encourages the reification of faculties and hence the conception of faculties as agents. We may rightly wish to distinguish the faculty of reason from the faculty of the will or the sense faculties. Nevertheless, faculties are *not agents* but classes of powers. Reason does not control the passions; rather *we* should control our feelings when they are, for one reason or another, irrational or unreasonable. The emotions are not intelligent, but *we* may display our intelligence (as well as our sensitivity) in our emotional responses, in their manifestation or in the suppression of their manifestation, and in the good judgement that we exhibit in acting out of our emotions.

Secondly, it fosters a misconception of the faculty of reason. Mesmerized initially by the model of geometry and more recently by the model of logical calculi, we are all too prone to conceive of our powers of reasoning as restricted to deductive reasoning, and to conceive of the activity of reason as deducing and inferring. Hence Hume's mistaken averral that reason is and should be no more than the slave of the passions. But not only does reason not engage in activities – deducing and inferring are not activities anyway. We deduce conclusions from premises, and draw inferences from evidence. But to do so is to *apprehend* conclusions as warranted by their *supporting reasons* – it is to come to view the transition from grounds (reasons) to conclusions as justified. The arguments in the law courts rather than the calculi devised by mathematicians are the proper models of much of human reasoning. For reasoning is more commonly a matter of examining pros and cons, weighing different considerations, and deciding which are more apt in the situation in which one finds oneself.

Thirdly, it obscures the relationship between reason, reasoning, and reasons. The power of reasoning should be understood by reference to *sensitivity to reasons*, and the ability to think, feel, and do things *for reasons*. We have *reasons for feeling* no less than reasons for thinking. It is mistaken to suppose that the passions are given by physical perturbations of the body and brain, and are then subjected to the dictates of reason. We have reasons for becoming angry with someone who is offensive, reasons for being fearful of what is threatening, reasons for feeling compassion, loyalty, or gratitude. Our reasonableness is not exhibited in our logical prowess (formal logicians are neither more rational nor more reasonable than other mortals) but in our ability to weigh reasons judiciously.

Fourthly, the picture (the conceptual iconography, as it were) of reason and the passions intimates that reason is always in the right, keeping the unruly passions on the right track (Plato), or guiding action down the rails that will lead to the satisfaction of the passions (Hume). This fails to do justice to that fact that reasons may themselves be good, poor, or even downright bad. Our powers of reasoning are reflexive. It often needs careful reasoning and dispassionate reflection to weed out the poor and the bad reasons. We may have reasons for being angry, and also reasons for forgiving the vexing offence. It may need sober reasoning and calm reflection to realize that we must curb our anger, or alternatively restrain our forgiveness (if the offence was unforgivable).

Consequently the picture of Reason and the Emotions as being in perpetual conflict, of the rectitude of the faculty of Reason and the irrationality of the Emotions, is a pernicious distortion of important truths. Our emotional responses are commonly rational and reasonable. But they may be irrational or unreasonable. They are then to be judged, criticized, and changed or restrained by *reasoning*. Conversely, our reasons for thinking or acting may be wrong, poor, or even bad, and they can be corrected by our feelings – especially by different forms of love and compassion. Forgiveness is often wisely motivated by love; deserved indifference is sometimes rightly mitigated by compassion; reasonable self-interest is sometimes overridden by feelings of fraternity and solidarity. Finally, one emotion may often correct another: hope may overcome despair; curiosity may master disgust; pride may control fear. But these are not conflicts between forms of unreason.

We caricature our abilities and liabilities when we contrast 'cold' reason with 'hot' passion, although it is true that passions warp good judgement. But there is nothing 'cold' about *reasons* for feeling gratitude or indignation, compassion or remorse, pride or shame, and nothing 'hot' about *feeling* indifferent or apathetic. To say that we are going to act in accordance with our heart, not with our head, is misleading. For that, if taken at face value, is tantamount to saying that we shall disregard good reasons and act out of unreasoned inclination. What is presumably intended is a declaration that we shall disregard cost–benefit considerations and act out of loyalty, love, or fraternity.

*Intuition*  We sometimes appeal to intuition (or to feminine intuition) against reason. This too is either unwarranted or misleading.

There is, for the most part, no warrant to favour groundless hunches or guesses over *good* reasons. Intuition can carry weight only when it is the product of tuition. Then 'intuition' (feminine or masculine) signifies not groundlessness, but the immediacy of the well-honed faculty of judgement of a connoisseur. To be sure, there may be circumstances in which we justifiably favour intuition over reasons, for example, when the reasons are indecisive or equivocal and one has a knack for good decision-making in conditions of uncertainty.

Reason may be presented as being in control of the passions, but not after the Platonic model of the charioteer in control of two steeds. We have reasons for caring about what we care about – but we may be wrong, or we may care to excess. We have reasons for our emotions – but they may be poor rather than good reasons, invalid rather than correct, and we may indulge to excess in the emotions we feel. Our emotions often provide us with motives – but whether we should act out of the emotion we feel requires judgement and understanding. In these ways, and in others, reflexive reason *is* needed to control the passions. Its task is to assess the rational warrant for our feelings when such warrant is meet, to curb excess in the emotions felt, to control their manifestation and expression, and to keep them within the bounds of reasonableness. It is not always up to the task.

## 3. The place of the emotions in human life

*Evolution of emotions*  Susceptibility to emotions is a feature of advanced forms of animal life. As we have seen, *one* thread that binds most, although perhaps not all, emotions together is *caring* about something – something's *mattering* to one, positively or negatively. Mere attraction and avoidance behaviour, although indicative of appetites, is – we have averred – too thin to warrant emotion-ascription in any but the thinnest sense. Even then it is limited largely to anger and fear. As one moves up the evolutionary tree, more plastic forms of behavioural response to circumstances become evident and more plastic facial features are exhibited. Once expressive behaviour is upon the evolutionary carpet, primitive emotions are in play – primitive in so far as they are pre-linguistic. That evolution should have selected for susceptibility to such feelings and for the manifest forms they take is unsurprising. The fight-or-flight response (also called the acute stress response), first identified and analysed neuro-pharmacologically by Walter Cannon in the 1920s, has obvious physiological utility in preparing an animal to meet a perceived threat with readiness to fight or to flee.

*Animal emotions* This is marked in territorial animals, where the tendency to attack is potent when the animal is within its own territory, the tendency to flee is dominant when it is on another's territory, and ritualized behaviour (simultaneous ambivalence, successive ambivalence, and displacement behaviour) is exhibited on the territorial border. The *manifestation* of rage and fear that is, among higher animals, a visible and audible somatic corollary of the fight-or-flight response, has an essential *communicative* function. The *forms* these emotions take – their manifestation in facial expression, raising of hair, arching of the back, twitching or erection of the tail, emission of sounds (howls, growls, and hisses), and tension of the limbs – *signal* to the threatening animal preparedness for fight. Among socialized pack or tribal animals, the combination of patent manifestations of fear and submission behaviour has evident utility in reducing the actual fighting and injury, and in strengthening group unity. In the case of animals that share the burden of rearing young, forms of bonding – exhibited in mutual grooming, sharing food, and manifestations of receptive pleasure in them – increase the likelihood of rearing successful offspring. In general, the care *of* offspring implies caring *for* offspring. Such forms of bonding and caring are the roots of feelings of reciprocal affection.

*Language extends the emotions* As we have seen, the range of emotions possible for non-language-users is very limited in comparison to human emotions. The objects of that limited range are similarly constrained by lack of linguistic, conceptual, abilities.

However, once language is in play, in the context of complex forms of social organization, the range of possible emotions and of their objects is vastly extended and becomes relieved of evolutionary selection. Emotions become attuned to social value systems, symbolic behaviour, and systems of belief, including religion and ideology – the transmission of which from one generation to the next is independent of gene transmission. Human history and the history of cultures are not shaped by sexual selection after the manner of humanoid development in prehistory. Emotions are now not only *manifest* in behaviour, but also articulated in language and *expressed* in linguistic behaviour. The normal user of any developed language can be said to *have reasons* for feeling the emotions he feels (save in pathological cases), for these are the factors he cites (or can cite) in answering the question *why*. And, if he can do that, he *can* also distinguish between emotions warranted by reason and those that are not. In this way, emotions become sensitive to reasons and answerable to reasoning. The horizon of the intentional objects of emotions expands with respect to time (to encompass the past and the future), with respect to generality (to encompass one, a few, some, most, and all), and with respect to value (to encompass emotional responses to the desired and desirable, the right and the good, the unwanted, the wrong, and the evil). Emotions of self-assessment become possible, such as pride, shame, and guilt. It becomes possible to feel self-directed anger at one's prior feelings of fear, shame at one's feelings of intimidation, pity and compassion for the grief or sorrow of others, gratitude for their solicitude and sympathy, and so on. The human world is indeed rooted in the animal world, but differs from it as the fruit differs from the seed.

    Many emotions are deleterious and detrimental to human
*Negative* felicity. The *victims* of hatred and anger, spite, malicious
*emotions* envy, and jealousy are countless. The *agents* of such emotions scar their own souls. Nevertheless, not even the Stoics, who aimed at *apatheia* (freedom from the passions) or *tranquilitas* (as Cicero averred), thought that *all* passions were evil and mere 'diseases of the soul'. While some of the Stoics deplored most human emotions precisely because they *are* passions and hence *imposed* upon us, they embraced *eupatheia*, which include feelings of joy, generosity, and affection. We may concede that there are emotions that, on the whole, one should not feel, such as rage, anguish, despair, hatred, terror, panic, malicious envy, spite, jealousy. If one does feel them when confronted with the manifold misfortunes, ills, and evils of human life, one should strive to control them by reflection, since they are inimical to good judgement in the particular case, and to a good life in general. They are *negative* emotions – emotional responses to something felt to be profoundly repugnant – that one would prefer not to feel.

But whether such feelings of repugnance are warranted should itself be subject to the judgement of reason. Such negative emotions are often *excessive feelings*, such as despair, panic, and rage, which commonly involve over-reacting to circumstances of life, or *wicked feelings*, such as spite and malicious envy.

Nevertheless, there surely are, as Aristotle averred, forms of anger that are warranted, absence of which would signify a defect of character, such as *indignation* at injustice or *resentment* at false imputations of evil to oneself or others. But one must concede that it is a feature of the unrefined, ill-educated, and uncontrolled human constitution often to over-react – with rage that deprives one of the powers of reflection and judgement. There surely are forms of fear that are warranted by danger to oneself and to those one loves, by threats to one's interests and the interests of others for whom one feels responsible, and by menace to things one cherishes. But, again, one must concede that it is an unavoidable feature of human physiology that the episodic fear one feels may be excessive. It may amount to paralysing terror, to ill-judged panic expressed in inutile behaviour. Instead of preparing one to face the looming danger or threat by putting one on one's toes, it blinds one's judgement and is exhibited in behaviour that is deleterious to oneself and others. Similarly, the persistent fear one feels may be disproportionate and in need of rational control. In so far as love is a blessing, then grief and sorrow are an unavoidable part of the human condition. One may, in Roman fashion, wish to suppress their manifestation. But to extirpate such feelings is to harden one's heart against love too. For one criterion for how much one loves another is the depth of the grief one feels when they die. However, for one's grief and sorrow to lead to despair and anguish is detrimental to one's life, damaging to those with whom one lives, and deleterious to one's ability to fulfil one's responsibilities. In short, the negative emotions often need to be curbed and controlled by reason and by reasoning. Systematic failure to do so in the course of one's life is to be a victim of one's feelings.

Spinoza sapiently remarked 'the impotence of man to *Human* govern or restrain the emotions I call bondage, for a man *bondage* who is under their control is not his own master ... So that he is often forced to follow the worst, although he sees the better before him' (*Ethics*, IV. 6). One can be released from bondage to one's emotions by striving to feel the right emotions, at the right times, towards the right people, for the right reasons, to the right degree, and to manifest or suppress their manifestation in the right way

(Aristotle). To teach this is one of the duties of moral education. A large part of moral education is, or should be, the education of the emotions. One must learn both 'to care and not to care' (T. S. Eliot) – and to grasp the reasons that make something worthy of care. One must learn to identify misguided or excessive emotion, and to curb and control it. Moreover, one must strive to sharpen one's sensitivity to the good, the true, and the beautiful, as well as to evil, falsehood, and the ugly.

*Aristotle on emotion*　　Aristotle applied his doctrine of the mean not only to the virtues, but also to the emotions. He thought that all emotions come in triplets of excess, deficiency, and propriety, these being connected with parallel triplets among the virtues and vices. So there is one way of hitting the target and two ways of missing it. What he is doing, I believe, is imposing a form of representation upon his descriptions of the emotions – a constant pattern in terms of which to represent them (as we represent knowledge as a possession, pain as an object, thinking as a process). It is not the result of examination of the emotions, nor is it the result of analysis of the concepts of the emotions. However, Aristotle has a much deeper and felicitous insight into the nature of the emotions, which can be detached from his conception of an emotional mean. He remarked of the emotions that 'There are many ways of going astray … whereas there is only one way of getting it right (which is exactly why the one is easy and the other difficult – missing the mark is easy, but hitting it difficult)' (Aristotle, *Nicomachean Ethics*, 1106$^b$29–33). This insight, which is at odds with the doctrine of the mean, is a nice conceptual observation. As we shall see in our investigations into specific emotions, we have a rich vocabulary for the *manifold* ways in which we can err with respect to our emotions. For there can be *many* inappropriate emotional responses (see list 3.1), many different ways of 'going astray' from occasion to occasion. To be sure, the suggestion that there is only *one* way of getting things right is true, at best, only of the polymorphous description that Aristotle offers. In the case of existential decisions, such as that made by Sartre's young man confronting a choice between fighting for the Free French or taking care of his old widowed mother, even that is incorrect.[9]

Aristotle emphasized the connections between the emotions and the virtues and vices. The former (the emotions), we have seen, may be temporary (either momentary or episodic) or enduring. The corresponding

[9] J. P. Sartre, 'Existentialism is a Humanism' (1946).

virtues and vices are character traits. These connections are not coincidental, but intrinsic, for the reasons for feeling an emotion are commonly also reasons for acting in response to the object of the emotion, and provide a motive for plans, projects, and actions in the longer term. Nevertheless, the immediate emotional reaction and response, as well as the indeterminate forms in which that very emotion may find expression in the future, are embedded in the flow of life. It is rendered intelligible by its history and by its occasion, and they in turn render intelligible the agent's subsequent thoughts, feelings, and action. To describe and explain the type-specific underlying physiology, neuro-pharmacology, and cortical processes of generic emotions is the province of neuroscience. But, as we have already seen, for a variety of reasons, a human being's emotions and emotional life must be *understood* idiographically – in terms of the particularities of the specific case and its antecedent history.[10]

---

[10] A later reckoning may reveal whether that person's emotional response on a given occasion exemplifies any significant generalization.

# 4

# The Dialectic of the Emotions

## 1. The Cartesian and empiricist legacies and their invalidation

Given the extensive discussion of the emotions by Plato and Aristotle, by Epicureans (Philodemus, Lucretius) and Stoics (Cicero, Seneca), and by the Christian Platonic (Augustine) and Aristotelian traditions (Aquinas), it is surprising to find Descartes announcing, at the beginning of his *The Passions of the Soul* (1649):

> The defects of the Sciences we have from the ancients are nowhere more apparent than in their writings on the passions. This topic, about which knowledge has always been keenly sought, does not seem to be one of the more difficult to investigate, since everyone feels passions in himself and so has no need to look elsewhere for observations to establish their nature. And yet the teaching of the ancients about the passions are so meagre and for the most part so implausible that I cannot hope to approach the truth except by departing from the paths they followed. That is why I shall be obliged to write just as if I were considering a topic that no one had dealt with before me.[1]

It may be that Descartes's remarks rest on his conviction that, whereas the ancients had no adequate account of the physiological basis of the

---

[1] Descartes, *The Passions of the Soul* (henceforth *PS*), in *The Philosophical Writings of Descartes*, vol. 1, trans. J. Cottingham, R. Stoothoff, and D. Murdoch (Cambridge University Press, Cambridge, 1985), I. 1; AT IX, 327–8.

*The Passions: A Study of Human Nature*, First Edition. P. M. S. Hacker.
© 2018 John Wiley & Sons Ltd. Published 2018 by John Wiley & Sons Ltd.

emotions, he did. His physiology, however, was no less defective than theirs. But it may also be that his contemptuous remarks rest on his advancing theses that repudiated the Aristotelian and scholastic tradition.

*Descartes's account of the emotions*    Human emotions, according to Descartes, are passions – ways in which the soul is affected. They are things we experience in ourselves and are unlike heat and movement, which we can attribute to things (material objects) outside us as well. But emotions must be distinguished from other passions (or passivities), such as sense perceptions, on the one hand, and appetites, on the other. Perceptions (passions), in the most general sense of the term, are all the thoughts that are not actions of the soul or volitions. Perceptions, thus understood, may be caused by and referred to things outside us. They may be sense perceptions, which we refer to the objects that we take to have caused them. They may be sensations (such as pain) or appetites (such as hunger), which are caused by and referred to our body. They may be emotions. The immediate causes of our emotions most commonly lie in neural agitations, about which we normally know nothing. Whereas we feel hunger in our stomach, and may feel pain in any part of our body, we do not refer our emotions to our body. Like our other perceptions, our emotions are things of which we are conscious. We apprehend our emotions infallibly: 'even if we are asleep and dreaming, we cannot feel sad, or moved by any other passion, unless the soul truly has this passion within it' (*PS* I. 26). So, emotions (in humans) are thoughts (*cogitationes*). Nevertheless, they are inextricably bound up with the body and agitations of the nervous system.

The gist of Descartes's rationalist analysis of the emotions consists of the following points:

(i)   What is, as it were, 'cogitatively felt', when an emotion *qua cogitatio* is felt, is not ascribable to the body of a human being – for the human body is an extended, not a thinking, substance. Thought in general is the defining attribute of the mind. Just as we cannot have a thought without knowing that we do, so too we cannot have an emotion without being conscious of it. Emotions, *qua 'thoughts'*, are attributes of the soul or mind *in so far as it is intimately conjoined to the body*. The question of whether disembodied minds can feel emotions is not addressed.

(ii)  The immediate cause of a cogitatively felt passion of the soul is a motion of the pineal gland, which Descartes thought to be suspended in the animal spirits in the ventricles. (Actually, it is in the epithalamus between the two hemispheres, in the quadrigeminal cistern.) The more remote cause may be some physiological irritation in the body (turbulence in the heart, blood, and animal spirits) – as when we experience an objectless mood. But it may be some external object acting upon the senses that causes such physiological perturbations. The perturbations drive animal spirits to the ventricles, where they cause motions of the pineal gland which affect the mind. So we feel fear because we feel (or seem to feel) our hyperventilating and trembling, feel anger because we feel (or seem to feel) our temples throbbing and heart pounding, in response to an external stimulus associated with the beneficial or harmful.

(iii)  The physiological perturbations that are causes of the felt emotion may also cause bodily movement directly – without any mental intervention in response to what is perceived, for example, of flight in the case of something previously harmful and so now frightening, or of movement towards something previously beneficial and so now appealing (*PS* I. 13, 37–8). So a behavioural response to an emotional stimulus may be generated along two distinct causal pathways, the first a rapid pathway that bypasses the mind and brings about non-voluntary emotional actions, the other a slower pathway that involves the conscious direction of the mind in the production of voluntary responses to the emotional stimulus.

Animal emotions are not 'cogitatively felt', and to ascribe an emotion to an animal is not to ascribe 'thoughts' to it. For, having no minds, animals cannot have thoughts. Rather, animal emotions are generated and give rise to behaviour purely physiologically, without consciousness (*PS* I. 36–8).[2] The pineal gland in animals is indeed active in directing the animal spirits, but it has no role in any two-way interaction with a mind.[3]

(iv)  Emotions that are cogitatively felt by human beings 'move and dispose the soul to want things for which they prepare the body.

---

[2] The difficulties Descartes confronts in trying to reconcile the fear, anger, or contentment of animals with their lack of minds and the body dependence of human emotions with the intelligibility of thoughts without a body, are meticulously described in J. R. Cottingham, '"A Brute to Brutes?": Descartes's Treatment of Animals' and 'Cartesian Trialism', repr. in his *Cartesian Reflections: Essays on Descartes's Philosophy* (Oxford University Press, Oxford, 2008), pp. 163–88, and 'Overview', in the same volume, pp. 29–36.

[3] See S. Finger, 'Descartes and the Pineal Gland in Animals: a Frequent Misinterpretation', *Journal of the History of Neuroscience* 4 (1995), 166–82.

Thus the feeling of fear moves the soul to want to flee, that of courage to want to fight, and similarly with the others' (*PS* I. 40).
Consequently, the soul is engaged in acting out of the emotion it feels
by causing the appropriate movements of the pineal gland that then
moves the body in a manner corresponding to the volition (*PS* I. 41).

(v)   Emotions are only *externally, causally, related* to their stimulus
and so too are only *externally related* to their behavioural manifestations. There is no logical or constitutive connection between
an emotion and its behavioural manifestation.

(vi)  Feedback effects of the bodily perturbations maintain the
emotion for however long it is cogitatively felt (see fig. 4.1) by

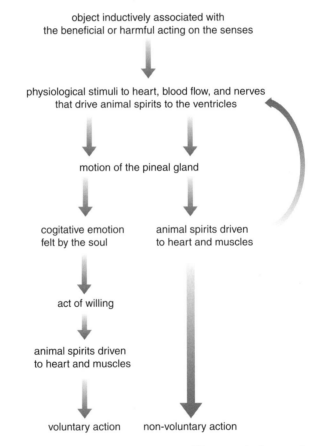

**Figure 4.1**   *A representation of Descartes's theory of
emotion (arrows signify direction of causal relations)*

persistent stimulation of animal spirits that act on the pineal gland. These causal chains exhibit the firm union of mind and body in human beings.

(vii) The cogitatively felt emotions serve the (divinely ordained) purpose of apprehending what is beneficial or detrimental to the living human composite and inducing voluntary and non-voluntary actions accordingly. Animals emotions are likewise subservient to survival, but without the intervention of acts of will or of thought.

*Comparison with Aristotle, Augustine, Aquinas*

Comparison with the Aristotelian tradition is instructive. For Aristotle the problem of mindless emotions in animals and bodiless emotions in disembodied minds cannot arise. In his analysis of the emotions, he invoked his distinction between form and matter. Whatever physical perturbations accompany each emotion are *the matter* of the emotion, as distinct from its *form*, which characterizes the emotion:

all the affections of the *psuchē* involve the body – passion [anger], gentleness [good temper], fear, pity, courage [confidence], joy, loving, and hating: in all these there is a concurrent affection of the body. ... Hence a physicist would define an affection of the *psuchē* differently from a dialectician; the latter would define, e.g. anger as the appetite for returning pain for pain, or something like that, while the former would define it as the boiling of the blood or warm substance surrounding the heart. The one assigns the material conditions, the other the form or account; for what he states is the account of the fact, though for its actual existence there must be embodiment of it in a material such as is described by the other. ... the affections of the *psuchē*, insofar as they are such as anger and fear, are inseparable from the natural matter of the animals.[4]

Furthermore, although Aristotle speaks of 'the affections *of* the *psuchē*', he rightly insists that to ascribe emotions to the mind or soul is to commit a category mistake: 'to say that the *psuchē* is angry is as if one were to say that the *psuchē* weaves or builds. For it is surely better not to say that the *psuchē* pities, learns, or thinks, but that the man does these with his *psuchē*.' It is not the *psuchē* that is the subject of emotions, but the living animal or human being *as a whole*.[5]

---

[4] Aristotle, *De Anima*, 403ª16–17, 29–30; 403ᵇ1–4, 16.

[5] Aristotle, *De Anima*, 408ª12–15. Note that doing things with one's soul or *psuchē* is like doing things with one's talents, not like doing things with one's hands.

For Aquinas too it would be unintelligible to ascribe human emotions to disembodied intelligences:

> In the functioning of the sensory orexis [*appetitus sensitivi*], however, physical modification is essential. Thus, in defining the various affections of the sensory orexis, one mentions the modification of the relevant bodily organ: anger, for instance, is said to be *the overheating of the blood around the heart*. One sees then that the notion of passivity, and so of the passions and the emotions, is more fully verified in the functioning of the sensory orexis than in that of sense-perception, even though each involves the action of some part of the physical organism. (*Summa Theologica*, 1ª2ᵃᵉ, q. 22, reply to Objection 3)

By contrast, Augustine, mindful of the notions of the wrath of God, of the love and compassion of Christ, and of the adoration of God by souls in heaven, had had no hesitation in detaching emotion from sensibility, and hence from the body, and in associating it instead with the will (*The City of God*, 14.3; see pp. 116–17 below).

Descartes, like Augustine, ascribed emotions to the soul or mind:

> The perceptions we refer only to the soul are those whose effects we feel as being within the soul itself, and for which we do not normally know any proximate cause to which we can refer them [i.e. we cannot ascribe anger or joy to anything other than the soul as we can ascribe shape and motion to objects we perceive]. Such are the feelings of joy, anger and the like, which are aroused in us sometimes by the objects which stimulate our nerves and sometimes also by other causes. ... We usually restrict the term [passion] to signify only perceptions which we refer to the soul itself. And it is only the latter that I have undertaken to explain here under the title 'passions of the soul'. (*PS* I. 25)

*An irresolvable incoherence in Descartes*     According to Descartes, a human being is a union, indeed an especially 'intimate' union, of two distinct substances, each possessed of categorially distinct attributes. In his view, the occurrence of emotions in man *qua* embodied mind is in general attributable to the *union* of mind and body (*PS* I. 46–7).[6] Nevertheless, it is the mind that loves or hates, feels joyful or sad, is overcome by wonder or desire, not the body-machine. For the emotions, *in human beings*, are 'thoughts' (*cogitations*) or modes of consciousness. Is it then not the human

---

[6] See also Descartes, *The Principles of Philosophy*, I. 48; II. 190. 'In general' because presumably one can feel overjoyed at having solved a new mathematical theorem.

being, as a composite union of distinct substances, that feels emotions? Only if Descartes relinquishes his thesis that emotions are thoughts, or his thesis that thoughts are *essentially* modes of the uniquely defining attribute of mind, namely thinking. Ascription of emotions to the mind is what I have elsewhere called 'a mereological fallacy', that is, the misconception of ascribing to parts of a being predicates that can be ascribed only to the being as a whole.[7] For it is no more the mind that feels emotions than it is the mind that weaves or builds. It is the living human being, not *qua* unity of mind and body, but *qua* substance. This mereological confusion regarding emotions was repeated by most early modern and modern philosophers as well as by scientists to the present day.

*A lacuna in Descartes: intentionality*

Unlike Aristotle and Aquinas, Descartes failed to investigate the intentionality of the emotions. He did not distinguish the causes of an emotion from what is signified by the object-accusative, nominalization- and infinitive-accusatives of an emotion verb. (To remind the reader of our previous example: The cause of my fear, when I am awakened at night by a noise downstairs, is the noise; the object of my fear (of whom or what I am afraid) is a burglar downstairs (who may or may not exist), and the intentional-accusative of my fear is *that I will be robbed and assaulted*.) Nevertheless, Descartes does attempt to explain the *telos* of our susceptibility to emotions. God has so created us that we have behavioural pronenesses that preserve our lives and are beneficial for us. So we are naturally caused to flee from what we have previously experienced as endangering us.

*Descartes on animal emotions*

Animals (the higher animals) are frightened or enraged no less than human beings. Unlike us, however, they cannot take themselves to be frightened or furious, let alone reflect on whether their fear or rage is warranted. These acknowledged truths are problematic for Descartes's substance dualism, and are not really resolved by his drift towards the view that some attributes are ascribable to the union of mind and body ('Cartesian trialism').[8] For, although he insisted that human emotions display the intimate union of mind and body, animals, in his view, are *not* a union of mind and body at all. So, in whatever sense *they* feel

---

[7] For discussion of the mereological fallacy, see M. R. Bennett and P. M. S. Hacker, *Philosophical Foundations of Neuroscience* (Blackwell, Oxford, 2003), pp. 12–16, and ch. 3.

[8] See Cottingham, 'Cartesian Trialism'.

emotions, it must be purely behavioural. This tension can be partly resolved only by suggesting that the word 'emotion' has two distinct although related meanings. So, although animals feel emotions, they do not do so in the sense in which human beings do.

*Consciousness, emotion, and privileged access*

In chapter 1 of *The Intellectual Powers*,[9] I challenged the coherence of the Cartesian conception of consciousness and self-consciousness. Here I merely note that, although some temporary emotional episodes that have genuine duration can be said to be *states* of consciousness, this does not imply that they are emotional states *of which one is conscious* or *aware*. It means that they are emotional states one is in *while one is conscious*, and not when one is asleep or unconscious. (To dream that one is angry or excited is not to be angry or excited.) It does not follow that whenever one is in an emotional state one is conscious of so being. *That* requires that one have realized that one is. But, just as one may be in a state of intense concentration without realizing it, so too one may feel jealous (see quotation from *Othello* (see p. 65)) without being aware of it, be in love without realizing it (like Prince Andrei (see p. 64)). It is true that human beings (unlike animals) can say how things are with them emotionally, but it does not follow that they are in a state of constant awareness or consciousness of how things are with them. Nor does it follow that, whenever someone does avow an emotion ('I love you', 'I'm frightened', 'I hope/regret she is coming'), his ability to do so rests on his being conscious of his emotion. To *express* an emotion (e.g. to exclaim 'I hate you!', 'I'm furious with you!', 'Oh, I'm so bored') is not to *describe* a thought (something of which, according to Descartes, one is conscious).

It is because Descartes held human emotions to be objects of consciousness that he held that the human subject of an emotion has 'privileged access' to his episodic emotions. Only the subject can *know* his own thoughts with complete certainty and infallibility. Hence only the subject can *really* know what emotions he is feeling. In this Descartes has been followed by mainstream thinkers to this very day. Antonio Damasio, an influential neuroscientist, asserted:

> the term *feeling* should be reserved for the private, mental experience of an emotion ... This means that you cannot observe a feeling in someone

[9] *The Intellectual Powers: A Study of Human Nature* (Wiley Blackwell, Oxford, 2013).

else, although you can observe a feeling in yourself when, as a conscious being you perceive your own emotional states.[10]

It is noteworthy that the Cartesian conception, especially in its concern with the physiology of the emotions and with their causal order, inspires neuroscientific investigation of the emotions to this day.

*Locke and Hume on the study of the emotions* A detailed empiricist account of the character of the *concepts* of the emotions and of their *mode of acquisition* is to be found in the writings of John Locke. In his view, all ideas are derived either from sensation (including therein perception) or from reflection, that is:

> The other Fountain [distinct from sensation] from which Experience furnisheth the Understanding with *Ideas*, is *Perception of the Operations of our own Minds* within us, as it is employ'd about the *Ideas* it has got; which Operations, when the Soul comes to reflect on, and consider, do furnish the Understanding with another set of *Ideas* which could not be had from things without ... This source of *Ideas*, every Man has wholly in himself; and though it be not Sense, as having nothing to do with external Objects; yet it is very like it, and might properly enough be call'd internal Sense. (*An Essay concerning Human Understanding*, II. 1. 4)[11]

This inspired the common conception of the British empiricists from the seventeenth to the late nineteenth centuries. The received view was that grasp of what an emotion is (and of what specific emotions are) is derived from introspective scrutiny of the operations of the mind by means of 'inner sense'. In order to give a name to an emotion, we need but focus our attention upon an appropriate passion we are feeling, and assign it a name. For each emotion has its own special character, which the subject of the emotion feels and can name.[12] The study of the emotions is therefore to be conducted by introspective means.

[10] A. Damasio, *The Feeling of What Happens* (Heinemann, London, 1999), p. 42.

[11] For critical analysis of Locke's account of emotions, see A. J. P. Kenny, *Action, Emotion and the Will* (Routledge & Kegan Paul, London, 1963), pp. 17–20.

[12] This conception anticipates modern *qualia*, which enjoyed a misguided popularity at the end of the last century. This might have some plausibility if, as both Plato and Aristotle suggested, it were true that all emotions are accompanied by pleasure or pain (suffering). For then there would be *an* answer to the question of what it is like to feel such-and-such an emotion (although not a different one for each emotion). But it is not true. There are emotions that have no particular hedonic tinge, for example, epistemic emotions such as curiosity and wonder, and such feelings of attachment as trust, devotion, and loyalty.

Investigators have to rely on the reports of the subject of the emotion, which constitute the data from which they can construct theories about the emotions. (It is as if the subject could peer into a Wilson cloud chamber, to which he alone has privileged access, and report back to the physicist something that only he can see.)

A somewhat similar sentiment is expressed by Hume in his examination of pride and humility.

> The passions of PRIDE and HUMILITY being simple and uniform impressions, 'tis impossible we can ever, by a multitude of words, give a just definition of them, or indeed of any of the passions. The utmost we can pretend to is a description of them, by an enumeration of such circumstances, as attend them: But as these words, *pride* and *humility*, are of general use, and the impressions they represent the most common of any, everyone, of himself, will be able to form a just idea of them, without any danger of mistake. (*A Treatise of Human Nature* (1739), II. i. 2)

It should be evident from our discussion in chapter 3 that it is mistaken to suppose that one can study the emotions thus. It is true that what the subject *says* about his feelings is a datum – a defeasible criterion for his acquaintances and for any investigating psychologist to ascribe emotions to him. But what he says is not a description of what he sees *in foro interno*. It may be an expression of his feelings or it may be a report of his feelings (the two are not always sharply distinguishable), but it is not a description resting on introspective 'observation'. Nor are his utterances, even if perfectly sincere, uniformly immune to error. He may not realize that he is, in fact, jealous. He may be deceiving himself when he avers that he is not in the slightest bit envious or the least ashamed of himself for what he has done.

It is equally mistaken to suppose that one can acquire an idea or concept of emotion, or of any of the emotions, in this way. In chapter 3, the manner of acquisition of the vocabulary of the emotions was delineated, not as an exercise in armchair learning theory, but as part of an analysis of the logical nature of these concepts. It was suggested that the rudiments of the use of some emotion words – for example, 'angry', 'frightened', 'excited', 'love' – are learnt as linguistic extensions of natural emotional behaviour of anger, fear, excitement, and affection in response to appropriate emotion-stimulating events and circumstances. Others, such as 'remorse', 'gratitude', and 'trust', are not. But they are not acquired by reflection on the operations of the mind *in foro interno* either. Grasp of these concepts of emotions involves understanding the character of the occasions that warrant them, the various forms of behaviour that express them, and the actions that may be motivated by them.

*The private language argument applied to the emotions*

Contrary to what seems implicit in Descartes's account, and is explicit in both Locke and Hume, it is logically impossible to give a meaning to, or to learn the meaning of, emotion words by attending to the emotions one feels and naming them (or learning to associate appropriate names with them). The early modern conception of the acquisition of concepts of the emotions presupposes the intelligibility of a *private ostensive definition* and so too of a *logically private language*.[13] These are forms of words that make no sense. This is not the place for elaboration and defence of Wittgenstein's arguments against the possibility of a private language.[14] I shall give only a thumbnail sketch of the conceptually incoherent consequences of the idea that we know the meaning of emotion words by association of emotion and name, or by means of a private ostensive definition employing the recollected emotion as a *defining sample*. We have inherited this conception from traditional philosophical thought, and, as we shall see, it is still presupposed in much contemporary reasoning and investigation in psychology and cognitive neuroscience.

*The need for a private ostensive definition*

On this conception, one would have to assign a meaning to an emotion word 'E' by associating the word with a currently felt emotion (a Humean impression) and resolving to call *this* emotion by the name 'E'. Subsequent uses of the word 'E' would have to be linked to the memory of the emotion one felt when one assigned a meaning to the name 'E'. For the meaning of the word 'E' could be given only by displaying for oneself alone the associated Humean idea (or contemporary 'mental representation') of the emotion *in foro interno*. For I can say of myself that I am feeling E only if I know what 'E' means. I know what 'E' means only inasmuch as I can display for myself what it means by conjuring up a mental representation of E

[13] A logically private language is conceived to be a language the words of which signify subjective experiences that no one else can have (since, it is held, no one can have another's experiences), and only their subject really knows what those experiences are (since only he has access to them).

[14] For a survey of his arguments, see P. M. S. Hacker, *Insight and Illusion: Themes in the Philosophy of Wittgenstein* (Thoemes Press, Bristol, 1997), ch. 9. For comprehensive examination, see P. M. S. Hacker, *Wittgenstein: Meaning and Mind* (Blackwell, Oxford, 1990): extensively revised edition (Wiley Blackwell, 2018).

and saying to myself that *this* → is E (the arrow here indicates the directing of one's attention). So anything that *is* what *this* → is is rightly characterized as E. So what I am currently feeling is E inasmuch as what I am feeling is *this* → (whereupon I focus my attention on the recollected mental representation (sample) of E).

*The consequences of a private ostensive definition*

The immediate consequence would be that no one else could know what the word 'E' meant. For, it is argued, no one can 'have access' to another's feelings. One person cannot have another's anger, fear, or love, but only his own. Consequently, no one else can know 'what it is like' for the subject to have the emotional experience he had.[15] A further consequence would be that the concept of an emotion would be logically detached from its constitutive grounds of application (criteria), that is, emotion-manifesting and emotion-expressing behaviour that warrants the application of the concept in second- and third-person cases. There would be no internal (conceptual, logical) relation between grief and tears, between delight and laughter, between fear and trembling. On the contrary, the emotional behaviour would have to be inductively correlated, as a matter of experience, with the 'inner' emotion. But, it was generally agreed, one can make this inductive correlation only in one's own case. Hence the traditional popularity of the argument from analogy (e.g. Berkeley, Mill) – but how irresponsible to generalize from only one case! Hence too the modern popularity of appeal to 'an inference to the best explanation' on the model of the theoretical sciences (e.g. J. L. Mackie) – but how bizarre to put others' feelings of fear and hope, anger and delight, on the same level as mesons and bosons! Hence, too, the current popularity of appealing to the fact that we are all 'wired up' in the same way in order to show that what goes for me goes for others too (e.g. John Searle) – but how curious to suppose that we had to wait upon these recent discoveries in order to be confident that others have any feelings!

---

[15] Of course, it is tempting to argue that one *obviously* knows what it is like for another to feel E (envious, jealous, angry): he just has to feel the same as one feels oneself when one feels E. But, as Wittgenstein noted, that is like arguing that we *obviously* know what it is to be five o'clock on the sun: it is five o'clock on the sun if it is the same time on the sun as it is here when it is five o'clock here! (*Philosophical Investigations*, §350). But for it to be the same time on the sun as it is here when it is five o'clock here, we have first to determine what it is to be five o'clock on the sun. Then, and only then, will it *make sense* to say that it is the same (or different) time there as it is here.

These are absurdities enough. They will not be discussed here. The deepest and least anticipated consequence of the standard conception is that *one would not be able to know what the word 'E' meant one- self* – in fact, it would have no meaning. There are three unobvious but fundamental reasons for this.

*The impossibility of a private ostensive definition 1*

First, there would be no criterion of correctness for the recollected sample the adducing of which is *meant to be* an essential element in giving the mean- ing of 'E' and in exhibiting to oneself that one knows what it means. According to this classic con- ception, the meaning of 'E' is determined by a private ostensive defini- tion that correlates a mental representation of a particular emotion with its name. Similarly, according to the empiricists, the meanings of colour words are determined by the mental colour image that comes to mind in association with 'red' (or 'green', or 'yellow', or 'blue'). But, although colour predicates *are* explained by *public* ostensive definitions by reference to samples, emotion predicates are not. They have a quite different logic from colour words. Moreover, neither colour words nor emotion words could possibly be defined by so-called private ostensive definition, since there is and could be no such thing. The very thought that one might exhibit to oneself what an emotion (or colour) word means by calling to mind a mental representation of, say, anger (or of 'green') is incoherent. For whatever pops into one's mind in association with the word 'E' (or 'C', in the case of a colour word) would be right – *and that means that nothing would be right* (Wittgenstein, *Philosophical Investigations*, §258). The point is not the fallibility of memory. It is rather that remembering correctly *the rule* that E is *this*, *which explains what 'E' means*, presupposes an independent criterion of correctness for the *this*. That is to say, we would need a criterion of correctness, not for whether we are currently experiencing the emotion E, but *for the sample or mental representation that allegedly determines what 'E' means*. But there is none. So the word 'E' would have no mean- ing for us. *A fortiori* we should not be able to *judge* that what we are now feeling is, as a matter of fact, emotion E.

To be sure, we speakers of a public natural language *can* remember what emotion we felt on some past occasion, and can *say* what emo- tion we are experiencing here and now *without any criterion* and *without employing any kind of sample*. But *we* possess the concept of the relevant emotion. We know what the word 'angry' (or 'jealous', or 'grateful') means. We know how to use such words correctly, both in first-person utterances (without any criterion) and in third-person ascriptions of emotion (warranted by behavioural criteria). Of course, we do not (and indeed *could not*) explain what it means by giving ourselves a 'private ostensive definition', since there is no such thing. Emotion names are not, and could not, be explained by reference to mental-sample-involving ostensive definitions.

*The impossibility of a private ostensive definition 2*

Secondly, a mental 'something' (an idea, impression, internal representation, *Vorstellung*) cannot fulfil the role of a defining sample in an ostensive definition. For a sensation, impression, idea, or representation cannot – logically cannot – fulfil the role of an object for comparison. An object for comparison, in this context, is an object (such as a metre rule) that can be used in order to judge whether something else has the property of being E (of being a metre long). One *cannot* hold up an internal representation of an emotion (a mnemonic image of what it feels like to be angry or joyous) and *juxtapose* it to a currently felt emotion (e.g. a flash of anger, a wave of joy, a pang of regret) in order to determine whether what one is now feeling *is* what the putative sample is supposed to be a sample of. (One might as well attempt to judge whether a piece of string is a metre long by trying to hold up a mental image of a metre length and to juxtapose it with the piece of string!)

In fact, things are even worse! For one cannot – logically cannot – simultaneously imagine what one is currently experiencing. One *cannot* conjure up a mental image of red while one is looking at a red object, in order to determine whether what one is looking at is red. So, too, one cannot imagine anger or fear while one is angry or fearful – and that is not because the impression is so vivid that it masks the idea! Of course, we can compare what we now feel with what we felt yesterday – as when we say that we are getting over our grief or resentment, or that the love we bear for another has not changed. But *we do not do so by juxtaposing mental images or representations* as measures, in order to make such a judgement of identity. We just sincerely say that our feelings have, or have not, changed – and *what we say* is a (defeasible) criterion *for others* to judge of the sameness or difference of our feelings.

*The impossibility of a private ostensive definition 3*

Thirdly, in the sense in which one *might* conceive of a sensation as an idea, impression, or 'internal representation' (*Vorstellung*), there is no such thing as an idea, impression, or internal representation *of an emotion*. One may feel intense joy or fear, love or detestation, but there is no inner *this* that *is* the joy or fear, love or detestation. One's pulses may sensibly race; one may feel one's breathing to be short and shallow; there may be butterflies in one's stomach or a lump in one's throat. But there is nothing here in the complex syndrome constituted by physical and somatic sensations, knowledge and belief, thought and intent, reasons and response, that might even be thought to function as a sample by reference to which one might define an emotion, or by reference to which one might determine whether what one now feels is an emotion, let alone what emotion it is.

This result is of great importance for the study and understanding of the emotions and the concepts of the emotions. It is not only early modern accounts of the emotions that presuppose the intelligibility of a private language and of private ostensive definition. The same confusion is implicit in many current psychological and neuroscientific theories of the emotions.

## 2. Philosophical and psychological confusions: James

The most influential psychological account of the emotions advanced in the late nineteenth century was the James–Lange theory. It dominated reflection upon the emotions among experimental psychologists until the rise of behaviourism, and it again had a substantial influence towards the end of the twentieth century upon the *somatic marker theory* of the emotions advanced by the cognitive neuroscientist Antonio Damasio. This conception in turn prevails among current twenty-first-century neuroscientists. Both theories have striking similarities to Descartes's. Both are worth scrutiny, as they vividly demonstrate how failure to attend adequately to conceptual questions concerning the nature of the emotions leads to conceptual confusions in the construction of what purport to be empirical theories of the emotions.

*James on the emotions*        James conceived of emotions as awarenesses of bodily reactions. Instincts, he thought, lead to action: 'emotional reactions, however, fall short of instincts, in that the emotional reaction terminates in the subject's own body, whilst the instinctive reaction is apt to go farther and enter into practical relations with the exciting object.'[16] He distinguished

---

[16] W. James, *The Principles of Psychology* (Henry Holt, New York, 1890), vol. 2, p. 442. The core of James's theory had been elaborated earlier in 'What is an Emotion?', *Mind* 9 (1884). C. Lange was a Danish physiologist. His similar theory was published in 1885. Lange's account will not be discussed here.

between the 'coarser emotions', namely grief, fear, rage, and love, which have 'strong organic reverberations', and the 'subtler emotions', with less pronounced bodily associations. In effect, he restricted the concept of an emotion to the felt perturbations of temporary emotions, in particular momentary ones. He screened out the rationality and intentionality of emotions, as well as their nexus with motivation, character, the virtues and vices. For this he provided no warrant.

James argued as follows:

> Our natural way of thinking about coarser emotions is that the mental perception of some fact excites the mental affection called the emotion, and that this latter state of mind gives rise to the bodily expression. My theory, on the contrary, is that *the bodily changes follow directly the perception of the exciting fact, and that our feeling of the same changes as they occur is the emotion.* Common sense says, we lose our fortune, are sorry and weep; we meet a bear, are frightened and run; we are insulted by a rival, are angry and strike. The hypothesis here to be defended says that this order of sequence is incorrect ... And that the more rational statement is that we feel sorry because we cry, angry because we strike, afraid because we tremble ... Without the bodily states following on the perception, the latter would be purely cognitive in form, pale, colorless, destitute of emotional warmth. We might then see the bear, and judge it best to run, receive the insult and deem it right to strike, but we should not actually *feel* afraid or angry. (*Principles of Psychology*, pp. 449–50; emphases original)[17]

On the next page, James elaborates the rationale for this radical supposition:

> the vital point of my whole theory ... is this: If we fancy some strong emotion, and try to abstract from our consciousness of it all the feelings of bodily symptoms, we find we have nothing left behind, no 'mind-stuff' out of which the emotion can be constituted, and that a cold and neutral state of intellectual perception is all that remains ... For us, emotion dissociated from all bodily feeling is inconceivable. The more closely I scrutinize my states, the more persuaded I become that whatever moods, affections, and passions I have are in very truth constituted by, and made up of, those bodily changes which we ordinarily call their expression or consequence ... each emotion is the resultant of a sum of elements, and each element is caused by a

---

[17] Note that what James calls 'expression' we denominated 'manifestation' in chapter 3, in order to distinguish non-verbal from verbal emotional behaviour. It is remarkable that James pays no attention whatsoever to the verbal expressions of emotions.

physiological process of a sort already well-known. The elements are all organic changes, and each of them is the reflex effect of an exciting object. Definite questions now immediately arise – questions very different from those which were the only possible ones without this view ... The questions now are *causal*: 'Just what changes does this object and what changes does that object excite?' And 'How come they excite these particular changes and not others?' We step from a superficial to a deeper order of inquiry. (*Principles of Psychology*, vol. 2, pp. 451, 453–4; emphases original)

James takes it that our unreflective way of conceiving of the coarser emotions is as shown in figure 4.2.

Perceptual stimulus — *causes* → Temporary emotion — *causes* → Bodily changes and behavioural manifestations

**Figure 4.2** *James's notion of our intuitive conception of emotions*

However, the correct way of conceiving of the emotions, he avers, is in the manner shown in figure 4.3.

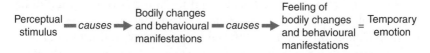

Perceptual stimulus — *causes* → Bodily changes and behavioural manifestations — *causes* → Feeling of bodily changes and behavioural manifestations = Temporary emotion

**Figure 4.3** *James's conception of emotions*

Thus represented, the account is overly condensed, although vividly revolutionary. Presented in greater detail, James's theory can be outlined thus: a perceptual stimulus affects a sense organ. The sense organ sends impulses to the brain. The brain immediately reacts, and sends neural impulses to the body, thus bringing about muscular and visceral effects. These bodily changes are relayed back to the cortex. Their reception then causes the emotional experience, which is *the feeling of these bodily changes*. So the felt emotion is not the cause of the bodily changes that characteristically accompany it – on the contrary, the emotional feeling is caused by them. Note that, according to James, the phrase 'bodily/visceral changes' subsumes physical sensations, somatic feelings (tension, felt pulse rate, felt changes in breathing, etc.), and overt somatic changes (flushing red or growing pale, gooseflesh, perspiring, frowning, trembling, clenching of teeth, dilation of nostrils). In his view, '*every one of the bodily changes, whatsoever it be, is* FELT, *acutely or obscurely, the moment it occurs*' (*Principles of Psychology*, vol. 2, pp. 450–1). To the multiplicity of human emotions answers the indefinite multiplicity of bodily/visceral changes that are felt.

The upshot of this theory is, as James observes, that we feel fear because we tremble; we feel anger because we clench our fists; and we feel sorrow because we weep. Our emotion just *is* the feeling of these bodily changes caused by 'an exciting fact'. James's account is, as he knew full well, counter-intuitive. Nevertheless, it is easy to see what drove him to this curious view. Two correct considerations weighed with him.

First, no purely 'intellectualist' account of emotions *2 merits to* can be satisfactory. Any attempt to characterize emo-*James's account* tions in terms of judgements, evaluations, and consequent actions alone would leave out the ardour of love, the heat of anger, the warmth of affection, the cold breath of fear, the agony of grief. 'Without the bodily states following on the perception, the latter would be purely cognitive in form, pale, colorless, destitute of emotional warmth' (James, *Principles of Psychology*, vol. 2, p. 450).

Secondly, committed as he was to the empiricist conception of introspection and privileged access, James noted correctly that all he can apprehend when he 'attends closely to his emotions' are somatic perturbations and agitations. If one is very angry, and attempts nevertheless to focus one's attention on one's feeling, what is there to attend to other than throbbing temples, tight chest, clenched jaw muscles? If one is beset with grief or sorrow, what does one, on 'introspective reflection', feel? Is there more to be found than the sensation of tears coursing down one's cheeks, the feeling of sobbing, the constricted feeling in the chest, and so forth? Such felt perturbations seem, on close scrutiny, to be all there is to the emotion. For once these are, as it were, abstracted from a given emotion-stimulating occasion; all that seems to be left is cold, detached judgement and behaviour.

These are not trivial considerations. Nevertheless, *6 criticisms of James* the Jamesian response to them is misguided:

(i)   James did not conceive of persistent anger, jealousy, hatred, gratitude, love, and affection as emotions at all. But this stipulation severs momentary emotional occurrences (e.g. a flash of anger, a stab of envy, a pang of fear) from episodic emotions (being in a state of anxiety, feeling joyful or excited) and from persistent or enduring emotions (such as love, hate, pride, regret, remorse, and guilt). He also cuts the deep connections between emotion, motivation, temperament, and character. That in turn disconnects emotions from vices and virtues. There is little to be said for this. The anger one feels in response to an offence is the same anger that festers all the afternoon. The jealousy that is aroused by the sight of one's beloved flirting shamelessly with another is the jealousy that keeps one awake all night and torments one for weeks. So James's account is not a general theory of the emotions at all but, at best, a theory of emotional perturbations. Emotions are not bundles of sensations. Persistent emotions are complex syndromes of grounds for the emotion, knowledge, and belief concerning the object of the emotion, sensation and somatic feeling, feeling pleased or distressed, thought and reason, intention and motive – not simply classes of felt bodily changes. Even momentary emotional occurrences (which are James's primary concern) are syndromes of interwoven features of which perturbations are but one element.

(ii) James takes it for granted that the analysis of the emotions *must* involve one or the other of two different causal chains (see fig. 4.2 and fig. 4.3). But it is by no means evident that we are forced to choose between these two alternatives. For the conceptual structure of the emotions, as we have seen, is far more complex than James allows for.

(iii) James (in fig. 4.2) misrepresents our unselfconscious use of the emotion vocabulary, and conflates it with our naïve conception of the emotions, informed by our unreflective conceptual intuitions. Are we really committed to the view that the characteristic bodily sensations and behavioural manifestations of an emotional occurrence are *caused by* our fear, anger, or jealousy? One may raise one's voice *in* anger, turn red *with* rage, shake one's fist angrily – but these are *expressions* or *manifestations* of anger. It is not part of our concept of anger that such forms of behaviour are *caused* by something 'inner' I-know-not-what called 'anger'. Rather, as we have seen, they are one *form* among others that anger may take. Heat certainly causes perspiration – it makes one sweat. One may also break out in *a sweat of fear* – but the cause of one's fear, what frightened one (a noise in the night), does not make one sweat. Nor is the perspiring *caused* by the fear; it is the form in which the fear is manifest on this occasion. Being tickled certainly causes laughter. One may also laugh *with* delight – but one does not laugh *with* tickles, even though the tickling makes one laugh. Onions may make one cry when one slices them; the death of someone one loves may also make one cry. But we cry *in* grief, not *in* onion slicing, and we shed tears *of* sorrow, but not tears *of* onions. These prepositional differences are not decisive in exhibiting fine grammatical differences between causation, on the one hand, and manifestation or expression, on the other. But they are suggestive.

(iv)    Like Descartes, James did not distinguish between the cause of a temporary emotion and its object (what is signified by the material object-accusative or the nominalization-accusative of the emotion verb), that is, he failed, for example, to differentiate between *what* frightened one, *of whom* one is frightened, and *what* one is frightened of. His account is devoid of intentionality, and hence too of rationality. But not only does this omit a large part of what is distinctive of emotions; it also renders it incomprehensible how we can be responsible for our emotions, and how it is that non-pathological emotion evaporates when an accompanying belief is recognized to be false. Consequently, he obscures the connection between the emotions and the virtues and vices of mankind, between pride and being a proud person, between fear and being cowardly or timorous, between anger and irascibility.

(v)    James insists that *all* bodily/visceral changes are felt. This is meant to be an empirical claim. As such, it is patently false – there is no reason whatsoever to suppose that one feels every change of one's facial expression as one intently watches an exciting episode, that one feels every movement of one's hands in debate, or every change to one's position or posture, let alone every change in our heartbeat or rate of breathing. James acknowledges that we are not *fully* aware of all such changes, but suggests that if we carefully attend to, for example, our facial musculature when we are excited, we shall see what a plethora of subtle and indescribably fine sensations we feel. But all that shows is what sensations we feel when we focus our attention, not what sensations we feel when we do not.

(vi)    As Walter Cannon, one of James's scientific critics, pointed out, (a) there are numerous forms of bodily and visceral changes that are unaccompanied by any emotion (e.g. those accompanying running or swimming); (b) there are different emotions that share much the same array of bodily changes (e.g. resentment and indignation, remorse and regret); and (c) the physiological reactions are often too slow in comparison with the immediacy of an emotional reaction (e.g. of fear to a clap of thunder) for the emotion to be the feeling of bodily changes.[18]

So, what purported to be scientific discoveries in the psychology of the emotions turns out to be no more than a morass of conceptual confusions. We may grant James that a purely intellectualist account of the emotions is inadequate. But it does not follow that the remedy to this defect is to identify the emotions with the 'perception' of bodily changes. We may grant James that attending to what one feels when one is in the grip of a momentary 'coarse' emotion will, *in one sense*, reveal nothing other than sensations. But that is because the instruction: 'Attend to your anger (fear, jealousy, love)!' is bizarre. To attend to what angers one is not to attend to one's anger; nor is attending to who angers one; attending to what one does *in anger* is not to attend to one's anger either. But that does not show that anger (fear, jealousy, love) consists of nothing other than a melange of felt bodily changes to which one may attend. On the contrary, it shows that there is a category mistake in the supposition that introspective attention can disclose what it is to feel an emotion. What is necessary is not to look into ourselves, but to remind ourselves of the use and circumstances of use of emotion verbs and their cognates, to bring to mind the criteria for ascribing emotions to people and the circumstances in which speakers express and report their own emotions. Any empirical investigation into the psychology or neuroscience of the emotions presupposes the concept of emotion. Any competent speaker of our language has mastered the use of a wide range of emotion words. But mastery of the use of a word does not imply possession of an overview of that use. It is precisely the latter that psychologists and neuroscientists lack. Lacking such an overview, they stumble from one conceptual confusion to another.

## 3. Neuroscientific confusions: Damasio and the somatic marker hypothesis

*Damasio's somatic marker theory*   The defective James–Lange theory of the emotions was vigorously revived by Antonio Damasio in the 1990s in his 'somatic marker theory'. This has now

---

[18] W. Cannon, 'The James–Lange Theory of Emotions: A Critical Examination and an Alternative Theory', *American Journal of Psychology* 39 (1927), 106–24.

become a dominant cognitive-neuroscientific theory of emotions,[19] and is assumed to provide a model for investigating decision-making in the domain of neuro-economics.[20] This variant of the James theory is straightforward.[21] The essence of emotion, according to Damasio, is 'the collection of changes in body state ..., which is responding to the content of thoughts relative to a particular entity or event'.[22] Damasio's conception of thoughts is a simplified variant of the conception characteristic of eighteenth-century empiricism. Thoughts, he claims, consist of mental images (*DE* 107–8). The images constituting thoughts are comparable to the images constituting perceptions. Thoughts differ from perceptions (as Hume had argued) inasmuch as thought images are fainter or less vivid than the images (Humean impressions) of which perceptions consist. If thoughts were not exhibited to us in the form of images of things or of words signifying things, Damasio avers, we should not be able to say what we think.

James distinguished the somatic changes in response to an 'exciting fact', which are not an emotion, from the emotion itself, which consists in the 'perception' of those somatic changes. Damasio distinguishes *an emotion* from *the feeling of an emotion*. An emotion is 'a collection of changes in body state connected to particular mental images that have activated a specific brain system'. A feeling of emotion is the experience of such changes in juxtaposition to the mental images that initiated the cycle. 'In other words, a feeling depends on the juxtaposition of an image of the body proper to an image of something else, such as the visual image of a face or an auditory image of a melody' (*DE* 145). Accordingly, an emotion is a bodily response to a mental image, and the feeling of an emotion is a cognitive response to the resultant bodily condition (*DE* 130). Feelings of emotion, Damasio asserts, are first and foremost *about the body*. They offer us,

---

[19] See A. D. Craig, 'How Do You Feel? Interoception: the Sense of the Physiological Condition of the Body', *Nature Reviews: Neuroscience* 3 (2002), 655–66.

[20] See M. Reimann and A. Bechara, 'The Somatic-Marker Framework as a Neurological Theory of Decision-Making: Review, Conceptual Comparisons, and Future Neuroeconomics Research', *Journal of Economic Psychology* 31 (2010), 767–76. 'The somatic marker framework', they write in their abstract, 'is still providing a unique neuroanatomical and cognitive framework that helps explain the role of emotion in decision making'.

[21] I here make use of my paper 'The Conceptual Framework for the Investigation of Emotions', *International Review of Psychiatry* 16 (2004), 199–208.

[22] A. Damasio, *Descartes's Error: Emotion, and the Human Brain* (Macmillan, London, 1994), p. 139. Henceforth *DE*.

he avers, the cognition of our visceral and musculoskeletal state that is generated by our thoughts (mental images):

> Feelings let us *mind the body* ... Feelings offer us a glimpse of what goes on in our flesh, as a momentary image of that flesh is juxtaposed to the images of other objects and situations; in so doing, feelings modify our comprehensive notion of those other objects and situations. By dint of juxtaposition body images give other images a quality of goodness or badness, of pleasure or pain. (*DE* 159)

Accordingly, Damasio proposes the somatic marker hypothesis that links his account of emotions with decision-making. The hypothesis is that positive and negative somatic responses to 'images' (perceptions and thoughts) serve to increase the accuracy and efficiency of decision-making processes. In virtue of their axiological associations, they screen out a range of alternative courses of action, thus allowing the agent to choose from fewer (*DE* 173, 175). Somatic markers, constituted by the somatic response to situations confronting us, assist deliberation by highlighting some options as beneficial and eliminating others as detrimental. The types of somatic response that we allegedly use in making decisions, Damasio claims, were probably 'created in our brains' during the process of education and socialization, by connecting specific classes of stimuli with specific classes of somatic state (*DE* 177). In short, 'gut reactions', often culturally dependent, provide the basis for rational decision-making. Hence, Damasio conjectures, decision-making deficiencies in patients suffering from lesions in the prefrontal cortices are explained by lack of somatic markers to guide them.

The connective analysis of the concept of emotion in chapters 2 and 3 facilitates the identification of the manifold errors and incoherences in Damasio's theory. It is, in fact, no more an empirical, scientific theory than William James's theory, which anticipated it. Like James's theory, so too Damasio's is not a general theory of the emotions, but only a theory of emotional perturbations. This restriction does not reveal the place of emotion in human life – it obscures it. The theory rests foursquare on failure to grasp the very concept of an emotion. This can readily be demonstrated

*7 criticisms of Damasio's theory*     (i)  An emotion is not an ensemble of positive or negative somatic changes caused by a 'thought' (mental image) of an object or event. First, even if a perturbation-involving emotional occurrence involves a manifold of somatic changes, what makes the experience of such changes *sensations of fear* as opposed to sensations of anger, and what makes felt blushes *blushes of shame* rather than of embarrassment or of love is not the mental image, *if any*, that causes them, nor the 'positive or negative' features of the somatic changes, but the circumstances of the emotion experienced and the reasons for it.

Secondly, if emotions were essentially ensembles of somatic changes caused by mental images – if that were what the word 'emotion' means – then learning the meaning of emotion words and learning how to use them correctly would be a matter of learning names of complexes of bodily changes with specific causes. It would be akin to learning the meaning and use of phrases such as 'sea-sickness' or 'giddiness', which do signify unpleasant ensembles of sensation with specific causes. But, as we have seen, we do not learn the use of emotion words by learning sensation names, names of overall bodily condition, and names of somatic feelings. Rather, we learn what are appropriate formal and material objects of given emotions: that what is threatening or dangerous is the formal object of fear; that what is annoying, offensive, or wrong is the formal object of anger; that worthy attributes, achievements, or possessions are formal objects of pride; and so forth.

Thirdly, if emotions were ensembles of somatic changes caused by thought-constituting mental images, then one could not have good reasons for feeling certain emotions and would not be answerable for one's emotions in the manner in which we are. For, although there may *be* a reason (a causal explanation of) why one has a headache, or why one's breathing rate or heartbeat increases, one cannot *have* a reason (i.e. a ground or warrant) for such bodily changes. We often say that someone ought to, and has good reason to, feel proud or ashamed, but we cannot say that he ought to increase his pulse rate or has a good reason for his psychogalvanic reflex reactions. To say that someone ought to be more excited is not the same as saying that he ought to hyperventilate.

Fourthly, one can feel an emotion E without feeling any E-type perturbations. One can love a person, a people, a country, an object (a piece of music, a book, a painting, a landscape, a house) or an abstract value (truth, justice, honour) without feeling any perturbations of love when one thinks about them. There need be no felt somatic changes accompanying the thought (image?) of a rise in the rate of inflation, although one may well fear such an event and take precautions against the threat it poses to one's finances. One may be forever grateful to someone for past kindnesses, but that does not imply that one breaks out in a battery of gratitude-constituting sensations whenever one thinks about one's benefactor.

To be sure, one might argue that, by definition, to feel a 'coarse' emotion does require some somatic changes. But, even if that were so, the somatic changes linked to a mental image do not identify the emotion and attending to them is certainly not identical with feeling the emotion. Moreover, it is an egregious confusion to suppose that one can study emotions experimentally by exposing subjects to pictures in a laboratory and investigating somatic changes (and cortical concomitants) dissociated from the stream of life within which emotions have their place. (This is like dropping a key in the road in the dark and then looking for it under a street lamp because the light is better there!) What one will discover is no more than the somatic changes and cortical accompaniments of reactions to pictures. (Studying the somatic changes and perturbations of cinemagoers to watching a first-rate film of *War and Peace* or *Anna Karenina* will not give one greater insights into the nature of human emotions than watching the film.)

(ii) Emotions are not essentially image-involving. Perceiving an object and perceiving that things are thus-and-so does not involve having images of anything.[23] To perceive Paris is not to perceive or to have an image of Paris. Conversely, to have a mental image of Paris in a dream or a daydream is not to perceive Paris. Neuroscientists and psychologists are prone to believe that perception is image-mongery because they cleave to the classical causal theory of perception, rooted in the distinction between primary and secondary qualities. Ignorant of history, they are prone to take this to be modern scientific discovery, rather than bad seventeenth-century metaphysics with no empirical basis or *experimentum crucis* to support it.

---

[23] The analysis of perception is given in *The Intellectual Powers*, ch. 8.

It is equally misguided to suppose that, in order to think something or to think of something, it is either necessary or sufficient to have an image of anything, let alone an image of what one thinks, or what one thinks of, or of words that would, if uttered, express what one thinks or refer to what one thinks of. As we have seen,[24] it is mistaken to suppose that one thinks in images or that, in order to speak with thought, one must first say to oneself in the imagination what one is going to say out loud. One can talk to oneself in the imagination (which involves auditory images) without thinking (as when one counts sheep in one's imagination in order to stop oneself from thinking). One can think without talking to oneself in the imagination – as when one talks thoughtfully to another. Since neither thinking nor perceiving need involve any images, the somatic changes that *may* be part of the syndrome of a momentary emotion and which *may*, but need not, be caused by a thought (in the proper sense of the term) or by perceiving something, need not be caused by mental images.

(iii)   While there can be a difference between feeling an emotion (e.g. jealousy) and realizing what emotion one feels (e.g. realizing that one feels jealous), there is, as we have seen in chapter 3, no difference between having an emotion and feeling an emotion, any more than there is a difference between having a pain and feeling a pain. Damasio's distinction between emotion and feeling an emotion, if taken as a *stipulation*, has nothing to recommend it. For there is no point in using 'emotion' to signify an ensemble of somatic changes associated with mental images – which would exclude what we call 'emotions'. Nor is there any point in using the phrase 'feeling an emotion' to signify a *felt* ensemble of somatic changes associated with mental images, since, given Damasio's conception of mental images, this would include sea-sickness and giddiness.

(iv)   Feeling an emotion is not a cognitive response to an emotion, and an emotion is not a bodily condition caused by thought-constituting mental images. As we have noted, if one is frightened by a noise in the night, one may feel frightened that there is a thief in the house, and one's pulses may race. But, contrary to James and Damasio alike, one's fear is not the perception of, or a response to, one's felt racing pulses – *even if it is true that one*

---

[24] The analysis of thinking is given in *The Intellectual Powers*, ch. 10.

*would not feel fear but for one's racing pulses.* What one was frightened *by* was the noise (not an imagined noise or an auditory image); what one was frightened *of* was a burglar; and one was frightened *that* a burglar had broken in and would threaten one. One may or may not notice one's racing pulses, but whether one does or not, one's fear of a burglary is not a response to one's racing pulses or even to one's racing pulses conjoined with an image of a burglar. Feelings of emotion are not *about* the body at all. What they are about or of is the *object* of the emotion, which, as we have seen, may be signified by the object-accusative or nominalization-accusative of the emotion verb.

(v) One's 'feelings of emotion' – one's love, hope, or pride – are not ways of finding out facts about 'our visceral and musculoskeletal state'. Indeed, emotions do not inform one either of the state of one's body or of the state of one's environment. But one's emotional perturbations may inform one of one's emotional attitudes. A pang of jealousy or a feeling of longing may indicate to one that one is falling in love. A blush of embarrassment may bring home to one how ashamed one is of some misdemeanour. One's tears of grief may make one realize how much one loved the deceased. Far from one's emotions (or felt emotions) informing one of the state of one's body, the state of one's body may often inform one about the intensity of one's emotions.

(vi) Damasio's somatic marker hypothesis is misconceived. First, emotions do not consist of 'positive' and 'negative' somatic images that tell one what is good or bad. Bodily reactions do not inform us of good and evil. If one feels indignant at an injustice, what tells one that the object of one's indignation is an evil is not that one feels unpleasantly flushed in association with the thought of the act in question. On the contrary, one is indignant at what was done because it is unjust, and one knows it to be unjust because it rides roughshod over someone's rights, not because one flushes in anger. Indeed, one's flush is a flush of anger only in so far as one is thus indignant. Moreover, one will feel indignant only to the extent that one cares about the protection of the rights of human beings or of *this* human being.

(vii) Part of the appeal of Damasio's account is his suggestion that there is a rational part of the brain and an emotional part of the brain, and that the former, without the latter, is woefully deficient for optimal decision-making. This suggestion has had considerable public appeal. But the argument is confused. For if 'better' means 'optimally rational', and if the 'emotional part' of the brain evaluates options 'better' than the 'rational parts' of the brain, then the so-called emotional parts of the brain *are* in fact the rational parts! (To be sure, parts of the brain are not in the decision-making business. It is human beings that make decisions, not their brains.)

*Axiological element in emotion is not somatic*     Damasio attempts to budget for the axiological element present in some emotions by reference to what he calls 'positive and negative somatic feelings'. But, first, pleasant and unpleasant bodily sensations are insufficient to guide one in one's evaluations. The mere somatic changes associated with fear can be quite pleasant as long as there is no apprehended danger in what would otherwise be a fearful situation (as is evident from the pleasure people take in riding roller-coasters or in watching horror films). The somatic changes associated with excitement can be repulsive if the object is inappropriate (one might feel disgusted with oneself for enjoying the excitement of a bull-fight or of boxing). Neither pity nor indignation is enjoyable, but the guidance they give to evaluation is altogether different. Some emotions, such as longing and nostalgia, are blends of pleasantness and unpleasantness, but they do not give rise to contrary evaluations. And there are many emotions and occasions upon which many kinds of emotion are felt that do not involve any somatic feelings at all, but do involve evaluations. Distrust may involve somatic changes on some occasion, but trust need not. One's fear of global warming or of a rise in the rate of inflation need involve no perturbations, only concern.

Secondly, it is altogether bizarre to suggest that the 'coarse' emotions should be proposed as guides to rational action, when it is they that typically disrupt and distort clear thinking and decision-making. Bodily perturbations of anger are hardly conducive to rational decision-making – that is why we are well advised to take a deep breath and to count to ten before responding to something offensive. Somatic markers of fear are, indeed, typically reactions to what is perceived to be threatening or dangerous, but it is precisely they that get in the way of rational responses to danger and threats. It is no coincidence that it is said that a person passionately in love is as fit to choose a spouse as a blind person is to choose a painting.

Damasio may be perfectly right in linking the capacity for rationality in practical reasoning and in pursuit of goals with the ability to feel emotions. But that is not because felt emotions are somatic markers that function as axiological litmus paper. Rather the linkage consists in a common feature underlying both emotion and practical reasoning, namely caring. Let me explain. The emotions do not let us 'mind the body'. So it is implausible to suppose that what is wrong with patients (such as the famous and pathetic Phineas Gage) who have suffered damage to the ventromedial sector of the prefrontal cortex and manifest difficulties in decision-making is that their somatic responses or their apprehension of their somatic responses are awry or uninformative. But what might be investigated is whether the brain damage in the kinds of patient Damasio investigated affects their ability to care or to persist in caring about goals and objectives. For such a deficiency would affect both their emotions and their ability to pursue goals over time. One feels no emotions about things to which one is indifferent, and one does not pursue goals efficiently or effectively unless one cares and persists in caring, for one reason or another, about achieving them.

## 4. Evolutionary accounts of the emotions: Darwin and Ekman

*Darwin's 3 aims*      Darwin's book *The Expression of the Emotions in Man and Animals* (1872) was the last of his great evolutionary trilogy.[25] He was motivated by his opposition to a form of an argument from design expressed by Sir Charles Bell in his *Anatomy and Philosophy of Expression* (1806, posthumous third edition 1844). Believing in the argument from design, Bell held that human beings were endowed with the facial musculature they possess in order to give them the ability to express their feelings. Although Darwin relied upon Bell's brilliant anatomical and physiological research (as well as upon the work of Pierre Gratiolet and G. B. Duchenne de Bologne), his purpose was to demonstrate that:

(i)   there are non-coincidental similarities between the behavioural expression of emotions in animals and in man;

---

[25] What Darwin called '*expression*' of emotion' is what was, in chapter 3, stipulatively characterized as 'manifestation' and distinguished from articulate expression. In the following discussion we shall abide by Darwin's use.

(ii)   certain forms of expression of human emotions are universal (pan-cultural), innate to the human species, and inherited;

(iii)  the recognition of facial expressions of emotion is, for the most part, transcultural.

His account of emotions was meant (a) to confirm his theory that mankind is continuous with animate nature; (b) to provide further evidence for his hypothesis of the descent of all races of man from a common progenitor; and (c) to support his account of natural selection and evolutionary adaptation.

Darwin's book was well received and highly influential. He laid the foundations for evolutionary psychology, and his book was pregnant with ideas that called out for further development and investigation. However, his views fell out of favour in the twentieth century. The most important anti-Darwinian ideas came from anthropologists, such as Margaret Mead, Gregory Bateson, and Ray Birdwhistell. They advanced the social constructivist view that the forms of expression of emotion among human beings are, for the most part, socially learnt and culturally relative. However, from the 1970s onwards, there was a powerful revival of Darwinian theories by Paul Ekman and his colleagues.

*Darwin's susceptibility to traditional misconceptions*

Darwin had not ventured to define the concept of an emotion, but took it for granted that there is a wide consensus about what counts as an emotion. Had the notion been available to him, he might have suggested that the concept of an emotion is a family resemblance one. It is unsurprising that Darwin went along with the received conception that the expression of an emotion is an outward sign of an inner mental state. Indeed, he uncritically adopted the received picture of the 'inner' and the 'outer'. In early notes, written in 1840, he observed that 'we cannot perceive the thought of another person at all, we can only infer it from his behaviour' – presumably assuming that the sincere expression of thought is mere words, and that the thought itself is still concealed no matter how sincere the speaker may be. He evidently also assumed that the thinker himself *can* perceive his own thoughts in all their non-linguistic purity! So it is not surprising that he thought that the relationship between emotion and its bodily expression is causal (external, contingent) – like that between fire and the smoke that signals it. He did not realize that the expressions of, say, fear or anger are *the forms* that fear and anger may take, rather than their effects. This in itself does not materially affect his often suggestive ideas. Nor, for that matter, does the fact that he pays but scant attention to persistent emotions and their motivating power, since the focus of his attention is upon the facial expression of momentary emotions. But there were two unfortunate consequences of Darwin's work. One was that it steered research, especially in the second half of the twentieth century, into an exaggerated concern with the recognition of the facial expression of emotions in humans. We shall examine this later. A second unfortunate consequence of Darwin's work was to impress upon many of his successors the idea that emotions *are* actually no more than momentary or very short-term emotional perturbations. This, as we have seen, is misconceived, especially (but not only) when it comes to the study of human emotions that are bound up with mastery of a language. If the empirical study of the emotions is to encompass the role of emotions in human life and the ways in which irrational, obsessive, and pathological emotions can be treated and ameliorated, it must recognize the inadequacy of restricting the concept of an emotion 'for scientific purposes' to emotional perturbations.

*Ekman's conception of an emotion*

This restriction is marked in the work of a distinguished contemporary evolutionary psychologist, Paul Ekman. He holds that 'emotions can begin so quickly that they can happen before one is aware that they have started ... Indeed, quick onset is fundamental ... to the adaptive value of emotions'. He acknowledges that 'emotions do not always begin so quickly. There are occasions when an emotion unfolds very slowly, taking a number of seconds or minutes for characteristic emotional responses to occur.'[26] It is indeed correct that an emotional response may be very quick, as when one jumps with fear in response to a noise, blushes with embarrassment, or responds angrily to an insult. But a slowly evolving emotion is not one that takes a few seconds or minutes. Love may take weeks or months to evolve slowly and unwillingly in the face of pride (Mr Darcy) or prejudice (Elizabeth Bennet). Hatred may take months to develop from loving admiration to dislike, from dislike to distrust, and from distrust to the hostility of hatred (Isabel Archer's evolving emotional relation to Gilbert Osmond in James's *The Portrait of a Lady*). Feelings of devotion, loyalty, and trust could hardly 'unfold' in a number of seconds or minutes. Although one may feel a stab of jealousy, jealousy may also evolve only gradually from detached amusement, to slight annoyance, to suspicion, before flowering slowly into jealousy.

[26] P. Ekman, 'An Argument for Basic Emotions', *Cognition and Emotion* 6 (1992), 185.

For how long was Othello jealous? For just one unbroken period from Iago's insinuations until his murder of Desdemona? Or was he jealous 672 times during this period? Ekman avers that emotional responses

> do not last very long unless the emotion is evoked again ... It may be that under exceptional circumstances a single emotion endures for more than seconds and minutes, but I think it more likely that close inspection would reveal that the same emotion is being repeatedly evoked.[27]

The evidence he advances for this claim is the measurement of the duration of both expressive and physiological changes during spontaneous events:

> When subjects have reported experiencing an emotion for 15 or 20 minutes, and I have had access to a videotaped recording of their preceding behaviour, I found that they showed multiple expressions of that emotion. My interpretation of such incidents is that people summate in their verbal report what was actually a series of discrete emotion episodes.[28]

But this is to tailor one's clothes to the length of one's tape measure. Love and hatred, according to Ekman, are not emotions but *emotional attitudes*; grief, jealousy, and infatuation he holds to be *emotional plots*. This is not a discovery, but a stipulation that cuts across our concept of an emotion. That, of course, is in principle licit. Ekman may stipulate as he pleases. But stipulations have consequences. The space carved out by the concept of an emotional attitude is already occupied. It includes contempt, disdain, respect, reverence, and admiration. These are emotionally coloured cognitive stances towards people or things. Attitudes, unlike emotions, can be taken up, adopted, or assumed. One may change one's attitude on further consideration, but one does not change one's anger, love, or jealousy *on further consideration*, even though they are information-sensitive and may change. The notion of an emotional plot or narrative is perfectly acceptable – indeed we have emphasized that emotions belong to a narrative or history. But the plot or narrative to which an emotion belongs is not the emotion felt, but the history that renders it intelligible, embeds

[27] Ekman, 'An Argument for Basic Emotions', 185–6.
[28] Ekman, 'An Argument for Basic Emotions', 186.

it in the life of the subject, and recounts its development. Love, hatred, jealousy, and grief, for example, are persistent emotions that lack genuine duration. As we have seen, they are not dispositions or tendencies to feel emotional perturbations or spasms. The love that is disclosed in a loving smile and tender voice, and manifest in an embrace or kiss, is not a different love from the love that is exhibited in care and concern, in longing and loyalty, in speech and in writing. The study of emotions is not the study of agitations and perturbations, and to strive to understand the emotions is not to strive to understand spasms.[29]

## 5. The quest for basic emotions

The idea that some emotions are basic, others derivative, goes back to the Stoics. Unlike Aristotle, they held emotions, for the most part, to be detrimental to human felicity and to the virtuous life. With the exception of *eupatheic* emotions such as awe, reverence, amity, and generosity, they thought emotions to be forces of unreason.

*Cicero on basic emotions*   It was the Stoics who introduced the idea that all emotions are variations on a set of basic ones. Cicero in the *Discussions at Tusculum* (III), held that emotions (*perturbationes*)[30] are disorders of the mind – forms of mental suffering. They are 'furies let loose upon us and urged on by folly', which we must learn to overcome if we are to live as befits mankind. There are, Cicero averred, only four basic emotions: distress (*aegritudo*: misery, grief), pleasure (*laetitia*: delight, joy), fear (*metus*: apprehension, trepidation), and desire (*libido*: lust, craving, appetite). All other emotions can be presented as species of these genera. The basic emotions are two pairs, one of which is directed to the present

---

[29] To be sure, one may hold, with P. E. Griffiths, that 'the general concept of emotion has no role in any future psychology. ... As far as understanding ourselves is concerned, the concept of emotion, like the concept of spirituality, can only be hindrance' (*What Emotions Really Are* (University of Chicago Press, Chicago, 1997), p. 247). Quine similarly argued that scientific epistemology should dispense with the concept of knowledge (W. V. O. Quine, *Quiddities* (Penguin, London, 1987), p. 109). What can one say, save, as Friedrich Waismann would have put it, that they are great dispensers before the Lord.

[30] Cicero translated the Greek *pathos* as *perturbatio*. He held that the Greek *pathos* signified distemper or disease, whereas the Romans more accurately conceived of the emotions as perturbations of the mind. Seneca chose *affectus*; others opted for *passio*.

and one to the future. One of each pair involves a judgement that something is a good, and the other a judgement of an evil.

The manifold species of emotions are differentiated by alternative pairings, often in conjunction with a further differentiating factor. So envy, for example, is alleged to be misery at a supposed good believed to belong to another that one desires oneself; despair is held to be fear of an unavoidable forthcoming evil. In general, the Stoics conceived of our susceptibility to emotions as a form of human bondage and strove to surmount the emotions in the endeavour to achieve *apatheia* or, as Cicero translated it, *tranquilitas*, that is essential to the virtuous life. The analytic reductionism appears to be motivated by the objective of *treating* the emotions (as one treats a disorder of the mind) by self-examination, reflection, and by exercises. In so far as all emotions can be analysed into beliefs concerning present and future good and evil and positive and negative responses to them, the cures for these disorders of the mind are more readily manageable. For they are to be focused upon achieving an understanding of the illusory character of the goods and evils with which fortune presents us, and their irrelevance to the life of virtue (see table 4.1).

|  | *Present* | *Future* |
|---|---|---|
| Good | Delight | Desire |
| Evil | Distress | Fear |

**Table 4.1**   *Cicero's basic emotions*

*Augustine's reduction of emotions*

Augustine followed the Stoics, but held that the basic Stoic emotions (*passio*) were all reducible to forms of willing (*City of God*, 9.4; 14). Desire and delight are forms of willing with consent those things we will for; fear and distress are willing in dissent from the things we will against. Reducing the emotions to the will was ideologically motivated. Unlike the materialistically inclined Stoics, Augustine believed in the survival of the soul after death. He also believed that a bodiless being could feel emotions, as God, who feels love and compassion, does, and as do the angels. Hence his dissociation of the emotions from the body. Having connected the emotions to the will, he then associated them all with love. Desire is a love that strains after a loved object; pleasure or joy a love that possesses and enjoys its object; fear a love that shuns what opposes it; and distress a love that feels that opposition when it happens. Consequently, Augustine rejected the Stoics' condemnation of the emotions. One ought to love one's enemies, to be angry at sinners, to fear God. Jesus patently felt emotions, and such emotions cannot but be proper to the human condition that Jesus assumed. In general, laudable emotions are those objects of love that are correctly chosen by the will. Concupiscent love must be controlled by the will and the path of charitable love must be chosen. But that requires grace.

*Aquinas on basic emotions*     Aquinas was more liberal in his list of basic emotions (*Summa Theologica*, 1ª2ᵃᵉ, q. 22–48).[31] He held emotions to be passive powers of the sensitive appetite common to man and beast. They are states of the human being as a whole, not of the mind or of the body. Unlike Augustine, but like Aristotle, he held that the somatic manifestations of emotion are essential to it. The somatic and physiological changes linked to an emotion are its material 'cause' or explanation, whereas its formal object provides its formal 'cause' or explanation. Aquinas identified eleven basic emotions (see list 4.1). There are six *concupiscible* emotions: love and hate; desire and aversion; delight and distress. These opposite pairs all involve an emotional response to the positive and negative value of the object of the emotion. Love and hate are inclinations or pronenesses of the sensitive appetite; desire and aversion are exhibited in movement towards or away from the object of the emotion, and delight and distress are responses to the satisfaction of the emotion. There are five *irascible* emotions: hope and despair; confidence and fear; and anger (which, contrary to Aristotle, has no opposite[32]). These are all emotional responses to

| Concupiscible emotions | Irascible emotions |
|---|---|
| Love—hate (proneness or tendency) | Hope—despair |
| Desire—aversion (movement to or away) | Confidence—fear |
| Delight—distress (response to attainment) | Anger |

**List 4.1**  *Aquinas's basic emotions*

---

[31] See P. King, 'Aquinas on the Emotions', in B. Davies and E. Stump (eds), *Oxford Handbook of Aquinas* (Oxford University Press, Oxford, 2012), and 'Emotions in Medieval Thought', in P. Goldie (ed.), *The Oxford Handbook of Philosophy of Emotion* (Oxford University Press, Oxford, 2009), to which I am indebted.

[32] The opposite of anger, according to Aristotle, is gentleness (*Eudemian Ethics*, 1222ᵇ1).

what we apprehend to be the difficulty in attaining or avoiding the object of our emotion. Hope and confidence are emotional responses in which we view the difficulties in the attainment of the beneficial as surmountable; fear and despair see the difficulties as probably or certainly unsurmountable and the evil as probably or certainly unavoidable. Anger is the response to the advent of an evil one has been unable to avoid. Each basic type subsumes further variants. Anger, for example, subsumes irascibility, ill-will, and rancour or vindictiveness, and love subsumes friendly love or benevolence and covetous or possessive love.

There are some concerns about this typology. First, while the distinction between concupiscible and irascible emotions is intelligible, it seems neither superior nor deeper than many other ways of classifying the emotions. One can differentiate between emotions of self-assessment and emotions that involve no self-assessment: social and solitary emotions, pre-linguistic emotions and language-presupposing emotions, backward- and forward-looking emotions, and so on. Secondly, some of Aquinas's basic emotions are not, by our standards, emotions at all – such as desire and aversion. Thirdly, Aquinas discusses a variety of emotions sequentially and enumerates their subvarieties. But what principles he employs is unclear. It is not obvious, for example, why there are just those two types of love. Love of beauty (of landscapes, of music and literature) seems neither a form of benevolence nor a form of possessive love. Nor is it evident why anger is to be subdivided into irascibility, ill-will, and vindictiveness, without investigating annoyance, irritation, and rage. Indeed, ill-will may characterize some forms of anger but not all, and ill-will may be manifest quite independently of anger (in hatred, for example). Other scholastics, such as Scotus, Ockham, and much later Suárez took issue with Aquinas. It is noteworthy that Suárez held that there are many different possible taxonomies of the emotions. None is privileged. All are purpose-relative.

*Early moderns on basic emotions* Philosophy in the early modern era was flooded with treatises on the emotions. These were much given to divergent reductive typologies that purported to show how all emotions could be *defined* in terms of a favoured basic set. Descartes argued that there are six simple and primitive passions: wonder, love, hatred, desire, joy, sadness (*PS* II. 69). Hobbes offers a similar list: appetite, desire, love, aversion, hate, joy, and grief (*Leviathan*, I. 6). Spinoza was more economical, arguing that all the emotions can be derived from the triad of desire, joy, and sorrow, by combining them severally with varying degrees of knowledge or belief (*Ethics*, III. 59). His exhaustiveness, subtlety, and sensitivity in part III of the *Ethics* is the high point in the history of reductive analyses of the emotions. Locke was similarly economical: 'Pleasure and pain and that which causes them, good and evil, are the hinges on which our passions turn' (*An Essay concerning Human Understanding*, II. 20. 3). He endeavoured to demonstrate the reducibility of all emotions to pleasure and pain associated with the thought of current/future possession/lack of possession and degrees of certainty/uncertainty thereof. Most emotions, he conceded, have 'operations on the Body, and cause various changes in it: Which, not being always sensible, do not make a necessary part of the *Idea* of each Passion' (*An Essay concerning Human Understanding*, II. 20. 17).[33] This philosophical endeavour continued into and throughout the eighteenth century, but no consensus was ever reached about a privileged set of emotions in terms of which all other emotions are to be defined. Nor were the definitions of emotions advanced by different philosophers agreed by all. In the nineteenth century the preoccupation with basic emotions gradually waned.

*Scientists on basic emotions*      As philosophers abandoned the quest for basic emotions, psychologists and later evolutionary psychologists and cognitive neuroscientists took it up. Their motivations were different. All were eager to show that there is a set of basic emotions in terms of which all other emotions can be *explained*. Different types of scientists selected different sets of basic emotions according to their concerns and the research methods available to them. One might distinguish the following:

(i)   neo-Jamesian theories, conceiving of emotions as the perception of somatic changes;

(ii)   cognitive and appraisal theories, emphasizing the roots of emotions in judgements and appraisals;

(iii)   social construction theories, stressing the dependence of emotions on social roles;

(iv)   neo-Darwinian evolutionary theories, conceiving of emotions as adaptations conducive to fitness;

(v)   cognitive neuroscientific theories that endeavoured to discover localized neural structures that generate a basic set of emotions

---

[33] This latter qualification distances him from Descartes and puts his conception of the emotions far removed from that of James and his successors.

in animal and man. Neuroscientists sought to discover the neural mechanisms that generate the felt 'inner emotion', on the one hand, and its determinate, pre-programmed, form of expression on the other.[34]

It is not surprising that these distinct investigations appeared complementary. Universality seemed to imply innateness. Innateness suggested genetic determination, on the one hand, and dedicated neural structures, on the other. Genetic determination presupposed evolutionary selection and adaptation. It is noteworthy that various theorists seized upon one or another of the constitutive elements of emotion, took this to be an empirical insight with theoretical import, and constructed a putatively empirical theory that exaggerated one aspect of an emotion at the expense of others. More effort spent on connective conceptual analysis might have spared us much conceptual confusion, futile theorizing, and pointless experimentation. We must look more closely at the various enterprises.

*Psychologists on basic emotions*     Psychologists, from the turn of the nineteenth century, engaged in a quest for basic emotions. The disagreements among them about the number of basic emotions and about which specific emotions are basic is as great as that among philosophers. This should give us pause. James (1890) recognized four 'coarse' emotions, based on their distinctive somatic components: fear, grief, love, and rage.[35] McDougall (1926) cited seven basic emotions: anger, disgust, elation, fear, subjection, tender-emotion, and wonder.[36] Watson (1930), the father of behaviourism, acknowledged but three: fear, love, and rage.[37] Ekman et al. (1969) listed six based on differences of universal facial expressions: anger, disgust, fear, joy, sadness, and surprise.[38] Izard (1971) hypothesized ten: anger, contempt, disgust, distress, fear, guilt, interest, joy, shame, surprise. On reconsideration (2007), he reduced his

[34] Neuro-pharmacological theories might well contend that the basic emotions are determined by the number and nature of specific neurochemical pathways that have been found in treating affective disorders, such as depression, anger, excitement, and so forth.

[35] W. James, *The Principles of Psychology*, vol. 2, p. 449.

[36] W. McDougall, *An Introduction to Social Psychology* (Luce, Boston, 1926).

[37] J. Watson, *Behaviourism* (University of Chicago Press, Chicago, 1930).

[38] P. Ekman, E. R. Sorenson, and W. V. Friesen, 'Pan-cultural Elements in Facial Displays of Emotions', *Science* 164 (1969), 86–8. Ekman later changed his mind and expanded his list.

list to six: interest, joy, sadness, anger, disgust, and fear.[39] Plutchik (1980) cited eight on adaptive evolutionary grounds: trust, anger, anticipation, disgust, joy, fear, sadness, and surprise.[40] Oatley and Johnson-Laird (1987) mention five on the grounds of not requiring any intentional content: anger, disgust, anxiety, happiness, and sadness.[41] Most recently Rachael Jack and colleagues, by ever more sophisticated investigations into facial expressions, has reduced the basic emotions to four: anger, fear, happiness, and sadness.[42]

*No consensus on what an emotion is*

There is no consensus among scientists on the elementary question of what an emotion is. Carroll Izard attempted to crystallize the degree of common understanding based on a survey of thirty-four contemporary scientists studying the emotions. The upshot was the following overview:

> Emotion consists of neural circuits (that are at least partially dedicated), response systems, and a feeling state/process that motivates and organizes cognition and action. Emotion also provides information to the person experiencing it, and may include antecedent cognitive appraisals and on-going cognition including an interpretation of its feeling state, expressions or social-communicative signals, and may motivate approach behaviour, exercise control/regulation, and be social or relational in nature.[43]

Without consensus on what an emotion *is*, that is, on the *concept* of an emotion, scientific investigations stumble from one confusion to another. Appetites, such as hunger, thirst, and lust, are treated as emotions (Rolls).[44] But we have seen ample reason to distinguish them from emotions (see pp. 7–12, 26–8). Agitations, such as surprise, are

[39] C. E. Izard, 'The Emotions and Emotion Constructs in Personality and Cultural Research', in R. B. Cattell and R. M. Dreger (eds), *Handbook of Modern Personality Theory* (Wiley, New York, 1969), pp. 496–510.

[40] R. Plutchik, 'A General Psycho-evolutionary Theory of Emotion', in R. Plutchik and H. Kellerman (eds), *Emotion: Theory, Research and Experience* (Academic Press, New York, 1980), vol. 1, pp. 3–31.

[41] K. Oatley and P. N. Johnson-Laird, 'Towards a Cognitive Theory of Emotions', *Cognition and Emotion* 1 (1987), 29–50.

[42] R. Jack, O. Garrod, and P. Schyns, 'Dynamic Facial Expressions of Emotion Transmit an Evolving Hierarchy of Signals over Time', *Current Biology* 24 (2014), 187–92.

[43] C. E. Izard, 'The Many Meanings/Aspects of Emotion: Definitions, Functions, Activation, and Regulation', *Emotion Review* 2 (2010), 363–70 (367).

[44] E. T. Rolls, *The Brain and Emotion* (Oxford University Press, Oxford, 1999).

assimilated to emotional perturbations (Izard). But surprise is *an epistemic response* to something unexpected that may be pleasant, unpleasant, or neither, depending on what one is surprised at. Emotional attitudes, such as contempt and disgust (not the agitation, but the standing attitude towards another for shabby behaviour) are held to be emotions.[45] Epistemic attributes, such as interest and anticipation, are held to be emotions (Plutchik). It is true that the boundaries between these categories is blurred. It is also true that some expressions, for example 'being pleased', may sometimes signify a mere affective response (an agitation) and sometimes a persistent attitude. Nevertheless, the widespread disagreements call out for conceptual clarification. Consensus about the subject under investigation is a precondition for fruitful empirical research.

There is similar lack of consensus on what a *basic* emotion is. Again, Izard attempted to delineate what scientists mean by the term:

> A basic emotion may be viewed as a set of neural, bodily/expressive, and feeling/motivational components generated rapidly, automatically, and non-consciously when on-going affective-cognitive processes interact with sensing or perception of an ecologically valid stimulus to activate evolutionarily adapted neurobiological and mental processes.[46]

Such an overview does not provide a perspicuous representation of what a basic emotion is. But it does make it patent that the concept of a basic emotion requires elucidation and determination. Further reflection will show that *there is no such thing* as a basic emotion *simpliciter*, for 'basic', like 'large' or 'small', is an attributive adjective, rather than a predicative adjective like 'red' or 'sweet'. So being basic is a relative rather than absolute notion. Something may be basic of its kind relative to one determination, and non-basic relative to another.

*Futility of the quest for basic emotions*    (i) As we have seen, philosophers from the Stoics until the nineteenth century held an emotion to be basic if it is a member of a set of emotions in terms

---

[45] It is noteworthy that happiness has wandered on and off lists of basic emotions. It seems to mean *being pleased* or *delighted*. It evidently does not signify a mental state with genuine duration (as in 'We were so happy together that afternoon on the downs') nor a dispositional state (as in 'Those three months in Greece were the happiest of my young life'), let alone the *summum bonum*.

[46] C. E. Izard, 'Basic Emotions, Natural Kinds, Emotion Schemas, and a New Paradigm', *Perspectives on Psychological Science* 2 (2007), 260–80.

of which all others may be defined. However, there is no reason to suppose that all emotions can be fruitfully and illuminatingly defined in terms of a subset of emotions. In so far as they can, there is no reason to suppose that there is a *unique* subset. One may construct a *geometry of emotions*, so to speak, in many different ways. If any enjoys priority, this will not demonstrate veracity to nature, but fruitfulness, elegance, or economy relative to a purpose.

(ii)    In the wake of Darwin's research, basic emotions have been understood by evolutionary psychologists to be those for which there are universal, transcultural, forms of facial expression. The criterion for this has been taken to be the alleged universality of the ability to recognize facial expressions exhibited in photographs as manifestations of emotions. The methodology and reasoning are bizarre. Evolution certainly did not select for the ability, under laboratory conditions, to recognize photographs of facial expressions of emotions independently of any context. The animal and human ability to recognize emotions is context-dependent. It does not depend solely on facial expression, but also on body language in the circumstances confronting the agent, and on recognition of those circumstances. These points will be elaborated.

If, despite the labours of Ekman and his followers, there is no universal, transcultural recognitional ability (and Ekman's results have indeed been challenged), then *in this sense*, there are no basic emotions. On the other hand, there is no doubt that the facial expression of emotion plays a crucial role (a) in animal (including human) behaviour and (b) in animal responsiveness to the play of facial features both of other animals of its own kind and of animals of other kinds. The degree to which the recognitional abilities are cross-cultural and transcend local physiognomic differences is an empirical question to be resolved by empirical investigations. If there are differences in cross-racial recognitional abilities, this makes little difference to the contention that emotions are common to mankind, let alone to the claim that many human emotions have correlates among non-language-using animals, or indeed to the claim that the modes of facial expression of emotions and the ability to recognize them are evolutionary adaptations genetically transmitted. If it is more difficult for members of one racial group to read the faces of members of another than to read the faces of members of their own, this does not affect Darwin's argument.

The modern scientific endeavour to *reduce* all emotions to a set of basic ones is a post-Darwinian concern. A primary focus of the research done by psychologists has been on the recognition of facial expressions. Apart from the fact that there is much to be measured here by means of the latest forms of instrumentation, there seems little to be said for using changes in facial expression to be *the* key to understanding the nature of the emotions and their role in human life. Facial expression is but one criterion among others for feeling an emotion. The same facial expression may express different emotions. Different facial expressions may express the same emotion. Many emotions can be felt without manifesting any facial expression.

*Constitutive grounds for emotion ascription* It is not an empirical truth that human beings laugh when amused or delighted, smile when pleased or overjoyed. It is not an empirical discovery that we frown or scowl when angry or irritated. It is not a natural law that we weep with grief, in sorrow and distress. These are *constitutive grounds* for whether the subject feels an emotion – they are *forms* an emotion takes in certain contexts and on certain occasions. So we need to bear in mind some features of the very notion of a logical criterion or of constitutive grounds:

*Logical features of criteria* (a)  Criteria *are* criteria only in appropriate circumstances. A scowl when one is insulted is a criterion of anger; a scowl when one is engaged in lifting or moving a very heavy weight is a criterion of effort. A laugh when one has been told a joke is a criterion for being amused, but when one is being tickled it is not. Tears with down-turned mouth and eyes squeezed shut are a criterion of sadness, grief, or disappointment. But, if such behaviour is manifest when one is on the winner's podium or is being given an award, they are tears of joy. The grimace of pain and of orgasmic ecstasy are very similar, but one is unlikely to mistake the one for the other.

(b)  Criteria are defeasible. One may laugh in response to a joke, but if one did not understand the joke, one does not laugh in amusement. One may laugh with joy, but in the absence of a joyous occasion and reason for feeling joy, one's laugh is not an expression of joy. One may smile in amity but, if one murders whilst one smiles, the smile is not a criterion of friendliness. One may weep with grief, but if one is cutting onions the tears may not be tears of grief at all – what one *says* may settle the matter.

(c)  Different emotions may be exhibited by the same facial expression in certain circumstances. It is not just 'happiness' that is expressed by a smile or laugh, but also, in appropriate contexts, being pleased (a reactive attitude), feeling cheerful (a mood), feeling delighted, being amused, sharing the amusement of others (smiles and laughter being infectious), being embarrassed. It is not just 'sadness' that is expressed by tears and sobbing, but, in appropriate contexts, joy or relief. The facial expression of fear and of horror may be identical.

(d)  The same emotion may be manifest by different facial expressions. One can express anger without scowling and going red in the face, but with tight lips and a pallid and rigid face. One can express embarrassment by blushing, but also by laughing uneasily. One may cry out and weep in fear, or simply go white, gulp, and grit one's teeth.

(e)  There are multiple criteria for a person's occurrent emotion. The *bodily demeanour* of someone who is enraged may be no less distinctive than his facial expression. The characteristic shrinking or cowering in fear is as marked as the frightened face. We recognize the *gestures* of love and affection as well as those of anger, fear, grief, triumph, relief, or joy. Most obviously, we recognize the *tones* of love and affection, of anger and rage, of anxiety and fear, of disappointment or sorrow no less immediately than we recognize facial expressions. We *understand* verbal expressions of emotion in the avowals and reports of others, irrespective of whether an emotion word is used. Our capacity for recognizing the emotions of our fellow human beings is dependent upon all of these, which are usually all taken in immediately. The absence of one criterion does not imply that the emotion may not be manifest and readily recognizable.

(f)  The forms that an emotion may take are culturally conditioned, both by way of inhibition and by way of substitution. If the expression of amusement or good cheer by laughter is held to be vulgar and beneath one's dignity (as

Lord Chesterfield informed his son), it may well be suppressed in certain social circles. If embarrassment is something that needs to be concealed (as it is in many Asian
societies), the standard form it takes may well be a broad
smile, which, in embarrassing circumstances, is not a criterion for amusement or friendliness.

*Perceiving the*        Indeed, our normal recognition of emotions in
*emotions of others*    others turns not only on the various kinds of criteria or constitutive grounds that warrant attribution
of an emotion, but on the circumstance in which the expression is manifest, the antecedent history, the knowledge or
belief of the agent, and the subsequent behaviour. For criteria are criteria only in appropriate circumstances. If someone engaged in a normal, amicable, and measured
conversation were suddenly to assume a facial expression
of terror, fury, ecstasy, or hilarity without any ostensible
object, we would not understand what was happening. If
no explanation were forthcoming, we would view the event
as a pathological aberration.

       So, with all this in view, what sense can be made
*Relativizing the idea*    of the idea that certain forms of facial expression
*of basic emotions*    determine some emotions as basic?

(iii)   Developmental psychologists may wish to use the expression
'basic emotion' to signify emotions exhibited by babies or very
small children prior to any language acquisition.[47] There is nothing wrong with such a suggestion. It would restrict the range of
basic emotions to those that are language-independent. So it
would exclude such emotions as regret, remorse, pride, and
shame. It would be plausible to include among the basic emotions thus conceived fear, rage, frustration, distress, feeling
'happy' (i.e. being pleased) – all of which commonly occur in
these lists. But it would also include contentment, affection, hostility, confidence, boredom, excitement, anxiety. Of course,
babies may also exhibit disgust, surprise, curiosity, expectation,
and disappointment. But these may well not be considered to be

---

[47] To be sure, there are different phases prior to the child's language acquisition.
Moreover, it is unclear how to draw a clear boundary between babbling and words,
between responding systematically to words and using words. But this need not concern us here.

emotions. Be that as it may, the list is not restricted by the neo-nate's or baby's ability to recognize or respond to the facial expressions of others. Indeed, it is not limited or determined solely by the parental ability to recognize the facial expressions of babies – recognition of vocal expressiveness is no less important.

(iv)    Evolutionary psychologists may wish to use the phrase 'basic emotion' to signify those emotions human beings share with other animals. These will be confined to emotions that presuppose no linguistic ability. So they will be similar to the previous list of the emotions of pre-linguistic children. But one may wish to add emotional corollaries of social hierarchies among social animals that occur in humans only at a later stage of maturation, subsequent to a child's mastery of a language.

Evolutionary psychologists are interested in basic emotions in this sense for different reasons from the developmental psychologist. Their concern is with the genetic transmission of the capacity to feel certain emotions, and with the characterization of the functions for the sake of which just these emotions were selected for by evolutionary pressures. The idea of emotions being *selected for* by evolutionary pressure is pregnant with potential confusion. Emotions are not kinds of things, since they are not things at all. So what evolutionary pressures may select is an innate tendency or proneness to respond in certain ways to the perception and recognition of other animals, their behaviour, and concurrent features of the environment. Among self-moving creatures, the most primitive forms of responsiveness is the behavioural manifestation of attraction and aversion in response to something that has caught the animal's attention. Where attention is focused upon food, we have the rudiments of liking and disliking, and the roots of disgust. Where it is focused upon perceived danger, we have the rudiments of fear. Where it is focused upon sexual competition for a female in heat, or upon the incursion of another member of the same species into marked territory, we find displays of combative rage. The criteria for the animal's perceptions are not independent of the criteria for its affective response, and the criteria for the affective response are not independent of the action the animal takes.

(v)    Cognitive neuroscientists invoke the notion of a basic emotion with yet another interest. They are concerned with identifying systems of interconnected parts of the brain that are active when an emotion is experienced. An emotion is accounted basic if its occurrence is explained by reference to an 'executive emotion system' in the brain. Such genetically programmed systems are held to integrate the physiological, psychological, and behavioural aspects of an emotion. Whether there are such 'systems' is a matter of controversy among neuroscientists. The criteria for what constitutes such a system are unclear. *A fortiori*, the number of such systems is disputed.

The constitutive complexity of human emotions, their diverse relation to time, to knowledge and belief of a neurologically uncircumscribable scope, to reasons and the evaluation of reasons, to somatic and expressive perturbations, to motivation and decision, guarantees that there can be no *simple* correlation between genetic, physiological, or neural facts and an emotion. The supposition that biological research could reveal that all emotions are variations upon a set of basic ones has no warrant. The underlying biological facts are *more*, not less, complex than the characteristic emotions felt in the stream of life. They surely provide no grounds for the reduction of emotions to a privileged set of basic ones. It is evident that there are manifold senses in which an emotion may be deemed to be basic or non-basic. It is also clear that there is *no* absolute sense in which an emotion can be said to be a basic emotion. So the quest for absolutely basic emotions is as chimerical as the quest for absolutely simple ideas.

# PART II

## Human, All Too Human

# 5

# Pride, Arrogance, and Humility

## 1. The web of pride

Pride is an emotion, an emotional attitude, a character trait, and a motive for action. It is an emotion of self-assessment and presupposes possession of a language that makes such reflexive evaluation possible.[1] We feel proud when we achieve something difficult for us and important to us and when we are congratulated and admired for our achievement. We take pride in the good results of our work, and also in the skill we have acquired, the judicious use of which enabled us to achieve what we achieve. But we also take pride in our good looks or figure, which are not achievements of ours at all. We take pride in our family and in the achievements of members of our family, in our treasured possessions, in our elevated status. Some people are characterized as proud. This is often thought to be a vice:

> Of all the causes which conspire to blind
> Man's erring judgement, and misguide the mind,
> What the weak head with strongest bias rules,
> Is pride, the never-failing vice of fools.[2]

---

[1] In the following discussion of pride I am much indebted to G. Taylor's illuminating *Pride, Shame, and Guilt* (Clarendon Press, Oxford, 1985) and *Deadly Vices* (Clarendon Press, Oxford, 2006).

[2] A. Pope, *Essay on Criticism*, II. 1.

*The Passions: A Study of Human Nature*, First Edition. P. M. S. Hacker.

Other writers disagree:

> He who would climb and soar aloft
> Must needs keep ever at his side
> The tonic of a wholesome pride.[3]

Indeed, we say that each person should have their pride – a proper sense of their worth and dignity. Improper pride is arrogance; proper pride, one might say, is necessary for self-respect. We also do things, and equally often refuse to do things, out of pride. These are some of the matters that we shall be concerned with in this chapter.

*Pride is not a mental state*
As an emotion, pride may take the form of a *momentary emotional occurrence*, as when, for example, one is complimented by people whose approval one appreciates on some achievement of one's own, of one's spouse, or of one's children. At their words one may 'flush with pride' and thank them for their congratulations. It may also take the form of a longer-lasting *emotional episode* as when, for example, one 'basks in pride' at a celebratory dinner in one's honour. Similarly, one may feel that one is 'bursting with pride' as one listens to the speeches in honour of one's beloved spouse or child. Nevertheless, the notion of *genuine duration* has only a weak grip here – the idea of *interrupting* one's feeling proud by distraction of attention and later *resuming* it limps. So there is no sharp boundary line between these two forms of a *temporary emotion* (momentary and episodic). Hence too the notion of being in a *mental state* of feeling proud gets no grip.

*Mien and posture of pride*
It is noteworthy that pride, unlike shame, has no distinctive sensational or somatic constitutive association. That we 'swell with pride' or are 'bursting with pride' are figurative descriptions. For to feel proud is neither to have a local sensation of pride (like a pain) nor a diffuse overall bodily sensation (like feeling exhausted). It might, however, be said to be infusive, and the figurative descriptions perhaps derive from the fact that the characteristic mien of pride (which one may adopt when informed of one's achievement and recognition) is of erect posture, raised chin, smile of delight, and expansive, confident gestures. The posture of arrogant pride is likewise erect posture, raised chin, and confident mien, with haughty or supercilious look (see, e.g., Van Dyck's portrait of the two Stuart brothers (sons of the Duke of Lennox) in the National Gallery, London).

---

[3] A. H. Clough, 'The Higher Courage', in *Ambarvalia: Poems by Thomas Burbridge and Arthur H. Clough* (1849).

Pride may also take the form of a *persistent,*
*Pride as a* *enduring, emotion,* as when one feels proud of one's
*persistent emotion* beauty and figure, or of the good looks of one's
spouse or children; of one's achievements; of some
admirable possession one owns; of one's dog or horse; of one's high
rank and office; and so forth. One does not cease taking pride in one's
children or spouse when one falls asleep, any more than one ceases to
know or believe whatever one knows or believes when one sleeps.
However, such pride is not a behavioural disposition. It is not, for
example, a disposition to speak well of oneself or one's family (proper
pride excludes boasting or showing off, and one can be proud of
oneself and one's achievements without telling anyone). Nor is it a
disposition for the thought of one's merits or of one's family's excellences to cross one's mind. To dwell excessively in thought upon one's
merits and achievements is itself a fault, and not a corollary of proper
pride; moreover, the judgement that someone is proud or proud of
something is not falsified by their rarely thinking of themselves or of
something they possess, but simply taking their superiority or the
superiority of what they possess for granted. Rather, to be proud of
something is to value and take pleasure in what one is proud of, to
take oneself to have *good reasons* for holding such-and-such a possession or quality or achievement of one's own or of a member of one's
family to be meritorious. It is for one's self-esteem to be maintained or
enhanced thereby, and, in the case of pride in one's family's merits, for
one to appreciate and take pleasure in one's enviable relationship to
them. (For a diagrammatic representation of the conceptual web of
pride, see fig. 5.1.)

Pride is linked to *motivation.* In an honour culture,
*Pride and* one acts *out of pride* when one acts for the sake of the
*motivation* demands of honour, which are the standards of the honour group to which one belongs.[4] Not to do so would
mean shame and contempt. It is the pride of a warrior-hero that
drives Beowulf in his old age to confront the fearsome dragon.
In Conrad's *Lord Jim,* Jim acts out of pride, when he knowingly
goes to his death at the hands of Doramin.[5] One may also act out of

[4] Of course, one may also act to avoid disgrace and humiliation. That is not to act
out of pride, although it is to act in accordance with the demands of honour.

[5] Marlow, the narrator, holds that Jim goes to his death 'at the call of his exalted
egoism. He goes away from a living woman to celebrate his pitiless wedding with a
shadowy ideal of conduct' (*Lord Jim,* ch. 45).

*injured pride* when one has become, or fears becoming, an object of ridicule and taunts. A cuckolded husband may act out of injured pride in killing his wife's lover (Baron von Innstetten, who kills Major Crampas (Fontane's *Effi Briest*); Othello, who endeavours to arrange Cassio's murder).

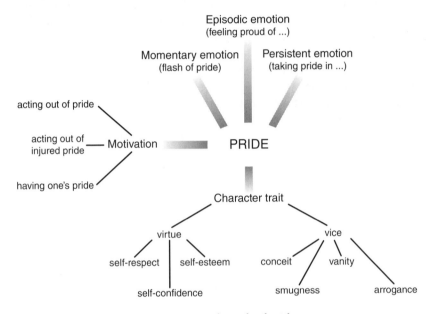

Figure 5.1   *The web of pride*

One may *take pride* in one's skill and its exercise, and in the successful results of one's productive skills (as did Halvard Solness in Ibsen's *The Master Builder*). One may *have one's pride* in maintaining one's self-respect. So, for example, one may refuse assistance from others who are better off, if one feels that the moral indebtedness would lower one's self-respect or the respect of others for one (Mrs Mary Dale in Trollope's *The Small House at Allington*). It is pride that informs a stiff upper lip. As George Eliot observed:

*Having one's pride*

> We mortals, men and women, devour many a disappointment between breakfast and dinner time; keep back the tears and look a little pale about the lips, and in answer to inquiries say 'Oh, nothing!' Pride helps us, and pride is no bad thing when it only urges us to hide our own hurts – not to hurt others. (*Middlemarch*, ch. 6)

Pride is also a *character trait*. Hector and Achilles
*Pride as a*  are proud men, acting out the role of heroes that was
*character trait*  their birthright, their self-esteem nailed to their code
of honour – the pride of one arising from self-respect
and that of the other from self-absorption. Shakespeare's Coriolanus
is the embodiment of unbridled patrician arrogance and contempt.
The Prince of Salina in Lampedusa's *The Leopard* exhibits the
self-confident pride of nobility coupled with the humility of one
who knows his faults. Mr Darcy, in *Pride and Prejudice*, exemplifies
an arrogant sense of superiority of a wealthy English landowning
aristocrat.

## 2. Shifting evaluations of pride

*Aristotle on*  Aristotle approved of the character trait of *megalopsuchia*
*megalopsuchia*  (great-souledness), holding it to be 'a mean between
*and hubris*  vanity and diffidence'. The Greek expression is commonly
translated as 'pride'. But although *megalopsuchia* is a
second cousin of pride, this is as misleading as translating *psuchē*
as 'soul'. To describe a man as *megalopsychic* is far more august a
characterization than to say of a person that he is proud. Great-
souledness, Aristotle held, 'seems indeed to be a sort of crown of the
virtues; for it makes them greater, and it is not to be found without
them. Therefore it is hard to be truly great-souled; for it is impossible
without nobility and goodness of character' (*Nicomachean Ethics*,
1123$^b$24–33). The great-souled man distinguishes between great and
small excellences and pursues only the former. His primary concern is
with honour in accordance with desert. He must therefore be good
in the highest degree, for greatness in all the virtues is characteristic
of him.

On the other hand, Aristotle was as critical as one can be of the vice
of *hubris* – arrogance, insolence, and conceit:

> *Hubris* is also a form of slighting, since it consists in doing and saying
> things that cause shame to the victim, not in order that anything may
> happen to yourself or because anything has happened to yourself, but
> simply for the pleasure involved. ... The cause of the pleasure thus
> enjoyed by the *hubristic* man is that he thinks himself greatly superior
> to others when ill-treating them. That is why youths and rich men are
> hubristic. (*Rhetoric* 1378$^b$22–29)

One of the roots in the Western cultural tradition *Old Testament* of the condemnation of pride as an emotion, charac- *on pride* ter trait, and motive are in the Old Testament. *Ge'eh* (proud), *ga'avah* (pride), and *l'hitgaot* (to take pride in) occur tens of times in the Old Testament, primarily in the Prophets and in the poetical and wisdom books. It is almost uniformly associated with the vices of the powerful – with arrogance or with challenging God and his laws (or, in effect, the priesthood). It is linked with supercilious looks (Psalm 101: 5; Isaiah 5: 15), with haughtiness of heart (Jeremiah 48: 29; Ezekiel 28: 2, 5, 17), and with arrogant speech (1 Samuel 2: 3). It is often said to precede downfall and disgrace (Proverbs 11: 2; 16: 18). In Isaiah 13: 11, God avers 'I will punish the world for its evil, and the wicked for their sins; and I will put an end to the arrogance of the haughty and will humble the pride of the ruthless.' It is patently a vice of autocrats, manifest in their treatment of the powerless, and in their threat to the priesthood. In Old Testament narratives, King Uzziah's leprosy and downfall after a spectacularly successful reign is ascribed to his pride in threatening the prerogative of the high priest in Jerusalem. Daniel explains Nebuchadnezzar's fall by reference to his pride: 'But when his heart was lifted up, and his mind hardened in pride, he was deposed from his kingly throne, and they took his glory from him' (Daniel 5: 20). Belshazzar is likewise damned for his pride.

Most importantly for subsequent developments, *Christian conceptions* the apocryphal book Ecclesiasticus (10: 13) writ- *of pride* ten in the second century BC, declares that 'pride is the beginning of all sin'. This is one of the sources of the Christian vehement condemnation of pride. The New Testament partly dissociated pride from autocracy and the powerful agents of the autocratic state, presenting it rather as the original sin of man and a ubiquitous vice of mankind in general, not only of the high and the mighty. The fathers of the church elaborated its doctrine. St Augustine, quoting Ecclesiasticus, argues that the first sin, eating of the tree of knowledge, stemmed from pride – the craving for undue exaltation. For Adam turned away from God towards himself, and away from the love of God to self-love (Augustine, *The City of God*, 14.13). St Gregory the Great, to whom we owe the list of seven deadly sins, held, without qualification, that pride (*superbia*) in its various forms was *the worst* of them all.[6] It was not merely exalting oneself above other human beings, but exalting oneself above one's lowly station *in comparison with God*. In their eagerness to damn pride, Christian theologians rested upon the authority of Galatians 6: 3: 'For if a man think himself to be something, when he is nothing, he deceiveth himself.' Aquinas held pride to be not merely a *capital sin*, from which others flow, but the 'common mother of all sins' (*Summa Theologica*, $2^a2^{ae}$, q. 153, art. 4, reply to objection 2). Dante presented the proud as condemned to tread a weary path in Purgatory, crushed under heavy stones on their backs that force them to bend in half and prevent them from looking upwards.

The late medieval conception of pride as a capital sin is elaborated by Geoffrey Chaucer's 'Parson's Tale' in *The Canterbury Tales* (late fourteenth century):

And though it be so that no man can completely tell the number of the twigs and of the harms that come from Pride, yet will I show a part of them, as you shall understand. There is disobedience, boasting, hypocrisy, scorn, arrogance, impudence, swelling of heart, insolence, elation, impatience, contumaciousness, rebelliousness, presumption, irreverence, pertinacity, vainglory, and many another twig that I can not declare. Disobedient is he that disobeys for spite to the commandments of God, and to his superiors, and to his spiritual father. Boaster is he that boasts of the harm or of the goodness that he has done. Hypocrite is he who hides showing himself such as he is and shows himself such as he is not. Scornful is he that has disdain of his neighbor – that is to say, of his fellow-Christian – or scorns to do what he ought to do. Arrogant is he that thinks that he has these good things in him that he

[6] The source of the list of seven deadly sins appears to be in the writings of Evagrius Ponticus, a fourth-century monk in the Eastern Empire, who listed eight evil kinds of thought. This was transmitted to Western Christianity by St John Cassian (ca. 360–435) in his *De Institutis Coenobarium* (Institutes of the Coenobia), which elaborated the rules for cenobitic (communal) monasticism. He listed gluttony, lust, greed (covetousness), pride, anger, despair (*tristia*), vainglory (boastfulness), sloth (*acedia* or *accidie*) – a list of monastic or monkish sins (hence the otherwise startling omission of cruelty). St Gregory revised this list and reduced it to seven deadly sins in 590. He assimilated despair (sorrow, despondency) to sloth (a corollary of what was probably chronic depression common among monks) and vainglory to pride, and added envy (but, strikingly, not jealousy – presumably because it was not a monastic sin, or because it is a virtue of the Almighty, who is 'a jealous God'). It remains curious that hatred is not listed.

has not, or supposes that he should have them by his deserts, or else he supposes that he is what he is not. Impudent is he that for his pride has no shame of his sins. Swelling of heart is when a man rejoices him for harm that he has done. Insolent is he that despises in his judgment all other folk, as compared to his value, and of his understanding, and of his speaking, and of his bearing. Elation is when he can tolerate having neither master nor fellow. Impatient is he who will not be taught nor reproved for his vice, and by strife wages war on truth wittingly, and defends his folly. Contumacious is he that through his indignation is against every authority or power of them that are his superiors. Presumption is when a man undertakes an enterprise that he ought not do, or else that he can not do; and this is called presumption. Irreverence is when men do not honor where as they ought to do, and expect to be reverenced. Pertinacity is when man defends his folly and trusts too much to his own wit. Vainglory is to have pomp and delight in his temporal high rank, and to exult in this worldly estate. Jangling is when a man speaks too much before folk, and clatters like a mill, and takes no care what he says.

*Iconography of pride*        In medieval pictorial representations of *superbia*, it is usually depicted as a youthful knight falling from his horse (pride brought low),[7] vanquished by humility, pride and humility being conceived to be contraries. In Renaissance representations of pride there is a striking gender switch. Pride is now symbolized by one of its species, namely *vanity*, and is represented by a *female figure* accompanied by a lion and eagle (rulers of earth and air), as well as a peacock, the proudest of the birds. This evolves over the next century or so into a female figure looking into a mirror (which in itself becomes a standard *vanitas* symbol). So, in Eichler's illustrations of 1758–60 for Hertel's edition of Cesare Ripa's *Iconologia* (1593), pride is indeed depicted as a beautiful woman admiring herself in a mirror, accompanied by a peacock. The associated *fatto* (the depiction of an illustrative biblical or classical tale) in the background is of St Michael driving the rebel angels out of heaven and casting them into hell, for it was their pride that led them to challenge God. Some depictions of pride have a devil holding the mirror (e.g. Hieronymus Bosch's *Seven Deadly Sins and Four Last Things* (ca. 1500) in the Prado); others have Satan looking out of the mirror. The colour associated with pride in iconography is red. According to the doctrine of the humours, the vice of pride is caused by an excess of sanguinity.

---

[7] A youthful knight, presumably, because of the careless arrogance of youth in a military aristocracy.

With the Age of Reason the evaluation of pride among philosophers began to change. Spinoza, writing in his *Ethics* (1674), observed that *superbia* is 'Love of oneself, or Self-esteem, insofar as it so affects a man that he thinks more highly of himself than is just' (III. 28), and held it, in accordance with theological tradition, to be a vice:

> For we usually call him proud who exults too much at being esteemed, who tells of nothing but his own virtues, and the vices of others, who wishes to be given precedence over all others, and finally who proceeds with the gravity and attire usually adopted by others who are placed far above him. (III. 29)

But he goes on to say that proper self-esteem that is fully warranted is 'really the highest thing we can hope for' (*Ethics*, IV. 52, schol.). Such proper self-esteem may well be said to be a proper form of pride.

Hume, in the Age of Enlightenment, went further. In *A Treatise of Human Nature* (1739), he broke with theological tradition and held that,

> tho'an over-weaning conceit of our own merit be vicious and disagreeable, nothing can be more laudable, than to have a value for ourselves, where we really have the qualities that are valuable. ... 'tis certain, that nothing is more useful to us in the conduct of life, than a due degree of pride, which makes us sensible of our own merit, and gives us a confidence and assurance in all our projects and enterprises. (III. iii. 2)

Fifty years later, Thomas Reid, in his *Essays on the Active Powers of Man* (1788) observed sapiently:

> Self-esteem, grounded upon external advantages, or the gifts of fortune, is pride. When it is grounded upon a vain conceit of inward worth that we do not possess, it is arrogance and self-deceit. But when a man, without thinking of himself more highly than he ought to think, is conscious of that integrity of heart, and uprightness of conduct, which he most highly esteems in others, and values himself upon this account; this perhaps may be called the pride of virtue, but it is not a vicious pride. It is a noble and magnanimous disposition without which there can be no steady virtue.[8]

---

[8] T. Reid, *Essays on the Active Powers of Man* (1788) (Edinburgh University Press, Edinburgh, 2010), III. 7.

To come to grips with these different conceptions and opposed valuations of pride, we must clarify the relationship between feeling proud of some person or institution and what one is proud of being or of having done; and between having one's pride and being a proud person. We shall have to investigate whether there is a proper form of pride, as opposed to degenerate forms such as arrogance, conceit, haughtiness, smugness, superciliousness, and vanity. We shall also have to attend to the relationship between pride and self-esteem, on the one hand, and self-respect, on the other, as well as to the relation of pride to humility. And this must be done with due sensitivity and attention to class, cultural, and historical differences between societies.

## 3. Pride: connective analysis

*Object-accusatives*     The notion of the object of a person's pride is ambig-
*of pride*            uous. It may be signified by the object-accusative
of a pride-ascription (see chapter 2, section 2), in
which case it is the person or item *of whom* or *of which one is proud*.
There are conceptual constraints on the objects of someone's pride.
One can intelligibly be proud of oneself; of past or present members
of one's family; of house or clan; of one's school and university, legion
or regiment; of an institution for which one works or with which one
is appropriately associated; of one's favoured charioteers (blues or
greens) or football team; and of one's country. But one cannot now
feel pride in Queen Elizabeth I, only admiration (although one may
feel proud to belong to a nation of which Queen Elizabeth I was monarch, as one may feel shame to belong to a nation of which Adolf
Hitler was Führer). One cannot feel proud of Italy, if one is not Italian
or a long term resident of Italy. One can intelligibly be proud of one's
children, but one cannot take pride in one's neighbour's children – only
admire them. How are the limits of the objects of pride, in this sense,
circumscribed? It would be misleading to hold that all forms of the
feeling of pride involve self-assessment and a real or supposed increase
in one's idea of one's worth or worthiness. To be proud of one's children involves not assessing oneself, but assessing the children. Nor
does having beautiful and talented children involve thinking that one
is therefore more worthy – only that one is more fortunate than many
other parents and that one's situation is enviable.[9] What one is proud

---

[9] To be sure, one may feel proud of having brought them up so well, in which case,
their excellences redound to one's credit. But this is not a necessary feature of taking
pride in one's children.

of must be someone or something with whom or with which *one's sense of identity is entwined*. I can be proud of my family, not of yours; proud of my school, not of other schools, no matter how admirable. I can be proud of my football team, which I have enthusiastically supported all these years, but not of other football teams. I can be proud of my country, not of other countries. One is proud to *belong to* or *to have* such a family, *to have attended* such a school or university, *to work for* or *to be associated with* such an institution, *to support* such a football team, *to be a member* of such a community or a *citizen* of such a country. The associative link is a constitutive element of one's conception of oneself. To be sure, one's sense of identity is nebulous. But the limits of the objects of pride, in this sense of the phrase, are nebulous too.

*Nominalization-accusatives of pride*

'Object of pride' may also be used to mean what is signified by a sentential or nominalized intentional-accusative of a pride-ascription. Such intentional-accusatives specify the answer to the question 'Of what is so-and-so proud?', where the wh-pronoun is interrogative rather than relative. So the object of pride in this sense is *that in virtue of which one is proud*. Such objects of pride include natural endowments (one is proud of one's good looks, figure, natural grace), august lineage and inherited status (in hierarchical societies), cultivated endowments (one is proud to possess such-and-such skills, knowledge, expertise), deeds and achievements (one is proud to have done such-and-such and proud that one achieved this-or-that), possessions, honours granted, and offices held. These may be one's own or may belong to others to whom one stands in an appropriate relation. How are such objects of pride circumscribed? What one may be proud of, in this sense, is some desideratum of which one approves. It is something in which one may take pleasure and delight. Usually one will think this to be the object of the approbation and esteem of others with whom one shares one's values. Sometimes one may be proud of something precisely *because* it is esteemed by others, such as honours, rank, social status. But one may be proud of something irrespective of the judgement and opinion of others, cleaving only to one's own standards. These may be impeccable or misplaced.[10] Not all objects of pride, in this sense, need enhance one's self-esteem. Some do – as when one is proud of one's beauty, skills, good taste,

---

[10] A wonderful example of a pride that cleaves to misplaced subjective standards of value is depicted in the conceit of Gilbert Osmond in Henry James's *The Portrait of a Lady*.

or achievements. But, as we noted, others may rather enhance one's awareness of one's good fortune, for example, in having such talented children or in being a citizen of such a great country.

*Approbation and objects of pride*        So, what one is proud of must be an object of one's own approbation. But one may have many things that one is glad to have without being proud of them, if, for example, these enviable things are not appropriately closely bound up with one's conception of oneself. No doubt it is *pleasing* to win the lottery, but it cannot *reasonably* be something of which to be proud. One must also be proud of and *value* the relationship that obtains between oneself and the object of one's pride – proud *to be* the spouse, parent, friend of such a lovely person, or proud *to have done* what one has done, *to have made* what one has made, *to have invented or discovered* what one has invented or discovered. The fact that one values the appropriate relationship to the object of one's pride in *this* sense determines the pleasures of pride.

It is tempting to suppose that what one is proud of must be something, some deed or achievement, that is rare or exceptional. But that would be mistaken. What one is proud of achieving is internally related to one's standards of expectation.[11] These are a function of one's conception of what is normal in one's social group, of what lies within one's power to do or achieve, and of one's idea of the expectations of others. One is proud of achieving or obtaining that which goes beyond one's own or others' expectations from or for oneself. Most of us are fortunate to have normal physical abilities, but someone who has had to struggle against disease and disability to achieve such ordinary powers may rightly be proud to be able to walk or run at all. In general, those who achieve something in the face of abnormal disabilities are warranted in taking pride where others would not be.

*Pride in gifts of nature*        Among the many things in which human beings take pride, natural gifts rank high.[12] We may be endowed with good looks, a good figure or physique, beautiful eyes or hair. To be beautiful or good-looking attracts admiration, and it is gratifying to be admired. Merely to possess such features does not imply that one is proud of them. One must

---

[11] See G. Taylor, *Pride, Shame, and Guilt*, pp. 37 ff.

[12] For a penetrating discussion of natural pride see A. Isenberg, 'Natural Pride and Natural Shame', *Philosophy and Phenomenological Research* 10 (1949), reprinted in his *Aesthetics and Theory of Criticism* (University of Chicago Press, Chicago, 1973), pp. 216–44, to which I am indebted.

know (or think) that one possesses these natural excellences of appearance, and conceive of them as excellences that attract admiration. Indeed, one must know (or think) that one possesses them to a greater degree than most others do – if all human beings were identical in appearance, no one would take pride in their looks. We can recognize and admire, and may envy, such gifts in others. With greater difficulty, due to our biased eye, we can recognize them in ourselves. To be proud of them, one must take pleasure in, and value, their possession.

We are not responsible for such gifts of nature. We may make the most of them, but cannot make them – only mar them. It is tempting to dismiss such pride as unwarranted or even reprehensible precisely *because* we can take no credit for the possession of such features. They are gifts of fortune for which we should be grateful. That is true, but does not preclude feeling some pride in one's appearance. We are not responsible for other gifts of nature either, such as sensitivity, intelligence, and will-power that we utilize in our praiseworthy endeavours, the fruits of which are admirable and are objects of legitimate pride. Rather, good looks – enviable and advantageous though they may be – are very much less significant in the constitution of an admirable human being and in living a good human life than those objects of pride that are achieved by the exercise of sensitivity, will, and intellect. Failure to appreciate this is one of the vices associated with pride in one's looks. One may overvalue personal beauty, thinking that one is superior to others who are less well endowed; one may feel contempt for those who are, or whom one thinks to be, ordinary or ugly.[13] One may think that one's beauty grants one both superiority and privileges over others less fortunate (as do Rosamond Vincy in *Middlemarch* and Lady Angelica Headingham in Maria Edgeworth's *Patronage*). One may dwell too long on one's appearance and care too much about it. Another such vice is the self-deception that goes with exaggerating the degree to which one possesses these natural excellences – as did the ageing Queen Elizabeth I. Her acceptance of the fawning and flattery of her courtiers was a blot on her dignity and

[13] Listen to Miss Bingley speaking to Darcy about Elizabeth Bennet: "'For my own part", she rejoined, "I must confess that I never could see any beauty in her. Her face is too thin; her complexion has no brilliancy; and her features are not at all handsome. Her nose wants character; there is nothing marked in its lines. Her teeth are tolerable, but not out of the common way; and as for her eyes, which have sometimes been called so fine, I could never perceive any thing extraordinary in them. They have a sharp, shrewish look, which I do not like at all; and in her air altogether, there is a self-sufficiency without fashion, which is intolerable"' (*Pride and Prejudice*, III. 3).

character. Vanity, conceit, and narcissism are character traits consequent on feeling disproportionate pride in one's appearance.

Similar considerations apply to pride in one's lineage – a common
emotion and emotional attitude in hierarchical societies. It was an
advantage to be *born* into the warrior aristocracy in a heroic society,
to be born into the senatorial class in Rome, or to be a member of the
feudal aristocracy – it entitled one to a wide range of privileges. This
was nothing for which one could claim credit. But it was a legitimate
source of pride in so far as it was linked to a proper sense of the duties
of the station into which one was born (*noblesse oblige*), to excellence
in the discharging of those duties, and, as we shall see, to complementary humility. However, it was always a fecund source of vainglorious
pride and patrician arrogance (as depicted in *Coriolanus*).

*Proper pride*     One may rightly object to condemnation of pride in
all its forms. Pride is an emotion that may be perfectly
proper to feel, when it is felt with regard to the right
object, for the right reason, and to the right degree. A *proper pride*
in something calls for a proper sense of values so that what one is
proud of warrants approbation. Secondly, it demands an unbiased
judgement concerning the extent to which one does indeed possess
the characteristic in which one takes pride. Thirdly, it requires a
correct estimate of the degree to which being or having whatever one
is proud of confers merit upon one. Finally, one's pleasure in what
one takes pride in must not be excessive nor its display immodest.
The terrible fate of Niobe and her children is a token of the ancient
Greeks' awareness of the hubris of flaunting one's blessings – to do
so is to challenge the gods themselves and to invite nemesis. For the
most part, what one is proud of enhances one's self-esteem and
increases one's self-confidence. A *false pride* involves taking pride in
the wrong kind of thing, or overvaluing what one is proud of, or
overestimating the extent to which one has it, or having an excessive
degree of pride.

*Forms of excess of*     There are many forms that an excess of pride may
*pride: vanity and*     take: vanity, conceit, superciliousness, smugness,
*conceit*     arrogance, haughtiness. Similarly, there are multiple
forms that deficiency of pride may take: lack of
self-confidence, lack of self-esteem, meekness, self-
contempt, lack of self-respect (see fig. 5.2). Vanity and conceit are
vices of the mirror ('Mirror, mirror on the wall, who is the fairest of
them all?'). Vanity is the vice into which pride in one's good looks
slides, when one is excessively occupied with, and overvalues, one's

**Figure 5.2**   *The target of pride: 'There are many ways of going astray ... only one way of getting it right'*

appearance (good looks and dress).[14] It involves an exaggerated concern with inducing the admiration and approval of others for one's appearance, and sometimes also with an excessive eagerness to be the object of sexual attraction. Vanity makes one's self-esteem dependent upon the judgement and flattery of others – they are the mirror in which one seeks one's worth. Narcissism is a more subject-dependent, solipsistic, variety of vanity. The narcissist is his own mirror, and is intoxicated with self-admiration.

Where vanity seeks to see *the reflection* of one's value in the eyes of others, conceit seeks to see one's worth *in comparison with others*. Their fellow human beings are the yardstick against which the conceited mis-measure their value. The conceited choose their own metric (superiority of lineage, of class, of wealth and ostentation, of office and rank, of intelligence and skill, and so on). Their excessive self-esteem is parasitic on comparison with those whom they deem to be inferiors. Conceit is commonly accompanied by boastfulness, and often requires the acclaim of others as confirmation of superiority. One can be vain without being conceited, if one's preoccupation with

---

[14] 'Vanity' also has a use to signify self-esteem (as in 'This rejection was a blow to my vanity').

one's appearance does not lead one to look down on others. But the two vices often go hand in hand. The combination of vanity in one's appearance and conceit in one's lineage is exemplified by Sir Walter Elliot in *Persuasion*:

> Vanity was the beginning and end of Sir Walter Elliot's character; vanity of person and of situation. He had been remarkably handsome in his youth; and at fifty-four, was still a very fine man. Few women could think more of their personal appearance than did he; nor could the valet of any new made lord be more delighted with the place he held in society. He considered the blessing of beauty as inferior only to the blessing of a baronetcy; and Sir Walter Elliot, who united these gifts, was the constant object of his warmest respect and devotion. (ch. 1)

One can be conceited without being vain if one's reasons for being conceited are independent of one's appearance. Intellectual conceit, for example, involves being supercilious in relation to others whom one holds to be less intelligent or less well educated (Casaubon in *Middlemarch*). The smirk of intellectual conceit is comparable to a swagger of bravado. Smugness is the form pride takes when a person is overwhelmingly self-satisfied and complacent, seeing neither the need nor room for improvement (Mr Brooke in *Middlemarch*).

*Arrogance*  Arrogance is the most grievous of the vices of pride. It is overweaning pride in oneself. Unlike vanity and conceit, it does not require the mirror of others to confirm or sustain self-esteem. It is wholly self-centred, and indifferent to the opinions and approbation of others. The arrogant see themselves as superior to others by birth, by nature, by talents, by possessions, by office, or by achievements, excelling in the only spheres that, in their judgement, matter. They expect more *for* themselves, in particular more deference, than they think should be due to others. They may (like Coriolanus), or may not (like Lady Catherine de Bourgh), expect more *from* themselves than from others. They do not view their birth, their talents, their possessions, or their achievements as grounds for their exaggerated self-esteem. Rather, they take these for granted. To be praised for what they have done is offensive to them. For, no matter how meritorious their deeds, they do not exceed their own expectations – praise would imply that they had done better than was to be expected. They do not question their value system, conceiving it to be the only correct one. They do not entertain the possibility of their being wrong in their judgements or in their conflicts with others. Their attitude to others, whom they do not consider their equals, is one of disdain, contempt, and inconsiderateness. The arrogant can improve themselves only by being humbled by others, as Mr Darcy was humbled by Elizabeth Bennet,[15] or by being humbled by harsh experience, as Edmund Talbot was in Golding's *To the Ends of the Earth*. For they need to renounce their excessive self-esteem, to reach a proper estimate of their merits, to bethink themselves that it is possible for them to be wrong in their judgements and deeds,[16] and to acquire respect for others.

*Pride and self-esteem*    It is patent from the survey that one is oneself the point of origin on the graph of objects of pride. Pride concerns the conception one has of oneself and of one's standing in relation to others. It is internally related to self-esteem, which is a ranking concept. Self-esteem is a function of one's favourable evaluation of that in which one takes pride. What one is proud of confirms or increases one's self-esteem and self-confidence or one's sense of good fortune in standing in an appropriate relationship to something admirable (one's spouse or children). Overvaluation, however, thinking too well of oneself, leads to conceit and arrogance. Where it leads to harmless conceit in one's newly acquired status, unaccompanied by disdain and contempt for others (as in Sir William Lucas in *Pride and Prejudice*), it is mere silliness. But, when it is accompanied by disdain and contempt for others (as in Sir Walter Elliot's pride in his lineage), it is offensive. To damage someone's self-esteem is to humble him. It is to make him 'eat humble pie' and to downgrade his conception of his merits and his unwarranted sense of superiority. Undervaluing one's merits engenders lack of self-confidence. One has then little joy in one's achievements or in one's blessings.

*Pride and self-respect*    The character trait of pride is internally related to self-respect. One's self-respect consists in unwillingness to do or suffer what would, in one's own eyes, derogate from one's conception of one's worth as a human being. 'To have one's pride' consists in one's recognition of limits beyond which one cannot go in one's actions and of requirements that one cannot meet without damage to one's conception of oneself. One kind

---

[15] 'Such I was, from eight to eight and twenty; and such I might still have been but for you, dearest, loveliest Elizabeth! What do I not owe you! You taught me a lesson, hard indeed at first, but most advantageous. By you I was properly humbled' (*Pride and Prejudice*, III. 16).

[16] Here it is important to distinguish the actuality of the possibility from the possibility of the actuality. What is required is recognition of one's fallibility, not of the probability of one's error.

of such pride is nicely sketched in Somerset Maugham's *The Explorer* where the protagonist cannot bring himself to defend himself against base accusations:

> at the bottom of his heart was a fierce pride. He was conscious of the honesty of his motives, and he expected that Lucy should share his consciousness. She must believe what he said to her because he said it. He could not suffer the humiliation of defending himself, and he felt that her love could not be very great if she could really doubt him. And because he was very proud perhaps he was unjust. He did not know that he was putting upon her a trial which he should have asked no one to bear. (ch. 17)

In general, voluntarily to humble oneself before another in supplication is painful and can be humiliating. In appropriate circumstances, a person with self-respect may be, or find himself to be, *too proud* to do something or to accept something from another person. To do so would, in his view, be dishonourable or beneath his dignity[17] – he would not 'sink so low' as to do such a deed or to accept such a favour. To force a person to do or to undergo what is beneath his dignity is to humiliate him and undermine his self-respect. To destroy someone's self-respect is to make his life meaningless and worthless in his own eyes (Shapur I's alleged treatment of the emperor Valerian, whom he treacherously captured after the battle of Edessa (AD 260), was to make him a living mounting block in the royal stables).

How then are self-respect and self-esteem related? The two commonly march hand in hand. Loss of self-respect typically implies loss of self-esteem, and loss of self-esteem may well involve loss of self-respect. But they are mutually detachable. One may have self-respect without either having or lacking self-esteem, if one is not concerned with judging and evaluating one's own merits (e.g. Joe Gargery in *Great Expectations*, Caleb Garth in *Middlemarch*).[18] One may possess self-esteem with little self-respect, as do those who are willing to grovel to their superior, while displaying the arrogance of office towards their

---

[17] The notion of dignity was originally associated with an elevated station in life. What was beneath one's dignity to do were the tasks of one's inferiors and subordinates. One of the great transformations in Western mentality has been the early modern and Enlightenment association of dignity and respect with human nature as such, irrespective of rank, birth, or property. This was vividly expressed in the great Putney debates on democracy in 1647 and is the cornerstone of Kantian ethics.

[18] G. Taylor, *Pride, Shame, and Guilt*, p. 78.

subordinates (Mr Slope in Trollope's *Barchester Towers*). For grovelling consists in obsequious flattery to curry favour. One may also possess self-esteem without self-respect, if one values one's achievements but nevertheless thinks of oneself as worthless. In such cases, one may still have one's pride, but deem oneself a contemptible sinner or moral weakling (something of this was, it seems, true of Dr Johnson and of Wittgenstein alike). One may possess self-respect but little self-esteem if one undervalues one's achievements, or if one has a realistic view of one's meagre achievements, or thinks of one's life as a series of lost opportunities and failures. Despite this, one may retain one's pride.

It is time to sum up the results of our investigation. It is evident that there are different forms of the emotion of pride, some laudable or at any rate harmless, others both offensive and vicious. One can be proud of one's beauty without being vain as long as one holds one's pride in just proportion and does not think that one's good looks make one any better than others. One can be proud of something without being conceited about it, if one's self-esteem is not overinflated and one's respect for others not diminished. One may legitimately be proud of one's achievements without becoming arrogant, if one retains due humility and modesty. There are likewise different senses in which one can be deemed a proud person, some of which betoken virtues. Self-respect that refuses obligation-incurring favours from the powerful or wealthy is, if judicious, no vice. The self-respect that limits one's entreaties to others and prevents one from grovelling for favours is an object of approbation. Such a person is too proud to stoop so low. So, too, the pride of the craftsman that forbids him to produce anything but his best is something to be admired rather than censured. The pride that goes with lineage and rank, when tied to a sharp awareness of the obligations they impose and a willing acceptance and effective discharge of them, is a virtue, not a vice – as long as it is accompanied by due humility.

*Humility* It may seem odd to suggest that certain forms of pride must be accompanied by humility, for these are commonly contrasted. Christian theologians have taken them to be contraries, the former a deadly vice and the latter a virtue. Hume too took pride and humility to be contraries, but held the former to be a virtue and the latter a vice:

> According as our idea of ourself is more or less advantageous, we feel either of those opposite affections, and are elated by pride, or dejected with humility ... 'Tis impossible a man can at the same time be both

proud and humble; and where he has different reasons for these passions, as frequently happens, the passions either take place alternately. (*A Treatise of Human Nature*, II. i. 2)

How then are they related? And is humility a virtue or a vice?

Humility is the herm among the virtues. It consists in knowing one's limitations, and in constraining one's self-esteem within proper boundaries. It is the virtue that demands that one acknowledge one's place as but one person among teeming millions, wending one's way through the world from birth to death. No matter how noteworthy one's qualities, others too possess great qualities. No matter how great one's achievements, others too have achieved glory. Many of one's qualities and powers will wither with age. All will sink into oblivion with time. If one deserves respect, so too do others, who likewise have the duties and rights of rational, free, beings. One must acknowledge that perfection is not given to any human being. One may be proud of one's merits, but one must also strive to have a right estimate of one's faults and weaknesses, and to shed one's pretensions. For only then can one see oneself in just proportion, and achieve the self-knowledge that Apollo demanded one strive for.[19]

Far from being the contrary of pride, humility is the complement of rightful pride. For just as proper pride consists in measured self-esteem, proper humility consist in knowing one's limitations. Just as pride admits of degenerate forms such as vanity, conceit, and arrogance, so too humility admits of degenerate forms such as self-abasement and self-denigration, on the one hand, and servility and obsequiousness, on the other. At one extreme is St Francis, who is held to have said that,

> forasmuch as those holy eyes have beheld among sinners none more vile, more imperfect, nor a greater sinner than I, therefore since He hath found no viler creature on earth to accomplish the marvelous work He intendeth, He hath chosen me to confound the nobility, the majesty, the might, the beauty, and the wisdom of the world: in order to demonstrate that every virtue and every good thing cometh from Him the Creator.[20]

---

[19] *Gnothi seauton* (know thyself) was, according to Pausanius, inscribed in the pronaos of the temple of Apollo in Delphi. It is a recurrent theme in Plato's dialogues.

[20] *Little Flowers of St Francis*, quoted by Isenberg, 'Natural Pride and Natural Shame', p. 226.

This seems to be false, and terrible self-denigration. Indeed, it may conceal a false pride, rooted in self-admiration for one's humility before God. At the other extreme is Dickens's Uriah Heep, who gave the adjective 'humble' a bad name. He lacked all self-respect, regarding no circumstance as shame-inducing. His assumed 'humbleness' was obsequiousness masking insincerity, deceit, resentment, and vaunting ambition.

The opposite of pride is not humility but shame, which is the subject of the next chapter.

# 6

# Shame, Embarrassment, and Guilt

## 1. Shame cultures and guilt cultures

*Contrasts between shame and guilt cultures* The distinction between shame cultures and guilt cultures is due to the anthropologist Ruth Benedict.[1] Homeric Greece and republican Rome are prototypes of shame cultures in the West. Ancient Israel is the prototype of a guilt culture. The form of the dominant norms of a shame culture determine what one ought *to be*.[2] The most forceful motivation is the quest for honour and the avoidance of shame before one's peers. If one is as one ought to be, then one is truly noble. That does *not* mean that there are no prescriptions and prohibitions.

[1] R. Benedict, *The Chrysanthemum and the Sword* (Houghton Mifflin, Boston, 1946). Benedict was concerned with the contrast between Japanese and Western cultures. Her distinction was applied to the ethos of the Homeric epics by E. R. Dodds in his *The Greeks and the Irrational* (University of California Press, Berkeley, 1951).

[2] G. E. Moore referred to such norms as 'ideal rules' ('The Nature of Moral Philosophy', in *Philosophical Studies* (Kegan Paul, Trench & Trübner, London, 1922)). G. H. von Wright follows him in *Norm and Action* (Routledge & Kegan Paul, London, 1963), pp. 14–15. The distinction is derived from the German distinction between *Seinsollen* and *Tunsollen* (e.g. N. Hartman, *Ethik* (de Gruyter, Berlin, 1925), I. 6. 18–19). M. Scheler used the terms *ideales sollen* and *normatives sollen* (*Formalism in Ethics and Non-formal Ethics of Values: a New Attempt toward the Foundation of an Ethical Personalism*, trans. M. S. Frings and R. L. Funk (Northwestern University Press, Evanston, Ill., 1973; originally published in German as *Der Formalismus in der Ethik und die materiale Wertethik*, 1913–16)).

*The Passions: A Study of Human Nature*, First Edition. P. M. S. Hacker.
© 2018 John Wiley & Sons Ltd. Published 2018 by John Wiley & Sons Ltd.

The moral education of the youth in a shame culture will involve a multitude of prescriptions determining how to conduct oneself.

The form of the dominant norms of a guilt culture is the imperative or dominative tense ('Thou shalt'), which determines what one is obligated *to do*. This is the typical form of the obligation-imposing commandments of God. If one abides by the commandments of God and does all that one must do and refrains from doing all that one must refrain from doing, one is truly righteous. Transgressing the commandments of God is sin, and acknowledgement of sin is guilt before God and shame before one's peers. This does *not* mean that there are no ideal norms. The moral education of a guilt culture will urge the ideals of *being* just, righteous, and God-fearing. The roots of guilt cultures in the Christian West lie in the Old Testament. God sees into our hearts – for one is unavoidably and inevitably *exposed*, not to the eyes of one's peers, but to the sight of God. As the Psalmist wrote:

> Whither shall I go from thy spirit?
>    or whither shall I flee from thy presence?
> If I ascend up into heaven thou art there;
>    if I make my bed in hell, behold thou art there.
> If I take the wings of the morning
>    and dwell in the uttermost parts of the sea:
> Even there shall thy hand lead me,
>    and thy right hand shall hold me.
>                                        (Psalm 139: 7–10)

It is striking that the motto on Hieronymus Bosch's painting *The Seven Deadly Sins and the Four Last Things*, which was mentioned in chapter 5, is *Cave, cave, Deus videt* (Beware, beware, God sees).

It is of paramount importance to realize that *both* guilt and shame cultures internalize the standards of behaviour of the society, but they severally view and value human beings and their behaviour from profoundly different viewpoints. A shame culture focuses upon *status* within a peer group, on acting *as becomes* one's position, on gaining public esteem and winning honour. A guilt culture focuses on acceptance of and compliance with authoritative norms, on fulfilling one's duties and obligations.[3] The predominant motivations of the one are

---

[3] It would be superficial to associate shame cultures with heteronomy and guilt cultures with autonomy, or a shame ethos with selfishness and self-centred concerns and a guilt ethos with other-regarding concerns, or shame culture with honour and guilt culture with dignity. These misleading contrasts are well discussed in B. Williams, *Shame and Necessity* (University of California Press, Berkeley, 1993), and A. Fussi, 'Williams's Defence of Shame as a Moral Emotion', in *Etica & Politica* 17 (2015), 163–79.

bound up with honour and avoidance of shame for failure to satisfy the demands of one's role, the other with conscience and the avoidance of guilt for transgression of the laws or commandments of God. Failure to live up to an honour code entails loss of face, ignominy, and ostracism – for the primary value is public esteem. *In extremis*, there is no redemption short of death.[4] By contrast, in a guilt culture there is room for remorse, repentance, atonement and expiation, and forgiveness. It is important to bear in mind that the notions of shame and guilt cultures are ideal types. Contemporary cultures, for the most part, can merely be said to be predominantly one or the other (Japanese and Chinese cultures are predominantly shame cultures) or more or less one or the other (as Britain is more of a shame culture than Germany). However, shame cultures do still survive, for example among the Pashtun warrior peoples in the tribal territories of northwest Pakistan, with their honour code of Pashtunwali.[5]

*Heroic societies and shame culture*      Heroic societies with a closed aristocratic warrior class are typically shame cultures. The standards of male behaviour are determined by the honour code of the ruling aristocracy and their military retainers. This included prowess and valour in battle, hospitality to guests, exchange of munificent gifts with one's host, the zealous guarding of honour against slight or insult, and generosity in giving bounty to one's military retainers ('I am a river unto my people', the Bedu chieftain Auda abu Tayeh exclaims in Robert Bolt's screenplay for *Lawrence of Arabia*). To fall short in any of these dimensions is a reason for shame. Self-respect is a function of membership in the honour group and of recognized compliance with its code of behaviour. Self-esteem is wholly dependent on public esteem, which is the imprimatur of individual worth. Failure to live up to the code of behaviour implies loss of honour. Loss of honour implies loss of public esteem. Loss of public esteem implies loss of self-esteem – as manifest in Hector's reply to Andromache when she pleads that he stay within Troy and fight upon the walls, rather than fight Achilles in face-to-face combat:

---

[4] Of the two guiltless Spartan survivors of Thermopylae, Pantites hanged himself out of shame, while Aristodemus suffered unbearable ignominy until Plateae, where he 'wiped away his shame' by suicidal valour (Herodotus, *Histories*, VII. 229. 1).

[5] R. Ullah, 'The Role of Shame, Honour and Pride in Gender Inequality in the Tribal Regions of North-West Pakistan', paper presented to the Second Conference of the European Philosophical Society for the Study of the Emotions, Edinburgh, July 2015. I am indebted to this thoughtful and informative paper.

All this weighs on my mind too, dear woman.
But I would die of shame to face the men of Troy
and the Trojan women trailing their long robes
if I would shrink from battle now, a coward.
Nor does the spirit urge me on that way.
I've learned it all too well. To stand up bravely
always to fight in the front ranks of Trojan soldiers
Winning my father great glory, glory for myself.

(*Iliad* VI. 522–9)

*Honour groups within a shame culture* One is dishonoured if one fails to live up to the code (of a hero in Homeric Greece, of chivalry in medieval Europe, of *bushido* in Shogunate Japan, of Pashtunwali among the Pashtuns). There is no moral space for individual conscience or private moral judgement that deviates from the code. The only remedy for dishonour in medieval Japan was for the samurai to commit *seppuku*. If a samurai's leader died in battle and he failed to get himself killed too, he was fated to become a *ronin*, a masterless sword for hire. For to lose one's status as a member of an honour group implied the loss of one's very status *as a person*. One's self-identity and self-respect were bound to one's role and to its rights and duties. In Viking society, expulsion from an honour group as a consequence of dishonour meant that one became a *nithing* – a man without a name. The decline and gradual disappearance of warrior aristocracies in the ancient world was co-ordinate with the emergence of a conception of individual identity that was no longer wholly submerged in public esteem for valour, charisma, cunning in leadership, hospitality to guests, and generosity to dependents.

*Transformation of honour in classical Greece* Despite the decline of military aristocracies, both pride and shame continued to be linked with honour in fourth-century Athens, although the concept of honour was significantly transformed, as is patent in Aristotle:

*Megalopsuchia*, then, is the best condition of character in relation to choice and exercise of honour and other honourable goods, and it is these rather than utilities that we assign as the sphere of the *megalopsuchos*. (*Eudemian Ethics*, 1233ᵃ4–7)

Shame [*aidos*] should not be defined as a virtue; or it is more like a feeling than a state of character. It is defined, at any rate, as *a kind of fear of dishonour*, and produces an effect similar to that produced by fear of danger; for people who feel disgraced blush, and those who fear death turn pale. (*Nicomachean Ethics*, 1128ᵇ9–12; emphasis added)

The conception of honour and of what is honourable changed further with the collapse of the Greek city-states and the rise of empires. In Hellenistic Greece, with the rise of Stoicism and the defensive psychological 'retreat into the inner citadel', the domain of the private expanded and withdrawal into the private was legitimized. The possibility of a good and honourable life that was neither that of a warrior nor that of an active member of a ruling elite could be contemplated.

*Honour code in republican Rome*     Less so for the ruling patrician class in republican Rome. Valour (*virtus*) in battle was the path to renown (*gloria*), and was rewarded with praise and recognition. This in turn, after ten years of military service, led to public office. Glory was familial and heritable, as is evident from the inscription on the tomb of Gnaius Cornelius Scipio Hispanus:

> By my character I increased the valorous deeds [*virtutes*] of my forebears. I have had children and emulated the exploits of my father. I sustained the praise of my ancestors, so that they rejoice that I was born to them. My office has ennobled my descendants.[6]

Distinguished military service was a condition for public office. Tenure of high office enabled those of noble birth to serve Rome, to benefit its citizens, and to win prestige (*dignitas*) and authority (*auctoritas*). It was, from a functional point of view, a highly successful competitive honour code that served Rome well for three centuries, but it also brought the republic to its internecine end.

*Emergence of guilt culture with rise of Christianity*     In the late Roman imperial world, with the decline of the power of a ruling aristocracy, the development of a semi-professional bureaucracy, and the existence of professional armies, the conception of honour and of shame shifted. A major role in this transformation was the rise and triumph of Christianity. This introduced a guilt culture into Rome, where, in the social and military crises of the fourth and fifth centuries, it rapidly took root for a multitude of convergent reasons. A primary focus of shame in the emerging guilt culture became sexuality and the body, and shame became forcefully riveted to the notion of sin.[7]

---

[6] Quoted by N. Rosenstein, 'Aristocratic Values', in N. Rothenstein and R. Morstein-Marx (eds), *A Companion to Republican Rome* (Blackwell, Oxford, 2006), p. 367.

[7] For detailed exploration of this theme, see P. Brown, *The Body and Society: Men, Women and Sexual Renunciation in Early Christianity* (Columbia University Press, New York, 1988), and K. Harper, *From Shame to Sin* (Harvard University Press, Cambridge, Mass., 2013).

Female honour was firmly bound to chastity and marital fidelity. This preoccupation persisted through and beyond the Middle Ages, concurrent with the re-emergence of the ethos of a warrior code after the fall of the West. This was gradually transmuted, by the genius of the Catholic Church, into the Christian chivalric codes of the High Middle Ages. Here shame culture and guilt culture coexist in considerable tension, torn between the secular authority of monarch and barons and the religious authority of papacy and priesthood.

*Chivalric ethos and the rise of bourgeoisie* The aristocratic/chivalric ethos of honour (ferociously caricatured by Cervantes) slowly declined with the rise of the bourgeoisie and was gradually replaced by that of the individual conscience answerable to God, given prominence in different ways by the various forms of Protestantism. That in turn became detachable from the notion of the inner voice of God and associated with the developing conception of moral autonomy and the inner voice of an autonomous conscience. The autonomous moral agent may feel ashamed of his deed if he has done something unworthy *in his own eyes* and before *the Tribunal of Reason*. He may still strive to conceal his offence from the eyes of others, but even if successful, he will still feel ashamed of himself and feel guilty for his transgression of the moral law. The high point of rationalist articulation of this conception is Kantian ethics.

Residues of the aristocratic and military conception of honour persisted in the West, in increasingly degenerate form, into the twentieth century, brilliantly caricatured by Mark Twain (in *A Tramp Abroad*) in his description of the duelling fraternities in late nineteenth-century German universities.

## 2. Shame and embarrassment: connective analysis

*Shame and loss of honour* Roughly speaking, shame is an emotion of concealment. It is prototypically a social emotion. The primitive roots of the emotion of shame lie in the loss of face felt to be incurred by *being seen* by others – primarily, but not only, by members of one's peer group – when one is in an indecorous condition that should be concealed from public eyes; or when one is engaged in an activity that reveals one's failure to attain standards of competence that others demand of one or that one demands of oneself; or when one fails to live up to the standards of the honour code of one's

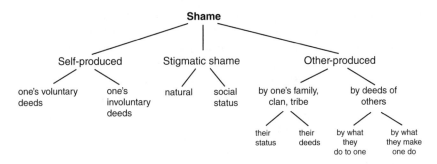

**Figure 6.1**   *The roots of shame*

peer group and that one accepts oneself (see fig. 6.1). Shame is linked to loss of honour, which may be due to one's own behaviour or to the behaviour of someone who is bound to one by familial, marital, or tribal links. One may bring shame upon one's house and one's name, or upon one's clan or tribe, by failing to live up to the honour code demanded of one. One's wife may bring shame upon one by casting her eyes upon another; one's children may bring shame upon one by their misdeeds and misconduct no less than they may bring honour to their parents by their heroic or noble deeds. One's (unmarried) daughters are a magnet for shame and must be zealously guarded from the eyes of others – if they bring shame upon one, the only way to expunge the shame is to kill them. The result of shame is loss of honour. Exposure leads to humiliation by others and to loss of pride and self-esteem. One is made an object of contempt and ridicule. One becomes exposed to the taunts and insults of others. One may be subjected to a life of abject misery from which, *in extremis*, the only escape may be suicide or becoming an outcast.

                      The Germanic etymology of the English word 'shame'
*Shame and* suggests a connection with the idea of exposure and
*genital exposure* that of covering up. Its proto-Germanic root is \**skamo*,
from a possible pre-Germanic \**skem*, derived from
\**kem*, meaning 'to cover'. Rembrandt's *Susanna and the Elders* could therefore be said to be an archetypal representation of the primal feeling of shame. Strikingly, the Old English *scamu* and *sceomu* meant not only feelings of disgrace and confusion caused by shame and loss of self-esteem, but also private parts. The Latin for shame – *pudor* – is linked to *pudenda*, meaning 'that of which one feels ashamed', in effect one's genitals. The Greek for shame is *aidos*, derived from *aidoia*, meaning literally *that which inspires shame* (as well as awe and reverence),

and hence too signifying the genitals.[8] The Hebrew for shame is *boo-sha* which is derived from the archaic biblical word *mevoshim* (Deuteronomy 25: 11), which means 'that of which one is ashamed', and hence signifying the genitals. The connection between shame and genital exposure that dominates the monotheistic theological tradition is articulated in Genesis 2: 25 and 3: 4–7.

> And they were both naked, the man and his wife, and were not ashamed. … And the serpent said unto the woman, Ye shall not surely die: For God doth know that the day ye eat thereof, then your eyes shall be opened, and ye shall be as gods, knowing good and evil. And when the woman saw that the tree was good for food, and that it was pleasant to the eyes, and a tree to be desired to make one wise, she took the fruit thereof, and did eat, and gave also unto her husband with her, and he did eat. And the eyes of both of them were opened, and they knew that they were naked, and they sewed fig leaves together, and made themselves aprons.

It is noteworthy that the doctrine of the Fall and original sin are later Christian additions, that we owe to St Paul (Romans 5: 12–21) and subsequently Irenaeus, but above all to Augustine in his anti-Pelagian writings. The probable ur-Genesis tale is Promethean in character, describing the rise of man, who, contrary to the will of God, learnt the difference between good and evil.[9] Adam and Eve not only acquired the moral knowledge that is unique to mankind among the creatures of the earth; they also learnt to dress as befits a human being and not to expose their genitals as animals do.

---

[8] Pseudo-Lucian, describing the Cnidean Venus in his book *Erotes*, uses the word *aidos* to signify her private parts: 'Nothing hides her beauty, which is entirely exposed, other than a furtive hand veiling her *aidos*.'

[9] A point mentioned in *The Intellectual Powers: A Study of Human Nature* (Wiley Blackwell, Oxford, 2013), p. 148n. I owe it to D. Daube's *Civil Disobedience in Antiquity* (Edinburgh University Press, Edinburgh, 1972), pp. 60–1. Daube was anticipated in this view by Hegel: 'For the state of innocence, the paradisaical condition, is that of the brute. Paradise is a park, where only brutes, not men, can remain. For the brute is one with God only implicitly [not consciously]. Only Man's Spirit (that is) has a self-cognizant existence. This existence for self, this consciousness, is at the same time separation from the Universal and Divine Spirit. If I hold to my abstract Freedom, in contraposition to the Good, I adopt the standpoint of Evil. The Fall is therefore the eternal Mythus of Man – in fact, the very transition by which he becomes man' (*Lectures on the Philosophy of History* (1837), trans. J. Sibree (Batochee, Kitchener, 2001), p. 340).

*Being ashamed of and being ashamed for*

Shame is a complex social emotion with multiple ramifications. So we must distinguish. We must distinguish between *self-produced shame* and *other-produced shame*, according to whether the source or reason for the shame originates with oneself or others. We must distinguish between *self-directed shame* and *other-directed shame*, according to whether one is ashamed of oneself or of another. We must distinguish between being ashamed *of* another and being ashamed *for* another. If one feels ashamed of another, one may or may not feel empathetic shame for the other – that depends on how much one loves them, and on the nature of their misdeed or misdemeanour. Biff, in Arthur Miller's *Death of a Salesman*, no doubt felt ashamed of his father Willy Loman, but perhaps he also felt ashamed for him. By contrast, in *All My Sons*, Ed surely felt ashamed of his father Joe Keller for selling faulty aircraft engines to the US Air Force, but did not feel ashamed for him.

*Self-produced shame: feeling shamed and feeling ashamed*

Self-produced shame entails that one is ashamed *of oneself*. The sources of one's shame are one's deeds. Deeds that make one ashamed of oneself may be voluntary and intentional, or involuntary (accidental, done by mistake, or in ignorance). But one may have shame *brought upon one*, either by the deeds of members of one's family, clan, or tribe (as is characteristic of a shame culture), or by what is done to one by others and by what they force one to do. If one has shame brought upon one by what others have done to one or by what they forced one to do, one may feel ashamed of oneself if one believes that one should have done more to resist the humiliation (even to the point of allowing oneself to be killed or to the point of inviting death). But, if that is not so, then one may feel *shamed* (and *non-transitively ashamed*) without feeling ashamed *of oneself*. One feels ashamed inasmuch as shame has been brought upon one. Susanna evidently felt shamed by the ogling eyes of the elders, and felt ashamed for her nudity to be exposed to their salacious gaze. But she had no reason to be ashamed of herself (see fig. 6.1).

*Feeling shame and feeling ashamed; natural shame*

We must further distinguish between *feeling shame* and *feeling ashamed*. The former implies the latter, but not vice versa. One feels self-directed shame if one realizes that one has done something *shameful*, something that is a stain on one's character and hence on one's self-esteem. However, in the case of what I shall call *stigmatic shame* one may feel ashamed without feeling shame.

For one may feel ashamed not at what one has done that brings shame upon one, but at one's natural features and deficiencies – one's ugliness or facial deformities, one's physical deformities and consequent limited abilities. This is *natural shame*. One may feel ashamed at one's *social status*, for example, at being an illegitimate child, or at being born into an inferior caste or class. One may feel ashamed of these, but feel no shame unless others mock and ridicule one. But one may also feel ashamed of what one has done, without feeling shame. An elderly person in a 'senior moment' may do something foolish or forgetful, and feel ashamed, without feeling shame. This is more than mere regret. It involves recognition of one's dwindling powers, of the fact that one can no longer rely on them as one used to, and of the fact that one is going to be a less reliable person. In that case, self-esteem may be damaged. Nevertheless, the deed of which one is ashamed in such a case need not affect one's self-respect. It is not something for which one would or should blush with shame – indeed, one may laugh at oneself. By contrast, to feel shame can be no laughing matter. Even in the case of serious misdemeanours, a person may feel ashamed without feeling real shame if the standard of conduct that has been violated has not itself been wholly accepted and internalized. In such cases, the agent may acknowledge guilt for the offence, but feel no shame. This is nicely exemplified in Effi's reflections on her past adultery with Major Crampas in Fontane's novel:

> What does weigh down on me is ... fear, mortal fear, and the constant dread that it will eventually come out after all. And then, apart from fear ... shame. I'm ashamed of myself. But just as I don't feel true remorse, I don't feel true shame. I just feel ashamed because of the eternal lies and deception; I always took pride in the fact that I couldn't lie and didn't need to lie; lying's so contemptible, and now I've had to lie all the time, to him and to the whole wide world, little lies and big lies, and Rumschüttel noticed and shrugged his shoulders; who knows what he thinks of me, certainly not very highly. Yes, I'm tormented by fear and shame at my deception. But shame at my guilt, that's something I *don't* feel, or not real shame, or not enough. (*Effi Briest*, ch. 24)

*'Shame' is Janus-faced: emotion or its object*     The noun 'shame' is Janus-faced. It may signify the painful emotion one feels, when one is aware of being, or of having been seen to be doing, something ridiculous, indecorous, or dishonourable; when one is humbled by what one acknowledges to be warranted criticism; or when one reflects on one's misdeed. It may, however, signify the disgrace

and ignominy constituted by what one has done or failed to do, which is *shameful*, or the humiliation to which one has been subjected, which *brings shame upon one*. It is in this sense that someone vile may be 'stained with a thousand shames'. It does not follow that he feels shame or feels ashamed. Despite the fact that his deeds were shameful in the extreme, Tito Melema in George Eliot's *Romola* feels none – any more than did some of the more odious Roman emperors or the great dictators of the twentieth century. Actions may be judged shameful by an agent who is actually applauded by his audience (as George Orwell was in 'Shooting an Elephant'). Someone may perform an action that *she* thinks to be meritorious, which is in fact shameful (Emma Woodhouse's meddling in the lives of others, in Jane Austen's *Emma*).

The verb 'to shame' has active and passive uses. *To shame another* is to expose his disgrace to public view; *to be shamed* is to be publicly humiliated. To inflict shame on another, or to bring shame upon one's family, clan, tribe, or country by one's ignominy and disgrace, doubtless makes them feel shame and feel ashamed of one, but the shame one brings upon them is not the shame they feel, but its reason – for what one has done is a shame and dishonour to them.[10]

*The temporal dimension of shame* — Shame may be felt for a moment (a sudden pang of shame). It may be felt for a more prolonged period of time, as when one is exposed to the contempt of others (e.g. when one is humiliated in the stocks, or shamed by a teacher in front of the class). But one may also feel the episodic emotion when lying sleepless in the small hours of the morning, writhing in shame at the thought of what one did or of how one was exposed to the eyes of others. Shame may also be a persistent emotion without genuine duration. For one may remain ashamed of the sins and misdemeanours of one's youth for the rest of one's days as St Augustine confesses himself to have been (see fig. 6.2).

*Shame and motivation* — Whereas pride is a character trait, shame, as Aristotle pointed out, is not – although being shameless (as Messalina and Theodora reportedly were) may be. However, like pride, shame too is a motive. For one may do various things *out of shame*, for example, withdraw from society to avoid the humiliation of the censorious looks and remarks of others (as does

[10] This is comparable to the distinction between one's belief *qua* what one believes (which may be true or false, well or ill supported, affirmed or denied) and one's belief *qua* one's believing of it, which may be passionate or stubborn, dogmatic or enlightened. For discussion, see *The Intellectual Powers*, pp. 203–5.

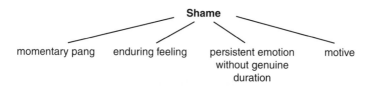

**Shame**

momentary pang    enduring feeling    persistent emotion        motive
                                      without genuine
                                      duration

**Figure 6.2**    *Different forms of shame*

Louis Trevelyan in Trollope's *He Knew He Was Right*), or, *in extremis*, commit suicide because the searing shame is intolerable (as does the Reverend Alfred Davidson, after fornicating with Sadie Thompson, in Somerset Maugham's 'Rain'). Just as honour and glory are powerful incentives to action, so too is shame (not the feeling but the shame one might bring upon oneself) a powerful disincentive. For the loss of honour may be unbearable. Just as feeling proud is the emotional upshot of meritorious achievement, so feeling shame is the emotional upshot of dishonourable, shameful, or indecorous behaviour, either one's own or another's with whom one's sense of identity is interwoven.

*The conceptual web of shame*    Feeling shame, like feeling pride, lies at the centre of a ramifying cluster of emotions and emotional attitudes. Shame bears a kinship to embarrassment. The expression 'embarrassment', like 'shame', can signify either an emotion ('He squirmed / She blushed with embarrassment') or the internal accusative of the emotion ('It will be a terrible embarrassment if they find out'). Embarrassment bears a kinship to shyness, which is both an emotion and a character trait. All three emotions involve self-attention. Shame is linked not to *being humble* (which, as we have argued, is a complement of proper pride), but to *being humbled*, on the one hand, and to *being humiliated*, on the other. Parallel to feeling proud, feeling shame too is internally related to self-respect and self-esteem. To have acted shamefully and to realize one has done so implies loss of self-esteem. For one has not lived up to the standards that one recognizes and accepts. To feel shame is to suffer a blow to one's self-respect, for one's feeling of shame implies that one realizes that one is of less worth as a human being than one thought one was, typically both in the eyes of others and in one's own.

*Humbling and humiliating a person*    As we noted earlier, to humble a person is to reduce his self-esteem, to show him to be less meritorious than he believed himself to be. One may feel humbled, and so ashamed of oneself, without feeling humiliated. To humble a person in public, however, is to shame *and* to humiliate him. For it demonstrates to onlookers that he is worth less than he was thought to be, that he merits less respect than he was wont to be given. To humiliate a person in public is to strike a blow at his self-respect. This is commonly done by depriving him of dignity. It is to present a person as an object of the emotional attitudes of contempt and scorn. Such deprivation of dignity is often institutionalized, for example, by the humiliating ceremonial stripping of military rank (e.g. Captain Dreyfus, after being found guilty of treason – wonderfully described by Robert Harris in *An Officer and a Spy*), by forcing humiliating costume upon the victim (as was done by the Spanish Inquisition, and in Nazi concentration camps), by displaying the person to public gaze in shameful circumstances (in a cage, pillory, or stocks), or by exposing them to degrading treatment (being spat upon, pelted with refuse, urinated on). It is to subject a person in public to ridicule, derision, and mockery intended to reduce his public esteem and, if successful, to reduce his self-respect too.

One may be humiliated by what other people do to one, by what they force one to do, or by circumstances of life and what they force one to do (beg, prostitute oneself, sell oneself into slavery). Extreme humiliation that is forced upon one characteristically deprives a person of dignity and self-respect – unless, like Aleksandr Solzhenitsyn or Primo Levi, one has the strength of character and will-power to 'retreat into the inner citadel' and to rise above the suffering and indignity inflicted upon one. One may also feel humiliated by having to reveal one's natural or acquired physical defects to public gaze (severe facial scarring, loss of limbs) and one's natural disabilities (Philip Carey in Maugham's *Of Human Bondage* suffers agonies of humiliation before others because of his inability (due to his club-foot) to walk without limping or to run), or one's acquired ones (Jake Barnes's humiliating impotence resulting from a war wound in Hemingway's *The Sun Also Rises*). One may also feel humiliated by realizing how badly one has behaved, irrespective of public exposure. Jane Austen portrays such a case in describing Elizabeth Bennet's rude awakening:

> She grew absolutely ashamed of herself. – Of neither Darcy nor Wickham could she think, without feeling that she had been blind, partial, prejudiced, absurd.
>
> 'How despicably I have acted!', she cried. – 'I, who have prided myself on my discernment! – I, who have valued myself on my abilities! Who have often disdained the generous candour of my sister and gratified

my vanity in useless or blameable distrust. – How humiliating is this discovery! – Yet how just a humiliation! Had I been in love, I could not have been more wretchedly blind. But vanity, not love, has been my folly.' (*Pride and Prejudice*, II. 13)

*Shame: neither*      While proper pride and self-respect are virtuous, and
*virtue nor vice*    arrogance and conceit are vices, shame is neither a
                     virtue nor a vice (see fig. 6.3). To be sure, it is right that
one should feel ashamed of one's misdeeds – 'He that hath no shame
hath no conscience.'[11] It is better that one should feel shame rather
than be shameless, for the shameless show contempt for accepted
standards of behaviour and honour, and often even flaunt their
disregard (like Nastasya Filippovna in Dostoevsky's *The Idiot*).
Nevertheless, feelings of shame too can be excessive. For being overwhelmed by shame can lead to mortification (as in the case of the
Reverend Robert Colley, in Golding's *Rites of Passage*, who literally
dies of shame) and to suicide (Ajax, in Sophocles' eponymous play;
Jocasta, in his *Oedipus Rex*). One should feel shame with regard to
the right objects (shameful deeds), on the right occasion, and to the
right extent. For feelings of shame and of being shamed are powerful
derivative *disincentives*,[12] curbing one's unruly and improper impulses,

Fear of exposure

Feeling embarrassed          Feeling ashamed

**FEELING SHAME**

Feeling humbled          Feeling humiliated

Feelings of guilt

**Figure 6.3**   *The web of shame*

---

[11] Thomas Fuller, *Gnomologia*, no. 2148.
[12] 'Derivative' inasmuch as shame is parasitic on the standards of attainment or behaviour failure to satisfy which is the reason for feeling ashamed.

and restraining one's devious and immoral deeds. However, to dwell on one's misdemeanours, to brood over one's sins, to wallow in one's shame (like the unnamed protagonist in Dostoevsky's *Notes from Underground*) produces despondency, morbidity, self-loathing, and self-flagellating guilt.

*Shame and social control*

Shame, functionally conceived, is a powerful and often terrible form of social control. It induces conformity to social norms and strengthens social identity. In Puritan New England in the seventeenth century an adulteress was forced to wear a large scarlet letter 'A' upon the front of her dress, the experience of which is brilliantly depicted in Nathaniel Hawthorne's *The Scarlet Letter*:

> The poor ... whom [Hester Prynne, thus condemned] sought out to be the objects of her bounty, often reviled the hand that was stretched out to succor them. Dames of elevated rank, likewise, whose doors she entered in the way of her occupation, were accustomed to distil drops of bitterness into her heart, sometimes through alchemy of quiet malice, by which women can concoct a subtle poison from ordinary trifles; and sometimes by a coarser expression, that fell upon the sufferer's defenceless breast like a rough blow upon an ulcerated wound ... When strangers looked curiously at the scarlet letter – and none ever failed to do so – they branded it afresh into Hester's soul; so that oftentimes, she could scarcely refrain, yet always did refrain, from covering the symbol with her hand. But then, again, an accustomed eye had likewise its own anguish to inflict. Its cool stare of familiarity was intolerable. From first to last, in short, Hester Prynne had always this dreadful agony in feeling a human eye upon the token: the spot never grew callous; it seemed, on the contrary, to grow more sensitive with daily torture. (ch. 5)

The use of the pillory in England as a punishment for crimes (until 1837) likewise involved deliberately shaming and humiliating the offender. In this way, the emotion of shame, coupled with ostracism, especially in closed societies, is harnessed as a means of expression of social solidarity in response to deviance from social norms. 'Naming and shaming' is still a potent but dangerous disincentive. It encourages bigotry, intolerance, and persecution of minorities.

*Manifestations of shame, shyness, and embarrassment*

The somatic and behavioural manifestations of shame are common to feeling embarrassed and to feeling shy as well. The boundaries between these three emotions are blurred. Shyness can slip into embarrassment when one is made the object of attention. Embarrassment readily slides into feeling ashamed (when one is caught farting,[13] for example) if the grounds of embarrassment impact upon one's self-esteem. Characteristic of all three emotions is blushing, which, according to Darwin, is a uniquely human non-voluntary response. Remarkably, it is not only a non-voluntary reaction, but the self-conscious wish to restrain it actually exacerbates it. Such blushing is normally accompanied by a degree of emotional perturbation, a sense of discomfort, and a wish to 'disappear' or to 'sink into the ground'. The characteristic behavioural accompaniments are eye-contact avoidance, either by deliberately averting one's gaze (especially in the case of feeling shame or embarrassment), or by casting one's eyes down (especially when feeling shy in company). In all three cases, one's movements are prone to be awkward and nervous. One's vocal reactions may involve stammering. Often hands will be put up to the face to conceal a blush or to cover the eyes. Such behavioural responses are the characteristic criteria for these three kinds of occurrent emotions, the differentiation of which depends upon additional behavioural criteria, upon the context and antecedent history of the episode, and upon the object and intention of the emotion.

*Differences between shame and embarrassment*   Embarrassment is distinguished from feeling shame in so far as it is *essentially* an audience-involving emotion. One cannot feel embarrassed in solitude. Feeling embarrassed is logically tied to a specific social occasion. So it has no duration beyond the time at which it is felt. Moreover, embarrassment, for the most part, is bound up with what used to called 'small morals' (see Hobbes, *Leviathan*, ch. 11) – inadvertent or, worse, ignorant failure to conform to etiquette and social mores – whereas shame stretches far beyond the compass of small morals. However, the two emotions commonly overlap and blur. The grounds for embarrassment, like the grounds for feeling ashamed, are commonly (but not uniformly) also reasons for others' ridicule, sneers, derision, and smiles of superiority. But the responses to shameful behaviour may be far more serious

---

[13] In *Brief Lives* (1693) John Aubrey tells a tale of Edward de Vere, Earl of Oxford, at the court of Queen Elizabeth I, who inadvertently broke wind loudly in the presence of the queen, and was so embarrassed and ashamed of himself that he fled to the continent, where he travelled for seven years. Upon his return, hoping the embarrassing event would not be remembered, he ventured to court again, only to be greeted by the queen with the words 'My Lord, I had forgotten the fart'.

than manifestations of social snobbery: they include the expression, by one's peers, of disdain, scorn, contempt, and abhorrence for failure to live up to the accepted standards of behaviour demanded of anyone with one's social standing (class, profession, gender, age). One may be embarrassed at spilling a glass of wine over one's hostess's tablecloth, at committing a linguistic infelicity, or at having forgotten the name of an acquaintance. One may be both embarrassed and ashamed at not knowing something anyone in *these* social circles is expected to know, or at showing incompetence when competence is expected (Phineas Finn – in Trollope's eponymous novel – at his first speech in the House of Commons), or at dropping a particularly bad clanger. But to be caught lying, stealing, molesting a child, raping a woman, or exhibiting cowardice is not *embarrassing*.

*Embarrassment*          Because of the temporal constraints on feeling embarrassed, it may give way after the event to feeling ashamed. If one commits a truly embarrassing *faux pas* at a dinner party, one may later lie in bed feeling deeply ashamed at the exposure of one's ignorance, clumsiness, or indelicacy. But one cannot blush with embarrassment after the event. So recollection of embarrassment can be painful but not embarrassing.[14] Table 6.1 enumerates some of the characteristic grounds for feeling embarrassed and compares embarrassment with shame with respect to them.

In some cultures, embarrassment may be manifest by embarrassed smiles, nervous laughter, or, especially among women, by giggling. These are socially sanctioned forms of an *embarrassment shield*. On some occasions, embarrassment may lead to a display of anger at the observer or at the person who is exposing one. Like feeling shame but unlike feeling shy, feeling embarrassed can readily slide into feeling humiliated if, for example, one is made the object of taunting, mockery, and ridicule.

It is a moot point whether one can be vicariously embarrassed by the behaviour of others with whom one's sense of identity is *not* bound up. Certainly one may be embarrassed to witness things that should be private, for example, husband and wife criticizing each other too vigorously in public, or revealing things to others that should be kept private. One may be embarrassed inadvertently to witness

---

[14] However, it need not be so: the embarrassments of one's youth may become objects of amused recollection in old age, when one realizes how foolish and unsure of oneself one was, and with what misguided values one tentatively approached the adult world.

|  | Embarrassment | Shame |
|---|---|---|
| Inadvertent or ignorant breaches of rules of 'small morals' | ✓ | × |
| Being seen performing natural bodily functions; seeing another performing natural bodily functions | ✓ | × |
| Exposure one's naked body or parts of one's body that convention requires keeping concealed in the circumstances | ✓ | ✓ |
| Exposure of one's ignorance in circumstances where knowledge is expected | ✓ | ✓ |
| Exposure of one's incompetence at tasks the ready performance of which is expected | ✓ | ✓ |
| Being seen eavesdropping, snooping, or deliberately observing something one should not observe | ✓ | ✓ |
| Being subjected to harsh criticism or being given a dressing-down in public | ✓ | ✓ |
| Having trivial aspects of one's private life revealed to others in one's presence | ✓ | × |
| Overhearing oneself being unfavourably or over-favourably discussed by others | ✓ | × |
| Not being drawn into the circle of others when one wishes or longs to be | ✓ | × |

**Table 6.1** *Comparison of embarrassment and shame with respect to grounds of embarrassment*

others performing private functions (sexual or lavatorial). More pertinently, one may, as it were, cringe at the embarrassing deeds of others – at their manifestation of lack of *savoir faire*, their embarrassing ignorance, or their inept behaviour. Curiously, one may react thus when watching a film or television, where one's discomfort is at *what* one witnesses, not at one's *witnessing* it. Nevertheless, one cannot blush with embarrassment at the conduct exhibited, nor wish, as it were, to 'sink into the ground' with embarrassment, even though one may deliberately cease look at the cringe-making scene. It is curious that English, unlike Spanish (*vergüenzajenea*), should, such argot apart, lack a word for this distinctive reaction.

*Object-accusatives of shame*

Let us return to shame. How are the object-accusatives of shame circumscribed? Of whom and of what can one be ashamed? Here pride and shame are homologous – one can be ashamed of oneself, of other people, and of institutions with whom one's sense of identity is bound up. To have a father who is a traitor, a mother who is a whore, a son who is a worthless drunk are grounds for shame, despite the fact that one bears no responsibility for their shameful condition. One may be ashamed of them, and ashamed of one's relation to them. One may feel ashamed of the behaviour of the institutions with which one is appropriately associated or the behaviour of one's country (if one's sense of identity is bound up with it). One can be embarrassed by, and ashamed of, the behaviour of a member of one's family if one is present, watching them behaving indecorously in public. Elizabeth positively cringes at her mother's behaviour when Mrs Bennet is talking to Bingley about Darcy:

> 'Aye – that is because you have the right disposition. But that gentleman,' looking at Darcy, 'seemed to think the country was nothing at all.'
>
> 'Indeed, Mama, you are quite mistaken,' said Elizabeth blushing for her mother. 'You quite mistook Mr Darcy. He only meant that there were not such a variety of people to be met with in the country as in town, which you must acknowledge to be true.'
>
> 'Certainly, my dear, nobody said there were; but as to not meeting with many people in this neighbourhood, I believe there are few neighbourhoods larger. I know we dine with four and twenty families.'
>
> Nothing but concern for Elizabeth could enable Bingley to keep his countenance. ... the general pause which ensued made Elizabeth tremble lest her mother should be exposing herself again. (*Pride and Prejudice*, I. 9)

And again, she whispers to her mother:

> 'For heaven's sake, madam, speak lower. – What advantage can it be for you to offend Mr Darcy? – You will never recommend yourself to his friend by doing so.'

Nothing that she could say, however, had any influence. Her mother would talk of her views in the same intelligible tone. Elizabeth blushed and blushed again with shame and vexation. (*Pride and Prejudice*, I. 18)

*Sharing shame*   One can *feel shamed* by the disgrace of members of one's family in virtue of one's relationship to them. Furthermore, one can *share* the shame and humiliation of another.[15] So, for example, Mrs Bulstrode, in *Middlemarch*, having found out about her husband's sordid past and its public revelation, resolves to share his humiliation:

> He had married her with that bad past life hidden behind him and she had no faith left to protest his innocence of the worst that was imputed to him. Her honest ostentatious nature made the sharing of a merited dishonour as bitter as it could be to any mortal.

> But this imperfectly-taught woman, whose phrases and habits were an odd patchwork, had a loyal spirit within her. The man whose prosperity she had shared through nearly half a life, and who had unvaryingly cherished her – now that punishment had befallen him it was not possible to her in any sense to forsake him ... She knew, when she locked her door, that she should unlock it ready to go down to her unhappy husband and espouse his sorrow, and say of his guilt, I will mourn and not reproach. But she needed time to gather up her strength; she needed to sob out her farewell to all the gladness and pride of her life ... she had begun a new life in which she embraced humiliation. (ch. 74)

*Nominalization-accusatives*   How are the nominalization-accusatives of
*of shame*                shame to be circumscribed? Shame again runs
parallel to pride. As there is natural pride in one's natural endowments, so too there is natural shame in ugliness, physical deformities of visage and physique, in being undersized, in suffering from weak health and consequently having limited physical prowess. A part of the motivation behind Richard III's wickedness in Shakespeare's play lies in his bitterness and shame over his deformities (*Richard III*, I. 1). Many objects of natural shame are *comparative* disadvantages. If no human being could run, no shame would be felt by children who cannot run. In the land of the hunchbacks, the straight-backed man would be an object of ridicule.

---

[15] Perhaps one cannot *share the pride of another* because the abstract noun 'pride' is unlike 'shame' in not approximating an internal accusative of the verb. One cannot 'share the pride of another', although one may bask in their pride and one may share the honours bestowed.

*Natural shame*

There can be similar responsibility-independent shame in being born out of wedlock or a member of a despised race or caste or of a disgraced family, as well as sexual shame in impotence, frigidity, or homosexuality. As there is pride in one's lineage, so too, in a class-conscious society, there may be shame in one's humble origins if one encounters disdain and contumely as one tries to gain access to the higher orders. In such cases, the person who is ashamed of some characteristic for which he bears no responsibility is responding to the ridicule, contempt, and aversion of others. To be ashamed of such a quality (as opposed to feeling only resentment and indignation) involves concurring with the judgement that it is shameful. So one feels oneself disgraced in the eyes of those who treat one with contempt, undermine one's self-respect and erode one's self-confidence. When one is subjected to mockery and ridicule, to humiliation and derision, it is tempting to respond with the thought that *it is not one's fault*, that one is not responsible for such natural misfortunes and disabilities, or for membership of such despised classes.

Although this is true, it is not the correct response. As Arnold Isenberg pointed out, the right response, difficult though it may be for one to accept it in the face of public opinion, is 'It is no disgrace!' One may be proud of one's good health, but it does not follow that one should be ashamed of one's ill-health. One may take pride in the beauty and grace of one's youth, but that does not imply that one should be ashamed of the decrepitude of age. That bigots treat one with contempt does not mean that being a Jew, black, lesbian, and so on is a reason for feeling ashamed. What is needed is the rejection of the standards by which one is wrongly disgraced, and *which one implicitly accepts in feeling ashamed*. One must strive for a proper set of values, and a balanced view of human merit. This will not ease one's resentment or make one any the less ill at ease in the company of those who accept and enforce a false set of values. It may not prevent one wishing that one did not have such-and-such a characteristic or that one had not been born into such-and-such a group. But it will prevent one from feeling ashamed, and assist one in finding one's proper balance in a bigoted and prejudiced world.

One may also feel ashamed of one's vices, one's unsavoury habits and pronenesses, ignorance, lack of *savoir faire*, mien and manner, incompetence, accent or form of speech. These are remediable, and one's shame may be a spur to improve oneself relative to the standard by reference to which one finds oneself wanting. One may be ashamed of one's expressive behaviour – one may be embarrassed to have laughed too loudly or inappropriately, or ashamed of having broken down in tears. One may be ashamed of one's acts and omissions, of one's voluntary deeds, and of what one voluntarily lets happen to one.

*Would life be better without shame?* Feeling shame and feeling ashamed are unpleasant. Would we not live happier lives without such negative feelings, as we should surely live happier lives if we were not susceptible to feelings of hatred, envy, jealousy, rage, or terror. We often try to treat people who have succumbed to such negative feelings as these, attempting to change their outlook upon life, their moral expectations, their self-control, and their exercise of reason. Should we similarly endeavour to eradicate feelings of shame, to mitigate their effects upon self-esteem and self-respect? The phenomenon of *misplaced* feelings of shame is familiar – especially in cases of natural shame – and we should certainly strive to ameliorate the effects of such emotion. But, in general, feelings of shame are a corollary of having, and having internalized, standards of moral and social behaviour. Indeed, a criterion for someone's having accepted such norms and ideals of conduct, of knowing what one ought to do and what one ought to strive to be, is that they feel ashamed (and often guilty) when they fail to conform to these norms and fall short of these ideals. To endeavour to eradicate our susceptibility to feeling ashamed of ourselves (and feeling guilty at our misdemeanours) would be tantamount to endeavouring to eradicate the norms and values that are constitutive of a good life.

## 3. Guilt: connective analysis

*Normativity of guilt* Guilt is a cousin to shame. Unlike shame, which is linked primarily to (but is detachable from) public disapprobation, to falling below what one's status requires, and hence to loss of self-esteem and self-respect, the core idea of guilt is normative[16] – bound up with the transgression of obligation-imposing rules (linked in ancient Jewish and later monotheistic cultures with the laws and commandments of God). Failure to comply with an obligation-imposing rule is to *be guilty* of breaking the rule. If one acknowledges the obligation and has internalized the rule, one will, other things

[16] As in *Human Nature: the Categorial Framework* (Blackwell, Oxford, 2007) and *The Intellectual Powers*, 'normative' means pertaining to a norm or standard of correctness and incorrectness, right and wrong. It does not mean prescriptive.

being equal, *feel guilty* for one's commission or omission. If the deed was heinous, one may be overwhelmed by *feelings of guilt*. However, beyond the primal normative idea of guilt, there are forms of guilt that are non-normative but linked to what one ought to be, rather than to what one ought to do (*Seinsollen* rather than *Tunsollen* in von Hartmann's terminology). The behavioural demands upon an agent are circumstance-specific and tied to polymorphous descriptions of behaviour. One may feel guilty for letting someone down (one ought to be faithful) or for inadvertently offending someone by a thoughtless remark or insensitive joke (one ought to be sensitive to the feelings of others). One may feel guilty for failure to stand up for a maligned friend, or for exposing one's family to risk. In such cases, the specific action or omission is not readily subsumable under an obligation-imposing rule, but is a moral requirement specified by the injurious consequences of one's deed or omission, or by the intrinsic qualities of what one did or failed to do and its incompatibility with one's valued relationships to others.[17]

*Defeasibility of guilt*    In certain circumstances, one's violation of an obligation-imposing rule may be justified by a weightier consideration that overrides the obligation. In such a case, one broke the rule but was not wrong to do so. So one need feel neither guilt nor remorse, although one may feel bitter regret. Alternatively, one may be excused for one's misdeed by the absence of one or another of the mental conditions of moral responsibility. In such cases, what one did was wrong, but there was no negligence and it was not one's fault. So, again, other things being equal, one need feel no guilt. However, other things may not be equal. Just as in law, where there are laws of strict liability for which absence of the mental conditions of criminal responsibility does not excuse (does not defeat liability), so too in the morality of both guilt and shame cultures there are circumstances in which absence of the mental conditions for liability carry no weight. It is, however, striking that, while our laws of strict liability are, on the whole, confined to relatively minor offences

---

[17] Of course, one might speak of a duty not to let people down or an obligation not to offend them. This is, I think, highly artificial. It favours a deontic form of representation. But, if we have no axe to grind, we should normally say that one *ought* not to let people down and *ought* not to offend them. By contrast, we have an *obligation* to keep our promises and to repay our debts, which is more emphatic than 'one ought to keep one's promises'. The path of duty, one might say, is characteristically laid down in advance (that is the point of *having* a duty), whereas virtue, where it does not coincide with duty, has no preordained pathway, but is occasion- and person-sensitive.

(traffic offences, making changes in one's passport, selling adulterated milk), strict liability in social mores, customary law, and morality is characteristic of the most serious offences and violation of the gravest social taboos (e.g. murdering members of one's family, incest (Oedipus)). So, one may be liable to feelings of guilt or of shame irrespective of whether one could help what one did or of whether one knew what one was doing.

*Feeling guilty*     If the *conceptual iconography* of feeling ashamed is *the eye of others*, that of feeling guilty is *the voice of conscience*. The focal point of *being shamed* is the esteem of others and its loss. The focal point of *feeling ashamed of oneself* is self- and peer-group esteem, and self-respect and its loss. But the focal point of *feeling guilty* is the deed done, the transgression of an obligation-imposing rule – the commandment of God, customary law, the moral law – or the failure to satisfy a serious moral requirement determined by the specificities of the occasion. There is no 'feeling guilty *of oneself*'. The searchlight of guilt shines *on what one has done*, and only obliquely on one's public standing and the judgements of others.

Feeling guilt is the emotion linked to a person's acknowledgement of the validity of an obligation-imposing rule or of a moral requirement (how one ought to be), to acknowledgement of transgression, and to acceptance of responsibility and liability. For this one is answerable above all to God or one's conscience. Contrary to what is sometimes claimed, the obligation-imposing rule and the moral requirement *need not* concern prohibitions on harming others. Feelings of guilt are not restricted to violating *other-regarding* obligation-imposing rules or failing to satisfy moral requirements. One may feel guilty for wasting one's talents, or for wasting one's time – which may harm one, but need not harm others. One may feel guilty for one's wicked, malicious, or sordid thoughts and wishes, as well as for one's base desires. No harm to others is thereby caused, but, for all that, these are potent sources of feelings of guilt.

*Guilt, responsibility,*     Nevertheless, guilt feelings are for the most *remorse, and expiation*     part linked to (moral) responsibility for *a deed*. Responsibility for one's deed is linked to liability. Liability, in a guilt culture, is linked to remorse, atonement,[18] and expiation, which may take the form of suffering retribution or endeavour

---

[18] Atonement ('at-one-ness') may be between someone guilty and the person he has offended, between the offender and the community, between the offender and God, or between the community and God.

to make reparation for one's misdeed. Remorse and expiation are needed to enable those who feel guilty to relieve themselves of the burden of guilt and to live with themselves again. Retribution makes the offender 'pay' for his offence in the currency of suffering. Reparation discharges the guilt by repairing the wrong done or by compensating for it in so far as possible. Metaphorically speaking, this 'restores the balance'. The Day of Atonement in Jewish practice and confession in Catholic practice, coupled with remorse and a retributive penance authoritatively imposed, are powerful devices for discharging feelings of guilt.

Of course, one may feel shame as well as guilt even in the most puritanical of cultures, such as that of Salem, Massachusetts, in 1692 – guilt for one's deed, shame in one's own eyes and in the eyes of others. John Proctor, in Arthur Miller's *The Crucible* is racked with guilt at his adultery, feels no shame for engaging in witchcraft, since he is innocent of the offence of which he is accused, but is willing, under pressure, to confess to it to save his life. What he cannot bear is to have his confession displayed in public for all to see his shame at buying his life with a lie, while others, equally innocent of witchcraft, go to their deaths with integrity.

PROCTOR:     I have confessed myself! Is there no good penitence but it be public? God does not need my name nailed upon the church! God sees my name; God knows how black my sins are! It is enough!

DANFORTH:     Mr. Proctor –

PROCTOR:     … I am John Proctor! You will not use me! It is no part of salvation that you should use me!

DANFORTH:     I do not wish to –

PROCTOR:     I have three children – how may I teach them to walk like men in the world, and I sold my friends?

DANFORTH:     You have not sold your friends –

PROCTOR:     Beguile me not! I blacken all of them when this is nailed to the church the very day they hang for silence!

DANFORTH:     Mr. Proctor, I must have good and legal proof that you –

PROCTOR:     You are the high court, your word is good enough! Tell them I confessed myself; say Proctor broke his knees and wept like a woman; say what you will, but my name cannot –

DANFORTH,     *with suspicion*: It is the same, is it not? If I report it or you sign to it?

PROCTOR,     *he knows it is insane*: No, it is not the same! What others say and what I sign to is not the same!

| | |
|---|---|
| DANFORTH: | Why? Do you mean to deny this confession when you are free? |
| PROCTOR: | I mean to deny nothing! |
| DANFORTH: | Then explain to me, Mr. Proctor, why you will not let – |
| PROCTOR, | *with a cry of his whole soul*: Because it is my name! Because I cannot have another in my life! Because I lie and sign myself to lies! Because I am not worth the dust on the feet of them that hang! How may I live without my name? I have given you my soul; leave me my name! |

*(The Crucible, IV)*

We noted earlier that one may feel shame for the deeds of one's fathers and one may feel ashamed of them. Equally, one may feel shame for the actions of one's children, who may bring shame upon one. Moreover, one may feel ashamed for them. But one cannot feel *vicarious guilt* for their offences. One may regret the wrongs they have done, but one cannot feel remorse for them.

*Guilt and mens rea*    It is noteworthy that the limits of guilt *and* of shame do not coincide with the conditions of *mens rea*. Oedipus did everything he could to avoid the dreaded fate the gods had ordained, but nevertheless unwittingly killed Laius his father (who was threatening his life) and unknowingly fell in love with, married, and had children by Jocasta, his mother. His shame was so great that he stabbed out his eyes with Jocasta's brooches. But surely, one may remonstrate, Oedipus was not responsible for his deeds. Why then did he feel such shame? Is it that he was merely *causally responsible*, and that this is both necessary and sufficient for shame? I think not. First, although he may be said to have brought about (caused) the death of his father by stabbing Laius, he did not bring about *his killing* of his father – this was a voluntary deed under his full control. Furthermore, he did not *bring it about* that he slept with his mother – he slept with her, although he can be said to have brought it about that she was with child.[19] For we do not bring about our own actions. So we have more than mere causal responsibility – which one bears if, in being knocked over, one falls against another person, causing him injury. Secondly, in doing what he did, Oedipus satisfied the requirements of *capacity responsibility*, that is, he possessed the requisite two-way powers to act or refrain over a wide sphere of competence, was in full command of his faculties, and

---

[19] For detailed discussion of the differences between doing, acting, and bringing something about, see *Human Nature*, ch. 5, section 8.

was a rational agent sensitive to reasons for acting, feeling, and thinking, and able to deliberate and form intentions. In addition, he satisfied the conditions of *act responsibility*.[20] That is, he not only possessed the requisite generic abilities, but was also able to exercise them on the occasion in question. Nevertheless, he did not know, and in the circumstances could not have known, that Laius was his father and Jocasta his mother. Normally non-culpable ignorance exculpates. Nevertheless, Oedipus felt utter horror and infinite shame. Irremovable stigma was attached to him. He had *polluted* Thebes and was condemned to leave the city.

*The limits of rationality*     Strikingly, feelings of guilt in our culture may also be felt despite absence of intent, malice, recklessness, or negligence. If a person, driving with utmost care, unavoidably runs over and kills a small child who suddenly darts across the road, he will, in all probability suffer terrible feelings of guilt for the rest of his days. Is this irrational? Even in cases in which he knows full well that there was nothing he could have done to prevent the accident. Should he then feel no guilt? Should he shrug his shoulders regretfully, and say 'What bad luck!'?

*Survivor guilt*     Are the blurred boundaries of rationality *crossed* in cases of *survivor guilt*? This was felt by many survivors of the Nazi Holocaust, and is sometimes felt by soldiers who have survived against the odds while their comrades fell (as in the trenches of the First World War). Here guilt is felt not for something one has done, no matter whether intentionally or unintentionally; nor is it for something one allowed to be done to one. It is felt simply for surviving, where others (who were one's people or one's comrades) died. It is an expression of solidarity with those who went through the valley of death with one and who perished. Is it rational? Perhaps here reason itself must be silent – it can go so far, but no further.

*Shame in a shame culture*     Deep differences between feeling shame and feeling guilt are evident when we turn to examine the forms of response to these reactive feelings. For regret – even bitter regret – belongs to shame, whereas remorse fits guilt. Deep shame that one has brought upon oneself can be expunged (in a shame culture) only by heroic death. Not to act as befits someone

[20] The terminology and categories are those of H. L. A. Hart, *Punishment and Responsibility: Essays on the Philosophy of Law* (Clarendon Press, Oxford, 1986). Continental legal systems, unlike the English legal system, distinguish *imputability* from *fault*.

of one's standing is to suffer a blow to one's self-esteem and self-respect. What one has done cannot be undone – and, in a shame culture, one cannot remove the stain. Hence Ajax's agonized cry when he discovers that he has run amok and slaughtered cattle instead of his enemies, thus making himself a laughing stock and losing all honour:

> Look at me! Me, the brave hero! The one who never trembles with fear in battle! Never afraid of enemies! Look at what I have done! I have killed these helpless animals, poor beasts that have never hurt anyone!
>
> Look at me!
>
> Is there anyone more shameful than me? Is there anyone who's suffered a greater insult?
>
> ...
>
> Darkness! You are my light! Hades' misery! You are my greatest hope!
>
> Take me! Take me, Hades, and let me live within your darkest halls!
>
> Here, I am no longer fit to seek the help of gods or mortals.
>
> Here, Zeus' daughter, that mighty goddess Athena, tortures me mercilessly.
>
> Where can I find refuge. Where can I go and live?
>
> If all my glorious past is gone, my friends, gone like those slaughtered animals, and all I'll be remembered for is having so mindlessly chosen to slaughter these innocent beasts, then let the whole army raise their swords and strike me dead![21]

As noted earlier, Aristodemus could wipe out his shame for not having died in battle with his 300 fellow Spartans at Thermopylae only by suicidal valour at Plataea. This should not be so alien to us as it may seem. Harry Faversham, in A. E. W. Mason's popular 1902 novel, *The Four Feathers*, can expiate shame and public shaming (by being given white feathers) only by acts of extreme heroism.

By contrast, feelings of guilt, if accompanied by remorse and repentance, may be annulled by atonement and reparation to the victim (if possible), forgiveness from the victim (if possible), and, in a religious guilt culture, forgiveness from God.

---

[21] Sophocles, *Ajax* (trans. G. Theodoris), 365–8, 395–400.

It is important to note that shame and guilt are not exclusive emotions. One can feel shame and guilt simultaneously for the same offence. One feels ashamed of oneself, has brought shame upon oneself, and one feels guilty for what one has done (see table 6.2).

*Regret and remorse*          How are regret and remorse related? The objects of regret, unlike those of remorse, are not limited to one's deeds – one may regret the passing of one's youth or the death of a friend. To regret something is to judge the object of regret as unfortunate, a mistake, or a necessary evil. If one is

| *Shame* | *Guilt* |
|---|---|
| One can be ashamed of oneself or ashamed of another appropriately associated with oneself. | Guilt is restricted to oneself – one cannot feel guilty for another. |
| The scope of shame extends much further than one's deeds and omissions | The scope of guilt is limited to one's deeds and omissions. |
| Feelings of shame are not defeasible by absence of *mens rea*. | Save in extreme cases, feelings of guilt are defeasible by absence of *mens rea*. |
| Fear of shame is a powerful disincentive. | Fear of feeling guilty is not a disincentive, save in degenerate cases.[a] |
| *In extremis* can be expunged only by extreme action demonstrating that one possesses the character trait one was shamed for not having | Can be atoned by admission and confession, expiation, reparation or retributive punishment |
| regret | remorse |
| Characteristic consequence of having brought shame upon oneself or of being shamed is loss of public esteem, leading to loss of self-esteem | Characteristic consequence of feeling guilty is the desire to atone for the deed done and 'restore the balance' one has disrupted |

[a] A degenerate case here is one in which one has abandoned a previously accepted standard of conduct (e.g. the dietary laws of a religion), but continues to comply with them simply because of an engrained sense of unease. Here the residue of guilt provides a reason for compliance with a norm, even though the norm itself does not.

**Table 6.2**   *Differences between feelings of shame and feelings of guilt*

ashamed of what one did, one regrets doing it – wishes one had not done it. But feelings of regret for one's deeds are compatible with thinking that what one did was right and not shameful at all. One may have chosen the lesser of two evils. One may then regret what one did, but insist that, given similar circumstances, one would do the same again. One may also regret lost opportunities, and acknowledge that one was wrong not to seize Fortune by her forelock.

Remorse, by contrast, does imply wishing one could undo what one has done, and does imply wanting to restore the *status quo ante*. Failing that possibility, one must seek atonement in deeds. One cannot feel remorse and continue to think that one was justified in doing what one did. Agamemnon may have felt bitter regret for the sacrifice of Iphigenia, but no remorse – since he viewed it as a necessary evil. Claudius, in *Hamlet*, is guilt-ridden, but cannot feel remorse and cannot repent, for he cannot bring himself to abandon the throne and his queen.

> O, my offence is rank, it smells to heaven,
> It hath the primal eldest curse upon't,
> A brother's murder. Pray can I not;
> Though inclination be as sharp as will,
> My stronger guilt defeats my strong intent,
> And like a man to double business bound,
> I stand in pause where I shall first begin,
> And both neglect.
> ...
> But O, what form of prayer
> Can serve my turn? 'Forgive me my foul murder'?
> That cannot be, since I am still possess'd
> Of those effects for which I did the murder,
> My crown, mine own ambition and my queen.
> May one be pardon'd and retain the offence?
>
> (*Hamlet*, III. 3)

Macbeth, after murdering Duncan, is horrified by his own deed and regrets the murder ('Wake Duncan with thy knocking! I would thou coulds't!' (*Macbeth*, II. 3). Nevertheless, he feels no remorse or shame. Instead, he changes his conception of himself, and therewith the grounds of his self-esteem and self-respect, and plunges ever deeper into blood in order to maintain his throne ('Things bad begun make strong themselves by ill' (III. 3)). Genuine remorse, therefore, is linked to motivation in a manner in which regret is not. In Judaeo-Christian ethics, sin and guilt may be atoned for. The sin may be forgiven, and the guilt expunged. This gives formidable power to synagogue and church in the control of individual lives. But guilt, remorse, and atonement also find a place in rationalist ethics that has severed the links between the requirements of morality and divine command. The burden is carried by the conscience of the individual.

# 7

# Envy

## 1. Envy and jealousy: a pair of vicious emotions

No one wishes to feel envious or jealous of another, any more than one would wish to feel sorrow or grief, disappointment or despair.[1] What one is envious or jealous of are things that matter deeply to one. The acclaim given to another person may be disturbing in the extreme to someone who feels robbed of due recognition, and who resents the actual recipient's being granted it. The love of one's spouse for another may be a torment to one. Feeling these emotions is painful – *in extremis*, even harrowing. But envy and jealousy are not negative emotions in this sense alone. They can motivate mean, malicious, and evil deeds. Actions done *out of* jealousy or envy are vicious. The corresponding character traits – having a jealous or envious disposition – are vices. These emotions can destroy the soul, inasmuch as they may numb the moral sensibility of an agent, mar the power of reason and reasonable judgement, undermine the self-respect that is necessary for

---

[1] I am much indebted, in this chapter and the next, to G. Taylor's *Pride, Shame, and Guilt* (Clarendon Press, Oxford, 1985) and *Deadly Vices* (Clarendon Press, Oxford, 2006).

*The Passions: A Study of Human Nature*, First Edition. P. M. S. Hacker.

one to live at peace with oneself, and often lead to self-deception and loss of integrity.[2]

*Envy as a*    That envy is a primary vice is evident from one of the
*primary vice*   most ancient myths of the Old Testament. The first murder, according to Genesis, was committed out of envy:

> And Abel was a keeper of sheep, but Cain was a tiller of the ground. And in the process of time it came to pass, that Cain brought of the fruit of the ground an offering unto the Lord. And Abel, he also brought of the firstlings of his flock and of the fat thereof. And the Lord had respect unto Abel and unto his offering: But unto Cain and to his offering he had not respect. And Cain was very wroth, and his countenance fell. ... And Cain talked with Abel his brother: and it came to pass, when they were in the field, that Cain rose up against Abel his brother, and slew him. (Genesis 4: 2–8)

Similarly, the Greeks conceived of envy as a vice that gives rise to catastrophe and misery. It was envy between Hera, Athena, and Aphrodite over Paris's award of the golden apple that was the distal cause of the slaughter of the Trojan Wars. Moreover, their envy was maliciously engendered by Eris, the goddess of Discord. Agamemnon, having been forced to return Chryseis to her father, envied Achilles' possession of Briseis and, as commander in chief, maliciously demanded her for himself, thus precipitating the quarrel between the two men that will cause thousands to die. And it was Ajax's envy for possession of the armour of Patroclus that lay at the root of his hatred of Odysseus, which led to his own madness and suicide.

In the Christian tradition, envy (*invidia*) is held to be both a deadly (or mortal) and a capital sin. The deadly sins are actions that spell the death of the soul. For they irremediably corrupt the soul unless the agent is redeemed by remorse, repentance, confession, expiation, and absolution. A capital sin, according to Aquinas, is one that is the fountainhead of further sins. It 'has a desirable end, so that through desire for that end, a man proceeds to commit many sins, all of which are said to arise from that vice as from a principal vice.'[3] In his examination of envy, Aquinas notes that envy is a mortal sin because someone

---

[2] In using the term 'soul' I am not referring to any part of a human being, let alone to an immaterial, immortal substance lodged within a human being. I am speaking of distinctive human powers associated with righteousness, love and compassion, the ability to see meaning in human life and the ability to live a meaningful life, moral self-knowledge, and guilt. These abilities can be marred or destroyed by vices.

[3] Aquinas, *Summa Theologica*, 2ª2ᵃᵉ, q. 153, art. 4.

who envies his neighbour rejoices in his neighbour's misfortunes. But this is contrary to charity, the supreme Christian virtue, which requires us to take joy in the good fortune of our neighbours.[4] Moreover it tortures and torments the envious themselves.

The Age of Reason too had no hesitation in condemning envy. Bacon, in his essay on envy, observed that 'It is also the vilest affection and the most depraved, for which cause it is the proper attribute of the devil'.[5] Baltasar Gracián wrote:

> The envious person dies not once, but as often as his rival lives in applause. Lasting fame for the envied means eternal punishment for the envious. The former lives forever in his glories, the latter in his punishment. The trumpets of fame play immortality for one and taps for the other, sentencing him to the gallows of anxiety.[6]

In view of received wisdom, it was, of course, shocking, and meant to be shocking, for Bernard Mandeville, in his *The Fable of the Bees; or, Private Vices, Public Benefits*, in 1714 to endorse envy in socio-economic life as beneficial to society. It is equally shocking to find modern socio-economic theorists advancing the view that envy is not a vice at all.[7] It is conceived to be the lubricating grease for the economic machine (the Moloch of our societies). Envy, it is said, motivates ever greater efforts in the pursuit of private wealth, and, coupled with greed and covetousness, stimulates acquisitive competition, thus benefiting the economy (now not merely reified, but vivified and conceived – like living things – to have a good, a welfare and an ill-fare). This clash with both Greek and Judaeo-Christian morality merits scrutiny. This will not be done here.

*Jealousy: less dominant a vice in antiquity* Jealousy in general, and the jealousy of lovers in particular, play little if any role in the Homeric epics. Menelaus' *honour* is besmirched by Paris' abduction of Helen; Achilles's honour is damaged by Agamemnon's confiscation of Briseis; but there is no mention of sexual jealousy.[8] It is striking that Homeric warriors are

---

[4] Aquinas, *Summa Theologica*, 2ª2ᵃᵉ, q. 36, art. 4. This, to be sure, is misleading, since to rejoice in one's neighbour's good fortune is not a form of charity at all.

[5] F. Bacon, 'Of Envy', in *Essays; or; Councils, Civil and Moral* (1625).

[6] B. Gracián, *The Art of Worldly Wisdom* (1647), trans. C. Maurer (Doubleday, New York, 1992), §162.

[7] As well as social Darwinist authors who glorify selfishness, such as Ayn Rand.

[8] Although, when Agamemnon returns her to Achilles, he hastens to assure him that he has not had sexual intercourse with her.

not described as given to jealousy – perhaps because it would be incompatible with their elevated status, honour, and pride. But their women sometimes are. Similarly, among the gods, it is Hera who is most commonly moved to vengeful jealousy by her husband Zeus's endlessly inventive extramarital infidelities with, for example, Leto, Callisto, Io, and Lamia, all of whom come to a sticky end at Hera's command. Sexual and marital jealousy of women is the theme of a few of the surviving classical Greek tragedies, such as Euripides' *Medea* and *Andromache*, and Sophocles' *Trachiniai*. It is striking that sexual jealousy is little discussed by philosophers in antiquity. Aristotle discusses envy and righteous emulation, but not the jealousy of lovers. It is equally striking that marital jealousy is not mentioned by the church fathers as being among the deadly sins, and rarely receives much attention. Aquinas examines the deadly sin of envy, but mentions marital jealousy only in passing.

Nevertheless, it is patent that jealousy has always been considered to be a particularly evil vice. It found its most hideous and deep literary expression in ancient and early modern theatre alike – in the *Medea* of Euripides and in Shakespeare's *Othello*. It has inspired many great novels in the canon of Western literature, such as Tolstoy's *Anna Karenina*, Trollope's *He Knew He Was Right*, and Proust's *In Search of Lost Time*, and some of the greatest poems, ranging from Sappho to Shakespeare's jealousy sonnets and on to Baudelaire's great poem 'To a Madonna', and beyond. The latter wonderfully characterizes the jealousy of love as a capital vice:

thy heel shall rest
Upon the snake that gnaws within
  my breast,
Victorious Queen of whom our
  hope is born!
And thou shalt trample down and
  make a scorn
Of the vile reptile swollen up with
  hate.
And thou shalt see my thoughts, all
  consecrate,
Like candles set before thy flower-
  strewn shrine,
O Queen of Virgins, and the taper-
  shine

Je mettrai le Serpent qui me mord
  les entrailles
Sous tes talons, afin que tu foules et
  railles
Reine victorieuse et féconde en
  rachats
Ce monstre tout gonflé de haine et
  de crachats.
Tu verras mes Penser, rangés comme
  les Cierges
Devant l'autel fleuri de la Reine des
  Vierges
Étoilant de reflets le plafond peint
  en bleu,

Shall glimmer star-like in the vault
   of blue,
With eyes of flame for ever
   watching you.
While all the love and worship in
   my sense
Will be sweet smoke of myrrh and
   frankincense.
Ceaselessly up to thee, white peak
   of snow,
My stormy spirit will in vapours go!

And last, to make thy drama all
   complete,
That love and cruelty may mix and
   meet,
I, thy remorseful torturer, will take
All the Seven Deadly sins, and from
   them make
In darkest joy, Seven Knives, cruel-
   edged and keen,
And like a juggler choosing, O my
   queen,
That spot profound whence love
   and mercy start,
I'll plunge them all within thy
   panting heart!

Te regarder toujours avec des yeux
   de feu;
Et comme tout en moi te chérit et
   t'admire,
Tout se fera Benjoin, Encens, Oiban,
   Myrrhe,
Et sans cesse vers toi, sommet blanc
   et neigeux
En Vapeurs montera Esprit orageux.

Enfin, pour compléter ton rôle de
   Marie,
Et pour mêler l'amour avec la
   barbarie,
Volupté noire! Des sept Péchés
   capitaux,
Bourreau plein de remords, je ferai
   sept Couteaux
Bien affilés, et comme un jongleur
   insensible,
Prenant le plus profond de ton
   amour pour cible,
Je les planterai tous dans ton Coeur
   pantelant,
Dans ton Coeur sanglotant, dans
   ton Coeur ruisselant![9]

## 2. Envy and jealousy: conceptual unclarity

To a first approximation, envy is the vice of wanting to acquire what another has, begrudging his possession of it, and taking malicious pleasure in his loss of it (*Schadenfreude*). Jealousy, by contrast, is wanting to keep the love that someone has granted one (or that one feels is due to one), fearing and profoundly resenting its loss to another. These characterizations require refinement and qualification, but they clearly pick out quite different centres of variation.

[9] 'To a Madonna', in *The Poems and Prose Poems of Charles Baudelaire*, trans. J. Huneker (Brentano's, New York, 1919).

Nevertheless, the relationship between the two emotions is generally held to be unclear.

*Historical difficulty in distinguishing envy from jealousy*

Unclarity regarding the English terms goes back a long time. Wycliffe's translation of Song of Songs 8: 6 reads: 'Love is as strong as death, envy as hard as hell.' In the King James translation this is transformed into 'Love is as strong as death, jealousy as cruel as the grave'. Neither is quite accurate, but 'jealousy' is the correct translation. Wycliffe was translating from the Vulgate, which uses the Latin *aemulatio* (zealous, imitative of, actuated by rivalry), which in turn was a questionable translation of the Hebrew *qin'âh*. Robert Burton, in *The Anatomy of Melancholy*, remarked that three things cause jealousy: a mighty state, a rich treasure, and a fair wife. It seems clear that he is speaking of envy. It is often remarked that modern and contemporary speakers find it difficult if not impossible to distinguish between jealousy and envy.[10] Indeed, only a little attention is needed to realize how commonly 'jealousy' is invoked to mean wanting to acquire what another possesses and/or grudging his possession of it. The following are randomly chosen examples: 'I am jealous of everything whose beauty does not die. I am jealous of the portrait you have painted of me. Why should it keep what I must lose?' (Oscar Wilde); 'A negative judgement gives you more satisfaction than praise, provided it smacks of jealousy' (Jean Baudrillard); 'Jealousy is the tribute mediocrity pays to genius' (Fulton J. Sheen); 'The thermometer of success is merely the jealousy of the malcontents' (Salvador Dali); 'There tends to be a jealousy in England towards countries that are successful' (Chris O'Dowd).

*Iconographic confusion*

The unclarity even invaded traditional iconography. In Eichler's 1760 illustration for envy in Hertel's 1758–60 edition of Cesare Ripa's *Iconologia*, the background *fatto* is of Joseph and his brothers. But Joseph's brothers sold him to Egyptian traders out of jealousy for their father's excessive love of Joseph, not out of envy of his many-coloured coat.[11]

*Common features*

So, we must examine the reasons for this indeterminacy and unclarity. It is patent that envy and

[10] P. Walcot, *Envy and the Greeks* (Aris & Phillips, Warminster, 1978), p. 1; G. M. Foster, 'The Anatomy of Envy: a Study in Symbolic Behaviour', *Current Anthropology* 13 (1972), 165–202 (167); P. Toohey, *Jealousy* (Yale University Press, New Haven, 2014), pp. 5ff.

[11] It is striking that the same misinterpretation of the tale of Joseph and his brothers is to be found in S. Brant's *Ship of Fools* (1494), ch. 53, 'Of Envy and Hate'.

jealousy share numerous features (see list 7.1). They are both *other-regarding emotions*, by contrast with self-regarding, reflexive emotions such as pride and shame. One cannot envy oneself or be jealous of oneself. One cannot envy without envying someone, or be jealous without fearing that someone may attract the affections of one's spouse or beloved. They are both *persistent emotions*. 'Envy never takes a holiday', Bacon quotes,[12] and the same can be said of jealousy. Although one may feel a brief pang of envy, both emotions are typically persistent. They are not mental states, since they lack the genuine duration that characterizes mental states. For they cannot be interrupted or broken off by distraction of attention and later resumed, and they persist through periods of sleep. Moreover, they are *pervasive emotions* that may take many forms. They invade one's thoughts, bedevil one's dreams, drive one's will, and take over one's imagination. They become obsessive, colouring and poisoning one's daily life.

Both are *complex blends* of further emotions. Envy is characteristically a blend of feeling aggrieved at not possessing what another has and/or feeling one degree or another of ill-will towards the person one envies and (often) wishing he did not have it – which may range from resentment to anger and rage. It commonly involves feelings of inferiority and a blow to one's self-esteem (which may or may not be acknowledged), and malicious feelings, and it can evolve into hatred.

---

Other-regarding
Persistent
Pervasive
Blends of multiple further emotions
Possessive
Involve varying degrees of hostility
Provide motives for action
Rooted in self-love
Undermine one's self-esteem
Commonly involve self-deception
Comparison-involving
Self-destructive

---

List 7.1  *Twelve features shared by envy and jealousy*

---

[12] F. Bacon, 'Of Envy'; he gives no source for his quotation, which is an Italian proverb.

Jealousy is typically a blend of love and an agonizing feeling of abandonment and betrayal. Prior to confirmation or apparent confirmation, sexual jealousy involves doubt and extreme suspicion, feelings of insecurity coupled with fear of loss of love. After confirmation or apparent confirmation, sexual jealousy commonly evolves into resentment, anger or rage, hatred, self-pity, feelings of inadequacy, loss of self-esteem (which may or may not be acknowledged), and feelings of shame and disgrace.

Both emotions are typically *possessive* – envy, when its object is a unique item that can be owned, often (but not necessarily) merges with covetousness and commonly involves wishing the other did not possess it, since their possession demeans one. Jealousy is typically a fear of losing to another person the love one possesses or thinks one's due. Both typically involve *varying degrees of hostility* towards another. Envy is often linked to *Schadenfreude*. Jealousy characteristically involves hostility if not hatred towards the person who is taking away the love one feels is due to one, and engenders bitterness, hostility, or hatred towards the person one loved. Like many emotions, envy and jealousy *provide motives for action*. For in both cases there are characteristic patterns of backward- and forward-looking reasons for action. One may blacken the name of another out of envy, or murder another out of jealousy. As Congreve observed, 'Heaven has no rage like love to hatred turned, Nor Hell a fury like a woman scorned' (*The Mourning Bride*, III. 8).

Both envy and jealousy are *rooted in fear of loss of esteem* (both self-esteem and the esteem of others).

*Envy, jealousy, and self-esteem*

Envy often implies the desire to possess for oneself the advantage possessed by another. But it may rather imply the thought that one's own standing is diminished by the other's advantage: that one feels humiliated by the other's possession of the envied good (glory, acclaim, *dignitas*). As Caesar says of Cassius: 'Such men as he be never at heart's ease / Whilst they behold a greater than themselves' (*Julius Caesar*, I. 2). However, things look different from Cassius's point of view: 'I had as lief not be, as live to be / In awe of such a thing as I myself.' This sense of belittlement and humiliation can provide the motive for destroying the envied person or for dispossessing him of the advantage he has. Jealousy has similar roots. La Rochefoucauld sapiently observed that jealousy contains more of self-love than of love. Indeed, far from protecting and preserving the love that is believed to be threatened, it often destroys it. As is already implied in the previous points, the intentional objects of both envy and jealousy undermine the agent's *self-esteem*, and the emotions, once aroused, gnaw away at it. Envy often involves a fear of losing the esteem of others as a result of not winning or possessing the desideratum one lacks. A feeling of diminution of status ensues, which in turn impinges upon one's self-esteem. Sexual jealousy involves a blow to one's pride inasmuch as one has been rejected by the person one loves in favour of another. The cuckolded husband is a traditional figure of ridicule. So jealousy commonly drags in its wake both shame and humiliation, which likewise reduce self-esteem. Acknowledging these forms of loss of self-esteem is itself painful, and various defence mechanisms commonly spring into place. Hence both envy and jealousy lead to *self-deception*. One may mask one's envy by deprecating the good for which one envies another. Similarly, one may attempt to mask one's jealousy and humiliation by affecting, to oneself and others, not to love the person for whose love one stills longs, or even never to have really loved him or her. One's love for the person who has betrayed one may transmute into hatred, which is sometimes a defence mechanism masking from oneself one's abiding love.

Both envy and jealousy are comparison-involving. In the case of envy, the envious person resents the desideratum that the envied person possesses or has been granted. He may feel that he should have had that benefit, or that the person he envies is less meritorious than he, and so should not have attained or been granted that advantage. Comparably, the person who is jealous of the love his beloved bears another may be tormented by the thoughts 'How is he (or she) better than I am?' and 'How could my beloved, after all we have shared together, possibly succumb to the charms of another?'

Finally, both emotions, like boomerangs, return to strike the agent – for they are essentially *self-destructive*. Both involve inflicting untold suffering upon oneself. As the well-worn idiom has it, one may 'eat one's heart out' with either envy or jealousy. 'As iron is eaten away by rust, so the envious are consumed by their own passion', Antisthenes rightly observed. Sexual jealousy, as just noted, commonly destroys the very love it craves, as well as destroying the humanity of those who are jealous. In Giotto's wonderful depiction (1305) of *invidia* among the seven deadly sins in the Scrovegni Chapel in Padua, the figure of *Invidia* has, instead of a tongue, the head of a snake that turns back to bite the very face from the mouth of which it protrudes. *Gelosia* is portrayed in Renaissance painting by a female figure tearing out her hair (as in Bronzino's *Allegory with Venus and Cupid* in the National Gallery, London (discussed in chapter 8)).

Despite their shared features (shown in list 7.1), envy and jealousy are very different. The tendency to conflate the two emotions needs further explanation. We must investigate the differences between them and whether these differences merit sharper demarcation in the study of the emotions than they commonly receive. We must provide connective analyses of both concepts, and enrich the concepts by elaborating, with the aid of examples drawn from literature, a clear conception of envy and jealousy respectively. We must investigate whether either of the two emotions and corresponding character traits and motives can assume beneficial forms. And we must raise the question of whether these emotions are unavoidable elements of human nature. We shall examine envy and jealousy in this chapter; the larger part of our discussion of jealousy, however, is deferred until chapter 8.

## 3. Envy and jealousy: their conceptual roots

*Conceptual*        Correctly to delineate a concept requires description of
*roots: English*   the current use and circumstances of use of the concept-
                    word in question, and needs no historical investigation
into the mode of concept acquisition of either an ontogenetic or a phylogenetic kind. Nevertheless, Austin was right that many a word in a language trails behind it clouds of etymology that are of interest in their own right and that often illuminate the evolution of the current concept and make evident its point and purpose. Such investigations can be valuable contributions to cultural and intellectual history, and shed light on the manifold conceptual connections disclosed by connective analysis.

The English 'envy' and its cognates (including 'invidious') are derived from the Latin *invidia* and *invidere*, the meaning of which is to look askance upon, to look with the evil eye, to envy or grudge, to be jealous. The Latin expressions are also the source of the Italian *invidia*, the Spanish *envidia*, and the French *envie*. It is noteworthy that classical Latin made no distinction between envy and jealousy. The lack of separate words clearly to differentiate the two emotions and corresponding vices is a feature classical Latin shared with ancient (as well as modern) Hebrew. Classical Greek had separate words – *phthonos* and *zelos* – but, as we shall see, they do not sharply distinguish envy from jealousy.

'Jealousy' and its cognates are derived from Middle English 'gelusie' or 'ielousy', which are importations from Old French *gelosie* and *jalousie* (later to evolve into *jaloux*), themselves derived from medieval Latin. In the post-classical era, Latin borrowed the Greek *zelotupia* and *zelos*, which gave rise to low Latin *zelotypia* and *zelosus*, from which the Romance languages and English derive their expressions. As we shall see, this mixed ancestry goes some way towards explaining the equivocation over the negative connotations of the word. So, I shall turn briefly to an archaeological excursus.

*Conceptual roots: Hebrew* In Hebrew there is only one word for envy, jealous, and zealous: the noun *qin'âh*, which occurs forty-four times in the Old Testament, and the verb *l'qaneh*, which occurs thirty-two times (according to Strong's *Concordance*). Whether what we conceive to be envy or jealousy is meant in a given utterance has to be gathered from the context. There are numerous biblical tales to illustrate the evils of envy, and others that demonstrate the vice of jealousy. For the most part, *qin'âh* is condemned as a serious and self-destructive vice. Narratives that exemplify envy are, for example, the tales of Cain and Abel, Rachel and Leah, and Saul and David. The Psalms and Proverbs frequently condemn envy: 'Envy not thou the oppressor, and choose none of his ways' (Proverbs 3: 31); 'Fret[13] not thyself because of evildoers, neither be thou envious against the workers of iniquity. For they shall soon be cut down like the grass and wither as the green herbs. Trust in the Lord and do good' (Psalm 37: 1–3); 'A sound heart is the life of the flesh: but envy the rottenness of the bones' (Proverbs 14: 30). The bitter voice of the Preacher (Ecclesiastes 4: 4) shares the view of modern socio-economic theorists, but is not bereft of the moral judgement they lack: 'And I saw that all toil and all skill in work comes from a man's envy of his neighbour, but this too is vanity and vexation of spirit.' The evils of jealousy are illustrated by the story of Joseph and his brothers, in which it is patent that the brothers are jealous of Jacob's love for Joseph:

> Now Israel [i.e. Jacob] loved Joseph more than all his children, because he was the son of his old age: and he made him a coat of many colours. And when his brethren saw that their father loved him more than all his brethren, they hated him, and could not speak peaceably unto him. (Genesis 37: 3–4)

[13] *Titchar*: to burn; to be kindled with anger.

It is out of jealousy that they betray their brother and sell him into slavery, lie to, and break the heart of, their father. Proverbs views marital jealousy consequent upon adultery as the source of revenge and pitilessness:

> But he who commits adultery with a woman lacks understanding: he that does so destroys his own soul. Wounds and dishonour shall he get; and his reproach shall not be erased. For jealousy arouses the rage of a husband: therefore he will not have pity on the day of revenge. He will not have regard for any ransom; neither will he rest content, even though you give him many gifts. (Proverbs 6: 32–5)

The word here is, of course, *qin'âh*, but it is obvious that the subject is jealousy, and not envy.

So far, one may think, so good. There is only one word in play, but it is so used as to subsume both concepts, and both are firmly associated with vice or sin. But the waters are muddied by the recurrent claim in the Old Testament that God himself is a jealous god (e.g. Exodus 20: 5; Deuteronomy 4: 24; 5: 9; 6: 15), even averring his name to be 'Jealous' (Exodus 34: 14).[14] The authors of the Pentateuch conceived of God's covenant with Israel to be akin to a marriage, and made use of this simile to represent idolatry as a form of adultery. Indeed, idolatry is described in derogatory sexual terms (*Vezanu akh'rei elim a'kher'im*: they went a whoring after other gods). An immediate consequence of this is that not all forms of *qin'âh* are vicious or sinful. This commitment would, in due course, be another root of unclarity about the boundaries of, and evaluation of, jealousy and envy.

*Conceptual roots: Greek*  It is striking that there was a similar unclarity in differentiating envy from jealousy in classical Greek.[15] *Phthonos* subsumes malicious envy, grudge, spite, and possessive jealousy, but apparently not marital/sexual jealousy. It is uniformly a negative attribute. *Zelos* signified enthusiasm, burning zeal, hot ardour, emulation, eager rivalry, and also envy and jealousy. It does not uniformly have negative connotations. Neither *phthonos* nor *zelos* means the same as 'jealousy', although either, in certain contexts, can be so translated. The negative connotations of *zelos*, understood as malicious envy,

[14] Jealous, but not envious; God, one presumes, cannot be envious.
[15] For a comprehensive discussion, see E. M. Sanders, *Envy and Jealousy in Classical Athens* (Oxford University Press, Oxford, 2014).

however, are powerfully expressed in early Greek poetry in Hesiod's *Works and Days* (ca. 700 BCE):

> The spirit of Envy [*Zelos*], with grim face
>   and screaming voice, who delights
> in evil, will be the constant companion
>   of wretched humanity,
> and at last Nemesis and Aidos, Decency and Respect
>   shrouding
> their bright forms in pale mantles, shall go
>   from the wide-wayed
> earth back on their way to Olympos,
>   forsaking the whole race
> of mortal men, that all that will be left by them
>   to mankind
> will be wretched pain. And there shall be no defense against evil.[16]

By contrast, approval is given to non-malignant rivalry, to the *zealous* pursuit of good objectives, and to *zeal* in emulating enviable characteristics. Indeed, much later Aristotle contrasted envy (*phthonos*) in *Rhetoric* (II. 10) with emulation (*zelos*) in II. 11:

> Emulation [*zelos*] is pain caused by seeing the presence, in persons whose nature is like our own, of good things that are highly valued and are possible for ourselves to acquire; but it is felt not because others have these goods, but because we have not got them ourselves. It is therefore a good feeling felt by good persons, whereas envy is a bad feeling felt by bad persons. Emulation makes us take steps to secure the good things in question, envy makes us take steps to stop our neighbour from having them. (*Rhetoric* 1388ª30–36)

It appears evident that classical Greek had no separate word for the jealousy of lovers or for marital jealousy. When post-classical Greek moved to fill this gap, it opted for cognates of *zelos* (such as *zelotupia*) rather than of *phthonos*. The great comic writer of the post-classical era, Menander, found sexual jealousy an appropriate topic for comedy in his play *Perikeiromene* (The Girl with Her Hair Cut Short', ca. 314 BC) in which he uses the adjective *zelotupos* to signify sexual jealousy. The lack of clarity in the boundaries of *phthonos*, *zelos*, and later *zelotupia* was to complicate matters when it came to translating

---

[16] *Hesiod*, trans. R. Lattimore (University of Michigan Press, Ann Arbor, 1991), ll. 195–201.

the Old Testament into Greek, and later into Latin, given that the God of Israel was a jealous God.

*Conceptual roots: Latin*

Classical Latin, like Hebrew, had only one multi-purpose word: *invidia*, signifying envy, malice, hatred, ill-will, grudge, and also jealousy. The verb *invidere* meant 'to look askance at', 'to look maliciously at', 'to cast an evil eye on', 'to envy or grudge', 'to be prejudiced against', 'to aspire to rival', 'to prevent, refuse or deny'. The associative link with eyesight was powerful and infiltrated ancient superstition. A malicious glare was endowed with magical powers to inflict evil. Plutarch explained that the eyes are a source of deadly rays emitted by the envious to damage the person envied.[17] Indeed, a symbolic apotropaic charm was necessary to disarm the evil eye. A victorious general, enjoying a triumph, had a small metallic phallic charm called a *fascinus* (from *fascinare*, to cast a spell) ceremoniously suspended below his chariot by Vestal Virgins as a *medicus invidiae* (remedy for envy (Pliny)).[18]

As we just noted, *zelotypia* and *zelosus* are the Low Latin roots of the English noun 'jealous' (derived from French), the French *jaloux*, the Italian *gelosia* (no earlier, it seems, than Petrarch and Boccaccio), and the Spanish *celoso*. This too contributed to the confusions and equivocations of medieval Latin in which being jealous and being zealous are not explicitly distinguished. Just because God is conceived to be a jealous God, the expressions for jealousy had to be capable of retaining positive connotations. Envy was, however, listed as one of the deadly sins. What has in current philosophical writing been characterized as harmless or even beneficial 'emulative envy' was denominated *aemulatio*.

It is evident that a fertile seedbed of equivocation, shifting boundaries, and indeterminacy was inherited by the moderns from the

---

[17] Plutarch, *Quaestio Convivialis*, V. 7. 2. This belief was long-lasting, even among the learned. Bacon writes in 'Of Envy': 'The scripture calleth envy an "evil eye", and the astrologers call the evil influence of the stars "evil aspects", so that still there seemeth to be acknowledged, in the act of envy, an ejaculation or irradiation of the eye. Nay some have been so curious as to note that the times when the stroke or percussion of an envious eye doth most hurt are when the party envied is beheld in glory or in triumph, for that sets the edge upon envy.'

[18] The superstition or its residue persist to this day in Muslim lands, where the apotropaic talisman is most commonly either a *nazar* (a disc consisting of blue and white concentric circles) or a *hamsa* (a vertical aversive hand), or a combination of both.

ancients in general, and from monotheism in particular. We must see whether there is any merit to this equivocation, or whether, for the sake of clarity in investigations of the passions of the soul, we should abandon it.

## 4. Envy: iconography, mythology, and iconology

*Dante on envy*    Envy, then, is a vice of the eye. For the envious look askance on their neighbours and competitors. This is vividly portrayed in Dante's *Purgatorio*, when his guide Virgil takes him to the circle in which 'the sin of envy is chastised', on seeing which Dante remarks:

> I do not think there is in all the world
> A man so hard, that he would not be pierced
> By pity for the people that I saw
> For when I had arrived so near to them,
> That I could clearly recognize their state,
> Great tears of grief were wrung forth from my eyes.
> They seemed to be with coarsest hair-cloth clad,
> And each upon the next one's shoulder leant,
> And all of them were leaning on the cliff.
> So do the blind men who are destitute
> Sit in row at pardons begging alms,
> And one man sinks his head upon the next,
> In order that compassion may be stirred
> Not only by the sound of their complaints
> But also by their looks which plead no less.
> As the sun's light does not help the blind,
> So to the spirits that I speak of now
> The light of heaven refuses its largesse;
> Their eyelids are sewn up with iron wire
> Like untamed hawks that will not settle down.[19]

The eyes of the envious are sewn up to teach them not to covet what is another's, not to be on constant watch for the benefits others receive. Equally, the envious take pleasure in seeing others brought low – hence they are deprived of their eyesight. In parallel manner,

---

[19] Dante, 'Purgatory', canto 13, in *The Divine Comedy* (trans. K. Mackenzie).

Spenser portrays envy wearing a cloak embroidered with eyes and chewing a venomous toad (*Faerie Queen*, I. 4. 32).

*Ovidian mythology of envy*      The iconography of envy is derived from classical mythology. The mythological representation of envy comes from Ovid's *Metamorphoses* (II. 4), in which he recounts the tale of Aglauros, who envied her sister Herses for attracting the love of Mercury. As a price for acting as go-between, Aglauros demands payment in gold. Minerva, with punishment in mind, flies swiftly to the Cave of Envy:

> Straight the doors
> flew open, and, behold, within was Envy
> ravening the flesh of vipers, self-begot,
> the nutriment of her depraved desires. –
> ...
> Her face is pale, her body long and lean,
> her shifting eyes glance to the left and right,
> her snaggle teeth are covered with black rust,
> her hanging paps overflow with bitter gall,
> her slavered tongue drips venom to the ground;
> busy in schemes and watchful in dark snares
> sweet sleep is banished from her blood-shot eyes;
> her smiles are only seen when others weep;
> with sorrow she observes the fortunate,
> and pines away as she beholds their joy;
> her own existence is her punishment,
> and while tormenting she torments herself.
> (Ovid, *Metamorphoses*, trans. B. More)

*Iconography of envy*      It is this remarkable description that inspired the representation of envy in Mantegna's engraving 'The Battle of the Sea Gods' (1485–8) and in Botticelli's renowned *Calumny of Apelles* (1494). Pieter Bruegel the Elder's engraving of envy in his series *The Seven Deadly Sins*' (1557), however, has no classical inspiration, but rather the northern European pedagogical iconography that informed the paintings of Hieronymus Bosch. Géricault's portrait *Woman Suffering from Obsessive Envy* (1819–20) has departed far from the Renaissance tradition, and depicts with deeply disturbing realism a pathetic inmate of a lunatic asylum, who is beset by pathological envy.

The Ovid-inspired iconography gave rise to analytic iconology, the most famous book of which we have already mentioned, namely

Cesare Ripa's *Iconologia* of 1593. Ripa describes *Invidia* as an aged woman, ugly – for she is the enemy of all virtue, which is beautiful. She is livid (grey-blue) in colour – owing to lack of any warmth. Her breasts are shrivelled since envy lacks all charity, and she has snakes instead of hair, signifying that her evil thoughts spread poison. She is eating a heart, which she holds in her hand, since she eats her heart out with envy and consumes herself. Her other hand rests on a hydra whose heads have poisonous breath. For just as cutting off a head of the hydra produces two in its place, so too quelling one source of envious suspicion merely produces two further ones. With its many heads, the hydra never sleeps, like envy itself. Envy is accompanied by a lean dog symbolizing envious selfishness.

*Symbolic colour of envy*    The iconographic representation of envy has a leaden or livid complexion. This was held to be the characteristic complexion of the envious. The received explanation was by reference to the doctrine of the humours, which originated with Hippocratic medicine and was further developed by Galen, Avicenna, and Renaissance physicians. The alleged fundamental bodily fluids, visible in four-layered blood precipitate, were red blood (unclotted red blood cells in suspension, associated with the liver or heart), yellow bile (clear yellow serum in the blood), black bile, and phlegm (white blood cells in the blood), correlated respectively with sanguine, choleric, melancholic, and phlegmatic personalities. Humoral imbalance was believed to be the cause of personality disorders. Envy was held to be the result of an excess, and consequent admixture, of yellow and black bile (which have nothing to do with what we call 'bile') that also gives rise to anger, aggression, and depression.[20] Quite apart from the iconographic association of envy with being livid, there is a literary association with the colour green. To this day we speak of being 'green with envy'. This may be rooted in a mistaken supposition that the archaic verb 'to grien (grene)', meaning 'to hanker after or to long for', was a cognate of the colour name 'green'. But this hypothesis is questionable since the same associative link obtains in French and Italian. It may be that the colour association is to be explained by reference to green bile, but this was not a part of the doctrine of the humours. In German, *Neid* is associated primarily with yellow (*gelb vor Neid*) – in all probability

---

[20] See, e.g., Descartes's *The Passions of the Soul*, III. 184: 'How it comes about that envious people are apt to have a leaden complexion'. This doctrine held sway until the nineteenth century.

owing to a variant of the doctrine of the humours that linked jealousy with yellow bile rather than with an admixture of yellow and black bile. But *grün vor Neid* also occurs.

## 5. Envy: connective analysis

*Envy and covetousness*     Envy is related to covetousness. Covetousness, prohibited in the Decalogue, is a desire to have another's possession (e.g. his wife, his house, his cattle, his servants). It is, as game theorists say, associated with zero-sum games. Envy, although it overlaps with covetousness, nevertheless differs with respect to four features. First, its scope is wider than covetousness, since one may envy another person's character traits, skills, looks, rank, or office, which are not *possessions* one might covet. Secondly, unlike covetousness, envy involves ill-will towards the person one envies. For if one envies another, one does not merely want what the other has (indeed, one may not want it for oneself at all), but one feels discontent, displeasure, or resentment that he has it. Hence, thirdly, envy is commonly, though not inevitably, associated with *Schadenfreude*, that is, taking malicious pleasure at the misfortunes of the person of whom one is envious.[21] Finally, envy is sometimes satisfied if the other loses what one envies him for having, whereas covetousness is satisfied only if one attains what he has.

The adjective 'enviable', however, muddies the *Envy and what* waters, for it has lost the association with malice. *is enviable* Something another has is said to be enviable if it is highly desirable. One may say that one envies another their holiday in Italy, without any implication of ill-will or any suggestion that one is vexed by the other's good fortune. This is a distinctive

---

[21] Aristotle groups together envy, spitefulness, and righteousness as emotional states concerned with the fortunes of our neighbours. Righteous indignation is pain at the undeserved good fortune of another. It is the mean between two vicious emotions: envy, which is pain at all good fortune of another, and spitefulness, which is pleasure at the misfortune of another (*Nicomachean Ethics*, 1108[b]1–5). This triadic form of representation is appealing, but misleading. Righteous indignation is not only chagrin at the undeserved good fortune of others, but also indignation at injustice. That is not a mean between envy and *Schadenfreude*. Moreover, as Aquinas pointed out, taking pleasure at the misfortune of another need not be spiteful or vicious, if the other is threatening one (when Sennacherib besieged Jerusalem, the capital of the kingdom of Judea, the Jerusalemites rejoiced when the plague struck the Assyrian army).

use of the verb 'to envy' to signify no more than that one views another's good fortune with approval. 'Oh, I do envy you your complexion / invitation to the ball / having seen that wonderful performance' is not an admission of guilt or confession of sin, but rather a compliment to another on his good fortune and a declaration that one too would like to be similarly fortunate. So it is an expression of admiration, coupled with an idle wish. It is perfectly understandable that usage should have drifted in this direction. However, it severs the notions of envy and being envious from their link with vice and sin. Strikingly, the expression 'invidious', from the same Latin verb *invidere*, fulfils the same role that 'enviable' would have fulfilled had it not cut its moorings. For an action, charge, or complaint is said to be invidious if it tends to excite odium, ill-will, or malicious envy. A comparison or distinction is said to be invidious if it is offensively discriminating. And an object is said to be invidious if it invites ill-feeling or envy against its possessor.

A further form of non-malicious and non-covetous

*Emulative envy* envy is *emulative envy* (i.e. *zelos, aemulatio*), which, as we have noted, Aristotle discussed in the *Rhetoric*. One may envy another his energy, efficiency, skills, or moral qualities. Such characteristics one views with admiration, wishing to have them too. With effort and dedication, one may acquire them oneself, without diminishing or impairing the other's enviable qualities. Wilfred Thesiger, in his *Arabian Sands*, tells of two Bedouin youths speaking *with envy in their voices* of an elderly and now impoverished man whose hospitality in his days of prosperity was proverbial. What they envied was his generosity.

In the following discussion, I shall disregard these forms of non-malicious envy. It is not they that are characterizable as deadly sins or vices. It is not they that are iconographically represented as a horrible old hag with snakes as hair, withered dugs, and livid complexion. That English evolved such usages that detach the notion of envy from the vicious and sinful is a matter of linguistic fact, and no philosophical investigation is going to change it. It does, however, muddy the waters. No one is going to speak of emulating the virtues of another *out of envy*, nor is one likely to describe another person who is prone to strive to better himself by emulating a good role model as being of *an envious nature* or as being an *envious person*. In investigating the conceptual character of the emotion, character trait, and motive of envy, we are interested in limpid waters in which the nexus of envy with vice is maintained.

*Roots of envy* Envy, unlike jealousy, is rooted in social comparison, self-love, and rivalry. One person envies another for his possession of something that is held, by the envier or by society at large, to be desirable. Commonly, the envier believes public esteem for himself to be reduced by comparison with the envied's possession of the desideratum (the granting of a triumph by the Senate of Rome, the award of a competitive prize). The envier must also *resent* the envied having whatever good he has, and want him not to have it. Typically, the envier wants the object of his envy for himself, for his own benefit and aggrandisement. But he *need not* actually covet it himself. He may merely maliciously want the other not to have it,[22] or to destroy the other who has it. Cassius's envy of Caesar's renown shines forth in his great dialogue with Brutus:

> I was born as free as Caesar; so were you,
> We both have fed as well, and we can both
> Endure the winter's cold as well as he:
> … and this man
> Is now become a god, and Cassius is
> A wretched creature, and must bend his body,
> If Caesar carelessly but nod on him
> …
> Why, man, he doth bestride the narrow world
> Like a Colossus, and we petty men
> Walk under his huge legs, and peep about
> To find ourselves dishonourable graves.
> Men at some time are masters of their fates:
> The fault (dear Brutus) is not in our stars,
> But in ourselves, that we are underlings.
> Brutus and Caesar: what should be in that Caesar?
> Why should that name be sounded more than yours?
> Write them together: yours is as fair a name:
> Sound them, it doth become the mouth as well:
> Weigh them, it is as heavy; conjure with 'em
> Brutus will start a spirit as soon as Caesar.
> Now, in the names of all the gods at once,
> Upon what meat does this our Caesar feed
> That he is grown so great? Age, thou art shamed.
> (*Julius Caesar*, I. 2)

*Who can be envied?* The thing envied – what the person envied supposedly has – may be a personality trait, character

---

[22] Gore Vidal self-mockingly remarked, 'Every time a friend succeeds, I die a little.'

trait, or ability. It may be a desirable object of a kind, in which case the envier may want another like it for himself, or it may be a unique object that he wants to possess himself. It may be a rank or office. Or it may be fame and glory (and, in ancient Rome, *dignitas*) and the consequent public esteem; or it may simply be the esteem of someone noteworthy. What are the constraints on whom one can, logically, envy? Aristotle made nice distinctions in this regard. The envied cannot be too far removed from the envier in time or place, or in envied feature. Rather, we envy our approximate equals 'in birth, relationship, age, disposition, distinction or wealth' (*Rhetoric*, 1387$^b$24).[23] Can a man envy the good looks of a woman? Can a Hollywood starlet envy the beauty of Helen of Troy, or only the beauty of a Hollywood star? A lesser multi-billionaire may envy Bill Gates, but can you or I? Envy is circumscribed by a reference group to which the envier belongs – beyond that, it is mere idle wishing. The envied person may be believed by the envier to merit the desideratum or not to merit it. The envier may believe himself to deserve the desideratum, or not to deserve it, but merely want it; or not want it but merely want the possessor not to have it (as Cousine Bette aimed to ruin Adeline Hulot). If the object desired is an instance of a kind, this may lead to no more than innocuous competitive emulation. But, if the object is unique and transferable, then there is a zero-sum game – wanting to obtain or attain what the other uniquely possesses. But this alone may be mere competitive rivalry, not envy. To be envious, the agent must *resent* the other's possession of the good. The envious *may* take pleasure in attaining it for themselves, and/or take malicious pleasure in the other's deprivation of it or in destroying the person envied.

*Motive of envy*  Envy, like many other emotions, can also function as a motive. For the emotion of envy furnishes a person with reasons for action that fit a general pattern of having a backward-looking reason specifying an undesired state of affairs, and action to remedy the situation, and a forward-looking reason for the attainment of the desideratum. The recurrent pattern is (very roughly) that another possesses something the envier desires him not to have, conceives of him as not meriting it, conceives of himself as more worthy of it, and (sometimes) desires to have it for himself.

---

[23] Aquinas follows Aristotle here: 'a man envies not those who are far removed from him, whether in place, time, or station, but those who are near him, and whom he strives to rival or surpass' (*Summa Theologica*, 2$^a$2$^{ae}$, q. 36.1, reply to obj. 2). Similarly, he adds, one competes with rivals within one's own class of ability.

So the envier acts to deprive the other of the object of envy and/or to attain it for himself or herself. Envy-motivated actions may range from mere malicious gossip against the person envied (nicely described by Flaubert in the Yonville ladies' gossip about Emma Bovary), to defamation, inflicting ruthless damage on the interests of the envied (as Cousine Bette destroys the fortune of the Hulot family), to bringing about their death (as Cassio brings about Caesar's). Where what is envied is a possession, the envier may drive himself to destroy the object the possession of which is envied rather than to let it fall into the hands of or be possessed by the person envied – better that no one should have it than that he should. This is spiteful destruction done out of envy.

*Self-destructiveness of envy*

Envy, carried to extremes, is also *self-destructive*, doing irreparable damage to the personality and character of the envier:

> Dame Envy is a wound infected;
> No healing is to be expected;
> Her growth, once she has set her mind
> Upon a thing, is unconfined,
> Relaxing neither night nor day
> Until she has achieved her way,
> And sleepless, cannot feel the smart
> Afflicting her in mind and heart.
> When envy sees a ship go down,
> She laughs as if she made it drown;
> She bites and gnaws to pass the hours
> And yet herself entire devours
> As Etna eats itself alone.[24]

The self-destructiveness of extreme envy is manifest in loss of self-esteem, consequent upon another's having something one lacks and on the possession of which one misguidedly hangs one's self-esteem. The envious person wants to 'be someone', and in the darkness of his soul thinks that 'being someone' amounts to possessing or attaining something that another has, and wanting to deprive him of it or to destroy him, since the other's possession shows the envier's own shortcomings. Iago remarks of Cassio that he 'hath a daily beauty in

---

[24] S. Brant, *The Ship of Fools* (1494), trans. W. Giles (Folio Society, London, 1971), ch. 53.

his life that makes me ugly' (*Othello*, V. 1). Envy involves fear of losing the esteem of others too. This engenders frustration, and sometimes gnawing self-doubt and feelings of inferiority that eat away at one's integrity.

*Envy and self-deception*   As noted, envy drags self-deception in its wake. Confronting the fact that one is envious is itself painful, since envy is indeed a vice. So a self-protective mechanism may be invoked to mask one's envy from the criticism of others and from oneself. This allows the envier to hide his envy. This may take one of at least two forms. First, one may hide one's envy from others and from oneself by apparent transmutation. One clads one's odious envy in the garb of disinterested righteous indignation at what one presents as the unmerited advantage of the person one covertly envies. This involves devaluing the other and besmirching his reputation, while elevating one's own. Thus Iago on Cassio:

> One Michael Cassio, a Florentine,
> A fellow almost damned in a fair wife,
> That never set a squadron in the field,
> Nor the division of a battle knows
> More than a spinster – unless the bookish theoric,
> Wherein the togèd consuls can propose
> As masterly as he – mere prattle, without practice,
> Is all his soldiership. But he, sir, had the election;
> And I, of whom his eyes had seen the proof
> At Rhodes, at Cyprus and on other grounds
> Christian and heathen, must be be-lee'd and calm'd
> By debitor and creditor. This counter-caster,
> He, in good time, must his lieutenant be.
> (*Othello*, I. 1)

A second way of masking one's envy, especially from oneself, and of mitigating it as well, is to devalue what one envies. Thus Proust's description of his grandmother:

> My grandmother's sisters having expressed a desire to mention to Swann this reference to him in the *Figaro*, my great-aunt dissuaded them. Whenever she saw in others an advantage, however trivial, which she herself lacked, she would persuade herself that it was no advantage at all, but a drawback, and would pity so as not to have to envy them.
> (*Swann's Way*, ch. 1)

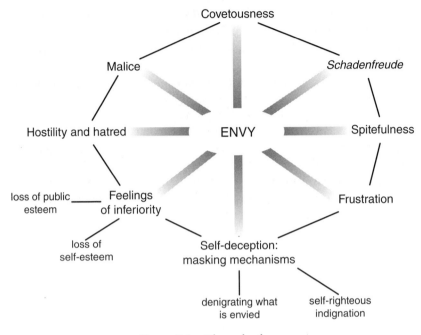

**Figure 7.1**   *The web of envy*

So 'sour grapes' sometimes conceal futile envy. Figure 7.1 gives a schematic overview of the web of envy.

*Is envy unavoidable?* Is envy an inevitable corollary of human nature? Herodotus wrote that 'Envy is natural to man and has been so since the beginning' (*Histories*, III. 80. 3). Spinoza elaborated:

> for the most part human nature is so constituted that men pity the unfortunate and envy the fortunate, and [envy them] with greater hate the more they love the thing they imagine the other to possess. We see, then, that from the same property of human nature from which it follows that men are compassionate, it also follows that the same men are envious and ambitious. (*Ethics*, III. 32, schol.)

Melanie Klein, in modern times, averred that 'envy is an oral-sadistic and anal-sadistic expression of destructive impulses operative from the beginning of life, and … it has a constitutional basis'.[25] It does indeed seem to be a natural corollary of the desire for and pursuit of

---

[25] M. Klein, *Envy and Gratitude* (Tavistock, London, 1957), p. ix.

what is, or is thought to be, valuable. If one pursues a good and finds that another has it or if one recognizes as a good something another has, one may wish for it. However, there seems no reason to suppose that envy is an inevitable or unavoidable consequence of this. For while merely wishing one had what another has is one of the roots of envy, it needs watering to grow into an acquisitive desire, and manure to evolve into resentment and malice.

# 8

# Jealousy

## 1. Different centres of variation

Having drawn a reasonably sharp dividing line to differentiate envy from jealousy, and having clarified the nature of envy, we can now focus our attention on jealousy. This possessive emotion often wreaks havoc among those who love each other. It can be the cause of deep unhappiness, and in its extreme forms it is destructive both of the soul of those who feel it, and of their relationship with those they love. There are many different forms of jealousy. These can be brought to light by scrutiny of grammar, which discloses the scope and limits of our concept of jealousy and hence too of the emotion it subsumes.

We noted in chapter 7 that 'jealousy' and its cognates are derived from the Late Latin borrowing of the post-classical Greek noun *zelotupia* and adjective *zelotupos*. From these origins (and from the older *zelos*) developed 'jealous', 'jealousy' (from Old French *gelosie* and *jalousie*), as well as 'zeal', 'zealous', and 'zealotry'.[1] With such mixed ancestry, it should not be surprising to find that jealousy has a number of different, though related, centres of variation (see fig. 7.1).

---

[1] German went down a different road, combining the word for zeal or passion: *Eifer*, with *sucht*, i.e. illness, mania, addiction. Hence Grillparzer's pun 'Die Eifersucht ist eine Leidenschaft, die mit Eifer sucht, was Leiden schafft' (Jealousy is a passion that zealously seeks that which causes suffering).

*The Passions: A Study of Human Nature*, First Edition. P. M. S. Hacker.
© 2018 John Wiley & Sons Ltd. Published 2018 by John Wiley & Sons Ltd.

A standard logico-grammatical form of the verb
*Logico-grammatical* 'to be jealous' is 'A is (or feels) jealous of B's love
*form* for C'. The object of B's love is commonly another
person, but it need not be: one may be jealous of one's beloved's love
for and dedication to their work or art, or of their affection for their
dog or horse, or of their love of honour (hence Lovelace's avowal to
his wife as he goes off to war: 'I could not love thee, dear, so much, /
Lov'd I not Honour more'). All that is necessary is that B's love or
affection for C, whoever or whatever C may be, is felt by A to dimin-
ish B's love and loving attentiveness to A, and to resent it.

'( ) is jealous of ( )'s love for ( )' is a three-place predicate, but it
does not signify either a triadic or a dyadic relation, since it does not
signify a relation at all. This is an intentional use of the verb 'to be
jealous' – B's love for C may not exist (and one cannot stand in a relation to what does not exist) and C may not exist. The *nominalization-
accusative* of this form of jealousy (*what*[2] A is jealous of) is *B's love
for C*. But that does not imply that jealousy is a dyadic relation
between A and B's love for C, since B may not love C. Othello was
jealous of Desdemona's love for Cassio, but in fact Desdemona did
not love Cassio at all. Louis Trevelyan was jealous of his wife Emily's
love for Colonel Osborne, although she did not in fact love him (in
Trollope's *He Knew He Was Right*). What is the *object-accusative*
(given in answer to 'Whom/what is A jealous of?')?[3] We typically
answer the question 'Of whom is A jealous?' by specifying A's rival,
who threatens (or appears to threaten) to deprive A, or has deprived
A, of the love he cherishes. The binary grammatical structure 'A is
jealous of C' is parasitic on the tertiary one. In this use we may say
that Othello was jealous of Cassio and Louis Trevelyan of Colonel
Osborne. Note that the object-accusative likewise *need not* exist for it
to be true that A is jealous of B's love or friendship for C. It is an
intentional object-accusative. In Wilde's *The Importance of being
Earnest*, Gwendolyn did not in fact feel jealous of Ernest's apparent
friendship for the imaginary Bunbury, but she might well have.

We also use the verb 'to be jealous' in a different
*Protective jealousy* logico-grammatical structure, namely, 'A is jealous
of his honour/name/reputation/privileges'. The
object-accusative of this form of jealousy need not be a material thing.
But one must believe oneself to possess it: one cannot be jealous of one's

---

[2] This is the interrogative wh-pronoun, not the relative pronoun.
[3] Here the wh-pronoun 'what' is the relative pronoun, not the interrogative one.

reputation if one believes one has none, or of one's honour if one believes one has lost it. I shall call this *protective jealousy of status*. Strikingly, the modifier 'feel' would be out of place here. A man or woman may *be* jealous of their honour (as was Isabella in *Measure for Measure*), but not *feel* jealous of their honour. Protective jealousy amounts to being *zealous* in the protection of some aspect of one's standing, either in the eyes of others or in one's own eyes. Isabella is jealous of her honour – zealous in the protection of her chastity with which her honour is bound up. Cyrano de Bergerac is likewise jealous of his honour, which is bound up with protecting his good name from the slightest insult. What they jealously protect is something on which their self-esteem rests. Protective jealousy for such non-material things that one has and values need not be vicious. To be jealous of one's good name (as was John Proctor in Miller's *The Crucible* (see pp. 176f.)) is no vice. Nor need someone who is jealous of his honour be acting wrongly (Isabella), although such jealousy may motivate various wrong-doings if it involves a distortion of values (Cyrano de Bergerac, despite Rostand's best efforts, is a bully and selfishly deceitful).

*Material protective jealousy*                          A related logico-grammatical form of protective jealousy involves a substantive object-accusative. The object accusative may signify (i) a material possession, or (ii) a person one views as belonging to one. The former kind of jealousy is manifest by those who *jealously* guard and protect material things they own – an estate, a garden, an art collection, or a library. There *need be* nothing vicious in that. Harold Nicolson and Vita Sackville-West lovingly created, over decades, their beautiful gardens at Sissinghurst, and doubtless lovingly and jealously protected them. I shall call this *material protective jealousy*. The latter kind is manifest, for example, by Othello and by Pozdnyshev in Tolstoy's *The Kreutzer Sonata*. I shall call this *personal possessive jealousy*.

Material protective jealousy may be *possessive*, *non-possessive*, or *mixed*. For what one values and protects may be above all one's *ownership* of what one values ('It's mine, *mine, mine!*'), or what one values above all may be *the treasured thing* one owns. These are two poles between which material protective jealousy may fluctuate. One may jealously guard one's great art collection, not allowing anything in it to be lent and but rarely showing it to others (e.g. Albert G. Barnes, who established the Barnes Foundation in Philadelphia). Even more perversely, a miser may jealously guard his hoard of gold (e.g. Silas Marner in George Eliot's eponymous novel). What he cares for above all is his *ownership* of it.

It may be that one is not so much jealous and jealously protective of *one's owning* whatever it is one is jealous of, but rather of *the integrity of what one owns*. This is nicely exemplified by Mrs Gereth in Henry James's *The Spoils of Poynton*, whose protective jealousy for her great collection of antiques is not for her ownership of it, but for the integrity of her collection, on the one hand, and its being in the hands of someone who will appreciate it, on the other. So her jealousy for Poynton Hall and its collection is not motivated by cupidity. Her young friend and protégé, Fleda

> saw how little vulgar avidity had to do with this rigor. It was not the crude love of possession; it was the need to be faithful to a trust and loyal to an idea. The idea was surely noble; it was that of the beauty Mrs Gereth had so patiently and consummately wrought. Pale but radiant, with her back to the wall, she rose there like a heroine guarding a treasure. To give up the ship was to flinch from her duty; there was something in her eyes that declared she would die at her post. ... Her fanaticism gave her a new distinction, and Fleda perceived almost with awe that she had never carried herself so well. She trod the place like a reigning queen or proud usurper; full as it was of splendid pieces, it could show in these days no ornament so effective as its menacing mistress. (*The Spoils of Poynton*, ch. 5)[4]

This non-possessive protective jealousy for material things, in Mrs Gereth's case, is the fruit of egotism, and leads to much grief and sorrow. But it need not be so. Many great collectors have donated their collection to their country in their lifetime, or given it to one who appreciates it. Others donate their cherished collection only after their death, jealously guarding it as their possession during their lifetime, but caring zealously for its integrity and preservation after their demise.

One is also said to be jealous of a person one views *Personal possessive* as *belonging to one*. This too is a form – arguably a *jealousy* morally degenerate form – of possessive jealousy.

It is manifest in one's description of someone as a jealous husband, wife, lover, father, or mother. In such cases, the husband, wife, or lover views their spouse or partner as belonging to them. In shame societies, the honour of the married man is bound up with the honour of his wife and daughters, who can bring shame upon him, his name, and his extended family by their failure to

---

[4] Poynton Hall is a successor to Thornfield Hall in *Jane Eyre* and an ancestral model for Manderley in Daphne du Maurier's *Rebecca*.

comply with the ethos governing the conduct of women. Hence a man must jealously – and zealously – guard his wife and daughters from contact with those who may endanger their honour, and hence his honour. Such possessive personal jealousy can be said to be morally degenerate in so far as the person jealously protected (and perhaps loved) is commodified and viewed as a *possession*, as an object *owned*. Honour killing is the sanction for female transgression. But the motive for honour killing is often not jealousy at love withdrawn, but injured pride.

An extreme of personal possessive jealousy and its evil is chillingly described in Robert Browning's great dramatic monologue 'My Last Duchess'.[5] It describes the projection of possessive material jealousy onto a marital relationship that is actually devoid of any love whatsoever. 'She is my wife' is perversely confused with 'She is *mine*', which in turn pathologically merges with 'It is *mine*'. Alfonso II, Duke of Ferrara, is showing his art collection to a visiting emissary from the Duke of Tyrol (with whom Alfonso is negotiating for the hand of his niece). He comes to a curtained portrait of his previous duchess, which he draws back to show his guest:

> That's my last Duchess painted on the wall,
> Looking as if she were alive. I call
> That piece a wonder now: Frà Pandolf's hands
> Worked busily a day, and there she stands.
> …
> … She thanked men, – good! but thanked
> Somehow – I know not how – as if she ranked
> My gift of a nine hundred year's old name
> With anybody's gift. Who'd stoop to blame
> This sort of trifling? Even had you skill
> In speech – (which I have not) – to make your will
> Quite clear to such an one, and say 'Just this
> Or that in you disgusts me; here you miss,
> Or there exceed the mark' – and if she let
> Herself be lessoned so, nor plainly set
> Her wits to yours, forsooth, and made excuse,
> – E'en then would be some stooping; and I choose
> Never to stoop. Oh sir, she smiled, no doubt
> Whene'er I passed her; but who passed without
> Much the same smile? This grew; I gave commands;

[5] The poem is based on the rumored murder of the sixteen-year-old Lucrezia de' Medici by her husband Duke Alfonso II of Ferrara in 1561.

Then all smiles stopped together. There she stands
As if alive. Will't please you rise? We'll meet
The company below then.

The duchess was evidently valued merely as a decorative chattel, so
the duke's pathological jealousy for her is in effect material possessive
jealousy – as for an object in his art collection. She was *his*. But there
is no hint that he felt any love for her. Nor is there any intimation of
sexual jealousy – he was not jealous of her love or even affection for
another. His murder of her was motivated merely by her cordial
attitude towards others, and for her failure to behave as he thought
befitted a wife he owned – for even her smiles should have been his
alone. The duchess, in the duke's corrupt eye, was merely a zealously
protected, exclusive, possession.

Whether protective jealousy in general is vicious or not depends on
what it is that is loved, cherished, or valued; why it is valued; whether
it merits being thus valued; the moral and psychological cost, to oneself
and to others, of one's protective feelings; and what one does in one's
zeal. (For a schematic representation of the varieties of jealousy, see
fig. 8.1: note that the two main branches are not exclusive: jealousy for
love may be accompanied by zealous protectiveness of person.)

So, in the form 'A is jealous of B's love for C', the use of the verb is
intentional, the nominalization-accusative is 'B's love for C' and the
object-accusative is 'C'. Such interpersonal jealousy is jealousy for the
love of another that one fears losing or fears one has lost to a third
person or to a distraction. It is an enduring, and often pervasive,
emotion. This may be of at least two kinds according to the character
of the love that is perceived to be threatened: rivalry for sexual love

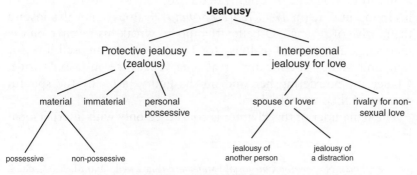

**Figure 8.1**  *Varieties of jealousy*

and affection, and rivalry for loving care. Rivalry for loving care is manifest, for example, in sibling rivalry for parental love. Rivalry for sexual love and affection is manifest between spouses and an extra-marital lover, or between lover, partner, and rival.

Protective jealousy is a proneness. Protective, imper-
*Categorial* sonal, immaterial jealousy is not a proneness to *feel*
*differentiations* jealous about anything, but to be zealous in the protection of one or another aspect of one's social status.
Material possessive jealousy is a proneness to guard and protect mate-rial possessions from others who might dispossess one, to keep these chattels for oneself alone, to resent others using them or borrowing them, or, in the case of land, to resent anyone trespassing upon it, no matter how harmlessly. Personal possessive jealousy, however, is not a proneness. It is an enduring emotion that is felt, and that is commonly pervasive. It is a complex blend – typically involving fear of loss of love, viewing the love another has bestowed upon one as a right, view-ing with suspicion the amiable advances of others towards the person whose love one thinks is threatened, and so forth – coupled with the obsessive thought that 'He/She is *mine*'. But, as we have seen, it *need not* involve love at all – in some forms it may involve only a perceived threat to one's honour and pride. Jealousy, as a character trait ('He has a jealous personality'), is a proneness – a disposition to be jealous, a tendency to be apprehensive of threats to the love given one by a per-son one loves, to fear the loss of that love to another. (But remember that a human disposition is very unlike inanimate dispositions.[6]

The noun 'jealousy' signifies not only an emotion, but
*Jealousy and* also a motive. For one may act 'out of jealousy'. It was
*motivation* jealousy that drove Marcel to spy upon Albertine
(in Proust's *The Captive*), and jealousy and resentment at his erotic bondage that motivated Pozdnyshev's horrific murder of his innocent wife (in *The Kreutzer Sonata*). Jealousy may also inspire the motive of revenge. Othello attempts to wreak his revenge on the innocent Cassio out of jealousy for Desdemona's supposed love for him, and Medea horrifically wreaks her vengeance on Jason's bride, Glauce, by murdering her, and on the guilty Jason by the spiteful murder of their two children.

The remainder of this chapter is concerned only with interpersonal jealousy.

[6] See *Human Nature: the Categorial Framework* (Blackwell, Oxford, 2007), ch. 4, sections 7–9.

## 2. Iconography

*Iconography and physiognomy*    It is striking that there appears to be no rich iconography, let alone iconology, of jealousy. Rather surprisingly, it seems as muted a theme in painting as it is in philosophy and theology. In Bronzino's fascinating painting in the National Gallery, London, that goes by the name of *An Allegory with Venus and Cupid*, the figure on the lower left is generally agreed to be Jealousy, tearing out her hair with a scream of anguish. Nevertheless, jealousy has few, if any, identifying iconographic attributes. In the eighteenth century, long after the decline in the use of identifying iconography, Charles Le Brun attempted to codify the physiognomy of jealousy for the guidance of painters:

> Jealousy is expressed by the wrinkled brow, the eyebrow drawn down and frowning, the eye sparkling, the pupil hidden under the eyebrow and turning towards the object which causes the passion, looking at it out of the corner of the eye while the head is turned away; the pupil must appear in ceaseless movement, and full of fire, as also are the whites of the eye and the eyelids; the nostrils are pale, open and more apparent than usual, and drawn back, which makes folds appear in the cheeks. The mouth may be shut, and showing that the teeth are clenched; the lower lip is thrust out beyond the upper, and the corners of the mouth are pulled back and downwards; the muscles of the jaw appear hollow ... One part of the face will be enflamed, another yellowish; the extremities livid; and the area around the eyes, and even the whites of the eyes will be of a fiery colour; the cheeks will be yellow, the lips pale or livid.[7]

Of course, a jealous person could not maintain such a facial appearance for long. What Le Brun is describing is *a jealous look* that a painter might wish to depict.

*Pictorial representations of jealousy*    The subject of jealousy in painting became prominent only in the nineteenth century, for example, in James Ward's *Ignorance, Envy and Jealousy* (1838) or in Anthony Frederick Sandys's *Jealousy* (1890). In the latter, the female subject of which *looks askance* at something or someone we cannot see; she is surrounded

---

[7] Charles Le Brun, *Méthode pour Apprendre à Dessiner les Passions* [Method for Learning How to Draw the Emotions] (Francois van der Plaats, Amsterdam, 1702).

with yellow marigolds, and a cartouche carries Robert Herrick's seventeenth-century poem 'How Marigolds Came Yellow':

> Jealous girls these sometimes were,
> While they liv'd or lasted here:
> Turn'd to flowers, still they be
> Yellow marked for jealousy'

At the turn of the twentieth century Edvard Munch produced a number of powerful paintings on the theme of sexual jealousy, as did Gustav Klimt, whose extraordinary decadent painting of Jealousy glows with gold and yellow. (The theme of Medea murdering her children was popular among late nineteenth-century Romantics and classical revivalists (e.g. Delacroix, Sandys, Evelyn De Morgan).)

*Jealousy and the humours*  In Bronzino's painting, Jealousy (like *Invidia*) has a livid complexion (a mixture of yellow and black bile).[8] Herrick's poem in Sandys's painting, however, associates jealousy with yellow. In this, he too was following the doctrine of the humours, which explained jealousy by reference to an excess of the choleric humour of yellow bile that causes anger, irritability, boldness, envy, jealousy, and courage (we noted, in chapter 7, the link, in German, between envy (*Neid*) and the colour yellow). The associated colours were rendered even more complicated by literary fancies. Shakespeare added to the confusion by his recurrent averral that jealousy is 'green-eyed'. Iago warns Othello: 'O beware, my lord, of jealousy; / It is the green-eyed monster which doth mock / The meat it feeds on' (*Othello*, III. 3), and Portia similarly refers to 'green-eyed jealousy' (*The Merchant of Venice*, II. 2). This has become a byword in English literature, although it appears to be unknown why Shakespeare made this curious connection between jealousy and green eyes.

## 3. Jealousy: connective analysis

*Jealousy and exclusive possession*  Interpersonal jealousy is essentially possessive. The person of whose love one is jealous is viewed as *belonging* to one – *my* husband/wife; *my* betrothed; *my* lover. One fears the loss of this relationship with the person one loves. One cannot bear the thought, let alone the fact,

[8] Note that the Latin *livor* (blue-grey – the colour of a bruise, a bruise) became an expression used derivatively to denote jealousy or envy (by both Descartes and Kant).

of sharing that love and/or losing that status. So jealousy characteristically involves an *exclusive relationship*, or a *desire* for an exclusive relationship, with someone loved. If it is merely a desire the fulfilment of which is threatened by a rival, then it must be accompanied by hope of fulfilment – otherwise it would merely be envying the other who gained the love. So Levin, in *Anna Karenina*, is jealous of Kitty's relationship with Vronsky even before he, Levin, has declared his love for her – for he hopes for her love and hand in marriage. If there is an established relationship of love with another, then jealousy involves a perceived or suspected threat to the exclusivity of that relationship. The jealous person then realizes or fears that what was an exclusive love will now either (i) *have to be shared*, as in the case of the jealousy of a first-born for his newly arrived sibling, or when a spouse or lover exhibits or appears to exhibit undue affection for another who is viewed as a competitor for attention (e.g. Louis Trevelyan's jealousy of Colonel Osborne and Levin's (post-marital) jealousy of Vasenka Veslovsky), or when a spouse is having an extramarital affair or a simultaneous affair with another; or (ii) *be lost altogether* (to another lover or prospective spouse). So there must be an actual or imagined rival for the affections of the beloved. This may be *non-personal* – as when the love and affection one craves from the person one loves is diverted from oneself into a passion for advancement, glory, creative work or even for a hobby. Alternatively, the rival may be *personal*. In such cases, the jealous person may *fear* the loss of love previously given, or, if it is actually lost, may still *harbour hope of regaining* the cherished relationship (Deianeira's jealousy of Heracles' love for Iole in Sophocles' *Trachiniai*). But the love that was cherished may be destroyed by the very thought that it has been unforgivably shared with another (as Angel Clare's love for Tess is destroyed on her post-marital confession that she had been raped by Alec d'Urberville). However, the love may transmute into hatred (Othello). When love is transmuted into hatred, accompanied by an overwhelming sense of betrayal, resentment at one's own sexual bondage, rage at sexual infidelity, outrage at the ingratitude for the intimacies of a previously shared life, then jealousy, may motivate murder (Medea, Othello, Pozdnyshev) or wanton cruelty (Louis Trevelyan, who denies his wife access to a beloved child).

*Jealousy of sexual love/ deprivation of love*
Jealousy may be *of* actual or suspected sexual love of another or *of* loving care and affection for another. The non-sexual love of which one might be or become jealous may take various

forms, according to the relationship between the people involved. One may be jealous of the other's relationship to (i) another person or persons, or (ii) to his engagement with an activity or concern. In such cases, one fears (or feels) deprivation of the loving attention to which one feels entitled. This may be exhibited in marital jealousy of a friendship (e.g. Louis Trevelyan's jealousy of his wife's friendship with Colonel Osborne, who was not a sexual rival at all). It may be manifest in a father's jealousy for the attention his wife gives to their newborn child and her loss of interest in him. It may be a son's rivalry with his father for his mother's love or a daughter's rivalry with her mother for her father's love (if Freud is right, this *is* a form of sexual love, albeit unconscious). It may be sibling rivalry for parental love (as in the tale of Jacob and Esau). It may involve a husband's or wife's jealousy of the friendships, interests, or concerns of their spouse. A wife may feel jealous of her husband's commitment to his work or art, or of the evenings spent in the pub with his mates, or of the time spent on his hobbies or interests. Here the jealousy arises out of felt deprivation of loving attention to which she has, or believes she has, a claim (e.g. Anna's jealousy of Vronsky's visits to his clubs and friends). Mrs Strickland's love for her husband, in Maugham's *The Moon and Sixpence*, turns from jealousy to bitter hatred when she discovers that he has abandoned her not for another woman (which she could have tolerated), but for the sake of painting. A mother's possessive love for her son may be transformed into jealousy when he, in due course, falls in love and brings his fiancée home. Similarly, a father's possessive love for his daughter may be manifest in jealousy when a young man falls in love with her. In both cases, the jealousy is in part fear of the loss of filial love. To what extent it may involve a degree of sublimated sexual love is moot. It is striking that one can be jealous of the dead, as the second Mrs de Winter was jealous of the dead Rebecca in Daphne du Maurier's eponymous novel, for she was jealous of Maxim's supposed love for Rebecca.

*Pathological possessiveness of jealousy*

Sexual jealousy may be between spouses, or lovers, heterosexual or homosexual. It is commonly a vice and, in its typical consequences, it is vicious. As Shakespeare nicely observed:

> For where Love reigns, disturbing Jealousy
> Doth call himself Affection's sentinel;
> Gives false alarms, suggesteth mutiny,
> And in a peaceful hour doth cry 'Kill, kill!'
>
> (*Venus and Adonis*)

Sexual jealousy is often pathologically possessive. The person loved is thought to *belong* to one. The love with which they have graced one is *a possession one owns*. One cannot bear the thought of sharing or losing it. The body of the person loved likewise belongs to one – it is *for one's use*, and the thought of sharing it with another is the stuff that the jealous person's nightmares are made of. In one of Othello's more repulsive revelations of his jealousy, he views Desdemona as a sheath for his masculine tumescence:

> I had rather be a toad,
> And live upon the vapour in a dungeon,
> Than keep a corner in the thing I love
> For other's uses. (*Othello*, II. 3)[9]

The onset of interpersonal jealousy may be swift, requiring only an occasion that induces realization – as when Emma hears of Harriet Smith's hopes of wedding Mr Knightley in Jane Austen's *Emma*: 'it darted through her mind, with the speed of an arrow, that Mr Knightley must marry no one but herself!' (III. 11).

*Pervasiveness and obsessiveness*    Like envy, jealousy is characteristically both pervasive and obsessive. Although it may be sparked off in an instant, it is not a sudden perturbation or spasm nor is it a series of perturbations or spasms. This, again, is nicely described by Jane Austen when characterizing Captain Wentworth's jealousy of Mr Elliot in *Persuasion* – for it 'had influenced him in everything he had said and done, or omitted to say or do, in the last four-and-twenty hours' (*Persuasion*, II. 11). Once the green-eyed monster is aroused, it may, *in extremis*, gnaw away constantly and there may be no respite.

*Epistemological pathology of jealousy*    Sexual jealousy breeds pathological suspicions, distrust, doubt, and uncertainty. So Othello cries out in his torment:

> By the world,
> I think my wife be honest, and I think she is not:
> I think that thou art just, and think thou art not:
> I'll have some proof.
>
> (*Othello* III. 3)

---

[9] As Spinoza dryly observes: 'he who imagines that a woman he loves prostitutes herself to another not only will be saddened, because his own appetite is restrained, but also will be repelled by her, because he is forced to join the image of the thing he loves to the shameful parts and excretions of the other' (*Ethics*, III. 35, schol.).

And Swann, in Proust's *Swann's Way*, describes the epistemological pathology of jealousy: the shame of spying outside a window, of putting adroitly provocative questions to casual witnesses, of bribing servants, of listening at doors. The pathological doubts and suspicions torture the jealous, nourishing their anxiety, fear of loss and insecurity – wonderfully depicted in *Othello*:

> Avaunt, be gone, thou hast set me on the rack:
> I swear tis better to be much abus'd
> Than but to know a little.
> What sense had I of her stolen hours of lust?
> I saw't not, thought it not, it harm'd me not:
> I slept the next night well, was free and merry;
> I found not Cassio's kisses on her lips:
> He that is robb'd, not wanting what is stolen,
> Let him not know't, and he's not robb'd at all.
> ....
> I had been happy, if the general camp,
> Pioneers and all, had tasted her sweet body,
> So I had nothing known.
> ...
> Villain, be sure thou prove my love a whore,
> Be sure of it, give me ocular proof.
>
> (*Othello*, III. 3)

In extreme cases, the anxieties of jealousy do not even need a suspected personal object-accusative, intentional nor non-intentional. The mere *possibility* of transfer of love suffices for the self-devouring torments of jealousy. So it is with Anna as she fears the loss of Vronsky's love:

> In her eyes the whole of him, with all his habits, ideas, desires, with all his spiritual and physical temperament, was one thing – love for women, and that love, she felt, ought to be entirely concentrated on her alone. That love was less; consequently, as she reasoned, he must have transferred part of his love to other women or to another woman – and she was jealous. She was jealous not of any particular woman but of the decrease of his love. Not having got an object for her jealousy, she was on the lookout for it. At the slightest hint she transferred her jealousy from one object to another. At one time she was jealous of those low women with whom he might so easily renew his old bachelor ties; then she was jealous of the society women he might meet; then she was jealous of the imaginary girl whom he might want to marry, for whose sake he would break with her. And this last form of jealousy tortured

her most of all, especially as he had unwarily told her, in a moment of frankness, that his mother knew him so little that she had had the audacity to try and persuade him to marry the young Princess Sorokina. (*Anna Karenina*, VII. 23)

What accompanies these self-inflicted tortures is (and in some cases may be primarily) hurt pride (see, e.g., Trollope's description of George Western's feelings about his young wife, Cecilia, who he thinks has betrayed him by failing to disclose her antecedent engagement to Sir Francis Geraldine (*Kept in the Dark*, ch. 18)).

*Consequent shame and humiliation*
A consequence of jealousy of an actual or imagined affair that one's spouse is having with another may be twofold. First, shame (consequent upon injured pride) and humiliation – the injured person, beset by jealousy, feels humiliated by sexual rejection or the loss of sexual exclusiveness, by the shattering of the exclusive relationship of the marital bond or the lovers' commitment, by the disvaluation of the shared life and intimacies previously enjoyed. So too the jealous husband may feel shamed by having the wreckage of the relationship exposed to public knowledge and gossip, and by incurring public derision and contempt for wearing the horns of a cuckold.[10] Secondly, the injured person may have recourse to subterfuges, lies, snooping, and spying to satisfy his pathological doubts and suspicions. This in turn breeds feelings of humiliation and shame at stooping so low, with consequent loss of self-respect (e.g. Louis Trevelyan's self-tormenting reflections on having hired a detective to spy upon his imagined rival for his wife's love (*He Knew He Was Right*, ch. 25)).

The fevered imagination of the sexually jealous conjures up images of sexual intimacies, hitherto shared with the beloved, being now granted to the rival. Such images are the salt with which the jealous rub their open wounds:

That was the worst period of all: it is my profession to imagine, to think in images: fifty times through the day, and immediately I woke during the night, a curtain would rise and the play would begin: always the same play, Sarah making love, Sarah with X, doing the same things we had done together, Sarah kissing in her own particular way, arching

---

[10] The terminology and imagery are interesting. 'Cuckold' is derived from 'cuckoo', by way of the idea that another man has planted an alien egg in the nest. It is much less clear why, in so many European languages, the cuckolded male is said to have had horns planted upon his head.

herself in the act of sex and uttering that cry like pain, Sarah in abandonment. I would take pills at night to make me sleep quickly, but I
never found any pills that would keep me asleep till daylight. (Graham
Greene, *The End of the Affair*, ch. 6)

This, almost unavoidably, leads to feelings of inadequacy, both sexual
and emotional. In what way had one failed the person one loves or
loved?

*Consequent resentment*
*and anger*
    A complementary consequence (sometimes
masking one's feelings of inadequacy) are feelings
of resentment and anger at one's lover's infidelity, and rage at the thought of his amorous
coupling with another. Euripides' Medea anticipated Congreve's 'Nor
Hell a fury like a woman scorned':

> Oh in all things but this,
> I know how full of fears a woman is,
> And faint at need, and shrinking from the light
> Of battle: but once spoil her of her right
> In man's love, and there moves, I warn thee well,
> No bloodier spirit between heaven and hell.[11]

And Tolstoy describes the murderous rage of jealousy run amok:

'Yes, offended, humiliated, and dishonoured, and after that to hold me
still responsible,' I thought, and suddenly a rage, such a hatred invaded
me as I do not remember ever having felt before. For the first time I
desired to express this hatred physically. I leaped upon her, but at the
same moment I understood my condition, and I asked myself whether
it would be well for me to abandon myself to my fury. And I answered
myself that it would be well, that it would frighten her, and instead of
resisting, I lashed and spurred myself on, and was glad to feel my anger
boiling more and more fiercely.

'Go away, or I will kill you!' I cried, purposely, and I grasped her by
the arm. She did not go away. Then I twisted her arm, and pushed her
away violently.

'What is the matter with you? Come to your senses!' she shrieked.

'Go away,' I roared louder than ever, rolling my eyes wildly, 'It takes
you to put me into such a fury. I do not answer for myself! Go away!'

---

[11] Euripides, *Medea*, trans. G. Murray (Oxford University Press, London, 1906).

In abandoning myself to my anger, I became steeped in it, and I wanted to commit some violent act to show the force of my fury. I felt a terrible desire to beat her, to kill her, but I realized that that could not be, and I restrained myself.' (Tolstoy, *The Kreutzer Sonata*, ch. 22)

The endless nagging suspicions, the feelings of inadequacy, the sense of betrayal, the feverish imagination of sexual infidelity, lead to helplessness, loneliness, and self-torment that may take different forms. In the repulsive case of Pozdnyshev, Tolstoy describes the horrors of extreme possessive sexual jealousy in which the person with whom one was previously in love has become a mere object for sexual satisfaction:

'I must consider,' I said to myself, 'whether what I think is true, whether there is any reason to torment myself.' I sat down, wishing to reflect quietly; but directly, instead of the peaceful reflections, the same began again. Instead of the reasoning, the pictures.

And again it all began. Ah, what torture! It is not to a hospital filled with syphilitic patients that I would take a young man to deprive him of the desire for women, but into my soul, to show him the demon which tore it. The frightful part was that I recognized in myself an indisputable right to the body of my wife, as if her body were entirely mine. At the same time I felt I could not possess this body, that it was not mine, that she could do with it as she liked, and that she liked to do with it as I did not like. And I was powerless against him and against her. (Tolstoy, *The Kreutzer Sonata*, ch. 25)

In a different key, Swann describes the same desolation of spirit at the enormous anguish of not knowing at every hour of the day and night what Odette had been doing, of not possessing her wholly, at all times, and in all places.

With this much to bear, it is not surprising that the *Jealousy and* jealous have recourse to self-deception, which is both *self-deception* part of their syndrome of the suspicions of jealousy and a mask to conceal their jealousy from themselves. To admit such jealousy, even to oneself, is sometimes intolerable. So we find Louis Trevelyan, when first seized by jealousy as he sits in his study, convincing himself that any such feeling on his part would be a monstrous injury to his wife, that what he felt was not really jealousy (Trollope, *He Knew He Was Right*, ch. 1). Similarly, the gentle Levin, soon after his marriage to Kitty, after seeing Veslovsky flirting with her, confronts his young wife with a complete lack of self-understanding:

'You must understand that I'm not jealous, that's a nasty word. I can't be jealous, and believe that … I can't say what I feel, but this is awful … I'm not jealous, but I'm wounded, humiliated that anybody dare think, that anybody dare look at you with eyes like that' (Tolstoy, *Anna Karenina*, VI. 7). Othello, having murdered Desdemona, and about to commit suicide after Iago's treachery has been disclosed, still cannot face the fact of his pathological jealousy. For he tells Lodovico:

> I pray you in your letters,
> When you shall these unlucky deeds relate,
> Speak of them as they are; nothing extenuate,
> Nor set down aught in malice, then must you speak
> Of one that lov'd not wisely, but too well;
> Of one not easily jealous, but being wrought,
> Perplex'd in the extreme.
>
> (*Othello*, V. 2)

But the scarlet threads running through the story of Othello are his own persistent self-deception, his egotism, and the role he unselfconsciously assumes as a protective persona for a black mercenary in an alien land. He had not loved well, let alone wisely. Indeed, it was not so much Desdemona that he had *ever* lov'd, as the *idea* of his loving her.

The self-deception invited by jealousy can stretch to cool and calm reflection on murderous intent. This is wonderfully described by Theodor Fontane in his *Effi Briest*. Baron von Instetten has discovered (while searching in his beloved wife Effi's's sewing table) that, seven years earlier, she had had a brief affair with a Major Crampas. Now, discussing the matter with his friend Wüllersdorf, he talks himself into the unavoidability of challenging that officer to a duel, in which he (being a first-class shot) will kill him:

> Wüllersdorf nodded. 'I'm with you there entirely, Innstetten. I might well feel the same. But if that is how you view the matter and you tell me, 'I love this woman so much, I can forgive her everything', and if we take that other aspect into account, the fact that it's all so far in the past, like something that happened on another planet, well, if that's the way it is, then why all the fuss, Innstetten?'
>
> 'Because, in spite of all that, it has to be. I've thought it through this way and that. We're not just separate individuals, we're part of a whole, and we must always consider the whole, we're entirely dependent on it. If it were possible to live in isolation, I could let it go. Then I would be the one bearing the burden I had taken up myself, true happiness would

be a thing of the past, but many, many people have to live without this "true happiness", and I would have to do that too – and I'd be able to. You don't need to be happy, and in no sense do you have a right to be, and it's not necessary to eliminate the person who has taken your happiness away from you. If you're willing to turn your back on the world for the rest of your life, you can let him go. But there's a something that has developed within our social existence, it's there and we have become accustomed to judging everything according to its laws. And disregarding it is not possible; society would despise us, and eventually we would despise ourselves as well and be unable to bear it and blow our brains out. ... It's not about hatred or anything like that, I don't want to have blood on my hands because of the happiness that's been taken away from me; but that – tyrannical, if you like – social something is not concerned with charm, nor with love, nor with the lapse of time. I have no choice. I have to.' (*Effi Briest*, ch. 27)

Here it is *arguable* that jealousy, injured pride, and desire for vengeance are given rein by a self-deceptive mask of social obligation, that is, in effect, invoked to warrant murder and, indeed, the destruction of his marriage and the very love he craved and now spurns.

Yet another form of self-deception consequent upon the sexual infidelity of one's spouse or lover is to deny the very love one bore the person whose love one has lost. So Karenin, after Anna has confessed her love for Vronsky, persuades himself that he had never really loved Anna at all:

'No honour, no heart, no religion; a depraved woman. I knew it and have seen it all along, though I tried out of pity for her to deceive myself,' he thought. And he really believed that he had seen it all along. He went on to recall incidents of their past life, and things in which he had never seen anything wrong before now plainly showed that she had been a depraved woman. 'I made a mistake when I linked my life to hers; but there was nothing blameworthy in my mistake, and therefore I am not to be unhappy. I am not the guilty one', he told himself, 'but she is. However, she is no concern of mine. She does not exist for me.' (*Anna Karenina*, III. 13)

It is easier to live with the thought that Anna had always been a depraved woman, and that he had never really loved her, than to confront the fact that he had loved her, but had taken her for granted and had failed to give her the love and attention she needed.

Once convinced that one has lost the love one was

*Consequent hatred*

given, the anger, sense of betrayal, and shame are prone to transmute into hatred for the very person whom one loved. This, indeed, is Karenin's first emotional reaction: 'I have done everything for this woman, and she has trodden it all in the mud to which she is akin. I am not a spiteful man, I have never hated anyone, but I hate her with my whole soul, and I cannot even forgive her, because I hate her too much for all the wrong she has done me!' (*Anna Karenina*, IV. 13). And the hatred rots his very heart. Out of hatred, he forbids Anna access to her beloved son Seriozha, and that very hatred and self-righteousness lead him to mar, distort, and destroy the loving character of the young boy. Similarly, Baron von Innstetten destroys his daughter Annie's love for her mother, Effi. The sins of the jealous are indeed visited upon their children.

*Consequent desire*       Injured pride, shame before the eyes of the world, the threat to one's self-esteem, and hatred conjointly *for revenge*       breed the desire to punish the person who has withdrawn their love, and to wreak revenge upon one's rival. Anna, racked with irrational fear of losing Vronsky's love, seeks death not merely to escape her suffering, but to punish Vronsky (*Anna Karenina*, VII. 26). But where Anna kills herself, Medea, driven by unbearable sexual jealousy, with deeply wounded sexual pride, at having been betrayed by Jason for whom she had sacrificed all – even to the extent of murdering her own brother to save Jason – is incandescent with desire for vengeance. If Jason is not to be hers, then he will be no one's – and she murders his betrothed, Glauce, as well as her father, King Creon of Corinth. Even this does not satisfy her. To inflict upon him yet greater suffering, even at the cost of her maternal love for her children, Medea murders their two sons. Triumphant in her revenge, she declares:

> This thing was not to be,
> That thou should't live a merry life, my bed
> Forgotten and my heart uncomforted,
> Thou nor thy princess: nor the king that planned
> Thy marriage drive Medea from his land,
> And suffer not. Call me what thing thou please,
> Tigress or Skylla from the Tuscan seas:
> My claws have gripped thine heart, and all things shine.

Similarly, Othello craves unlimited vengeance and cries out to slake his jealousy with Desdemona's blood:

> O, that the slave had forty thousand lives!
> One is too poor, too weak for my revenge.
> Now do I see 'tis true. Look here, Iago:

All my fond love thus do I blow to heaven ... 'tis gone.
Arise, black vengeance, from thy hollow cell!
Yield up, O love, thy crown and heart'd throne
To tyrannous hate! Swell, bosom, with thy fraught,
For 'tis of aspics' tongues!

(*Othello*, III. 3)

*Self-destructive and*     It is patent that jealousy is an emotion pregnant
*self-defeating*           with further evils. It was surely only medieval
                           respect for Gregory the Great (see chapter 5, note 10)
that prevented the scholastics, including Aquinas, from classifying
jealousy as a capital sin. It is, indeed, a fountainhead of evil (see fig. 8.2).
Moreover, it can destroy the very soul of the jealous person. It is not
only *self*-destructive, but also self-*destructive*, that is to say, it is intrinsically self-defeating.

That jealousy *can* destroy the soul should be evident from the profound viciousness to which it can lead, which we have now surveyed.
It has also been made evident by the quotations from great literary
works whose authors have so eloquently described the manifold ways
in which uncontrolled feelings of jealousy can infiltrate the mind,
dominate the will, and blacken the very soul of the jealous. It is a
malignant emotion that feeds upon itself – the more one succumbs to

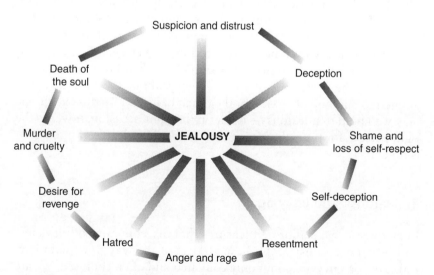

**Figure 8.2**  *Jealousy as a capital vice: one possible cycle*

feelings of jealousy, the stronger they grow. The more one indulges the emotion, the greater the torment one inflicts upon oneself.

It should also be evident that jealousy, *in extremis*, is intrinsically self-defeating. For, in order to preserve a cherished love, it proceeds to destroy the very love it craves as well as the love it bears. Its roots, when they are deep, involve profound moral confusions, namely that the person one loves belongs to one, that their love is akin to a commodity that one can possess, that one has a right to the love of another, and that their love is one's due. But lovers do not own each other. Love is not a possession. The person whose love one fears to lose does not *owe* one their love and one has no *right* to it. It is given as an act of grace, not as the fulfilment of an obligation.

This is not to say that love does not involve reciprocal commitments and recognition of requirements, that the shared life and intimacies of lovers (whether married or not) does not create moral bonds (see chapter 10). The severance of those bonds and abandonment of those commitments is grievous – and the occasion for great sorrow and suffering. There may be much cause for resentment at the subterfuge and deception of betrayal, and for grief at the devaluation of all that has been shared.

*Susceptibility to jealousy a criterion of love* Jealousy, in appropriate contexts, is doubtless one of the (defeasible) criteria for loving another. If a husband or wife were to avow that they would feel no jealousy at all if their spouse were to have an extramarital affair, one might well be puzzled. For fidelity is a constituent element in a good marital relationship. Resentful jealousy need not be a criterion of overwhelmingly possessive love, but it is a criterion of a sense of broken faith and distress. For it may be indicative of caring deeply about the love that was granted to one, and of anxiety at the threat of its loss. To this extent one may well hold that jealousy – if felt on the right occasion, towards the right person, for the right reason, and to the right degree of intensity – is no evil.

## 4. Jealousy and envy again

In chapter 7, we elaborated features that are common to both envy and jealousy (see list 7.1). These go part of the way to explain why jealousy and envy are commonly conflated and often confused. We are now in a position to elaborate the manifold differences between these two emotions and the corresponding character traits and motives. The comparison, as should now be evident, unavoidably involves numerous *for the most parts*, and *normallys*.

*Jealousy and envy contrasted* One envies another their having some character trait, office, material possession, or public esteem, but one is jealous of a relationship that obtains or that one thinks obtains between two other people. So envy may involve admiration and a desire to emulate the other, or resentment at not having what the other has as well as resenting his having it, or malicious destruction of that for which one envies the other. By contrast, jealousy typically implies fear of losing the love of another, or resentment and anger at having lost it. So envy usually implies a desire to gain or destroy what another has, whereas jealousy characteristically implies a desire to retain the love that is threatened. Envy does not involve an exclusive relation to another person. Jealousy does. Envy leads to malice, spitefulness, and hatred. Jealousy leads to resentment at the deprivation of exclusive love and anger at the transfer or threat of transfer of love and intimacy to another. Only when the love is irremediably lost or thought to be irremediably lost does jealousy lead to hatred and sometimes even to the desire for revenge and punishment (but there is no place for revenge and punishment in envy). Envy is an emotion that emerges as a consequence of comparison with another in respect of public esteem, social advantage, and status. But jealousy emerges from actual or imaginary threat to love (or, as in the case of the Duke of Ferrara, from marital possession). Consequently, envy commonly involves injured pride, loss of face, and diminution of public esteem by comparison with the envied. Jealousy too involves injured pride and loss of face, but also a feeling of shame in the face of public knowledge of one's lover's faithlessness, and a sense of being an object of ridicule and contempt. Envy is not a socially sanctioned emotion, and so is commonly masked by righteous indignation or denigration of what is envied and of the person envied. Both emotions may involve a sense of humiliation. In the case of envy, one may feel humiliated by competitive failure in which one bitterly envies and resents the success of one's rival. In the case of jealousy one may feel humiliated by loss of love and betrayal of intimacy, both psychological and sexual – for one has bared one's soul and body to the gaze of the person one loved (see table 8.1).

| Envy | Jealousy |
| --- | --- |
| The person envied is the possessor of the desideratum one craves or wishes to deprive him of. | The person one is jealous of is the rival for the love one fears to lose or resents having lost. |
| What one envies are possessions, characteristics, rank, office, etc. | What one is jealous of is the actual or suspected love of one's beloved for another. |
| Desire to gain something one lacks (or to ensure that the other does not have it). | Desire to retain what one already has. |
| No exclusive relation to another person. | An exclusive relation to another person. |
| Leads predominantly to malice and hatred. | Leads predominantly to resentment and anger – and to hatred only when the love has been lost. |
| No question of *punishing* the person envied (since he has done no wrong). | May lead to desire to punish the lover who betrayed one. |
| No vengeance (since there is nothing to revenge), but may lead to desire to destroy the person envied or to destroy what he has and one covets | May lead to desire for vengeance against one's rival (and against the person one loved). |
| Emerges from comparison with another in respect of self-esteem and public esteem consequent on possession of the envied good. | Emerges from threat or imagined threat to the love one was granted by one's beloved. |
| Involves actual or imagined loss of esteem by comparison with the person envied. | Involves a sense of shame in the loss of the valued relationship and injury to one's pride. |
| Involves a sense of humiliation by competitive failure. | Involves a sense of humiliation at loss of love.and at being shamed in the eyes of society. |
| Not intrinsically self-defeating. | Intrinsically self-defeating since jealousy destroys the very love that is valued. |
| Socially reprehensible emotion and motive. | Socially admissible emotion and motive. |
| Masked by denigrating what is envied or by righteous indignation at the envied person's having undeservedly obtained the desideratum. | Masked by denying one's previous love, as well as the love one received, and by denigrating the person one loves or loved. |

**Table 8.1** *Thirteen differences between envy and marital jealousy or jealousy between lovers (excluding 'for-the-most-part' differences)*

These differences are deep enough and significant enough to recommend to us a sharper differentiation between envy and jealousy, which we saw, in chapter 7, to be blurred in common usage. Our recommendation is indeed to 'snip the ragged edges of common usage' (as Sidgwick nicely put it), not for theoretical purposes – we are not engaged in theory construction of any kind – but for the purpose of rational discussions of our emotional lives.

# 9

# Anger

## 1. The phenomena of anger

Anger, like fear, is one of the most common of human emotions. When we wake up, we may be *annoyed* for having overslept; we may be *ill-tempered* because we have a hangover from last night's party; we may *become angry* with the children at breakfast because they make so much noise; we may *lose our temper* with the motorist who weaves from lane to lane in front of us as we drive to work. We may be *irritable* when we arrive at work. If we are a chief executive with an *irascible* personality, we may work ourselves into a *rage* with our staff, and enjoy making them cower. If someone accuses us of a misdemeanour of which we are innocent, we may feel *indignant*. If someone mocks us, we may feel *resentful*. The offense may *rankle*; we may brood on it and on the offender for a prolonged period of time, *bearing rancour* and *feeling vindictive*. And so on.

*Anger: a primitive emotion*
Anger is not merely a ubiquitous emotion; it is also a primitive one, in three different senses. First, beasts become irritated, angry, and enraged no less than we do (although not indignant or resentful). Secondly, and as a corollary of the ascribability of anger to beasts, anger in some of its forms, unlike pride or remorse, is independent of mastery of a language. Thirdly, the criteria for the elementary forms

*The Passions: A Study of Human Nature*, First Edition. P. M. S. Hacker.
© 2018 John Wiley & Sons Ltd. Published 2018 by John Wiley & Sons Ltd.

of human orgetic[1] behaviour are non-linguistic. Small children roll on the ground on their back or belly in rage, screaming, scratching, biting, and kicking. An adult may turn red with anger, scowl, flare his nostrils, clench his fists, grind his teeth, thump the table, or stamp on the ground.

*Evolutionary selection for anger*

        Inasmuch as our concept of anger applies to beasts no less than to man, we can and do speculate on the evolutionary role of anger. It is patent that animals that have a disposition to become angry when challenged enjoy an advantage relative to those members of its kind that do not. First, the behavioural manifestations of anger signal to a challenger awareness of the challenge and readiness to fight. This functions as a warning, and may induce backing off, thus diminishing the chances of mutual injury. Secondly, the typical stance of anger signals to an aggressor that the threatened animal is too large or fierce to take on, thus, again, inducing withdrawal. Conflict reduction is conducive to survival. Thirdly, the physical and physiological accompaniments of anger – the raised blood pressure, the increased heartbeat, the deep breathing and consequent increased oxygen supply – prepare the animal for conflict and, if necessary, for flight.

    It does not follow from these evolutionary advantages of irascibility that anger therefore has a warrant in a society of rational beings. There is no *a priori* reason why an emotional disposition that has served the survival of a species in the long march of mindless evolution should continue to be of similar advantage to language-using beings, with the ability to reason and to give reasons, living in societies governed by laws, in states that have a monopoly on the legitimate use of force. That is something that requires investigation.

*Accompaniments and manifestations of anger*

        The phenomena of anger can in general be distinguished into:

(i)   physical and physiological accompaniments, such as increased heartbeat, rise in blood pressure, secretion of adrenaline and noradrenaline, release of glucose (stored in the muscles and liver in the form of glycogen), increase in blood flow to the limbs, deep breathing to increase blood oxygen;

(ii)   somatic feelings, such as felt rise of heartbeat, pulsing temples, felt experience of panting and deep breathing, impulse to swallow, and felt musculoskeletal tension;

---

[1] From the Greek *orgē*, which is the term Aristotle uses in his analysis of anger. 'Orgetic' is modelled on the pattern of the accepted adjective 'orectic' (concerning desire or appetite).

(iii) behavioural manifestations of anger: these are varied; in the case of both beast and man there are changes in:

(a) stance, preparatory for combat: the big cats crouch in readiness to spring; bulls lower their horns and deer their antlers in preparation for a charge. Men square up, clench their fists, stiffen and tense their muscles; they may wave their arms aggressively or thump their fists against an object or against their chest (as do gorillas), and they may stamp their feet.

(b) apparent size: animals commonly endeavour to magnify their occlusion size. Dogs raise their hackles, cats' fur bristles, elephants wave their ears to make themselves appear even larger, bears rise up on their hind legs, and kangaroos raise themselves to their full height. Men too tend to rise to their full height in a threatening posture.

(c) facial expression: baring of teeth as a threat, ears laid back to avoid injuring them or getting caught by them. Men are prone to go red in the face (but may turn white with anger too), frown, flare their nostrils, stare, clench their teeth, jut out their jaw, and scowl.

(d) vocalization: animals characteristically spit, snarl, growl, screech, or trumpet. Human orgetic vocalization is diverse. They may shout in rage, scream or shriek in anger, growl threateningly or in bad temper. But they may speak in icy tones of 'cold anger', with harsh, clipped, enunciation.

(e) verbalization: only humans are language-users, so only humans can *express* their anger in utterances. Characteristic utterances of anger are swearing in all its diversity, profanities, insults, threats, expressions of righteous indignation at affronted dignity or of resentment at insult, sarcasm, and irony.

Much of this is wonderfully described by Shakespeare in Henry V's Harfleur speech, as he whips up battle rage in his troops:

> But when the blast of war blows in our ears,
> Then imitate the action of the tiger.
> Stiffen the sinews, conjure up the blood,
> Disguise fair nature with hard-favoured rage.
> Then lend the eye a terrible aspect,
> Let it pry through the portage of the head
> Like the brass cannon, let the brow o'erwhelm it

As fearfully as doth a gallèd rock
O'erhang and jutty his confounded base,
Swilled with the wild and wasteful ocean.
Now set the teeth and stretch the nostril wide,
Hold hard the breath, and bend up every spirit
To his full height.

(*Henry V*, III. 1)

*Anger embedded in*    Anger, like all emotions, is embedded in the circum-
*personal history*    stances of life. The circumstances characteristic
    of an animal's becoming angry are such things as
combat, trespasses upon its demarcated territory, threats to its offspring, attempts to deprive it of its food, challenges to male or female
leadership (where a pack has an alpha male or female), a male's being
in rut, challenges to a male's sexual dominance in a pride or herd, and
offspring nuisance. Human life is infinitely more complex. Unlike
animal anger, human anger is, as it were, a part of an autobiography – for it is part of the life of a self-conscious being. Unlike animal
anger, it is concept-saturated, for human beings can normally say
what angered them and why, can reflect upon their reasons for being
angry, and can modify their responses accordingly. They can remember what angered them and why, and the memory of the offensive
behaviour may rankle long after the event. They are responsible for
what they do in anger. They can cite the fact that doing something will
anger another person as a reason for not doing it, and refrain from
doing it accordingly (or, sometimes, act for the very reason that doing
*this* will make so-and-so furious). Human anger is rendered intelligible
by reference to the history out of which it grows and the circumstances in which it arises. It is conceived to be warranted, even though
acting in anger is rarely warranted. The circumstances that give rise to
human anger are far more complex and variegated than those that
give rise to animal anger.

## 2. The vocabulary of anger

*Variety of orgetic*    Given the ubiquity of the phenomena of anger
*vocabularies*    and the roots of the emotion in our animal nature,
    it is not surprising that human languages have a rich
vocabulary to express, report, describe, and evaluate the various
manifestations and expressions of anger. Different cultures and different languages have evolved their distinctive orgetic vocabularies.

Given the common orgetic forms of human reactive behaviour in recurrent kinds of situations and provocations, leading to distinctive kinds of responses, there was an obvious need for an appropriate vocabulary. So too, the differences between human beings –

(i)   in the forms of their responsiveness;
(ii)  in the frequency with which they are aroused to anger;
(iii) in the intensity of their anger;
(iv)  in the nature and degree of provocation needed to call forth an angry reaction; and
(v)   in degrees of self-control

– demand a classification of human temperaments, pronenesses, and susceptibilities. The orgetic vocabulary is needed in order to help us make sense of ourselves and of each other, to make it possible for us to reflect on the patterns of feelings and behaviour (of ourselves and of others), and to subject them to rational scrutiny and criticism. Different languages have drawn different fruitful distinctions. There is no presumption that they should discern, and draw attention to, the same patterns in the manifold phenomena of anger, the circumstances that give rise to anger, the reasons for becoming angry, the duration of anger, and the different orgetic pronenesses and temperaments. It is patent that there is more than one way of drawing distinctions, and that there is no privileged way. So, although there is much to be learned from the reflections of the ancients upon anger, translation is sometimes problematic, and we must be wary of attributing error in analysis, where what is before our eyes is a slightly different concept with somewhat different boundary lines, or an explication (in Carnap's sense of the term) that diverges from ordinary use for philosophical or theological purposes.

*English orgetic vocabulary* We are concerned with the family of concepts of anger, as expressed in English. The vocabulary we have inherited is rich and diverse. List 9.1 puts some order into it.

This is but a small selection gleaned from a thesaurus. There are many more expressions, but this list suffices to remind one of the richness and diversity of the orgetic vocabulary in English and to intimate the kinds of distinctions that seemed worth drawing.

*Anger and the humours* It is striking how deeply embedded in our orgetic vocabulary is the ancient medical doctrine of the humours, for example, in such expressions as 'choleric', 'splenetic', and 'bilious'. The Greek *kholē* (whence 'choleric') signified

| | |
|---|---|
| Expressions for momentary, acute anger (classified by degrees of intensity) | in a frenzy; mad (raving or roaring mad); in a paroxysm of rage; to throw a tantrum; to fume; to rage; to be furious; to rant and rave; to be beside oneself with anger; to see red; to lose one's temper; to be angry, vexed, annoyed, exasperated, irritated, indignant; wrath, ire |
| Expressions for temporary mood-like forms of anger | cross; cantankerous; irritable; grumpy; testy; cranky; petulant; sulky; peevish; bilious; seethe; fume; boil with anger (some of these also function as names of temperament and character traits) |
| Expressions for enduring orgetic emotions | bearing rancor; feeling offended, resentful, aggrieved, embittered; rankling; brooding |
| Expressions for orgetic temperament and character traits | choleric; splenetic; bilious; irascible; touchy; rancorous; farouche; short-tempered; quick-tempered; bad-tempered; hot-tempered |
| Expressions for orgetic behavioural reactions (in order of degree of lack of control) | go berserk; run amok; be in a frenzy of rage or fury; be resentful, indignant, snappish, waspish |
| Expressions for the generation of anger | inflame; enrage; infuriate; make one's blood boil; incense; make one's hackles rise; drive to distraction; vex; provoke; rile; affront; irritate; annoy; offend; goad; nettle; prick; ruffle one's feathers; rub one up the wrong way; gall |

**List 9.1** *The vocabulary of anger*

yellow bile (which is not bile at all but yellowish blood serum), allegedly produced in the spleen (whence 'splenetic'). *Melaina kholē* signified black bile (which is not bile either but coagulated blood). A fiery, choleric temperament was explained by reference to a predominance of yellow bile in the blood. The general connection between anger and bile, thus understood, is manifest in our adjective 'bilious', that is, peevish, irritable, cranky. The four humours were linked to the four elements: fire, air, water, and earth. Anger was associated with fire, as is evident from such expressions as 'to make one's blood boil', 'to inflame', 'to flare up', 'to be incandescent with rage'. The colour associated with the choleric temperament was not yellow (as might be expected from the yellow bile, excess of which was held be its primary cause) but red, because of the connection of choler with the element of fire, hence physiologically with heat and burning in the vicinity of the heart – as Aristotle conjectured (*De Anima*, 403ª31).

*Iconography of anger*

The doctrine of the humours is reflected in the iconography of anger. Eichler's engraved illustration for Ripa's iconological analysis of *Cholericus*[2] depicts an angry youth – for the young, Ripa explained, like the choleric, lack judgement. The youth's sword is drawn, since the choleric are always ready for a fight. On the ground before him lies a large shield with a flame emblazoned on it, since the choleric give off much heat when enraged. His complexion is yellowish, since there is an excess of yellow bile in his blood. He is accompanied by a fierce lion, since the lion is the boldest and proudest of the beasts – quick to anger and always ready to fight. The *fatto* in the background is a duel in which one of the combatants falls wounded or dead. Hertel's Latin superscript (in translation) reads 'Letting ourselves go and persisting in our inconsiderate rage, we often damage others, and ourselves run into trouble'. The German doggerel at the bottom of the page runs, in translation, 'A man who oft in rage doth burn / May find it back on him can turn'.

*Pictorial representation of anger*

The depiction of anger in European art occurs primarily in mythological and history painting. It is not surprising that these should concentrate upon extremes of anger – rage and fury. The depiction of the physiognomy of battle rage was brought to perfection by Leonardo (e.g. the now lost *Battle of Anghiari*, known primarily from Rubens's copy of it), and his inventions were utilized during the period of Baroque painting (e.g. by Rubens himself in numerous battle or lion-hunting paintings). The representation of Cain's murderous fury in killing Abel was a standard theme in the ever popular horror paintings of the Baroque (Titian, Tintoretto, Palma Giovane, Crespi). Goya, in the early nineteenth century, was a master of depiction of murderous rage. Nineteenth-century neo-classical painters, especially in France,

---

[2] See Hertel's 1758–60 edition of Cesare Ripa, *Iconologia*, 107.

were much taken with the subject of the wrath of Achilles, and produced many truly dreadful paintings (e.g. those by Charles-Antoine
Coypel, Asher B. Durand), but Delacroix compensated for them.
Painting lends itself to the portrayal of rage, but not to the subtler
physiognomic dynamics of mild forms of anger as when a shadow of
irritation flits across the face, nor, of course, to the subtle and varied
tones of voice that exhibit varying degrees of irritation, exasperation,
and annoyance.

*Literary representations of anger*     The literary representation of anger constitutes a cornucopia. The first great literary work
in Europe, Homer's *Iliad*, remains the most powerful tale ever written of wrath; of brooding,
rankling anger; and of battle rage. Anger is one of the primary themes
of many of the great Greek tragedies. Oedipus, Creon, Medea, Eteocles,
and Pentheus are gripped by it. Even the gods, such as Artemis,
Aphrodite, Athene, and Dionysus succumb to it. In the case of mortals,
such as Creon, Ajax, Theseus, and Pentheus, they are brought to catastrophe by their anger and rage. The Norse sagas, from the *Haraldskvæði*
(ninth century) to the Icelandic *Ynglinga saga* (thirteenth century),
contain descriptions of the battle frenzy (the *wut*) of the well-nigh
invincible bearskin-clad or wolf's-head-wearing berserkers. At the
acme of medieval literature, Dante's *Divine Comedy* (canto 8) pays
due attention to the deadly sin of anger, representing the wrathful as
enmired in a filthy, stagnant bog outside the City of Dis, rending their
own flesh with their teeth. One of the greatest masterpieces of
Renaissance literature, Ariosto's *Orlando Furioso*, is largely dedicated
to a description of an insane rampage of rage. The theme of anger is
explored by Shakespeare in many of his history plays (e.g. *Henry V*,
*Henry VI*), in his tragedies (e.g. *Macbeth*, *Lear*, and *Othello*), and in
some of his problem plays (e.g. *The Merchant of Venice*). In the flowering of the novel in the nineteenth century, anger receives its rightful
attention from a very wide range of authors in many different countries
(e.g. Tolstoy, Dostoevsky, Emily Brontë, Trollope, Dickens, Balzac,
Zola). *Look Back in Anger* and *Who's Afraid of Virginia Woolf* are
two noteworthy mid-twentieth-century plays on marital anger.

## 3. Anger: connective analysis

*Dimensions of anger*     Anger is an emotional response to the thwarting
of one's will or the flouting of one's authority or
instructions; to physical conflict; to an offense to one's status, pride,

or dignity; to challenges to one's judgement or opinion on matters close to one's heart; to the offenses of others that one considers to be wicked or otherwise unwarranted; to stupidity and incompetence (of another or one's own). This is not a *definition* of anger, merely a preliminary circumscription of the domain of our conceptual investigation. The social norms governing the propriety of feeling angry, the legitimacy of manifesting anger, and the forms and occasions in which it may be manifest vary from society to society, from one epoch to another, from one social class to another, and between men and women (for much of history and in most societies, anger is primarily a male prerogative, agitation and tears being more appropriate to women, save in relation to equals or subordinates, on whom anger could be vented). Like other emotions, anger can be characterized by reference to its manifold dimensions of duration and the variety of the temporal forms it takes; its degrees of intensity, which may wax or wane; its behavioural manifestations and linguistic expression; the range and limits of its material object-accusatives and nominalization-accusatives; the circumstances and frame of mind in which one's orgetic susceptibilities or liabilities are exposed; the general character of the reasons for anger and the amenability of anger to reason; the relationship of anger to motivation; and the orgetic dispositions and pronenesses characteristic of human beings (see fig. 9.1). To survey these will constitute a connective analysis of this ubiquitous emotion.

What are the proper subjects of anger? Clearly not *Proper subjects* inanimate objects – we do not, save in fairy tales, *of anger* conceive of sticks and stones, chairs or tables, as being possible subjects of orgetic attributes.[3] It is, however, striking that we readily conceive of the forces of nature as exemplifying wrath – for example, earthquakes, volcanic eruptions, tsunamis, avalanches, hurricanes, and tornados, as well as severe storms, thunder, and lightning. They display great destructive powers that both terrify us and strike awe in our hearts. We are powerless before such phenomena and may be in great danger – small wonder that primitive man viewed them as manifestations of the wrath of the gods of nature. We do not find it intelligible to ascribe anger in any of its forms to plants and trees. We do, however, comfortably and non-figuratively ascribe anger to animals that possess sufficient behavioural plasticity

---

[3] But they may be improper *objects* of anger. Herodotus relates that, when a Persian-built bridge across the Hellespont was destroyed in a storm, Xerxes was so full of wrath that he ordered that the Hellespont receive 300 lashes and bade the branders take their irons and brand the waters (Herodotus, *Histories*, VII. 35). Children similarly vent their anger upon their toys.

**Figure 9.1**  *The dimensions of anger*

to exhibit anger in mien, facial expression, and behaviour. It is striking that some ancient philosophers denied that animals can be angry. Seneca was perfectly explicit: 'We must admit, however, that neither wild beasts, nor any other creature except man is subject to anger [*ira*]' (*De Ira*, I. 3). Since the ancients were far more familiar with wild and domesticated beasts than we are, we may not put this down to woefully blinkered observation. Rather, a conceptual distinction is being made, and a boundary is being drawn, in a place where we draw none. Be that as it may, it is above all to human beings that we ascribe the varieties of anger. Our connective analysis is of the concept of anger as applied paradigmatically to mankind. But we should also bear in mind that many religions conceive of their god or gods as being no less susceptible to this emotion than mankind. The God of the Old Testament is frequently aroused to wrath. Christ loses his temper with the moneylenders in the Temple. The Olympians often get angry with each other, and furious with human beings. Whether divine wrath makes sense is debatable, but will not be debated here.

*Temporal dimensions of anger*      Anger may be temporary or persistent. If it is temporary, it may be momentary or episodic. In both cases, it may be accompanied by and manifest in intense perturbations. We may flare up with anger, explode with fury, burn with rage. As noted, in the case of such extreme orgetic reactions, we typically grow red in the face, clench our fists, rise to our full height, and assume a threatening and intimidating posture. We characteristically raise our voice, shout, or scream. But we may also manifest extreme anger in a cold fury, speaking with icy and controlled voice, with deliberately controlled movements of limb, and with frozen face. I know of no better example of icy anger and of the transition from it to an explosion of wrath than Shakespeare's depiction of Henry V replying to the French ambassador on receipt of the insulting gift of tennis balls from the Dauphin:

> We are glad the Dauphin is so pleasant with us.
> His present and your pains we thank you for.
> When we have matched our rackets to these balls,
> We will in France, by God's grace, play a set
> Shall strike his father's crown into the hazard.
> Tell him he hath made a match with such a wrangler
> That all the courts of France will be disturbed
> With chases. And we understand him well,
> How he comes o'er us with our wilder days,
> Not measuring what use we made of them.
> ...
> And tell the pleasant Prince this mock of his
> Hath turned his balls to gunstones, and his soul
> Shall stand sore charged for the wasteful vengeance
> That shall fly from them – for many a thousand widows
> Shall this his mock mock out of their dear husbands,
> Mock mothers from their sons, mock castles down;
> Ay, some are yet ungotten and unborn
> That shall have cause to curse the Dauphin's scorn.
>
> (*Henry V*, I. 2)

A momentary form of anger may be no more than a flash or twitch of irritation and annoyance. But one's anger may persist as long as the encounter or angry exchange of words go on. Similarly, battle rage may last as long as one is fighting. However, episodic anger may continue for a time in more than one form. One may continue to be angry with the person who thwarted one long after the end of the altercation, still fuming inwardly, going over his offensive remarks and threats in one's imagination, thinking of what one should have said, feeling vindictive, and planning how to even the score. A different form in which one's anger may continue is that it leaves behind a residue of irritability – one may be in a bad temper the rest of the day. If asked why, one may well reply, 'I am furious with so-and-so.'

Anger may also be persistent and enduring, as was the wrath of Achilles. The offence that is the ground of one's anger may rankle obsessively, breeding bitterness and hatred. So, when, many weeks after the quarrel, Odysseus and Ajax come to Achilles pleading in Agamemnon's name that he overcome his wrath, Achilles replies:

> My heart still heaves with rage
> Whenever I call to mind that arrogance of his –
> How he mortified me, right in front of the Argives –
> That son of Atreus treating me like some vagabond,
> Like some outcast stripped of all my rights!
> You go back to him and declare my message:
> I will not think of arming for bloody war again.
>
> (*Iliad*, XI. 789–95)

One mark of enduring anger is unwillingness or inability to forgive or forget. Enduring anger is not irascibility. Nor need it be (as Achilles' anger is depicted as being) a disposition to periodic outbreaks of rage with the offender. Rather it may consist in obsessive thoughts, in feeling vindictive, in imagining revenge with pleasure, in growing resentment and hatred, in *Schadenfreude*, and in hoping for an opportunity to retaliate. It may be manifest in severing of hitherto amicable relations, in a proneness to speak ill of the person who offended one or not to speak of that person at all, and in vengeful plans.

*Intensity of anger*   Because outbreaks of anger can be so frightening, we think of its intensity largely in terms of the perturbations of orgetic reactions. These range from the extremes of a frenzy of rage, an outburst of wrath and a paroxysm of fury, to minor annoyance and passing irritation. But to think of such manifest perturbations as the sole criterion for the intensity of someone's anger is as misleading as thinking of the intensity of fear as being exhibited only in the physical perturbations one experiences when encountering what one fears. As was remarked in chapter 3, the intensity of fear is no less manifest in the lengths one will go, and the sacrifices one will make, to avoid the fear-inducing circumstance or person. So too, in the case of anger we must note the longer-term effects of an anger-generating incident. To focus exclusively upon the perturbations of anger as a measure of orgetic intensity is to overlook the sense in which the degree of anger may be manifest in abiding resentment, persistent bitterness, inability to forgive or forget, and a long-lasting desire to do ill to, or inflict vengeance on, the offender. (In *Les Misérables*, Monsieur Gillenormand's anger with his grandson Marius Pontmercy persists for some years in the form of bitterness, resentment, indignation, prohibition on the mention of his name, and so forth.)

*Suppression of anger*    We have discussed the physiognomy, behavioural manifestations, and verbal expressions of anger. These, in appropriate circumstances, are our criteria for judging a person to be losing his temper, becoming angry, and perhaps erupting in wrath or revealing a flash of anger, a spark of irritation, or a shadow of annoyance. Such behavioural manifestations of anger, for the most part, are suppressible. But, except in cases of iron self-control, the suppression of anger is itself manifest in clenched jaws, frozen visage, and cold tone of voice. With respect to episodic anger that may last for some time in the course of the day, the criteria for someone's continued anger are the person's utterances and reports, and enduring bad temper.

*Orgetic excess*    The large majority of epithets for character traits and temperament associated with anger indicate forms of orgetic excess to which mankind is liable. Human beings are said to be *quick-tempered* if they become angry too swiftly; they are held to be *irascible* if they are too prone to become angry, if they lose their temper too frequently and too readily, or if but little provocation is needed for them to fly into a rage. They are *hot-tempered* if their anger is too intense and out of proportion to its grounds. They are said to be *violent* and *abusive* if they express their anger too vehemently, without appropriate self-control. And, if people retain their anger for too long, they are said to be *sulky* and hard to appease, *resentful* and harbouring rancour, or *embittered* and simmering with animosity. These tendencies and dispositions are all vices. It is patent that we are all the more susceptible to anger when subject to a range of somatic conditions or external circumstances. Unfulfilled appetites (such as hunger, thirst, and lust) and overall somatic states (such as weariness and feeling unwell) commonly make us more irritable or irascible than normal. Environmental conditions, such as extremes of heat, torrential rain (monsoon), and wind (sirocco, khamsin (or khamaseen)), affect the temper (the hot, dry, and dusty khamsin winds were, in Middle Eastern and North African societies, treated as a mitigating condition for an offence committed in anger). Being preoccupied with some exacting task, concentrating intensely upon a problem or goal-directed activity, is apt to make people prone to irascibility, and to be more likely to be irritated, annoyed, or angered by intrusion or interruption.

*Is anger always wrong?* Our vocabulary intimates that not all instances of anger are wrong. In this sense, our concepts of anger guide us down Aristotelian pathways. As he observed of *orgē*, 'The man who is angry at the right things and with the right people, and further, as he ought, when he ought, and as long as he ought, is to be praised' (*Nicomachean Ethics*, 1125ᵇ32). There *are* reasons for getting angry, but, according to Aristotle (when speaking, perhaps more generally, of actions spurred by *thumos*), we are prone to evaluate them wrongly:

> Anger seems to listen to reason to some extent, but to mishear it, as do hasty servants who run out before they have heard the whole of what one says, and then muddle the order, or as dogs bark if there is but a knock at the door, before looking to see if it is a friend; so anger, by reason of the warmth and hastiness of its nature, though it hears, does not hear an order, and springs to take revenge. For reason or imagination informs us that we have been insulted or slighted, and anger, reasoning as it were that anything like this must be fought against, boils up straight away. (*Nicomachean Ethics*, 1149ᵃ25–33)

We shall discuss Aristotle's analysis of anger later, and investigate the question of whether anger is indeed sometimes meritorious, or whether it is always a vice – a cardinal, if not a mortal, sin.

*Anger is not a motive* Although there are reasons for becoming and being angry, the word 'anger' (unlike, say, 'love', 'compassion', 'remorse') does not have the further role of the name of a motive that signifies a pattern of backward- and forward-looking reasons. Rather, temporary anger, both momentary and episodic, characterizes the *mode* of reaction and response rather than a motive for action. Hence the adverbial forms 'irritably', 'angrily', 'furiously', 'indignantly', 'resentfully', and 'waspishly'. As previously noted, one may act *in* anger but not *out of* anger, just as one may act with courage but not out of courage. One might wonder why. After all, one typical orgetic pattern is: a backward-looking reason for action, namely a painful insult or slight, and a rectifying purpose, namely to inflict pain on the offender, acting for which will enable one to 'get one's own back', 'right the balance', and 'wipe out the offence'. (The now defunct military aristocratic practice of the duel institutionalized this pattern in order to bring familial blood-feuding under control.) But this pattern already has a motive name – 'vindictiveness'.

Moreover, as we shall see, it is quite mistaken to suppose that what we call 'anger' necessarily implies a desire for punishment and vengeance, as Aristotle held *orgē* to do. One can be angry at disagreement without wanting to punish one's interlocutor; one can be angry at another's mistake but want merely to rectify it, not to punish for it; one can be angry with oneself without craving self-mortification. While the kinds of reasons that provoke anger can be roughly circumscribed and the criteria for feeling angry can be specified, there is no characteristic purpose that is pursued by those who are angry. Nevertheless, anger is entwined with other emotions that do furnish a person with motives. It is, as we have seen, enmeshed with pride. If someone mocks us, jeers at us, shows lack of respect for us, we are prone to respond with anger, and are often inclined to reciprocate angrily out of injured pride. Jealousy is commonly accompanied by anger for the actual or supposed betrayal of love (see Tolstoy's description of Pozdnyshev's rage, quoted on p. 222–3), and jealousy is indeed also a motive. Although one can hate without anger, anger at an offence may grow into hatred, which then provides a motive for vengeful retaliation.

*Material object-accusatives of anger*

Circumscribing the material object-accusatives of anger presents various problems. It is moot whether one can be angry with an inanimate object. To be sure, we often become angry when a tool fails us –we feel frustrated by its inadequacy to our purposes. But are we angry *with* the tool or angry at not having an adequate tool? Is the tool making us angry because of something it does or obstinately fails to do? We may throw the tool to the ground in anger, or even break it. But that appears to be frustrated displacement behaviour. After all, we cannot *tell* the tool how annoyed we are with it any more than Xerxes could tell the Hellespont how angry he was that the storm had wrecked his bridge. We may indeed be angry *that* we do not have an adequate tool (but no one would say 'I'm angry with the screwdriver'); we may be angry *that* we cannot open the door (and we may curse it – but we should not say 'I'm furious with the door!'); we may be enraged *that* the slot machine does not reward us with a shower of coins (and we may then kick it out of frustration, since it makes us angry). In such cases, we may not infer a material object-accusative from the intentional nominalization-accusative. Similarly, we may be angry *at* our fate, that is, angry that we find ourselves in such-and-such circumstances, but not angry *with* fate.

*Being angry with an animal* Animals are sometimes the objects of our anger. This was implicitly denied by Aristotle in so far as he limited genuine anger (*orgē*) to a desire for revenge for what appears to one to be a slight – and animals cannot slight one. However, as *we* conceive of anger, it certainly makes sense, and it is often true, that we get angry with beasts. We may get angry with our pets (e.g. when they make a mess on the carpet), with our horse or cattle (e.g. when they frustrate our will), with wild animals (e.g. when they destroy our crops), and so forth. We also vent our anger, sometimes in merciless rage, upon dumb brutes.[4] But Seneca was surely correct to remark that it is the act of a madman to be angry with dumb animals, who are not able to do us a wrong (as opposed to a harm) or to insult us (*De Ira*, II. 26).

*Being angry with oneself* Human anger, for the most part, is directed at human beings. One may be angry with oneself or angry with others. Self-directed anger may be for one's follies; for one's failures, when one believes one could have suc-ceeded with more care, effort, or wit; and for one's incompetences and inabilities, which frustrate one in one's pursuit of one's projects and goals. In such cases, one not only blames oneself for one's unto-ward act or omission, but feels annoyed at oneself. One may even feel exasperated with oneself. However, one cannot feel indignant or resentful towards oneself. Can one be enraged or furious with one-self? It might seem that one cannot, for one cannot shake one's fist at oneself or provoke oneself into a rage, as another might, by insulting oneself. Nevertheless, one *can* be enraged with oneself, although there are distinctive asymmetries between being enraged with others or by others, and feeling enraged with oneself. So, for example, Philip Carey, in Maugham's *Of Human Bondage*, after having been forced by the pain inflicted on him by his vicious schoolmates in the dormi-tory to show them his deformed club-foot,

> had got his teeth in the pillow so that his sobbing should be inaudible. He was not crying for the pain they had caused him, nor for the humili-ation he had suffered when they had looked at his foot, but with rage at himself because, unable to stand the torture, he had put out his foot of his own accord. (ch. 10)

---

[4] Ivan Karamazov, in explaining to his brother Alyosha why he is respectfully 'return-ing the ticket' to God, cites, among a series of examples of hideous evil inflicted upon the innocent and defenceless, a poem by Nekrassov about a peasant in a rage who flogs a horse to death for not being able to pull an overloaded cart, 'lashing the poor defenceless creature across its weeping "gentle eyes"' (Dostoevsky, *The Brothers Karamazov*, V. 4).

Similarly, reflexive anger cannot be self-righteous. Rather, it is always accompanied by regret for one's deeds and self-recrimination for one's omissions. This is well depicted in Hamlet's speech after the players withdraw to their quarters:

> O, what a rogue and peasant slave am I!
> Is it not monstrous that this player here,
> But in a fiction, in a dream of passion,
> Could force his soul so to his own conceit
> That from her working all his visage wanned,
> Tears in his eyes, distraction in's aspect,
> A broken voice, and his whole function suiting
> With forms to his conceit? And all for nothing.
> For Hecuba!
> ... Yet I,
> A dull and muddy-mettled rascal, peak
> Like John-a-dreams, unpregnant of my cause
> And can say nothing – no, not for a king
> Upon whose property and most dear life
> A damned defeat was made. Am I a coward?
> ... For it cannot be
> But I am pigeon-livered and lack gall
> To make oppression bitter, or ere this
> I should ha' fatted all the region kites
> With this slave's offal. Bloody, bawdy villain!
> Remorseless, treacherous, lecherous, kindless villain!
> O vengeance –
> Why, what an ass am I? Ay, sure, this is most brave,
> That I, the son of the dear muderéd,
> Prompted to my revenge by heaven and hell,
> Must, like a whore, unpack my heart with words
> And fall a-cursing like a very drab,
> A scullion! Fie upon 't, foh!
>
> (*Hamlet* II. 2)

These asymmetries between the first-person case and the second and third person are as striking as the parallel asymmetries between being afraid of others and being afraid of oneself (as was young Bertrand Russell, when he discovered with horror that he was capable of harbouring murder in his heart).

*Constraints on the material object-accusatives of anger*

Anger with others may be with a particular person or with a specifiable list of individuals. Are there any conceptual constraints on the intelligible objects of anger? One cannot, as Aristotle pointed out, be angry with an open class of persons. One may hate or despise social classes (the plebs or patricians, the proletariat or the bourgeoisie), peoples, or nations. Racialists may *hate* blacks, anti-Semites may *hate* Jews, and misogynists may *hate* women – but it is not evident what could be meant by *being angry* with blacks, Jews, or women in general. There is nothing such a class of people can do that would provide grounds for anger, since such a class is not an agent. Can one not speak of being angry with the Americans, the Russians, or the British? Yes – but only in so far as one thinks of them as a nation-state capable of collective action (in the form of governmental or military action). For, to be sure, one can be angry with an artificial person – a company or institution, a government or a state. Similarly, one can be angry with God (as Moses was, for allowing the maltreatment of the people of Israel (Exodus 5: 22); as Naomi was for the death of her husband and sons (Ruth 1: 20–1); and as Job was, for the sufferings so unjustly inflicted upon him (Job 30: 20–3)).

It is moot whether one can be angry with the dead, with whom one was never acquainted. One may be distressed to discover that Erasmus wrote polemical works in a most repulsively scatological form (as was customary in his day). One may feel deeply disturbed to learn that Sir Thomas More condemned people to be burnt alive at the stake for heresy (in accordance with the law). One may feel profoundly disappointed to find out that Wittgenstein harboured a repulsive anti-Semitic streak. But one surely cannot *feel irate* with them now. One may dislike, despise, or feel contempt for figures of the past, and deplore their deeds, feelings, and opinions – but one cannot intelligibly *be angry* with them. However, one may be angry with a recently deceased person who has failed to live up to one's expectations in his will – as are Mr Featherstone's relatives in *Middlemarch* (ch. 35) when his second will is read out to them.

Nevertheless, the range of material object-accusatives of anger is very wide indeed – it *makes sense* to say, truly or falsely, that one is angry with oneself, with another person or specifiable list of persons, with artificial persons and organizations, and with God or the gods. Are there any conceptual constraints on the personal objects of one's anger that are determined by one's relationship to the person? Or can one intelligibly be angry with *anyone* living? At first blush, it might seem that one can be angry only with those with whom one is acquainted. One may be angry with members of one's family, with one's personal acquaintances, with people one casually encounters who act offensively before one's eyes in the street, on the road, in the department store, in the park, or in the cinema or theatre. But it is not evident that one can be angry with someone with whom one is not even remotely acquainted. Members of the cabinet or of the party may be angry with the prime minister, but can a citizen who has never met the prime minister? If one reads in the press that some celebrity (pop star or footballer) has expressed such-and-such an offensive view, one may feel angry, indignant, and outraged *at the view expressed* – but can one feel angry with the person who expressed it? One may feel outraged at the policy of some foreign tyrant towards his own people (President Assad of Syria or President Kim Jong-un of North Korea), but can one feel *angry* with him? One may feel contempt for this person, as one feels contempt for *anyone* who holds such reprehensible views or does such horrendous deeds – but surely not anger! One may be angry at their outrageous utterances and heinous deeds – but can you or I be *angry* with the tyrants of the world? We must be careful not to conflate the material object-accusative of anger (namely a person) with the nominalization-accusative of anger that specifies what angers us, rather than with whom we are angry.

However, it seems that one can be angry with one's prime minister for breaking the promises he or she made during the election. Similarly, one may be angry with the president of Ruritania, which is an ally, because the policy he is pursuing endangers the security of one's country. That seems correct. One might explain this stretching of the range of material objects of anger by reference to the idea of obligation. For the prime minister has obligations to the electorate, and the president of Ruritania has an obligation not to endanger his allies. But one may be angry with a head of state who is no ally, but who appears to be harming one's country – a common refrain in contemporary crowd emotion in some countries being 'Death to NN' or 'Death to the Great Satan'. Is this individualized anger, or is it rather hatred? Can an irreligious liberal be angry with the pope for his pronouncements on contraception or is he only angry at the papal judgement? Here matters blur. Anger with acquaintances is evidently the focal case, around which the designations of other material object-accusatives can be arranged.

*Nominalization-accusatives of anger*

Now let us turn to examine the nominalization-accusatives of anger that specify why one is angry or why someone else is angry. The kinds of reasons that can intelligibly be adduced for being angry are evident from the *intentional objects of anger expressed by nominalization accusatives*. A person may be angry *that such-and-such has been done* (or omitted), or *at the doing* (or omitting) *of such-and-such*. In such cases, the nominalization-accusative specifies an intentional object of anger that specifies what makes one angry, the ground or reason why one is angry. The affront or apparent affront that may move a person to anger may be (i) impersonal (non-subjective), or (ii) personal (subjective) – an affront *to oneself*. It is noteworthy that one may be angry with, annoyed with, or irritated by (iii) features of a person.

(i)   In the case of impersonal, non-subjective affront, the range of possible grounds for anger include offences against morality (actual or supposed injustices, dishonesties, cruelties, meannesses, wanton destruction of nature, maltreatment of animals, and so forth), and affronts to mores (actual or supposed discourtesies to guests, visitors, members of the public or officials of state; forms of disrespect in the context of displays of public solidarity such as funerals, Remembrance Day ceremonies; public profanities and indecencies; and so on). They also include foolishnesses and incompetences in general by public or private authorities.

(ii)   In the case of personal, subjective affront (or affront to those close to one), the range of possible grounds for anger include:

(a)   failures of reciprocity: failure of a friend to realize the ill consequences for oneself of his or her deed, broken promises, omission of a reciprocal gift (especially important in gift cultures), non-repayment of debts, letting one down, or lack of good neighbourliness;

(b)   spite: the maliciously thwarting of one's will by interference with one's projects; frustrating, impeding, or preventing one's pursuit of one's goals;

(c)   slights: publicly showing contempt for one, insulting one, or manifesting *Schadenfreude* at one's misfortunes; failures of appropriate hospitality;

(d)   disrespect for one's authority: insultingly reluctant obedience, disobedience, or overt challenge;

(e)   foolishnesses and incompetences that impinge upon one, causing inconvenience.

(iii)   A person may be intensely irritated by *features or mannerisms* of people – especially (but not only) with those of people close to one. One may be annoyed by their dress or ornaments; by their personal features – such as abnormalities of face, limb, or posture; by their automatisms (such as sniffling, lisping, stuttering);

by peculiarities of voice (such as intonation, accent, inflection, sighing, kind of laughter); by their gestures, gait, or posture; or by their habits (such as manner of eating, unpunctuality, untidiness). These may irritate, anger, or even infuriate. The infuriated response to such angry-making stimuli may be cruel – mockery, sarcasm, malicious emulation, and outbursts of rage – as exemplified by Jimmy Porter in his tirades against his bourgeois wife Alison in John Osborne's *Look Back in Anger*. But one may be equally annoyed by features or mannerisms of people one does not know (political figures, celebrities) but merely sees on television.

These lists are worth bearing in mind, for, in so far as they correctly present the kinds of grounds for anger as we conceive it, they also serve to show errors in contemporary analyses of anger or differences in the concepts or conceptions of anger evident in the works of writers on the subject in different cultures and in the past.

*Anger and reasons*   It is possible for a person to be angry for no reason, just as one may be afraid for no reason. He may be bubbling with sullen rage. This may be termed pathological anger. It is the task of psychology to discover the causes of such mood-like anger.

Save in cases of pathological anger, there must be some *reason* (good or bad) for being angry with a given person – as opposed to simply venting one's anger upon a person, which is a form of displacement behaviour. The reason for someone's anger may be given by an observer, or avowed by the subject himself. Orgetic behaviour, including what is said and the manner of saying it, provides the circumstance-dependent criteria for ascribing anger to others. Being criteria, the grounds of ascription are defeasible. Sometimes someone may successfully pretend to be angry (just as sometimes one may not reveal one's anger or annoyance). But, if the criteria are not defeated, they warrant the ascription of anger and justify a knowledge claim. The orgetic behaviour is the form that anger takes on this occasion – it is not hidden behind the behaviour.

The first-person case, however, is more, not less, problematic. Although a person's avowal of anger and of his reasons for anger are defeasible, other things being equal, his word carries special weight. He is not *an authority* on his own anger (the idea of first-person 'authority' is a philosophical myth or misnomer). Rather, his word, unlike the word of others, is an *expression of his anger* (or an *ex post facto* report or recollection of his anger). But, in some cases, a person may not be able to say why he is angry (although someone who knows him very well – perhaps his wife – may be able to do so, and, once he has calmed down, he may acknowledge that she is right). In other cases, a person may sincerely avow his reason for being angry, but nevertheless be mistaken. He may be deflecting his own anger with himself onto another. Or, for want of a better target, he may be venting his anger on one innocent of all offence. Or he may be masking his fear, humiliation, or failure with an outburst of anger. And so on.

## 4. Conceptions of anger in antiquity

So much for the connective analysis of anger. Our understanding of the place of anger in human life can be deepened and enriched by scrutiny of some of the ancient literary and philosophical descriptions and analyses of the phenomena. This will both highlight different attitudes towards the various forms that anger may take and demonstrate different ways in which orgetic concepts may be moulded. I shall turn first to the Old Testament.

*Anger in the Old Testament* The Old Testament has a rich vocabulary of anger (*ka'as*), ire or irascibilty (*rogez*), and fury (*za'am, za'aph*). The conceptual iconography is readily intelligible to us. Wrath (*kharon*) links this form of anger with burning. Frenzy (*katsaph*) incorporates a picture of foaming at the mouth, and of snorting in anger or flaring one's nostrils in anger (*kharon aph; anaph*), linking hot anger with the nose and with breathing heavily in anger.

God is commonly angry, wrathful, or enraged with some particular person for his sinfulness, with alien peoples for their attacks upon the children of Israel, or with the children of Israel for their lapses from fidelity to God and from justice in the community, and for their disobedience. The wrath of God is presented either on the model of parental anger with wayward children, or on the model of a ruler confronting the enemies of his people or facing disobedient subjects who have broken his laws or are challenging his authority. Idolatry, a common ground for divine wrath in the older books of the Bible, is represented as a form of disloyalty, or as the breaking of a covenant between God and the Hebrews (as noted in chapter 8, the analogy with marriage is also commonly invoked in association with divine jealousy).[5]

[5] The conception of an angry god is equally alive in Christianity, uneasily juxtaposed with the conception of a god of love. Jesus displays anger himself, and God's wrath is emphasized in Romans 1: 18; 2: 5, 8; 9: 22–3, as well as in Revelation (e.g. 6: 16).

Anger plays a part in many of the Old Testament tales. Cain murders Abel in a rage of envy (Genesis 4: 5–8). Jacob, on his deathbed, curses his sons Shimon and Levi on the grounds of their ferocious destruction of Shechem in revenge for the rape of their sister Dinah: 'Cursed be their anger, for it was fierce; and their wrath, for it was cruel' (Genesis 49: 7). Samson vents his rage upon the Philistines for his wife's betrayal of his riddle (Judges 14).[6] Saul's envious anger at David's military successes and the consequent adulation of the people leads him to attempted murder and plots of assassination (1 Samuel 18–19). David is outraged at Amnon's rape of his sister Tamar (2 Samuel 13). And so on. Some of these outbursts of anger and rage are implicitly approved (Samson's), but most are condemned. The wisdom books of the Old Testament uniformly condemn wrath and anger as impediments to good judgement and harbingers of wrongdoing. The Psalmist instructs us to 'Cease from anger, and forsake wrath: fret not thyself in any wise to do evil' (Psalm 37: 8). Proverbs reiterates the folly of anger: 'He that is slow to wrath has great understanding, but he that is hasty to anger exalteth folly' (14: 29), and 'A wrathful man stirreth up strife, but he that is slow to anger appeaseth strife' (15: 18; cf. 16: 22; 29: 22; 30: 33). And Ecclesiastes associates anger with stupidity: 'Be not hasty in thy spirit to be angry; for anger resteth in the bosom of fools' (7: 9). As we noted, human anger with God is not condemned or damned for *hubris*, impiety, or blasphemy, but taken as a natural human response to the blows of fate.

*Anger in the Iliad*   When we turn to the *Iliad*, we find a very different world and a very different attitude towards anger.

The theme of the epic is indeed wrath, the wrath of Achilles. But ire is also the leitmotiv of the poem, exemplified in the internecine rage of many of the other heroes, such as Hector, Odysseus, Patroclus, Ajax, and Diomedes, and indeed in the anger of the gods for each other and for the humans in whose fates they interfere while pursuing their own feuds. Here too there is a rich vocabulary for different forms of anger. *Mênis* is used to describe the wrath of Achilles. There appears to be no exact equivalent of this expression in English, since it subsumes both deep-seated, long-lasting wrath *and*

---

[6] Samson is the primary archaic hero of the Old Testament, and the fury that enables him to perform superhuman acts of strength, valour, and slaughter is explained (like the Greek *mênis* of the Homeric heroes) by reference to divine intervention, for 'the spirit of the Lord' comes upon him when he rends the lion, slays the Philistines by their hundreds, and finally pulls down the temple of Dagon.

battle frenzy (*lyssa*). The latter aspect is conceived to be of divine origin, for it enables a warrior to perform superhuman deeds of valour and slaughter upon the battlefield.[7] It is given to a hero by a god, who infuses the hero's *thumós* (the manly passions located in his breast) with *mênis*. *Thumós* signifies both the spiritedness of a man – the fire in his belly, as we might colloquially put it – and its manifestation in natural rage. Both Achilles and Hector are said to be possessed of and by deadly *lyssa* (*Iliad* IX. 304–6; XXI. 537–43). Warriors are said to *breathe* fury. Achilles describes *kholos* as 'waxing like smoke in the breasts of men' (*Iliad* XVIII. 110–11). Less ferociously, *khótos* signifies anger, and *kótos* means long-lasting and smouldering rancour or resentment.

The *Iliad* opens by characterizing the wrath (*mênis*) of Achilles as 'accursed', 'fatal', and 'destructive'. For his anger and rancour are said to have

> Cost the Achaeans countless losses,
> hurling down to the House of Death so many sturdy souls,
> great fighters; souls, but made their bodies carrion,
> feasts for the dogs and birds.
>
> (*Iliad*, I. 2–5)

Nevertheless, wrath, rage, and anger are celebrated throughout the epic as the root and source of great deeds of valour that earn heroes what they most crave, namely everlasting fame and glory. Achilles himself characterizes battle rage thus:

> passionate anger [*kholos*], too, which incites
> even the prudent man to that sweet rage,
> sweeter than trickling honey in men's throats
>
> (*Iliad* XVIII. 108–9)

---

[7] The Homeric heroes fight better in battle if they are seized with battle frenzy (*lyssa* or *mênis*), in which they are immune to fear and pain. The same reverence for battle rage is manifest in the Norse sagas' attitude to berserkers. This sentiment is characteristic of an age of heroes – an aristocratic warrior class whose primary social role is warfare and raiding, and whose form of combat is individual face-to-face fighting. Warriors who were able to whip themselves up into such intoxicated states of bloodlust were held to be superhumanly inspired. In ancient Greece, once the hoplite (heavily armoured infantryman) shield wall was invented, it replaced individual combat and the day of the aristocratic hero and his divine battle-frenzy was over.

So anger may have disastrous consequences, but it is also glorious and manly.

Turning from the Homeric epics to the much later philosophical reflections of the fourth century, we find a great change in description and evaluation, as well as a change in vocabulary.[8] Aristotle provides one of the most comprehensive connective analyses of anger presented by a philosopher. He uses the post-Homeric expression *orgē*, which is derived from *orgáō*, meaning 'to swell up', 'to oppose', and is used to signify abiding anger and settled indignation, rather than an outburst of rage. He also uses the much older expression *thumós* to signify, as Plato had done, the spirited part or aspect of the *psuchē*. *Thumós* is derived from *thyō*, meaning 'to rush along', 'get heated up', 'breathe violently'. When a person is host to *thumós*, this signifies boiling up or being inflamed with anger that will soon subside. While *thumós* was said to be like fire in straw, quick to blaze up and quick to burn out, *orgē* is stable and persists, and is prone to grow into hatred and bitterness.

Unlike the dualist tradition that holds emotions to be attributes of the mind (conceiving of the mind as separable from the body), Aristotle sapiently insisted that it is not the *psuchē* that feels emotions, but the human being as a whole. Physical perturbations and somatic manifestations are the matter of an emotion. The reasons for and the intentional objects of an emotion are features of its form. As with body and *psuchē*, one cannot have the latter without the former. Aristotle defines *orgē* thus as 'a desire [or impulse], accompanied by pain, for what one takes to be revenge for what appears to be an offense at the hands of men who have no cause to offend one or one's friends' (*Rhetoric*, 1378ª31). He adds that *orgē* must always be accompanied by pleasure that arises from the expectation of retaliation. Strikingly, he contends that one cannot be angry with those who are superior in power to us (*Rhetoric*, 1370ᵇ13–15), with those whom we fear (*Rhetoric*, 1380ª33), or with social inferiors who cannot slight one.

As already noted, Aristotle applied his doctrine of the mean to the emotions in general. With respect to anger, he observed that

> with regard to anger also there is an excess, a deficiency, and a mean. Although they can scarcely be said to have names, yet since we call the

---

[8] Plato was highly critical of Homer's depiction of Achilles as being mercenary and greedy, with overweening arrogance towards gods and men, and wicked in his mal-treatment of Hector's corpse and in demanding human sacrifices at Patroclos' funeral (*Republic*, 390ᶜ–391ᵈ).

intermediate person good-tempered let us call the mean good temper; of the persons at the extremes let the one who exceeds be called irascible and his vice irascibility and the man who falls short an inirascible sort of person and the deficiency inirascibility. (*Nicomachean Ethics*, 1108$^a$4)

Subsequently he notes the praiseworthiness of the good-tempered man, who is angry at the right things and with the right people, as he ought, when he ought, and for as long as he ought. For the good-tempered man acts as reason dictates. By contrast, the bad-tempered, choleric, sulky man is to be condemned, as is the man who does not get angry at insults and slights. Such a man, according to Aristotle, is slavish or foolish (*Nicomachean Ethics*, 1125$^b$32–1126$^a$2). However, with the example of the noble Socrates' lack of anger at the wrong done him in his trial and at the insults thrown at him, Aristotle should perhaps have distinguished explicitly between the servility of one who accepts slights without any angry response and one who rises above them with nobility.

Aristotle's detailed discussion is exemplary in its scope and systematicity (indeed, it has provided the model for our present investigation). But it is debatable whether he is concerned with anger as we understand it, as opposed to a close cousin of it for which there is no precise English equivalent. It is also debatable whether he is primarily concerned with the common Attic understanding of *orgē*, as opposed to explicating or regimenting it. The latter question will not be discussed here. The former, however, is important, since numerous thinkers continue to cleave to Aristotle's analysis without being aware of its failure to circumscribe the bounds of anger as we understand it. Let us turn to examine his definition of *orgē* not in order to criticize it, but in order to register how deeply *orgē* differs from *anger.*

*Orgē and anger compared*      First, one might say that it is unpleasant to become and be angry. Unlike joy and delight, it is not an emotion for which one would wish. It is not generally true that anger is accompanied by pleasure at the expectation of retaliation (But it is noteworthy that there are those who enjoy fits of rage at their subordinates in order to boost their sense of self-importance and to confirm for themselves their power and superiority.)

Secondly, it is false that anger, as we understand the term, is aroused only by slight or insult to ourselves or our friends. One may be angry with one's spouse for not having done the washing up or for having forgotten to get some bread (which are neither insults nor slights), or with one's young children or aged parents for repeatedly making the same elementary mistake on the computer.

Thirdly, anger is not always aimed at retaliation or retribution, at inflicting suffering or punishment upon another. Marital, parental, or filial anger and annoyance may aim merely to correct or to object. Aristotle, in the *Rhetoric*, may have been thinking exclusively of the emotion aroused in the law court, where the plaintiff does indeed wish to retaliate or to inflict retribution (particularly in a legal system that does not distinguish tort from criminal law). But it is evident, in the *Ethics*, that Aristotle's claims extend beyond that context.

Fourthly, since anger need not involve any punitive or retaliatory desire, there is no reason why it should always be accompanied by any pleasurable thoughts of future vengeance and retribution – even though it may well have done so in the Athenian law courts, as it does in ours.

Fifthly, Aristotle's circumscription of the personal objects of *orgē* do not fit our notion of anger. We *can* intelligibly be said to be angry with an animal, and we surely are very commonly angry with small children (even though they cannot slight one). We *can* be angry with and feel resentful towards our superiors for their slights and insults, their meanness or ingratitude for our services. And we *can* be angry with our servants and employees, even though they may not be able to slight us.

Finally, we unhesitatingly speak of being angry with ourselves, but it is by no means obvious that Aristotle would find reflexive *orgē* intelligible. For we cannot literally slight or insult ourselves – although we may curse ourselves for our misdeeds and weaknesses – nor can we wish to take vengeance upon ourselves for a slight we have inflicted on ourselves.

Despite these marked deviations between *orgē* and our conceptions of anger, many great thinkers in the past, and some thinkers in the present, have felt no hesitation in unreflectively adopting Aristotle's analysis. Aquinas wrote: 'An angry reaction arises only when one has endured some pain, and desires and hopes for revenge' (*Summa Theologica*, $1^a2^{ae}$, q. 46, art. 1). Anger, he thought, both requires and impedes rational activity: it is reason that recognizes an offence, and reason that provides a motive for action. So animals can be angry only in a secondary sense, since they lack the powers of reason and reasoning. Similarly, he argues, we cannot properly, but only metaphorically speaking, be angry with ourselves. Descartes too followed the Aristotelian tradition: 'Anger is also a kind of hatred or aversion that we have towards those who have tried to harm not just anyone they happen to meet but us in particular ... it is based on an action that affects us and for which we have a desire to avenge ourselves' (*Passions of the Soul*, III. 199). Spinoza followed Descartes: 'The striving to do evil to him we hate is called Anger' (*Ethics*, II. 172).

It seems clear that we should be wrong to criticize Aristotle for having given a mistaken analysis of the ubiquitous emotion of anger. Rather he gave an analysis or perhaps an explication of the Greek emotion of *orgē*, which is not synonymous with 'anger'. The words express overlapping but nevertheless somewhat different concepts belonging to different times and different cultures.

## 5. Is acting in anger warranted?

*Approval of some*    Both Plato and Aristotle thought that some form of
*forms of anger*    anger was sometimes warranted and often useful
(e.g. in battle). Plato held it to be an intrinsic aspect of the spirited part of the tripartite soul, and, as long as it is governed by reason (the charioteer controlling the two-horse chariot of spirit and appetite), it is meritorious. It is, figuratively speaking, a good servant but a bad master. Aristotle, as noted, did not contrast anger and reason in the same manner as Plato, for anger too has its reasons. He thought that a man who is angry for the right reason, with the right person, to the right degree, on the right occasion, and in the right manner is praiseworthy.

    By contrast, Cicero, Seneca, and other Stoics
*Stoic condemnation*    insisted that anger is always to be condemned.
*of anger*    Cicero averred that 'Anger [*ira*] ... when it disturbs
the mind at any time, leaves no room to doubt its being madness.' Citing the hideous tale of Atreus and Thyestes,[9] Cicero objected to Plato's conception of anger and of the role of the spirited part of the *psuché*:

> Therefore we say, properly enough, that angry men have given up their power, that is, they are beyond the power of advice, reason, and understanding; for these ought to have power over the whole mind ... Where

---

[9] Atreus, in his anger at his brother Thyestes for his adulterous relation with Atreus' wife. Aerope, murdered Thyestes' two sons and served them up for dinner to their father.

then are they who say that anger has its use? Can madness be of any use? (*Tusculaneum Disputations*, IV. 36, 37)

Seneca developed the argument. He objected to Aristotle's claim that anger may be warranted and useful (e.g. in battle) as long as there are good reasons for being angry, that it is directed at the right person, and so on. For, Seneca averred:

> if it listens to reason and follows whither reason leads, it is no longer anger, whose characteristic is obstinacy ... If, therefore, anger allows limits to be imposed upon it, it must be called by some other name, and ceases to be anger, which I understand to be unbridled and unmanageable. (*De Ira*, I. 9)

One need but observe the faces of those who are enraged, Seneca added, to perceive that they are temporarily mad. The good man will not be angry if he sees his father murdered and his mother outraged, but will protect them or avenge them out of filial duty rather than impulsively in a frenzy. Indeed, Seneca declares, no plague has cost humanity more dear than anger, which has so often caused slaughter, the sacking of cities, and the ruin of peoples.

*Christian views of anger*      To some extent, as Aquinas pointed out, they were arguing at cross purposes (*Summa Theologica*, 1ᵃ2ᵃᵉ, q. 24, art. 2, reply). Plato and Aristotle argued that there were forms of anger that were warranted, being under the control of Reason (Plato), or reasonable in themselves (Aristotle). Cicero and Seneca argued that anger by definition is not under rational control and cannot be reasonable. Neither Plato nor Aristotle would have endorsed acting in a rage or frenzy of anger. Plato thought of rage metaphorically as the upshot of the charioteer of Reason losing control of the spirited white horse of the passions. Aristotle conceived it as exemplifying bad reasons overwhelming good judgement that is swamped by the agitations and perturbations of anger and the accompanying *phantasmata* (mental images). Aquinas's examination of anger endeavours both to do justice to Aristotle's account, and to accommodate the Christian view that anger is a deadly sin and a capital vice. Contrary to St Jerome, St John Cassian, and St Gregory the Great, Aquinas asserts that if one is angry with good reason and to the right degree, then anger is praiseworthy. For emotions may be vicious in two different ways: in respect of their end (as envy is), and in respect of their degree. But zealous (righteous) anger aims at just retribution (warranted vengeance), and reasonable anger is well controlled. Nevertheless, in so far as it is unjust, uncharitable, and inordinate, anger is a deadly sin. It is also a capital vice in so far as it is productive of blasphemy, abuse, rancour, and quarrels.

*Spinoza on anger*    Quite different from these disagreements between Peripatetics and Stoics, and Christian compromises with Aristotle, was Spinoza's attitude towards anger. Where we might, with good reason, say that anger is prone to grow into hatred, Spinoza defined anger in terms of hatred. Hatred, he held, was 'nothing but *Sadness with the accompanying idea of an external cause*' (*Ethics*, III. 13, schol.). To hate is to desire to remove or destroy what is hated. One may hate something or someone because of the evil they have caused one, or by association with some such cause. *Indignation* is hatred of someone who has done evil to another person. *Anger* is the striving to do evil to someone one hates; *vengeance* is the striving to return an evil done to one; *scorn* is thinking less highly of someone than is just, out of hatred. With these propositions in place, Spinoza declares uncompromisingly that 'Envy, Mockery, Disdain, Anger, Vengeance and the rest of the affects which are related to Hate, or arise from it, are evil' (*Ethics*, II. 45, cor. 1). A corollary of this judgement is that whatever we want because we have been affected with hate is dishonourable. In proposition 46 of *Ethics* II, Spinoza draws an anti-Aristotelian conclusion: 'He who lives according to the guidance of reason strives, as far as he can, to repay the other's Hate, Anger and Disdain toward him, with Love, or Nobility.' His demonstration is straightforward: all the emotions of hate are evil. So to live according to reason means striving not to be beset with hatred, and striving that others too should be free of it. Spinoza had no doubt that hatred and anger destroy the very soul of a person (in Aquinas's terms, they are deadly sins):

> He who wishes to avenge wrongs by hating in return surely lives miserably. On the other hand, one who is eager to overcome Hate by Love, strives joyously and confidently, resists many men as easily as one, and requires the least help from fortune. (*Ethics*, II. 46, schol.)

This is undoubtedly beyond most of us. The moot question is whether it is an intelligible ideal.

*Buddhist condemnation of anger*    The Buddha would have judged Spinoza to be one of the enlightened. Holding on to anger, he held, is like grasping a hot coal to throw at someone else. Anger is not a sign of strength, but of weakness. It is a form of self-inflicted harm. Like the Stoics, he thought that the idea of righteous anger is akin to that of beneficial disease. Anger is always wrong. Whether or not one is punished *for* one's anger, one is inevitably punished *by* one's anger. Susceptibility to anger, both agreed, is a form of human bondage. Unlike the Stoics, but like Spinoza, the Buddha believed that the proper response to hatred is love. For hatred does not cease through anger. The enlightened person *cannot* be slighted or insulted – for he will see the slights and insults of others as manifestations of the flaws and weaknesses of their personality, and will beware of being contaminated by them. A fictional character who exemplifies this ethos (albeit within the framework of Christian faith) is Alyosha Karamazov, whose response to insults and abuse is no more than a troubled but sympathetic look.

*Warranted anger*     Against this one might point out that indignation is often an expression of one's concern and care. To observe another's gross maltreatment of an animal or child without becoming indignant and indeed outraged would surely show culpable indifference. Resentment may indeed be an appropriate response to false accusations, innuendo, and other attacks on one's proper pride and self-respect. Indifference to such treatment would, at least in some cases, manifest excessive humility or servility. (Even that model of gentleness, Mr Harding, the precentor of Barchester Cathedral, becomes angry at the insulting rebukes of Mrs Proudie and Mr Slope (Trollope, *Barchester Towers*, ch. 5).) Furthermore, anger may spur the sides of one's intent when one fears to protest against offence. It may fortify one's courage to take a stand against injustice or wrong-doing.

*The evil of anger*     So, we must endeavour to get the vexed question of whether anger can be warranted into focus. Aristotle was surely right in his account of the manifold vices essentially associated with anger. There are many ways in which anger in some of its forms manifests a vice. An *irascible* man gets angry too quickly, and works himself into a destructive rage. In such cases, one allows one's temper to gain control of oneself and reason is flung to the winds. The history of rulers succumbing to rage attests to its madness (e.g. Alexander's drunken and infuriated murder of Cleitus; Valentian's envious and enraged murder of Aetius ('the last of the Romans'), and Henry II's outburst of rage against Becket,[10] which precipitated his

---

[10] His words, recorded by Roger Grim, were 'I have nourished and promoted in my realm idle and wretched knaves, faithless to their lord, whom they suffer to be mocked thus shamefully by a low-born clerk.'

murder by Roger fitzUrse and his comrades). The *hot-tempered man* is beset with a vice that wreaks havoc and reduces himself to the level of a beast. He acts out of control, without regard to consequences, and will often regret his murderous outburst. A *bad-tempered man* may become angry with the wrong person, for a mistaken or a wrong reason, in disregard of excuses or justification. This may lead to gross injustice. Seneca tells a terrible tale of Gnaeus Piso, an arrogant and irascible military commander. A soldier goes on leave with a comrade, and returns alone. Piso assumes that he must have murdered his comrade and sentences him to death. Just as the trooper is about to be executed, his comrade turns up. The centurion orders the execution to be stopped, and goes to Piso, pleased to have saved the life of an innocent man. Piso flies into a rage and orders the execution of both soldiers – the one because he had already been condemned, the second because he was the cause of his comrade's condemnation – and also of the centurion for disobedience. Here, Seneca observes, anger concocted three charges because it had grounds for none (*De Ira*, I. 16).[11] The *sulky* and *petulant child* is father to the *surly* and *resentful* man. The resentful man is prone to brood on what has angered him, to allow the slight or insult to him to rankle. He harbours his sullen anger, making his own life and the lives of those around him a misery (as does Jimmy Porter in *Look Back in Anger*). A man humiliated, insulted, and maltreated may well become *rancorous* and embittered, as does Heathcliff in *Wuthering Heights*. He may indeed rend himself with his ire. He may feed his anger with fantasies of vengeance, as one feeds smouldering coals with further fuel. His resentment may become obsessive, and grow into boundless, self-destructive hatred.

*Controlling anger*  It is because of this dreadful progression of bottled-up rage that one is often advised to express, rather than suppress, one's anger (see Blake's 'A Poison Tree' in *Songs of Experience*). It is said that anger should not be an overnight guest – left to rankle, it may never leave the house. But this is only a half-truth. There are no general rules that can guide one in the choice between suppressing one's anger and expressing it. (George and Martha, in *Who's Afraid of Virginia Woolf?*, constantly express their anger – doing so has become a ritualized game they play to relieve their self-contempt by blaming their spouse for their pain. Their expression of their anger does not relieve them of their torment.)

---

[11] This horrible tale is repeated, to illustrate the same point, by Montaigne in his essay 'On Anger' (*Essays*, II. 31).

Often suppressing one's anger may minimize damage, and the anger fades away overnight without more ado. In other cases, expressing one's anger may clear the air. Only good judgement can avail one, but anger is a poor seedbed for good judgement.

*Warranted anger*

Anger is a natural human emotion. It is easy to see its evolutionary warrant, but there is very little reason to think that this warrant is retained in civilized life. In the form of battle rage, it may have had its place in the heroic ages and in face-to-face combat to this day, but has little merit in disciplined warfare (as Seneca pointed out). Aristotle held there to be reasonable and meritorious *orgē* (with the right person, for the right reason, to the right degree of intensity) that is rightly expressed (on the right occasion, in the right manner). Reason is indeed needed to apprehend what is offensive, to oneself or to others. Indignation or resentment may indeed be appropriate emotional responses to slight and insult, to false accusations, or to various forms of offence. That is a proper mark of concern and care. Annoyance and irritation are natural reactions to various forms of disturbance, and natural expressions of frayed nerves. But these natural responses need to be dampened and kept under control lest they feed the flames of fury. Even if anger is warranted, it does not follow that any form of manifestation of anger is warranted. We often have an obligation to control, moderate, or suppress the manifestation of our anger.

Anger is a warranted response to wrong-doing in its manifold forms. It may fuel one's courage to oppose what is wrong. Nevertheless, to act *in anger* is never well advised. One may castigate without rage, censure and deplore without fury. The greater one's wrath, the more likely it is that one's judgement be led astray, one's utterances be inappropriate or worse, and one's action be unjust and harmful. One may rightly seek redress. It is good to endeavour to destroy evil. But reason needs no support from rage and anger in heightened forms in its quest for the right and the good.

There is, then, good reason to consider *proneness* to anger as something to be discouraged. For anger can destroy friendship and love. It may feed rancour and paranoia. It may blacken the very soul of man, twist his temperament into ever more ugly shapes, and even leave its brand upon an embittered face. It is equally evident that, if it takes root, it can become a capital vice, for it *can* feed hatred and nourish cruelty.

# PART III

## The Saving Graces:
## Love, Friendship, and Sympathy

# 10

# Love

## 1. Concepts and conceptions of love

*Biological roots and*   The manifold phenomena of love exhibited in
*social framework*    diverse human societies during different periods
of recorded history are rooted in biological fea-
tures of human beings. But the trunk, foliage, and fruits of the trees
that grow out of these biological grounds vary greatly from society
to society, from one social class to another, and from one period to
another. There are multiple ways of coping with these characteristic
features of the human species – different ways of channelling and
controlling the needs, desires, susceptibilities, and dispositions that
are evident in love. Different social, economic, and legal arrangements are the climate and weather that condition the nature of the
love that can develop at any given time. It would be mistaken to
suppose that the forms of human love have progressed until their
final culmination in current patterns of amatory relations in the
West. It would be equally mistaken to suppose that any form of loving relation exhibited by any society throughout history is as good
as any other. Not all the forms in which love has been realized (or
theorized) in different societies are equally conducive to human
flourishing and felicity. But no one of them is *uniquely* superior to
all others. The human need for love and care may well seek satisfaction in the future in relationships very different from the marital,

*The Passions: A Study of Human Nature*, First Edition. P. M. S. Hacker.
© 2018 John Wiley & Sons Ltd. Published 2018 by John Wiley & Sons Ltd.

parental, and filial love with which we are familiar in Western culture
in the late twentieth and early twenty-first centuries.

The different forms in which the human
*Different concepts and*    disposition to love is realized and in which the
*conceptions of love*      human need for love is accommodated are asso-
                           ciated with different *conceptions* of love, differ-
ent ways of thinking about love. Here, even more than in the case of
other emotions that we have examined so far, the distinction between
concepts and conceptions is needed. Possession of a concept is mastery
of the use of an expression. A concept is an abstraction from the use
of an expression. We have relatively little difficulty and, for the most
part, little hesitation in translating *l'amour, Liebe, amor, eros*, and
*ahava* (and their siblings and cousins) as 'love'. Whether the concepts
expressed are the same or different depends upon the context of their
use and on our fluid criteria for concept identity in this domain. There
are, to be sure, differences in the uses of the expressions in the different
languages and at different times; whether these differences are to be
counted as essential or inessential depends on the purposes at hand.

There is no doubt that the ways in which thinkers, novelists, dramatists, and poets in different times or societies have *conceived* of love
have been profoundly different. Some have thought of it as an ennobling emotion; others have conceived of it as a deplorable form of
madness. Some have thought of it as a relation between equals, incon-
ceivable as obtaining between superior and inferior. Some have
thought of it as a relationship between two human beings; others
conceived it as perfected only when directed at a non-human object,
such as God or the Idea of the Good. In classical Greece paederastic
love between a teenage boy and an adult young man was thought
to be a normal phase in adolescence and a prototype of love (*eros*).
Many of the church fathers (e.g. Tertullian, Cyprian, Ambrose,
Jerome) conceived of genuine love (*agape*) to be primarily a reciprocal
relationship between a person and God, and of sexual love (*eros,
concupiscentia*) between man and woman as a manifestation of
human weakness to be constrained within the marital relationship
and indulged in, if at all, only for procreative purposes. Courtly love
(*fin'amor*), in the form it assumed within the court circles of Provence
and Aquitaine in the eleventh and twelfth centuries, was conceived to
be primarily a redemptive and ennobling relationship between a
well-born man and a married noblewoman, normally not to be consummated. Romantic conceptions of love, as they erupted in Europe
in the late eighteenth and early nineteenth centuries, presented erotic

love as a transcendent and sublime relationship constituting the acme of human experience (for detail, see appendix).

The boundary lines between concept (expressed by the use of an expression) and conception (how the phenomena subsumed under the concept are thought of) are blurred here – much more so than in the case of other emotions. This is no coincidence. There is no analytic definition of love that captures in its net the use of the word. To define love as a steady will for the good of the person loved, for example, would exclude the love of God as well as various forms of passionate erotic love,[1] not to mention love of activities and possessions, of nature, and of art. The use of 'love' and its cognates is neither taught nor learnt by means of a fixed set of necessary and sufficient conditions. Nor are misuses of it corrected by reference to any agreed analytical definition. Rather, we can cite a variety of marks of love, some members or disjunction of members of which are arguably necessary features of love, others of which characterize most cases. Similarly, we can cite behavioural criteria for someone's loving another person or thing – but they are defeasible. We might establish agreement in concepts by an agreement on paradigm cases, although we do not define 'love' by reference to paradigm cases. For the paradigm cases of the wide variety of forms of love on which we might agree presuppose the concept and do not explain it. They do not function as a rule for the use of the expression, inasmuch as they do not function as a surveyable set that provides a guide for its application. Love is not obviously a family resemblance concept. One could not say 'This, this, and this, and other things like these, are cases of love', and expect this to be a guide and a standard for the use of the word. The penumbra of love is vague; and what belongs to the concept and what to varying conceptions of love is indeterminate.

With this brief preliminary, let us turn first to the *biological roots of love* and subsequently to the *social constraints* within which its various forms are possible.

## 2. The biological and social roots of love

*Biological roots of love*   It is a brute fact about *Homo sapiens* that members of the species typically have a very powerful sexual drive. Like other mammals, we reproduce sexually,

---

[1] Catullus, e.g., seems not the least concerned with the good of Lesbia (who, it is conjectured, was Clodia Metelli, the infamous sister of the rabble-rousing Publius Clodius Pulcher).

feel sexual appetite, copulate, and take pleasure in copulating and in orgasm. Males and females, especially in youth, are erotically attracted to each other by their respective somatic characteristics. Unlike most mammals, adult human males do not go into rut for an annual mating season, and females are receptive not only in a breeding season. No other mammals blush, and consequently other mammals do not blush when attracting sexual attention. Few other mammals appear to take pleasure in exploring each other's bodies prior to or while coupling, and manifest little if any desire to give pleasure during intercourse. Such biological features of human beings play a role in the transformation of lust into directed sexual desire and into erotic love.

*Sexual urge, directed lust, erotic love*      The sexual drive and the need to satisfy it are persistent, and may be triggered physiologically, cogitatively (by imagination), or externally (by perceived stimuli). The brute sexual urge is animal – an appetite similar to the other natural appetites of hunger and thirst. It is a felt sensation blended with desire, it is localizable, and it is recurrent. Satisfying lust, like satisfying other appetites, is a relief, although the pleasure is far more intense. Unlike hunger, thirst, and addictions, lust is person-involving. For one slakes one's lust on or with another human being. The feeling of lust *need not* involve a *specific* object. One may simply desire sexual relief through copulation (e.g. the rape rage of soldiers after capturing a city). But, unlike the other appetites that *cannot* have any specific object, sexual desire *may* be directed at a specific person (as Tarquin lusted after Lucretia and not just any noblewoman, or Potiphar's wife after Joseph and not just any slave in court). It is a characteristic feature of civilization to tame explosive human sexual appetites, transforming particularized sexual desire that may constitute no more than directed lust into erotic love and the forms of mutual respect that characteristically accompany it.[2] The moralization of sexuality, its valorization, the manner in which it is regulated by moral norms, and the forms of its institutionalization are both marks and measures of a culture.

*Maternal love*      The human procreative urge among women is natural to our species. The procreative urge among men, as opposed to lust and sexual desire, is much less the product of biology and much more a function of social psychology and social mores. Maternal love is rooted in mammalian nature.

---

[2] The most intelligent and sensitive discussion of this theme that I have encountered is R. Scruton's *Sexual Desire* (Continuum, London, 2006), to which I am indebted.

Maternal attachment or bonding is normally instinctive, beginning during pregnancy and typically strengthening during lactation.[3] It does not rest on reasons, but provides reasons – for thought, feeling, and action. The ideal love of a mother for her child is a common transcultural paradigm of selflessness. In dire circumstances, maternal love may go to its ultimate limit in suicidal self-sacrifice. To be sure, this is a behavioural proneness shared with many other animal species, save for the self-consciousness involved in maternal self-sacrifice, which renders it a form of love. Maternal feelings and behaviour weave together three characteristics: first, a self-conscious, selfless concern for the requirements of the child; secondly, a similar concern for the benefit of the child; and thirdly, the reciprocal bonding between mother and child, of which the mother is aware. The idealized love of a mother for her child, in childhood and adulthood alike, is a prototype of devotion, tenderness, care, protection, and forgiveness.[4]

*Parental, filial, and sibling love*     The prolonged period of dependency of neonates upon maternal care and of children upon parental care, protection, and teaching is a further conditioning *socio-biological* fact. The process of physical maturation is slow, and the transmission of essential knowledge and skills characteristic of any human society takes many years. The forms

---

[3] Lactation produces oxytocin, which increases parasympathetic activity. The evolutionary explanation for the innate maternal disposition to love the neonate, and for mutual bonding is evident.

[4] Finely articulated by Heinrich Heine:

| | |
|---|---|
| I sought love far and near, unrespited, | Die Liebe suchte ich auf allen Gassen, |
| I stretched my hands to every kindly soul, | Vor jeder Thüre streckt' ich aus die Hände |
| And begged crumbs of love as for a dole: | Und bettelte um g'ringe Liebesspende – |
| Laughing they gave me chilling hate instead. | Doch lachend gab man mir nur kaltes Hassen. |
| And ever did I search for love – yes, ever | Und immer irrte ich nach Liebe, immer |
| Pursued the quest of love, but found it never, | Nach Liebe, doch die Liebe fand ich nimmer, |
| And came back home, dejected and downcast. | Und kehrte ich nach Hause, krank und trübe. |
| But there you came to welcome me again, | Doch da bist du entgegen mir gekommen, |
| And oh! Within your eyes I saw it then – | Und ach! Was da in deinem Aug' geschwommen, |
| There was the sweet, the long-sought love at last. | Das war die süsse, langgesuchte Liebe. |
| | 'To My Mother, B. Heine' |
| | (trans. Hal Draper) |

parent–child relationships may take are moulded by the size of the prevailing social groups, by economic imperatives, by social convention and law, and they vary between different periods of history, different cultures, and different social classes.

A child's attachment to both parents naturally involves trust if the child is brought up by its parents with care and love. Sibling attachment or bonding is typical in the common familial structure of most human societies. Sibling love is a natural growth out of common parentage and upbringing, shared experience, natural empathy and sympathy. It is fostered by mutual dependency and reciprocal advantage, but may war with competition for parental love and attention, as well as competition for distinction. Parents are typically sources of authority, solace, and advice, and role models for the children. Accordingly both mother and father may become objects of filial respect, love, and affection. This may be weakened by the separation of small children from their mother (their early allocation to a wet nurse and subsequent upbringing by slaves, nannies, or tutors) or by their early removal from the parental home (boys in Sparta were sent to the barracks at the age of seven; aristocratic boys in medieval Europe were sent to the household of another nobleman for training; upper-class boys in Victorian, Edwardian, and post-Edwardian England were sent to boarding school). The persistence of paternal authority over adult children may have deleterious consequences (in ancient Rome, it included unconstrained rights of disinheritance, which inadvertently encouraged patricide during periods of social upheaval (e.g. under Sulla)).

*Love: an emotion of language users* Language is a uniquely human social practice. Other animals may communicate with each, but they do not talk. *Homo sapiens*, I have suggested in earlier volumes,[5] is a misnomer, but the description *Homo loquens* characterizes our essential nature. Human beings are essentially language users, and it is our nature as language users that makes it possible for humans beings to love another. For only a language user can exercise the reproductive imagination in daydreaming about past encounters with someone loved, and exercise the productive imagination in fantasizing on the next encounter. Only a thinking being can realize that he or she is in love or find himself or herself obsessed with love. Only a rational creature can conceive of love as being of *intrinsic value* and as *imposing moral demands* upon those bound by ties of

---

[5] *Human Nature: the Categorial Framework* (Blackwell, Oxford, 2007) and *The Intellectual Powers: A Study of Human Nature* (Wiley Blackwell, 2013).

love. Love can be a motive for action, that is, provide a pattern of back-ward- and forward-looking reasons, only for creatures that *can* reason and can *weigh reasons*. That is why it is mistaken, even though natural, to speak of an animal's loving its mate or its young. It is mistaken inasmuch as the complexity of the emotion of love involves cognitive, cogitative, mnemonic, and imaginative abilities that are beyond the powers of non-human animals that lack a developed language. Animals may be attracted to each other at first sight but cannot fall in love at first sight, nor can they realize that they are in love. They may bond for life, but they cannot wish to share their lives. They may demonstrate affection for each other but not persistent love. Pets may show great affection for their master or mistress, and even pine away on their death. But it does not follow that they love them.

The concept-laden character of love, as we conceive it, is made vivid by the fact that *realization* that one loves another typically involves *recognition* of requirements thereby imposed on one. Loving another person or thing generates reasons for acting that would otherwise not obtain. These requirements are typically met without any reluctance, and fulfilled willingly. Coupled with recognition of the requirements of love is a powerful desire, characteristic more of women than of men, *to be desired* (especially in the courting stage) and to be needed (especially in companionate marriage or partnership). A further conceptual node in the web is the *desire to please*. Moreover, one wishes the person one loves to recognize one's endeavours to please *as* expressions of love, and to value them as such. *Inspired by love*, the lover wants to please in surprising and unexpected ways. (This, to be sure, applies to parental and filial love too.)

Marriage is the most common human institution for

*Marriage: the institutional framework* the regularization of sexual relationships, for the generation of children, and for the allocation of responsibility for their upbringing. It provides for the possibility of different forms of mutual dependency and mutual protection, and furnishes the framework for the possibility of satisfying the widespread human need to be cared for and to care for. The forms of love and affection, of attachment and trust, of intimacy (both physical and psychological), of intergenerational love that can evolve and flourish within the marital framework are, to be sure, a function of prevalent mores and morals, and of a multitude of social, economic, and legal conditions and conventions that frame the institution of marriage in any social class, at any time or place. Throughout European history, monogamous marriage between members of propertied classes was a contractual relationship designed to unite two distinct social groups, rather than merely two people. Its purposes were predominantly procreative, reticular,[6] and acquisitive. Love was not held to be a prerequisite for, or to be the normal antecedent to, marriage.

*Social frameworks of love*  The family is the minimal social unit of mankind. It may be nuclear or extended, the core of a household (e.g. the Roman aristocratic household) or of a clan. Extended family relations and the manifold relations within a large household typically involve forms of affection, loyalty, and dependency. The extended family or familial household was a part of a larger social grouping – of a patriciate, aristocracy, feudal nobility; or of tribe, clan, village, or town. Social relations of labour, craft, or commerce commonly engender mutually beneficial cooperative activities that may blossom into forms of friendship. Proximate relations with neighbours often foster amicable relations between children. Relations between post-pubescent youths typically lead to passing amity. In the warrior societies that characterize much of human history, shared battle experience and mutual trust and reliance in battle were powerful forms of male bonding. Friendship (or, as Aristotle called it, 'primary friendship') has often been conceived to rise to the level of a form of love (*philia*), without the encumbrances of *eros* (see chapter 11).

Tribal and regional bonds (strengthened by common sociolect) and identification with a people or state engender loyalties to specific authority figures, as well as to the larger social unit. The personal loyalty of servant to master or mistress, of squire to knight, and of soldier to commander can (but need not) grow into a form of love. The human capacity for attachment to a larger social unit is likewise the root of local, regional, tribal, and national loyalties. Thence grows the love of the people for their country and for their ruler. (It is a remarkable and disturbing fact that the most evil leaders and rulers of the twentieth-century, Hitler, Stalin, and Mao, were also the most loved.)

## 3. The objects of love

*Objects of love*  The possible objects of love as we conceive it are manifold. The range of items that can intelligibly be said to be loved apart from human beings and social groups is wide

---

[6] i.e. aimed at fostering a network.

(see fig. 10.2). Domestication of animals characterizes most known human societies, and the use of animals for transport and for hunting naturally leads to bonding between owner and animal, especially dogs and horses. The bonding is mutual – since the animal may display not only recognition and attachment, but also affection. It is therefore unsurprising that we speak of loving one's horse or dog, and of loving a pet, although, as we have seen, it would be mistaken to conceive of our pet as loving its master or mistress.

Love of nature and of the beauty of nature, although common in modern culture, by no means characterizes all human societies at all times (there is little trace of it in surviving early medieval texts or paintings).[7] It is, for the most part, a privilege of those who do not need to extract a living from nature by the sweat of their brows and do not, accordingly, view nature with hostility. It is manifest in admiration of landscape and of fauna and flora, in the desire to travel to see and spend time in natural beauty, in love of hiking in the countryside for pleasure (elevated to an ideal by the Romantics), and in landscape painting, which in the post-classical world, evolved into a genre in the West only in the sixteenth and seventeenth centuries.

The notion of loving one's work is perfectly familiar, and we think of those who love their work and dedicate their efforts to it as singularly fortunate. At a higher level of abstraction, the attachment to one's culture, and the striving for ideals, such as honour, justice, or beauty, are conceived to be severally forms of love.

The idea of loving God originated in the religion of ancient Israel, was developed throughout the centuries of composition of the books of the Old Testament, and further refined by the rabbinical schools. It was taken over and variously modified by the subsequent two monotheistic religions, Christianity and Islam. Why the idiom of love

---

[7] Petrarch, in 1336, was exceptional in wanting to climb a mountain (Mount Ventoux) in order to see the view from the summit. His consequent feelings of guilt at his pleasure in the beauty of the landscape is notorious. It was generated by his reading in his pocket edition of Augustine's *Confessions* when seated on the summit. As he later wrote: 'I closed the book, angry with myself that I should still be admiring earthly things who might long ago have learned from even the pagan philosophers that nothing is wonderful but the soul, which, when great itself, finds nothing great outside itself. Then, in truth, I was satisfied that I had seen enough of the mountain; I turned my inward eye upon myself, and from that time not a syllable fell from my lips until we reached the bottom again. We look about us for what is to be found only within ... How many times, think you, did I turn back that day, to look at the summit of the mountain which seemed scarcely a cubit high compared with the range of human contemplation' (*Epistolae Familiares*, IV. 1).

should be extended to the relation between human beings and their god, and what exactly might be meant by loving a supernatural omnipotent being is problematic. It is connected to loyalty love of a subject to a superior and to filial love of a father (and hence to loving obedience), and to the abnegation of one's own selfish will (see appendix).

It is a very general fact about human beings that they are *attracted* to material things, dwellings, and places, and become *attached* to family houses, objects, estates, and locations. These forms of attachment, if sufficiently intense and lasting, are, in numerous languages, subsumed under the concept of loving – of loving one's birthplace or home, the countryside in which one grew up or in which one chooses to live, the mountains one views, the river or lake in which one fishes or swims. Human beings are attracted to artefacts for a wide variety of different reasons – their utility, their beauty, the social prestige of their possession, and so forth. If such an artefact is duly acquired, one often becomes deeply attached to it for an equally wide range of reasons – who gave it to one, who made it, to whom it previously belonged, what has been done with it and what one has done with it oneself, and so on. One may also become attached to a thing (e.g. the kitchen table of one's childhood) or location (e.g. the slum in which one grew up, such as the East End) not because one is or ever was attracted to it, but because of familiarity with it and the community that lived there. So it is entirely natural to speak of loving things to which one is thus attracted or attached, for one values them, does not wish to part with them, and takes care of them. Human beings have strong appetitive desires and marked preferences for their objects. So we talk of loving such-and-such foods or beverages. This is, to be sure, no more than a case of intense liking. But it is a natural (but non-necessary) extension of the idiom of love. For one likes them, prefers them to others, goes out of one's way to get them, and takes pleasure in consuming them. Similarly, likings for distinctive activities or passivities (doings as opposed to watchings) may grow into a passion.

What knits all these together? Not a determinate set of necessary and sufficient conditions, but a variety of threads that duly knotted together at nodes form a web (see fig. 10.1). To be sure, one stable component in the emotion of love in all its forms is the subjective *importance* (i) of the object of love, and (ii) of one's loving it. Loving someone or something is never trivial or insignificant to the subject. It occupies an important place in one's life, and in some of its forms (such as erotic love, companionate love, parental love) an overwhelmingly dominant place. Although other emotions, such as vengeful

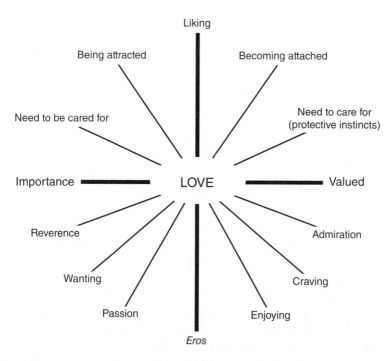

**Figure 10.1** *Connecting threads in the web of the objects of love*

hatred, jealousy, or envy *may* assume monstrous proportions, dominating the lives of their subjects (literary examples abound, e.g. Walter Herries in Walpole's *The Fortress*; Marcel in Proust's *The Prisoner*; Cousine Bette in Balzac's eponymous novel), these are exceptions rather than the rule. But, in the case of the love of another human being, it is the rule. A further characteristic feature of love, as we heirs of the Romantics conceive it, is that it is normally valued. We (unlike, say, typical Romans of the first century BC) think of a life bereft of love as flawed. Other things being equal, we think of the experience of falling in love, of being in love, and of loving another person as intrinsically valuable and as a constituent part of a good and fulfilled human life.

*Limits of love: concepts and conceptions*

What it makes sense to say of one kind of love may make no sense of another. One can be infatuated or besotted with a man or woman, but with God one can only become intoxicated, and with one's country none of these. One can dote on one's spouse or children but

**Figure 10.2**   *A synopsis of objects of love*

not on a book. One can worship God, one's inamorata, one's parent, or a leader but not a pet or neonate. One can feel amorous towards one's lover, but not towards other objects of love. One may have reasons for loving a work of art, a city, or an activity, for in such cases the value we apprehend in what we love provides us with a reason for loving it. But other kinds of love are independent of reasons for loving. We shall explore the peculiarities of the nexus between inter-personal love and reasons later in the chapter.

Other, somewhat different, concepts or conceptions of love would doubtless exclude some of the items we have mentioned as possible objects of love. In some societies or in some circles of society, the idea that a man should *love* his wife would have seemed bizarre, either because all true love is between equals (and husband and wife were not held to be equals in, e.g., ancient Greece or early medieval Europe) or because all true love is extramarital (*fin'amor* in twelfth-century Aquitaine). In some societies (ancient Greece or Rome), the thought that human beings should *love* their gods, as opposed to fearing and revering them, would have been as ridiculous as the thought that one should love the plague. We incorporate material things to which we are attached into the class of things we love. In other cultures, this might seem absurd – one can love another human being, but how on earth might one love an *object*? Some of these exclusions may properly be classified as conceptual in so far as they transgress the bounds of intelligibility (akin to 'My three-year-old child is an adult').

From the late sixteenth century onwards, sexual passion was increasingly conceived *in literature* to be not only an admirable form of love but also the natural prelude to marriage. But in ancient Rome, it seems, erotic love was commonly viewed as an unfortunate appetite, best slaked as soon as possible with a prostitute:

Ah, cursed images!

| | |
|---|---|
| Flee them you must and all the food of love | sed fugitare decet simulacra et pabula amoris |
| Reject, and turn the mind away, and eject | absterrere sibi atque alio convertere mentem |
| The pent-up fluid into other bodies, | et iacere umorem coniectum in corpora quaeque |
| And let it go, not with one single love | nec retinere semel conversum unius amore |
| Straitjacketed, nor storing in your heart | et servare sibi curam certumque dolorem; |
| The certainty of endless cares and pain. For feeding quickens the sore and strengthens it, | ulcus enim vivescit et inveterascit alendo |
| And day by day the madness grows and woe | inque dies gliscit furor atque aerumna gravescit, |
| Is heaped on woe, unless the first wounds by new blows | si non prima novis conturbes volnera plagis |
| Are deadened and while the wound's still fresh you cure it | volgivagaque vagus Venere ante recentia cures |
| By wandering with Venus of the streets. | aut alio possis animi traducere motus.[8] |

We are inclined to separate friendship, especially non-erotic friendship between men, from love. But Aristotle thought that true (non-erotic) friendship between men of excellence was the epitome of love (*philia*), and Montaigne held his friendship with Étienne de La Boétie to be the most perfect form of love. We would find the common ancient Greek relation between adult male *erastes* and teenage male *eromenos* a reprehensible form of paedophilia. The Athenians (or at least the aristocrats in Plato's circle), Megarans, and Boeotians held it to be a natural and laudable stage in male maturation.[9]

## 4. Historico-normative constraints

*The historicity of love*    Let us now turn from the multiple kinds of possible objects of love and the threads connecting them, to a brief reminder of the framework of moral, social, and

---

[8] Lucretius, *The Nature of Things* (trans. R. Melville), IV. 1062–72. This view is by no means confined to Lucretius (see appendix, section 4).

[9] A brilliant attempt to render this intelligible to us is to be found in Mary Renault's depiction of the love between Alexias and Lysis in her novel *The Last of the Wine* (Longmans, Green, London, 1957).

legal norms within which human love is realized. The evaluation and propriety of a given relationship affects, and is in turn constrained and moulded by, custom and law. So love, *unlike other human emotions* such as fear and anger, has a long and convoluted history (some moments of which are examined in the appendix). What is emotionally possible in one society, at one time, or in one class, may not be possible or even conceivable in another. The phenomena of love, one might say, are moulded by the conception, and the conception is in turn moulded by the phenomena. It is in this sense that love, unlike most other emotions, has a history.

To this it might be objected that the history of the emotion of love is no different in principle from the histories one might tell of other emotions. Shame too, one might argue, has a history, since the objects of shame vary from period to period and from society to society. Not to meet an insult with a challenge to a duel was once a reason for shame, but it no longer is. For a woman to show her thighs, in some societies, was and is a ground for shame; in others it is no more shameful than showing one's hands. The emotion does not change, it might be argued; only its objects change. It is the very same emotion, namely shame – but what one ought to be ashamed of is a function of social mores. Is it not like this with love?

It seems not. The historicity of love is not merely a matter of different objects of love, but different emotions of love. The love of God, for example, is not 'just like' the love of a man or woman, but for the fact that what one loves is God, not a human being. The *criteria* for loving God are very different from the criteria for loving a man or woman. A troubadour's courtly love of a married lady is not just like the love of an *erastes*, only with a lady as its object rather than a good-looking youth. The *responses* that characterize these forms of love are altogether different, and so too are the ways in which such love is *expressed* in word and deed. The loyalty love of a squire for his knight, of a soldier for his captain, of a servant for his or her master or mistress, is not just like erotic love, only with different objects. The *requirements* recognized in such forms of love are unlike those of erotic love. The differences between these social and historical forms of love are altogether unlike the differences in possible objects of fear at different times (devils, witches, spells, plagues, inflation, bombing), where one might indeed say that the emotion is the same, the criteria for its ascription are the same, the web of subjective feeling and expression is the same, and only its objects change. The love of God, in both Judaism and Christianity, was a reason for martyrdom.

The love between *erastes* and *eromanos* demanded constant display of virtue and valour in order to be worthy of love. These are not merely the same emotion with historically variable objects; they are different kinds of love with historically conditioned forms of reaction, expression, and response, as well as historically different motives for different kinds of action.

*Social constraints on love*    The roles and social position of men and women in a given society constrain and enable the possible forms of heterosexual love. The social class of a person has always been a constraint on possible spouses, lower-class women, and even more so men, being typically debarred from marrying above their class. Whether the determination of a spouse is free or arranged and what the customary ages of the couple are (in Rome girls of thirteen often were married off to thirty- or forty-year-old men) constrain the nature of possible relations within a marriage. Differences between the educational possibilities available to men and to women condition the relationship between spouses. Legal rights to wealth and property determine women's liberty as well as their equality or subordination in marriage, as does the free and equal availability of divorce and possibility of remarriage, and the fair regulation of custody of children after divorce. The availability or unavailability of means of contraception and abortion conditions female independence and freedom. All these in turn affect attitudes towards sexual desire and love, marital, and extramarital love. They determine the conceptions of love alive in any given society.

Complementary constraining features pertain to the structure of daily life. These mould and are moulded by preconceptions concerning social and marital life, the roles of husband and wife, the status of children and the responsibilities for their care, and the position of other members of the household and of servants. Architectural arrangements condition relations within a home. In early medieval Europe, all members of a household slept in the same great hall, the space for the lord and his wife being perhaps curtained off from the rest. Only later did they have separate quarters of their own, but other members of the household had none. From the Renaissance until the eighteenth century, rooms in the houses of the aristocracy opened directly into other rooms. Only later did the idea of having a corridor that gives access to individual rooms arise. Such architectural differences determine the possibilities of privacy and are determined by prevailing conceptions and needs for privacy. Attitudes towards privacy, and the need and desire for privacy, were accordingly different, and such differences modulate the manner in which erotic love and intimacy can develop and flourish.[10]

Attitudes towards bodily cleanliness, dress, and nudity – indeed deeply rooted attitudes towards the body as such – also play a role in guiding the forms in which erotic love may find expression.[11] Christianity not only transformed late imperial Roman attitudes towards sexuality; it also induced an attitude of shame in respect of the human body as such, especially of women (not merely shame at being *seen* naked), as well as linking sexual shame with sin (a nexus previously absent in Roman culture).[12] This was to affect European social, moral, and sexual life for the next two millennia. As Nietzsche remarked, 'Christianity gave Eros poison to drink; he did not die of it, certainly, but he degenerated into vice' (*Beyond Good and Evil*, §168).

So, both the different concepts of love that have evolved in the West over the past 2,500 years and the different conceptions of love characteristic of Western societies and cultures from one period to another must be understood in relation to changing moral and religious belief systems; to different legal and economic relationships; to the age of marriage and to life expectancy; and to the expectation of successive marriages. The concepts are *deeply* embedded in different ways of living that determine and are determined by distinct conceptions of love.

## 5. The phases of love

Love is a paradigm of a *developing emotion*. We can put some order into our thought about it by distinguishing the possible phases in the development of interpersonal love between sexually mature human beings, both in youth and in maturity (see fig. 10.3).

[10] For detailed historical surveys, see the five-volume work of *A History of Private Life*, under the general editorship of P. Ariès and G. Duby, trans. A. Goldhammer (Harvard University Press, Cambridge, Mass., 1987–91), originally published as *Histoire de la Vie Privée* (Editions du Seuil, Paris, 1985–7).

[11] P. Brown, *The Body and Society: Men, Women, and Sexual Renunciation in Early Christianity* (Columbia University Press, New York, 1988).

[12] K. Harper, *From Shame to Sin: the Christian Transformation of Sexual Morality in Late Antiquity* (Harvard University Press, Cambridge, Mass., 2013). It is striking that, after the fall of Rome, there is no sculptural representation of the beauty of the human nude, as opposed to the depiction of the shivering and pathetic nakedness of the sinner, until the thirteenth or fourteenth century (see K. Clarke, *The Nude* (John Murray, London, 1956)).

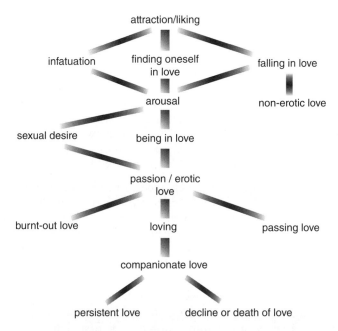

attraction/liking

infatuation    finding oneself in love    falling in love

non-erotic love

arousal

sexual desire    being in love

passion / erotic love

burnt-out love    loving    passing love

companionate love

persistent love      decline or death of love

**Figure 10.3**   *Courses of erotic love*

*Liking*   *Personal liking* commonly precedes love. But one may love someone without liking them (as Catullus loved Lesbia: 'Odi et amo' ('I hate and I love')). Liking a person, which is an attitude, is distinct from *falling in love* with someone, which may be an event, if one falls in love *at first sight* (as Isaac fell in love with Rebecca, Troilo with Criseide (in Boccaccio's *Il Filostrato*) or Romeo with Juliet).[13] Victor Hugo gives a powerful description of Marius's falling in love with Cosette as he passes her sitting on a park bench with Jean Valjean:

The girl looked up at him and their eyes met.

What message was to be read in her eyes? Marius could not have said. Nothing and yet everything. A spark had passed between them.

She looked down and he continued on his way. What he had encountered was not the frank innocent gaze of a child. It was as though a door had suddenly opened and then had been as swiftly closed. There

---

[13] Nevertheless, Christopher Marlowe erred in declaring 'who ever loved that loved not at first sight' (*Hero and Leander*, repeated by Shakespeare in *As You Like It*, III. 5).

comes a day when every girl has this look in her eyes, and woe to him who encounters it.

That first gaze of a spirit that does not yet know itself is like the first glow of sunrise, the awakening of something radiant but still veiled. Nothing can convey the perilous charm of that unexpected gleam, shedding a sudden, hesitant light on present innocence and future passion. It is a kind of unresolved tenderness, chance-disclosed and expectant, a snare laid unwittingly by innocence, which captures a heart without intending or knowing what it does, a maid with the sudden gaze of a woman.

Rarely does it happen that a gaze such as this does not profoundly affect its victim. All purity and ardour is concentrated in that magical but fateful gleam which, more than the most calculated oglings of a coquette, has the power to implant in another heart the ominous flower, so loaded with fragrance and with poison, that is called love. (*Les Misérables* (trans. N. Denny), III. 6. 3)

This is one human possibility – one recognizable form which falling in love at first sight may take. There are others. Nevertheless one may fall in love with another person, without doing so at first sight (as Jane Eyre slowly grows to love Mr Rochester). Falling in love is not the sole route to *coming to love* another person. For one may *find oneself in love*, sometimes even against one's will (as Mr Darcy reluctantly finds himself in love with Elizabeth, who is his social inferior), or, indeed *realize* that one already loves someone (e.g. as Emma realizes that she loves Mr Knightley).

*Passionate love*, involving adoration, submission to, *Infatuation* and enchantment with, the person loved, appears to occur in most human societies. What attitude is taken towards the phenomenon of being 'smitten by love', how it is evaluated, varies. It has sometimes been viewed as the acme of human experience (e.g. by the proponents of courtly love and the Romantics). But *eros* has also been thought of as a 'sickness', a 'madness', a cruel god who robs us of our wits (e.g. Euripides, Menander, Catullus, Propertius, Lucretius).[14] We distinguish between *falling in love* and *becoming infatuated*, and

[14] Similar sentiments are expressed in the early modern era. Francis Bacon acidly remarked: 'The stage is more beholding to love, than the life of man. For as to the stage, love is ever the matter of comedies, and now and then of tragedies; but in life it doth much mischief; sometimes like a siren, sometimes like a fury' ('Of Love', in *Essays; or, Councils, Civil and Moral* (1625)). In the nineteenth century, Byron wickedly rhymed: 'Think you, if Laura had been Petrarch's wife / He would have written sonnets to her all his life' (*Don Juan*, III. 3).

between *being in love* and *being infatuated* – the former pair signifying transitions and the later pair emotional states. *Being in love* and
*being infatuated* have in common attraction, arousal, desire, and (in
cases of falling passionately in love) urgency and intensity. Whether
the desire be erotic *love* or merely the *sexual desire* of infatuation is
often impossible for the subject to judge. What is distinctive of infatuation is the reckless commitment to satisfying one's desire; elation and
euphoria; abandonment of all other projects and commitments for
the sake of what seems to one to be love (all is thrown to the wind);
inability to make rational choices (inasmuch as nothing seems of
value in comparison with one's passion); and hence opting for high-
risk choices (e.g. elopement, no matter what the costs). Tolstoy's
description of Natasha Rostova's disastrous infatuation with Anatole
Kuragin (as well as Kuragin's infatuation with her) is a brilliant
description of this youthful condition. For example:

'No, I can't believe it,' insisted Sonya. 'I don't understand. How can you
have loved someone for a whole year and suddenly ... Why, you have
only seen him three times! Natasha, I don't believe you. You're joking.
In three days to forget everything and be like this ...'

'Three days?', interrupted Natasha. 'It seems to me as if I'd loved him a
hundred years. It seems to me as if I had never loved anyone before.
You can't understand, Sonya, wait – sit here.' Natasha threw her arms
around her and kissed her. 'I have heard of this happening – and so
have you, surely? But it's only now that I feel such love. It's not what
I felt before. As soon as I saw him I felt he was my master and I his slave,
and that I couldn't help loving him. Yes, his slave! Whatever he bids me
do, I shall do. You don't understand that. What am I to do, Sonya?' cried
Natasha, with a blissful yet frightened face. (*War and Peace*, VIII. 15)

The inevitable fall after the infatuation produces a profound sense of
emptiness, of the valuelessness of all, and suicidal depression.

*Being in love* is the natural sequel to falling in
*Being in love and* love. It involves wanting to be with the person loved,
*erotic passion* a strong desire to please, to share experience, and to
delight in shared experiences. It is characteristically
accompanied by *erotic passion* – which is a desire for, and the excitement of, kisses, caresses, and embraces, and for the exploration of the
other's body. It involves the mutual breaching by the lovers of the
space with which we all surround ourselves and upon which others
may not encroach without offence. It is no coincidence that erotic

passion is described in terms of 'craving' the embrace and kisses of the beloved, and of 'hunger' for sexual possession. These epithets mark the connection between erotic passion and appetite.

However, seducers may feel sexual desire and even erotic passion for someone without being in love with their victim (Don Juan; Pechórin in Lermontov's *A Hero of our Time*). Conversely, there may be love between man and woman without any erotic passion or yearning, as in cases of what has, since the Renaissance, mistakenly been called Platonic love (e.g. Michelangelo's love for Vittoria Colonna which is expressed in his sonnets). One may love someone without the person with whom one is in love *reciprocating* (as Beatrice did not, in fact, reciprocate Dante's love, and, in fiction, Roxane did not reciprocate Cyrano's love). The pain of disdained, disprized, or rejected love echoes throughout the ages in the poetry of the suffering lover and in a multitude of romantic novels.

*Companionate love*     Being in love, with us, commonly yields to *sharing life*. With time, sexual and temperamental compatibility, faithfulness and shared joys and hardships, mutual respect and considerateness, and the ability to compromise, being in love may evolve into *companionate love*. Companionate love may persist throughout a shared life, strengthened by common experience, by physical and psychological intimacy, by shared activities and responsibilities, and by parenthood. But love that has persisted for some time may cease. It may fade away, through the grating of the rough edges of personality incompatibilities. It may rupture through boredom or the loss of erotic attraction (as Oblonsky has lost interest in Dolly in *Anna Karenina*). Or it may crack under the pressure of insufficient space for autonomy (Nora Helmer in Ibsen's *A Doll's House*). Love may get diverted, when one of the pair falls in love with a third person and has an affair, the discovery of which inevitably strains the existing partnership (as in the case of Oblonsky's disloyalty to Dolly) and may rupture it irremediably. In some cases, the discovery of infidelity may immediately destroy the pre-existing relationship (e.g. von Instetten's reaction to learning of Effi's previous affair with Major Crampas in *Effi Briest*). Love may also be abruptly destroyed through the disclosure of some wickedness (past or present) that manifests lack of honesty and openness in the failure to disclose the past and that outweighs fidelity in the grossness of the evil. But it may survive the blow (as does Mrs Bulstrode's loyalty love to her husband after his disgrace, in *Middlemarch*).

So much for the different pathways down which interpersonal erotic love *as we conceive it* may tread (see fig. 10.3). Which pathway it goes down depends upon the personalities involved, the circumstances, good and bad fortune, and mutual knowledge and understanding, as well as upon self-knowledge and self-understanding. For loving another is not a state that one passively enjoys. Love imposes requirements upon one. It has to be sustained, fostered, and cultivated by expression, action, and attention.

## 6. The web of concepts of love

English is blessed with a very large vocabulary of love, fine-tuned to the nuances that characterize this most important of emotions and motives (see table 10.1 and table 10.2).[15] Having sketched in the possible courses of interpersonal love, we may now turn to examine the fine web of words available to us for characterizing love in its manifold forms.

| | |
|---|---|
| From liking to loving and to loving an activity | attracted by; take pleasure in; take delight in; find agreeable/pleasant/enjoyable; have a passion for; become obsessed with |
| From liking to friendship | liking; affection; affinity; rapport; fondness; amiability; warmth; congeniality; cameraderie; comradeship; fellowship |
| Falling in love | smitten with love; pierced by love; head over heels in love; swept off one's feet; lose one's heart; bewitched; enthralled |
| Being in love | adore; adulate; idolize; worship; besotted with; captivated by; entranced with |
| Erotic love | passionate; ardent; swept away by; burn with desire; consumed with desire/lust; enraptured; melt with desire |

**Table 10.1**  *A selection from the vocabulary (1)*

[15] I shall not survey the huge vocabulary of masculine bawdy and obscenity. It is a disturbing fact that so much of it is aggressive or even sadistic, which perhaps betokens the permanent difficulty of refining and civilizing the male sexual drive. For an illuminating survey of Shakespeare's bawdy, see E. Partridge's eponymous book, rev. edn (Routledge & Kegan Paul, London, 1968).

| Loving | fondness; feelings of protectiveness; feelings of reliance; affection; tenderness; warmth; intimacy; attention; devotion; to cherish; to treasure; to trust; to hold dear; to be uxorious |
|---|---|
| Idealized object of love | good-looking; attractive; beautiful; gorgeous; fabulous; stunning; like an angel; divine; like a goddess; sweet; adorable; gentle; exquisite; charming; sensitive; enchanting; engaging; fascinating; ravishing; alluring; enthralling; bewitching |
| Maternal/paternal love | tenderness; devotion; protectiveness; affection; warmth; dote on; adore; treasure |
| Absent or rejected love | yearning; pining; lovesick; moping; lovelorn; unrequited love; crossed in love; jilted; rejected; spurned; disdained |
| Love of one's neighbour (*caritas*) | considerateness; compassion; pity; care; concern; kindness; charity; solicitude; sympathy; fellow feeling; benevolence; fraternity; solidarity; altruism; selflessness |

**Table 10.2**  *A selection from the vocabulary (2)*

*The lexical web of liking*

The general concept of liking someone or something is linked to the *hedonic*. What one likes one enjoys and takes pleasure in. One element in the objects of liking is their *attraction*, which is a pivotal node in the web of concepts of love (see fig. 10.1). One may like, and be attracted to, people and other living things, material objects and possessions, landscapes and seascapes, activities and passivities. One may like something immediately, on first encountering it. But one may come to like something only after repeated encounters. One normally likes a thing for a reason, which is given by specifying a characteristic possessed by the thing liked. One may like a characteristic for no reason (preferences for sensible qualities, such as colour, taste, and sound, are characteristically non-rational). But one may like a thing because it possesses an intrinsic desirability characteristic, such as beauty. Whom one likes one may come to love. But, as noted, one can be in love with someone without liking him. By contrast, one cannot feel friendship for someone one does not like. What one likes is something in which one *takes pleasure* and may *delight in*, finds *agreeable* and *pleasant* and *enjoys*. If liking a thing or an activity modulates into loving it or loving doing it, what one is thus attracted by and attached to may also become something one is *obsessed with* and has *a passion for*. The liking of another person that is reciprocated may grow into feelings of friendship and the hedonic vocabulary of liking is naturally extended to the sphere of friendship and feelings of amity. One enjoys being with a friend, takes pleasure in the company of a friend, and enjoys doing things together. Friendship, like love, involves *attachment*. It also involves *affection*, *fondness*, *warmth*, *devotion*, and *loyalty* (see chapter 11).

While liking may modulate into loving (*eros* or *philia*), the love of God does not grow out of liking God, for one cannot like God. The reasons are threefold. One cannot merely *like* what one knows to be perfect. One cannot be commanded to like someone or something, as one *can* be commanded to love God (see appendix, pp. 395–400). The love of God is not linked to the hedonic in the manner in which liking is. One cannot enjoy being with God as one can enjoy being with those one likes. Nor can one take pleasure in God as one can take pleasure in what one likes, save in the case of eroticized religious ecstasy. The love of God, in Kant's terminology, is *practical* rather than *pathological* (a form of *pathos*).

*The lexical web of erotic passion*  Falling in love has its distinct vocabulary. One may be 'smitten with love', be 'swept off one's feet', or 'lose one's heart' in a moment. If this happens to one, one may then be 'bewitched' and 'enthralled' by one's beloved. These epithets also characterize infatuation. The sequel to falling in love is the period of 'being in love', which fascinated the Romantics, being conceived to be the acme of human experience, redemptive and transcendent. Here too English offers a rich vocabulary: the lovers may 'adore', 'adulate', or even 'idolize' and 'worship' each other. They are, we say, 'head over heels in love', 'besotted', 'captivated', and 'entranced' with each other. The vocabulary of concupiscent love borrows freely from the language of (i) enslavement, (ii) magic and witchcraft, (iii) loss of reason, and (iv) religion. This is not surprising. The love-making, in both the older sense of the phrase (to court or woo) and in the modern sense (to copulate) may be 'passionate' or 'ardent', and the lovers may be 'swept away' or 'burn' or 'be consumed' with desire. They may be 'amorous', 'enraptured' with each other, or 'yearn to melt' in each other's arms, craving to lose their separate identities in erotic union. The incendiary and liquescent vocabulary too is no coincidence.

*The lexical web of companionate love*  Erotic passion, as we noted, may or may not grow into mutual love. Marriage may or may not be preceded by falling in love and being in love. It may or may not evolve into companionate love. In Western culture today, we have a determinate conception of the progress of love from encounter to steady companionate marriage or partnership (see fig. 10.3). At other times and in other cultures marriage was not expected to be preceded by passionate love or even by any love at all, and marriage itself was rather characterized by fidelity (especially female fidelity), mutual obligations of care and loyalty, perhaps reciprocal confiding (as in Rome), and, in due course, in shared parental love and pride. Marital relations in the West today are describable by means of a rich vocabulary of 'caring', 'trusting', 'cherishing', 'protecting', and of being 'devoted' to each other. Spouses in a successful marriage may enjoy varying degrees of 'emotional intimacy' in addition to the intimacy of sexual relations. They may exhibit varying degrees of 'warmth', 'fondness', 'affection', 'tenderness', and 'concern' for each other. In fortunate cases, spouses may 'dote on' or 'treasure' each other.

The love of another, both in courtship and in marriage, is manifest in the acts, actions. and activities motivated by love. Lovers characteristically wish to do things together, to share their enjoyments, to take pleasure in joint activities, and to please each other. A mark of love is the desire to share not only pleasures, but also the burden of sorrows and hardships. Those who resolve to share their lives in marriage or partnership characteristically wish to undertake joint projects and to make a home together, and typically wish to have children and to share in their upbringing. One feature of selfless love is to be open to the needs and requirements of the person loved, and to treat them as weighty reasons for action.

*The lexical web of idealization*      Falling in love and being in love typically lead to *idealization* of the loved person (as does *being infatuated*). Idealization seems to be an engrained feature of courtship. Stendhal described this process in detail, and called it 'crystallization'.[16] It informs most love poetry, reaching ever greater heights in *fin'amor* poetry, in Dante and Petrarch, in Renaissance poetry, and in the poetry of the Romantics. For in their imaginations, the enamoured paint rough pebbles with all the shimmering colours of jewels, endowing their lover with perfections not possessed. In their wooing, men and women are prone to elevate the

---

[16] Stendhal, *Love* (1822). By 'crystallization' he did not mean the transformation of the inchoate, but rather the manner in which the mundane may take on the appearance of the sublimely beautiful, as when a twig is left for a while in a salt mine and becomes encrusted with salt crystals.

object of their love beyond reason. Similarly, since the troubadours, on the one hand, and the Renaissance poets, on the other, being in love itself is sublimed.

The larger part of the vocabulary of amorous idealization is tailored for the enamoured youth's adulation of his young woman, for it is he who woos her and it is she who is warmed, flattered, and beguiled by his adoration. The vocabulary concentrates upon three focal points: good looks, traits of temperament, and allure. The woman loved may be 'graceful', 'exquisite', 'beautiful', 'a goddess'. She may be 'sweet', 'adorable', 'charming', 'delightful', 'captivating', 'enchanting', 'angelic'. She may also be 'seductive', 'ravishing', 'stunning', 'fabulous', 'bewitching', 'alluring', 'fascinating'. Of course, when we turn to poetry, the hyperbole becomes even more extreme.

The vocabulary for the description of a loved youth is strikingly different, being focused less on looks ('good-looking', 'attractive', 'handsome') and more on physique, temperament (in particular, 'self-confidence', 'good humour', 'warmth', 'passion') and character traits ('attentiveness', 'faithfulness', 'reliability', 'generosity'). These differences in forms of attraction have an obvious socio-biological explanation – women by and large having an innate disposition to seek in a mate characteristics that will ensure healthy offspring and a permanent stable relationship in which to bring them up – reliability and protection.

Correlative to the wide vocabulary of love, we unsurprisingly have a battery of epithets to signify disappointed love. Whereas friendship is necessarily reciprocal, love need not be. For love may be unrequited. A lover may be 'disdained', 'jilted', 'rejected', or 'spurned'. The lovesick youth or girl may 'pine', 'mope', and 'languish' in the absence of the person they love. They may be 'forlorn', 'wretched', and 'desolate' in the face of disprized love. Loss of love (or death of the person loved) may be 'heart-breaking' or 'heart-rending', leaving one 'inconsolable' and 'heart-broken'.

*The lexical web of compassionate and parental love*  A different centre of variation in the vocabulary of love focuses on the more impersonal love of one's fellow men and women. This is the love of *caritas* (in the Christian tradition) or of its ancestral *khesed* (in Judaic ethics), which is described in the appendix (see pp. 400, 419f.). In its *selflessness* it is linked to parental, in particular motherly, love. Maternal love ideally involves 'care', 'concern', 'tenderness', 'cherishing', 'devotion', and 'doting on' the child. It has had the most powerful pictorial representation from the

Renaissance onwards (following Leonardo's and Raphael's inventions). However, maternal love *can* be selfish, as in the case of the possessive love of Mrs Morel for her son Paul in Lawrence's *Sons and Lovers*, or of Judith Paris for her son Adam in Walpole's *The Fortress*. The relationship between the elderly Prince Nikolai Bolkonsky and his daughter Princess Maria is an equally powerful example of self-centred, possessive, paternal love.

Parental love (one form of *philia* in classical Greek writings) was characterized by Aristotle as an unequal relationship, akin to that between benefactor and beneficiary. In general, he thought, parents love their children more than children love their parents. For the children are the creations of the parents and the product of years of care and tutoring. The intensity of parental grief at the loss of an adult child is wonderfully expressed by King David's agonized cry on hearing that Absalom, who was in revolt against him, had been slain: 'O my son Absalom, my son, my son Absalom! Would God I had died for thee, O Absalom, my son, my son!' (2 Samuel 18: 33). Similarly, the pietà, depicting Mary lamenting the death of Jesus, is one of the most potent of Western images from the Middle Ages until the eighteenth century, giving solace to mothers grieving for their dead child.

The *love of one's neighbour*, however, does not have the particularity and uniqueness of personal object that characterizes parental love. The Good Samaritan was not concerned with the specific identity of the injured wayfarer he encountered lying on the road – he would have behaved with similar charity towards any other helpless and suffering person. This form of love involves motivating feelings of *compassion, concern, solicitude, care*, and *kindness*, the rationale of which is the ill-fare, misfortune, and suffering of another. Generalized even further, such selflessness, conceived as a form of love, merges with feelings of *fraternity, sympathy for*, and *solidarity with*, one's fellow human beings, motivated by general *benevolence* and *altruism*.

*The intrinsic value of love* To love another human being is today widely held to be intrinsically valuable. Indeed, the nineteenth-century Romantics conceived love to be a uniquely self-transcending emotion that gives meaning to human life. 'Loving or having loved is enough', Victor Hugo observes, 'Ask for nothing more. There's no other pearl to be found in the sombre folds of life' (*Les Misérables* (trans. N. Denny), V. 6. 2). In our culture, never to have loved another and never to have been loved are reasons for pity and compassion. Not only are loving and being loved of intrinsic value, but the *ability to love* is a distinctive human power that is itself valuable. Its absence is sometimes held to be catastrophic. 'What is hell?' Father Zossima queries, 'I maintain that it is the suffering of being unable to love' (*The Brothers Karamazov*, ch. 41).

*Compatibility of love and hate*

It is noteworthy that we are inclined to think that the opposite (*contrary*) of love is hate. Certainly love may turn to hate, as depicted by Lermontov's description of the transformation of Princess Mary's feelings for Pechórin, once he tells her that he has merely been playing with her. Nevertheless, emotions are not propositions: contrary propositions cannot both be true, but contrary emotions may coexist. As has already been noted, it is perfectly possible both to love and to hate the same person at the same time. One may hate the person to whom one is enslaved by one's passion (Catullus), or resent the lack of reciprocity or its non-exclusiveness (Swann). The combinatorial possibilities of the passion of erotic love with various forms of revulsion are patent in Somerset Maugham's description of Philip Carey's bondage:

> it seemed impossible that he should be in love with Mildred Rogers. Her name was grotesque. He did not think her pretty; he hated the thinness of her, only that evening he had noticed how the bones of her chest stood out in evening-dress; he went over her features one by one; he did not like her mouth, and the unhealthiness of her colour vaguely repelled him. She was common. Her phrases, so bald and few, constantly repeated, showed the emptiness of her mind; he recalled her vulgar little laugh at the jokes of the musical comedy; and he remembered the little finger carefully extended when she held her glass to her mouth; her manners like her conversation, were odiously genteel. He remembered her insolence; sometimes he had felt inclined to box her ears; and suddenly, he knew not why, perhaps it was the thought of hitting her or the recollection of her tiny, beautiful ears, he was seized by an uprush of emotion. He yearned for her. He thought of taking her in his arms, the thin, fragile body, and kissing her pale mouth: he wanted to pass his fingers down the slightly greenish cheeks. He wanted her. He had thought of love as a rapture which seized one so that all the world seemed spring-like, he had looked forward to an ecstatic happiness; but this was not happiness; it was a hunger of the soul, it was a painful yearning, it was a bitter anguish, he had never known before. (*Of Human Bondage*, ch. 57)

*Incompatibility of love and indifference*

Elie Wiesel suggested that the opposite of love is not hatred but indifference. It is certainly true that one cannot love anyone or anything and not care about whom or what is loved. The *contradictory* of love in general, and of the love of mankind (respect for humanity, and compassion for the suffering of others) in particular, is indifference.

*Love and the heart*
Just as we link thinking with the head, even though we do not think with our head (or brain) and do not think in our head either (but in our armchair, in the library, or on the train),[17] so too we associate love with the heart, even though we do not love with or in our heart. We say that our heart *melts with love, overflows,* or is *warm with love.* If our love is rejected or our beloved dies, we are *heart-broken.* To feel pity or compassion is for *one's heart to bleed* for another. To lack compassion is to be *heartless* or to have *a cold heart.* Presumably the reason for this cardiac association is the strongly felt increase in heartbeat when falling in love or when being passionately in love and encountering the person with whom one is in love; also the tightening of one's chest and painful feeling of pressure in the area of the heart when love is lost; and perhaps also the acculturated inclination to put one's hand upon one's heart when declaring one's love and troth. So the conceptual iconography of love incorporates the heart in its heraldic blazon.

## 7. The iconography of love

*Iconography of Aphrodite*
As in the case of previous emotions that we have examined, the literal iconography of the emotion of love in European art is both instructive and interesting in its own right. The symbolism often illustrates tales from Greek and Roman mythology, and is commonly used in the pictorial representation of Plato's philosophy of love and Renaissance neo-Platonism. Aphrodite (Venus), the goddess of love, and Eros (Cupid, Amor), the god of sexual desire, determine the large part of the iconography of love in European painting. The three graces, Agaia, Euphrosyne, and Thalia, are, according to Hesiod, handmaidens of Aphrodite. They represent, according to Seneca, the threefold facets of generosity: *giving, receiving,* and *reciprocating* gifts. According to the Florentine humanists, they either symbolize the three phases of love (*beauty, desire,* and *fulfilment*), or are personifications of *chastity, beauty,* and *love.* The identifying attributes of Venus are a pair of doves (symbols of love and fidelity) or swans (symbols of grace and beauty), which commonly draw her chariot, a scallop shell, and dolphins, which allude

[17] See *The Intellectual Powers*, ch. 10, section 7.

to her marine genesis (from the foam (*aphros*) of the waves, produced by the semen from the castrated genitals of Uranus cast upon the sea by his son Cronos). Her magic breast-band, which enthrals the observer (lent to Hera to enchant Zeus (*Iliad*, XIV. 235 ff.)) and a flaming torch signifying the kindling of passionate love are further attributes. The flower of Aphrodite is the red rose (alluding to the death of Adonis), and her sacred plant is the evergreen myrtle, symbolizing constancy.

*Iconography of Eros/Cupid*

Eros (or Cupid in Eros's Roman incarnation (from the Latin *cupido* (desire)) was of uncertain parentage. Hesiod presents Eros as primordial, like Chaos and Gaia. Later Greek writers assigned him various parents: Ares and Aphrodite, Heaven and Earth, Strife and Zephyr. The Romans conceived of Cupid as the son of Venus, but his paternity was disputed. By the Renaissance, following one of Pausanias's suggestions, he was held to be the son of Mars and Venus. Both in antiquity and in the Renaissance, Cupid is presented as winged. As Shakespeare explained, he is often depicted as blindfolded:

> Love looks not with the eyes, but with the mind,
> And therefore is winged Cupid painted blind.
> Nor hath love's mind of any judgement taste;
> Wings and no eyes figure unheedy haste.
> And therefore is love said to be a child
> Because in choice he is so oft beguiled.
> (*A Midsummer Night's Dream*, I. 1)

His attributes are his bow, golden arrows, and quiver. His victims are struck down by love, pierced by irrational passion. He sometimes possesses a burning torch with which to inflame the hearts of lovers. Extinguished and upturned, it signifies the absence or the passing of love. Most representations of Eros in Greece are of a youth, but in Rome Cupid also appears as a chubby boy. During the Renaissance and, subsequently, the Baroque, the youthful Cupid was progressively replaced by a chubby, winged child with bow and arrow (Cranach). At the same time, Cupid tended to multiply into *amorini*, which then degenerate into a mass of putti (Titian, Rubens), by which time the iconography began to lose both power and interest. Nevertheless, the youthful Cupid survived (e.g. Caravaggio's cheeky homoerotic Cupid (1602) in Berlin; Thorvaldsen's sculpture (1814) in Copenhagen; and Gilbert's aluminium cast sculpture (1892) in Piccadilly Circus (which is, strictly speaking, a statue of Anteros, Eros' chaste sibling)).

The Christian iconography of love is focused upon
*Iconography of* the representation of *agape* or *caritas*, on the maternal
*caritas/agape* love of the Virgin Mary for her son, and on religious
ecstasy. *Agape* combined the love of god and the love
of one's neighbour. Only in conjunction with the love of God was the
charitable love of one's neighbour of absolute value. The latter was
depicted by a figure (often of a woman) performing one or more of
the six works of mercy: tending the hungry, the thirsty, the stranger,
the naked, the sick, and the prisoner. In the thirteenth century,
Bonaventure's appeal to divine illumination granted in ecstatic loving
union with God associated the supreme form of the love of God with
light and fire.[18] This had a rapid impact on iconography. Thenceforth,
in Italy, the figure of love (*agape*, *caritas*) was depicted as holding a
flame issuing from a vase, or a candle, or as offering a flaming
heart to God. From the fourteenth century onwards the older
image of *Virgo Lactans* inspired the representation of *caritas* by
means of a woman suckling two infants. Renaissance paintings,
above all Raphael's, gave prominence to maternal love by sublime
paintings of maternal tenderness. The transformation of the hieratic
representation of Virgin and Child as the *Sedes sapientiae* (throne of
wisdom) in the eleventh century (in which the Virgin becomes the
*cathedra* (seat) for the *Logos* incarnate, with the Child standing on
the enthroned Virgin's knee staring steadfastly at the observer) to
the representation of divine loving maternity of the fifteenth and
sixteenth centuries (Leonardo, Raphael, Andrea del Sarto) betokens a
change in Western *mentalité*.

One of the most philosophically interesting themes
*Sacred and* of Renaissance love painting is exemplified by Titian's
*profane love* *Sacred and Profane Love* (1514), perhaps better named
*Human and Divine Love*, in the Galleria Borghese in
Rome. The former title was first recorded in an inventory of 1693
and is disputed. Since the carving on the marble fountain on which
the two female figures are seated represents the chastisement and
chastening of sexual passion, it is improbable that the serene,

---

[18] Its most dramatic and notorious representation in art is Bernini's sculpture (1652)
of the ecstasy of St Teresa of Avila. His sculptural ensemble, at the Cornaro Chapel in
Santa Maria della Vittoria in Rome, is faithful to her own description of her vision.
Bernini depicts her, illuminated by golden light streaming from above, being pierced
by the arrow of an angel, and experiencing divine ecstasy (*ekstasis*) in the form of an
overwhelming orgasm.

elegantly clothed female figure on the left without any adornment of jewellery represents the profane love of *Amor bestiale*. (The tripartite distinction between *amor celeste*, *umano*, and *bestiale* is Pico della Mirandola's, who attempted to reconcile Plato, Plotinus, and Christianity.) Edgar Wind argued persuasively that she represents *Amor umano*, which has been purged of uncontrollable desire.[19] The beautiful female opposite her is nude, her nakedness representing innocence, purity, and truth. She is more ardent than her correlate, holding in her raised hand a vase in which burns the sacred flame of divine love. She represents celestial love – the most elevated and sublime form of love that synthesizes the ultimate stage of Plato's *scala amoris*, namely the detached and abstract form of *eros*, the object of which is the pure Idea of Beauty, with the passionate sublimity of the love of God.

For more general iconographic representations of love in its various forms, we may turn, as in previous chapters, to Cesare Ripa's *Iconologia*. In the 1758–60 Hertel edition, the love of God (43) is represented by means of an image of Simeon praising God, with a *fatto* of the presentation in the Temple. The love of one's fellow man (44) is represented by a rich man giving alms to a beggar, with a *fatto* of the Good Samaritan. Enforced love (*Amor coactus*, 45) is represented by a blindfolded infant Cupid sitting on a broken column, holding an hourglass (time overcomes passion), with a *fatto* of Joseph fleeing from Potiphar's wife). Lewdness (*Impudicitia*, 70) is represented by a beautiful woman, scantily dressed, sitting on a richly decorated and rumpled bed, fondling a blindfolded Cupid. She holds a sprig of colewort (an aphrodisiac), and at her feet sit a partridge (the most libidinous of birds) and a goat (the most potent and easily aroused of animals). The *fatto* is Sardanapalus dallying with two nude women in bed.

It is a striking testament to the influence of Renaissance neo-Platonism that the theme of Cupid overcoming Pan became so popular among Baroque painters of the late sixteenth and seventeenth centuries. The subject, sometimes illustrating Virgil's oft-quoted line 'Omnia vincit amor' ('Love conquers all') and sometimes simply depicting the triumph of true love over mere carnal love, shows Cupid assaulting and subduing the god Pan, who, in Renaissance art, represented lust.

---

[19] E. Wind, *Pagan Mysteries of the Renaissance*, enlarged edn (Faber, London, 1967), pp. 141–51.

## 8. Connective analysis I: categorial complexity

Philosophers, psychologists, and cognitive scientists commonly attempt
to subsume love under a very general categorial concept. Some hold it to
be a feeling; others deny that. Some aver that it is an emotion; others
dispute this. Some contend that it is a disposition; others contest that.
Some assert it to be a persistent mental state; others challenge that. Part
of the point of the quest for categorial classification is the idea that, if we
can correctly locate love within such a general category, we would be
able to read off the salient features of love from the general categorial
form under which it is subsumed. I shall argue that these attempts are
futile. Love is categorially complex, with affinities to many categories,
but it is not readily subsumable under any save, trivially, that of feeling
and, less trivially, that of an emotion. Moreover, it can rightly be held to
be a feeling or an emotion precisely because these categories are so diffuse and imprecise that they provide little categorial guidance. To gain
an overview of the concept of love, and hence too of the emotion it signifies, there is no short cut by way of reading off the salient features of love
from the category under which it is subsumed. We need to engage in
detailed connective analysis. This is our purpose in the following discussion. Given that interpersonal love is essentially *a developing emotion*,
its multifaceted categorial character should not be surprising.

*Categorial analysis:
love and states*

It is evident that falling in love is not a mental
state, but may perhaps be classified as an event or
process. It can be said to be an event if it occurs at
first sight. It can be said to be a process if it occurs
slowly over a plurality of encounters – a gradual falling in love.
Sometimes its time is indeterminate. Is falling in love a *mental* event
or process? That would be a confusion of categories. Falling in love is
not a matter of intellect and will alone. But, as we have seen in *Human
Nature: the Categorial Framework* (ch. 8, section 3), it is these that
are the proper province of attributes of mind. It is striking that one
can deceive oneself about the occasion on which one fell in love with
the person one is now in love with, as Natasha did.[20] It is something
that happens to one, and it may happen without one even being aware
of it at the time. *En passant*, it is striking that young lovers are prone
to see the hand of destiny in their falling in love at first sight. That is
a natural projection of their sense of wonder at their having met at all.
'You were meant for me' or 'You were made for me' are characteristic

---

[20] 'You know that from the very day you first came to Otradnoe I have loved you,'
she cried, quite convinced that she was speaking the truth' (*War and Peace*, VI. 23).

expressions of the lovers' experience, echoing Plato's Aristophanic myth in the *Symposium* (see appendix, pp. 407f.).

Being in love (the natural sequence to falling in love), like being infatuated, may be said to be a state, but not a mental one. It lacks genuine duration, inasmuch as it cannot be disrupted by distraction of attention and later resumed (as the mental state of intense concentration can) and it persists through states of sleep and unconsciousness (as do knowledge, belief, and understanding, which, as has been shown in *The Intellectual Powers* (ch. 3, section 5; ch. 4, section 4; ch. 5, section 7), are not mental states). One does not cease to be in love when one falls asleep. So being in love is not a *mental state*, but, if it is a state at all, then it is a *state of a human being*, of a person. However, being in love has a close kinship with *states of mind*, inasmuch as being in love colours the way we view the world. To young lovers, the world is gilded with their happiness.

Love is said to be a feeling – and so it is, inasmuch
*Love and feeling*   as love is a *passion* (in the traditional sense of the word: see chapter 1) or affection, not an action. One cannot *order* another to fall in love with someone any more than one can order someone to feel ill. Nor, indeed, can one decide to love someone, any more than one can decide to feel giddy (the relation of loving to the will is examined later). However, being in love with someone, and indeed loving someone, involve an indeterminate variety of intentional actions done *out of love*. So love is commonly a motive, as are many other emotions (e.g. envy, jealousy, compassion).

Love is not a sensation, although falling in love and
*Love and ability*   being in love involve a multiplicity of sensations. Love is not a perception, but falling in love and being in love are perception-involving. Lovers delight in the beauty of the person they love, and find joy in touching and caressing each other. To remove human love from the physical intimacy that it naturally seeks and from the joy and delight of physical intimacy, and to focus it upon Platonic or neo-Platonic love of the Good or upon the Christian love of God, is to dehumanize it. It is in human erotic love that our *whole* nature is involved, our nature as living human beings. The point is well made by John Donne in 'The Ecstasy':

> So must poor lovers' souls descend
> T' affections, and to faculties,
> Which sense may reach and apprehend,
> Else a great Prince in prison lies.
> To our bodies turn we then, that so

Weak men on love reveal'd may look;
Love's mysteries in souls do grow
But yet the body is his book.

Love itself is not a power or ability, although *being able to love* is. But it is not an evenly distributed ability among mankind. Many people do not know how to love. It is not given to all to love well, for not all have the gift. Some have a greater capacity for the intense passion of being in love. Not all human beings are equally sensual, and a mismatch of sensuality may lead to much grief. Some have a greater ability than others *to give themselves* in love, to transcend their own self-centred (although not necessarily selfish) concerns, to understand and encourage the interests and concerns of the person they love, to delight in their joys, and to share in their sorrows. Similarly, the ability *to respond to being loved*, to recognize and to manifest one's recognition and appreciation of adoration, tenderness, or affection is likewise not equally shared by all.

In a quite different sense of power, namely power *Love and dominion* as *dominion*, being loved may provide the possibility of intense joy in the exercise of power over the person who is attracted to one (Signora Neroni in *Barchester Towers*). Being sensually attractive and alluring, and knowing that one is, gives men and women seductive abilities. In some cases, the experience of such power may in itself be intoxicating and addictive. It is manifest in the archetypal male seducer, Don Juan, who collects conquests as a butterfly collects nectar, driven by an insatiable desire to sample the fruits of seduction but once in each defloration. It is differently exhibited in the great French novel of libertinage, Laclos's *Dangerous Liaisons*, by the cynical seducer, Vicomte de Valmont, who delights in his seductive powers and aims only to humiliate and degrade the young women who fall in love with him. The seductive powers of the *femme fatale* is a recurrent theme in romantic literature, wonderfully expressed in Turgenev's *Torrents of Spring*, where Maria Nikolaevna, having seduced Sanin, who was about to go to Frankfurt to join his fiancée, asks him whether he will follow her to Paris instead:

'Where are you going, dear? To Paris or to Frankfort?'

'I am going where you will be, and will be with you till you drive me away,' he answered with despair and pressed close to him the hands of his sovereign. She freed her hands, laid them on his head, and clutched at his hair with her fingers. She slowly turned over and twisted the unresisting hair, drew herself up, her lips curled with triumph, while her eyes, wide and clear, almost white, expressed nothing but the ruthless and glutted joy of conquest. The hawk, as it clutches a captured bird, has eyes like that. (*Torrents of Spring*, ch. 42)

And therewith Sanin's life was destroyed. Similar sentiments are expressed by Heine in the prefatory poem to the third edition of his *Buch der Lieder* (Book of Songs) (trans. H. Draper):

| | |
|---|---|
| Before the gate there lay a Sphinx – <br> Terror and lust cross bred! | Dort vor dem Thor lag eine Sphinx, <br> Ein Zwitter von Schrecken und <br> Lüsten, |
| In body and claws a lion's form, <br> A woman in breast and head. <br> A lovely woman! Her white eyes <br> Spoke of desire grown wild; <br> Her lips gave silent promises, <br> Her mute lips arched and smiled. <br> ... | Der Leib und die Tatzen wie ein Löw', <br> Ein Weib an Haupt und Brüsten. <br> Ein schönes Weib! Der weisse Blick, <br> Er sprach von wildem Begehren; <br> Die stummen Lippen wölbten sich <br> Und lächelten stilles Gewähren. <br> ... |
| I yielded, passion-tossed – <br> And as I kissed that lovely face, <br> I knew that I was lost. | Ich konnt' nicht widerstehen – <br> Und als ich küsste das holde Gesicht, <br> Da war's um mich geschehen. |
| The marble image came alive, <br> Began to moan and plead – <br> She drank my burning kisses up <br> With ravenous thirst and greed. | Lebendigward das Marmorbild <br> Der Stein begann zu ächzen – <br> Sie trank meiner Küsse lodernde Glut <br> Mit Dürsten und mit Lechzen. |
| She drank the breath from out my <br> breast, <br> She fed lust without pause; <br> She pressed me tight, and tore <br> and rent <br> My body with her claws. | Sie trank mir fast den Odem aus – <br> <br> Und endlich, wollustheischend, <br> Umschlang sie mich, meinen armen <br> Leib <br> Mit den Löwentatzen zerfleischend. |
| O rapturous torment and exquisite <br> pain! <br> Anguish and bliss evermore! | Entzückende Marter und wonniges <br> Weh! <br> Der Schmerz wie die Lust <br> unermesslich |
| While the kiss of her mouth was <br> thrilling joy, <br> Her lion claws ripped and tore. | Derweilen des Mundes Kuss mich <br> beglückt, <br> Verwunden die Tatzen mich <br> grässlich. |

Within the marital relationship, too, love has commonly been interwoven with competition for power and dominance. For 2,500 years,

first Greco-Roman pagan culture and, subsequently, Christian monotheistic culture endorsed the superiority of male over female, emphasizing the biological and moral inferiority of women, and demanding
obedience from wife to husband. Although marriage was a contractual relationship, it was, for the most part, not one conceived to be
between equals, and, with the advent of Christianity, not one that
could be dissolved. For more than sixteen centuries thereafter, the
wife was legally and morally subordinate to her husband. That is
not to say that women of strong character did not domineer their
husbands. Viragos no doubt did. It is not for nothing that the hen-pecked
husband is a figure of comedy (written by men) throughout the ages.
Nor is it to say that love, loyalty, and affection did not sometimes
characterize marriages.

*Love and disposition*   Is love a disposition? It is tempting to think so,
since it is neither a sensation nor a perception,
neither an activity nor a process, and it is not a
mental state. Must it not then be a so-called dispositional state or
just a plain disposition? It shares some features with dispositions,
but it would be misleading to characterize it thus. We must call to
mind our earlier distinction between a distinctively *human* disposition,
that is, a trait of character or temperament, and a disposition *qua*
tendency or proneness (*Human Nature*, pp. 118–21). A person may
be of a prudent, kindly, benevolent disposition or of a tidy, orderly,
reliable one. Evidently, someone may be of a loving disposition. This
disposition (character trait) is manifest in the loving care and tenderness that the person exhibits to others. But, obviously, *loving* another
person is not such a disposition, although if one loves another
one may (but need not) have a tendency to exhibit loving care and
tenderness.

Is loving another then a tendency or proneness? That would be
misleading, since tendencies and pronenesses are characterized by
reference to what they are tendencies or pronenesses *to do*. But it
is far from obvious that for someone to love another is to have a
tendency or proneness to perform individual acts belonging to any
*identifying* act-category. Doubtless, if one loves another, one will
often show tenderness and care, or act to promote and protect their
interests and welfare. But these polymorphous specifications do
not provide an act-category that identifies the putative disposition.
Moreover, good doctors do not love their patients and conscientious
shepherds do not love their sheep, although they care for them and

protect them.[21] Similarly, there can be selfish, self-centred lovers (in *The Forsyte Saga*, even when wooing Irene and showering her with gifts, Soames was trying to *gain a possession* with the purpose of producing a son).

There *are* affinities between the idea of love and the notion of a disposition. But the connection is not as direct as that between being irascible (a patent disposition) and being prone to lose one's temper, or between being indolent (another patent disposition) and tending to avoid work and effort. One typically (but not necessarily) desires one's beloved. One typically (but not inevitably) fantasizes about making love to the person with whom one has fallen in love. That one loves another provides one with a motive for action. For one then typically (but not ineluctably) takes the interests and welfare of another as a reason for one to act to benefit or protect the person one loves. To love another, as we conceive of love, is characteristically to want to be with the person one loves, to share one's life with him or her, to engage in joint projects, to care for, protect and cherish this person. Furthermore, there is a period in human life when human beings are prone, have a tendency, *to fall in love* – often more than once, namely when they are young. But *actually loving* another person is not a disposition – merely disposition-involving.

So, let us draw the threads together. Interpersonal love in general, and erotic love in particular, are categorially complex. Erotic love is essentially tied to sensations. It is necessarily connected to perceptions, indeed, to all five senses. Love has a connection with human dispositions (even though loving another is not a disposition of character or temperament). To love another is not a tendency or proneness to perform an act of any determinate act-category, even though there are amatory tendencies and pronenesses. To fall in love may be an event, but need not be. To be in love has affinities with a state of mind, but it is not a mental state. However, to characterize loving another person for a prolonged period of time as a state of a person or dispositional state would be as misguided as characterizing knowing or believing something as a state of a person. The upshot of these considerations is that the attempt to pigeonhole love within our standard array of categorial concepts is, at the very least, unhelpful. For there is no single

---

[21] The shepherd's relationship to his sheep is a singularly inept metaphor or simile for love. This is patent as soon as one remembers to ask *why* the shepherd takes such good care of his sheep.

category under which love may be subsumed *off which we can then read the salient, defining characteristics of love.*[22] Love is many-faceted. Different categorial concepts get a grip upon only one facet or another of this complex emotion. It has to be examined in detail in its own right.

## 9. Connective analysis II: peculiarities of love as an emotion

*Love qua emotion*    Love is an emotion – which category, as argued in chapters 1 to 3, is disorderly, with multiple centres of variation. Like other emotions, love has no bodily location. It is an attribute of human beings as wholes, not of their parts. Like all emotions, it admits of degrees, and can wax and wane. It has both intensity and depth. Its intensity may be exhibited in essentially associated emotions: the intensity of joy at reciprocated love, the intensity of the anxiety felt when the person one loves is endangered, the intensity of the delight in joint activities and successful projects, the intensity of the longing for the person one loves when absent and of the joy when reunited, in the grief of bereavement, and so forth. The depth of love is revealed by the manner in which it penetrates manifold levels of the personality of the lover, by its grip on the imagination, by the weight of the reasons for thought and action with which it furnishes the lover, by the extent to which it motivates behaviour, and by its giving meaning to one's life.[23] The ultimate test of the depth of love,

---

[22] Attempts to investigate the neural correlates of romantic and maternal love (see A. Bartels and S. Zeki, 'The Neural Correlates of Maternal and Romantic Love', *NeuroImage* 21 (2004), 1155–66) by showing patients under an fMRI scanner pictures of their lover or child can at *most* disclose neural activity correlative to seeing photographs of one's lover or child. These experiments shed no light whatsoever on what neural structures or processes (if any determinate structures or processes exist) are correlative to the love one bears one's lover or child when they are absent, missing, or in danger; when one wants to please them (present or absent), longs for them, caresses them, or embraces them with one's eyes closed, speaks to them lovingly (directly or on the telephone), writes to them, writes a sonnet to them, acts out of love for them, and so on.

[23] This has been given (perhaps inflated) expression by Elizabeth Barrett Browning:

> How do I love thee? Let me count the ways.
> I love thee to the depth and breadth and height
> My soul can reach, when feeling out of sight
> For the ends of being and ideal grace.
> I love thee to the level of every day's
> Most quiet need, by sun and candle-light.

perhaps, is one's willingness to sacrifice one's life for the person one loves, either by one's death (e.g. Soames Forsyte in saving the life of his daughter Fleur) or by dedicating one's life to the loving care of an invalided spouse (e.g. Jane Eyre for the blinded Rochester), parent, or child. Like other emotions, love is intentional (it is 'directed' and its object need not exist (the atheist need not deny that believers love God)), and the verb 'to love' takes both material object-accusatives and nominalization-accusatives.

*8 peculiarities of the emotion of love*

Nevertheless, love is unlike most other emotions in its overwhelming importance in the lives of those who love and in the way in which it informs their lives. It is also distinctive in the manner in which it weaves together the following eight features:

(i) it essentially runs a course and has a history;
(ii) it is institutionalized;
(iii) there is no *occasion* for loving another person;
(iv) it can be put to the test;
(v) it is essentially interwoven with many other emotions;
(vi) there is no clear formal object for love;
(vii) the relationship between love and reasons for loving is idiosyncratic;
(viii) the object of love possesses a distinctive particularity or uniqueness.

These merit investigation.

(i) Unlike emotions that *can* take a momentary, reactive form, such as fear, anger, ecstasy, or pride, love necessarily runs a course. To be sure, one may experience a sudden wave of love towards the person one loves, occasioned perhaps by a momentary glimpse or the sound of his or her voice, or by something said or

---

I love thee freely, as men strive for right.
I love thee purely, as they turn from praise.
I love thee with the passion put to use
In my old griefs, and with my childhood's faith.
I love thee with a love I seemed to lose
With my lost saints. I love thee with the breath,
Smiles, tears, of all my life; and, if God choose,
I shall but love thee better after death.

(*Sonnets from the Portuguese*, sonnet 43)

done, or even just hearing something said of that person. But this experience presupposes that one already loves the person for whom one suddenly feels a rush of love. There is no such thing as feeling a flash, spark, or moment of love towards someone one does not already love – one cannot love another person for fifteen seconds, as one may feel intense fear for fifteen seconds. In this respect, love resembles emotions like trust or grief. Indeed, unlike episodic forms of emotion, such as episodic anxiety, it would need very special circumstances to render intelligible the idea that one might love another for three hours in the manner in which one might be anxious for another person for three hours. Other things being equal, love is a *persistent* emotion, lacking genuine duration. Moreover, it is an emotion that has a *history* in the course of which it changes as the loving couple, or the mother and child, change with the passing of years. The love between a man and a woman *may* last a lifetime, persisting through youth and marriage, through childbirth and the joys and trials of parenting, through middle age and the gradual waning of passion but perhaps ever-growing and deepening affection, to old age, when all passion is spent and yet, despite knowledge of the approach of death, which informs thought and feeling, love endures.

(ii) Unlike other emotions, different phases and forms of love can be and typically are institutionalized. Most formally, love is institutionalized in marriage and the formal roles of husband and wife. But it is also moulded by the semi-formal social roles of suitor and wooed, lover and mistress, or recognized 'partners' in an unmarried union. These roles are, to a greater or lesser degree, governed by social convention, and determine forms of behaviour and legitimate expectations. Other forms of love, such as parental love and filial love, as well as loyalty love, can be and typically are institution-dependent and normative.

(iii) There are occasions for feeling fear, namely when confronted by something dangerous and threatening to one's well-being or the well-being of those whom one loves. There are occasions for feeling angry – when another intentionally does something untoward, offensive, or wrong. There are occasions for feeling remorse, when one recognizes that one has done something wrong, wishes one hadn't, and seeks to make amends. But what is an occasion for feeling love? Surely not encountering a beautiful youth or girl! Nor is it recognizing the beauty or excellence of their souls. These are occasions for admiration, not for love. Is it not when Eros' arrow hits one's heart, as when Levin sees Kitty in a passing coach:

> She recognized him, and a look of wonder and delight lit up her face.
>
> He could not be mistaken. There were no other eyes like those in the world. There was only one creature in the world that could concentrate for him all the light and meaning of life. It was she, it was Kitty. (*Anna Karenina*, III. 12)

But this is the occasion *on which* Levin falls in love with Kitty, not an occasion *for* him or for anyone in a like situation to fall in love with her or to love her in the sense in which great danger is an occasion for anyone in a like situation to feel fear, or a vile insult an occasion for anyone thus insulted to feel affront or anger.

(iv)   Love, like friendship and loyalty, may be tested, as was Hugh Stanbury's in Trollope's *He Knew He was Right*, who withstood disinheritance for the sake of his love for Dorothy. It was tested in the case of John Willoughby in *Sense and Sensibility* who abandoned Marianne at the prospect of an heiress, and lived to rue his decision. Natasha's love for Prince Andrei was tragically tested by her being made to wait for him for a year, and she succumbed to an infatuation with Anatole Kuragin. True love, we may hold, *should* withstand the temptations of selfishness and cupidity, the loneliness of separation, as well as the temptations of attraction to others. But we may also hold that in some cases the test may have been too great, so that failure should be forgiven – as Pierre believed that Natasha truly loved Prince Andrei, and that Andrei should forgive her.

(v)   Love is essentially interwoven with a multitude of other emotions. To love another is to increase one's hostages to fortune. It is to crave reciprocity, which may not be forthcoming (Tatiana's love for Onegin) – and the rejection may be heart-breaking. It is to place trust in another – and that trust may be betrayed (Marianne's trust in Willoughby in *Sense and Sensibility*). It is to care for another beyond most if not all things (Francis Herries's love for Mirabell, in Walpole's *Rogue Herries*). Hence it is to lay oneself bare to fear for the person one loves in sickness or in danger, to anxiety when there are grounds for worry, to jealousy should his or her love be turned in other directions, and to guilt should one's own heart be captured by another. Some loves may not survive de-crystallization and the realism that replaces the imagined perfections with true appraisals (Lydgate and Rosamond Vincy in *Middlemarch*). The pain of realization may be sore indeed. Some great loves, through misfortune or tragedy, are severed, leaving a lasting and unassuageable longing and sorrow (Yuri and Lara in *Doctor Zhivago*). Above all, to love is to confront the possibility of great grief at the death of those one loves. These are among the vulnerabilities of love.

*The cornucopia of love*  The cornucopia of long-lasting love, however, *can* be generous. Whether it will be lies in the natures of the lovers, in their capacity for understanding and self-understanding, and in the hands of the fickle goddess Fortuna. Requited love, *as we conceive it*, involves reciprocity of respect and gratitude for the gift of love. Lovers who have chosen to share their lives *may* find joy in the company of their spouse or partner, in their joint activities (including the making of a home) and shared interests, and in joy and pride in their children. With due cultivation and attention these joys *may* persist. To love is to feel pride in the spouse, to take pride in his or her achievements. To give and to receive affection, to share tenderness and intimacy, are the *possible* jewels of human life *as we conceive it* (but they *can* turn into old stones and tawdry glass). Above all, we hold, it is in love that human beings can achieve part of the *summum bonum*, the self-transcendence of love, in which selfishness and self-centredness are cast aside. This web of interwoven emotions associated with love at its best, in its various possible courses, and in its various stages in life, is far richer than can be found with respect to most other emotions (see fig. 10.4).

(vi) The formal object of anger can be said to be the annoying and offensive; that of fear the dangerous or threatening; that of remorse a wrong-doing of one's own one wishes one had not done; and so on. But what is the formal object of love? Is it *the lovable*? Surely not: as noted, a person is lovable if he or she is sweet-tempered, gentle, good-willed and good-humoured, kind and attentive, in short, endearing. But one may recognize someone's lovable character without loving them, and not every person loved is lovable or is believed to be lovable (Fleur certainly loved her father Soames Forsyte (*The White Monkey*), Princess Maria loved her father Prince Nikolai Bolkonsky, and Rose loved Pinkie

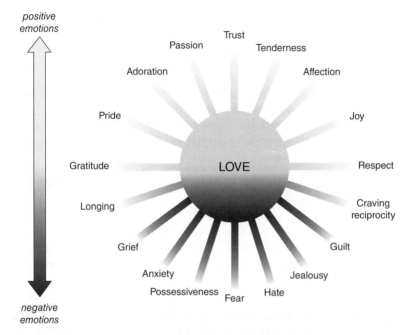

Note: by 'ownership' I mean feelings of possessiveness and domination; by hate I mean to indicate love–hate relationships.

**Figure 10.4**   *Positive and negative emotions potentially interwoven with love*

(*Brighton Rock*), but these men were anything but lovable). The concept of the lovable has been allocated a place in our conceptual web that is quite different from that of a formal object of love.[24] Plato held that the formal object of ideal love is the Idea of Beauty, and Augustine held it to be the Good. But such idealization deliberately abstracts from *human love* and its objects. It prescribes an ideal that dehumanizes human love but sheds no light on the formal object of interpersonal love.

It appears then that love has no formal object. Erotic love presupposes being *attracted* by the person loved. However, being attracted by the person whom one loves is not an intrinsic property of one's beloved, *a fortiori* not a formal property, but being *attractive* is. But one may well fall in love with another, be *attracted*, and love, without any

---

[24] See G. Taylor, 'Love', *Proceedings of the Aristotelian Society*, 76, 147–64.

process of Stendhalian crystallization yielding the idea that the person loved is *attractive*. As Shakespeare noted:

> My mistress' eyes are nothing like the sun;
> Coral is far more red than her lips' red.
> If snow be white, why then her breasts are dun;
> If hairs be wires, black wires grow on her head.
> I have seen roses damasked, red and white,
> But no such roses see I in her cheeks.   (Sonnet 130)[25]

One may be attracted by another and love her obsessively (as Philip loved Mildred Rogers in *Of Human Bondage*) without thinking her attractive and without her being attractive.

(vii)   One can generally answer the question of why one feels a certain emotion. One normally has reasons for fearing something, for being angry with someone, for feeling embarrassed or proud, and so forth – and one fears, is angry, feels embarrassed or proud *for* those reasons. One has reasons for admiring or esteeming someone, as one has reasons for being grateful or resentful – and, accordingly, one admires, esteems, is grateful, or resentful *for* those reasons. But does one love someone *for* a reason? A child grows to love his parents without reasons, quite irrespective of how admirable his parents are or are thought to be. Parents do not love their children for the characteristics the children possess, no matter how delightful they may be. Do they not love them for the simple reason that they are theirs? *Being one's own* is a reason for being responsible for the child. It is less than clear whether it is a reason for the parents to love their child. Of course, they may love the child *because* the child is theirs, but it is not obvious that *being one's own* is a reason *for* loving one's child. 'I love her because she is my child' may be an explanation. It may perhaps be a warrant. But it may rather be a terminal block to the demand for reasons (akin to 'I just want it').

*Love and reason*   Do lovers love each other for no reason? – If young lovers are asked why they love, they can give a multitude of reasons, as poets attest. It is, on occasion, the beautiful features of the beloved that attract the lover, that enchant, intoxicate, bewitch, and enthral. It may be the character traits, the

---

[25] It has been suggested that this sonnet is primarily and perhaps even a cheap five-fingered anti-Petrarchan exercise of intentionally amusing virtuosity.

masculinity or femininity, the masterfulness or the gentleness and sensitivity, the intelligence and perceptiveness, the generosity and protectiveness, the sensuality and adoration, that entrance the lover. Love, even when it originates in love at first sight, involves *appraisal* of the loved person – which may be realistic or falsely idealized ('crystallized'). The moot question, however, is whether such reasons are reasons *why* one person loves another, or whether they are the lover's reasons *for* loving. In the former case, they explain why the lover is so deeply attracted to the person loved and may in turn be subjected to aetiological analysis which may disclose affinities and connections of which the lover is unaware (her smile is like his mother's (of whom he has no memory), her askant eye is akin to that of the long-forgotten little girl he loved in kindergarten (as Descartes related of himself)). If the reasons are reasons *for* loving, they warrant the emotion. If the putative reason turns out to be false, then the emotion will cease (as with gratitude: if Jill finds out that it was not Jack who sent her the roses, she will cease to feel grateful to him). It is true that sometimes love may falter or fail on discovery that, contrary to one's first impression, the person with whom one fell in love has a mean, cruel, deceitful, or cowardly streak. But what this amounts to is that love may be undermined by reasons for dislike or contempt – it does not show that love is supported by reasons in the manner in which belief is normally supported by reasons for believing.

(viii)  Reasons have a degree of universality: if one admires or esteems another, one has, and can cite, reasons for one's admiration and grounds for esteeming the person. Other things being equal, one would admire and esteem *anyone* who had such qualities or had done such things.[26] But love felt for another is focused upon just *that* person. Another person with the same admirable features would not, as it were, 'do just as well' (Leah was no substitute for Rachel, no matter how beautiful and graceful she may have been). The relationship is not captured merely by saying that it holds between two unique individuals. After all, *all* binary human relationships are between two unique individuals, since human beings *are* severally unique. Rather, one is inclined to say, it is the very uniqueness that is loved. As Montaigne said when pressed to explain his friendship-love

[26] Of course, reasons may be relativized, e.g. if someone else had said *that* to me, I would be a little annoyed, but that *you* should say it to me is mortifying. But even this possesses a degree of universalizability: for anyone who stands to me in the relationship in which you stand to me were to say what you did, I should be likewise mortified.

for La Boétie, 'I can say no more than because it was him and because it was me' (*parce que c'était lui; parce que c'était moi*). The thought remains opaque. What *is* the uniqueness of the person loved, and how is this focus upon specificity to be characterized?

If one is angry with another, one is indeed angry *with that very person*. This says no more than that the relationship is transitive, that is, that 'angry with' demands an object. If one is angry with someone, that person, like every human being, will be specific and, like all human beings, unique. But much more than that is being indicated by pointing out that interpersonal love involves love *of the uniqueness of the person*. It is not that the lover does *not* love the eyes, the smile, the voice of the beloved. He loves the way she moves, her gestures, the particular way in which she bends her neck and the way she laughs. And she loves his strength and protectiveness, his adoration and worship of her, his concern for her, his gentleness or manliness and his caresses or urgency. But these are not conceived merely as general characteristics that might equally be instantiated in others, who would similarly arouse one's love.[27] One loves just *this* person, who cannot be replaced by another sharing similar characteristics. What does this mean?

*Individuum est ineffabile*, the scholastics said. Another person might have these very characteristics too. But what attracts one, what one loves to see and feel, to hear and taste, are conceived to be *constitutive* of the person loved here and now.[28] Of course, they will change with age: the alabaster skin will fade, the raven or golden locks will turn grey, and the young god or goddess will be gone. But the person will remain the same person through change, and the love, if it flourishes, will grow ever stronger through shared life and experience. This sentiment is sometimes expressed by saying that one wishes to be loved *for one's own sake*. The tension between loving a

[27] It is striking to see how Pascal painted himself into a corner on this matter: 'Does he who loves someone on account of beauty really love that person? No; for the small-pox, which will kill the beauty without killing the person, will cause him to love her no more. And if someone loves me for my judgement, memory, he does not love *me*, for I can lose these qualities without losing myself. Where, then, is this Ego, if it be neither in the body nor in the soul? And how love the body or the soul except for these qualities which do not constitute *me*, since they are perishable? For it is impossible and would be unjust to love the soul of a person in the abstract and whatever qualities might be therein. We never, then, love a person, but only qualities' (*Pensées*, V. 323).

[28] What is truly terrible about the deception that Cyrano and Christian de Neuvillette practise upon Roxane is that they deceive her into thinking that Christian's good looks are the manifestation of the beauty of his soul as expressed in Cyrano's poetic eloquence.

woman for her beauty and loving her for herself is articulated in all
its paradoxical nature by Yeats in his poem 'For Anne Gregory':

> 'Never shall a young man,
> Thrown into despair
> By those great honey-coloured
> Ramparts at your ear,
> Love you for yourself alone
> And not your yellow hair.'
> 'But I can get a hair-dye
> And set such colour there,
> Brown, or black, or carrot,
> That young men in despair
> May love me for myself alone
> And not my yellow hair.'
> 'I heard an old religious man
> But yesternight declare
> That he had found a text to prove
> That only God, my dear,
> Could love you for yourself alone
> And not your yellow hair.'

The sentiment is echoed by Friedrich Rückert in his poem 'Liebst du
um Schönheit', which is part of Mahler's song cycle *Rückert Lieder*:

| | |
|---|---|
| If you love for beauty, | Liebst du um Schönheit, |
| O love me not! | Oh nicht mich liebe! |
| Love the sun | Liebe die Sonne, |
| with its golden tresses! | Sie trägt ein gold'nes Haar! |
| | |
| If you love for youth, | Liebst du um Jugend, |
| O love me not! | O nicht mich liebe! |
| Love spring-time, | Liebe die Frühling |
| that is young each year! | Der jung ist jedes Jahr! |
| | |
| If you love for wealth, | Liebst du um Schätze, |
| O love me not! | O nicht mich Liebe. |
| Love the mermaid, | Liebe die Meerfrau, |
| with luminous pearls! | Die hat viel Perlen klar. |
| | |
| If you love for love's sake, | Liebst du um Liebe, |
| O yes, love me! | O ja, mich liebe! |
| Love me forever, | Liebe mich immer, |
| you I love forevermore! | Dich lieb' ich immerdar. |

Elizabeth Browning likewise expressed the conception of the unique *quiddity* of the beloved by means of the thought that one loves *for love's sake*.[29]

What are we to make of this? Of course, the young are prone to love the features of the person they love. To be sure, those features will alter with age (although, if love persists, one will love the aged features no less). The beauty of her face is enchanting because of the sweetness of her smile and the loveliness of her laugh. The attraction of her smiles or laughter cannot be separated from the objects and occasions that give rise to them, for it is these that reveal the sensibility and character (the frigid beauty of Griselda Grantly in Trollope's *Framley Parsonage* and the majestic beauty of Jennifer Cards in Walpole's *Judith Paris* is deceptive, for they mask vapid personalities). Similarly, the beautiful figure that can be captured in a portrait or photograph is not, in the circumstances of life, sharply separable from the grace with which the individual moves and the dignity which she displays. These are exhibited under a variety of circumstances, including joy, abandon, stress, anger, sorrow, insult, and offense – through which character shines. *One* aspect for which the notion of loving someone *for her own sake*, for her unique and ineffable *quiddity*, or *for the sake of love*, is perhaps fumbling is that what one loves is the unique personality that will persist when the beauty has faded, when the gay laughter has gone, when the grace of movement and gesture has given way

---

[29] If thou must love me, let it be for naught
Except for love's sake only. Do not say,
'I love her for her smile – her look – her way
Of speaking gently, – for a trick of thought
That falls in well with mine, and certes brought
A sense of pleasant ease on such a day' –
For these things in themselves, Beloved, may
Be changed, or change for thee – and love, so wrought,
May be unwrought so. Neither love me for
Thine own dear pity's wiping my cheeks dry:
A creature might forget to weep, who bore
Thy comfort long, and lose thy love thereby!
But love me for love's sake, that evermore
Thou mayst love on, through love's eternity.
(*Sonnets from the Portuguese*, sonnet 14)

to the arthritic movements of old age.[30] We can perhaps extend this thought further.

*The love of a person*

What one loves is not merely this man or woman, with just these features, whose *Doppelgänger* would do just as well, but this person *as possessor of a history*, indeed a *unique* history, since every human being necessarily traces a unique autobiographical route through the world. That history has moulded that person and their personality. In loving another, one loves a unique person with *an intrinsic character, temperament,* and *personality*, and, as it were, an *autobiography*, not merely a substance instantiating a set of synchronic properties, let alone a set of properties possessed by a bare substance. Some of the properties are indeed mere accidents, which will change. Love, lovers hope, will transcend such changes, and the vows of lovers are a commitment to constancy through such change.

There is a temptation to *define* love, or 'true' love, by reference to its ability to withstand time and change:

> Love is not love
> Which alters when it alteration finds,
> Or bends with the remover to remove.
> O no, it is an ever-fixed mark
> That looks on tempests and is never shaken.
>
> (Shakespeare, Sonnet 116)

That would be either an unwarranted stipulation or the prescription of an ideal. It is true that if the lovers are dedicated and fortune favours them, their love will grow and flourish through shared experience. It is, after all, with *this* person and with no one else, that one will trace a (partly) common autobiographical route through

---

[30] When you are old and grey and full of sleep,
And nodding by the fire, take down this book,
And slowly read, and dream of the soft look
Your eyes had once, and of their shadows deep;
How many loved your moments of glad grace,
And loved your beauty with love false or true,
But one man loved the pilgrim soul in you,
And loved the sorrows of your changing face.
(W. B. Yeats, 'When You are Old')

the world, the memories of which cement the relationship. Attraction may in due course be overlain by devotion, and adoration by trust and mutual dependency, and erotic intimacy may become the accompaniment of persistent psychological intimacy and mutual understanding. But Eros is a fickle god. What seemed a good match, a happy marriage, or an ideal partnership may become a painful clash of personalities; the erotic attraction may fade and not be replaced by loving companionship but by ever-increasing estrangement and recognition of misfit. What seemed gold may turn to iron, and rust.

## 10. Connective analysis III: some characteristic features of love

*Love and reciprocity*   Love normally *craves reciprocity*.[31] Unlike friendship, which *essentially* involves reciprocity, love does not – for it may be unrequited. Courtship, which in our society is common between young lovers, seeks a response of love. It manifests attraction, and craves to inspire reciprocal attraction and love. Reciprocity in love must be freely given, otherwise one is dealing with manipulation and seduction. The lover strives to induce reciprocity by attention, care, and concern, by the exercise of social graces such as charm and wit, and sometimes by revelation of his past life and deeds that lay bare his heart, inducing admiration or compassion.[32] Lack of reciprocity in courtship may

---

[31] 'Normally' because there may be constraints of propriety or commitment. Pierre falls in love with Natasha, but he is already married to Helena. Sydney Carton loves Lucie Manette, but considers himself unworthy of her and is aware of her love for Darnay. Here the lover does not crave reciprocity but service, recognition, and appreciation.

[32] Othello, accused of having induced Desdemona's love by magic and drugs, explains to the Duke of Venice and to Brabanzio how he had wooed Desdemona by telling her the tale of his adventurous life: 'She loved me for the dangers I had passed, / And I loved her that she did pity them. / This is the only witchcraft I have used.' To be sure, his stories included fanciful lies about 'men whose heads do grow beneath their shoulders', told merely to impress her and to foster his sense of superiority (*Othello* I. 3).

lead to the natural fading of love. But it may lead to persistent anguish and suffering (as it does for Sonya, whose love for Astrov is unrequited, in Chekhov's *Uncle Vanya*) or even to suicide (young Werther in Goethe's *Sorrows of Young Werther*). Lack of reciprocity in marriage may lead to great suffering (Francis Herries's anguished relationship to Mirabell in *Rogue Herries*) and sometimes to the death of love (as Karenin's love for Anna, which flares up when she almost dies in childbirth, but subsequently turns to hatred[33]). It is noteworthy that unreciprocated love, despite the agonized and often humiliating craving to be loved, may nevertheless be preferable to no love (as it was for Francis Herries). That, in itself, is puzzling. How can such suffering be preferable to its absence? Only because the deep love of another, even though rejected, is held to be redemptive and of intrinsic value. (Here, perhaps, we have a surviving residue of *fin'amor*.)

*Love and union of lovers*  Carrying, as we do, the heavy burden of romanticism, we can readily understand the belief that love, for those who are open to its intense forms, is inseparable from the thought of *union with the beloved*. But what does this mean? The most obvious interpretation of this sentiment is that the connection between love and the notion of the union of two persons or two souls is made by the idea of sexual intercourse. This metaphor was already alive in the minds of the authors of Genesis 2: 24: 'Therefore shall a man leave his father and his mother and shall cleave unto his wife: and they shall be one flesh.' The widespread cross-cultural idea that the craving for union with the beloved is exhibited in frenetic copulation was fiercely caricatured by Lucretius:

---

[33] Comparable switches may occur in the case of admiration (an emotional attitude), which can swiftly turn to contempt when the object of one's admiration fails to meet the standards one expects and is seen to have feet of clay. In both cases, high expectations are disappointed, and one may feel cheated and perhaps humiliated by one's previous love or admiration.

| | |
|---|---|
| They cannot satisfy their eyes with looking, | nec satiare queunt spectando corpora coram |
| Nor with hands wandering aimlessly o'er the body | nec manibus quicquam teneris abradere membris |
| Can they glean anything from tender limbs; | possunt errantes incerti corpore toto. |
| And when at last with body clasped to body | denique cum membris conlatis flore fruuntur |
| They pluck the flower of youth, when body knows | aetatis, iam cum praesagit gaudia corpus |
| The bliss to come and Venus is ready, poised | atque in eost Venus ut muliebria conserat arva, |
| To sow the fields of love, they cling together | adfigunt avide corpus iunguntque salivas |
| Mouth pressed to watering mouth and lips to lips | oris et inspirant pressantes dentibus ora, |
| Drawing deep breaths as body calls to body. | ne quiquam, quoniam nihil inde abradere possunt |
| In vain. For they can rub nothing off from it, | nec penetrare et abire in corpus corpore toto; |
| Neither can body be absorbed in body. | nam facere inter dum velle et certare videntur. |
| For that sometimes they seem to want and strive for, | usque adeo cupide in Veneris compagibus haerent, |
| So ardently in Venus' toils they cling | membra voluptatis dum vi labefacta liquescunt. |
| Their limbs with rapture liquefied and melted. | (*The Nature of Things* (trans. R. Melville), IV. 1102–14) |

This is to take literally what is at best a metaphor. Most lovers, despite Andrew Marvell, would not truly wish it.[34] Indeed, the literal merging of bodies is not possible. More plausible is the thought, presumably engendered by an intense co-ordinated orgasmic experience, that in sexual ecstasy there is a union of souls. (This is echoed in the

[34] Marvell, in 'The Definition of Love' proclaims that his love 'was begotten by Despair upon Impossibility' since although a union of minds is attainable, the ultimate merging of bodies, for which love craves, is not:

> For Fate with jealous Eye does see
> Two perfect Loves; nor lets them close:
> Their union would her ruin be,
> And her Tyrannick pow'r depose'

See E. Greenwood, 'Marvell's Impossible Love', *Essays in Criticism* 27 (1977), 100–109, for an insightful interpretation of this poem).

religious experience of a mystical union with God.) Here, one may suspect, the temporary *loss of a sense of identity* in orgasmic ecstasy is interpreted as an experience of *union of two souls*. It is striking that Tertullian remarked that 'in that last breaking wave of delight, do we not feel something of our very soul go out from us'.[35] But a misconceived *union of souls* should not be confused with a *harmony of souls*. That is often an idea characteristic of being in love, and an ideal of companionate love.

Love and completion

Related to the idea of a union of souls is a further ubiquitous picture, namely of *finding completion* in the love of another. This too is part of Aristophanes' myth in Plato's *Symposium*. One source of the idea is a characteristic feature of new love in which a lover is intensely aware that aspects of his or her nature that have hitherto been suppressed and stultified are brought out by reciprocated love. In loving and being loved, lovers may think, the best side of their nature is liberated and allowed to flourish. And that may well be no illusion, even though it may not be permanent. Those who love well are less selfish and self-centred than they otherwise might be, are more open (and hence, too, more vulnerable) and more attentive. For when in love, one's caring and protective instincts may be powerfully aroused, one's considerateness and generosity may increase, and one's capacity for self-transcendence may be enhanced. When loving another and being blessed with reciprocal love in a shared life, aims, and purposes, pleasures and joys converge. The capacity for joy and delight is enhanced by its being shared joy and shared delight. Such consequences of the reception of love may then be experienced as *a completion of oneself*. Only with one's beloved, one may feel, is one's nature fully realized. Given that loving another person can be so transformative and life-enhancing, it is natural that we should see it as the most important of human emotions. For many, it is the flowering of devoted interpersonal erotic love and its maturation into companionate love, which endows their lives with meaning (*this* grace is beyond the reach of Don Juan in his frenetic pursuit of erotic conquest). It is important to realize that this conception of human felicity and of human amatory relationships would, by and large, have been alien to ancient Greece and Rome. In Greece, it was above all virtue (courage, temperance,

---

[35] Tertullian, *De Anima*, XXVII. 5. Freud conceived of the male experience of union in love-making as a regression to the womb, a craving for the primary prenatal unity with the mother.

justice, and wisdom) and service to the polis that were constitutive of a well-lived life. In Rome, it was primarily personal and familial standing and esteem (*dignitas* and *auctoritas*) in the service of the republic or empire, and the fathering of children to carry on the line. It would, to a considerable degree, have been unintelligible in early and medieval Christian Europe (see appendix, pp. 419–26). To be sure, there was room for loyalty and affection between superior and inferior.

*Love and the will*     Like all emotions, human interpersonal love is a passion. One cannot be ordered to love another human being, only to be charming and kind to another (as Pierre instructed Prince Andrei to dance with Natasha at the ball). Falling in love is not a voluntary action, nor an involuntary one either, since it is not an action. It is non-voluntary. Nevertheless, it is not wholly beyond one's control, for one can decide *not* to succumb to the temptations of attraction and arousal. One may stifle one's nascent feelings and avoid any further engagement. Although one cannot *decide* to love another, one can decide to woo or make love to someone (in the old sense of the phrase). This may be done by suitor, lover, or seducer. Winning love is inducing attraction and arousal, as well as trust. Because loving another human being is not a voluntary *action*, there can be no duty or obligation to love. Hence, too, reciprocity is not a right. Rather, love is a gift. But how can that be? After all, the giving of gifts *is* a voluntary action. And what *is* the gift one gives? To be sure, one cannot love at will, although one may *try* to love another (as Mirabell tried unsuccessfully to love Francis Herries), that is, to try by one's deeds and engagement with another to bring it about that one loves that person. If one does love another, *then* one may give one's love as a gift. What does one then give? One might say that one gives oneself. But what does that mean? One gives one's attention to the person one loves, in care, thoughtfulness, and interested concern. One opens one's heart to the other, for lovers *reveal* themselves to each other. Truthfulness and candour are tokens of love. One gives, and indeed invites, physical intimacy, for one permits one's lover into the normally inviolable space with which human beings surround themselves. One puts one's hopes for happiness in the hands of the person one loves.

*Love and possession*     In our culture, a loving relationship involving erotic love (unlike friendship-love and parental, filial, and sibling love) lays claim to exclusivity and possessiveness. But the possessiveness is not a matter of *possession* but rather of commitment. 'I am yours' expresses an undertaking and confers an erotic permission, but it is not a transfer of rights of ownership. Nevertheless, it is striking how much of the language of sexual intercourse has a misleading form ('to take', 'to have', or 'to possess'). In polygamous or polyandrous societies exclusivity is waived as a matter of course. But then the psychological space for loving relations has a very different form from Western monogamous love.

*Erotic love*  Erotic love runs a course. This incorporates attraction, arousal, and desire. Reciprocity, if granted, magnifies desire, excitement, and urgency. These can be overwhelming. The normal course to consummation of sexual desire and erotic love involves the invitation to explore the beloved's body, expressed by Donne in his passionate poem 'To his Mistress Going to Bed' and by Shakespeare in *Venus and Adonis*, where the female voice is heard:

> 'Fondling', she saith, 'since I have hemm'd thee here
> Within the circuit of this ivory pale,
> I'll be a park, and thou shalt be my deer;
> Feed where thou wilt, on mountain or in dale:
> Graze on my lips; and if those hills be dry,
> Stray lower, where the pleasant fountains lie.
> 'Within this limit is relief enough,
> Sweet bottom-grass, and high delightful plain,
> Round rising hillocks, brakes obscure and rough,
> To shelter thee from the tempest and from rain;
> Then be my deer, since I am such a park;
> No dog shall rouse thee, though a thousand bark.'

Passionate erotic love may veer from uncontrolled physical passion to tenderness, *adoration*, and *worship*. The naturalness *to us* of the latter pair of religious epithets is a legacy of *fin'amor* and of Renaissance and Romantic poets and thinkers. What is worshipped and adored is the living human being as a whole – not an embodied soul or a psycho-physical unity, but an ensouled body. The mutual delight of lovers is a joy in their physical nature, in the intimacy it permits and in the consummation it invites.

*Companionate love*  Being in love may burn itself away in passion. Love affairs may cease in friendship, in indifference, or in enmity. But being in love, in our culture, may lead to a desire for commitment and a shared life. The conventional form for its fulfilment is marriage, conceived as the paradigmatic institution for having and rearing children. As the urgency and intensity of erotic love fades, loving friendship in the persisting relationship may, ideally, replace it. In companionate love, the lovers are no longer *in love*, but *love* each other. Passion is replaced by trust, affection, shared life and common projects, mutual loyalty, and (usually) children. As the crystals of idealization fall away, the lovers may attain a more realistic idea of each other. The weaknesses and character failings have to be accepted as given, and willingly tolerated and compensated for by loving care and attention, otherwise they may progressively erode respect, esteem, and finally love itself. Companionate love is a human possibility in our culture, a form of intrinsic value that we can hope for and pursue.

*The creativity of companionate love*    Although falling in love and consequently being in love are in the fickle hands of Eros, the mutual love that may grow between lovers once the passion of being in love has been burnt away is not. It is in the hands of the lovers. If it is to flourish, it must be fostered by loving concern and attention, by sympathy and understanding. It has to be constantly replenished by affection, thoughtfulness, and gift-giving within the framework of a shared life. The companionate love that obtains between lovers is not only intrinsically valuable; it is itself a creative force in three respects.

(i)   It is in itself life-enhancing, but not in the manner in which falling and being in love are. It is life-enhancing in depth rather than in intensity. It does not paint the world in glowing colours, as being in love does. Rather, it puts down roots that grow deeper as time goes by. It is constituted not merely by the sharing of life, but also by the transcendence of selfishness and self-centredness.

(ii)  Consequently, it provides the setting within which the loving couple can *create themselves* in forms of loving openness to each other, and of mutual dependency and joy in each other. It involves self-transformation and character development.

(iii) Companionate love is itself a relationship of intrinsic value that is created in the daily lives of a loving couple by indefinitely many deeds expressing love and affection, by sharing daily experiences both under stress and in delight, in sorrow, and in joy.

Companionate love intrinsically involves and generates moral requirements and commitments. The acceptance of ordinary gifts changes one's standing to the gift-giver, whose generosity benefits one. How much more, then, does the gift of love generate commitments, if the lovers are able to *give themselves* to each other. They may bare their souls to each other, revealing their vulnerabilities in complete trust – and that trust demands respect, those vulnerabilities beseech protection, and the love requires cherishing. The shared joys and travails, the shared projects and goals, are severally emotionally and rationally binding factors in the relationship. The forms in which the requirements of love are naturally expressed are modal ('ought', 'should', and 'must') but not deontic ('obligation' and 'duty'). When rights and duties are invoked in times of stress and strain, what was a loving relationship is in danger or has already foundered (see Heloise's first letter to Abelard in appendix, pp. 424f.).

*Love and morality*        Nevertheless, the relationship between love and morality is moot. Although we may grant love intrinsic value, and conceive of love as endowing our lives with meaning, it is not in itself an intrinsically moral emotion either (i) in its objects or (ii) in what it motivates. In this respect, it resembles loyalty. Contrary to the conception of love advanced by Plato, love, as we conceive it, is not essentially directed at the good and the virtuous. Even more disturbingly, it can be directed at evil and the wicked. Wicked tyrants throughout history have been loved by women to the point of suicidal self-sacrifice (Hitler and Eva Braun; Mussolini and Clara Petacci), and men have loved wicked women (as Antony loved Cleopatra, or Claudius Messalina).) One might concede this, but still insist that, even when someone loves a wicked person, the lover cannot believe the person he or she loves to be wicked. One must either be ignorant (perhaps culpably so), or avert one's eyes from the evil deeds of one's lover (self-deception), or positively condone them. While these are indeed possibilities, there seems no reason to suppose that it is either logically or psychologically impossible to love a person one knows to be wicked. (Did Macbeth not love his wife? Or Rose not love Pinkie, in *Brighton Rock*?) What *is* impossible is to love someone *for* their wickedness.

*Love as a motive*        There is no doubt that love is a motive, determining a pattern of reasons and action, and equally there can be no doubt that it can motivate evil deeds. The determination may be direct or indirect. King David brings about the death of Uriah, motivated by his love for Bathsheba and his desire to possess her. Medea murders her brother out of love for Jason. Indirect determination is patent in the cases of fear of disloyalty or infidelity, which may inspire jealousy, which in turn may lead to the murder of the actual or suspected lover or to the murder or maltreatment of the beloved (Browning's duke). (Notoriously, Gian Lorenzo Bernini attempted to murder his brother Luigi for having a love affair with his mistress, and had the beautiful Costanza Bonarelli's face slashed several times with a razor by one of his servants.) In less dramatic and horrifying forms, love can and does give rise to a multitude of evils. Love may degenerate into possessiveness, which in turn may provoke contempt and disgust (as in Louis Trevelyan's love for Emily in Trollope's *He Knew He Was Right*). Imperfections in the marital relationship may lead to domination (even well-intentioned domination) of one spouse by the other and to the crushing of autonomy (e.g. Torvald and Nora Helmer in *A Doll's House*). Sexual mismatch of need and sensual responsiveness may cause great distress (Madame Bovary). Love may wane, and the relationship may be threatened and undermined by extramarital affairs. These, in our culture, cause much suffering, a sense of ingratitude for all that has been freely given, and grief at the dismissal of the years of shared happiness enjoyed and common sorrows endured and surmounted. Infidelity breeds resentment and jealousy. Abandonment may inspire hatred and vengeance.

## 11. Self-love

Self-love is commonly conceived to be a form of love. It is widely assumed that it is a universal feature of mankind that we love ourselves. That idea is embedded in the 'Great Commandment' of Leviticus 19: 18, 'Thou shalt love thy neighbour as thyself', endorsed by Jesus and adopted by Christianity. We have no hesitation in employing the phrase, either ironically, as in Oscar Wilde's witticism in *An Ideal Husband*, 'To love oneself is the beginning of a lifelong romance' or as a serious and critical character description, as when Judith Paris describes her husband George as loving 'no one at all but himself' (*Judith Paris*, II. 1). The moot question, however, is whether self-love is a form of love at all. Hume sapiently pointed out that 'When we talk of *self-love* 'tis not in a proper sense, nor has the sensation it produces any thing in common with that emotion, which is excited by a friend or mistress.'[36] But how can this be? Reflect that, if asked to make a list of the people I love, I would not put my own name on the list – and that is not because it is so obvious that I am among those whom I love that it is not worth listing. The term 'self-love' in itself is as innocuous

---

[36] Hume, *Treatise on Human Nature*, II. ii. 1 (Selby-Bigge edn, p. 329); note that he uses 'mistress' rather than 'wife'.

as the term 'self-deception', that is, it has a perfectly good use. It is also as misleading, inasmuch as just as the expression 'self-deception' has a grammar quite different from that of 'deception of others',[37] so too 'self-love' has a quite different grammar from that of 'love of others'.[38]

*Logical asymmetry of self-love*

One cannot fall in love with oneself, let alone become infatuated with oneself. Nor can one yearn for reciprocity from oneself as one yearns for reciprocity from the person with whom one has fallen in love. Similarly, one cannot sacrifice oneself for oneself, as one may sacrifice oneself for one's lover. One cannot wish to share one's experiences with oneself as one wishes to share one's experiences with the person one loves, and that is not because one *necessarily* shares one's experiences with oneself. One can no more share an experience with oneself than one can resemble oneself. One cannot be charmed by oneself as one can be charmed by the person one is in love with. One cannot miss oneself, long for oneself, or long to be reunited with oneself. One cannot grieve over one's departure and welcome one's return. One cannot be disinterestedly concerned with one's own interests as one may be disinterestedly concerned with the interests of the person one loves, nor can one sacrifice one's own interests for oneself. In short, self-love is not a form of love. This insight is nicely illustrated by the myth of Narcissus. He is besotted with his own beauty, but he cannot touch the image that enchants and fascinates him. He cannot kiss the lips of the lovely face he sees in the water. When he tries to caress the face he sees, it dissolves into ripples.[39] Not only is self-love not a form of love, it is not an emotion at all.

Self-love involves a concern with one's own interests in disregard of the interests of others. But self-interest is not a form of love, nor is acting out of self-interest motivated by love. Rather, it is motivated by selfishness – which is one form self-love takes. Vanity is another form of self-love. As we have seen (chapter 5, section 3), vanity involves not only an excessive pride and preoccupation with one's appearance, but an overestimation of one's abilities and worth. So another possible facet of self-love is arrogance. Self-love also implies egocentricity or

---

[37] See *The Intellectual Powers*, pp. 251–3.

[38] Here I take issue with H. Frankfurt's *The Reasons of Love* (Princeton University Press, Princeton, 2004), ch. 3.

[39] The point is nicely made by S. Blackburn in *Mirror, Mirror: the Uses and Abuses of Self-Love* (Princeton University Press, Princeton, 2014).

self-centredness – a persistent preoccupation with one's interests and concerns to the exclusion of those of others (nicely depicted by Tolstoy in the character of Boris Drubetskoy in *War and Peace*). In extreme cases, self-love involves self-obsession – a complete immersion in one's own thoughts about oneself, in self-evaluation, in introspective reflection. But one may be self-obsessed without the vanity and self-admiration of self-love, as in the actual cases of Augustine, Rousseau, or Wittgenstein. Indeed, self-obsession may be wedded to self-hatred, as in the character of the narrator in Dostoevsky's *Notes from Underground*.

# 11

# Friendship

## 1. Friendship and love

In antiquity the subject of friendship occupied centre stage in discussions of the good life. It again moved to centre stage in Renaissance and post-Renaissance axiological reflections that were inspired by, and that emulated, the classics of the ancient world.

*Aristotle on friendship* — 'We consider having a friend', Aristotle wrote, 'to be one of the greatest goods, and friendlessness and solitude to be quite terrible'; indeed, he added, 'without friends no one would choose to live, though he had all other goods'.[1] Friendship 'is not only necessary, but also noble; for we praise those who love their friends, and it is thought to be a fine thing to have many friends'.[2] Aristotle's detailed investigations of friendship in the *Nicomachean Ethics* set the stage and determined the questions to be addressed in all subsequent discussions. It is important to bear in mind that the vocabulary he used does not coincide exactly with ours. The abstract noun *philia* brackets both love and friendship. The noun *philos*, unlike our noun 'friend', subsumes *those who are dear to us*,

---

[1] *Eudemian Ethics*, 1234$^b$32–3 (henceforth *EE*). Doubtless Aristotle would have found the life of an anchorite or hermit degenerate inasmuch as it forecloses the various forms in which the distinctive nature of man as a rational and social being can be fully realized.

[2] *Nicomachean Ethics*, 1155$^a$5 (henceforth *NE*).

*The Passions: A Study of Human Nature*, First Edition. P. M. S. Hacker.
© 2018 John Wiley & Sons Ltd. Published 2018 by John Wiley & Sons Ltd.

that is, not only extra-familial relationships of amity, but also the desirable, albeit (in his view) asymmetric, marital relationship between husband and wife, the maternal relationship between mother and child, and the paternal and filial relationships within the family. It also includes the homoerotic relationship between *erastes* and *eromenos* (*NE* 1164[a]3–11). The verb *philein* can accordingly mean to love, to hold dear, to feel fond of, or to feel the affection of friendship with, another.

*Cicero and Plutarch on friendship*                    Cicero, in his dialogue *Laelius: On Friendship*, writing some 300 years later in 44 BC, averred that 'Friendship [*amicitia*] is the noblest and most delightful of all the gifts the gods have given to mankind' (XIII. 69), and recommends that we 'place friendship above every other human concern that can be imagined! Nothing else in the whole world is so completely in harmony with nature and nothing so utterly right, in prosperity and adversity alike' (IV. 35–40). Plutarch, a century and a half after Cicero, voiced much the same sentiment: 'friendship', he wrote, 'is the most pleasant of all things, and nothing more gladdens the heart of man.'[3]

*Augustine on friendship*                    Augustine evidently enjoyed close and warm friendships in his youth, describing one such relationship in his *Confessions*:

> We could talk and laugh together and exchange small acts of kindness. We could join in the pleasures that books can give. We could be grave or gay together. If we sometimes disagreed, it was without spite, as a man might differ with himself, and the rare occasions of dispute were the very spice to season our usual accord. Each of us had something to learn from the other, and something to teach in return. If any were away, we missed them with regret and gladly welcomed them when they came home. Such things as these are heartfelt tokens of affection between friends. They are signs to be read on the face and in the eyes, spoken by the tongue and displayed in countless acts of kindness.' (IV. 8)

Despite a natural gift for friendship, Augustine had qualms. This should not be surprising, since they run parallel to his qualms

---

[3] 'Friends and Flatterers', in *Moralia*, §5. It is noteworthy that Plutarch had a much more instrumental conception of friendship than Cicero, writing that we should choose our friends carefully, and 'attach ourselves to those who are worthy of our friendship and likely to be serviceable to us' ('On Having Many Friends', *Moralia*, §4). Utility friendships were the norm in the fiercely networked and networking Roman elite even in Plutarch's times.

about human love in general that we have already examined. He thought that friendship and friendship-love stand in the way of the love of God:

> The bond of human friendship has a sweetness of its own, binding many souls into one. Yet, because of these values, sin is committed, because we have inordinate preference for these goods of a lower order and neglect the better and higher good. (*Confessions*, II. 5)

He tried to reconcile friendship-love with the love of God in *Confessions*, IV. 12:

> If the things of this world delight you, praise God for them but turn your love away from them and give it to their Maker, so that in things that please you, you may not displease Him. If your delight is in souls, love them in God, because they are too frail and stand firm only when they cling to Him.

And again in *Confessions*, V. 19:

> You only love your friend truly, after all, when you love God in your friend, either because he is in him, or in order that he may be in him … There is no true friendship unless God welds it between souls that cling together by the love that is poured into their heart by the Holy Spirit.

*Similarities between love and friendship*   We have no term comparable to *philia* that subsumes both love and friendship. The moot question for us is whether friendship, *as we understand it*, is simply one form of love, or whether only some kinds of friendship are. So we shall commence our examination of friendship by investigating its relationship with love, *as we conceive the two*. There are, to be sure, significant similarities. Both are indisputably important in our lives. Both can be put to the test. It is well said that only time and fortune can determine who are one's friends (and whether someone really loves one), and that misfortune reveals friends (and true love) more than good fortune. Neither relationship is transitive: one's love of one's spouse does not imply love of one's mother-in-law, and one's friend's friend is not necessarily one's friend – it has indeed been sapiently observed that 'we are all someone's awful friend'.[4]

---

[4] By Jack Gallagher, sometime professor of commonwealth history at Balliol College, Oxford.

Just as *not* loving, and *not* being in love with a certain person, may be crucially important to one, so too *not* being someone's friend may be of great importance. So, for example, it is important to Marguerite Gautier (in Dumas the Younger's *The Lady of the Camellias*) that she is *not* in love with her aristocratic lovers, and it is important to her that Armand Duval, whom she does indeed love, should know this. Similarly, it may often be important to one (in politics or high society) that, although one is acquainted with so-and-so, he is *not*, and *is known not to be*, a friend. The distribution of one's affections is a constituent element of one's conception of oneself as well as the conception others have of one (e.g. Lucien Chardon in his attempts to climb the social ladder in Restoration Paris, in Balzac's *Lost Illusions*). Both love and friendship admit of degrees, for just as one may love a certain person more than another, so too one may feel greater friendship for, and feel closer to, one friend rather than another. Similarly, both love and friendship may wax or wane. Just as one's love for another may grow greater with time, so too one's friendship with another may grow stronger and deeper as one weathers misfortune with the support, or in support, of one's friend. Conversely, just as one's love may wither as the years go by, so too a friendship may grow weaker and ultimately dissolve with time and separation.[5] Just as a lover, *in extremis*, may be willing to sacrifice his life for the sake of the person he loves (as Sydney Carton sacrificed his life for the sake of the felicity of Lucie Manette in *A Tale of Two Cities*), and lovers commonly express their feeling that they would not wish to continue to live without the other (*Romeo and Juliet*), so too friends may risk

---

[5] Well expressed by Nietzsche, ruminating on a lost friendship (possibly with Wagner, Paul Ree, Rohde (the friend of his student days), or even Burckhardt): 'We were friends and have become estranged. But this was right, and we do not want to conceal and obscure it from ourselves as if we had reason to feel ashamed. We are two ships each of which has its goal and course; our paths may cross and we may celebrate a feast together, as we did – and then the good ships rested so quietly in one harbour and one sunshine that it may have looked as if they had reached their goal and as if they had one goal. But then the almighty force of our tasks drove us apart again into different seas and sunny zones, and perhaps we shall never see each other again; perhaps we shall meet again but fail to recognize each other: our exposure to different seas and suns has changed us. That we have become estranged is the law *above* us; by the same token we should also become more venerable for each other – and the memory of our former friendship more sacred' (*The Gay Science*, ed. and trans. W. Kaufmann (Random House, New York, 1974), IV. 279).

their lives for each other (Jack Aubrey for Stephen Maturin in Patrick O'Brian's seafaring novels) or sacrifice their lives for the other's sake (as the Marquis of Posa sacrificed his life for the sake of his friend Don Carlos in Schiller's eponymous play).

The capacity for friendship, like the capacity for love, is not equally distributed. Some people are fortunate enough to have a talent for friendship, just as they may have a gift for love. Both love and friendship need cultivating with attention, with expressive behaviour that confirms and reinforces the relationship, with the pleasures of discourse and joint activities, and with deeds of love or friendship, if they are to flourish. Both may wane through inattention and unwillingness to make the effort of expressing the emotion properly and of perpetuating the relationship; and both may fade away as a result of lengthy separation. Both are susceptible to possessiveness and jealousy (e.g. in the early phases of Sebastian's friendship for Charles Ryder in Waugh's *Brideshead Revisited*, Sebastian fears to introduce Charles to his family, lest they rob him of the friendship). Both can turn to indifference, resentment, or even enmity (e.g. the friendship between Henry II and Thomas Becket, both in fact and in drama (Anouilh's *Becket*)). Both can involve deception and treachery (e.g. the friendship between Lucien Chardon and David Séchard in Balzac's *Lost Illusions*).

So far, so substantial similarities – which seem to warrant subsuming the concept of friendship under that of love, and conceiving of friendship in general as but one form of love. But many voices in the past are to be heard in protest against this. Montaigne spoke for others too in ranking male friendship far above heterosexual erotic love *as he conceived it*:

> You cannot compare friendship with the passion men feel for women ... Nor can you put them in the same category. I must admit that the flames of passion ... are more active, sharp and keen. But that fire is a rash one, fickle, fluctuating and variable; it is a feverish fire, subject to attacks and relapses, which only gets hold of a corner of us. The love of friends is a general universal warmth, temperate moreover and smooth, a warmth which is constant and at rest, all gentleness and evenness.[6]

---

[6] Montaigne, 'Of Friendship', in *The Essays of Michel de Montaigne*, trans. and ed. M. A. Screech (Penguin, London, 1991), pp. 208–9.

Other, more modern voices, Romantic and post-Romantic, conceiving differently of love, would think of friendship as *inferior* to true love in intensity, depth, and endurance.

*Differences between love and friendship* Bearing this in mind, let us turn to examine differences between friendship and love. Friends are typically chosen – it makes perfectly good sense to say of certain fastidious people that they 'choose their friends carefully'. By contrast, love is not *chosen*, even though one may choose *not* to allow oneself to pursue an initial attraction and stirring of erotic love. It makes sense to say 'I fell in love with her at first sight', but not 'I chose (decided) to fall in love her at first sight'. Nor can one *choose* to continue or to cease to love another, which is why one may pray for the renewal of marital love (as Christians do), but not for the renewal of one's feelings of friendship with another. One does not *fall into* the relationship of friendship, as one falls in love, even though two people may 'take to' each other on first acquaintance. Falling in love (prior to the establishment of a long-lasting loving relationship) may change one deeply 'through the power of love', but, save in cases of unusually intense degrees of friendship-love (e.g. Montaigne and Étienne de La Boétie), one does not change deeply through the power of friendship at the commencement of a friendship, but only through experiences of comradeship. Friendship, unlike love, cannot be known to be unrequited. For it is part of the grammar of friendship that the affection of friendship is reciprocated and is known to be reciprocated. (If it merely seems to be, as in the case of Isabel Osmond (née Archer) and Madame Merle in James's *The Portrait of a Lady*, then it is not truly a friendship, but was merely thought to be so by Isabel, until she discovered the horrible truth.) Although love normally begins with liking and attraction, as we have seen, it is possible to be in love with, be sexually attracted to, and indeed infatuated with another without even liking them (e.g. Catullus' attraction to Lesbia; Philip Carey's infatuation with Mildred in *Of Human Bondage*). However, it is not possible to feel friendship with a person whom one does not like. Friendship, as Aristotle pointed out, requires not merely reciprocal feelings of attraction, but also mutual recognition of those feelings. One may love another without any hope of reciprocity (Sonya has not ceased to love Astrov at the end of *Uncle Vanya*). One may be an admirer, benefactor, or well-wisher 'from a distance', so to speak, without even being personally acquainted with the object of one's admiration, good will, or largesse. Can one enjoy a friendship 'from a distance' in the same manner? It seems not. But one may be a friend *to* someone, even though one no longer enjoys friendship *with* that person. So, for example, by the end of *Brideshead Revisited*, when Sebastian has become an alcoholic and drug addict in Morocco, the friendship between him and Charles Ryder has died away, but Charles is still a good friend *to* Sebastian.

Although interpersonal love, ideally, involves mutual trust, it need not (e.g. Marcel certainly does not trust Albertine, in *The Captive* and *The Sweet Cheat Gone*), but friendship does involve trust, which if known to be betrayed or felt to be betrayed, terminates a friendship. Love, we have seen, is extensively institutionalized and determines social roles (husband and wife, fiancé and fiancée, partners, *eromenos* and *erastes*, lover and mistress, and so on). But friendship, although certainly socially recognized, for the most part is not institutionalized and by and large does not presuppose social roles, save in the case of some forms of friendship, such as loyalty-friendship and warrior-friendship. There are striking differences between the possible objects of love in general and those of friendship: one can love a city (as Dr Johnson loved London), a garden (as Vita Sackville-West loved Sissinghurst), a landscape (as Wordsworth, Coleridge, and Walpole loved the Lake District), or a work of art (as one might love a work of music, a novel, a painting, or a building). To love such things is a form of attachment or attraction that may, *in absentia*, involve longing, and does involve pleasures of intellect and senses, of anticipation and recollection). But, because they are inanimate objects, there can be no reciprocal feelings nor mutual recognition of reciprocated feelings. One cannot *befriend* a city or landscape, or *be friends with* a beautiful house or garden. It is noteworthy that, while parents may love their small children, they cannot befriend their children until (if at all) they are well into maturity. In general, adults, no matter how affectionate they may feel towards a child, cannot enjoy a friendship with a child, the inequality of age and experience being too great. But, to be sure, reciprocal love may exist between the old and the very young, as between the aged warden Septimus Harding and his granddaughter Posy in Trollope's *Last Chronicle of Barset*, or between Jean Valjean and Cosette in Hugo's *Les Misérables*. The bonds of friendship are typically more fragile than the bonds of love inasmuch as they lack extraneous support. Quarrels between lovers, and marital tiffs, are common enough, and commonly remediable. The determination and institutionalization of the social roles involved plays a large part in cementing such relationships and protecting them from rift. But friendships may be ruptured by a casual, thoughtless remark.

While an insult from an enemy is to be expected, an insult or perceived insult from a friend may fester and destroy the friendship, unless reconcilement and forgiveness follow swiftly.[7] Friendships may more readily break over differences of opinion or political judgement than love. Finally, love is, whereas friendship is not, intentional: one can love fictional characters, such as Elizabeth Bennet or Pierre Bezukhov, but one cannot be friends with them. One can love God, even though there is no God, but one cannot befriend him (although Christianity, peculiarly, holds that Jesus, unlike God the Father, may be one's friend).[8]

The differences are as marked as the similarities (See table 11.1). Our concepts of love and friendship are indeed different from the Greek concept of *philia*. It would be mistaken to assert that friendship

---

[7] Finely articulated by Edward Greenwood in his poem 'Reconciliation':

> What an unlucky day can bring,
> As all that was so bright turned grey
> When what occasioned quarrelling
> Were tactless words too late to unsay,
> That drove all harmony away.
>
> And so it is at each day's end
> Reflection must return again
> To how our folly wronged a friend
> With tongue too quick for the slow brain
> To stop, and think, and so restrain.
>
> A luckier day may yet restore
> A warmness where there now is frost
> And friendship's bond be as before,
> When what a thoughtless moment cost,
> Left reconciliation lost.
>
> 'To err is mortal, to forgive
> Divine' is what the poet said.
> Let reconciliation live,
> To right the wrong which folly fed,
> Make harmony in discord's stead.

[8] To be sure, Abraham was said to be the friend of God (Isaiah 41: 8, alluded to in the epistle of James 2: 23). Curiously, the Genesis Florilegium (4Q252), one of the Dead Sea Scrolls, and the so-called Cairo–Damascus document (CD II. 18 ff.) say of Abraham (in the same context) that he was 'beloved of God'. Exodus 33: 11 says, 'And the Lord spake unto Moses face to face, as a man speaketh unto his friend.' These passages originate in early Hebrew texts that are monolatrist rather than monotheist. But, even in this context, God does not *make friends* with Abraham, nor does Abraham *befriend* God – he obeys him faithfully, and trusts him completely. God is in effect declared to be a friend *to* Abraham, rather than a friend *of* Abraham, as Athene could be said to be a friend *to* Odysseus and Zeus a friend *to* Hector. But even that supportive relationship of friendship sits ill with the notion of a non-physical, omnipotent, omniscient, and omni-benevolent deity. It is noteworthy that Aristotle denied that human beings can be friends with the gods (*NE* 1158[b]35).

|  | *Love* | *Friendship* |
|---|:---:|:---:|
| Can it be put to the test? | ✓ | ✓ |
| Is it transitive | × | × |
| Does it admit of degrees? | ✓ | ✓ |
| Can it wax or wane? | ✓ | ✓ |
| Are natural capacities for it equally distributed? | × | × |
| Is it susceptible to jealousy and possessiveness? | ✓ | ✓ |
| Can it turn to enmity and betrayal? | ✓ | ✓ |
| Can it motivate self-sacrifice? | ✓ | ✓ |
| Is reciprocity or believed reciprocity necessary? | × | ✓ |
| Can it be chosen freely? | × | ✓ |
| Can it be felt at first sight? | ✓ | × |
| Can one be immediately changed by its onset | ✓ | × |
| Can one hope or pray for its renewal | ✓ | × |
| Can it be unrequited? | ✓ | × |
| Does it require liking? | × | ✓ |
| Does it require mutual recognition? | × | ✓ |
| Does it require trust? | × | ✓ |
| Can it be institutionalized in social roles? | ✓ | × |
| Are children objects of adult …? | ✓ | × |
| Does it include inanimate things as possible objects? | ✓ | × |
| Is it relatively fragile? | × | ✓ |
| Can one stand in this relation to something non-existent? | ✓ | × |

**Table 11.1** *A comparison of love (erotic and non-erotic) with friendship*

in general is a form of love, although it can be said of some kinds of friendship that they *are*.

## 2. The roots and marks of different forms of friendship

Aristotle argued (*EE* 1242ᵃ) that the origins of *philia* lie in the house-hold (as it obtained in Greece). That is debatable on anthropological grounds. But it would surely be right to suggest in an Aristotelian spirit that friendship, in its various forms, springs from our social nature, on the one hand, and from the benefits of division of labour as well as of cooperative labour, on the other.

*Roots of friendship in childhood bonding*

The source of one kind of friendship lies in the bonding that occurs in childhood and youth in the context of play, and of playing games (described in innumerable children's stories, most vividly and amusingly in Mark Twain's *Tom Sawyer* and *Huckleberry Finn*). The friendships of childhood merge with the subsequent friendships of youth, as the maturing child makes his hesitant or abrasive attempts to find a foothold in the world of adulthood (depicted, e.g., by Shakespeare's descriptions of the golden youth of Verona in *Romeo and Juliet*). These were most commonly unisexual relationships between the young, who found delight in adventure and escapade, in breaking the behavioural codes of childhood and pushing up against the behavioural norms of adult-hood, and in shared experience of early forays into sexuality and erotic love (Hero, Margaret, Beatrice, and Ursula in *Much Ado about Nothing*, or Mercutio and his circle of male friends in *Romeo and Juliet*). Aristotle, it seems, thought of such relationships as *pleasure friendships*. They are indeed sustained by the enjoyment of play and joint activities in pursuit of pleasure, as well as the need for discussion of novel experiences of youth and girlhood and the need for peer approval, either with *a* friend or with friends. But it would be mistaken to suppose that such non-erotic relationships, unisexual or bisexual, do not run deep. The emotional engagement between children or teenagers may involve much more than mere compan-ionship for the sake of fun – for example, in opening their hearts to each other, in a genuine concern for each other, in appreciation of each other's personality, and in strong affection. To be sure, such relationships may not persist. But they are not less authentic for that, nor is their value impugned thereby.

*Roots of friendship in division of labour* A different source of a different kind of friendship, into which children and teenagers are inducted, turns on division of labour and joint productive activities for family and community. This applied in prehistoric times to hunting (groups of hunters being more efficient than solitary hunters, as long as mutual trust and reliability obtain, and fairness in division of spoils is ensured). It applied equally within the household, where friendships between servants eased the burden of labour and often provided not only a form of solace but also mutual protection. Interdependency in agricultural activity, on the one hand, and artisanship, on the other, constituted a further form of adult cooperation, often leading to mutually beneficial friendly relationships. Similar forces are evidently at work in subsequent times in commercial, financial, and industrial life, where 'business friendships' emerge. Following Aristotle, all these may be characterized as 'utility friendships'.[9] But business friendships converge on friendships among colleagues at work, which are commonly an admixture of hedonic and utility friendship. Similar to these are convenience friendships established between neighbours, especially between women bringing up children of the same age. But it is important to note, despite Aristotle, that all these kinds of friendship, if they are indeed friendships rather than mere friendly and cooperative acquaintanceships, are sustained by congeniality and the mutual advantages of cooperation and interdependency, which in turn depend upon trust and reciprocity of favour characteristic of friendship in general. A further form of friendship is the friendship of social companionship. This kind of friendship is characteristic of modern forms of sociability and entertainment of mature adults. Its typical form in the West in the twentieth-century is dining and wining together, playing games indoors or outdoors, going out to public entertainments, and going on holidays together. Such friendships may fade off into mere

---

[9] It is, as La Rochefoucauld wrote, 'a reciprocal conciliation of interests and an exchange of good offices; it is a species of commerce out of which self-love always expects to gain something' (*Maxims*, 83). But only a cynic like La Rochefoucauld would aver that this is all that friendship ever amounts to.

acquaintanceship, but they may also develop into stronger affinities and closer bonds.

*Roots of friendship in political activity*

A further domain in which mere utility friendships play a dominant role in society is the political sphere of activity and the struggle for power. To climb up the greasy pole of power in any society requires mentors and supporters, nowhere more so than in the political life of republican Rome, with its elaborate system of patrons and clients, in which favours granted are the rungs of the ladder to power, each of which constitutes a debt that will subsequently be called in. Though less systematic and institutionalized, mutually advantageous networking is patent in any political system (well described for the court of Henry VIII by Hilary Mantel's *Wolf Hall* and *Bring Up the Bodies*, and for mid-Victorian politics by Trollope in *Phineas Finn* and *Phineas Redux*). No doubt, political friendships *may* involve a degree of liking and congeniality. They are, to be sure, the most precarious form of friendship, liable to betrayal when advantageous. As Cicero remarked (and he knew at first hand):

> We should be hard put to it to find anyone at all who would not be prepared to sacrifice his friend to his political or military career. Place the lucrative attractions of office on one side, and the claims of friendship on the other, and far too often the former will easily come first. For human nature is too weak to refrain from coveting power.[10]

Just how friendship may be compromised and betrayed in the scramble for power is well depicted in Robert Harris's novels on Cicero and his times: *Imperium*, *Lustrum*, and *Dictator*. (It is also well exemplified in current political affairs.)

*Comradeship*

A different and much deeper form of friendship (predominantly male) is *comradeship*, the roots of which are shared experience of hardship and danger in common endeavour, and willingness to risk or sacrifice one's life for one's comrade. Sharing the hardships of war and the dangers of the battlefield, having another to guard one's back and to extricate one from peril, and being able to talk to another about the experiences of danger jointly undergone have always constituted a powerful form of male

[10] Cicero, *Laelius*, XVII. 5. Similarly, 'In men at the top, competitive ambition for jobs and distinctions is what causes the deadliest enmities, even between those who have been the most intimate friends hitherto' (*Laelius*, IX. 32.) Caesar and Pompey, and Octavian and Mark Antony, are good examples.

bonding (and today, in some societies, of female bonding too). This form of friendship is recorded and celebrated in epic poetry from the tale of Gilgamesh and Enkidu, through Homer's Achilles and Patroclus, to the *chansons de geste* (e.g. Roland and Olivier), in innumerable war novels (and memoirs) and tales of adventure (e.g. the friendship that grows between young David Balfour and the much older Alan Breck Stewart in *Kidnapped*), and in poetry (e.g. Robert Graves's 'Two Fusiliers'). It may, or may not, endure after the end of the war in which it was forged, as the erstwhile comrades separate to return to their distant homes. But it is neither a mere hedonic friendship, nor a utility friendship, even though such warrior friends take pleasure in each other's company, and certainly benefit from reciprocal protection in battle, from mutual attachment and affection. Very often it amounts to a form of love. Something similar applies to the friendships formed in the course of hazardous endeavour, such as dangerous expeditions (even fiction cannot display greater comradeship in adversity than that described in Captain Scott's diaries[11]).

Such are the varieties of friendship and their

*Aristotle on the value of friendship*

roots. The boundaries between them are blurred. One may often not know how sound or deep the friendship one enjoys runs. Nevertheless, this classification (others are possible) explains why such forms of bonding should emerge between human beings. However, more needs to be said on why true friendship is an ideal human relationship, and why it is 'one of the greatest goods' and one of the 'noblest gifts' the gods have given to mankind. According to Aristotle, utility friendships and pleasure friendships are (typically) passing relationships and instrumental goods, dependent on circumstances and contingent on benefits that accrue and on pleasures derived. *Primary friendship*, as Aristotle refers to the prototypical form of friendship (*philia*) that he envisaged, is of *intrinsic* value.[12] The relationship is not merely instrumentally and hedonically good, but it is valued for itself. It is such friendships, he held, that are a constituent of a good life. True friends, he averred,

---

[11] In particular, Captain Oates's sacrifice of his life in the hope that his comrades would be able to save themselves when unencumbered by him (see *Scott's Last Expedition: Being the Journals of Captain R. F. Scott*, ed. L. Huxley (Smith, Elder, London, 1913)).

[12] 'Primary' in the sense of prototypical. Aristotle suggested that friendship was a focal concept, the focal point of which was the perfect friendship that obtains between virtuous men. Other kinds of friendship are deemed such because of analogies and resemblances to the primary kind (*NE* 1157$^b$3–5).

are valued for themselves alone and not for their utility or for the pleasure one derives from their company, even though true friends may well be useful, in so far as they will aid one when one needs support; to spend time with a true friend is a pleasure and a joy.[13] Perfect friendship, Aristotle argued, is possible only between men of excellence (*arete*, *virtù*) and between equals. One loves one's friends for the sake of their character and temperament, for the excellences they possess. Friendship is possible between people who are not equals in virtue, status, power, or intellect, but then, Aristotle argues, it is a less than perfect form of friendship. We shall examine Aristotle's method of analysis and resultant view further. As has already been noted, his tripartite classification and implied sharpness of boundaries between the three categories does not do justice to the varieties of friendship and to the absence of sharp boundaries between them. But, to render matters clearer, we must first describe the marks of true friendship as understood in the modern world (see fig. 11.1).

Friendship, *for the most part*, requires liking and
*Friendship and*     congeniality of temperament – 'for the most part'
*congeniality*       because the role of liking may be fulfilled by respect
                     and devotion (one could hardly describe Wittgenstein's
devoted younger friends among his pupils, e.g. Malcolm, von Wright, Drury, as *liking* him). Friends must get on together, enjoy or at least feel the need for each other's company, and take pleasure in or derive satisfaction from conversation, sharing meals, and joint activities. True friendship incorporates what Aristotle thought of as mere hedonic friendship, but reaches far deeper than that. It flourishes when the friends share interests and tastes, have broad agreement in opinions (as well as some differences) and a common sense of humour, so that they may share gaiety and laughter (see Augustine's sensitive description quoted earlier, p. 328). For laughter and merriment are among the joys of friendship. These are, to be sure, distinctive marks

---

[13] Beautifully articulated by Nietzsche in a letter to Franz Overbeck, November 14, 1881: 'My dear friend; what is this our life? A boat that swims in the sea, and all one knows for certain about it is that one day it will capsize. Here we are, two good old boats that have been faithful neighbours, and above all your hand has done its best to keep me from "capsizing"! Let us then continue our voyage – each for the other's sake, *for a long time yet*, a long time! We should miss each other so much! Tolerably calm seas and good winds and above all sun – what I wish for myself, I wish for you too, and am sorry that my gratitude can find expression only in such a *wish* and has no influence at all on wind or weather' (quoted by Kaufmann in his edition of Nietzsche, *The Gay Science*, p. 226 n.).

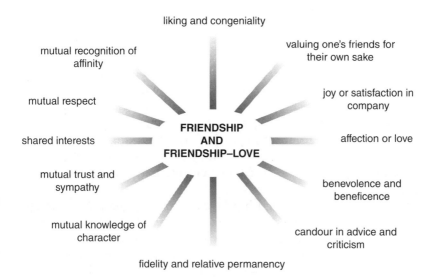

liking and congeniality

mutual recognition of affinity

valuing one's friends for their own sake

mutual respect

joy or satisfaction in company

**FRIENDSHIP AND FRIENDSHIP–LOVE**

shared interests

affection or love

mutual trust and sympathy

benevolence and beneficence

mutual knowledge of character

candour in advice and criticism

fidelity and relative permanency

**Figure 11.1** *Attributes of friendship and of friendship-love*

of hedonic friendship but also constituents of deeper friendships that may include the exuberance and revelries of youth. Comradeship requires not only liking and participation in joint endeavour, but also sharing of hardship, labour, danger, mutual assistance, and self-sacrifice for the sake of one's comrade or comrades. As Aristotle noted, 'a man becomes a friend when he receives and returns *philia*, and when each of the two is fully aware of this' (*EE* 1236ᵃ). Friendship requires both reciprocity and recognition of reciprocity.

*Friendship: self-respect and self-love*

Friendship presupposes self-respect and requires mutual respect. Aristotle averred that friendship grows out of self-love. If this means that friendship is a form of selfishness, it is mistaken – and surely not what Aristotle had in mind (as is patent in *NE* 1169ᵇ1–2), since that would equate friendship in general with mere utility friendships. What he meant was that a true friend acts in such a manner as always to achieve nobility, and that to desire nobility is the higher form of self-love. This seems sophistry. But one might employ 'self-love' not to mean selfishness but rather to mean self-respect. To link self-respect with friendship is indeed insightful. Someone who holds himself in contempt, who is obsessed with his failings (both moral and practical), is, it seems, unlikely to have a significant capacity for friendship (or for love). For true friendship requires surmounting self-interest and self-concern, and this conflicts with the self-concern and self-obsession characteristic of those who despise themselves (one cannot imagine Dostoyevsky's Underground Man, in *Notes from Underground*, having friends). Equally, friendship requires mutual respect. If that is missing (as it is in Charles Ryder's later relationship with Sebastian Flyte, when Sebastian sinks ever deeper into alcoholism), it has to be compensated for by some other feature (e.g. by the compassion Ryder feels for his erstwhile friend). So, too, when one of two old friends succumbs to dementia. In such cases, as we have noted, one partner may well be a friend *to* the other.

*Friendship, mutual admiration, and trust*  Friendship involves an engagement of personalities. For friends must feel affection for each other because of the personality each takes their friend to have – even though they may not articulate or be able to articulate their esteem. It would be mistaken to think that true friends must discern *perfections* in each other, but they must find *some* admirable characteristics in their friend. Indeed, a condition of trust between friends is a reasonable degree of mutual knowledge of character and temperament. That is one reason why friendship, unlike typical cases of erotic love, usually grows slowly, taking time to emerge from congeniality and amicable acquaintanceship. For it takes time to get to know someone and to place one's trust in him. Indeed, friendship flourishes and grows stronger with the memories of shared experience (both hardships and joys) – for these are the cement of long-lasting friendships.

Friends share in each other's joys and successes. A friend will rejoice selflessly at the good fortune of his friend for no reason other than the fact that the friend has enjoyed good fortune. Indeed, one may rejoice overtly in one's friend's successes more than in one's own. It is unseemly to crow over one's own triumphs, but no such modesty is required in the case of a friend's.[14]

The trust between friends must suffice for one to be able to open one's heart to the other on occasion. The principal fruit of friendship, Bacon averred, 'is the ease and discharge of the fullness and swellings of the heart, which passions of all kinds do cause and induce'.[15]

---

[14] Mores are changing: on the fields of sport what would once have been considered to be gross exhibitions of triumph are positively expected.

[15] Bacon, 'Of Friendship', in *Essays; or, Councils, Civil and Moral* (1625).

Without confidence, Epicurus remarked, there is no friendship. For in baring one's heart to a friend, one makes one's friend privy to one's vulnerabilities – trusting the friend not to reveal them to others. The sharing of the pains of ill fortune presupposes both sympathy and empathy between friends (see chapter 12).

*Philia and friendship-love*

The closest terms we have in English for *philia*, that both fall short of love and signify an emotion, are 'affection' and 'fondness'. Anything that falls short of affection amounts to no more than amicable acquaintanceship. The moot question is whether the noun 'affection' suffices for the deepest forms of friendship that we may be fortunate enough to enjoy. It is patent that the exceptional friendship that Alexander and Hephaestion enjoyed, or the uncommonly close friendship between Montaigne and La Boétie, or, to turn to fiction, the comradeship between Gottfried Lenz, Otto Köster, and Bobby Lohkamp (in Erich Maria Remarque's *Three Comrades*), or the relationship between Lady Glencora and Madame Max (in Trollope's *The Pallisers*), are much more than merely affectionate friendships. These are instances of *friendship-love*, for the friends are *dear to each other*. They involve deep and strong feelings that constitute powerful motives for action. They are characterized by joy and pleasure in each other's company and in joint activities, by reciprocal trust, respect, and mutual confidence; by a readiness to open their hearts to each other; and by a willingness to sacrifice self-interest and perhaps even life for each other's sake. The boundary line between the affection of friendship and friendship-love is blurred. The extent and depth of friendship-love may vary. It does not require the singularity and intensity of such friendships as Alexander's or Montaigne's.

*Friendship, benevolence, and beneficence*

Friendship presupposes benevolence – wishing one's friend well, and finding joy in one's friend's good fortune and success. It also involves a concern for one's friend's welfare – as charmingly, although exaggeratedly, represented in La Fontaine's fable 'The Two Friends'. Similarly, it implies beneficence. For, when an occasion arises, one will choose to benefit one's friend *for one's friend's sake*. It is important to recognize that, although the beneficence of friendship is reciprocal, this does not imply that true friendship is what anthropologists call a 'gift-reciprocity' relationship. For gift exchanges generate forms of mutual indebtedness, involving calculation, self-interest, and the establishment or maintenance of social equality or hierarchy. But it is true that business friendships and political friendships often operate in a manner akin to relationships in a gift-exchange culture.

*Friendship and criticism*

Although, as argued in chapter 3, the emotions in general are misrepresented as being non-rational, they are often irrational. The reasons that warrant our feeling what we feel may be poor. Our emotional response may be warranted but misdirected. It may be warranted, but indulged in to excess or exhibited too weakly. It may be warranted, but exhibited on the wrong occasion. It may be exhibited on the right occasion, but in the wrong manner. It is to our friends that we may then turn for solace, advice, and, *ex post actu*, for approval or correction. One characteristic feature of true friendship is candour, benevolent advice, impartial appraisal, and, where required, criticism. That which is not another's business may well be the business of one's friend *if asked*, and sometimes even if *not* asked. It is one of the obligations of friendship to warn one's friend that he is doing wrong. We are rightly inclined to think that if my friend will not tell me that I am doing wrong, who will? Black Cleitus was indeed a good friend to Alexander, although he paid for his criticism with his life.[16]

*Friendship, fidelity, and permanency*

Finally, friendship is characterized by fidelity and relative permanency. A personal relationship that is turned on and off at whim, or according to other attractions, is no friendship. Relative permanency is an aspect of friendship, and a requirement of mutual trust and reliability. But such constancy should not be exaggerated. Durability may be missing from a child's relationships with playmates (which rarely outlast a change of kindergarten or school). But that need not impugn the friendship and its closeness. Permanency is often absent from the friendships of youth (which may not outlast job changes, university days, general maturation, or settling down in marriage). Warrior friendships may not outlast the terminus of war. But that does not imply that these passing friendships are not genuine or that they are of no intrinsic value.

---

[16] Cleitus criticized Alexander publicly at a feast in Persia, when Alexander was in his cups. In uncontrolled rage Alexander flung a spear through his heart. On some accounts, Cleitus criticized him angrily both for his boasting that he was a greater king than his father Philip, and for his demand that Macedonians adopt the demeaning Persian habit of *proskynesis* (prostration before a great king). Evidently, Cleitus chose the wrong occasion and wrong manner in which to criticize his comrade.

Which of these various characteristics, or which disjunctions of these characteristics, have to be present, and to what degree they must be present, in order for a relationship to count as friendship is indeterminate. So the very concept of friendship is intrinsically vague and its boundaries essentially contestable (see fig. 11.1).

So much for laying bare the ground. Now we may turn to further analysis.

## 3. Analysis of the relation

*Friend with and friend to*  It is evident from our discussion thus far that friendship is a relationship, not an emotion. That relationship may be deep or superficial (casual), depending upon the strength and depth of the feelings that obtain. We have surveyed its prominent characteristics above. It is *the feelings of friendship*, for which we have no single expression akin to *philia*, that are an emotion. In English, as we have noted, we must make do with 'affection', 'fondness', and 'the love of friends'. *Friendliness*, like *amiability*, is a character trait, rather than an emotion. A relationship of friendship obtains whenever there are mutual feelings of friendship between people that are recognized as such. One cannot be a friend *with* another without feeling affection, fondness, or love for one's friend. But one may be a true friend *to* another without an erstwhile friendship persisting (as Charles Ryder is a true friend to Sebastian after Sebastian's disintegration in Morocco). One may enjoy a true friendship without being in general a friendly person but, perhaps, a shy recluse.

*Polyadicity of friendship*  The question arises of whether friendship, being a relation, is necessarily binary or may involve more than two people. The most famous friendships of antiquity and of the mythology of antiquity are binary: for example, David and Jonathan, Orestes and Pylades, Achilles and Patroclus, Ruth and Naomi, Alexander and Hephaestion, Scipio and Laelius. Plutarch held that 'friendship is a creature that goes in pairs, and is not gregarious, or crow-like, and to think a friend a second self ... shows that friendship is a dual-relation' ('On Having Many Friends', §2). But it is by no means clear that this is a conceptual or grammatical feature of friendship. It would surely be mistaken to suppose that there *cannot* be a deep friendship between three or even more people (see the earlier quotation from Augustine). Certainly the friendship described by Remarque in *Three Comrades* is convincing, and it is deep enough for Otto to sacrifice his most treasured possession for the benefit of Robert and his lover Pat, and to risk his life to avenge the death of Gottfried. But one may readily concede that such triadic friendships are, as a matter of fact, rare, and require special circumstances of antecedent bonding and joint endeavour. Much more common in contemporary culture are friendships between two (usually married) couples, who enjoy each other's company and joint activities, and perhaps take holidays together. It is characteristic of such friendships that they are between bonded couples. The close friendship may not survive they death of one of the spouses.

Can one have many friends? As we noted *Aristotle: utility, hedonic,* above, Aristotle observed that 'it is thought to *and true friendships* be a fine thing to have many friends' (*NE* 1155ª5). But, as he himself wrote, we must distinguish: no doubt it is good to have many utility friendships, for these involve reciprocal benefits and forms of cooperation and mutual assistance in the business of life. But they are conditional on the forms of dependency, and contingent upon the duration of dependency. These are not cases of primary *philia*. Similarly, it is good to have many hedonic friendships, especially in youth, when merrymaking and adventures give zest to life. These are conditional on the enjoyment derived. They may often involve generosity of spirit and delight in the friendship, and so approximate primary friendship more closely than most utility friendships. However, like business friendships, Aristotle averred, they are rarely lasting. When it comes to primary (proper, true, deep) friendships, however, one can have a few, but not many, true *philoi*. Such friendships require exceptionally attuned people. Aristotle further held that both friends must be men of excellence (and such men are rare); moreover, such friendships demand time and attention, mutual trust and reliability, as well as a past rich in shared experience. We shall challenge this idealization later.

According to Montaigne, the supreme kind *Montaigne on perfect* of friendship, which is passing rare, must be *and common friendships* unique. Evidently thinking of his friendship with La Boétie, Montaigne wrote that in this kind of friendship:

> Love takes possession of the soul and reigns there with full sovereign sway: that cannot be duplicated ... The uttermost cannot be matched. If anyone suggests that I can love each of two friends as much as the

other, and that they can love each other and love me as much as I love them, he is turning into a plural, into a confraternity, that which is the most 'one', the most bound into one. One single example of it is moreover the rarest thing to find in the world.[17]

These kinds of extraordinary friendship Montaigne contrasted with 'common friendships'. In such cases, he wrote:

I am seeking the companionship and society of such men as we call honourable and talented ... The end of intercourse with such men are simply intimacy, the frequenting of each other and discussion – exercising our minds with no other gain. In our conversation, any topic will do: I do not worry if they lack depth or weight: there is always grace and propriety: Everything in it is coloured by ripe and sustained judgement mingled with frankness, good will, gaiety and affection.[18]

This seems a perfectly good characterization of one aspect of common friendships.

Are true binary friendships solely unisexual or can they be bisexual? Deep bisexual 'Platonic' friendships do surely obtain, even though they are less common than unisexual ones. They are most common between the elderly (in fiction, see, e.g., Vita Sackville-West's *All Passion Spent*), or between a very old and a much younger person (as that between Old Jolyon and Irene as described in *The Forsyte Saga*), or between a homosexual man and a heterosexual woman (e.g. Michelangelo and Vittoria Colonna, or Henry James and Edith Wharton), or between a lesbian and a man (as depicted in the relationship between Stephen Hall and Jonathan Brockett in Radclyffe Hall's *The Well of Loneliness*). There are both socio-historical and socio-psychological explanations for this, as well as psychosexual ones. These we shall not discuss here.

*Friendship, inequality, and loyalty friendship* Aristotle held that primary friendships can obtain only between equals, but he himself saw that less perfect forms of *philia* can obtain between father and son, between an older and a younger man, between man and wife, and even between master and slave. These are relationships between unequals, and the feelings of the one for the other, according to Aristotle, should be in inverse

[17] Montaigne, 'On Friendship', p. 215.
[18] Montaigne, 'On Three Kinds of Social Intercourse', in *Essays*, p. 928.

proportion to their relative status. This is an oversimplification of very different asymmetrical relationships of friendship.

Although there is a form of friendship between old age and youth (e.g. Mrs Gereth and Fleda Vetch in James's *The Spoils of Poynton*, Mrs Wilcox and Margaret Schlegel in Forster's *Howards End*), the disparity of experience is too great for there to be complete open-heartedness between the older and the younger person. An older man or woman may befriend a younger one, and an elderly teacher a pupil, but the solid ground of shared experience and memories that characterize friendship between equals is likely to be missing. That places constraints on the possibility of the older person opening his heart to the younger one in the manner in which two equal friends may do. Similarly, the younger person, if indeed a true friend, may well be constrained by respect, and is often intimidated by the experience, knowledge, and perhaps wisdom of the older friend.[19] But none of this implies that such relationships are not true friendships, and sometimes indeed loving friendships.

There are, of course, many forms of inequality that may militate against friendship: inequalities of power, of wealth, of social class, of intelligence, and of education. Nevertheless, renowned friendships of antiquity, such as those between Jonathan and David, Achilles and Patroclus, Alexander and Hephaestion, Scipio and Laelius, were not between equally powerful friends. They were between comrades in arms of disparate status. The possession of supreme power in any domain (possessed not only, e.g., by a monarch or autocrat, but also by a ship's captain) is notoriously lonely. The authenticity of the friendship of political subordinates is a source of anxiety, for, on the one hand, treachery often lurks in the wings, and, on the other hand, favouritism must be avoided if power is to be exercised wisely. To be sure, where it is not, the role of favourites at the courts of the mighty is commonly precarious and often mortally dangerous. It is not surprising that the friendships of the high and the mighty are often wisely with people who are completely detached from the arena of power (e.g. between Hamlet and Horatio, or between Jack Aubrey and Stephen Maturin in fiction (Patrick O'Brian's novels), and between Cicero and Atticus in fact).

The loneliness of power gives rise to a distinctive relationship, namely loyalty friendship or loyalty love, that may obtain between

---

[19] As one imagines Aristotle was for Plato, and maybe also Plato for Socrates. But also the old soldier for the young one, the veteran politician or master-craftsman for the novice, and so on.

the powerful and a favoured servant (historical examples are Louis XIV and Bontemps, Queen Victoria and John Brown) or even a master and slave (Cicero and Tyrro). This is a top-heavy relationship that is characterized not merely by the loyalty of the subordinate, but also by his personal devotion and love. Loyalty alone may be blind. It may also sacrifice principles of right (notoriously so in the ethos of the German officer class in the twentieth century). Then it may become terrible. But loyalty friendship is neither blind nor impervious to what is right and just. That is precisely because it *is* a form of love, and so involves the subordinate's concern not merely for the welfare of the master or mistress, but also for their good. A loyal and loving servant or subordinate will not endorse what he sees as wrong-doing or contemptible conduct by the person they serve. For devoted servants or subordinates who stand in the relationship of loyalty friendship both love their superior and care for their superior's moral standing. To what extent they can advise or restrain depends on the character of the relationship and the circumstances (Jeeves provided a benevolent guiding hand for Bertie Wooster). Disparities of wealth are similarly constraining. Inequalities of education and intellect narrow the scope of common interests and shared opinions, as well as the joys of discourse and debate. Inequalities of social status often (but not always) constitute a barrier to the possibility of friendships. The difficulties of establishing genuine friendships in the face of differences in social ethos, in wealth, and in education is brilliantly characterized by E. M. Forster in *Howards End* (namely, in the Schlegel sisters' attempt to befriend Leonard Bast), and by Jane Austen's description of Emma's interference in Harriet Smith's personal relationships in *Emma*. The additional constraints imposed by an environment of bigotry and racial prejudice are described in *A Passage to India*, in Forster's depiction of the friendship between Cyril Fielding and Dr Aziz.

*Friends as second selves*     In what should have been understood to be a fairly innocuous, more or less metaphorical, remark, Aristotle wrote that, in a perfect friendship, 'a person is to his friend as he is to himself, for his friend is another self [*allos autos*]' (*NE* 1166ª31–2). Aristotle was investigating the extent to which the sentence form 'I V myself' (where 'V' is, roughly speaking, a verb of benefiting) applies truly to cases of friendship, when 'myself' is replaced by 'my friend'. We needn't pursue the exercise here. It is far from satisfactory (it is reprehensible to admire myself, but not so to admire my friend; it is objectionable to praise myself in public, but not so to praise my friend; it is appropriate that a man decide things for himself, but unacceptable (other things being equal) that he should decide things for his friend; and so on) – but that matters little. For the important point is that between true friends there is neither *selfishness* nor *self-centredness*. A true friend is as eager to protect the interests of his friend when he can as he is to protect his own. Close friends are *kindred spirits*. Between friends, there is likely to be widespread agreement in opinions and widespread convergence of taste (but not of identity, for the joint exploration and examination of differences of judgement is one of the pleasures of friendship).

Unfortunately, Aristotle's remark was picked up by his successors and made pivotal to the characterization of true friendship. Cicero wrote that in the face of a true friend we see a second self (*alter ego*), so that where a man's friend is, he is; if his friend be rich, he is not poor; if he is weak, his friend's strength is his; and in his friend's life, he enjoys a second life after his own is finished. This is rhetorical hyperbole.[20] Taken literally, it is patently either nonsense or false. A true friend is not an *alter ego*, since the very notion of 'an ego' or 'a self' is questionable.[21] If my friend is in New York, I am not with him, save perhaps 'in thought'. If my friend is rich, that does not lessen my poverty, though it means that he will aid me if I let him. And, although my friend may outlive me, that does not extend my life, but only ensures my commemoration. All of which, to be sure, are a great solace – but involve no metaphysical mysteries of merging of souls.

## 4. Friendship, virtue, and morality

*Aristotle on primary friendship*    Aristotle asserted emphatically that primary or perfect friendship obtains only between men of excellence or virtue. This conception is moot. Let me recapitulate before challenging his view. Unlike utility and pleasure friendships, Aristotle averred, the friendship of men of excellence is not instrumental. Such friends love each other for their own sakes,

---

[20] Augustine likewise seized upon the figure, writing that in the course of the great friendship of his youth 'I felt that our two souls had been as one, living in two bodies.' Montaigne, a millennium and more later, expressed the same confused idea: 'In the friendship I am talking about, souls are mingled and confounded in so universal a blending that they efface the seam which joins them together so that it cannot be found' (p. 211). The same idea is at work in Ben Jonson's poem quoted on p. 351.

[21] See *Human Nature: the Categorial Framework* (Blackwell, Oxford, 2007), ch. 9, sections 1–2.

not for the sake of the mutual benefits they derive from the relationship, nor for the sake of the pleasures of companionship. The usefulness of a man is a contingent, passing quality, and mere utility friendships wane with the change of business and terminus of usefulness. Hedonic friendships decline as men mature and grow out of the riotous pleasures of youthful irresponsibility and gaiety. But the virtues of men of excellence are not contingent on circumstances or age. They are persistent character traits. The formation of friendship consists not merely in congeniality, but in mutual recognition of excellence or virtue. The friendships of such men endure. Primary friendship, Aristotle held, involves complete trust, which takes time to establish. Such friendship is the product of slow growth of confidence in mutual good will, and mutual knowledge of excellences of character. It is stable, and not subject to fluctuation in changing circumstances. To be sure, perfect friendship involves joy. But the delight is not simply in the pleasures of joint activities, but the delight in the company and the friendship-love of a man of excellence *because* he possesses the excellences proper to man. Similarly, such friendships are indeed often beneficial, as one can turn to one's friend for advice and assistance in times of trouble and misfortune. But the benefits thus granted are freely given, typically without even the need to request. They are not given in the expectation of reciprocity (that would be demeaning and ignoble), but out of generosity. Reciprocity goes without saying.

This rich conception of primary friendship had a profound influence upon subsequent European reflections on friendship. It is well expressed by Ben Jonson 2,000 years later, in the following stanza of his poem 'To the Immortal Memory and Friendship of that Noble Pair, Sir Lucius Cary and Sir Henry Morison':

> And shine as you exalted are,
> Two names of friendship, but one star:
> Of hearts the union. And those not by chance
> Made, or indenture, or leased out t' advance
> The profits for a time.
> No pleasures vain did chime
> Of rimes, or riots, at your feasts,
> Orgies of drink, or feigned protests,
> But simple love of greatness and of good;
> That knits brave minds and manners more than blood.

Such perfect friendship, Aristotle admits, is rare, since men of excellence are rare. Despite its rarity, he presents it as the prototype of friendship. Friendship, he in effect suggests, is a focal concept, the focus of which is the friendship of men of excellence and virtue who are, in relevant respects, equals. Other forms of friendship are so called because of their affinities with the primary form (*EE* 1236ª16–32).

*Ideal analysis or connective analysis*

Aristotle chooses as the primary or focal form of a concept one the exemplification of which, as he admits, is singularly rare. Even if one grants that utility friendships, pleasure friendships, and loyalty friendships are derivative forms – the first two because of their instrumentality, the third because of its asymmetry – it does not follow that the only genuine, true, or proper friendships are between men of perfect excellence or virtue. That presents primary friendship as an asymptotic ideal (as '2πr' *presents itself* as the description of an ideal circle). To aver that primary friendship obtains only between perfectly virtuous friends is to lay down a form of representation (just as '2πr' is not a description of a perfect circle but a norm of description). It is to conflate a description of a form of friendship with a form of description of friendship. What Aristotle has in effect done is to adopt a Platonist strategy of accounting for the nature of friendship by reference to an Idea of Friendship, as it were. Around this idea of perfect friendship, actual types of human friendship can be arranged according to their proximity to or distance from this ideal form. The connective analysis that I have proposed follows a quite different course by mapping the conceptual links of friendship, in all its varieties, with a network of associated concepts (see fig. 11.1). I believe that this gives us a clearer insight into the nature of friendship and feelings of friendship than Aristotle's method of idealization.

*Friendship and virtue*

There is indeed a conceptual link between the notion of true friendship and the virtues, and between the notion of true friendship and the good. But true friendships may obtain between people who are themselves less than perfectly virtuous, and indeed, if there is honour among thieves, may perhaps obtain between people who are, in many respects, wicked. What true friendship demands is congeniality; benevolence and beneficence; affection or indeed friendship-love; mutual respect and trust; and delight in each other's company. All of these associated attributes admit of degrees, and correspondingly friendship admits of degrees. But nothing here indicates that true friendship can obtain only between the truly virtuous or only between men of surpassing excellence. The friendship between Alexander and Hephaestion satisfied all these conditions, but Alexander himself was anything but a flawless man. So too, it seems, was the friendship between William Marshal and Henry FitzHenry, but although the earl marshal was indeed a paragon of medieval virtues, the young king was certainly not.[22] This is convincingly brought out in fiction: Jack Aubrey and Stephen Maturin were evidently the closest of friends, but they were far from perfectly virtuous; Madame Max was well nigh flawless, but Lady Glencora was not – yet their friendship was true.

If our qualms are warranted, we must explore further the relationship between friendship and virtue. For there seems little doubt that we think of true friendship as intrinsically valuable. Friendship in itself involves a distinctive range of virtues and excellences, such as fidelity, trustworthiness, benevolence, and a willingness to make sacrifices for the sake of one's friend in appropriate circumstances (see fig. 11.1). Anyone who is seriously lacking in these cannot be a true friend to another, but perhaps only a business colleague, however amiable, or a chum whose company one enjoys. So possession of these virtues, to a greater or lesser degree, is a constitutive feature of friendship.

*Friendship between bad men?* In so far as bad people are malignant and distrustful, and altogether lack the intrinsic virtues of friendship, there can indeed be no true friendship between bad people (cf. *EE* 1237ᵇ). Can there not be 'honour among thieves'? There certainly can be *a perversion* of the very concept of honour, as among mafiosi, who, like Nazi officers, identify honour with unqualified and unlimited loyalty. Whether there can truly be *honour* is unclear. Can there be friendships between wholly evil people (committed Nazis, concentration camp officers, or guards)? It seems that they could be loving spouses and parents (Goebbels and Göring apparently were). Could they be true friends? That seems much more doubtful, since for that they would have to possess virtues that are incompatible with their viciousness. There may, however, be degrees and forms of friendship among bad men, who are not bad without qualification. Such friendships then depend upon the saving graces of the only partly wicked. Of course, bad men

---

[22] The history of the friendship is well recounted in Thomas Asbridge, *The Greatest Knight* (Simon & Schuster, London, 2015).

may enjoy instrumental friendships for the sake of utility or pleasure (*NE* 1157ª16–19; 1157ᵇ1–4).

*Rupturing friendships*          Various manifestations of vice and certain kinds of misdemeanour are inimical to friendship, and commonly destroy it. Aristotle put his finger on the salient point: true friends do not wrong each other (*EE* 1234ᵇ25–30). Friendships are broken by injustice or wrongness between the friends. For one cannot be friends with someone who has maltreated one, or who one thinks has maltreated one. Indeed, as we have noted, a friendship can be broken by an ill-judged or even inadvertent word. If the friendship can be mended, it is only through admission of fault, forgiveness, and reconcilement (see n. 6). Cicero spelled out the link between friendship and injustice as he saw it: it is more terrible to defraud a friend than a fellow citizen, more terrible not to help a brother than a stranger, more terrible to wound a father than anyone else (cf. *NE* 1160ª3–9, from which it is derived). To wrong a friend, as Lucien Chardon wrongs David Séchard (in Balzac's *Lost Illusions*) by forging a cheque in his name, is indeed disgraceful. It is a breach of the trust intrinsic to proper friendship.

Friendship may similarly be broken by the discovery that one's friend was in fact wicked, as when Rollo Martins discovers that his lifelong, debonair, and charming friend Harry Lime was a racketeer who had made a fortune by selling diluted penicillin on the black market in postwar Vienna, causing the deaths of, and brain damage to, hundreds of children (Greene's *The Third Man*).[23] The discovery not only breaks the

---

[23] In the novella, Greene depicts a striking difference between erotic love and friendship. When Martins, still believing that his best friend Harry Lime is dead, is shown the results of Lime's criminal activities, he goes to see Anna, Harry's lover, to tell her:

> He said hopelessly, 'I feel as though he had never really existed, that we'd dreamed him. Was he laughing at fools like us all the time?'

> 'He may have been. What does it matter?', she said. 'Sit down. Don't worry.' He had pictured himself comforting *her* – not this other way about. She said, 'If he was alive now, he might be able to explain, but we've got to remember him as he was to us. There are always so many things one doesn't know about a person, even a person one loves – good things, bad things. We have to leave plenty of room for them'

> 'Those children –'

> She said angrily, 'For God's sake stop making people in *your* image. Harry was real. He wasn't just your hero and my lover. He was Harry. He was in a racket. He did bad things. What about it? He was the man we knew.' …

friendship, but leads Martins to re-evaluate its whole history. The shock of discovery brings about a change of aspect, as he realizes that he had always been cast in the role of the 'fall guy' throughout the whole span of their friendship. But whether there is one *right* aspect is by no means clear. Nor is it *obvious* that Martins was right to help the police in cornering and killing Harry Lime, as opposed to leaving them to get on with their job. But it is not *obvious* that he was wrong either. However, it does not need anything as extreme as that to rupture a friendship. Deep political disagreement that emerges in response to the changes of the day (e.g. civil rights, women's suffrage, foreign policy, fascism, or communism) may also do so.

*Doing wrong for a friend* — A moot point discussed extensively by Cicero is whether friendship is compatible with doing wrong (or what one conceives to be a wrong) for one's friend's sake. His answer is unequivocally negative. Wrongdoing (or, we should perhaps add, what is conceived to be wrongdoing) is the limit of proper friendship. One should, accordingly, never ask a friend to do something that one knows to be wrong, and a friend should never comply with a request to do (what he conceives to be) wrong for the sake of friendship. This principle brings with it a host of difficulties associated with social or rational determination of wrong and subjective (existential, volitional) determination of wrong. These difficulties did not arise within the framework of Cicero's world-view. It is striking to juxtapose Cicero's judgement with E. M. Forster's, who famously averred that if asked to choose between betraying a friend or betraying one's country, he hoped that he would have the courage to betray his country.[24] This characteristically Bloomsbury view, Cicero would have found unintelligible. It seems to many a modern eye not to be a matter on which one can confidently advance a general principle. It is surely an idiographic, rather than nomothetic question. Each case must be examined in its individual

---

He said, 'As soon as they've cleared up this Koch murder, I'm leaving Vienna. I can't feel interested any longer in whether Kurtz killed Harry – or the third man. Whoever killed him, it was a kind of justice. Maybe I'd kill him myself under these circumstances. But you still love him. You love a cheat, a murderer.'

'I loved a man', she said. 'I told you – a man doesn't alter because you find out more about him. He's still the same man.' (*The Third Man*, ch. 11)

[24] E. M. Forster, 'What I Believe', in *Two Cheers for Democracy* (Penguin, Harmondsworth, 1965), p. 76.

and historical uniqueness, and the actual decision is often existential. In deciding thus or otherwise, one is deciding what sort of person to be or become.

*False friendships*    Implicit in our discussion thus far is the thought that friendships may be false, inasmuch as what appears to one of the protagonists to be a true friendship is in fact not so at all. We must distinguish this case from the breaking of a friendship through wrong-doing (e.g. the friendship between June Forsyte and Irene, broken by Irene's taking June's fiancé Bosinney from her) and from lop-sided friendships (e.g. that between Martins and Harry Lime in *The Third Man* or between David Copperfield and Steerforth in Dickens's novel). A false friendship is manifest when one person pretends friendship for self-serving purposes. This is brilliantly described in Henry James's depiction of the relationship between Madame Merle and Isabel Archer in *Portrait of a Lady*, in which Isabel is a mere tool in the hands of Madame Merle, manipulated by her for her own purposes. This is not a case of a failed friendship – it never was a friendship, but only appeared so to Isabel. False friendships are essentially wicked, for the deceitful partner is dishonest and manipulative, and violates fundamental trust, treating the gullible would-be friend only as a means.

# 12

# Sympathy and Empathy

## 1. Sympathy: the historical background

Sympathy, empathy, and compassion are strands in the network of love and essential corollaries of friendship. They are among the benevolent emotions. Together with love and friendship, they are the saving graces of mankind. Despite our self-centredness and selfishness, our cruelty and rapacity, our prejudice and bigotry, there is 'infused into our bosom some spark of friendship for human kind; some particle of the dove kneaded into our frame, along with the sentiments of the wolf and serpent'.[1]

*Unclear relationship between sympathy and empathy*   The relationship between the concepts of sympathy and empathy is controversial and their analysis has been much disputed in recent decades. The concept of *empathy*, introduced into English only in 1909 as a quasi-technical term in empirical psychology, has increasingly displaced its venerable relative *sympathy* from the domains of psychology, social psychology, practical medicine, and cognitive neuroscience. Indeed, the use of 'sympathy' today appears to be giving way to 'empathy' on the stage of public discourse as well. Whether this is a refinement of our thought about ourselves is

---

[1] D. Hume, *An Enquiry concerning the Principles of Morals*, IX. i.

*The Passions: A Study of Human Nature*, First Edition. P. M. S. Hacker.
© 2018 John Wiley & Sons Ltd. Published 2018 by John Wiley & Sons Ltd.

moot. Since sympathy has plausibly been held to be essential for the very possibility of morality (Hume and Adam Smith), and empathy (or, more accurately, its ancestor *Einfühlung*) has been held to be essential for hermeneutics, anthropology, and aesthetic experience (Herder, Vischer, Lipps), attaining clarity about the concepts is a worthy goal. Both have been yoked to the problem of knowledge of other minds. As we shall see, that yoke needs to be removed.

*Origin and development of concept of sympathy*     The concept of sympathy is a well-worn instrument in our conceptual toolkit. It was forged in ancient Greece (*sun* (with) + *patheia* (feeling, undergoing, suffering)). The word occurs frequently in ancient Greek literary texts and in philosophical writings. It appears in Late Latin as 'sympathia', and this usage was transmitted to the Romance languages. However, the word did not enter English until the mid-sixteenth century. Its earliest uses signify concord, agreement, harmony, or consonance. The *Oxford English Dictionary* informs us that one might write of '*sympathia* or equalitie of friendshipp' (1567) and of 'sympathy of manners [making] the coniunction of mindes' (1578), or, in biology, of '*Simpathia*, unity, agreements of spirits, humors and members' that preserve health (1574). It was also used to signify concord between the senses and their objects, or harmony between sounds. Another early usage was manifest in alchemy, astrology, and medicine to signify an occult affinity, mutual attraction, or common susceptibility. Hence, reporting Pliny's natural history, one might speak of '*Sympathie*, a fellow-feeling, used in Plinie for the agreement or amitie naturall in divers senseless things, as beteene yron and the loadstone'. This background informed the extension of usage to human relationships in order to signify affinity, concord of temperament and feelings, and harmony of disposition. Thus Spenser in his Platonist 'Hymn in Honour of Beauty' (1596):

> But, in your choice of loves, this well advise,
> That likest to yourselves ye them select,
> The which your forms' first source may sympathize,
> And with like beauty's parts be inly deckt;
> For, if you loosely love without respect,
> It is no love, but a discordant war,
> Whose unlike parts amongst themselves do jar.
> For love is a celestial harmony
> Of likely hearts compos'd of stars' concent,
> Which join together in sweet sympathy,

To work each other's joy and true content,
Which they have harbour'd since their first descent
Out of their heavenly bowers, where they did see
And know each other here belov'd to be.

Shakespeare, in *The Merry Wives of Windsor*, likewise used 'sympathy' to signify concord or happy agreement:

You are not young, no more am I;
Go to then, there's sympathy:
You are merry, so am I; ha, ha!
Then there's more sympathy:
You love sack, and so do I;
Would you desire better sympathy?[2]
(II. 1)

From this it was but a short step to apply the idea to *fellow feeling*, to being affected by the feelings of another with a feeling similar to or corresponding to the other's, and to the capacity to enter into or share the feelings of another, and thence to a feeling of compassion or commiseration with another's misfortune. So, by the mid-seventeenth century it was possible to speak of 'faithful and true sympathy and fellow-feeling with' someone (1662), and Milton wrote of 'answering looks of sympathie and love' (1667). It was in the eighteenth century, however, that the notion of sympathy came into its own in aesthetics, epistemology, philosophy of mind, and moral philosophy. The most important contributions to the analysis of sympathy were Hume's *A Treatise of Human Nature* (1739) and Adam Smith's *The Theory of Moral Sentiments* (1759). It was they who provided the first extensive phenomenological description and philosophical anatomy of sympathy.

*Hume on sympathy*     Hume introduced the notion of sympathy into his idealist philosophy in order to explain:

(i)   how we attain knowledge of the thoughts and emotions of other people; and
(ii)  how it is possible for creatures such as us to have moral sentiments.

---

[2] The Shakespeare concordance shows only ten occurrences of the word in his works, all of which are limited to concord of feeling and temperament.

In general, he held, perception involves reception of impressions, which are then converted into ideas, on which the mind variously operates. We cannot, Hume reasoned, *have* another person's ideas (another man's idea, Frege would later insist, is another idea). So 'No passion of another discovers itself immediately to the mind'.[3] Nor can we *enter* into another man's mind. How then can we know what others think, opine, and feel? Not the least tempted by Berkeley's argument from analogy,[4] Hume held that sympathy is 'the conversion of an idea into an impression by the force of the imagination' (*THN* II. iii. 6, para. 8).

> When any affection [of another] is infus'd by sympathy, it is at first known only by its effects, and by those external signs in the countenance and conversation, which convey an idea of it. This idea is presently converted into an impression, and acquires such degree of force and vivacity, as to become the very passion itself, and to produce an equal emotion, as any original affection. (*THN* II. i. 11, para. 3)

> Our affections depend more upon ourselves, and the internal operations of the mind, than any other impressions; for which reason they arise more naturally from the imagination, and from every lively idea we form of them. This is the nature and cause of sympathy; and 'tis after this manner we enter so deep into the opinions and affections of others, whenever we discover them. (*THN* II. i. 11, para. 7)

> 'Tis indeed evident, that when we sympathize with the passions and sentiments of others, these movements appear at first sight in *our* mind as mere ideas, and are conceiv'd to belong to another person, as we conceive any other matter of fact. 'Tis also evident, that the ideas of the affections of others are converted into the very impressions they represent, and that the passions arise in conformity to the images we form of them. (*THN* II. i. 11, para. 8)

In short, human beings resonate to each other's affective tunes. Hume pictures the process as shown in figure 12.1, where the arrow signifies causal generation. As we shall see, in this hypothesized process Hume

---

[3] Hume, *A Treatise of Human Nature Treatise*, III. iii. 1, para. 6 (henceforth *THN*).

[4] Berkeley, *The Principles of Human Knowledge* (1710), CXLV. Berkeley failed to realize that within the system he had constructed there is room only for tea for two, himself and God, not for other spirits. The argument from analogy can be invoked only by a dualist or physicalist (mind–brain identity theorist), not by an idealist, for the body of a human being other than myself is merely a set of ideas in my mind. The only spirits that inform such ideas are their subject – me and God.

**Figure 12.1** *Hume's theory of sympathy*

anticipated 'simulation theory' in contemporary psychology and cognitive neuroscience. (Deep confusions never die, nor do they fade away – rather they mutate.)

*Criticisms of Hume* Hume's account is convoluted, due to the exigencies of his associationist mental physics. He proudly modelled his 'experimental method' in psychology on Newtonian physics, with ideas being analogous to point masses and principles of association to laws of gravity. But it is not too difficult to penetrate the convolutions and apprehend the deficiencies of Hume's tale. Were it correct:

(i)   It would be impossible to *ascribe* to another an emotion one had not felt oneself. But one can attribute jealousy to another without ever having been jealous (just read Proust's *Swann's Way* or *The Prisoner* and *The Sweet Cheat Gone*). Never having experienced jealousy does not imply that one's ascription of jealousy to another is unintelligible to oneself.

(ii)  It implies that one cannot *sympathize* with another without feeling the very same emotion, albeit perhaps less vividly. But one may sympathize with a grieving friend without grieving or with a remorseful friend without feeling remorse. Not feeling the emotion for which one sympathizes with another does not imply that one's avowal of sympathy with the other is insincere.

(iii) It implies that one cannot even *apprehend* the emotion of another without concurrently feeling the same emotion oneself. But, as Wittgenstein rhetorically queried, 'Do you look into *yourself* in order to recognize the fury in *his* face?'[5]

---

[5] Wittgenstein, *Remarks on the Philosophy of Psychology*, vol. 1, ed. G. E. M. Anscombe and G. H. von Wright (Blackwell, Oxford, 1980), §927.

Moreover,

(iv)   If I assign meaning to emotion names by reference to my emo-
       tions alone (since they are allegedly the only emotions with
       which I am 'acquainted'), how could I project the emotions I feel
       onto another person? I would have to imagine emotions *I do
       not feel* on the model of emotions *I do feel.*[6] Would I be doing
       more than imagining myself feeling emotions in the breast of
       another? This is of doubtful intelligibility, but, as we shall see, it
       became the mainstay of German projectionist accounts of
       *Einfühlung*.

Hume noted the difference between contagious emotions and sympathetic emotions. In emotional contagion, by contrast with sympathy, the emotion felt, though caused by another's emotion, is not
conceived to be the other's emotion and is not ascribed to the other.
Sympathy involves imagination, contagion does not. It is noteworthy
that the scope of sympathy, according to Hume, is wide, encompass-
ing passions, emotions, opinions, sentiments, and aesthetic appreciation. 'In general', he remarked, 'the minds of men are mirrors to one
another' (*THN* II. ii. 5, para. 20).[7]

       Edmund Burke, in his *Philosophical Enquiry*
*Burke on sympathy* *into the Origin of our Ideas of the Sublime and*
       *Beautiful* (1757, 2nd edn 1759), was much influ-
enced by Hume in his conception of sympathy, to which he allocated
a pivotal role in his analysis of the empirical nature of our appreciation of beauty and of the sublime. It is by this emotion, he wrote,

> That we enter into the concerns of others; that we are moved as they are
> moved, and are never suffered to be indifferent spectators of almost any-
> thing men can do or suffer. For sympathy must be considered as a sort of
> substitution, by which we are put into the place of another man, and
> affected in many respects as he is affected ... It is by this principle chiefly
> that poetry, painting and other affecting arts, transfuse their passions
> from one breast to another, and are often capable of grafting a delight on
> wretchedness, misery and death itself. It is a common observation, that
> objects which in reality would shock, are in tragical, and such like pres-
> entations, the source of the highest degrees of pleasure. (I. 13)

---

[6] Compare Wittgenstein, *Philosophical Investigations*, §302.

[7] In the *Enquiry*, Hume changes his analysis of sympathy and subordinates it to
compassion and taste. This need not concern us here.

This subjectivization of aesthetic qualities, which presaged the rise of Romanticism, was to have considerable influence on the philosophy and psychology of aesthetics over the next century.

*Adam Smith on sympathy*      Adam Smith, a close friend of Hume's, made sympathy the fulcrum of his explanation of the origin and nature of morality. In his *Theory of Moral Sentiments*, he gave an extensive phenomenological description of sympathy. Like Hume, Smith held that susceptibility to sympathy is an original endowment of human beings:

> How selfish soever man may be supposed, there are evidently some principles in his nature, which interest him in the fortune of others, and render their happiness necessary to him, though he derives nothing from it except the pleasure of seeing it. Of this kind is pity or compassion, the emotion which we feel for the misery of others, when we either see it, or are made to conceive it in a very lively manner. (*The Theory of Moral Sentiments*, I. i. 1, para. 1)[8]

Remarking that 'sympathy' may originally have been restricted to our feelings for the misfortunes of others, that is, to pity and compassion, he declares that he will extend it to 'fellow-feeling' with any passion (emotion) whatever. Accordingly, one may feel sympathy with someone's joy no less than with their grief.

Like Hume, Smith allocates a central role to the imagination, both in our apprehension of other people's psychological attributes and in our feelings of sympathy for others.[9] He held that:

> As we have no immediate experience of what other men feel, we can form no idea of the manner in which they are affected, but by conceiving what we ourselves should feel in the like situation. Though our brother is upon the rack, as long as we ourselves are at our ease, our senses will never inform us of what he suffers. They never did, and never can, carry us beyond our own person, and it is by the imagination only that we can form any conception of what are his sensations ... By the imagination we place ourselves in his situation, we conceive ourselves enduring all the same torments, we enter as it were into his body, and become in some measure the same person with him, and thence form some idea of his sensation, and even feel something which, though weaker in degree, is not altogether unlike them. ...

[8] Pity and compassion, according to Smith, are forms of sympathy.
[9] For a detailed analysis of the concept of imagination, see *The Intellectual Powers: A Study of Human Nature* (Wiley Blackwell, Oxford, 2013), ch. 11.

> That this is the source of our fellow-feeling for the misery of others, that it is by changing places in fancy with the sufferer, that we come either to conceive or to be affected by what he feels, may be demonstrated by many obvious observations. (*The Theory of Moral Sentiments*, I. i. 1, paras 2–3)

Smith's account of sympathy, like Hume's, weaves together a proposed resolution of the so-called problem of other minds, an analysis of the emotion of sympathy, and an explanation of the moral sentiments. But this was a mistake. The problem of other minds needs dissolving, not answering by reference to psychological hypotheses.

*Problem of other minds*

The very phrase 'problem of other minds' is misleading, because it already contains the misguided presuppositions that set the problem, namely that the perceptions, sensations, feelings, and emotions of other human being are

(i)   attributes of *minds*;
(ii)  logically, inalienably, *owned* by minds;
(iii) essentially *hidden from view*;
(iv)  *accessible* to their subject alone (who has 'privileged access' to them);
(v)   *known immediately* to their subject by means of *direct perception* or *introspection*.

These are deep confusions, rooted in the picture of 'inner' and 'outer' discussed in chapters 2 and 3. Both Hume and Smith were victims of this conception, which they inherited from Descartes and Locke. It is muddled, although still alive and flourishing to this day in psychology and cognitive neuroscience. As already demonstrated, emotions are attributes of human beings and other animals, not of minds or brains. To be angry or to feel jealous is not to own anything. The emotions of others are not 'hidden' unless they are intentionally suppressed. Not telling someone what one feels or thinks is not ordinarily hiding anything. Sincerely telling another what one feels or thinks *is* to exhibit one's emotion and express one's thought. The emotion expressed in a person's responses *is* the emotion that is felt. Cries, tears, and excited saltations of joy are not mere behaviour behind which joy is hidden; rather they are the different forms which joy may, from occasion to occasion, take. To feel angry or joyful and to be able to say so is not to have access to anything, and if one manifests one's anger or joy in what one says and does, then it is fully observable by others. Of some psychological attributes, it makes no sense to say that the subject knows or indeed does not know them to be self-ascribable (being in pain, believing something to be so, or expecting someone). Of others (such as understanding) it does, but 'direct perception' and 'looking into oneself' play no role in confirming that one understands something. In short, the philosophical conundrums associated with knowing how things are with others should be separated from the analysis of sympathy. Sympathy plays no role in their resolution. So, separating the confusions surrounding knowledge of other people's psychological attributes from the analysis of sympathy, I shall briefly sketch Adam Smith's contribution to the phenomenology of sympathy.

*Sympathy, imagination, judgement, and understanding*

Smith noted that it is not only the faculty of the imagination that is active in producing feelings of sympathy, but also the faculties of understanding and judgement. For to sympathize with others, he averred, one must, at least to some degree, feel that their emotional response is warranted in its nature, its extent, and its intensity. One must feel that their suffering is undeserved, either altogether or in its extent and intensity – if someone brought their misfortune on their own head through folly or wrong-doing, they may not deserve our sympathy. Similarly, one must judge their good fortune to be merited or at least not reprehensible, and their joy warranted (no one will sympathize with the good fortune and joys of those they hold to be wicked). So sympathy arises not simply from the view of the passion observed, but also from understanding of the situation that excites it and from a degree of approval or disapproval. This is an important observation. Of course, the thought that the misfortune of another with whom one sympathizes need not cross one's mind, and one's judgement need not be explicit. But one would naturally adduce such considerations if challenged.

*Smith on irreducibility of sympathy to selfishness*

Smith was eager to emphasize the irreducibility of sympathy to any form of selfishness (perhaps with Hobbes or de Mandeville in mind). Accordingly, he wrote:

> But though sympathy is very properly said to arise from an imaginary change of situations with the person principally concerned, yet this imaginary change is not supposed to happen to me in my own person and character, but in that of the person with whom I sympathize. When I condole with you for the loss of your only son, in order to enter into your grief, I do not consider what I, a person of such a character and

profession, should suffer, if I had a son, and if that son was unfortu-
nately to die; but I consider what I should suffer if I was really you; and
I not only change circumstances, but I change persons and characters.
My grief, therefore, is entirely upon your account, and not in the least
upon my own. It is not, therefore, in the least selfish. (*The Theory of
Moral Sentiments*, VII. iii. 1, para. 4)

Smith did not advance a Humean projectivist account of sympathy,
whereby one projects *one's own feelings* onto someone else and conceives of them as his. Rather, one has to project *oneself* into another.
One has to imagine oneself in the other's shoes, or, indeed, not imagine *oneself* in another's shoes but imagine oneself *being the other*.

*Flaw in Smith's account
of self-projection*

Although he was quite right to repudiate the
Selfishness School, he went far too far. In order
sincerely and unselfishly to sympathize with
you in your grief, I do not have to transgress
the bounds of intelligibility: I do not have to consider what I would
feel 'if I were really you', since I could not really be you – there is no
such thing as me being you, or Julius Caesar, or Michelangelo, hence
there is nothing to imagine or consider. The phrase 'if I were you' is to
be taken figuratively to mean 'If I were in your position' or 'If I were
faced with your predicament', both of which are characteristically
employed to herald advice. In order to feel sympathy with you or
anyone else, I need not perform any impossible feats of imagination.
I need only be aware of what delight or suffering you must be enjoying or undergoing or what predicament you are facing, feel approval
or disapproval, and care about it as well as about you. For that, imagination *may* be necessary. But I don't have to imagine *being you*;
I have to imagine *what you must be feeling*, given *your* concerns
and values – I have to *bethink myself*, not, as it were, *project myself*.
And often I do not even have to do that, because I can *see* the joy in
your behaviour on your hearing of your success, *hear* your grief in
your broken voice when you tell of your bereavement. I do not *infer* your
emotion from your behaviour, I apprehend it *in* your behaviour – even
though emotion is not behaviour. Rather, certain kinds of behaviour
(in appropriate circumstances) are the forms emotions take.

*Smith on sympathetic
sensations and emotions*

Smith's phenomenology of sympathy is
richer than Hume's and has the merit of not
being interwoven with Hume's mental physics.
He notes the phenomenon of sympathetic sen-
sations (as one has when one reads tales of the illnesses of others, for

example, Solzhenitsyn's *Cancer Ward* or Roger Martin du Gard's description of old Thibault's long-drawn-out death in *The Thibaults*). He correctly observes that we can feel sympathetic emotion for another, which the other does not feel himself – as when we blush with embarrassment for his rudeness or impudence, although, of course, that does not imply that we sympathize with him. Smith similarly draws our attention to the fact that we may feel sympathy for a wretch who is not even aware of his plight and could not be, as when we feel sympathy for the insane (or, today, for sufferers from Alzheimer's disease). He also points out that our expression of sympathy for the successes of our friends commonly adds to their joy, just as our sympathetic commiseration with their misfortune may alleviate it. Finally he notes the intentionality of our feelings of sympathy, in the sense that we can and do evince sympathy, often intense sympathy, with fictional characters in novels, drama, and opera, and with personages in paintings.

So much, then, for a brief sketch of the British eighteenth-century school of sympathy, which purported to provide an analysis and phenomenology of sympathy, to resolve the 'problem of other minds', to describe the glue that holds society together, and to characterize the roots of morality. Our sketch provides a historical background against which to present the conceptual analysis of sympathy and locate it within the web of concepts where it belongs.

## 2. The analysis of sympathy

There are different ways in which human beings are homologously responsive to the emotions of others. We must distinguish contagious responses from infectious emotions and both from sympathy.

*Infantile contagious responsiveness* — Infant contagious responsiveness is exhibited by babies who commence to cry on the stimulus of other babies' crying. This is a non-cognitive innate response, which might well be compared with the sympathetic vibration of taut strings – a comparison that Hume misleadingly used to explain the nature of sympathy itself: 'As in strings equally wound up, the motion of one communicates itself to the rest; so all the affections pass from one person to another and beget correspondent movements in every human creature' (*THN* III. iii. 1). But this, like the neonate's behaviour, is a mere causal reaction, with no intentional component. The infant's resonating response is not itself an emotion at all, although there is no doubt that the baby's crying engenders its own distress. But, while the baby is reacting to another infant's cries of pain, it is not itself in pain and is not responding in sympathy to the other infant's pain but reacting automatically to its cries. No contagious resonating response is necessary for genuine sympathy – one may sympathize with another's pain, fear, or anxiety without feeling pain, fear, or anxiety oneself.

Contagious responsiveness among adults is patent in reactive yawning and laughter, although here, too, the emotional component may be nugatory – infectious yawning does not betoken boredom, and infectious laughter need not betoken amusement, since one may laugh without understanding the joke. But, to be sure, infectious laughter may raise one's spirits. (Here the James–Lange account of emotion (see chapter 4) gets some grip.)

*Motor mimesis*  A further form of infectious reaction to the behaviour of others is *motor mimesis*, as when spectators at boxing matches move their shoulders or even arms and fists in tune with the movements of the competitor they favour, or shrink when another is struck in the face; or when spectators at horse trials rise slightly in their seats as they watch a competitor approaching a fence. This resonating reaction is not an infectious *emotion*, although it is essentially linked to emotional attitudes, inasmuch as it typically occurs in the course of observing those whom one supports or favours. (It might be deemed to be *motor empathy*.) It is not intentional, but it is partly voluntary. One does not do it on purpose, but one can suppress it at will if it is drawn to one's attention.

*Infectious emotions*  *Infectious emotions* are powerfully manifested by the various forms of crowd or mob reaction to which human beings are susceptible. These range from the joy and excitement of celebrating victory or triumph (in sport, politics, and war) to the fierce crowd delight in the spectacle of cruelty (at gladiatorial combat, public executions, bear-baiting or cock-fighting, and, today, at boxing matches and bull-fights), through cries of indignation and anger induced both by rhetoric and by chanting at mass demonstrations, to adulation of a leader and rhetorically stimulated hatred of an enemy (religious, racial, national). Here emotions really are involved, for the joy, excitement, indignation, anger, adulation, love, and hatred have perfectly explicit objects. These may be people (as in adulation of the Führer in Nazi rallies (accompanied by thunderous mass cries of *Sieg Heil*), or God in the mass hysteria and blood lust of holy wars (*Deus vult* and *Allahu akbar*)) or an enemy against whom one's anger is aroused by rhetoric. Or they may be intentional objects signified by nominalization-accusatives (joy and excitement at victory or triumph, anger, and indignation at alleged treachery or blasphemy and heresy). Fear is similarly contagious in mob panic at an alarm (fire) or at danger (terrorism), where fear reactions may be stimulated by the crowd's behaviour without the reacting subject's even knowing the nature of the danger. Although resonance plays a major role in generating and sustaining such crowd emotions, they are not forms of sympathy. They are characterized by loss of a sense of one's own individuality, by self-identification with the crowd, and by succumbing to the contagious mass emotion exhibited. Suppression of critical faculties and abandonment of a sense of moral responsibility are corollaries of hysteria and loss of self-control in such circumstances. The consequent sense of anonymity, which, in certain kinds of case is accompanied by a sense of collective power, is commonly felt to be cathartic. Individuals, swamped by such mass emotions, are highly suggestible and susceptible to the rhetoric of political leaders, who may or may not be malignant. Crowd emotions at sporting activities can be said to vary between contagious, identity-effacing, collective emotions and consciously concurrent individual emotions which do not involve submergence of the sense of one's identity in the expression of enthusiasm for the triumph of the competitor or team one favours and of sympathy for their misfortune or defeat.

*Different uses of 'sympathy'*

Now let us turn to various uses of 'sympathy'. Some distinctions that may prevent later confusion are apt.

(i)   The use of 'sympathy' that will be our primary concern is to signify an *emotion* – concern for the plight of another. This use is manifest in such utterances as 'She felt sympathy for her sister' (as Elizabeth Bennet did for Jane) or 'Her gentle words were full of loving sympathy for him' (Cordelia for Lear on his awakening). Sympathy, in this sense, is something expressed in utterances of consolation and concern, manifest by an embrace and exhibited in deeds of compassion. We must distinguish between the object-accusative of sympathy, that is, the person *with* whom one sympathizes, and the nominalization-accusative, which specifies *what* one sympathizes with another *for*, for example, as when one sympathizes with her *for the loss of her husband,* or sympathizes with him *for the suffering he is undergoing.* The opposite of feeling sympathy for someone is *feeling no sympathy* or *being indifferent*. There is no sharp dividing line between feeling the emotion of sympathy when confronted by another person's current plight and the attitude of sympathy when one *sympathizes with* another person's standing misfortune and suffering.

(ii) We speak of people responding *in sympathy* with another person when they react *in concord* with the joy of another. This is not to feel sympathy *for* the other, let alone to sympathize with the other. It is to react *in* sympathy *with* the other's behaviour – as when one exhibits delight at their joyous responses to their success (e.g. teenage girls responding to each other's successful examination results; footballers responding to a teammate's scoring a goal), or joy at their happiness on hearing good news. This use is focused on spontaneous concordant reactive behaviour to another's spontaneous reactive behaviour. It is not, however, a matter of *feeling sympathy*, or *feeling sympathetic*, for the other's success (no one would say 'I feel sympathy with him in his triumph' or 'I felt sympathy with her for her success'). It is a momentary emotion, accompanied by emotional perturbations. It is followed not by a more prolonged emotion of sympathy but by an attitude of being pleased or delighted. As we shall see, the notion of empathy can equally be invoked in these contexts.

(iii) We further distinguish between being *in sympathy with*, or *feeling sympathy for*, someone's ideas and having no sympathy for, or being *out of sympathy* with, them. This use does not signify an emotion but rather a judgement – an attitude of agreement, which may amount to an emotional attitude. To feel *sympathetic towards* someone's policies or proposals implies that one *approves*, *favours*, or *supports* them. But this is defeasible, as is patent in the common response, 'I feel much sympathy for this proposal, but …'. Closely related to this is feeling *in sympathy* with the art or mores of an age, as when we say that we feel in sympathy with neo-classical architecture. This signifies *feeling comfortable with* and *approving of*. The contrary to feeling in sympathy with something is feeling *out of sympathy*, as when the elderly aver that they are out of sympathy with the informality of modernity or with the lack of emotional self-control of the youth. This signifies *being in discord or disagreement with* and *disapproval of*.

(iv) A 'sympathetic person' signifies a character trait of congeniality. Its contrary is *being antipathetic* and *uncongenial*. Someone who is congenial may, but need not, be a sympathetic person in a further sense, namely, they may have a disposition to feel sympathy for others and their misfortunes and hence be likely to show sympathy for one in one's distress ('Go and talk to Granny – she'll be sympathetic' or 'You can go to her for tea and sympathy').

(v) A further use that has survived the centuries is to speak of a place as 'sympathetic', meaning congenial. Its contrary is *being unsympathetic*.

It should be evident that the concept of sympathy is not determined by characteristic marks, nor is it a family resemblance concept. It is best presented as a centre of variation (see fig. 12.2).

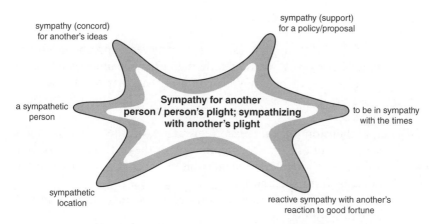

**Figure 12.2** *Sympathy as a centre of variation*

Our main concern in what follows will be with the analysis of feeling sympathy for or with another person for or in their ill fortune. Sympathy (like one of its its contraries, *Schadenfreude*[10]) is an emotional or attitudinal response

*Object- and nominalization-accusatives*

---

[10] A quite different contrary is antipathy for another's emotional response, perhaps because it is felt to be disingenuous or exaggerated.

to the plight of another. The object-accusative of sympathy is the person (or animal) *for whom* one feels sympathy or *with whom* one sympathizes. The nominalization-accusative of sympathy specifies *the reason* the subject has *for* feeling sympathy. This may take take two forms: first, specifying the distress the other feels or is assumed to feel – the suffering, the grief, the disappointment, the anger or indignation, the shame or humiliation. So we may feel sympathy *with* others *for* the pain they are suffering, *for* the grief that they are experiencing, *for* the disappointment they feel, and so forth. Secondly, the nominalization-accusative may render our sympathy transparent. We may feel sympathy for others *in* their grief at having lost their spouse, *in* their disappointment at not attaining their goal, *in* their indignation at being unfairly treated. These more explicit characterizations specify not only the person and their emotional or attitudinal response to their circumstances, but also the object of *their* emotion and hence, too, their *warrant* for their emotion.

*Seven implications of sympathy*　　　　Sympathy normally implies:

(i)　apprehension (or believed apprehension) of another person's distress or suffering: it may be immediately seen, heard or felt, or one may hear of a mishap that one knows will cause great distress, or one may learn by hearsay of another's distress;

(ii)　apprehension of the reason or cause of the other person's distress (but one may feel sympathy for the distress of those one loves even though (as teenagers often do) they refuse to disclose the reason for their suffering);

(iii)　understanding the other person's response (even if it is, in one way or another, awry);

(iv)　feeling sorry for the person with whom one sympathizes;

(v)　feeling concern and often anxiety for the other's welfare;

(vi)　reactions of solicitude, commiseration, compassion, and, where appropriate, tenderness;

(vii)　an implicit judgement of desert or warrant, made explicit by such negative and critical restraining responses as 'She does not deserve your sympathy; she brought it all on herself by her wilful behaviour' (as one might say of Jane Austen's arrogant, interfering Emma) – but one may feel compassion for another despite their not deserving one's sympathy (as does Monsigneur Bienvenue towards the wretched Jean Valjean, who stole his silver while being given safe haven in the bishop's house, in *Les Misérables*).

*Behavioural manifestations of sympathy*

Characteristic behaviour that manifests sympathy with others depends upon one's relationship with them, the plight to which they are responding, and their spatial proximity. If one is in the presence of another person who is in pain, then sympathy is typically exhibited by holding their hand and perhaps stroking it (or, in the case of one's child, by cuddling). In other cases, where the suffering of another is an emotional response to misfortune, sympathy is also manifest in physical contact: in holding hands or embracing the person who is in distress, in gently patting on the shoulder, sometimes in (non-erotic) kissing, in encouraging the sufferer to talk through his predicament, and in supportive commiseration and remedial advice (Walpole depicts this well in *Judith Paris*). The proximity of sympathy to love in such cases is patent. But the person with whom one sympathizes may not be present. One will then not be stirred by their evident distress but by one's apprehension of how distressed they must be. So the form one's sympathy takes may be one's own distress, making contact with the unfortunate person, deciding to cancel one's engagements and to travel in order to be with the distressed friend. In the case of complete strangers, perhaps en masse (as in the case of natural disasters or man-made catastrophes), the form that sympathy may take ranges from verbal expressions of pity, to donations to appropriate charitable organizations and similar acts of compassion. Such patterns of behaviour, in appropriate circumstances, are criteria for someone's feeling sympathy with another or with others.

*Why self-pity is not a form of sympathy*

Who and what are the possible objects of sympathy? One may feel sympathy for other human beings, but not for oneself. Whereas feeling proud of oneself is a form of pride and feeling ashamed of oneself is a form of shame, feeling sorry for oneself (self-pity) is not a form of sympathy. Why not? Sympathy with the plight of another is a virtue, but self-pity is a vice. One may *wallow* in self-pity but not in sympathy, let alone in 'sympathy for oneself'. Those who face misfortune with fortitude are to be admired, for they do not *indulge* in self-pity. We do not criticize them for lack of 'sympathy for themselves', as we may criticize them for lack of sympathy for others. The leader who drives himself in adversity even harder than he drives his men may be said to be merciless, or even pitiless, towards himself – which shows strength of character, but not lack of sympathy for himself. One may commiserate with a foreigner about the state of his country, saying 'I sympathize with you about the ghastly referendum or election results / civil war / economic crash', but the foreigner may not reply 'Yes, I sympathize with myself too'. In short, sympathy *cannot* be self-directed. Pity *can* be self-directed but *should not* be. Feeling sorry for oneself is a weakness of character. Pity for others is a form of sympathy, but self-pity is not.

*Limits of sympathy*        One may feel sympathy for a social or political movement (the Chartists or suffragettes), or for a nation or people who are suffering or being persecuted. One may feel sympathy for animals that are suffering, for one's pets or horses, for animals being tormented before one's eyes or otherwise visibly suffering (the bull in the corrida; caged animals in inhumane zoos; factory-farmed animals; injured animals). But one cannot feel sympathy for the damage done to and the destruction of non-sentient life, let alone inanimate objects, no matter how distressed and indignant one may feel at the destruction of great trees (the Californian redwoods) and forests (of Amazonia and Indonesia) or at the wilful damage to stalagmites or stalactites in wondrous caves.

*Degrees of sympathy*        Sympathy, like other emotions, comes in degrees. The degree of sympathy felt is a function of the agent's sensibility in general and of the agent's attention to the object of sympathy on the occasion, of the degree of suffering apprehended, and of the strength of the agent's positive relationship to the sufferer. As Hume pointed out, people tend to feel more sympathy for those who are dear to them than for mere business friends and acquaintances; more sympathy for such business friends than for strangers; and more sympathy for fellow countrymen than for foreigners. Similarly, as Hume also noted, one's sympathy seems inversely correlated with one's distance from the unfortunate. This feature, has, to some degree, changed due to modern mass media of communication, in particular television and smartphones. For the sympathetic imagination is more readily stirred by pictures than by description. Nevertheless, it is true that people are more distressed at the deaths and injuries of their fellow countrymen in wars, earthquakes, or tsunamis than at those of foreigners. This appears to be a brute fact about our nature that can be explained by evolutionary theory.

*Evolutionary roots*        The capacity for sympathy seems to be innate.
*of innate sympathy*        There is evidence to suggest that, in general, women are more prone to feel sympathy, and to feel it more acutely, than men. That has a plausible evolutionary explanation in terms of maternal care for the suffering or distress of her neonate and subsequently for her growing child. Sympathy for

others would then be an evolutionary offshoot of selection for maternal care. Male sympathy for neonates would appear to be culturally conditioned and largely a very recent phenomenon (decisions on neonate exposure in ancient Greece and Rome were the father's prerogative). Paternal sympathy for children is a corollary of paternal love – where the latter is socially encouraged, the former will develop. Sympathy between men has evolutionary roots in the cooperative benefits of comradeship among tribal creatures. To be sure, there can be no *philia*, or friendship-love, without sympathy, and only exceptionally can there be erotic love without it. In general, one criterion for love is sympathy in adversity.

Whatever capacity for sympathy one may be endowed with, it may be fostered or stifled. It may be encouraged by parental example and teaching, but it may be positively discouraged and extinguished. E. M. Forster's portrayal in *Howards End* of the male members of the Wilcox family (Henry and his sons, Charles and Paul) depicts the stunting of human sympathy for the unfortunate as a result of wealth, aggressive acquisitiveness, and a sense of social superiority.[11] Forster's portrayal of the British colonial rulers and their wives in *A Passage to India* depicts the complete absence of sympathy among the closed imperial classes for the native Indians. Here the capacity for sympathy and the sensitivity to the plight of others is destroyed by peer-group pressure, racial prejudice, bigotry, a sense of imperial superiority, and wilful ignorance of an alien culture. (Fielding's sympathy for the falsely accused Dr Aziz stands out as a boycott-incurring exception.)

---

[11] In discussing the fate of Leonard Bast with Helen Schlegel, Henry Wilcox remonstrates against Helen's sympathy for Leonard's increased impoverishment as a result of a casual economic prediction made by Henry, transmitted to Leonard by Helen, and which proved mistaken: 'Don't take up that sentimental attitude over the poor. ... The poor are poor, and one's sorry for them, but there it is. As civilization moves forward, the shoe is bound to pinch in places, and it's absurd to pretend that anyone is responsible personally. Neither you, nor I, nor my informant, nor is the man who informed him, nor the directors of the Porphyrion, are to blame for this clerk's loss of salary. It's just the shoe pinching – no one can help it; and it might easily be worse. ... By all means subscribe to charities – subscribe to them largely – but don't get carried away by absurd schemes of Social Reform. I see a good deal behind the scenes, and you can take it from me that there is no Social Question – except for a few journalists who try to get a living out of the phrase. There are just rich and poor, as there always have been and always will be. ... Our civilization is moulded by great impersonal forces ... And there always will be rich and poor. You can't deny it ... And you can't deny that, in spite of it all, the tendency of civilization has on the whole been upward' (*Howards End*, ch. 22).

Natural sympathy for human beings can be destroyed by bigotry, racism, and the dehumanization of the victims – as in concentration camps, coupled with peer pressure and fear of stepping out of line in mass murder on military orders. Fellow feeling for humanity – a sense of fraternity among victims – may be eroded through fear and suffering. It requires exceptional integrity and heroism to rise above such terror, as Primo Levi and Bruno Bettelheim evidently did, and doubtless many other nameless heroes who were slaughtered. Sympathy may be momentarily blocked, as Aristotle observantly noted, in cases of the severe plight of those one loves, through horror at their physical suffering.

It is in virtue of sympathy that we are able to view the misfortunes and suffering of others *as reasons* for our sympathetic responses and emotions, and *as reasons* for attempting to ameliorate their suffering or to resolve their predicament. Although our instinctive emotional response is not itself voluntary, its expression is partly voluntary (for we can sometimes suppress the response) and the subsequent motivated behaviour is intentional.

*Is acting out of sympathy always good?* Is action done out of sympathy always morally good and praiseworthy? We must distinguish acts *of* sympathy and acts *done out of* sympathy. Acts of sympathy are always benevolent in intent. They are *expressions* and *manifestations* of sympathy. Nevertheless, they may misfire in various ways. In Aristotelian spirit one may say that they must be done on the right occasion, in the right manner, and to the right extent. *Expressing* sympathy on the wrong occasion (e.g. in the presence of others) may be offensive, inducing shame in the recipient. Expressing it when unwanted may enrage (as it often does teenagers, who react violently to well-meant parental sympathy). *Manifesting* sympathy in the wrong manner may be harmful and even insulting, calling forth indignant rejection that takes the sympathy to be pity and its expression to be condescending. *Exhibiting* it to the wrong extent, as when Helen Schlegel (in *Howards End*) sends Leonard Bast a cheque for five thousand pounds (a great fortune in Edwardian England), merely leads to rejection out of pride and unwillingness to accept so great a gift. (In general, Helen's sympathy for the Basts is disproportionate in every way, and leads to catastrophe.) The impulse behind behavioural manifestations of sympathy for the plight of another may be meritorious and the reason for the sympathy may be sound, but, unless acts of sympathy are controlled by reasoned judgement, they may cause more harm than good. Acts *motivated by sympathy*, on the other hand, are a much wider category. They need not be acts *of sympathy*. Though commonly beneficial, sympathy for the plight of others has sometimes motivated horrendous acts of terrorism – by anarchists in the late nineteenth and early twentieth century, and by Muslim jihadists in the late twentieth and twenty-first centuries.

## 3. Empathy: from *Einfühlung* to mirror neurons

The term 'empathy' is a very recent addition to our vocabulary. Although derived from the Greek *en* (into) + *patheia* (feeling), *empatheia* occurs very rarely indeed in ancient Greek texts, and where it does it signifies no more than intense passion or emotion. In modern Greek *empatheia* means bias, hostility, or meanness. *Empathie* was introduced into German by Herman Lotze in 1858 as a Greco-German variant of *Einfühlung*. The word 'empathy' was introduced into English only in 1909 by the experimental psychologist Edward Titchener as a translation of Theodor Lipps's use of *Einfühlung* in his psychological theory of aesthetic experience and of knowledge of 'other minds'. So, if we are to get a grip on the evolution of the notion of empathy, we must first briefly investigate the eighteenth- and nineteenth-century uses of *Einfühlung*.[12]

*Herder's introduction of Einfühlung*  *Einfühlung* was first deployed by Johann Gottfried Herder (1744–1803) in his reflections on understanding alien cultures and the uniqueness of their conceptions of the world. Contrary to the Enlightenment notion of universal laws of human nature and development, and contrary to their nomothetic (subsumption theoretic) conception of explanation and understanding of human affairs, Herder moved down paths parallel to those pioneered by Vico in *Scienza Nuova*. There are no laws of human development: historical understanding is idiographic and ethnography has to understand

---

[12] I am indebted to G. Jahoda, 'Theodor Lipps and the Shift from "Sympathy" to "Empathy"', *Journal of the History of the Behavioural Sciences* 41 (2005), 151–63; M. Nowak, 'The Complicated History of "Einfühlung"', *Argument* 1 (2011), 301–26; and L. H. Edwards, 'A Brief Conceptual History of *Einfühlung*', *History of Psychology* 16 (2013), 269–81.

alien cultures in their own terms. Ancient texts (e.g. Homer, Ossian (then still thought to be authentic), the Old Testament) must be read in the spirit and context in which they were written. One must imaginatively enter into the age one studies, into the geography of the region of the peoples one investigates (for the mentality of plains people differs from that of desert dwellers, who in turn differ from mountain or riverine people), and into their history. But *Einfühlung* is not a peculiar psychological activity; it is a laborious scholarly one of studying texts in the context of other related writings by their author as well as writings of related authors, and in the socio-historical context in which they were written. To be sure, it involves imagination, but the imagination it involves is the cogitative imagination: the ability to think up novel possibilities. It is not a technique for *identifying with* the presuppositions of the thought of other cultures, but for *eliciting* them. In this, Herder had an important influence upon German hermeneutics, especially through his pupil Schleiermacher. It is noteworthy that, in this hermeneutical sense, *Einfühlung* is not an emotion at all, but a form of understanding. However, Herder also invoked *Einfühlung* in describing our responses to nature, which are emotional, in explaining our inclination to read psychological attributes into nature (*raging* storms; *menacing* rumbles of thunder; *tranquil*, *ominous*, or *brooding* landscapes), and in describing our emotional responses to works of art.[13] It is noteworthy that he does not appear to have intended to differentiate *Einfühlung* from *Sympathie*.

The idea of 'feeling one's way into' something proved enticing in many humanistic disciplines, among them philosophical aesthetics, art history, and the interpretation of works of art. Its primary appeal in these domains was to philosophers and psychologists of aesthetics reacting against the aesthetic formalism advanced by Johann Friedrich Herbart and his later followers. Herbartians aimed to discover the key to aesthetic pleasure in content-indifferent mathematical relationships and pleasing shapes, proportions, and structure. The countermovement to formalism sought to restore human emotions to the analysis of aesthetic experience. The three leading figures in rehabilitating the role of content in aesthetic experience and to do justice to

---

[13] Herder's unsystematic methodological reflections were to reverberate through the nineteenth and twentieth centuries in the philosophy of history (Droysen; Ranke; Rickerts; Dilthey, who drew the contrast between *Erklärung* (explanation) and *Verstehen* (understanding); as well as Collingwood, who emphasized the historian's 're-enactment' of the past). They were also echoed in twentieth-century anthropology and in the philosophy of the social sciences.

the spectator's psychological 'immersion' into a work of art and 'self-projection' into the art object were Friedrich Theodor Vischer (1807–87), his son Robert Vischer (1847–1933), and, most important of all, Theodor Lipps (1851–1913), who influenced Husserl and the phenomenological school. It is noteworthy that Lipps had translated Hume's *Treatise* into German. Arguably his account of empathy had its roots in Hume's projectivism. In parallel with Hume and Smith, Lipps wanted to yoke *Einfühlung* to the problem of the knowledge of other minds. Like Hume's account of sympathy, Lipps's analysis of *Einfühlung* was a forerunner of present-day simulation theory.

*Titchener's introduction of 'empathy'*   The confusions in their reflections on aesthetics and knowledge of other minds need not concern us now. What *is* important for our purposes is the next step. Edwin Titchener (1867–1927), an Englishman who spent two years working with Wundt in Leipzig before taking up a post at Cornell University, where he taught for the rest of his life, read works by Theodor Lipps. Much impressed by them, and by Lipps's extension of the idea of *Einfühlung* from aesthetics to human psychology and the 'problem of other minds', Titchener introduced the term 'empathy' into English:

> Not only do I see gravity and modesty and pride and courtesy and stateliness, but I feel or act them in the mind's muscles. This is, I suppose, a simple case of empathy, if we may coin that term as a rendering of *Einfühlung*; there is nothing curious or idiosyncratic about it; but it is a fact that must be mentioned.[14]

In his *Textbook on Psychology* (1910), Titchener explained: 'Empathy (a word formed on the analogy of sympathy) is the name we give to the process of humanizing objects, of reading or feeling ourselves into them.'[15] Like Lipps's *Einfühlung*, empathy was conceived to be an imitative/projective process.

The notion of empathy was of little interest to the school of behaviourists that displaced William James's introspective psychology and Titchener's Wundt-inspired introspective structuralism.[16] Behaviourism

---

[14] E. J. Titchener, *Lectures on the Experimental Psychology of Thought Processes* (Macmillan, New York, 1909), pp. 21–2.

[15] Titchener, *Textbook on Psychology* (Macmillan, New York, 1910), p. 417.

[16] Introspective structuralism consisted, roughly speaking, of Hume married to physiological psychology: namely, the analysis of the mind in terms of combinatorial structures made of the psychologically simplest components evident to introspection.

came to dominate Anglo-American psychology from the 1920s until the so-called (and misnamed) cognitive revolution in the 1970s.[17] But the notion of empathy found a home elsewhere, both in psycho-analysis and in phenomenology.[18]

*Post-behaviourist introduction of theory of mind*

With the demise of behaviourism in the 1970s, the notion of empathy again became an object for reflections of experimental and practical psychologists and therapists. Their interest in empathy was given substantial boost by two extraneous developments, one in the domain of philosophy and so-called cognitive science, the other subsequently in cognitive neuroscience. Within philosophy, in the United States, ordinary psychological words were held to be a theoretical vocabulary belonging to a primitive theory of the mind denominated 'folk psychology'. The two main figures whose writings underpinned this misconception were W. V. O. Quine and Wilfred Sellars.[19] It was not long before philosophers were advancing the view that our ascription of psychological attributes to others presupposed possession of a theory of mind. The mental attributes of others being unobservable, according to such 'theory-theorists', they have the status of theoretical entities postulated by a theory.

This idea was seized upon by psychologists, ethnologists, and cognitive neuroscientists. It seemed to many that this was the only way to explain what was referred to as 'mind-reading' – even though what is read, if anything, is not the mind, but expressive behaviour.[20] This putative explanation of the ability to respond to emotion-manifesting behaviour of others was rapidly extended to neonates and indeed to

---

[17] Misnamed because, as Jerome Bruner, one of the founding fathers of the movement, came to realize in his old age, it did not really reintroduce belief, thought, hope, fear, etc. into empirical psychology at all. It introduced *computation*, indeed it introduced *neuro-computational psychology*. It was, however, too late for Bruner to put the genie he had conjured up back into the bottle.

[18] For a detailed discussion of the history of the notion of empathy among early phenomenologists, see D. Zahavi, *Self and Other: Exploring Subjectivity, Empathy and Shame* (Oxford University Press, Oxford, 2014), ch. 10.

[19] W. V. O. Quine, *Word and Object* (MIT Press, Cambridge, Mass., 1963), and W. Sellars, 'Empiricism and the Philosophy of Mind' (1956), repr. in *Science, Perception and Reality* (Routledge & Kegan Paul, London, 1963).

[20] C. D. Frith and U. Frith compared our ability to apprehend the mental attributes of others to mind-reading ('Interacting Minds: a Biological Basis', *Science* 286 (1999), 1692–5). But this is a mistaken comparison. The expression 'mind-reading' is rightly used for intuitive apprehension of what another is thinking, feeling, or intending. Identical twins appear to have a gift for mutual mind-reading. They know each other's personalities exceedingly well and are perhaps sensitive to what are, for others, subliminal clues. But when we see another person, in appropriate contexts, scream in pain, shout in rage, jump with joy, nothing that can be dignified by the name 'mind-reading' is in question in our apprehension.

non-human animals, all of whom must allegedly evolve and then possess and employ a rich 'theory of mind'. A salient feature of theory-theories, such as those advanced by D. Premack and G. Woodruff,[21] S. Baron-Cohen,[22] and S. Stich, is that assertions about the psychological attributes of others are inferences – theoretical inferences, just as the argument from analogy holds such assertions to be analogical inferences, and the 'inference to the best explanation' holds them to be explanatory inferences.

*Simulation theory and mirror neurons*  In reaction to these absurdities (see chapters 2 to 4), simulation theorists, both philosophers such as Peter Goldie and Alvin Goldman, and experimental psychologists such as Paul Harris insisted, along lines parallel to Hume, Smith, and Lipps, as well as subsequent phenomenologists such as Scheler, Husserl, Edith Stein, and Merleau-Ponty, that our judgements about other people's psychological attributes are not inferential but simulative/projective.[23] This conception was given a substantial boost by the discovery by Rizzolatti, Gallese, and Fogassi in the 1980s and 1990s of so-called *mirror neurons*.[24] These are neurons, variously located in the cortex, whose heightened activity is associated with observation of sensation, perception, purposive action, and emotion of others, *and* with one's own sensations, perceptions, purposive actions, and emotions. So, when one observes another person picking up a teacup, mirror neurons in

---

[21] D. Premack and G. Woodruff started the hare in a paper on chimpanzees written in 1978, 'Does the Chimpanzee Have a Theory of Mind?', *Behavioral and Brain Sciences* 4 (1978), 515–26. They declared that 'an individual has a theory of mind if he imputes mental states to himself and others. A system of inferences of this kind is properly viewed as a theory because such states are not directly observable and the system can be used to make predictions about the behaviour of others.' They go on to claim that chimpanzees have a theory of mind. But, as I have argued, chimpanzees are not in the theory-constructing business, and they do not *impute* mental states either to themselves or to others.

[22] A pupil of Uta Frith whose work on autism is renowned. Unfortunately he supposes that autistic children are deficient in acquiring a theory of mind.

[23] For example, 'When seeing a target's expressive face, an observer involuntarily imitates the observed facial expressions. The resulting changes in the observer's own facial musculature activate afferent neural pathways that produce the corresponding emotion. This emotion is then classified according to its emotion-type and finally attributed to the target whose face is being observed' (A. Goldman, *Simulating Minds* (Oxford University Press, Oxford, 2006), p. 208).

[24] G. Rizzolatti, V. Gallese, and L. Fogassi made these discoveries, first in the premotor centers in macaque monkeys where mirror neurons were found to be active in observation of the movements of others, and subsequently in responses to facial grimaces. Later, further research was non-invasively done on human beings.

the premotor cortex will display much the same activity as they would if one were about to pick up a teacup oneself. Similarly, if one observes a smile or scowl, mirror neurons exhibit heightened activity as they would if one were about to smile or scowl oneself. This encouraged scientists to hypothesize that apprehension of the mental attributes of others involves *neural replication* or 'mirroring'. So Rizzolatti and Sinigaglia aver that

> The *mirror mechanism* ... is a basic principle of brain functioning. This statement becomes less surprising once it is acknowledged that the brain acts, first and foremost, as a planning and control system for organisms ... observing others' actions and emotions recruits different brain networks, each of which transforms the sensory information concerning others' actions and emotions into one's own motor and visceromotor representations of those actions and emotions ... what is common to all kinds of mirror-based processing is that they provide a route to knowledge of others, one which can be taken up just by capitalizing on one's own motor or visceromotor representations.[25]

So the twenty-first century moved from the empathetic/projective *mind* hypothesized by Hume, Smith, Lipps, and the phenomenologists to the mirroring/projective *brain* of neuroscientists, who not only repeated the old confusions but added further incoherences. For they supposed that brain can intelligibly be said to *plan* things, and that it is intelligible to describe the brain as transforming the *information* that another is moving his hand to pick up a teacup into heightened neural activity in the ventral premotor cortex and the inferior parietal lobule. But this makes no sense. Brains do not make plans or fail to make plans; they do not reflect on plans and revise them in the light of good reasons, let alone shelve them for another day. *I* can 'transform' the information that it is raining into the information that I shall get wet if I venture outside, that is, I can reason and draw inferences, but this is not something brains can intelligibly be said to do.[26] Rizzolatti and Sinigaglia further contend that 'the mirror mechanism operates in the emotion domain and plays a key part in processing and understanding the emotions of others'.[27] Mirror neurons, they

---

[25] G. Rizzolatti and C. Sinigaglia, 'The Mirror Mechanism: a Basic Principle of Brain Function', *Nature Reviews: Neuroscience* 17 (2016), 757.

[26] See M. R. Bennett and P. M. S. Hacker, *Philosophical Foundations of Neuroscience* (Blackwell, Oxford, 2003), ch. 3.

[27] Rizzolatti and Sinigaglia, 'The Mirror Mechanism', 760.

hold, provide the neural basis for *understanding* the behaviour and emotions of others. Indeed, they define mirror-based understanding as 'an understanding from the inside': The mirror mechanism may provide a route to knowledge of others, which can be exploited just in ways that depend on one's own motor and visceral processes and representations.[28] But this is confused.

First, since *there is no such thing* as a brain understanding anything (any more than there is any such thing as a brain getting married or wanting a divorce), it makes no sense to try to explain how it is that we can have knowledge of the emotions of others by reference to the inaccessible and unknown activities of our own mirror neurons. (Whatever *my* mirror neurons may be up to, that is not information available to me, and, even if it were, it would not provide me with the grounds for an inference or with a reason for projecting any feelings onto others.) There *could be* no such thing as mirror-based understanding of the emotions of others. So, too, there can be no such thing as 'understanding from the inside' if that means 'understanding that rests on knowledge of activities of one's own mirror neurons'. For we have no such knowledge. Secondly, just as the sympathists and empathists of the nineteenth century were conceptually confused in their doctrine of projection, so too are contemporary neuroscientists. To repeat, in order to realize that you are angry, jealous, or grieving, *I* do not have to feel a shadow of anger, an echo of jealousy, or a colourless reprint of grief (no matter how my motor neurons are behaving). Thirdly, the neural phenomena in question are far more readily intelligible as a response to *perceived affordances*: neural anticipatory activity to environmental possibilities for action and response. It is surely no surprise that the sight of fear in another should immediately activate a part of the brain associated with readiness to respond with fear. Fourthly, since the reaction of mirror neurons by definition does not differentiate between the other's action or emotion and the subject's own action or emotion, it cannot in principle determine sympathy or empathy. For both sympathy and empathy are *essentially directed at another person*. All mirror neurons could do would be to reinforce a 'me too' reaction (to eat the dinner of the starving, feel attracted to the wife of the happily married, and so forth). Fifthly, mirror neurons could not account for our ability to feel sympathy for an unobserved unfortunate (e.g. when we

*Confusion of linking mirror neurons to projectivism*

---

[28] Rizzolatti and Sinigaglia, 'The Mirror Mechanism', 763.

hear that our friend's spouse has died), whose woes we can readily imagine. Nor could they explain the persistence of our sympathy over time (e.g. when a suffering person for whom we feel intense sympathy is not in view), let alone the fact that sympathy is a motive – providing a pattern of reasons for the amelioration of suffering.

It is crucial, for our purposes, to separate neuroscientific questions from conceptual ones. It is patent that both theory-theorists and simulation theorists are enmeshed in conceptual confusions.[29] Neuroscientists rightly investigate what neural activities are necessary for normal neonate responsiveness to the current behaviour of other neonates, children, and adults. Such investigations are important not only for their own sake, but also for the light they may shed on ameliorative treatment in cases of defective responsiveness in pathological cases (e.g. Asperger's syndrome, autism). However, no matter what the results may be, they can shed no light on the

[29] The following examples (all quoted in Zahavi, *Self and Other*, p. 174) make this patent to anyone who has followed the reasoning of this book thus far:

(i) 'Normal humans everywhere not only "paint" their world with color, they also "paint" beliefs, intentions, feelings, hopes, desires, and pretences onto agents in their social world. They do this despite the fact that no human has ever seen a thought, a belief, or an intention' (J. Tooby and L. Cosmides, 'Foreword', in S. Baron-Cohen, *Mindblindness: an Essay on Autism and Theory of Mind* (MIT Press, Cambridge, Mass., 1995), p. xvii).

(ii) 'Mental states, and the minds that possess them, are necessarily unobservable constructs that must be inferred by observers rather than perceived directly' (S. C. Johnson, 'The Recognition of Mentalistic Agents in Infancy', *Trends in Cognitive Science* 4: 1 (2000), 22).

(iii) 'Normal adults attribute to one another (and to themselves) unobservable internal mental states, such as goals, thoughts, and feelings, and use these to predict behaviour. This human capacity for reasoning about the mental causes of action is called a theory of mind' (R. Saxe, S. Carey, and N. Kanwisher, 'Understanding Other Minds: Linking Developmental Psychology and Functional Neuroimaging', *Annual Review of Psychology* 55 (2004), 87).

(iv) 'The central concepts implicated in mindreading, for example, *belief*, *desire*, *intention*, are remarkably sophisticated concepts referring to unobservable states' (S. Nichols and S. Stich, *Mindreading: an Integrated Account of Pretence, Self-Awareness, and Understanding of Other Minds* (Oxford University Press, Oxford, 2003), p. 4).

(v) 'Mindreading is mysterious because there are genuine conceptual puzzles about how it is even possible to know the minds of others. Most obviously, we do not have direct access to what other people know, want, intend, believe, but must infer these mental states on the basis of what they do and what they say' (I. Apperly, *Mindreaders: The Cognitive Basis of Theory of Mind* (Psychology Press, Hove, 2011), p. 1).

conceptual conundrums associated with the problem of knowledge of other minds. For that is a tangle of purely *conceptual* problems that can be resolved only by conceptual means, that is, by systematic connective analysis of a whole field of interlocking concepts.

Psychologists rightly investigate infant learning, both in respect of responsiveness to the behaviour of others and in respect of the stages in the acquisition and use of the psychological vocabulary. Doubtless the conceptual pitfalls are numerous (see chapter 4). Conceptual clarity is a *sine qua non* for any advance, and the jettisoning of theories, such as theory-theories and simulation theories, is essential for intellectual coherence. Once that has been attained, *then* there is room for empirical theories that are subject to the normal canons of validation and falsification.

## 4. Empathy and sympathy

*Domain of sympathy/empathy and its limits*  Our task is to clarify the relationship between sympathy and empathy. It may be helpful first to list the relevant dispositions, tendencies, powers, and feelings (see list 12.1).

Note that understanding the mental condition of another that is preparatory to harming the other or which involves taking pleasure in the misfortune of another is excluded from the field of operation of empathy and sympathy. Consequently we exclude the understanding that the interrogator has for his victim (depicted in two different forms in Arthur Koestler's *Darkness at Noon* in Rubashov's successive interrogation by Ivanov and Gletkin). We similarly exclude a torturer's understanding of the victim's ability or inability to withstand further pain, even though that too may involve insight into the feelings of another (Room 101 in Orwell's *1984*). We also exclude emotional reactions to the manifest emotions of others that are independent of our own commiserative or ameliorative response: as when we withdraw in fright from another's rage, or react resentfully to another's contempt for us. In such common cases we certainly recognize the emotion or emotional attitude with which we are confronted, but no question of sympathy or empathy arises.

*Desert belongs with sympathy but not with empathy*  We have noted one major conceptual difference between sympathy and empathy: namely, that one may or may not

(i)   Infectious crowd emotions.
(ii)  Emotional responses to the plight and joys of others:
      (a)   to their plight:
            • by feeling distress for them;
            • by sharing the same emotion with them;
      (b)   to their joys and delight:
            • by being pleased for them;
            • by sharing the same emotion with them.
(iii) Attaining an understanding of the feelings of others with
      whom one is confronted:
      (a)   a single person;
      (b)   a multiplicity of persons, a crowd.
(iv)  Identification with another in their predicament, which
      may or may not be emotional:
      (a)   an actual person;
      (b)   a fictional personage in a novel, poem, drama, or film.
(v)   Hermeneutical understanding:
      (a)   of historical texts;
      (b)   of other cultures:
            • past;
            • present;
      (c)   of other people.

**List 12.1**   *The field for sympathy and empathy*

*deserve* the sympathy of another, but one cannot deserve or fail to
deserve the empathy of another. So sympathy is bound up with axiological judgement in a way in which empathy is not. That is patent in
our use of the verb 'to sympathize with', which, at least in some contexts, implies understanding the predicament of another, coupled with
the supportive judgement that the distress of the other person is warranted by the magnitude of their misfortune and that the misfortune
is undeserved.

It is noteworthy that the sentiment viewed with sympathy is understood as having practical consequences. These one may not wish to
endorse. That is why one can say, 'I sympathize with the Ruritanians,
but I don't condone their use of violence.' By contrast, one could not
say, 'I empathize with the Ruritanians, but I don't endorse their use of

violence.' In this use of 'sympathy' or 'sympathize', the notion is located in the vicinity of emotional attitude and judgement.

*Mitfühlen and einfühlen* Despite the efforts of Hume and Smith, the concept of sympathy does not have the good fortune of others as its object: one may be delighted at the success of one's friend, but one is not sympathetic with Jack because he got an award, nor is one full of sympathy with Jill because of her promotion – rather, one is pleased or overjoyed. A *fortiori*, one does not sympathize with them in their good fortune. But one may be said to *respond empathetically*, that is, to share in their joy. If one says that one responds *in sympathy* with the joy of another, that is a use of 'sympathy' (i.e. sympathetic reverberation) that signifies no more than concord. In this use and this context, there is no difference between an empathetic response and a sympathetic one. Here 'empathy' signifies concordance of positive emotion in response to the positive emotion of another person – finding joy in their joy, for example.

*Feelings* of sympathy are not intrinsically linked to understanding (in the manner in which empathy typically is), but are rather an emotional response to another's plight. (If empathy is *einfühlen*, then, one might say, sympathy is *mitfühlen*.) The behavioural expression of a feeling of sympathy is the manifestation of concern and distress at the lot of the other person, and consolatory action intended to mitigate their suffering. One's heart, metaphorically speaking, may 'bleed with sympathy' for a suffering child. But one could hardly be said to 'bleed with empathy'.

*Sympathy and imagination; motive; susceptibility* Sympathy may on occasion involve imagination, inasmuch as one has to imagine how another person is feeling in the predicament and circumstances at hand. Indeed, someone may lack sympathy for another through lack of imagination. Nevertheless, there are numerous occasions in which one needs no imagination to apprehend the plight of another, since it is patent. One's indifference then (watching public executions, boxing matches, bull-fights, abject poverty, human suffering) does not stem from lack of imagination. While *sympathetic understanding* of, and sympathizing with, the plight of another is primarily a cogitative response, the *feelings of sympathy* that one may have for another are primarily a commiserative emotional one. To be sure, the two commonly coincide.

Sympathy is a motive for action, since it provides a pattern of backward- and forward-looking reasons. The pattern is straightforward.

It involves recognition (or supposed recognition) of the plight of another, which one views with distress, and one acts in order to ameliorate or mitigate their distress. The pattern is indeed homological with compassion.

As we noted earlier, the capacity for sympathy is a power (not equally distributed) that may be cultivated or crushed. Feeling sympathy for another is a susceptibility – a passion rather than an action. Showing sympathy for another in one's facial expression or voice is often only partly voluntary (not displayed on purpose, let alone intentionally, but capable of being suppressed), but the expressions of sympathy in consolatory behaviour is intentional.

*'I sympathize':*
*a quasi-performative*

Finally, 'I sympathize with you' or 'You have my sympathy' are quasi-performative utterances in the sense that to utter these sentences on appropriate occasions *is* sympathizing with the addressee and indeed is *giving* the addressee one's sympathy. By contrast, to say 'I like you' is not liking the addressee. The former utterance, one might say, *is* a sympathizing, whereas the latter is not a liking. 'I sympathize with you' is only a *quasi*-performative inasmuch as, unlike promising (which is a paradigmatic performative utterance), insincerity defeats the performance. To say 'I sympathize with you' insincerely is to pretend to sympathize, whereas to say 'I promise' insincerely is still to make a promise, not to pretend to make one.

*Empathy not typically*
*an emotion*

Empathy, by contrast, is primarily an active power of the understanding and of the cogitative imagination. For the most part, it is not an emotion at all. In its legitimate use, it is linked with the ability to understand the thoughts, feelings, and experiences of others. There is little use for 'I empathize with you' (as opposed to 'I feel empathy for her') and it is not a quasi-performative utterance. If we are going to employ the expressions 'empathy' and 'empathetic understanding' as rough translations of *Einfühlen*, then empathy is a prerequisite of hermeneutics: the interpretation of texts and of the thoughts expressed in them. But it is not obvious that, pomposity apart, the readily available expressions 'having a feel for what he says/writes/thinks', 'knowing how his mind works', or 'having a gift for penetrating these (ancient/obscure) texts' do not achieve what is wanted with greater perspicuity. To be sure, we have further metaphorical phrases here, such as 'working one's way into his mind' and 're-enacting his thought and experience', but these are misleading. For nothing mysterious is involved – only sensitive scholarship and imagination aimed at coming to understand how the author thinks and reasons, and what he values. It is a moot point whether a writer can have an empathetic understanding of an obnoxious and morally repulsive text. Does a translator of Heinrich Kramer's *Malleus Maleficarum* (*The Hammer of Witches*) need empathy with the mind of a witch-hunter? The editors of the recent heavily annotated edition of *Mein Kampf* certainly display an understanding of an evil mind. Does their editorial work display empathy or empathetic understanding? That is doubtful. To be sure, nothing of that kind was suggested by those who introduced the expression, nor is it intimated by current usage. The matter is, therefore, at best indeterminate. What is certain, however, is that one may understand an evil mind without feeling or displaying sympathy or, indeed, sympathetic understanding.

*Sympathetic/empathetic understanding* Herder's introduction of the term *Einfühlung* in association with hermeneutics enabled subsequent thinkers, such as Schleiermacher, to isolate, elaborate, and describe the kinds of skills necessary to reach an understanding of problematic texts. Here it is surely useful to speak of *empathetic understanding*. But it should be noted that *sympathetic understanding* would have been equally appropriate, and would have met with Herder's approval or at least quiescence. *These* two notions surely coincide, save for the case of reaching an understanding of repulsive or evil writings, where sympathy is definitely excluded. The received expression 'feeling one's way into the author's mind' is a mere metaphor for the ability to elicit the best or most plausible interpretation of the text.

From trying to understand ancient or alien texts and trying to interpret problematic early modern or modern texts it is but a short step to trying to understand other human beings – their behaviour, their plans and projects, their emotions. We must distinguish between (i) understanding an individual whom one confronts in discourse, as a patient, or as a subject for painting; (ii) understanding a multitude (a crowd) that one addresses; (iii) understanding a fictional character in a novel, opera, or drama that one watches, or that constitutes a role one performs on stage or film.

*Being empathetic as a power* One person may be much more sensitive than others in apprehending what another person feels and thinks, how another is likely to respond to such-and-such circumstances. He is, we may then say, exceptionally empathetic – having, as it were, more refined antennae than the rest of us. This signifies not an emotion but a power or character trait. To be empathetic in this sense does not imply being sympathetic or readily feeling sympathy for others who are in distress. What it implies is a heightened sensitivity to the character, personality, and feelings of a person one encounters. One may encounter unpleasant people, with whom one has no sympathy at all. One may be a ruthless and ambitious person eager only to use people, not to ameliorate their suffering. But one may nevertheless have the power to grasp quickly what makes others 'tick', what kind of person they are, what moves them to action. Similarly, an empathetic portrait painter may have the gift of apprehending the character and temperament of the subject they are depicting, but they need not feel sympathy for their subject (Goya is a paradigm here).

Very different are the sympathetic and empathetic powers of those whose vocation it is to treat people in person in order to cure them or to ameliorate their suffering. One may say of a doctor, a psychiatrist, or a clinical psychologist that they need, or that they have a gift for, empathy. For this and for its exercise, identification with the patient or subject of investigation is neither necessary nor desirable. What is sought is *understanding the patient's mental condition* – since the therapist must treat a patient, a person, not merely a disease that happens to have settled onto a bearer. For that, the ability *to listen* to the patient is paramount, as is the ability to inspire the patient's confidence. It is difficult to discern any difference here between *empathetic understanding* and *sympathetic understanding*. Among those who treat and attempt to *ameliorate* the lot of the sick and suffering, empathy should go hand in hand with sympathy for their suffering.

*Rhetoric and empathy*          A good rhetorician may have empathy with or for ('a feel for') the crowd he addresses. Indeed, rhetoricians *need* such empathy with their audience if they are to play successfully on their heart strings. Hitler, an evil genius, undoubtedly understood the mentality of his audiences, knew what moved them and how to move them. (So does Mark Antony, unlike Brutus, in the funeral address in *Julius Caesar*.) Does having empathy in this sense imply sympathy? Not at all. When De Gaulle addressed the Algerian *pieds noirs* in 1958, famously telling them to their delight 'Je vous ai compris' (I have understood you), he might be said to have had empathy with the settlers, but to have concealed his lack of sympathy. And Antony certainly had no sympathy whatsoever for the Roman plebs, either in Shakespeare's historical drama or in fact. One should, however, note that *to have empathy for* one's audience does not imply *empathizing with* them.

Human beings have the power to identify with another, either with another person whom they know and love, or with someone they admire, or with imaginary characters in fiction, poetry, drama, and cinema. Is this a form of empathy or of sympathy? It is not obvious that it is either. It certainly seems possible to have marked susceptibility to the emotions expressed by music and opera, and an ability to identify with fictional protagonists in drama and fiction, while showing total indifference to actual human suffering. We do not enrich the notion of *the ability to identify with another* or the notion of *identifying with another* by subsuming either under the concept of empathy, nor do we illuminate them.

*Einfühlen and acting/art of biography*

Similarly, actors need *to feel their way into* a role. They need to understand the character presented by the playwright. But here, one may say, *einfühlen* is one thing, *einsfühlen* another. It is only Method actors who feel the need to identify deeply with the role they play. Lawrence Olivier is said to have remarked to Dustin Hoffman, who had starved and gone sleepless for three nights in order to identify fully with the role he was playing, 'Dear boy, why don't you try acting? It's so much easier!' Certainly actors do not have to sympathize with or to feel sympathy for the character they play (Iago, Lady Macbeth, Claudius), but they do have to understand the role. Does that imply that they must be *in empathy with* the role or *empathize with* the character they are playing? Nothing seems to be gained by forcing the phenomena into this straightjacket. But it is true that playing an evil or distraught character night after night on the stage may be a great emotional strain.

Hermeneutical understanding of another person 'at arm's length', as it were, is exhibited in the art of biography. It may or may not involve sympathy with and sympathetic understanding of the person about whom the author writes. It is not true that *tout comprendre c'est tout pardoner* (to understand all is to forgive all), and biographers of Hitler, Stalin, or Mao surely do not need sympathy in order to understand their subjects. Biographers need to understand how their subject's mind worked, how he thought and reasoned, what he valued and believed, how his character was formed and developed. In this sense it can be said to demand *einfühlen*. It is not clear, however, whether the newcomer to English, *empathy*, is rightly invoked in the case of a biographer's understanding an evil person. 'Empathize' seems definitely excluded.

In anthropological engagement with other societies, empathy is likewise an interpretive skill, not of alien texts, but of an alien culture. The anthropologist strives after an understanding of the ways of living, thinking, and feeling characteristic of a different form of life. Not only must ways of behaving be understood, but also belief systems and values. Here too, empathy is not an emotion but a form of understanding. This is a major theme in the philosophy of anthropology and of the social sciences.

## 5. Envoi

The capacity for fellow feeling, as we have noted, is unevenly distributed. Some people are more sensitive than others to the woes and joys of human beings. Fellow feeling may easily be washed away under stress. Sympathy may easily be destroyed under peer pressure. It is not a rock upon which morality is built, any more than is pure practical reason, for morality is not built on rock. Hume and Smith were surely right to suppose that without a natural power of sympathy there would be no morality. But they were mistaken to subordinate reason to the passions, for the heart too has its reasons that may be perfectly clear to the understanding, even though understanding and good judgement are necessary to monitor and guide them. Kant was surely right to link morality to reason, for without the power to reason, and the power to examine and weigh reasons for and against different courses of action, there could be no such thing as responsible moral agency. But he was mistaken to suppose that beings that lacked natural sympathy and the power of empathy could recognize the good of others as reasons for action.

This, however, is a tale for another book, which will examine human nature and its relationship to the good of man; human character, personality, and temperament and their relationship to good and evil; the nature of happiness and of a good human life; and the place of death in human life.

# Appendix:
# Moments in the History of Love

## 1. The history of love

*Love itself has a history* As we have seen in chapter 10, the love between individual human beings runs a course. It has a developing history, some of the possible forms of which we have examined. But over and above that, there is an important sense in which the *emotion* of love as such has a history. This could not be said of such emotions as fear or anger, joy or sorrow. Different concepts and different conceptions of love condition and mould the forms which the emotion of love takes. Love of God would have been unintelligible to the ancient Greeks and Romans. To do something for the sake of the love of Zeus or the love of Aphrodite was not a possible motive in Periclean Athens. The thought that the gods might *love* humanity as such (as opposed to individual gods fornicating with chosen girls and boys) would have struck the Romans as utterly bizarre. When love is held to be above all the love of youthful and beautiful boys, then the idea of marital love of a man to an inferior being, namely his wife, is not going to find much space. If the love of God is conceived to be the only form of perfected and pure love – as it was in early Christianity, then interpersonal erotic love may be, and was, relegated to a vice or conceived to be a weakness that may be tolerated.

*The Passions: A Study of Human Nature*, First Edition. P. M. S. Hacker.
© 2018 John Wiley & Sons Ltd. Published 2018 by John Wiley & Sons Ltd.

This appendix is a historical supplement to chapter 10. Western conceptions of love have their roots in Jerusalem, Athens, and Rome. To grasp not only where we are now, but also why we are where we are, it is illuminating to examine where we came from. For we are heirs to conflicting conceptions and shifting concepts of love. The discussion that follows is an attempt to give a much simplified synoptic view of what is a very complex weave of philosophical, psychological, physiological, and theological doctrines and social practices, and very different notions of relationships between human beings, their gods, this world, and the supposed afterworld. It is not a history of love – that is a subject for a whole book or series of books.[1] Rather, what I have done is to pick out a few 'moments' in the evolution of ideas of love in our culture, which, on the one hand, changed the course of human sentiment and experience in the West, foreclosing certain emotional possibilities and opening others, and, on the other hand, moulding the concept and creating new conceptions of love.

I have selected the following six moments in the evo-
*Six moments* lution of our concepts and conceptions of love: (i) the
*in its history* notions of love in the Old Testament and early rabbinical doctrine; (ii) Plato's conception of love and the socio-
historical context in which it was advanced; (iii) late republican and early imperial conceptions of love in Rome, which provided the seedbed for Christianity; (iv) early Christian concepts and conceptions of love; (v) the emergence of the idea of courtly love that elevated women as never before and sanctified unconsummated erotic love of a married noblewoman by an aristocratic youth or knight, and the impact of this idea upon medieval Italy and later upon the Renaissance; and (vi) the deification of love itself as it emerged in Romanticism in the late eighteenth and nineteenth centuries.

This will, I hope, serve to illuminate the extent to which the strands woven together to form our own twentieth- and twenty-first-century concepts and conceptions of love in the West are arbitrary (without being haphazard). It is not *necessary* to view the premarital passions of infatuated youth as being the same emotion as those associated with marriage, companionate or otherwise – but we do. Intergenerational love could well be conceived to be a different emotion from sexual love. It is not *necessary* to detach

---

[1] For example, I. Singer, *The Nature of Love*, 3 vols. (University of Chicago Press, Chicago, 1987–94); S. May, *Love: a History* (Yale University Press, New Haven, 2011). I am indebted to both.

friendship from love – but to a large extent we moderns do (few of us will tell our close friends that we *love* them). It is surely inessential to link intense liking and admiration of art or nature by means of the concept of love with the erotic relation between human beings – but we do.

## 2. Ancient Israel

*Ancient Hebrew* The primary Hebrew noun for love is *ahava*, the
*vocabulary of love* infinitive of which is *le'ehov*. The expression and its
cognates apply to God's love of his creation, of mankind in general, and of the covenanted people of Israel in particular; to the love of God; to erotic love (as in Song of Songs); to marital love (as in tales of the patriarchs and in Proverbs); to parental love (Genesis 22: 2; 25: 28; 37: 3); to devoted love between friends of the same sex (1 Samuel 18: 2; 20: 17); and to the love of one's neighbour – *re'ekha*, one who is nigh unto one (Leviticus 19: 18). It also applies to love of a place, for example Jerusalem (Isaiah 66: 10), and of abstract values, such as justice (Psalms 33: 5; 37: 28). The expression *khesed* signifies loving kindness, steadfast love, affection, and compassion (hence comparable to the Christian use of *caritas*). *Re'ut* is a more specialized term, meaning love of a friend or companion.[2]

The ancient Hebrews were the originators
*Love of God and of one's* of monotheism. Initially, like the Atonists in
*neighbour in the Torah* Egypt, they were monolatrists. By the sixth
century, monotheism was displacing monolatry. Among the commandments of the Torah,[3] two were paramount. The first is, as it were, the presupposition of all the others. It is the requirement that 'Thou shalt love the Lord thy God with all thine heart, and with all thy soul, and with all thy might'[4] (Deuteronomy 6: 5),[5]

---

[2] There are also other expressions, such as *kheshek* (desire, passion), *dodim* (sexual love, love-making), *t'shuka* (intense passion, erotic yearning), *ta'avah* (appetite), *yad'a* (to have sexual intercourse, 'to know').

[3] The word 'Torah' is ambiguous, sometimes referring to the Pentateuch, sometimes, as earlier, to the commandments of God.

[4] 'Soul' here is not the Platonic *psuchē*, an immortal spiritual substance, but rather the principle of life, as it were: vitality. 'With all your might' is a slightly misleading translation of *m'odekha*, which is simply an intensifier (roughly 'as much as you can').

[5] See also Deuteronomy 10: 12; 11: 1, 13, 22; 30: 6, 16, and Joshua 22: 5, with slightly different phrasing. Deuteronomy is generally considered to have been written in the seventh century BC during the reign of King Josiah.

a command coeval here with the recognition of the uniqueness and
unity of God ('Hear, O Israel: the Lord is our God, the Lord is one'
(Deuteronomy 6: 4)). Whether and how it is possible to command
*love*, which is a passion, not an action, needs to be clarified. So too
does the very idea of loving *God*, as well as the commitments involved
in loving God. The second is: 'Thou shalt love thy neighbour (*re'ekha*)
as thyself' (Leviticus 19: 18).[6] Both Hillel the Elder (first century BC)
and his school (the House of Hillel) and the great Rabbi Akiva (ca. AD
40–ca. AD 137) held this to be *the* fundamental principle of the
Torah – the Great Commandment. Who is to count as one's neighbour, what loving one's neighbour is supposed to amount to, and
what is meant by loving one's neighbour as one loves oneself, given
that self-love is not a form of love at all, are all contentious matters
that needed clarification (which was duly given by rabbinical commentary). What the relationship between these two commandments is
also calls out for elucidation, for they are not textually connected.
This too was clarified by rabbinical interpretation. Although the
Golden Rule does not occur in the Old Testament, it was well known
in the first century BC. Hillel, when asked to explain the Torah to a
pagan in a word, famously replied, 'What is hateful to you, do not do
to your neighbour [*re'ekha*]. This is the whole of the Torah. The rest
is commentary. Now go and learn.'

*How love of God can be commanded*     The command to love God is strange for numerous reasons. First, it presupposes the intelligibility
of the very idea of God in one form or another (the
idea of God in Judaism underwent extensive development between the monolatrist conception in the twelfth century BC
and the transcendent monotheist conception of the first century BC).
Secondly, the very idea that God, an all-perfect being, might *love* anything is (as Aristotle, and many centuries later, Spinoza noted) highly
problematic. Among other things, love, as we have seen, craves reciprocity, betokening the lack of something, which, if not received, constitutes a form of suffering incompatible with the perfection of God.
This was to be the subject of extensive rabbinical and Christian theological debate that continues to this day. Thirdly, the idea of *loving* a
god, as opposed to fearing and revering one is bizarre, and seemed so

[6] The dating of Leviticus is problematic. It is generally agreed to contain elements
dating back to the late seventh century BC, some elements from the Babylonian exile
and post-exilic period of the sixth and fifth centuries.

to pagan polytheists of those times. These three problems or clusters of problems will not be discussed here.

*Covenantal love*     The fourth problem *does* concern us, since it is a conceptual problem about the nature of love, rather than about the nature of God. The command to love God seems strange if we conceive of it as an order to feel an emotion (what Kant was later to call *pathological love*). But that would be misguided. The commandment is a requirement of *covenantal love*. The form of the commandment, together with the use of cognates of *ahava*, is modelled on ancient Near Eastern treaties between a vassal king and a great king, in which the former swears exclusive loyalty and service.[7] Here the people of Israel are conceived to be in the position of the vassal, and God in that of the supreme king. The Sinaitical covenant is a conditional one, unlike the Abrahamic covenant, which is a solemn pledge by God to the father of the people of Israel. The latter contains no stipulations about how Abraham's descendants must behave. The Sinaitical covenant, by contrast, demands of the people of Israel exclusive loyalty and service to God that is to be expressed in obedience to his commandments. The emphasis upon *commandments* (*Mitzvot*) rather than *laws* is important, for the notion of law is impersonal (its general form, one might say, is: 'All so-and-so's are to do thus-and-so'), whereas that of commandment is personal, addressed by God to the people of Israel both collectively and severally (its general form is: 'Thou shalt do thus-and-so'). The conditionality is expressed in Exodus 19: 5–6: 'Now, if ye will obey my voice indeed, and keep my covenant [*briti*], then ye shall be a peculiar treasure unto me above all people: for all the earth is mine. And ye shall be unto me a kingdom of priests, and an holy nation.' The people of Israel were chosen to bear the burden of the commandments of their God, and to live virtuous and holy lives – a conception later articulated as 'being a light unto the nations'.

However, what is required is not mere obedience but willing obedience rooted in reverence. For the commandments must be accepted and followed with good will. To be sure, protection and rewards are promised for fidelity. But to obey the commandments out of

---

[7] See M. Weinfeld, *Deuteronomy and the Deuteronomic School* (Oxford University Press, Oxford, 1972), and J. D. Levenson, *The Love of God: Divine Gift, Human Gratitude, and Mutual Faithfulness in Judaism* (Princeton University Press, Princeton, 2015).

self-interested considerations, that is, for the sake of the munificence of God, would not exhibit *loving obedience* at all. Rather, obedience must be as a loving son obeys his father, not reluctantly but eagerly. Loving obedience is the manifestation of unconditional and enthusiastic *commitment* ('with all your heart, with all your soul, and with all your might'). The parental analogy is carefully chosen. It is expressed in Moses's final address to his people: 'Know then [*v'yadata*] in thine heart, that, as a man chasteneth his son, so the Lord thy God chasteneth thee. Therefore thou shalt keep the commandments of the Lord thy God, to walk in his ways, and to fear [revere?] him' (Deuteronomy 8: 5–6).[8] In general, the paternal simile emphasizes reciprocal love between father and son. This is not love between equals. It is compatible with filial reverence and with fear of disapproval, of disappointment, or of giving offence. It is also compatible with fear of God's chastisement in the event of disobedience, with awe of his infinite power, and with fear of his omniscience. However, the *motive* for obedience to God should never be fear, but always love. Love of God, therefore, is not 'pathological love' but 'practical love'. Primacy is given to the *deeds* of obedience. The affective element comes from the relationship to God, for the obedience expresses personal fidelity, faithfulness, trust, and reverence. It is these that constitute the love enjoined upon the people of Israel in their covenantal relation to God. Rational conformity to the Kantian categorical imperative is considered, by pious intellectual Jews today, to be far inferior to the performance of the same deed out of love of God.

*Old Testament analogies for love of God* The analogies invoked throughout the Old Testament to illuminate the reciprocal relation of God and the people of Israel are suzerain and vassal, father and son, shepherd and flock, husband and wife, and lover and beloved. The marital analogy emphasizes love, obedience, fidelity, and reciprocal trust; it enables the presentation of reversion to idolatry as infidelity to God (going a whoring after other gods), which is akin to adultery (prominent in Hosea,

---

[8] The King James translation is perhaps misleading here. The Hebrew that has been translated as 'fear' is *yir'ah*. This word occurs more than forty times in the Old Testament. It can mean terror or fear, but also reverence and awe. Associated with God, as in *Yir'at Adonai* (*Elohim*, *Shaddai*), it commonly means reverence of God. Which it means here is a matter of interpretation. Note also that there is no 'Therefore' in the original.

Jeremiah, and Ezekiel). The analogy with the erotic relation of young lovers is paramount in the rabbinical interpretation of the Song of Songs. This interpretation, to be sure, postdates the composition of this sequence of secular erotic love poems, the date of which is highly contested (between the eighth and second centuries BC). But its late adoption into the canon of the Old Testament (ca. first century AD) and its evident appeal as a symbolic representation of the relation between God and Israel sheds light upon the rabbinical conception of the love of God in the first and second centuries AD. It served to *ekstasize* and eroticize the love of God, a peculiar feature common both to Jewish and to Christian mystical theology throughout subsequent centuries. Nevertheless, the *expression* of the loving relationship to God is not a craving for trance-like unity with God (as later mystical theologians, both Jewish and Christian, claimed), but rather willing obedience to his laws and commands. The covenantal love and the trust demanded must be unconditional and unlimited, *in extremis* even, transcending morality (as exemplified by the tale of the sacrifice of Isaac, which was the inspiration of Kierkegaard's *Fear and Trembling*). For the love of God involves submission to fate and necessity (elaborated in the book of Job). However, it does not require self-abasement, let alone self-inflicted pain (e.g. flagellation) or self-mutilation (e.g. castration), or annihilation of 'the self'. In these respects it differs from some subsequent Gnostic and Christian doctrines and practices.[9]

The Jewish conception of the love of God in the diaspora after the fall of the Second Temple is powerfully expressed in a poem by the great Sephardic scholar and poet Yehuda Halevi (1070–1141):

> With all my heart, in truth, and with all my might
> I have loved You, outwardly and inwardly.
> Your name is before me: How could I walk alone?

[9] Castration and self-castration, practised in the cult of Baal in Canaan, was strictly forbidden in Judaism, as were flagellation and any form of mutilation. It was practised in the Egyptian cult of Isis, the Greek mysteries of Dionysus, and the Roman cult of the Phrygian goddess Cybele. Self-castration became a practice among early Christians (the most famous being Origen and Melito, Bishop of Sardis) on the basis of their interpretation of Matthew 19: 12, Romans 8: 13, Galatians 5: 24, and 1 Corinthians 9: 27. The practice was sufficiently widespread to need explicit condemnation at the Council of Nicaea in AD 325, despite which it persisted for another century. Flagellation, of course, persists in Catholicism in various countries to this day. It is common among Shi'a Muslims too. In general, self-abasement emphasizes to oneself the vast gulf between oneself, with all one's weaknesses (real and imaginary), and the all-perfect God. This resonated among Calvinists.

He is my beloved: how could I sit solitary?
He is my lamp: How could my light go out?
How could I slip? He is a staff in my hand.
They have held me in contempt, who do not understand
That the shame I endure for the glory of Your name is my glory.
Fountain of life to me, I shall bless You while I live.
My song I shall sing to You as long as I exist.[10]

*How love of neighbour can be commanded*     The commandment to love your neighbour presents a similar problem as the commandment to love God, namely that feelings of love cannot be generated at will, and therefore cannot be ordered. So the commandment needs interpreting. What is demanded of one is that one treat one's neighbour with respect, righteousness, and impartial justice. To comply with these demands with good will (without reluctance) *is* to love one's neighbour. The charitable laws that are laid down for the benefit of the neighbour are numerous, ranging from permitting the gleaning of the harvest, supplying food and clothing, to access to impartial justice. One's neighbour, it is clear, is not simply the family living next door, so to speak, but anyone one might encounter. Nor is the commandment restricted to one's own people or co-religionists. For Leviticus 19: 34 elaborates the command of verse 18: 'the stranger [*ger*, alien] that dwelleth with you shall be unto you as one born among you, and thou shalt love him as thyself, for ye were strangers in the land of Egypt.' This is echoed in Deuteronomy 10: 18–19, which articulates the commandment in the form of *imitatio Dei*: God himself 'doth execute the judgement of [*oseh mish'pat*, gives judgement for] the fatherless [*yatom*, orphan] and the widow, and loveth the stranger, in giving him food and raiments. Love ye therefore the stranger, for ye were strangers in the land of Egypt.' The extension of 'practical love' to one's enemy is also striking. Exodus 23: 4–5 commands: 'If thou meet thine enemy's ox or his ass going astray, thou shalt surely bring it back to him again. If thou seest the ass of him that hateth thee lying under his burden, and wouldst forebear to help him, thou shalt surely help him.' Proverbs adds: 'Rejoice not when thy enemy falleth, and let not thy heart be glad when he stumbleth' (24: 17) and 'if thine enemy be hungry, give him bread to eat; and if he be thirsty, give him water to drink' (25: 21). It is noteworthy that the practical love of one's neighbour that is commanded in the Old Testament differs from Plato's *eros* and

---

[10] Quoted in Levenson, *The Love of God*, p. 74.

Aristotle's *philia* in two important respects: (i) it is not limited to one's social equals, and (ii) it is not limited to those who are virtuous.

*Marriage and erotic love in Old Testament*

Throughout the centuries of the composition of the Old Testament, and in the multitude of legends and histories in its books, it is evident that the ancient Hebrews were patriarchal and polygynous (although the practice declined during the period of the Second Temple). Despite the patriarchalism, prior to the first millennium BC, the tribes of Israel accepted Deborah as a judge over them; Atalya became queen of Judah after the assassination of her son Ahazyah and reigned for seven years (842/1–836/5 BC); and in the first century BC Queen Salome Alexandra (Shlom-Tsion), widow of King Alexander Yannai, ruled Judea as queen regent for nine years (76–67 BC). This conforms with the practices of other Near Eastern kingdoms, but not with the later practices of Greece and Rome. Marriage and erotic love within marriage were permitted not merely as a concession to human weakness (a view later advanced by Paul), but were regarded as natural, and were exalted.[11] Nor was erotic love confined to reproductive purposes. Divorce was permissible, as was remarriage. Adultery was strictly forbidden and was punishable by death. There is no hint of the profound anxiety about erotic love that characterizes Christianity from Paul onwards and comes to dominate early Christianity and hence late Roman conceptions of human, social, and religious life. Nor is there any attempt to elevate *eros* beyond what is human, as is characteristic of Plato and neo-Platonism. The temptations of extramarital love and its dangers are highlighted by the amorous adventures of Samson and his betrayal by Delilah. The passion of adulterous love and the wickedness to which it can lead is illustrated in the tale of David and Bathsheba. Erotic love is celebrated in the Song of Songs.

*Friendship-love in Old Testament*

Loving friendship between man and man is exemplified by the relationship between David and Jonathan. The soul of Jonathan is described as being 'knit with the soul of David' and Jonathan is said to have 'loved him as his own soul' (1 Samuel 18: 1). David's lament for the death of Jonathan is of surpassing beauty, some of which survives translation:

Saul and Jonathan were lovely and pleasant in their lives,
And in their death they were not divided:

[11] Indeed, a newly wed man was not liable for military service for one year, but should dwell at home in order to make his wife happy (Deuteronomy 24: 5).

They were swifter than eagles,
They were stronger than lions.
...

How are the mighty fallen in the midst of the battle!
O Jonathan, thou wast slain in thine high places.
I am distressed for thee, my brother Jonathan:
Very pleasant hast thou been to me:
Thy love to me was wonderful,
Passing the love of women.

(2 Samuel 1: 23, 25–6)

Comparable love, expressed with great power and simplicity, is that between Ruth and Naomi. Ruth, a Moabite, the widow of one of Naomi's sons, accompanies her adored widowed mother-in-law on her return to the land of Judah. She swears an oath of loving loyalty:

Whither thou goest, I will go;
And where thou lodgest, I will lodge;
Thy people shall be my people,
And thy God my God:
Where thou diest, will I die,
And there will I be buried.

(Ruth 1: 16–17)

Both these examples manifest deep non-erotic friendship-love. It is akin to Aristotelian *philia*, save for three features. First, in neither case is the love between social equals. Secondly, such love is not conceived to be restricted to men. Thirdly, it does not demand the perfect virtue of the Aristotelian *megalopsuchos*.

However, homosexuality, irrespective of consent between adult partners, was punished by death. Lesbian love is unmentioned. Unlike other countries in the vicinity, no distinction was drawn in ancient Israel between the passive and active role among homosexuals – both were equally abhorrent. Erotic relationships between free men was not, as in Rome, a matter of immeasurable and irremediable shame for the passive partner, but an 'abomination' irrespective of gender role. It is not evident what motivated this stringent moral prohibition.

## 3. Ancient Greece

The conceptions of love that dominated classical Greece differ fundamentally from those that informed ancient Israel. Greek culture was polytheistic, in which the gods were revered and worshipped, but not loved. Far from the gods of Olympus loving mankind, human beings were the playthings of the gods, hence a tragic sense of life and its fragility permeate Greek thought. There was no room for a theodicy in ancient Greek thought.

*Status of women in ancient Greece* The position of women in classical Athens was in many ways similar to that of women in traditional Islamic societies today. They were part of the household (*oikos*) governed by the head of the household, the *kyrios* (master), who was responsible for all women in the household. The *kyrios* arranged marriages for his daughters and any other female relatives in the household, and provided the necessary dowry. On marriage, the bride's husband became her new *kyrios*. Divorce was licit by mutual consent or by individual initiative, although a woman needed the help of her father or other male member of her family to represent her in court. After divorce, her dowry was returned to her *kyrios*, together with half the goods she had produced during her marriage. Any children remained in paternal custody. Women could neither speak nor vote in the assembly. They had very limited property rights: only to their dowry, gifts, and inherited property, and they could engage in only minor financial transactions. A wife's *kyrios* could dispose of her property and was responsible for any debts she might incur. Respectable women lived secluded lives within the household in the *gynaikon* (women's quarters), venturing forth in public only to get water from the well (a place for women to meet and gossip), for funerals, and to participate in the processions and rituals of public festivals such as the Panathenaia (for Athena), the Eleusinian Mysteries (Demeter and Persephone), the Anthesteria (Dionysus), and a few other festivals that were exclusively for women. Women were allowed to attend (but not to participate in) public speeches, to visit sanctuaries, and to bring offerings to family tombs. When in public, they were clothed from shoulders to ankle, and their neck and long hair veiled. Their role was to run the household, to spin and weave, and to produce children. The average marriage age for women appears to have been around thirteen, for men thirty. Prostitution was institutionalized in brothels, the prostitutes (*pornai*) being for the most part slaves. Courtesans (*hetairai*) were educated and cultivated women (similar to geishas in shogunate Japan). It was only they who could enter society and mix with the male aristocracy. Against this social and legal background, it should not be surprising to find Thucydides putting into Pericles' great funeral speech the words 'the greatest glory of a woman is to be least talked about by men, whether they are praising you or criticizing you'.[12] Aristotle lists the virtues of a woman as being beauty and stature, self-control and industry (*Rhetoric* 1361ª6–8). Apollodorus, as reported by Demosthenes, described the role of Athenian women candidly: 'We keep *hetairai* for the sake of pleasure, female slaves for our daily care, and wives to give us legitimate children and to be the guardians of our household.'[13] Despite this, Athens

---

[12] Thucydides, *The Peloponnesian War*, trans. R. Warner (Penguin, Harmondsworth, 1954), II. 4.

[13] Demosthenes, Oration 59, 'Theomnesta and Apollodorus against Neaera'. The contrast with Sparta, a culturally barren, eugenic, militaristic state, could not be greater. From the Lycurgan Reforms at the end of the seventh century BC (after the Second Messenian War, in which the Messenians were finally broken and subjected to helotry), Spartan women could inherit, bequeath, and own property. By the fourth century they are said to have owned 40 percent of the land. They were publicly educated at the expense of the state, enjoying some degree of literacy and numeracy, knowledge of music, dance, and poetry. They learnt to ride, run, wrestle, throw discus and javelin – their physical fitness being held to be conducive to successful child-bearing. As children, they were as well fed as boys (unlike Athenian practice). They were married between the ages of eighteen and twenty to men aged roughly twenty five, being then of sufficient age to enjoy sexual relations (thought to be necessary for conception) and to bear healthy children, and sufficiently mature to administer an estate. The whole of the male population between seven and sixty were in constant battle training. Marriage for both men and women was a duty owed to the state to ensure the supply of warriors. The young bridegrooms, however, lived in barracks and were not allowed to cohabit (pernoctate) with their wives until the age of thirty or to dine outside the barracks until the age of sixty. Divorce was possible (although a wife's adultery was not a ground for divorce) and remarriage licit. Male children were under the mother's control until the age of seven, after which they lived communally in barracks. Girls remained under their mother's care until marriage. Domestic work, including weaving, knitting, and sewing was done by *perioikoi* (non-citizen, but free, employees), freeing the wives for the administration of the estate (cultivation patterns, breeding stock selection, obtaining good seed stock), which was worked by helots. All business transactions associated with the agricultural estate was in their hands. Married women wore the Dorian peplos with slit sides, exposing their thighs. Their hair was cut short (it was adult men who had long hair) but not covered with a veil. While women were not members of the assembly, they lived public lives and engaged in public discussion and debate. They could travel freely without a male chaperone. Their primary *raison d'être* was to produce healthy warriors for the state and to administer the agricultural estates. Polyandry was not uncommon, since lineage was for the most part insignificant, all male children belonging to the state. Three or four brothers might share a wife in order not to break up a family estate. It is noteworthy that homosexuality, far from being approved as in Athens, was, according to Xenophon, condemned. One result of this female autonomy was a slow but persistently falling birth rate, which, by the fourth century led to the defeat and decline of Sparta (since it could no longer field a sufficiently large army).

invented and brought to perfection the idealized female nude (or semi-clad female) sculpture of surpassing beauty and sensuality.[14] So celebration and appreciation of female beauty was not lacking, and the public display of such sculpture was a source of civic pride. (Paradox in attitude and behaviour is close to the human heart.)

*Paederastia*     In Athens, and some other Greek city states, it was normal (at any rate among the aristocracy) for there to be a homoerotic relationship (*paederastia*) between a freeborn teenage (aged twelve to seventeen) youth (*eromenos*) and an older freeborn man (*erastes*), who, with the youth's consent, became his mentor and role model. The older man (usually in his mid- or late twenties) had to court the youth who attracted him by his beauty and character. There was no Greek expression for homosexuality, since Greek classifications cut across ours. Love of the physical beauty of youth was a natural human tendency, irrespective of its sexual orientation. What did matter crucially was the gender orientation, masculinity being associated with power and dominance. So copulation between *eromenos* and *erastes*, if any, was intercrural, penetrative copulation being strictly prohibited, since it involved a free boy assuming the subordinate role of a woman. This was irremediably shameful effeminacy, and any free male found guilty of such an ignominious offence (known as a *kinaidos*) was barred from holding any public office, and held in contempt.

*Ancient Greek vocabulary of love*     Different expressions in classical Greek converge on our notion of love, although accurate translation that will capture their subtle overtones is problematic. *Eros* and its cognates signified sexual love, infatuation, and loss of self-control in passion. *Philia* (verb *philein*, to hold dear) was used for affectionate regard, amiable hospitality, parental love, friendship, and the love of friends. *Philautia* approximates self-love, but two different kinds were distinguished: first, selfish and narcissist self-love (i.e. self-love as we might understand it (see chapter 10, section 11)); and, secondly, self-confidence, absence of self-doubt, and self-hatred. (That is perhaps one (subordinate) reason why Aristotle could say that friendship-love (*philia*) is rooted in self-love (*philautia*).) *Agape*, in early works, such as the Homeric epics, occurs only in verbal form to indicate affectionate greeting or showing affection. Subsequently it came to signify the liking of an activity and the positive relation to wife and family. Later it is used in the

---

[14] It was left to Christian Gothic art to depict the naked, as opposed to the nude, and to twentieth-century art (Schiele, Spencer, Lucian Freud) to perfect it.

Septuagint in noun form to translate the Hebrew *ahava*. Throughout the New Testament it is the primary term for love and signifies the self-sacrificial love of Jesus, the human love of God, as well as impersonal love of mankind (*caritas*). *Storge* was sometimes used to signify familial, especially parental, love. *Epithumia* meant desire, sexual longing, or lust, and *suneinai* meant sex.

*Misogynous strand in Greek thought*

It is noteworthy that from Hesiod onwards we find a degree of misogyny coupled with a streak of masculine fear of women that runs through the thought and attitudes of later centuries in Greece and Rome. Unlike the creation tale of Genesis, according to Hesiod (*Works and Days*, 54–89) woman was not created as a helpmeet for man, but as a punishment. Men had accepted the gift of fire from Prometheus, and for this Zeus punished them by ordering the creation of Pandora. She was formed out of earth by Hephaestus, in such a manner that everything visible was beautiful and irresistible, but within she was full of lies and crafty words, and had a deceitful nature. All the ills of mankind stem from her opening the box of gifts of the vengeful gods. Hence Hesiod advises, 'Do not let a flaunting woman coax and cozen and deceive you; she is after your barn. The man who trusts womankind trusts deceivers' (*Works and Days*, 373–5). Similar sentiments are expressed by Simonides ('On Women') and Euripides (in *Medea*). Aristotle held that women, like the females of other species, are inferior to males. They fall short in strength, intellect, emotional restraint, and character.

*Plato on love*

It is against this social background and belief system, that we should view *the most influential* of Greek philosophical reflections on love, namely Plato's. There is no reason to suppose that his ideas are representative. Nevertheless, his ideas were to shape both Christian and Renaissance conceptions of love. The primary source for the various views he examines is the *Symposium*.[15] The most important of the seven voices in the dialogue is that of the priestess Diotima, but some of the others articulate important ideas. Pausanias distinguishes between earthly and heavenly love (Aphrodite *Pandemos* and Aphrodite *Urania*), a distinction that

---

[15] It should be noted that Plato changed his mind about homosexual intercourse towards the end of his life. In the *Laws* (836$^b$–842), he condemned it as 'contrary to nature' and advocated complete abstention from sex save for procreative purposes within marriage. He conceded that conformity to such a law could be achieved in his ideal polity only by inculcating the fear of God. Christianity was to follow his advice.

was to enjoy a vigorous afterlife in Renaissance neo-Platonism.[16] Agathon contributes the idea that the proper object of love is beauty, and that love is the source of all virtue. It is to the figure of Aristophanes in the dialogue that we owe the comic but highly suggestive and influential myth of the unitary origin of man and woman. According to Aristophanes' tale, human beings were originally composite spherical, two-headed, four-legged, and four-armed creatures of three different kinds (men and women, men and men, and women and women). Since they planned to assault Olympus, Zeus split them into halves, each half thenceforth being fated to seek its complement. That is why lovers crave *for union* (fusion with one's 'other half') and *for completion* into a whole by their lover. Comic though this is meant to be, it articulates seriously what was fated to become a perennial refrain of romantic love, on the one hand, and of mystical love of God, on the other.[17]

All love, Plato avers, is love of the Good and the Beautiful, and a craving to possess it permanently. The most esteemed kind of earthly love is the love between the *erastes* and the *eromenos*. However, physical erotic love is the lowest and least admirable form, although, even in such homoerotic love, the striving for virtue is paramount, as each lover strives to be worthy of his beloved by his behaviour in the polis and in warfare. To attain the Good (identified with the Beautiful), each lover must ascend the ladder of love. Worldly erotic love must be purified from all particularity and humanity. Love must evolve from the love of *this* beautiful youth to the generalized love of the beauty of youth as such; from the generalized love of physical beauty to the love of the beauty of the individual soul, and thence to the love of beautiful souls. But this too is no terminus. For the quest for love must lead to the love of beautiful laws and institutions, to the love of the beauty of learning in general. The ultimate purification of love transcends all that is human, frees it of all desire for reciprocity, emancipates it from all particularity, and brings the enlightened lover to the contemplation of the Idea of Beauty in itself.

> And if, my dear Socrates, Diotima went on, man's life is ever worth the living, it is when he has attained this vision of the very soul of beauty.

---

[16] Strikingly, Pausanias asserts that, while earthly love encompasses desire for both women and boys, heavenly love is limited to *paederastia* (*Symposium*, 181$^{c-d}$).

[17] It echoes down the ages at least as far as Coleridge: 'Love is a desire of the whole being to be united to some thing, or some being, felt necessary to its completeness, by the most perfect means that nature permits, and reason dictates' (*Lectures on Shakespeare*).

> And once you have seen it, you will never be seduced again by the charm of gold, of dress, of comely boys, or lads just ripening to manhood ...
>
> And remember, she said, that it is only when he discerns beauty itself through what makes it visible that a man will be quickened with the true, and not the seeming, virtue ... And when he has brought forth and reared this perfect virtue, he shall be called the friend of god, and if ever it is given to man to put on immortality, it shall be given to him. (*Symposium*, 213$^d$–214$^b$)

In this way, love attains timelessness and transcends mortality.

This conception of love, rooted in Athenian (Megaran, Boeotian, etc.) homoerotic love, on the one hand, and general Greek attitudes towards women and marital relationships, on the other, was predicated upon Plato's dualism of mind and body, and corresponding disdain for our somatic nature. There is nothing akin to this in ancient Judaic thought. According to Plato, sexual desire is merely the animal beginnings of the journey of the soul in its quest for the Good and the Beautiful. Interpersonal love is of only instrumental value, to be transcended in the ascent towards perfect love. Complete virtue is the pathway to Love, and true love culminates in the intellectual contemplation of Beauty itself ('the Good and the Beautiful are one').

*Limitations of Plato's conception*

This sublime vision, when conjoined with Christianity, greatly influenced European thought on love and on the good life. Plato's discourse abstracts all humanity from love:

(i)   It abandons the individuality and uniqueness of the beloved – any lover is as good as any other, since all individuality is to be transcended.

(ii)  It repudiates the essential reciprocity of a perfect loving relationship, since the perfection of love transcends any loving relation to an individual. Perfected, love is a relation to an Idea.

(iii) It abstracts from our human nature as rational *animals* ensouled *bodies*.

(iv)  It excludes women from those capable of achieving true love.

While it is true that we are *rational* animals, and that our rationality determines our nature, it is also true that we are rational *animals* and that our animality likewise determines our nature. Indeed, despite almost two thousand years of indoctrination and consequent conceptual illusion, we have a unified, not a bifurcated, nature – no matter how much we strive to delude ourselves. We are not a unity of mind and body, nor are we a psycho-physical unity. We are human beings, a distinctive, and uniquely language-using, animal species.[18] So we are *essentially* sexual beings, with the power to civilize and moralize our sexual drive and to transform it into love, and its consummation into the expression of love.

Plato's conception of love (actual and ideal) deviates from ours in four further respects. First, it is mistaken to suppose that the object of love *as we conceive it* is essentially beauty. This is neither necessary nor sufficient for love. Beauty, even if perceived, does not have to inspire love (only admiration). And it is perfectly common to love someone – spouse, parent, sibling, child, or friend – who is ugly. Secondly, it would be equally mistaken *for us* to suppose that a lover, in loving, essentially pursues the Good, or that the Good (or virtue) necessarily inspires love. Not all people who are loved are also good or even thought to be. There is no reason to suppose that the wives or mistresses of the tyrants that besmirch the face of history, or gangster molls, think their lovers to be morally good human beings (Rose, in Greene's *Brighton Rock*, loves Pinky passionately, while knowing him to be a murderer and believing him to be damned for all eternity). Sometimes it is power, brutal power, that generates love (exemplified, horribly, by the final fate of Winston in Orwell's *1984* in which he finally loves Big Brother[19]). Thirdly, love of the Beautiful, as we conceive it, is not essentially connected with virtue and with love of the Good. One can be a refined art collector with an impeccable eye for beauty, while being cruel and inhumane (Gilbert Osmond in Henry James's *Portrait of a Lady*). Finally, Plato links true love with immortality, presenting true love as a transcendent emotion. This conflates the atemporal value of love with the putative sempiternality of the loving soul and its ultimate object.

As a counterweight to Plato's investigations into the nature of love, we should note Aristotle's down-to-earth scrutiny of *philia*, which, as we have seen, incorporates in its extension both friendship-love, parental love, affection, and marital affection. It is noteworthy that he conceives of marriage as a relation of *philia* that obtains between

---

[18] See *Human Nature: the Categorial Framework* (Blackwell, Oxford, 2007), chs 8 to 10.

[19] Equally horrifically, by the ending of Miloš Forman's brilliant film *Goya's Ghosts* (2006).

ruler and subject. In such cases, there is at most modified reciprocity in love, for 'The role of the ruler is to receive, not to give, love, or at least to give it in another way' (*Eudemian Ethics*, 1238ᵇ24–30). Elsewhere he remarks that both utility and pleasure are to be found in the marital relationship, for human beings live together not merely for the sake of reproduction but for various purposes of life. The functions of a household are divided between man and wife, and they accordingly help each other (*Nicomachean Ethics*, 1162ᵃ20–30).

None of this shows that, in classical Greece, men and women did not sometimes fall in love, were not sometimes seduced and betrayed, did not sometimes have affectionate marriages into old age or extra-marital partnerships (Pericles clearly adored his mistress Aspasia), or did not undergo the grief of loss. These possibilities are depicted in myth and drama – of Alcyone and Ceyx, Hero and Leander, Galatea and Acis, Theseus and Ariadne, Medea and Jason, Phaedra and Hippolytus, Orpheus and Eurydice, Philemon and Baucis. These were evidently fully intelligible, and presumably played a part in the fantasy lives of Greeks. Similarly erotic relations were, then as now, the subject of comedies and the object of mirth of varying degrees of vulgarity (Aristophanes' *Lysistrata*). Affectionate loyal marriages may indeed have befallen the fortunate as is suggested by funeral stele and by funeral pottery. But we must be careful. There is no reason to suppose that the myths and dramas were any closer to depicting Athenian social reality than Shakespeare's romantic comedies reflect premarital and marital relationships among the Elizabethan aristocracy. As for funeral stele and pottery, they should perhaps be viewed as formal expressions of affectionate recognition of loyalty (comparable to that for a faithful servant), and their reliability is arguably no greater than that of eighteenth- and nineteenth-century tombstones in English churches. Our concern has been with how articulate Greeks conceived of love and, in particular, how Plato did – for his reflections were destined to have far reaching influence.

## 4. From pagan Rome to Christian Rome

*Impact of Christianity on Rome*   Christianity effected a profound change in Western conceptions of sexual desire, love, and marriage. It undermined Greco-Roman morality and mores, producing a radical transvaluation of values the like of which would not be seen again until the Romanticism of the late eighteenth and early nineteenth centuries and the social revolutions of the twentieth century. In the second century, the emperor Hadrian's youthful and beautiful male lover, Antinous, met an early death by drowning. He was deified, a city was founded in his honour, temples were built for his cult, and some two thousand statues erected in his memory all over the empire. Four centuries later, under Justinian, the pagan gods were dead, God was love, homosexuality was illegal, and those found guilty of it were burnt at the stake. A new relationship between sexual morality and society was created, and a new conception of love evolved to displace the classical Roman one. The framework within which love and sexual morality were viewed shifted from city and empire to God and the afterlife. Roman civilization changed from the pagan shame culture of the republic and early empire to the Christian guilt culture of the fifth and sixth centuries. What was the norm in one age became a vice in the other. New conceptual distinctions were drawn (e.g. homosexual and heterosexual) and old ones disappeared (*paederastia*). The concept of the love of God, derived from Judaism but variously modified by the worship of Christ as God incarnate and sacrificial son of God, assumed a centrality undreamt of in, and unintelligible to, classical Greek and Roman thought and morality.

*Three explanatory features of Roman views* Three features of Roman civilization over the period from roughly the first century BC to the third century AD need to be kept in mind if we are to grasp the social context in which Christian conceptions of love, sexual desire, and marriage took root.

First, Rome was a slave society. In late republican and imperial Rome, the sexual exploitation of young male and female slaves was the social basis of sexual morals and mores.[20] For a young male member of the family to slake his momentary lusts upon a slave girl or boy was as straightforward and unproblematic as relieving himself. The availability of brothels for fornication was as natural and common as the availability of taverns for drinks. Young upper-class males, prior to marriage in their mid- to late twenties, were a threat to the marital relationships of older members of the ruling elites. An adulterous

---

[20] For detailed discussion of this point, see K. Harper, *From Shame to Sin* (Harvard University Press, Boston, Mass., 2013). In the following discussion, I am much indebted to his book as well as to P. Brown's *The Body and Society* (1988; 2nd edn, Columbia University Press, New York, 2008) and R. Lane Fox's *Pagans and Christians* (Viking, London, 1986).

relationship with a married woman was akin to theft from an equal, and accordingly condemned. Prostitutes, and slave boys and girls, provided a safety valve. So too, for the more fastidious, did a sexual relationship with a courtesan. An alternative, more permanent and potentially affectionate, relationship was concubinage with a woman of a lower class.

Secondly, Greek and Roman medical doctrines played an important role in Roman conceptions of marriage and erotic relationships within marriage. Women were conceived to be biologically failed males, and therefore as inferior to men. Female foetuses were the result of insufficient heat of the male and female semen and of uterine blood, leading to deficiency of vital spirits in the foetus, which consequently failed to achieve its full potentiality. Sex, in moderation, was held to be beneficial for health, since excessive retention of male or female seed leads to humoral imbalance and consequent illness. Copulating was thought to mitigate melancholia, epilepsy, and headaches in the young. But excessive concupiscence was detrimental, since it was held to lead to cooling of the seed. Women were thought to be more subject to erotic desire than men, less capable of self-restraint and less rational. Early teenage marriage for girls was warranted both on grounds of health (lest their unfulfilled erotic needs lead to illness) and to ensure virginity on marriage. Female orgasm was held to be a necessary condition for conception. Given that the primary justification for marriage was procreation, this supposition conditioned sexual relationships within marriage.

Thirdly, the dominant ethos of the Roman elites was Stoicism. Its primary aim was *apatheia* – independence from subjection to passions. *Virtus* – masculine self-discipline in the service of the right – would give the Stoic inner harmony within the soul as well as outer harmony with nature. A virtuous life was one governed by the exercise of reason in conformity with nature. This would give the Stoic *eupatheia* – the positive emotions consequent on, and not in conflict with, virtue. The greatest fear was human bondage to the passions or runaway emotions. Self-control and fortitude were characteristic of the Stoic and the aspiration of the ruling Roman elites. Self-control applied also to gesture, voice, and gait, which are vehicles for the expression of unruly passions. In Rome (as in classical Greece, and unlike Byzantium and high medieval Europe) it was not ostentatious clothing that was the mark of the male elite, but deportment and speech. Sexual desire, the Stoics held, was an inevitable response to the beauty of youth, but the pleasures of sexuality being of no value, desire was not worthy of indulgence. Sexual longing, they held, is inimical to reason and leads to poor judgement. However, one's restraint should not be flaunted (contrary to the later practice of Christian asceticism and abstinence). The most powerful, highly personal, expression of Stoic ethos is Marcus Aurelius's *Meditations*. It is striking that he expresses gratitude to the gods that in his youth he did not 'touch Benedicta or Theodotus' (a female and male slave in the imperial household) and that he adds, 'but that even in later years when I experienced the passion of love, I was cured' (*Meditations*, I. 17).

Falling in love and being passionately in love *Roman conception* were, on the whole, viewed as passing forms of *of passion* derangement in which the lover, a man in the hands of Atë (goddess of mischief and ruin), is not elevated by passion (as the poets of *fin'amor* and the nineteenth-century Romantics believed) but held in abject bondage (Cicero,[21] Lucretius,[22] Catullus, Propertius). Love, Catullus suggested, is hell:

> O gods, if yours be pity, yours compassion
> Given to falling men even on the road
> Leading to death, dispel this black obsession,
> Rescue my soul from hell. Support its load –
> ...
> I look no more for her to be my lover
> As I love her. That thing could never be.
> Nor pray I for her purity – that's over.
> Only this much I pray, that I be free,
> Free from insane desire myself, and guarded
> In peace at last. O heaven, grant that yet
> The faith by which I've lived may be rewarded.
> Let me forget.
> (Catullus, 76; in a very free translation)

The passionate love of youth was more likely to be a subject for wit and irony, as in Ovid's *Ars Amatoria*, rather than being presented as a

[21] See *Tusculan Disputations*, IV. 32–6, e.g. 'above all things, the man thus afflicted should be advised what madness love is: for of all the perturbations of the mind, there is not one which is more vehement; for (without charging it with rapes, debaucheries, adultery, or even incest, the baseness of any of these being very blameworthy; not, I say, to mention these) the very perturbations of the mind in love is base itself.'

[22] Admittedly, Lucretius opens *De Rerum Natura* with a paean to Venus, mother of Aeneas and patroness of Rome. But this is more a celebration of nature and procreation than a reflection of his views on love and passion, which are expressed in book 4.

fitting prelude to marriage. Marriage *may* lead to *philia* (and evidently did in the case of Marcus Aurelius). Its primary warrant, however, was not the fulfilment of interpersonal love, but reproductive duty to the state. This austere aspect of Roman mores and association of love with erotic infatuation was to provide a congenial seedbed for the Christian derogation of sexual desire and erotic love in the doctrines of many church fathers.

*Marital relations in Rome*      The purposes of marriage could be manifold, but the culmination of erotic love and its transformation into the persistent love of a companionate marriage does not appear to have been a major one. First, marriage for procreative purposes was conceived to be a civic duty during the late republic and early empire. Procreation within marriage fulfilled a dual obligation: (i) to provide for the continuity of the state and, if one was an aristocrat, of the ruling elites;[23] (ii) a direct, personal obligation to one's ancestors, namely, to ensure the survival of the ancestral line.[24] Secondly, marriage (for a man) was warranted in order to obtain wealth in the form of the wife's dowry that could then be used to further the husband's career (notoriously, Cicero required Terentia's wealth for his advancement). Thirdly, the wife's main obligation, apart from child-bearing, was to run the household. Her primary virtue was held to be modesty (*pudicitia*).[25]

The age gap between bride and bridegroom in a first marriage among the elite was typically considerable. Girls, partly for medical reasons, were usually married off between thirteen and fifteen years of age (plebeian women married at a later age). Upper-class men were normally in their mid-twenties on their first marriage, with experience of military service overseas and, if older, perhaps of civic office too. Infatuation might *follow* marriage (and notoriously did in Pompey's marriage to Julia) and a paternal kind of love might evolve (he was thirty years older than she). The age gap between wife and husband (especially if the girl was marrying an older man), and the bride's immaturity on her first marriage, must normally have precluded the

---

[23] In 100 BC, a censor is recorded as saying 'Marriage, as we all know, is a source of trouble. Nevertheless, one must marry, out of civic duty' (quoted in P. Veyne, 'The Roman Empire', in *A History of Private Life*, vol. 1, *From Pagan Rome to Byzantium*, ed. P. Veyne (Harvard University Press, Cambridge, Mass., 1987), p. 37.

[24] In the absence of children, adoption of an adult male (with change of name) would discharge this obligation to perpetuate one's lineage.

[25] See S. Treggiari, *Roman Marriage* (Clarendon Press, Oxford, 1991).

companionship and shared life moderns in the West take for granted.[26] Treating one's wife well was laudable but not compulsory. Companionate love *might* evolve, but that would be good fortune rather than an expected part of the institution of marriage, and was probably more common in a second marriage with a divorced or widowed woman. However, a mature wife had *parrhesiac* privileges – she had the right to give her husband frank and candid advice (which, in the brutal arena of Roman politics, he could not always rely upon from friends). Despite Augustus's legislation against adultery in his *leges Iuliae* (18 BC), marital fidelity was not expected from the husband, but was from the wife. However, the idea of cuckoldry did not exist. A wife's infidelity was a misfortune (akin to one's unmarried daughter becoming pregnant), and not a ground for public mirth and mockery. A wife's infidelity would reflect on her husband not as being a laughing stock, but only as being too indulgent or lacking in vigilance. He might himself denounce and divorce her. Women could own property and engage in commercial transactions. A wife's property could not legally be amalgamated with her husband's.

Divorce was easy for both parties during these centuries. Moreover, in the event of divorce, the wife reclaimed the dowry she had brought with her and any property she possessed or might have acquired during marriage. Although the husband normally had custody of any children, the wife's property rights and right of divorce gave her a formidable degree of independence that would not recur until the twentieth century. Marriage to divorcees incurred no social stigma, and remarriage was urged upon widows in Augustus's *leges Iuliae*. Unlike women in ancient Greece, Roman women were not segregated within the home. They joined their husbands for dinner and moved freely about the atrium in the morning where the well-to-do husband was receiving clients. Women were not confined to the house, did not wear veils, wore jewellery and elaborate hair-dress, attended public events, including theatre and games, and went to public baths. However, they had no statutory political power, and could neither vote nor hold public office (save for the Vestals), even though they were often influential behind the scenes.

Latin, like ancient Greek, had no words for 'homosexual' and 'heterosexual'. The sexual act was not classified according to the sex of

---

[26] Quintilian, the great first-century rhetorician, lost his wife when she was but eighteen, after she had borne him two children. Her death, he wrote, 'was like the loss not merely of a wife, but of a daughter'.

the partners, but according to the masculine (active) and feminine (passive) role. Sexual relations with a boy or girl were viewed as perfectly normal. The attraction and source of arousal was the young body, irrespective of sex. Romans did, however, share the Greek disgust with a male's assuming the passive role in copulation. That would be an unforgivably shameful derogation of masculinity and manifestation of effeminacy. Accordingly, violation of freeborn boys was a serious legal offence. Hence slavery and the availability of attractive slave boys were essential to the socio-sexual life of a Roman city. Greek *paederastia* had been a relationship between social equals of different ages, involving elaborate courtship by the *erastes* of the *eromenos*, in which the *erastes* assumed the social role of mentor. In Rome this disappeared completely and was replaced by the relation of the sexually aroused master and the submissive slave boy or girl. The slave was not an object of erotic love, but a fungible object for relief of sexual desire.

*Emergence of ideal of companionate marriage in Rome* In the late first and second centuries a change in Roman ideas of love and marriage appears to have taken place.[27] This coincided with the declining power of the aristocracy in the early empire, and the rising role of provincial elites with marked civic pride. Their duties were primarily to the city and urban community in which they lived and held office, and only then to the empire, ruled from Rome by the emperor and the imperial bureaucracy. Companionate marriage, incorporating conjugal *eros*, was now advocated as appropriate for free citizens and conducive to the welfare of the city and empire by Plutarch in his *Moralia*, Pliny in his letters, and Musonius Rufus (the first-century Stoic teacher of Epictetus) in his lectures. Marriage was thought, at least by some, to have a moral mission. It should cultivate *concordia* and *homonoia* (a union of Aphrodite and Hermes). The idea that *eros* is a threatening passion or even a disease was repudiated, at any rate by those susceptible to these novel ideas. Instead, love was viewed as a condition for the development of *amicitia* (*philia*). Marriage was not merely cohabiting for the purpose of procreation and the running of an efficient household, but was rather the

[27] Treggiari dates the change much earlier, to late republican and Augustan Rome (*Roman Marriage*, pp. 119–21). Other historians disagree. The evidence of the few surviving Roman comedies and novels is no more reliable than are Shakespearean comedies for engagements and marital relations among the Elizabethan and Jacobean aristocracy, although in both cases the beginnings of a shift in conception may be indicated.

sharing of life. Ideally, it was the mirror of well-run civil society. Adultery was immoral and prohibited to both spouses. Being a good husband became a part of the role of the well-born male. To what extent this new ideal of love and marital relations was accepted, let alone pursued, is, it seems, impossible to judge. However, even within this novel framework of values, the partners to marriage were held to be unequal, and wives were required to submit to their husbands, who made the final choices. A wife should not make sexual advances to her husband (that would be overeager, like a whore), nor should she reject his advances (that would be cold and unaffectionate). A wife, Plutarch superciliously suggested, should not have friends of her own, but enjoy her husband's friends together with him! ('Advice on Marriage', *Moralia*, 138ᵃ–146ᵃ).

The ethos of the provincial elites appears to have changed further. Not only did they recognize a primary obligation to their city (*philopatros*), but they also began to see themselves as having an obligation to alleviate the suffering of the poor (*philotōchos*). This apparently spread to the wider population of the relatively well-off. One can find a second-century pagan tomb of a Greek pearl merchant on the Via Sacra with the inscription 'Here lie contained the bones of a good man, a man of mercy, a lover of the poor'.[28] As Christianity spread throughout the empire, it found the most fertile soil within which to grow among the modestly well-off and relatively well educated, rather than among the slave population.

## 5. Early Christianity

*Jesus and Paul on human love*  Jesus of Nazareth was a Galilean teacher in the tradition of the prophets of Israel, and no less wrathful.[29] Like his predecessors, his purpose was not to destroy the moral order of Judaism, but to restore it:

> Think not that I am come to destroy the law, or the prophets: I am not come to destroy but to fulfil. For verily I say unto you, till heaven and earth pass, one jot or one tittle shall in no wise pass from the law, till all will be fulfilled. (Matthew 5: 17–18)

[28] Quoted by P. Brown in 'Late Antiquity: the "Well-Born" Few', in *A History of Private Life*, vol. 1, *From Pagan Rome to Byzantium*, p. 261.

[29] See Matthew 10: 34–8: 'Think not that I am come to send peace on earth; I come not to send peace, but a sword. For I am come to set a man at variance against his father, and the daughter against her mother, and the daughter in law against her mother in law. And a man's foes shall be they of his own household.'

In conformity with the school of Hillel, Jesus is held to have quoted Deuteronomy 6: 5 and Leviticus 19: 18 as the two great commandments of the Torah (Mark 12: 29–31). Affirming the primacy of the love of God, he did not aver that such love is above the Law (the Torah), but rather held it to be a presupposition of the Law. His primary concern, and the object of his wrath, is hypocrisy, avarice, arrogance, disregard for the poor, and neglect of the helpless. Like Hillel, he affirmed the Golden Rule, but had little new to say on interpersonal human love, and even less on erotic love. Where he clearly broke with Jewish law, in matters that concern us, is over divorce and remarriage, which, according to the Gospels, he prohibited.

The instigator of the fundamental break with Judaism, Jewish law, and the Jewish conception of marriage and marital love, was Paul. Unlike Jesus, he elevated love (*agape*) above the Law. Like the Stoics of his day, he had a dim view of *eros*. Both sexual desire and death, he intimated, were a consequence of the Fall: 'Wherefore, as by one man sin entered into the world, and death by sin; and so death passed upon all men, for that all have sinned' (Roman 5: 12).[30] He did not conceive of *eros* as a source of value in love between human beings: 'It is good for a man not to touch a woman' (1 Corinthians 7: 1). He advocated chastity and virginity as the best forms of Christian life for those who, like himself, had the will power to renounce sex and live a life of abstinence: 'I would that all men were even as I myself … I say therefore to the unmarried and widows, It is good for them if they abide even as I' (1 Corinthians 7: 7–8).

Nevertheless, he countenanced marriage for those too weak to withstand the lusts of the flesh – 'it is better to marry than to burn' (1 Corinthians 7: 9). But, *if* one marries, one must love one's wife as one loves oneself, and a wife must revere her husband and submit to him in all things (Ephesians 5: 22–33). Paul did not consider sexual relations within marriage as an expression of erotic love but rather of *agape* (*caritas*). It was, in effect, the charitable mutual servicing of the

---

[30] The doctrine of the Fall was developed by Irenaeus and made central to Christian thought by Augustine. The Fall was the fault of Eve, and the source of concupiscence. It marks the beginning of the conflict between spirit and flesh, since, prior to the Fall, sexual desire, he thought, must have been under control of the will. But, as a punishment for disobeying God, the human body, as well as sexual arousal and desire, was thenceforth rendered disobedient to, and independent of, the will. According to Augustine, original sin is transmitted by conception, so that children are born in sin. None of this has any parallel in Judaism or Stoicism.

irrepressible demands of the flesh.[31] Contrary to Roman conceptions, marriage was not held to be a civic obligation warranted by procreative ends (after all, he expected the world to end in the near future). Rather, Paul averred, it is merely a concession to human frailty and a defence against fornication (1 Corinthians 7: 2). Sexual desire, he thought, cannot be elevated to the expression of intrinsically valuable interpersonal love, but only tamed and defused. Extramarital sexual relations were declared illicit, and homosexuality condemned. Divorce and remarriage were prohibited (1 Corinthians 7: 10–11).

*Early Christianity*  Throughout the first and second centuries, as Christianity strove to establish itself in various cities of the empire, numerous different doctrines concerning love, sexual desire, and marriage were advanced and hotly contested; some were condemned as heretical. Many left a long-term mark upon Christian European *mentalité* or *Weltanschauung*. To do justice to the complexities of the evolving doctrines is impossible here, so all that will be ventured is an overview.

Christianity, like Platonism, moved love to centre stage in the conception of the good life. Like Platonism, Christianity held that the supreme form of love is not between human beings. Unlike Platonism, it is not the love of transcendent ideas, such as the Good or the Beautiful, but rather love of God. This kind of love, unlike the love of the Good advocated by Plato, is not rooted in *eros* at all, but is characterized as *agape*.[32]

---

[31] It is striking that this chilling conception is repeated by Kant in the eighteenth century: 'Sexual union is the reciprocal use that one human being makes of the sexual organs and capacities of another. ... Sexual union in accordance with law is marriage, that is, the union of two persons of different sexes for lifelong possession of each other's sexual attributes. ... the natural use that one sex makes of another's sexual organs is enjoyment, for which one gives oneself up to the other. In this act a human being makes himself into a thing, which conflicts with the right of humanity in his own person. There is only one condition under which this is possible: that while one person is acquired by the other *as if it were a thing*. The one who is acquired acquires the other in turn; for in this way each reclaims itself and restores its personality' (*Metaphysics of Morals*, 'The Doctrine of Right, Part 1: Private Right', III. §§24–5 (6: 277–8)).

[32] Nevertheless, the subsequent synthesis of Christianity with neo-Platonism, introduced *eros* into the notion of the *agapic* love of God. The relationship between *agape* and *eros* in the Christian conception of the love of God was to be a source of contention throughout the centuries, made ever more prominent by Protestantism. Furthermore, the love of God was sometimes eroticized by Christian mystics, in particular by some of the desert ascetics in Egypt in the third and fourth centuries, who inflicted unspeakable sufferings upon themselves as forms of therapy for their souls that would enable them to achieve the exaltation and ecstatic mystical union with God which they craved. This was a motif that was to recur throughout the centuries.

John the Evangelist had declared obscurely that 'God is love'. Christianity held that virtue is nothing other than the love of God, since love of mankind flows from the love of God. The power to love God was held to be given to mankind through the grace of God and through his love. For, unlike perfect Platonic love (and unlike Aristotelian love of the Prime Mover), but, like the Judaic conception of the love of God, the Christians conceived of the love of God as being reciprocal. To receive God's love, however, demanded humility, for only humility, and even abasement, will allow the Holy Spirit to enter one's soul. Love (*agape*, *caritas*) was conceived to be redemptive.

Christolatry broadened and modified the conceptions of the love of God and the love for God inherited from Judaism. God, it was held, so loved mankind (or Christian believers) that he sent his son Jesus to suffer self-sacrificial crucifixion in order to atone for the sins of mankind (or Christian believers) and to redeem mankind from sin and its consequences in the afterlife. The love of Christ (*christos*, the anointed, the messiah) therefore introduced new elements into the notion of the love of God, precisely because Jesus was incarnate, a different person, but the same substance as God. The theme of the love of Christ dominates the Gospel of John and the First Epistle of John, and is also given prominence in Paul's letters. The intelligibility of these doctrines is moot. We shall not discuss them here.

Needless to say, quite apart from their general intelligibility, numerous tensions were locked up in Christian attitudes towards love: between the voluntariness of the Christian's love of God and the dependence of love on grace; between interpersonal and marital love and the love of God; between loving one's neighbour and loving one's Christian neighbour; between God's endowing mankind with the power to love him and the patent fact that not all human beings have an equal capacity for love in any of its forms; between man's love of God and the problematic idea that God, a perfect being, might love anything (other than himself). These were to provide ample material for centuries of disputation and disagreement.

*Christianity and erotic love*  One strand in early Christianity, originating with Paul and becoming ever more powerful over the next two centuries, was a distaste for, and fear of, erotic love (1 Corinthians 7). Sexual renunciation was held to facilitate single-minded focus upon the love of God. Male continence was elevated to an ideal of life, indicative of mastery of the body and freedom from servitude to *eros*. Chastity and virginity were conceived to be forms of moral purity, the maintenance of which is indicative of aspiration to the state of the angels and to the prelapsarian condition of mankind.

Extensive debate occurred between the second and fifth centuries over the relative merits of celibacy and marriage, the point and purpose of marriage, and the constraints on marital sexuality. Already by the second century AD, Christianity had broken with mainstream rabbinical Judaism, which had sanctified the marital household and lauded companionate marriage. Some church fathers, following Paul, held that a celibate life was indeed morally superior to marriage, but permitted marriage as a concession to weakness. Marital sex was allowed, but *only* for procreative purposes. If otherwise indulged in and enjoyed, it was a form of adultery (Jerome).[33] Some, accepting the fact that most of their congregations were already married, advocated the maintenance of chastity and abstinence (as between brother and sister) *within* marriage (Clement of Alexandria, Tertullian). Origen (a third-century Christian Platonist) and his followers advocated perpetual continence, and idealized virginity. What is most striking about these debates is the widespread dissociation of sexual desire from love.

*Changes in mentalité*    Adultery was forbidden to both husband and wife. However, double standards were maintained in so far as a husband could divorce his wife on grounds of her adultery, but not vice versa. The prohibition of divorce on any grounds other than adultery broke with Judaic and Roman law alike. Whereas Roman law encouraged the remarriage of widows within two years of the decease of their husband, Christian leaders urged widows not to remarry (or even forbade remarriage (Tertullian)) but to dedicate themselves to the love of God, to charitable works, and, in the case of upper-class women, to becoming patronesses of the poor under the guidance of the local bishop. Women were given no role in the hierarchy and administration of the church. The general prohibition on divorce had the effect of reducing female autonomy. The subordination of women to their husbands progressively eliminated their economic independence. This in effect reintroduced patriarchy – the despotic authority of husband and father – which in

---

[33] *Against Jovinianus*, book I, St Jerome quotes Xystus' *Sentences*: 'omnis ardentior amator propriae uxoris aduter est' (any man who is too ardent a lover of his wife is an adulterer). This dictum was commonly repeated by medieval churchmen such as Peter Lombard and Albertus Magnus.

one form or another was to persist until the eighteenth century and the rise of affective individualism with its advocacy of the pursuit of happiness.[34]

Prostitution, which was part of the Roman social order, was adamantly condemned by Christianity, as it was in the late first century by pagan Romans such as Plutarch, Pliny, Musonius Rufus, and Dio Chrysostom. But, whereas such Roman thinkers condemned prostitution for the damage it did to society – encouraging lack of self-restraint and cultivating sexual addiction, the church fathers rejected it because it was sinful. Homosexuality was held to be unnatural, depraved, and categorically forbidden. For the first time in Western history, penitential disciplines were introduced to regulate sexual relations. Slowly but surely the Roman categories of shame and reputation were displaced by the Christian conceptions of sin and salvation.[35] This manifested a fundamental shift in motivation in human relationships. (It should also serve to remind us of the non-triviality of conceptual change. Concepts carve out channels down which thought flows, and, where thought goes, emotion and behaviour follow.)

*Augustine*  The most influential of the church fathers after Constantine's Edict of Milan in 313, which legitimated Christianity in the empire, was Augustine (354–430). He attempted to find a middle way between the excessive asceticism of Jerome (347–420) and Ambrose (340–97), who advocated celibacy as an ideal form of life superior in virtue to marriage, and the more liberal view of Jovinian (d. 405), who denied that a married couple who enjoyed erotic love and who did not limit it in marriage to procreative purposes were any less virtuous than the celibate. Augustine argued that, although celibacy is indeed better than marriage, marriage is nevertheless good since it involves natural companionship and preserves the human race. In *De Bono Coniugali* (*On the Good of Marriage*), Augustine advanced the view that companionate marriage had three benefits: (i) procreation, (ii) fidelity,

---

[34] For discussion of the decline of patriarchy in England in the eighteenth century and a description of the changes in ideology, in marital and inheritance law, see L. Stone, *The Family, Sex and Marriage in England 1500–1800*, abridged and revised edn (Harmondsworth, Penguin, 1979), ch. 6. For a countervailing view, see R. A. Houlbrooke, *The English Family 1450–1700* (Longman, New York, 1984) and, for a more general overview that lies between them, B. Gottlieb, *The Family in the Western World* (Oxford University Press, Oxford, 1993).

[35] For detail, see K. Harper, *From Shame to Sin*.

and (iii) sacrament (the marital bond symbolizing the relationship between the church and God).[36] Sexuality in marriage is not an expression of *eros* (reciprocal erotic love) but of *caritas*. It is a means of controlling concupiscence by diminishing the temptations of adultery and fornication. The sacramental character of Christian marriage implies that it is indissoluble. In the event of divorce (still permitted under Roman law), remarriage is prohibited for a woman as long as her husband is still alive.

*Augustine on flesh and spirit*      In his personal life, however, Augustine struggled desperately with desire and lust. In his *Confessions* he displays his anguish:

> Love and lust together seethed within me. In my tender youth they swept me away over the precipice of my body's appetites and plunged me into the whirlpool of sin ... I was tossed and spilled, floundering in the broiling sea of my fornication. ... The brambles of lust grew high above my head ... I walked the streets of Babylon. I wallowed in its mire as if it were made of spices and precious ointments, and to fix me all the faster in the very depths of sin the unseen enemy trod me under-foot and enticed me to himself. (II. 2–3)

Augustine, like other church fathers, was given to representing his sexual drive as strife between soul and flesh (which is not the same as that between mind and body; concupiscence, gluttony, and greed are likewise desires of the flesh). This is *a form of representation*, and arguably one that inclines thought to go down paths inimical to human felicity. It is striking that Augustine, as we have noted, was the main proponent of the doctrine of the Fall. In *The City of God*, he represented sexual arousal as a sign of original sin, since one consequence of the Fall is that the sexual organs are no longer under the control of the will. The sexual act is the triumph of the flesh over the spirit, a reminder of our mortality, a symbol of original human alienation from God, and a manifestation of our punitive enslave-ment to the flesh. The good of marriage is to relieve one's spouse's

---

[36] More than a millennium later, Luther would take issue with this conception. Protestantism marks an important break in the Western conception of marriage, sexu-ality, and marital love and their value. Far from viewing marital love as inferior to chastity and abstinence, Luther, Calvin, and Zwingli held it to be sanctified. They advocated companionate marriage, lauded conjugal erotic pleasure, and did not limit erotic relationships between spouses to procreative purposes. Subordination of wife to husband, however, changed but little.

concupiscence by *caritas*, and to transform something essentially bad into a manifestation of virtue.

*Abelard on flesh and spirit*    The distaste for, and fear of, sexuality is a distinctive strand in Catholic thought on the subject of love (in the tapestry of which, to be sure, there are other strands). The debasement of erotic love is a persistent theme for many centuries. It is striking that in Abelard's *Historia Calamitatum* (1132), which he wrote to console a friend, he recounts his passionate and tragic love affair with Heloise twelve years previously in these very terms:

> I yielded up to the lusts of the flesh. Hitherto I had been entirely continent, but now the further I advanced in philosophy and theology, the further I fell behind the philosophers and Holy Fathers in the impurity of my life ... Since, therefore, I was wholly enslaved to pride and lechery, God's grace provided a remedy for both these evils, though not one of my choosing: first for my lechery by depriving me of those organs with which I practised it.

He presents his love as no more than lust, and Heloise as no more than a victim of his vile appetites. After his castration at the hands of her uncle's hirelings, Abelard had induced her, despite the fact that he had secretly married her and that they had had a son, to enter a convent, against her will. Thereafter, he broke off all contact with her, leaving her to suffer alone. His *Historia Calamitatum* fell into her hands. Bitter to read the manner in which he presented their love, and deeply injured by his twelve-year silence, she wrote to him. Her love for Abelard, self-consciously contrary to all Christian doctrine, is patently unabated, guiltless and unrepentant, selfless and self-sacrificial. But she craves for some reciprocity, for a word of tenderness, and for recognition of the great love they had had and for what she had sacrificed for him:

> Yet you must know that you are bound to me by an obligation which is all the greater for the further close tie of the marriage sacrament uniting us, and are deeper in my debt for the love I have always borne you, as everyone knows, a love which is beyond all bounds.

> You know, beloved, as the whole world knows, how much I have lost in you, how at that one wretched stroke of fortune that supreme act of flagrant treachery robbed me of my very self in robbing me of you ... Surely the greater the cause for grief the greater the need for the help of

consolation, and this no one can bring but you; you are the sole cause of my sorrow, and you alone can grant me the grace of consolation. You alone have the power to make me sad, to bring me happiness or comfort. ... God knows I never sought anything in you except yourself; I wanted simply you, nothing of yours. I looked for no marriage-bond, no marriage portion, and it was not my own pleasures and wishes I sought to gratify, as you well know, but yours. The name of wife may seem more sacred or more binding, but sweeter to me will always be the word mistress, or, if you will permit me, that of concubine or whore. I believed that the more I humbled myself on your account, the more gratitude I should win from you, and also the less damage I should do to the brightness of your reputation. ...

I beg you then to listen to what I ask – you will see that it is a small favour which you can easily grant. While I am denied your presence, give me at least through your words – of which you have enough and to spare – some sweet semblance of yourself. (Heloise's first letter to Abelard)

Abelard, however sincere he may have been, was concerned primarily to shield his shame and humiliation with self-deception, to view his castration as a divinely ordained punishment for sin. Consequently, he scorned and degraded what was, for Heloise, the sublime passion of her life – her self-sacrificial erotic love for him. So he preaches to her. In his second letter to her, he pours insult upon injury:

You know the depths of shame to which my unbridled lust had consigned our bodies, until no reverence for decency or for God even during the days of Our Lord's Passion, or for the greater sacraments, could keep me from wallowing in this mire ... So intense were the fires of lust which bound me to you that I set those wretched, obscene pleasures, which we blush even to name, above God as above myself.

The self-centredness, self-deception, and complete disregard for Heloise's suffering and love are a token of the power of this dark Christian vision of *eros*. Just how extreme it could become is manifest in the late twelfth-century, Middle English poem 'Hali Meidhad' (Holy Maidenhead) addressed to anchoresses:

> that vice begot thee of thy mother, that same
> improper burning of the flesh, that fiery itch of
> that carnal excitement before that disgusting work

that animal intercourse, that shameless togetherness,
That filthy, stinking and wanton deed.[37]

This strand in early Christian reflection on human love made a deep impression upon European thought that lasted for centuries, foreclosing human possibilities, and moulding emotions and behaviour. Its traces are still evident in our own association of sexuality with dirt ('dirty jokes', 'a dirty weekend') and of pornography with filth.

## 6. The deification of love

*Beginnings of change: Mariolatry*     The beginnings of a far-reaching revolution in *mentalité* is manifest in the eleventh- and twelfth-century love poetry of Aquitaine and Provence. This coincided both with the rise of the ideals of chivalry and with the sudden eruption of Mariolatry in the west. The cult of the Virgin in the form of *Theotokos* (bearer of God) was sanctioned by the church at the Council of Ephesus in 431. It evidently answered a need for an influential, sanctified female figure to replace the earlier cults of such female divinities as Cybele, Tanit (Ishtar, Astarte), Diana (Artemis), and Venus (Aphrodite). The first Marian churches in Rome were built in the fifth and sixth centuries, but her cult was not greatly different from the cult of other Christian saints. However, in the twelfth century, Bernard of Clairvaux (1090–1153) presented Mary as the bride of God in the Song of Songs and elevated her worship as mediatrix for the salvation of souls. She was worshipped as the Queen of Heaven, the Mother of God, the Virgin of Mercy (Madonna della Misericordia) sheltering supplicants under her cloak, the Mater Dolorosa grieving for the death of her son, and as patroness of cities (e.g. Sienna). The divine mother figure appealed to warriors and monks, to men and women, to young and old, alike. The forgiving motherly love, the loving motherly protection, the sympathetic mother who herself knew the griefs of loss and suffering, was the perfect figure for an intercessor and object of loving worship. Between 1150 and 1250 over eighty cathedrals and five hundred churches were built and dedicated to the Virgin. This manifests a fundamental

---

[37] Quoted and translated by R. Scruton in his *Sexual Desire* (Continuum, London, 2006), p. 132.

shift in Western thought and sensibility, a taming of the warrior ethos of the earlier Middle Ages, and an acknowledgement of emotional needs hitherto suppressed.

*Chivalry*    Chivalry emerged between the eleventh and thirteenth centuries in northern France and the Low Countries, whence it spread to the rest of Europe as the aristocratic ethos of the mounted knight within the feudal order. It humanized the savage warrior code of honour, military prowess, courage, loyalty, and largesse to followers that characterized the Franks, Norse, and other Germanic peoples of the eighth to eleventh centuries. It encouraged *courtoisie*, magnanimity, civilizing rules of war (as it were, a Geneva Convention for the Middle Ages), and developed extensive initiation rites and ceremonies that brought knighthood within the sphere of influence of the church. It generated, among the nobility, a brotherhood of arms that transcended feudal loyalties, served as a life-insurance policy in battle and tourney, and produced a welcome source of income for younger knights subject to the rules of primogeniture (e.g. William Marshal, later Earl of Pembroke, whose renown rested on his prowess and chivalry). Ransom replaced slaughter.

The *chansons de geste*, celebrating the deeds of Charlemagne, his followers, and successors, had their roots in the eighth- and ninth-century Frankish victories against the Moorish infidels. They were sung in the royal court in the Ile de la Cité, in Abbot Suger's court at St Denis, and in the halls of military leaders and their uncouth warriors in northern France. They celebrate such quasi-legendary figures as Roland and Olivier and their heroic deeds at Roncesvalles, or the prowess of Guillaume d'Orange. In these tales, love plays as little a role as in the *Iliad* – courage, loyalty, and the quest for fame and reputation are the ideals that move their heroes. In the twelfth century, such warrior epics gave way to the *romans courtois* (romances of chivalry) of such poets as Marie de France in England and Chrétien de Troyes at the court of Champagne, where Countess Marie, daughter of Eleanor of Aquitaine, was an ardent follower of the southern poets of Languedoc. Tragic love tales of Tristan and Iseult, of Lancelot and Guinevere, Percival, King Arthur, and other tales of the 'Matter of Britain', with roots in Celtic Britain and Welsh mythology, replaced stories of heroic last stands.

*Courtly love*    It was in the courts of eleventh- and twelfth-century Provence and Aquitaine, during periods of relatively prolonged peace, within a society in which noblewomen could inherit property in their own right and be great landowners that the troubadour poetry of *fin'amor* (refined love) developed.[38] It is, above all, to Eleanor of Aquitaine (herself the granddaughter of the first of the troubadour poets, Guillaume IX, Duke of Aquitaine and Count of Poitiers[39]), her daughters, daughters-in-law, and grand-daughters, at a variety of royal and ducal courts throughout the Angevin empire and beyond, that we owe this transformation in the thought and sentiment of the West.

It is mistaken to represent the troubadours and the southern courts of Languedoc as having invented both the idea and the celebration of passionate erotic *love* between man and woman.[40] Erotic love poetry goes back as far as records survive (e.g. Sumerian erotic love poetry of Enhedduana, princess and priestess of the goddess Inanna, in the third millennium BC). Moreover, there are numerous examples of medieval love poetry from Persia, Andalusia, Georgia, and Byzantium representing the beloved lady as a veritable goddess of grace and beauty, conceiving of her as secular redeemer and saviour, presenting love as increased by suffering, as put to the test by deeds of valour, and as demanding virtue, humility, and obedience. Nevertheless, in terms of the medieval Christian European tradition, the troubadour poetry does mark a highly influential shift in Western conceptions of love. The *fin'amor* poetry of Guillaume IX, Bernard de Ventadour, Jaufre Rudel, Marabru, Peire Vidal, and others, sanctified earthly love of a well-born man for a married aristocratic lady. No longer was woman conceived as the eternal temptress, the source of concupiscence and the sins of the flesh. On the contrary, for the first time in European culture, the beloved woman was enthroned on high as the pinnacle of all virtues and of sublime beauty. Inverting both Christian doctrine and the feudal order, the lover presents himself as a feudal vassal sworn to the service of his noble lady.

The idea of courtly love stood in contrast to the Christian conception of love of its day and to the Greco-Roman one that preceded it, although it borrowed from both traditions. It had both Celtic and Almohavid–Hispanic roots. It presented Aquitaine with a novel concept

---

[38] 'Courtly love' (*amour courtois*) is a nineteenth-century coinage, introduced by Gaston Paris in 1883.

[39] Who wrote not only sublime *fin'amor* poetry, but also campfire songs of extreme bawdiness.

[40] As was suggested by Gaston Paris, Ernst Robert Curtius (1949), Reto Bezzola (1960), and C. S. Lewis (in *The Allegory of Love* (Clarendon Press, Oxford, 1936)). This thesis was decisively refuted by P. Dronke, in his *Medieval Latin and the Rise of the European Love Lyric* (Clarendon Press, Oxford, 1965).

and conception of love that, in due course, spread throughout Europe. It is far removed from modern conceptions, yet it contains the seeds of the deification of love of nineteenth-century Romanticism.

(i) Unlike the love of God, *fin'amor* is rooted in the sublime erotic attractiveness of the beloved lady (hence not simply in the subjective sexual attraction the knightly lover feels towards her). Like the first step of the Platonic ladder of love, its object is human beauty – but the beauty of a lady, not of a boy. Unlike Platonic *eros*, it never cuts itself off from its erotic roots or from its particularity and individuality.

(ii) It is essentially extramarital – the love of a well-born youth or knight for a married noblewoman. True love cannot exist within Christian marriage, for if passion in marriage is sinful (as the church held), then, Countess Marie of Champagne argued, there can be no true love in marriage. In marriage, the wife is subordinate to her husband, who has negotiated her marriage with her father, and she is bound to obey him in all. But in true love, it was argued, the lady is superior to her suitor, who adores and praises her, addressing her as *midons* (as he would his feudal lord). Moreover, a married couple are duty bound to give in to each other's desires – they are obliged to grant their favours. But true love is freely bestowed. Marital affection and the true love of lovers are wholly different, arise from different sources, and are incomparable.

(iii) In the most sublime variants of *fin'amor*, it is of the essence of true love that it should *not* be consummated – it is the asymptotic goal that the lover craves, the unattainability of which spurs him on to ever greater virtue and nobility. It involves no physical adultery, but, so to speak, only spiritual adultery. (There appears to have been an implicit recognition that illicit consummation of courtly love would destroy it, putting an end to its ennobling qualities, and besmirching its beauty.)

(iv) It is a secretive form of love, not to be shared with others (comparable perhaps to incestuous love even to this day, or to the love of a nymphet, as in Nabokov's *Lolita*).[41] The troubadour's poems to his lady, addressing her as *midons*, conceal her identity from others. Secret though the love is, it requires complete fidelity.

[41] This helpful analogy is suggested by Scruton in *Sexual Desire*.

(v)  It demands sacrifices from the lover, for his love must be put to the test. So it is inspiring, elevating, and ennobling. The lover must prove himself to be pure and truthful, loyal and faithful, courageous and generous, modest and adoring, *cortes* (courtly and courteous), and a model of *joy d'amour* when in the presence of his lady.

(vi)  The true love of the troubadour for his lady is an obsessive passion, involving suffering and heart-rending longing. It also produces ecstasy, not of consummation, but of awe and devotion.

(vii)  The love in itself is beautiful. Its moral quality lies in the lover's sacrifices for the sake of love, in his fidelity, selflessness, and adoration of his lady.

Courtly love can indeed be presented as a secularization of, although not a substitute for, the love of God. Indeed, God is often beseeched to bless and grant the troubadour's goal. Like the Christian mystic, who must go through the sufferings of *purgatio* (*catharsis*) to attain the union with God he craves, so too the lover must undergo suffering to win his lady's love. Just as God puts his worshippers to the test, so too the lover's adoration of his lady is put to the test. As God's grace is achieved only through the attainment and exercise of *virtù*, so too the love of the supplicant's lady is achieved through *virtù*. And, as God is revered by his worshippers, so the lady is revered by her lover.

*Internal tensions of courtly love*

Internal tensions and contradictions are patent in the ethos of courtly love. The love that it elevated into an ideal is also an illicit extramarital love, the consummation of which would be a sin. It idealizes extremes of passion, while at the same time demanding complete self-restraint, both in stifling the desire to consummate the passionate erotic love, and in demanding secrecy. On the one hand, it presents courtly love as ennobling, and, on the other hand, it demands of the knightly lover that he abase himself before his lady, begging for a token of her favour. It presents itself as a love between human beings (so singularly missing in the Christian doctrines of the day and in aristocratic marital arrangements), but ends up with a love from a distance that finds its expression not in tenderness and intimacy, but in poetry. The ideal of love it advances is profoundly perverse, at best the prerogative of a small minority of an aristocratic elite at royal and ducal courts, cultivating an emotion that it is committed to frustrating, detaching love from any viable social form and rendering it wholly parasitic on existing forms, and detaching love between man and woman from marriage and the bearing and bringing up of children.

To what extent courtly love was a mere conceit, an amusing game for an idle aristocracy, and to what extent it actually changed manners and mores, thought and feeling, it is difficult to judge. The practices of courtly love and the public presentation of the poems of *fin'amor* in the courts of Aquitaine were highly formalized and ritualized. How deeply they affected the thought and emotional lives of the participants in these rituals is impossible to say. But there can be little doubt that the poetry of courtly love played a significant role in transforming the European *conception* of love.

Troubadour poetry did not last long in the south. By the end of the twelfth century it was fading. The culture of Languedoc was largely wiped out by the rapacious barons of northern France in the terrible crusade against the Albigensian heresy (1209–40). But its literary influence was great. The troubadour tradition spread to northern France in the watered-down form of the poetry of the *trouvères*, and thence to England, the Low Countries, and the Germanic lands, where it gave rise to the minnesinger tradition. It migrated south to the poets of the Sicilian court of Frederick II, and thence to Florence, where it influenced the Tuscan *dolce stil novo* of Guido Cavalcanti (ca. 1250–1300), his friend Dante (1265–1321), and Petrarch (1304–74). Unlike the Greek and Roman conception of love, and equally unlike the Christian conceptions of its time, it placed the beloved lady upon an elevated throne, sanctifying the nobility of knightly love.

*Dante and Petrarch*    The *dolce stil novo* had a much weightier philosophical grounding than did the poetry of courtly love. Cavalcanti's secular love poetry was influenced by Averroes, as Dante's was by Aquinas and Petrarch's by his study of the classics. All three presented the suffering of permanent yearning and unfulfilled love as both elevating and redeeming, and idealized their beloved and her surpassing beauty. Both Dante and Petrarch were inspired by a passionate and unquenchable love for a barely known and wholly unattainable married lady (Beatrice and Laura, respectively), whom they sanctified and indeed deified.[42] Both ladies died young, but continued to be the objects of the poets' intense love and the subjects of two of the greatest love-cycles in European

---

[42] In sonnet 10 of *La Vita Nuova* (1295), Dante wrote: *Ecce Deus fortior me, qui veniens dominabitur michi* (Behold a deity stronger than I, who coming, shall rule over me).

poetry, Dante's *La Vita Nuova* and Petrarch's *Il Canzoniere*. In Dante's subsequent *Divine Comedy*, Beatrice is his semi-divine guide through Paradise. The *dolce stil novo* is rooted in the communes of the Italian city-states. Hence it differs from its *fin'amor* origins in its detachment from aristocratic courts and the artificialities of courtly behaviour, and in its dissociation from chivalry. Its theme is not courtly love, but love itself. Petrarch and the Petrarchan sonnet was to be *the* major formal influence and *a* major ideological influence in the formation of Renaissance love poetry and the Renaissance conception of love throughout Europe (in particular, France and England).[43]

*Renaissance neo-Platonism*   The other major influence, also Italian, was the humanism of the Florentine Renaissance, in particular the neo-Platonism that flourished at the Medici academy under the guidance of Marsilio Ficino and Pico della Mirandola. They attempted to synthesize Plato (stripped of all homoerotic concerns) with Christianity, merging the love of the Good with the love of God, elevating intellectual love over human and erotic love. Florentine neo-Platonism was in turn a major influence upon Baldassare Castiglione's *Il Cortegiano* (*The Book of the Courtier* (1528)), which paid tribute to church doctrine while idealizing love, and returned it to royal and ducal courts. 'In my opinion', Castiglione writes:

> Although sensual love is bad at every age, yet in the young it may be excused and perhaps in some sense even permitted. For although it

[43] Thomas Wyatt (the elder) and Henry Howard, Duke of Surrey, translated Petrarch and introduced the sonnet form to England. They were followed, during Elizabeth's reign, by Spenser and Sidney. Shakespeare, however, excelled at the sonnet form and developed it further, altogether abandoning its ideological roots in courtly love and Petrarchan idealization. The first 126 of his 154 sonnets are addressed not to an unattainable lady, but to a young nobleman. They are homoerotic – whether 'Platonically' so or not is moot. The final sonnets to the 'dark lady' are as anti-Petrarchan as can be, and arguably designed to be so. They are not addressed to a virginal or married noblewoman of surpassing beauty and virtue. They do not express elevating and ennobling erotic craving, but disgust with erotic gratification, jealousy, and misogyny. (How much of this is authentic expression of emotion and how much merely scintillating artifice is moot.) Nor is human interpersonal love conceived as a route to divine love and spiritual enlightenment. At the same time, Shakespeare's comedies present romantic love between aristocratic youth and maiden as a normal route to marital bliss, even though this was incongruous with the character of the aristocratic marriage in Elizabethan and Stuart England. Their appeal was, perhaps, that of wish fulfilment. But, if so, that already represents a highly significant shift in the emotional world of the audience.

brings them afflictions, dangers, exertions and all the unhappiness we have mentioned, yet there are many who perform worthy acts in order to win the favour of the women whom they love, and though these acts are not directed to a good end, they are good in themselves ... So just as I think those young people who subdue their desires and love in a rational manner are truly heroic, I excuse those who allow themselves to be overcome by the sensual love to which human weakness inclines them, provided that they then display gentleness, courtesy, worthiness and all the other qualities these gentlemen mentioned, and when they are no longer young they abandon it completely and leave sensual desire behind them, as the lowest rung of the ladder by which we can ascend to true love. (*Book of the Courtier*, 4)

The synthesis of Plato's conception of the ladder of love, the Stoic and Christian repudiation of sensual love, elements of the ethos of courtly love, and a merging of love of God and love of the Good are patent here. Castiglione's book was among the most widely translated and read books of the sixteenth century among the European aristocracy.

The flood of literature that ensued in western Europe throughout the sixteenth and seventeenth centuries, coupled with the decline of feudalism, the rise of the mercantile classes, the increase in literacy, and the invention of printing, on the one hand, and the rise of Protestantism and the Counter-Reformation, on the other, meant that debates about the nature of love, its merits and drawbacks, its role in a good human life, and the relationship between interpersonal love and the love of God, were more widespread than ever.

The final moment in European thought that I wish to
*Romanticism* touch upon very briefly (since the tale is much more familiar) is the Romanticism that swept Germany, Britain, and France between the 1770s and 1870s. This too constituted a transvaluation of values on a grand scale, a seismic shift in the European *Weltanschauung*. It displaced the Enlightenment, with its confidence in reason, order, restraint, and self-discipline and its distrust of emotional excess and 'enthusiasm'. Instead, Romanticism offered heroic individualism rather than conformity to received morals and mores or to rationality and reasonableness. It represented the triumph of the emotions over reason, of the will over the intellect, of imagination over cogitation, of spontaneity and 'naturalness' over measured reflection and convention (deemed, often with good reason, to be 'artificial'), of flamboyance over restraint. It advocated authenticity, self-expression, freedom, and self-realization. Within the scale

of human emotions, it was given to extremes of passion (Heathcliff in *Wuthering Heights*), to unrestrained sensibility (critically depicted in *Sense and Sensibility* (Marianne)), to unbridled enthusiasms, and to an uncompromising 'all or nothing' attitude towards the predicaments of human life (Michael Kohlhaas, in Kleist's eponymous novella, or, later in the nineteenth century, Brand in Ibsen's eponymous play).

*Deification of love*   The Romantic movement did not place the beloved lady upon a pedestal for adoration, but rather placed love itself there. Christianity had declared that 'God is love'. Romanticism avowed that 'Love is God'.[44] Plato had advocated transcending interpersonal erotic love in order to attain the love of the eternal Good (merging the Good and the Beautiful). Christianity had downgraded erotic love and replaced it by the transcendent love of the eternal God. Courtly love and Renaissance neo-Platonism had elevated the unattainable love of a lady to the point of mirroring the love of God. Romanticism deified love, detaching love from both God and the Good.[45] It is love itself that is transcendent, redemptive, provides meaning to life, transcends space and time, and is eternal and unlimited.

The Romantics secularized the love of God and projected its salient features onto the human plane of passionate youthful love. The Christian conception of union with God through love is replaced by the union of the souls of lovers. Cathy, in *Wuthering Heights* exclaims to Nelly: 'He's more myself than I am. Whatever our souls are made of, his and mine are the same' (ch. 9). Heathcliff, in his anguish, exclaims:

> 'Be with me always – take any form – drive me mad! Only do not leave me in this abyss, where I cannot find you! Oh God! It is unutterable! I cannot live without my life! I cannot live without my soul.' (ch. 16)

Strikingly, the passionate, destructive love of Cathy and Heathcliff has nothing to do with the goodness of their hearts or souls. Indeed, Cathy is selfish and Heathcliff a monster of hatred and revenge. But the depth of their passion is conceived to be redemptive for all that.

---

[44] This felicitous formulation is Irving Singer's in *The Nature of Love*, vol. 2, p. 294.

[45] Keats wrote to Fanny Brawne (October 13, 1819): 'Love is my religion – I could die for that.'

Where the religious were willing to die for the love of God, the Romantics *avowed* willingness to die for their beloved:

> With both elbows on the table and both hands pressed against his face, he cried in a sad and choked voice, 'I love her, love her madly!' and he was all aglow within, like a fire when a thick layer of dead ash has been suddenly blown off. ... he was utterly unable to understand how he could have sat beside her ... her! – and talked to her and not to have worshipped the very hem of her garment, that he was ready, as young people express it, 'to die at her feet.' ... Now he considered nothing, reflected on nothing, did not deliberate, and did not look forward; he had done with all his past, he leaped forward into the future ... he plunged headlong into that glad, seething, mighty torrent – and little he cared, little he wished to know, where it would carry him, or whether it would dash him against a rock! ... These were mighty, irresistible torrents! They rush flying onwards and he flies with them. (Turgenev, *Torrents of Spring*, ch. 25)

Falling in love is itself, as it were, a religious experience:

> How my heart beats when by accident I touch her finger, or my feet meet hers under the table! I draw back as if from a furnace; but a secret force impels me forward again, and my senses become disordered. Her innocent unconscious heart never knows what agony these little familiarities inflict upon me. Sometimes when we are talking she lays her hand upon mine, and in this eagerness of conversation comes close to me, and her balmy breath reaches my lips, – when I feel as if lightening had struck me, and that I could sink into the earth ...

> She is to me a sacred thing. All passion is still in her presence: I cannot express my feelings when I am near her. I feel as if my soul beat in every nerve of my body.[46]

Not only is love deified, but marriage is presented as a time-transcending return to Eden:

> The femininity of your soul ... consists in its regarding life and love as the same thing. For you all feeling is infinite and eternal; you recognize no separations, your being is an indivisible unity ... I am all yours; we

---

[46] Goethe, *The Sorrows of Young Werther*, entry of June 16. Subsequently Werther writes in his diary: 'What is to become of all this wild, aimless, endless passion? I cannot pray except to her. My imagination sees nothing but her: all surrounding objects are of no account, except as they relate to her.'

are closest to each other and we understand each other. ... Marriage is
the everlasting unity and alliance of our spirits, not only for what we
call this world and that world, but for the one, true, indivisible, nameless, endless world of our entire being, so long as we live. (Friedrich
Schlegel, *Lucinde* (1799))

This conception manifests little understanding of the emotion of love
as we understand it. Conceiving of the intensity of love as redemptive,
the Romantics were prone to confuse the intensity with the depths of
love. For them it is the erotic love of youth that gives life its meaning.
Such love is the source of sublime happiness (or the route to suicidal
despair). The two souls of the lovers are completed to form a single
one (echoes of Plato's Aristophanes), and merge to form a sublime
unity of spirit.

*Legacy of Romanticism* The Romantic conception of love arguably
embodies a vision no less inimical to human
felicity than the Platonic, early Christian,
Provençal, and Renaissance conceptions. It is misguidedly confined to
youthful love. It conflates the intoxication of infatuation with the tenderness of being in love. It misguidedly supposes that intensity of love
is the same as depth. It conceives of loving another person as transcending time; but loving another is a temporal phenomenon of
human life. What may be thought of as transcending time is not loving another person, but the *value* of loving another person, since that
value, like all absolute value, is atemporal.

Romanticism left the twentieth century a baneful legacy, placing
demands upon love that it is rarely able to meet and encouraging a
vision of love that bears but little relation to the reality of the complex
emotion of human interpersonal love. Popular literature, the
Hollywood dream factory, and the development of mass advertising
in which eroticism is the pivotal attraction for the purchase of a product all embedded superficialities of romantic love in the texture of
contemporary life and culture.

The twentieth century saw a further revolution in the conception of
sexual desire and erotic love, and in the manner in which they find
expression in social norms. The changes were as profound as those
that heralded the triumph of Christianity. Their roots lay in legal and
economic changes, in medical and technological discoveries, and in
ideological transformations. The most important legal changes concerned women's property rights, the availability of divorce and custo-
dianship of children, universal suffrage, and the legalization of

abortion. Economic changes, due largely to the two world wars, opened the labour market to women and made financial independence possible for them as well as choice of work or profession. Advances in technology and medicine made available effective means of contraception. Freud, irrespective of the correctness of his theories, made the discussion of sexuality licit. Marie Stopes (and others in her wake) contributed to the elimination of the deeply harmful ignorance characteristic of the nineteenth century. The twenty-first century has seen the introduction of same-sex marriage, the proliferation of single-parent families, and a soaring divorce rate – the apparent progressive disintegration of the traditional institution of marriage. How this will affect conceptions of human love and its axiological potentialities is for future generations to determine.

# Index

Pages containing significant discussions appear in bold.

Abelard, P., 37, **424f.**
addiction, 7
*aemulatio*, 188, 196
aesthetic formalism, 378
Aetius, Flavius, 262
affections, **13f.**
*agape*, 296, 405f., 419
agitation, **14–16**
*ahava*, 395, 406
*aidos/aidoia*, 158
Akiva, Rabbi, 396
Albee, Edward
    *Who's Afraid of Virginia Woolf*,
      239, 263
Alexander, of Macedon, 262, 343, 344n.
Alexander Yanai, King, 401
Alfonso II, Duke of Ferrara, 212
Ambrose, St, 422
*amor* (*bestiale, celeste, coactus,*
    *umano*), 297
analogy, argument from, 94
anger, **212–64**
    animal, 233, 235, 240f., 258f.
    as capital sin, 264
    constraints on objects of, 249
    and desire for punishment, 246
    and doctrine of humours, 236–8
    evil of, 262f.
    evolutionary selection for, 233
    excess of, 244f.
    and first-person authority, 252f.
    iconography of, 238
    intensity of, 243f.
    and jealousy, 222f.
    material object-accusatives,
      246–50
    momentary, temporary/persistent,
      241–3
    nominalization-accusatives of,
      250–2
    phenomena of, 233f.
    pictorial representations of, 238f.
    a primitive emotion, 232f.
    and reason/reasons, 245f., 252, 264
    self-directed, 247
    social norms of, 240
    suppression of, 244
    vocabulary of, **235–8**
    warranted, 262, 264
animal emotions, 4, 26, 42, 77f., 85, 87,
    89f., 231, 233, 235, 240f., 258f.,
    273, 381n.

*The Passions: A Study of Human Nature*, First Edition. P. M. S. Hacker.
© 2018 John Wiley & Sons Ltd. Published 2018 by John Wiley & Sons Ltd.

Anouilh, Jean
 *Beckett*, 331
Anteros, 295
Antisthenes, 191
*apatheia*, 79, 412
appetite, 4f., 7–12
 and emotion, 26–8
Aquinas, 24n., 88, 431
 on anger, 258f.
 on basic emotions, 118f.
 on capital sin, 137, 184f., 227
 on envy, 184f., 200n., 203n.
Ariès, P., 282n.
aristocracy, military, 154–6
Aristodemus, 154n., 179
Aristophanes, myth of, 299, 319,
 407, 436
Aristotle
 on anger, 80, 117n., 245f.,
 256–60, 264
 on envy (*zelos*), 195, 200n., 203
 on form and matter of emotion, 87
 on friendship, 327f., 336f., 339–41,
 346, 347f., 349, 350–4
 on friendship with gods, 334n.
 on love (*philia/philotia*), 279, 402,
 405, 409f.
 on the mean, 81f.
 on pride (*megalpsuchia*), 135, 155
 on *psuchē*, 87
 on shame, 155, 162f.
 on women, 404, 406
arrogance, 146f., 325
Asbridge, T., 353n.
ashamed, of oneself, 160
ashamed of/ashamed for, 160
Atalya, Queen, 401
atonement, 175f.
attitudes, 12f., 16, 35f.
Aubry, John, 167
Augustine, 72, 88, 136, 159, 162,
 275n., 309, 422
 on basic emotions, 116f.
 on friendship, 328f., 350n.
 on original sin, 418n.
 on sex, 423f.
Austen, J.
 *Emma*, 162, 219, 284, 349, 372
 *Persuasion*, 146, 219

*Pride and Prejudice*, 66, 113, 135,
 143, 147, 164f., 170f., 284, 369
*Sense and Sensibility*, 69, 307

Bacon, Francis, 185, 189, 196n.,
 284n., 342
Balzac, Honoré de
 *Cousin Bette*, 70, 204, 277
 *Lost Illusions*, 330, 331, 354
Bánffy, M.
 *Transylvanian Trilogy*, 38
Barnes, A. G., 210
Baron-Cohen, S., 381
Bartels, A., 304n.
Bateson, G., 112
battle rage/frenzy, 255
Baudelaire, Charles
 'To a Madonna', 186f.
Bechara, A., 104n.
behaviourism, 379f.
Bell, Sir Charles, 111
Bellini, Giovanni, 54
Benedict, Ruth, 152
Bennett, M. R., 89n., 382n.
Berkeley, G., 360n.
Bernard of Clairvaux, 426
Bernini, Gian Lorenzo, 323f.
 *St Teresa of Avila*, 296n.
Bezzola, R., 428n.
bile, 199f.
Birdwhistle, R., 112
Blackburn, S., 325n.
Blake, William
 *Songs of Experience*, 263
blush, blushing, 167, 169f., 270
Boccaccio, Giovanni, 283
Bolt, Robert, 154
Bonaventure, 296
*boosha/mevoshim*, 159
Bosch, Hieronymus, 138, 153, 198
Botticelli, Sandro, 198
Brant, Sebastian
 *Ship of Fools*, 188n., 204
Bremer, J., 53n.
Breughel, Pieter, the Elder, 198
Brontë, Charlotte
 *Jane Eyre*, 284
Brontë, Emily
 *Wuthering Heights*, 69, 263, 434

Bronzino, Agnolo, 192, 215, 216
Brown, P., 156n., 282n., 411n., 417n.
Browning, Elizabeth Barrett
   *Songs from the Portuguese* (sonnet
      14), 314
   *Songs from the Portuguese* (sonnet
      43), 305
Browning, Robert
   'My Last Duchess', 212f.
Bruner, Jerome, 380n.
Buddha, on anger, 261f.
Burke, Edmund, 362f.
Burton, Robert, 188
*bushido*, 155
Byron, George Gordon
   *Don Juan*, 284n.

Cannon, W., 78, 102f.
Caravaggio, M., 54, 295
caring, 3, 24, 73, 77
*caritas*, 291f., 395, 406
Cassian, St John, 137n.
Castiglione, B., 54f., 432
Catullus, Gaius Valerius, 269n., 281,
      332, 413
Cavalcanti, Guido, 431
certainty and doubt, possibility of, 66f.
Cervantes, M., 157
*chansons de geste*, 427
character trait, 19
charity, 185
Chaucer, G., on pride, 137f.
Chekhov, Anton
   *Uncle Vanya*, 317, 332
chivalry, 157, 427
Christianity
   on anger, 260
   and erotic love, 401, 420f.
   and guilt culture, 156f.
   impact on Roman conception of
      love, 410f.
   on love and marriage, **417–26**
   and love of God, 420
   on spirit and flesh, 423f.
   and subordination of women, 421f.
   and virginity, 420f.
Cicero, Marcus Tullius, 414
   on anger, 259f.
   on basic emotions, 115f.

on expression of emotion, 51, 52, 53
on friendship, 328, 338, 348, 350, 354
on love, 413
Clarke, K., 282n.
Clough, Arthur
   'The Higher Courage', 132
Coleridge, Samuel, 407n.
   'Dejection: an Ode', 17
Collingwood, R. G., 378n.
Commandment, the Great, 396
compassion, 291f.
comradeship, 338f.
conceit, 145f.
concept/conception, 268f.
concupiscence in ancient Rome, 412
congeniality, 340f.
Congreve, William, 190, 222
Conrad, Joseph
   *Lord Jim*, 71, 133
conscience, voice of, 175
Cottingham, J., 85n., 89n.
courtly love (*amour courtois*), **427–31**
covetousness, 200
Craig, A. D., 104n.
Cranach, Lucas, the elder, 295
craving, 11
criteria, 61, 124f., 126
cuckold/cuckoldry, 221, 415
Curtius, E. R., 428n.

Damasio, A., 90f., 97, **103–10**
Dante Alighieri, 286, 290, 431
   *Divine Comedy*, 197, 239
   *La Vita Nuova*, 431f.
Darwin, C., 26n., 111–13, 123, 167
Daube, D., 159n.
defeasibility, 61
Delacroix, Eugène, 216, 239
Della Casa, G., 54f.
De Morgan, Evelyn, 216
Demosthenes, 404n.
Descartes, R., 311
   on emotion, 83–7, 88–90, 118, 199f.
developmental psychologists, on basic
      emotion, 126f.
Dickens, Charles
   *Christmas Carol*, 71
   *David Copperfield*, 151, 356
   *Tale of Two Cities*, 316n., 330

dignity, 148
Dilthey, W., 378n.
Diotima, 407f.
disposition/proneness/tendency,
    18n., 32–4
Dodds, E. R., 74n., 152n.
*dolce stil novo*, 431f.
Donne, John
    'The Ecstasy', 299f.
    'To his Mistress Going to Bed', 321
Dostoevsky, Fyodor
    *The Brothers Karamazov*, 247n.,
        262, 293
    *The Idiot*, 165
    *Notes from Underground*, 166,
        326, 342
Dreyfus, Captain A., 164
Dronke, P., 428n.
Droysen, J. G., 378n.
Duby, G., 282n.
Duchenne de Bologne, G. B., 111
Dumas, Alexandre, the Younger
    *The Lady of the Camellias*, 330
duration, genuine, 12, 17n., 30
duty, path of, 174n.

ecstasy, religious, 296
Edgeworth, Maria
    *Patronage*, 143
Edwards, L. H., 377n.
Eichler, Gottfried, the Younger, 138, 188,
        199, 238, 297
*Eifersucht*, 208n.
*einfühlen*, 377, 387
*einsfühlen*, 391
Ekman, P., 113–15, 120n., 123
Eleanor of Aquitaine, 428
Eliot, George
    *Middlemarch*, 66, 134, 143, 146, 148,
        171, 249, 286, 308
    *Romola*, 162
    *Silas Marner*, 210
embarrassment, 163, 167–70
emotion, 22–36
    animal, *see* animal emotions
    and appetite, 26–8
    basic, 115–28
    and caring, 3f., 24f.
    causation of, 41f.

classification of, 22f.
complexity of, 35f.
and consciousness, 84, 90
constitutional uncertainty/
    indeterminacy of, 61–3, 66f.
contrasted with mood, 18
control of, 50n., 73f.
conventional signals of, 55
criteria for, 47, 61
developing, 282–7
and duration, 29f., 31f., 34,
    114, 115
epistemology of, 60–7
etymology of, 23
and evaluation, 58
evolution of, 9, 77–9, 111–15, 233,
    271f., 374f.
expression (manifestation) of, 45–56,
    69, 111f.
and facial expression, 46, 51,
    113, 125
formal object of, 27, 57
form taken by, 48, 78
and ignorance of one's feelings, 67
and imagination, 58f.
infectious, 368f.
infinitive-accusative of, 43
intensity of, 27, 69
intentionality of, 42–4, 79
and irrationality, 72
and judgement, 58
knowledge and belief, 57f.
and mastery of language,
    42, 78f.
and mental images, 105–10
misinterpretation of, 50
and motive, 15, 25, 41f.
and music, 39f.
neural associations of, 46f.
nominalization-/object-accusative
    of, 42–4
observability of, 364f.
opacity/transparency of, 62
and pretence, 50f.
and privileged access, 90
and reason/reasons, 57f., 67–77
representation in art, 39
responsibility for, 68–70, 72f.
self-control, *see* self-control

emotion (*cont'd*)
  and self-knowledge, 65–7
  somatic accompaniments of, 47
  understanding of, 37f.
  verbal expression of, 48
  vocabulary, learning of, 44f., 92
  vocabulary of, 41f.
  and will, 56f., 68
emotional attitudes, 35f., 114
  deficiency, 71f.
  history, 33f.
  narrative, 114f.
  perturbations, 30f., 105–7, 113
  self-consciousness, 45
emotions, crowd, 368f.
  education of, 73f., 81
  negative, 79f.
  philosophical problems of, 41
*empatheia*, 377
empathy, **377–85**
  and art of biography, 392
  compared with sympathy, **385–92**
  (*Einfühlen*), not an emotion, 388
  *qua* power to understand, 389f.
enviable, 200f.
envy
  colour of, 199f.
  conceptual roots of, 192–7
  emulative, 201
  evils of, 183f.
  iconography of, 197–200
  and jealousy, **187–92**, **228–31**
  material object of, 202f.
  as mortal sin, 184
  and motive, 203f.
  roots of, 202
  and self-deception, 205
Epicurus, 343
Erasmus, D., 54f.
*erastes/eromenos*, 281, 328, 405,
    407, 416
*Erklärung/Verstehen*, 378n.
*eros*, 284, 294, 295, 297, 401, 419
*eupatheia*, 79
Euripides
  *Andromache*, 186
  *Medea*, 186, 214, 222, 226
  *Phaedra*, 68
evidence, imponderable, 63

expiation, 176
eye, evil, 196n.
eyes, green, 216

facial plasticity, 51f.
Fall, doctrine of, 159, 418, 423
*fascinus* (phallic charm), 196
feelings, 4f., 13f., 104–9
feeling shame/feeling ashamed, 160f.
Ficino, Marsilio, 432
fight-or-flight response, 78
*fin'amor*, 290, 317, **428–31**
Finger, S., 85n.
Flaubert, Gustave
  *Madame Bovary*, 204, 324
Fogassi, L., 281
folk psychology, 380
Fontane, Theodore
  *Effi Briest*, 134, 161, 224f., 286
form
  contrasted with sign, 49
  and what it is a form of, 49
Forman, Miloš
  *Goya's Ghosts*, 409n.
Forster, Edward Morgan, 355
  *Howards End*, 348, 349,
    375, 376
  *A Passage to India*, 349, 375
Foster, G. M., 188n.
frame of mind, 17
Francis of Assisi, 150f.
Frankfurt, H., 325n.
Freud, S., 319n.
friendliness, 51f., 345
friendship
  capacity for, 341f.
  between equals/unequals, 348
  intrinsic value of, 339f.
  and love, similarities and
    differences, **329–36**
  loyalty-, 349
  and permanency, 344
  Platonic, 347
  pleasure-, 336f., 346
  political-, 338
  roots of, **336–9**
  and self-respect, 341f.
  of social companionship, 337f.
  utility-, 337, 338, 346

and virtue, 352f.
  between the wicked, 353f.
  with/of God, 334
friendship-love, 343, 401f.
friend to/friend of, 334n., 342, 345
Friesen, W. V., 120n.
Frith, C. D., 380n.
Frith, U., 380n., 381n.
Fuller, T., 165
Fussi, A., 153n.

Gallagher, Jack, 329n.
Gallese, V., 381
Galsworthy, John
  *The Forsyte Saga*, 303
  *The White Monkey*, 308
*gelosia*, 191f.
Géricault, Théodore, 198
gift-reciprocity, 343f.
Gilbert, Sir Alfred, *Anteros*, 295
Giotto di Bondone, 191
God
  anger of, 241, 253
  commandment to love, 395f.
  friendship of/with, 334
  human love of, 269, 280f., 289,
    334, 399
  jealous, 194, 196
  obedience to, 398
God's
  love of Israel, 395
  love of mankind, 395, 396
Goethe, Wolfgang von
  *The Sorrows of Young Werther*,
    317, 435
golden rule, 396, 418
Goldie, P., 33n., 381
Golding, William
  *Rites of Passage*, 165
  *To the Ends of the Earth*, 147
Goldman, A., 381
Gottlieb, B., 422n.
Goya, Francesco, 53f., 238
Gracián, B., 185
Gratiolet, Pierre, 111
Graves, Robert
  'Two Fusiliers', 339
Greek vocabulary
  of anger, 236f., 254f.

of envy, 192, 194f.
  of love, 405f.
Greene, Graham
  *Brighton Rock*, 308f., 323, 409
  *The End of the Affair*, 221f.
  *The Third Man*, 354f.
Greenwood, Edward
  'Marvell's Impossible Love', 318n.
  'Reconciliation', 334n.
  'The Story', 36
Gregory the Great, Pope, 136f., 227
Griffiths, P. E., 115n.
Grillparzer, Franz, 208n.
Guercino, Giovanni Francesco Barbieri, 54
Guillaume IX, Duke of Aquitaine,
    427, 428
guilt, 153, **173–80**
guilt, survivor-, 178
guilt and shame compared, 180
guilt-culture, 152–4, 156, 411
*gynaikon*, 401

Halevi, Yehuda, 399f.
Hall, Radclyffe
  *The Well of Loneliness*, 347
Hampshire, S., 72n.
*hamza* (apotropaic symbol), 196
hands, expressiveness of, 54
Hardy, Thomas
  *Tess of the d'Urbervilles*, 217
Harper, K., 156n., 282n., 411n., 422n.
Harré, R., 33n.
Harris, P., 381
Harris, Robert
  Cicero trilogy, 338
  *An Officer and a Spy*, 164
Hart, H. L. A., 178n.
Hartmann, N., 152n., 174
hatred, 225f., 261
Hawthorne, N.
  *The Scarlet Letter*, 166
Hebrew vocabulary
  of anger, 253
  of envy, 193
  of love, 395
Hegel, G. W. F., 159n.
Heine, Heinrich
  *Buch der Lieder* prefatory poem to, 301
  'To My Mother', 271

Héloïse, 37, **424f.**
Hemingway, E.
    *The Sun Also Rises*, 164
Herbart, J. F., 378
Herder, J. G., 377
hermeneutics, 378, 389
Herodotus, 240n.
heroic societies, 154f.
Herrick, Robert
    'How Marigolds Came Yellow', 216
Hertzberg, L., 52n.
Hesiod
    *Works and Days*, 195, 294, 406
*hetairai*, 403
Hillel, the Elder, 396, 418
Holbein, Hans, the Younger, 54
'Holy Maidenhead', 425f.
Homer
    *Iliad*, 74–5, 135, 154f., 179, 184,
       185f., 239, 243, 254f., 334n., 339
*Homo loquens*, 272
homosexuality, 281, 328, 402, 406n.,
    411, 415f., 422
honour, 153, 154–6, 157f.
Houlbrooke, R. A., 422n.
Howard, Henry, Duke of Surrey, 432
*hubris*, 135
Hugo, Victor, *Les Misérables*, 70, 244,
    283f., 292, 333, 372
human beings, opacity/transparency of, 62
humble, being/humbled, 163f.
Hume, D., 76, 92, 104, 139, 149f.,
    324, 357
    on sympathy, **359–62**, 366, 367, 379
humility/humiliation, 148, 149–51,
    163f., 221
humours, doctrine of, 138, 199f., 236–8

Ibsen, Henrik
    *A Doll's House*, 286, 324
    *The Master Builder*, 134
*ideales sollen*, 152n.
ideal rules, 152
idiographic/nomothetic, 37f., 377
idolatry, 194, 253
imagination, 58f.
indignation, 262
infatuation, 284f.
inference to the best explanation, 60f., 94

Ingres, Jean-Auguste-Dominique, 54
inner/outer picture of the mind,
    55f., 364f.
insincerity, 55
introspection, 91f.
intuition, 77
*invidere*, 192, 196
*invidia*, 184, 191, 192, 196
Irenaeus, 159
Isenberg, A., 142n., 150n., 172
Israel, people of, why chosen, 397
Izard, C. E., 121f.

Jack, R., 121
Jahoda, G., 377n.
James, Henry
    *The Portrait of a Lady*, 113, 141,
       332, 356
    *The Spoils of Poynton*, 211, 348
James, W., on emotion, **97–103**, 104,
    105, 120
jealousy, 10f., 185–7
    categorial analysis of, 214
    colour of, 216
    conceptual roots of, 208
    criterion of love, 228
    and envy, **187–92**, **228–31**
    grammatical form of, 209
    and hatred, 225f.
    and humours, 216
    iconography of, 215
    nominalization-accusatives of,
       209, 213
    object-accusatives of, 209, 213
    obsessiveness of, 219f.
    personal possessive, 211–13, 214,
       **216–23**
    physiognomy of, 215
    protective, 209–11
    and resentment/anger, 217, 222f.
    and revenge, 214, 226f.
    and self-deception, 223–5
    self-defeating, 217f., 219–21, 227f.
    self-destructiveness of, 227
    sexual, 191, 195, 214, **216–28**
Jerome, St, 421, 422
Johnson-Laird, P. N., 121
Jonson, Ben, 'To the Immortal
    Memory ...', 351

Kant, E., 397, 398, 419n.
Keats, John, 434n.
Kenny, A. J. P., 8n., 15n., 91n.
*khesed*, 291, 395
*kholē, kholos*, 236f., 255
King, P., 117n.
Klein, Melanie, 206
Klimt, Gustav, 216
*kótos*, 255
*kyrios*, 403

Laclos, Pierre Choderlos de
  *Dangerous Liaisons*, 300
La Fontaine, Jean de, 343
Lampedusa, Giuseppe Tomasi de
  *The Leopard*, 135
Lane Fox, R., 411n.
Lange, C., 97n.
La Rochefoucauld, François de,
  190f., 337n.
Latin vocabulary
  of envy, 196
  of jealousy, 208
Lawrence, D. H.
  *Sons and Lovers*, 292
Le Brun, Charles, 215
Leonardo da Vinci, 54
Lermontov, Mikhail
  *A Hero of our Time*, 286, 293
Lesbia, 269n.
Levenson, J. D., 397n., 400
Levi, Primo, 164
lewdness, 297
Lewis, C. S., 428n.
liability, 175f.
liking, 288f.
Lipps, Theodore, 377, 379
literature and emotion, 38
Locke, J., 91, 119
Lotze, H., 377
love, **267–326, 437**
  and ability, 299f.
  ancient Greek conceptions of, **402–10**
  of animals, 275
  and appraisal, 311
  biological/social roots of, 267f.,
    **269–74**
  categorial analysis, **298–304**
  commandment to, 395–400

commitments of, 320f.
companionate, 286, 289f., 321f.,
  416f.
concepts and conceptions, 268f.,
  278, 282
courtly, *see* courtly love (*amour
  courtois*)
covenantal, 397
and craving for union, 317f.
creativity of companionate-, 322f.
crystallization of (Stendhal), 310
deification of, **426–31, 434–6**
a developing emotion, **282–7**
and dispositions, 302, 303
and dominion, 300, 301
earthly/heavenly, 406f.
erotic/sexual, 278f., 284–6, 299f.,
  317f., 321, 331, 401, 407f.
formal object of, 308
and friendship, differences, **332–6**
and friendship, similarities, **329–31**
of God eroticized, 399, 419n.
and the heart, 294
historicity of, 280f., **393–437**
human, of God, 269, 275f., 280f.,
  289, 297, 299
iconography of, 294f., 296f.
idealization of, 290f.
and importance, 276f.
and indifference, 293f.
institutionalization of, 306f.
language dependence of, 272f.
limits of, 277f.
loyalty, 274
marks of, **304–16**
maternal, 270f., 291f., 301
and morality, 323
as motive, 273, 323f.
of nature, 275
of neighbour commanded, 400f.
objects of, **274–8**
parental, 271f., 291f.
passionate, 284f., 285f.
pathological, 397
permanence of, 315f.
practical, 398, 400
and reason/reasons, **310–12**
and reciprocity, 316f.
relations to time, 305f.

love (*cont'd*)
  and self-completion, 319
  social constraints on, 281
  and the *summum bonum*, 308
  tests of, 307
  uniqueness of person loved, 312–16
  vocabulary of, **287–94**
  and the will, 320
loving someone for their own sake/for
  love's sake, 312–15
Lucretius
  *The Nature of Things*, 279, 317f., 413
lust, 8f., 270, 297, 301, 411f., 413,
  416, 424f.
Luther, M., 423n.
*lyssa*, 255

Mackie, J. L., 94
Mahler, Gustav, 313
man, rise of, 159
Mandeville, B., 185
Mann, T.
  *Felix Krull*, 55
Mantegna, Andrea, 198
Mantel, Hilary
  *Bring up the Bodies*, 338
  *Wolf Hall*, 338
Marie, Countess of Champagne,
  427, 429
Marie de France, 427
Mariolatry, 426f.
Marlowe, Christopher, 281n.
marriage, 273f., 290, 302
  in Athens, 403–5
  in early Christianity, 421–4
  in Old Testament, 401
  Pauline conception of, 418f.
  in Rome, 412–17
  in Sparta, 404n.
Marshal, William, Earl of Pembroke,
  353, 427
Martin du Gard, Roger
  *The Thibaults*, 367
Marvel, Andrew, 'The Definition of
  Love', 318n.
Masaccio, Tomasso, 53
Mason, A. E. W.
  *The Four Feathers*, 179

Maugham, W. Somerset
  *The Explorer*, 148
  *The Moon and Sixpence*, 218
  *Of Human Bondage*, 70, 164, 247,
  293, 310, 332
  'Rain', 163
Maurier, Daphne du, 211n.
  *Rebecca*, 218
May, S., 394
McDougall, W., 120
Mead, M., 112
Medici, Lucrezia de', 212n.
Melito, Bishop of Sardis, 399n.
Menander
  *Perikeiromene*, 195
*mênis*, 254
mental images, 107f.
mental state, 17, 30
mereological fallacy, 87, 89
Michelangelo Buonarotti, 286
Miller, A.
  *All My Sons*, 160
  *The Crucible*, 176f., 210
  *Death of a Salesman*, 160
Milton, John, 359
mimesis, motor, 368
mind, 364f.
  frame of, 17
  state of, 17
  theory of, 380–5
mind-reading, 380
Mirandola, Pico della, 297
mirror neurons, 381–5
*mitzvot* (commandments of God (Old
  Testament)), 397
monolatry/monotheism, 395
Montaigne, Michel de, 263n., 279,
  311f., 331, 332, 343, 346f.
mood, **16–22**
  causes and objects of, 16f., 20
  contrasted with emotion, 18
  neural substrate of, 21f.
  nominalization-accusative of, 17
  objectless, 16f.
  occurrent/dispositional, 18
  reasons and causes of, 19f., 21
  and temperament, 19
  and will, 21f.

Moore, G. E., 152n.
moral autonomy, 157
Munch, Edvard, 216
Musonius Rufus, 416

Nabokov, Vladimir, 429
naked/nude, 405n.
narcissism, 145, 325
*nazar* (apotropaic symbol), 196n.
Nicaea, Council of, 399n.
Nietzsche, F., 330n., 340n.
*nithing*, 155
normative, 173n.
*normatives sollen*, 152n.
Norse sagas, 239, 255n.
Nowak, M., 377n.

Oates, Captain Lawrence, 339n.
Oatley, K., 121
obedience, loving-, 397f.
obligation-imposing rules, 175
O'Brian, Patrick
    Jack Aubrey novels, 331, 348, 353
obsession, 10f.
Old Testament
    analogies for love of God, 398f.
    on anger, 241, 249, 253f.
    on covetousness, 200
    on envy, 184
    on friendship-love, 401f.
    on friendship with God, 334n.
    on guilt, 153
    on jealousy, 188, 193f., 218
    on marriage and erotic love, 401
    on pride, 136
    on shame, 158
*orgē* (orgetic), 233n., 245
*orgē* contrasted with anger, 257f.
orgetic behaviour, 252
Origen, 399n., 421
Orwell, George
    *1984*, 409
    'Shooting an Elephant', 162
Osborne, John
    *Look Back in Anger*, 239, 263
other minds, knowledge of, 60–3, 126,
    363–5, 366, 380
ought to be/ought to do, 152, 174

Ovid
    on envy, 198
    on love, 413f.

*paederastia*, 405, 411, 416
Pantites, 154n.
Paris, G., 428n.
Partridge, E., 287n.
Pascal, B., 312n.
*Pashtunwali*, 154f.
'passion', uses of, 5n.
passions, 5f., 13
Pasternak, Boris
    *Doctor Zhivago*, 308
*pathos*, 5n.
pattern, formed by elements of
    emotions, 61f.
Paul, St, 159, 418f.
Pausanias, 150n., 295, 406f.
perturbations, 30f.
Petrarch, Francesco, 275n., 284n., 290,
    310n., 431
    *Il Canzoniere*, 432
*philia*, 327f., 334, 336, 339, 343,
    346, 405
phobias, 72f.
*phthonos*, 192, 194f.
Pico della Mirandola, Giovanni, 432
*pietà*, 292
pineal gland, 84f.
Piso, Gnaeus, 263
Plato, 24n., 76, 256n., 259, 260, 406n.
    on love, 299, 309, 319, 407, 408f.
Platonic love, 299, 323
Pliny, the Younger, 416
Plutarch, 196n., 345
    on friendship, 328
    on marriage, 416f.
Plutchik, R., 121f.
Ponticus, Evagrius, 137n.
Pontormo, Jacopo da, 54
Pope, A.
    *Essay on Criticism*, 131
Premack, D., 381
pride, **131–51**
    and approbation, 142
    Christian conception of, 136–8
    iconography of, 138

pride (*cont'd*)
  in lineage, 144
  and mental states, 132
  mien of, 54, 132
  and motivation, 133
  natural/in natural gifts, 142f.
  nominalization-accusatives of, 141
  object-accusatives of, 140f.
  Old Testament on, 136
  as persistent emotion, 133
  proper/improper, 132, 144
  and self-esteem, 133, 141f., 147–9
  and self-respect, 147–9
  and sense of identity, 141
  and standards of expectation, 142
privacy, 281
private language argument, 91–7
projectivism, 359–66, 379, 383f.
prostitution in ancient Rome, 422
Proust, Marcel
  *The Captive/The Prisoner*, 214,
    277, 333
  *In Search of Lost Time*, 186
  *Swan's Way*, 205, 220, 223
  *The Sweet Cheat Gone*, 333
*pudor/pudenda*, 158
Pushkin, Alexander
  *Eugene Onegin*, 307

*qualia*, 91n.
*quin'ah*, 188, 193
Quine, W. V. O., 115n., 380
Quintillian, Marcus Fabius, 415n.

Rand, Ayn, 185n.
Ranke, Leopold von, 378n.
Raphael, Sanzio, 54, 296
Raz, J., 72n.
realization, 65f.
*re'ekha*, 395
Reid, Thomas, 139
Reimann, H., 104n.
Remarque, Erich Maria
  *Three Comrades*, 343, 346
Rembrandt van Rijn, 54, 158
remorse, 175f., 181f.
Renault, Mary
  *The Last of the Wine*, 279n.
resentment, 263

responsibility
  for beliefs, 72f.
  mental conditions for, 174f.
  varieties of, 177f.
responsiveness
  contagious, 367f.
  infant, 367
retribution, 176
*re-ut*, 395
revenge, 226f.
Rickerts, H. J., 378n.
Ripa, Cesare
  *Iconologia*, 138, 188, 199, 238, 297
Rizzolatti, G., 381, 382
Rolls, E. T., 121
Roman conception of love, **411–17**
*romans courtois*, 427
Romanticism, 433–6
Romantics, 292
Roodenburg, H., 53n.
Rosenstein, N., 156n.
Rostand, Edmond
  *Cyrano de Bergerac*, 210, 286, 312n.
Rubens, Peter Paul, 54, 238, 295
Rückert, Friedrich
  'Liebst du um Schönheit', 313
Ryle, G., 34n.

Sackville-West, Vita
  *All Passion Spent*, 347
Salome Alexandra (Shlom-Tsion),
    Queen, 401
Samaritan, the Good, 292, 297
Samson, 254n.
samurai, 155
Sanders, E. M., 194n.
Sandys, Anthony Frederick, 215, 216
Sarto, Andrea del, 296
Sartre, J. P., 81
*scamu/sceomu*, 158
*Schadenfreude*, 35, 66, 187, 190,
    200n., 203, 243
Scheler, M., 152n.
Schiller, Friedrich
  *Don Carlos*, 331
Schlegel, Friedrich, 435f.
  *Lucinde*, 435f.
Schleiermacher, F. D. A., 378
Schopenhauer, A., 39f.

Scipio, Gaius Cornelius Africanus, 156
Scott, Captain Robert, 339
Scruton, R., 270n., 426n., 429n.
Searle, J., 94
second self, 349f.
*Seinsollen/Tunsollen*, 152n., 174
self-abasement, 399
self-castration, 399
self-control, 12, 50, 56, 69, 73f., 412f.
self-deception, 191, 205, 223f.
self-destruction, 191, 204
self-esteem, 147–9, 161, 163f., 191, 204
self-love, **324–6**
self-pity, compared with sympathy, 373
self-projection, 366, 379
self-respect, 147–9, 161, 341f.
Sellars, W. R., 380
Seneca, 115n., 241, 247, 260, 263,
  264, 294
sentimentality, 25n.
sentiments, 12, 16, 25n.
sex, as *caritas*, 424
sex and slavery in ancient Rome, 411f.
sexual desire, 217–19, 270, 321
sexual/erotic passion, 278f., 284–6, 289,
  299f., 317f., 321
sexual infidelity, **218–27**, 415
sexuality
  early Christian view of, **419–23**
  moralization of, 270
Shakespeare, William
  *As You Like It*, 283n.
  his bawdy, 287n.
  *Coriolanus*, 48, 135
  *Hamlet*, 181, 248, 348
  *Henry V*, 234f., 239, 242
  *Henry VI*, 239
  *Julius Caesar*, 190, 202, 390
  *Lear*, 72, 239, 369
  *Macbeth*, 18, 71, 181, 239
  *Measure for Measure*, 210
  *Merchant of Venice*, 216, 239
  *Merry Wives of Windsor*, 359
  *Midsummer Night's Dream*, 295
  *Much Ado about Nothing*, 336
  *Othello*, 10, 18, 44, 48, 65, 68, 71,
    134, 186, 204f., 209, 210, 214,
    216, 217, 219, 220, 224, 226f.,
    239, 316n.

  *Richard III*, 171
  *Romeo and Juliet*, 18, 38, 48, 283,
    330, 336
  *Sonnet 116*, 315
  *Sonnet 130*, 310
  his sonnets, 432n.
  *Venus and Adonis*, 218, 321
shame, 152f., **157–73**, 280
  and embarrassment compared, 167f.
  feeling, 178f.
  genital exposure, 158f.
  and guilt compared, 178, 180
  and humiliation, 221
  Janus-faced, 161f.
  life without, 173
  and motivation, 162f.
  natural, 161f., 171f.
  neither virtue nor vice, 165
  nominalization-accusative of, 171
  object-accusative of, 170
  shared, 171
  and sin, 156
  and social control, 166
  stigmatic, 160f.
  and temporality, 162
'shame', etymology of, 158f.
shame-culture, 152–6, 411
shamed, being/feeling, 162, 171
shaming and naming, 166
shaming another, 162
Shapur I, 148
shyness, 163, 166f.
sibling attachment, 272
Sidgwick, H., 231
Sidney, Philip, 432n.
sign, and what it is a sign of, 49
simulation theory, 379
sin, 153, 156
  capital, 137, 184
  mortal/deadly, 184
  original, 136, 418f.
Singer, I., 394n., 434n.
Sinigaglia, C., 382
sins, seven deadly, **136f.**
sleep, desire to ... not a craving, 11
smile, 51f.
Smith, Adam, on sympathy, **363–7**
Solzhenitsyn, Aleksandr, 164
  *Cancer Ward*, 367

somatic marker hypothesis, 109
Sophocles
  *Oedipus Rex*, 165, 177f.
  *Trachiniai*, 186, 217
Sorenson, E. R., 120n.
soul, 184n., 395n.
  death of, 227f.
  union of, 319
Spenser, Edmund, 432n.
  'Hymn in Honour of Beauty', 358f.
Spinoza, B., 80f., 118f., 139, 206, 219n.,
  259, 261, 396
state of mind, 17
Stendhal, 290n.
Stevenson, Robert Louis
  *Kidnapped*, 339
Stich, S., 381
Stoicism in Rome, 42f.
Stoics
  on anger, 259f.
  on emotion, 79, 115–17, 156
  on love, 412f.
Stone, L., 422n.
Suger, Abbot, 427
sympathetic person, 371
sympathize, quasi-performative, 388
sympathy
  acting out of, 376, 387f.
  behavioural manifestations of, 373
  being out of, 370
  compared with empathy, **385–92**
  compared with self-pity, 373
  conceptual history of, **358–67**
  degrees of, 374
  and desert, 385f.
  evolutionary roots of, 374f.
  field of, 386
  and imagination, 365f., 387
  implications of, 372
  limits of, 374
  nominalization-accusatives of, 372
  object-accusatives of, 372
'sympathy', uses of, **369–72**
sympathy for/sympathy with, 370, 372

Taylor, G., 142n., 148, 183, 309n.
temperament, 19
Tertullian, 72, 319, 421
theory-theory (in psychology), 380

Thermopylae, 154n., 179
Thesiger, Wilfred, 201
Thorvaldsen, B., 295
Thucydides, 403f.
*thumós*, 255
Titchener, Edward, 377, 379
Titian, 238, 295
  *Sacred and Profane Love*, 296f.
Tolstoy, Nicolai Lev
  *Anna Karenina*, 38, 61, 65, 186, 217f.,
    220f., 223f., 225f., 286, 307, 317
  *Kreuzer Sonata*, 70, 210, 214, 222f.
  *Resurrection*, 38, 71
  *War and Peace*, 18, 38, 49, 61, 64f.,
    70, 285, 292, 298, 307, 308, 316n.,
    320, 326
Toohey, P., 188n.
Torah, 395, 396
Treggiari, 414n., 416n.
Trollope, Anthony
  *Barchester Towers*, 149, 262, 300
  *Can You Forgive Her?* 61
  *The Duke's Children*, 71
  *Framley Parsonage*, 314
  *He Knew He Was Right*, 18, 38, 69, 70,
    163, 186, 209, 217f., 221, 307, 324
  *Kept in the Dark*, 221
  *Last Chronicle of Barset*, 333
  *The Pallisers*, 343, 353
  *Phineas Finn*, 69, 168, 338
  *Phineas Redux*, 338
  *The Small House at Allington*, 134
troubadours, **428–31**
Troyes, Chrétien de, 427
trust, 342f.
Turgenev, Ivan
  *Torrents of Spring*, 300f., 435
Twain, Mark
  *Huckleberry Finn*, 336
  *Tom Sawyer*, 336
  *A Tramp Abroad*, 157

Ullah, R., 154n.
understanding, idiographic/
  nomothetic, 37f.
urge, **11f.**

Valentian III, Emperor, 262
Valerian, Emperor, 148

Van der Weyden, Rogier, 54
Van Dyke, A., 132
Van Hoogstraten, Samuel, 54
vanity, 144f., 325
Venus, 294f.
Verrocchio, Andrea del, 54
Veyne, P., 414n.
Vico, Giambattista, 377
Vidal, Gore, 202n.
Virgil, 297
virginity, 420f.
Virgin Mary, cult of, 296, 426f.
Vischer, F. T., 379
Vischer, R., 379
Von Wright, G. H., 61n., 152n.

Waismann, F., 115n.
Walcot, P., 188n.
Walpole, Hugh
   *The Fortress*, 292
   *Herries Chronicles*, 277
   *Judith Paris*, 314, 324, 373
   *Rogue Herries*, 307, 317, 320
Ward, James, 215
Watson, J., 120
Waugh, Evelyn
   *Brideshead Revisited*, 331, 342, 345
Weinfeld, M., 397n.
White, A. R., 15n., 49n.

Wiesel, E., 293
Wilde, Oscar, 188
   *An Ideal Husband*, 324
   *The Importance of being Earnest*, 209
Williams, B., 153n.
Wind, Edgar, 297
Wittgenstein, L., 51, 61n., 94, 249,
   340, 361
women
   conceived as failed men (ancient
     Rome), 412
   status in Athens, 403–5
   status in early Christianity, 421f.
   status in Old Testament, 401
   status in Rome, 414f.
   status in Sparta, 404n.
Woodruff, G., 381
Wycliffe, J., 188

Xerxes, 240n.

Yeats, William Butler
   'For Anne Gregory', 313
   'When You are Old', 315
*yir'ah* (fear/reverence), 398n.

Zahavi, D., 380n.
Zeki, S., 304n.
*zelos*, 192f., 194f., 196, 208